REPRESENTING RAPE IN MEDIEVAL AND EARLY MODERN LITERATURE

THE NEW MIDDLE AGES

BONNIE WHEELER, *Series Editor*

The New Middle Ages presents transdisciplinary studies of medieval cultures. It includes both scholarly monographs and essay collections.

PUBLISHED BY PALGRAVE:

REPRESENTING RAPE IN MEDIEVAL AND EARLY MODERN LITERATURE

Edited by

Elizabeth Robertson
and Christine M. Rose

palgrave

*In memory of our fathers—
who helped us become feminists
James David Robertson (1922–1995)
Lloyd Ernest Rose (1924–1993)*

REPRESENTING RAPE IN MEDIEVAL AND EARLY MODERN LITERATURE
© Elizabeth Robertson and Christine M. Rose, 2001

First published 2001 by
PALGRAVE
175 Fifth Avenue, New York, N.Y.10010 and
Houndmills, Basingstoke, Hampshire RG21 6XS.
Companies and representatives throughout the world.

PALGRAVE™ is the new global publishing imprint of St. Martin's Press LLC Scholarly and Reference Division and Palgrave Publishers Ltd (formerly Macmillan Press Ltd).

ISBN 0–312–23648–4 hardback

Library of Congress Cataloging-in-Publication Data
Representing rape in Medieval and early modern literature / edited by Elizabeth Robertson and Christine M. Rose.
    p.   cm.—(The new Middle Ages series)
    Includes bibliographical references.
    ISBN 0–312–23648–4
    1. Rape in literature.   2. Literature, Medieval—History and criticism.
3. Literature, Modern—15th and 16th centuries—History and criticism.
I. Robertson, Elizabeth Ann, 1951-   II. Rose, Christine M., 1949-
III. Series.

PN56.R24 R47   2001
809'.93355—dc21

                                                        2001021878

A catalogue record for this book is available from the British Library.

Design by Letra Libre, Inc.

First edition: November 2001
10 9 8 7 6 5 4 3 2 1

Printed in the United States of America.

CONTENTS

SERIES EDITOR'S FOREWORD

The *New Middle Ages* contributes to lively transdisciplinary conversations in medieval cultural studies through its scholarly monographs and essay collections. This series provides focused research in a contemporary idiom about specific but diverse practices, expressions, and ideologies in the Middle Ages; it aims especially to recuperate the histories of medieval women. *Representing Rape in Medieval and Early Modern Literature,* a focused collection of essays edited by Elizabeth Robertson and Christine M. Rose, is the twentieth volume in this series. Few subjects cut as close to the bone as this, the topic of rape. The scholars who have collaborated in this project have culled their sources to show how the representation of rape fuels Medieval and Early Modern literary culture. Woman is both the primary subject and object of rape, yet rape is insidiously woven into the body of art that looks to women as patrons and audiences. The essays in this volume face this conundrum squarely, seeing rape not only as a trope from which we can attain comfortable distance but also as a fact that remains uncomfortably up-close and personal.

Bonnie Wheeler
Southern Methodist University

ACKNOWLEDGMENTS

This volume has emerged after a series of panels that we organized on the subject of rape in the early periods. We are grateful therefore to the other members of that first Modern Language Association panel on "Chaucer and Rape," Carolyn Dinshaw, Harriet Spiegel, Gail Berkeley Sherman, and Linda Lomperis, for providing the foundational moment for this volume through their collegial conversations about rape, their wonderful papers, and their responses to this volume. Thanks also to the presenters and enthusiastic audience of the "Rape in Medieval Literature" panel at the 27th International Congress on Medieval Studies, Kalamazoo, 1992, especially Kathryn Gravdal and Pamela Benson for helping us to broaden and focus our discussion, and to our students, for often hearing us out on this topic. We are indebted to Karen Robertson for her perspicacious advice in the formulation of this introduction. We are grateful to Colleen Anderson for her editorial assistance on this volume. Without the continual generous and astute advice of Jerome Singerman this volume would never have coalesced. And a final thanks to our husbands, Jeffrey Robinson and John Coldewey, for their support of our endeavor in every way. This volume is dedicated to our fathers, but it is for our mothers, our daughters, and all of our sisters.

PERMISSIONS

INTRODUCTION

REPRESENTING RAPE IN MEDIEVAL AND EARLY MODERN LITERATURE

Elizabeth Robertson and Christine M. Rose

> *Nemesis fled to the ends of the earth to escape Zeus, transforming herself into one animal after another, just as the manifest flees and scatters before being caught and pinned down by its principle. The same sequence of flight with metamorphoses followed by rape is repeated when Peleus chases Thetis and finally couples with her in the form of a cuttlefish. The repetition of a mythical event, with its play of variations, tells us that something remote is beckoning to us. There is no such thing as the isolated mythical event, just as there is no such thing as the isolated word. Myth, like language, gives all of itself in each of its fragments. When a myth brings into play repetition and variants, the skeleton of the system emerges for a while, the latent order, covered in seaweed.*
>
> —*Roberto Calasso,* The Marriage of Cadmus and Harmony

Feminist analyses of rape have only just begun. This volume engages in a conversation with earlier studies of rape to argue that stories of sexual violence against women serve as foundational myths of Western culture. Our collection of essays has two functions. First, the volume explores the resistance that representations of rape in Medieval and Early Modern literature generate and have generated for readers, especially for the female reader. Second, it investigates what early representations of rape tell us about social formations governing the relationships between men and women in those periods, and, more specifically, those cultures' notions of women as subjects. The editors and essayists of this volume seek to highlight the repetition of rape in art, and brush aside, as Calasso suggests, the "seaweed" of trope to reveal the skeleton of the system that perpetuates it. This is not to say that rape is only one thing; rather, in its extremity, rape makes manifest the specifics of a given culture's understanding of the female subject in society.

The omnipresence of images of rape in Western literature illustrates how the rapable body has been woven into the very foundations of Western poetics. The intertwining of poetics and the impulse to rape is displayed in the myth of Daphne and Apollo, where the laurels are the leaves of the body of Daphne, transformed into a tree by her own wish to escape the unwanted sexual advances of Apollo, the god of lyric poetry; thus, the lyric prize that celebrates poetic virtuosity also signals a violent escape from rape.[1] This image of rape, forever running away from poetry, yet forever symbolizing it, transformed and united to it, is a powerful and uneasy one. Furthermore, the lyric voice is itself often identified with the lamenting and sometimes vengeful voice of the raped and transformed body of Philomel, the nightingale. Paradoxically, Medieval lyrics even invoke the nightingale as an aid to lovers or represent her as sexual love itself, as in the Middle English debate poem "The Owl and the Nightingale." Over time, and perhaps because of its ambiguous classical history, the nightingale loses its strict gender association and becomes interchangeably male or female, simply a voice—but that voice, male or female, although sometimes cheerful, is more often than not associated with melancholy, even if it does not recall explicitly the words the Medieval French nightingale sings: "Oci" [kill]. Keats, for example, explores his own poetic vocation through his travels with the nightingale in the "Ode to a Nightingale." Yet the voice evoked in the figure of the nightingale is inescapably the voice of Philomel, a woman brutally raped and whose tongue is torn from her mouth. The laurel and the nightingale, our cultural images of poetry, are also images of rape.

Why, then, should the male poet's voice be associated with this suffering female figure? Because so many of our essays concern the work of male authors (Chaucer, the Gawain-Poet, Shakespeare, Sidney, Spenser), most of our essayists grapple with the various issues raised by this question. Consider the familiar example of John Donne's holy sonnet, Sonnet XIV ("Batter My Heart"), which concludes " . . . for I / Except you enthrall me never shall be free / Nor ever chaste, except thou ravish me."[2] In this poem, rape becomes a means to express self-knowledge and the speaker's desire for God. We must also inquire, however, how self-consciously Donne understands the violence and brutality of his image: Does he appropriate an experience without recognizing its implications and consequences for those who actually endure rape? Does he employ the word "ravish" only in its older sense as "abduction"? Or, does he acknowledge the traumatic power of rape by trying to convert it into an image of the extremity of religious desire? Donne's oxymoronic evocation of the pleasurable pain of being taken to a realm without consent skims over the trauma, degradation, and humiliation of real rape; and his emphasis on masochistic pleasurable pain bears a resemblance to Medieval misogynistic tracts and contemporary male fantasies, both of which emphasize female desire for rape.[3] To what degree, we might ask further, is Donne, a poet with a vexed relationship to the hegemony, identifying with suffering women? Such questions are evoked by the male poet's use of the figure of rape.

Rape is not only bound with notions of the aesthetic, but is also deeply implicated in the social and epistemological structures of Western culture. Thus, while representations of rape reveal how violence against women pervades culture—and yet is easily elided—at the same time such violence constitutes how we come to know ourselves and our world. After all, to "know" [cognoscere] a woman in the Vulgate Bible means to have sexual relations with her. Ovid's *Metamorphoses,* for example, recounts one rape after another, demonstrating that the world is set in motion through the rape of women—and sometimes men—by the gods. Europe in Ovid's depiction actually comes into being marked by the tracks left by Europa bemoaning her rape by Jupiter. If male contact and exploration results in knowledge, that is, the "mapping" of women's bodies, we need to ask what knowledge is procured for women in such transactions? The incidents of rape that pervade Ovid's work encode figures of how we know the world. Rape stands not just for the experience of women, but for "the human condition," human helplessness in the face of a capricious, chaotic cosmos.

Given the fact that incidents of rape are integral to the very structures of knowledge in society, rape must be understood and studied not simply in itself and by itself but also as systemic, that is, as embedded within the language, institutions, and social practices of Medieval and Early Modern culture. Catharine MacKinnon's controversial assertions about rape deserve further consideration in the light of Medieval and Early Modern representations of it:

> If sexuality is central to women's definition and forced sex is central to sexuality, rape is indigenous, not exceptional to women's social condition. In feminist analyses a rape is not an isolated event or moral transgression or individual interchange gone awry, but an act of terrorism and torture within a systemic context of group subjection, like lynching.[4]

MacKinnon here claims that rape inheres within the system, rather than is aberrant to it. Our book explores to what degree rape makes up the larger cultural framework within which it occurs by historically grounding our

studies in the legal statutes and social practices that shape Medieval and
Early Modern culture concerning the surveillance of women's bodies. In
our understanding, rape must be considered in its place on a continuum of
other acts concerned with the control of the sexuality and reproduction of
women, including marriage. While we are nowhere claiming that only
women are raped, it is generally agreed that the rapable body—even a
man's—is that one which is socially constructed as "female" and in a position of weakness or ambiguity, able to be taken by force and objectified by
those in power. Our essayists in the main take as their examples literary
rapes of female characters, since rapes of women are the most prevalent and
famous, but the essays often problematize the issues of gender by pointing
out the association of the raped and rapable body with that of the male
artist who through his art renders himself "feminized," objectified, gazed
upon, and liable to be violated. Furthermore, because rape rests on Medieval and Early Modern understandings of the legitimacy of consent, rape
crystallizes not only each era's particular understanding of female subjectivity, but its understanding of larger epistemological questions applicable
to men and women alike, such as free will and the nature of the individual agency in an unpredictable universe. Our book explores the cultural,
aesthetic, and social consequences and the meanings of the continued representation of an event that violates individual women's bodies. If we are
to move forward in reducing the pervasiveness of actual rape, we must advance beyond bemoaning its presence to discover its various *functions*
within Western society.

Surprisingly few books have been devoted to theorizing rape, and those
that have became classics, such as Susan Griffin, *Rape and the Politics of Consciousness* (1979); Susan Estrich, *Real Rape* (1987); Susan Brownmiller,
Against Our Will: Men, Women and Rape (1975); and Sylvia Tomaselli and
Roy Porter, *Rape: An Historical and Cultural Inquiry* (1986). Little theoretical work has been done on representations of rape—as opposed to historical accounts of events of rape, although we of course recognize that these
too are "representations"—in relationship to these contemporary theories.
In this volume, we hope to provide evidence both to challenge and to
complicate theories that have been developed by focusing on contemporary rape by examining it within the historical contexts of those eras that
have profoundly shaped rape as it occurs in the present—the Medieval and
Early Modern periods.

Despite a proliferating number of panels at literary conferences such as
the Modern Language Association meetings, the International Congress on
Medieval Studies, and meetings of the Shakespeare Association devoted to
discussions of the representation of rape in Medieval and Early Modern literature, few published studies have considered rape in these earlier periods

or in literature in general. This volume continues a conversation initiated in 1991 by Lynn Higgins and Brenda Silver in their superb collection of essays, *Rape and Representation* (Columbia University Press). That volume demonstrates the prevalence of rape in a wide variety of periods and genres from Ovid's ur-text, the story of Philomela, to Wordsworth's "The Solitary Reaper," and moves on to consider modern works such as E. M. Forster's *A Passage to India* (that work whose central act of rape was not mentioned in our college classrooms) and the film, "Last Year at Marienbad." We suggest that such studies of sexual violence can benefit from an investigation of its representation in the earlier periods alone because those early social formations concerning female identity profoundly shape our own.

Important theoretically informed studies of representations of rape from eras that have influenced the Middle Ages and the Early Modern period, that is rape in the Bible and the Classics, highlight images and themes that our volume recognizes as crucial. Mieke Bal was one of the first to consider portrayals of rape as aspects of patriarchy's self-construction in her notable work on rape in the Bible, especially in the Book of Judges.[5] Other biblical scholars such as Phyllis Trible, have done similar groundbreaking feminist work.[6] Until recently, however, scholars have failed to focus on how such biblical figures as Tamar, Susannah, Dinah, and Bathsheba—women who were either raped or subject to patriarchal seduction—resurface in Medieval and Early Modern works—indeed are fundamental to the literary modeling of female identity. Victims of rape in classical literature and history—such as Helen and Lucrece—as opposed to biblical rape victims, have received some critical attention, but again, more investigation is needed to trace what their different manifestations can tell us about changing notions of female subjectivity within various interconnected webs of social arrangements that support rape.

Three important works have appeared that have begun the study of representations of rape in the Medieval and Early Modern periods. They not only provided fuel for our discussions, but convinced us of the timeliness of our endeavor to gather scholars from these early periods to write and talk about rape in the works we study: Stephanie Jed's *Chaste Thinking: the Rape of Lucrece and the Birth of Humanism* (Indiana University Press, 1989) explores the implications of Salutati's Early Modern version of the legend of the rape of Lucrece for the *grand récit* of the foundations of Western culture. Building on her *Chaucer's Sexual Poetics* (University Press of Wisconsin, 1989), the first book-length feminist study of Chaucer's work, Carolyn Dinshaw, in her article "Rivalry, Rape and Manhood: Gower and Chaucer" (1991), posits homosocial rivalry between two poets as intimately linked to their representations of rape.[7] Kathryn Gravdal's study, *Ravishing Maidens: Writing Rape in Medieval French Literature and Law*

(University of Pennsylvania Press, 1991) confronts directly the violence against women that has been too long overlooked in medieval representations of rape. In her analysis of the French pastourelle and medieval poets such as Chrétien de Troyes, Gravdal explores representations within their legal, social, and linguistic contexts. As the first book-length study of rape in Medieval literature, *Ravishing Maidens* bravely exposes what has been ignored in generations of literary classrooms: the presence of brutal representations of violence against women in the earliest European literary traditions, a violence often troped as love. Gravdal's work, along with Higgins's and Silver's book, Jed's book, and Dinshaw's article, reflect a growing desire on the part of feminists to grapple with the inscription and subsequent erasure of sexual violence against women in a multitude of early literary works.[8]

Evelyn Vitz's recent critique of the work of feminist medievalists studying rape (especially Gravdal), published in both *Partisan Review* (1996) and *Romanic Review* (1998), urges feminist medievalists not to impose their modern assumptions about rape on a past culture without care to situate claims and opinions historically.[9] Although Vitz rightly calls for "historical, cultural and textual" support for arguments about past representations of rape, she paradoxically engages in just the kind of unhistoricized emotional statement of opinion that she describes as characteristic of feminist work, providing little other than textual evidence for her views. For example, she asserts that modern assumptions about the role consent plays in rape are inapplicable to medieval concepts of rape, seemingly unaware of the fact that, as several of our essayists discuss, while women were indeed not the legal persons they are today, consent nonetheless played a crucial role in Medieval and Early Modern rape cases, and was a hotly debated issue with a long theological as well as legal tradition in the period. She also alleges that medieval women readers enjoyed rape narratives, ignoring contemporary evidence to the contrary in the categorical denial by at least two famous medieval women writers that literary rape has anything of the game about it. Both Christine de Pizan and Marie de France forcefully criticize rape in their fictive worlds.[10] Our essayists explore representations of rape using just the historical, cultural, and textual evidence called for, but not practiced, by Vitz. The visibility of Vitz's essay and the relative invisibility of historicized studies of rape lead us to believe in the urgency of a collection that addresses literary rape from a historical perspective.

Vitz complains that feminists have clearly asserted a definition of rape without recognizing the difficulty of such a definition. Rape is indeed difficult to define, especially so when historical considerations are taken into account. Furthermore, if rape is viewed as systemic, its definition becomes harder to formulate, since our very tools of analysis are implicated in the production of rape. It is not so much that the works we discuss here—courtly love poems, royal entertainments, plays, or fabliaux—mask rape, or that they titillate while pretending to hide rape. Rather, rape is difficult to isolate for the purposes of analysis because, as this volume argues, it is deeply embedded in the assumptive practices of the culture. Because rape may underlie, as MacKinnon has argued, the foundations of our social structure, separating it from its construct may cause the structure to crumble. The very word in its original form is slippery to define: in the Middle Ages, the word "raptus," found most commonly in legal documents, applied equally to forced coitus and abduction for the purposes of marriage, sometimes with the consent of both partners. The related term "ravish" is similarly double (an ambiguity caught perfectly in Gravdal's witty title *Ravishing Maidens*), with its meaning ranging from sexual violence to a metaphorical delight in God. Many of the essays in this volume explore possible definitions of the term, trying to disentangle the act of rape from the larger connotative web within which it operates.

Yet, inevitably such disentanglement is complicated and will lead to different, sometimes apparently contrary, interpretations, as a number of our essays on the same subject matter reveal. Paradoxically, rape simultaneously exists as always one thing—a savage act against a woman, whether physical or psychological—and never one thing, since it inevitably constitutes a thread in a complex network of interconnected cultural institutions and practices that changes from one historical moment to the next. Rape is about bodies, and, like the body, it must be understood as it is socially constructed.[11] For example, while the Middle Ages and the Early Modern period in England shared basic legal understandings of women as marriageable commodities subject to damage as male possessions through rape, the relationship between Church and State control of female sexuality shifts dramatically after the Reformation, resulting generally in what we see as tighter controls over female self-determination. Incongruously, this tightening of control over women occurs at a time when Elizabeth I's position as queen affords women unprecedented opportunities, if only imaginative ones. Many of our essays articulate the complexity of these institutional debates about female identity as they seek to determine how rape operates in Medieval and Early Modern Europe. The essays in this collection contribute to a definition of rape by offering precise historically based legal definitions; at the same time, the essays explore the artistic thread that links early depictions of rape to contemporary rape, a thread that although twisted in different ways, at different times will remain unbroken as long as sexual access to women is controlled by patriarchal structures. With the help of these essays, we urge readers to face squarely the literal violence against women so often represented and too often easily passed over as merely metaphoric in Western art, while stressing our need to scrutinize the ways in which these representations reveal the deep structures of cultures that tolerate rape.

We begin this exploration of rape in the early periods with a discussion of the aestheticization of rape, a theme that recurs in this collection. Christine Rose discusses the problem of reading rape and teaching it in the classroom in texts that seem to displace sexual violence for other agendas. Her essay espouses a paradigm of reading that is relevant for feminist scholars and teachers and is implicitly or explicitly articulated throughout this volume. Choosing a canonical author, Chaucer, as her focus, Rose argues that he, like many canonical authors, uses rape as a plot vehicle repeatedly and variously, but consistently displaces the sexual violence of rape or the threat of rape for trope, for negotiations about and between men. Generations of scholars have taught these poems and written about their richness, while at the same time overlooking their sexual violence. Rose asks how feminists are to recognize, read, and teach rape in these tales. How are feminists to interpret the rape and sexual violence that forms so much a part of Chaucer's corpus, which in fact seems to be often the "subject" of Chaucerian narratives, however displaced? Articulating the complex aesthetic response required of readers attuned to reading rape, Rose urges us to recover the female body's lived experience of rape and not read the rapes only as tropes for masculine interaction. Through her discussion and readings of a number of Chaucerian "rape-tales," she asks that we make the tension between both rape *and* metaphor *part* of the meaning, privileging neither, resisting neither in our readings. Such a critical reading practice ensures the empowerment of readers who must see the real rape *and* its figurative meanings as a part of the art of Chaucer and of how, as a man of his age, he reinscribes the anxiety over sexual control of women prevalent in his culture. Engaging the gradually increasing body of criticism that grapples with rapes in individual tales, Rose raises many of the questions—about female consent, desire, subjectivity, and so on—with which we must contend when we study and teach rape and its use in Chaucer's work and that of other canonical writers.

Mark Amsler's essay presents a literary-historical context for understanding how medieval—as opposed to contemporary modern—audiences responded to the difficulties representations of rape pose for readers. This is an essay about how medieval readers were taught to read/interpret rape in the texts they inherited from the ancients, especially Ovid. Amsler studies mythographical commentaries on Ovid from the twelfth to the fifteenth centuries and demonstrates the various ways those readers elided or erased sexual violence against women and transformed it into something else: into moral exemplums, for example, or euhemeristic narratives of origins. Constructing a frame for reading based on ethical utilities, official commentaries, and allegorical mythographies, Amsler argues, helped shape later medieval discourses about rape by downplaying legal questions about rape, by silencing sexual violence within hermeneutic and aesthetic discourse, and by presenting rape narratives as "readings" to be decoded in terms of moral allegories based on gendered narratives of virtue and vice. Focusing especially on the three paradigmatic rape stories of Daphne, Proserpine, and Philomel, Amsler shows how some later writers (Chaucer, Gower, and Christine de Pisan) challenge in different ways such commentators' assumptions of what it means to read for pleasure and moral edification.

Enacting just such a double vision of reading rape in *Sir Gawain and the Green Knight,* as Rose argues for, Monica Brzezinski Potkay reveals this poem's advocacy of a new kind of hermeneutics in which the letter and the spirit are not to be violently divided as they are by St. Jerome's notions of how to read a text, but instead must be understood as indivisible. The romance first exposes Gawain as an inadequate reader who fails to see the aggression inherent in courtly language until that language is directed towards him. By ascertaining the constraints intrinsic to courtly conversation, and then by being metaphorically raped, as Potkay demonstrates, Gawain learns from the female characters of the work, Morgan Le Fay and Lady Bertilak, the inadequacy of his heironymian engagement with the world. The poem thus exposes the self-destructive nature of any reading practice that envisions reading as an act of rape. Rather than turning to an alternative mode of interpretation that avoids the courtly altogether and that denies the body, however, Potkay shows that the poem celebrates a hermeneutics based on the inseparability of the letter/body and the spirit.

Keeping Rose's model of double reading in mind—trying to understand how the trope of rape functions in a given work of art while at the same time keeping the horror of sexual violence against women at the forefront of our minds—we turn to four studies of that most pervasive and influential of rape narratives, the story of Philomel, an account that was known most fully in the Middle Ages and Renaissance through Ovid. This quintessential account of rape captures the brutality of female victimization inherent in rape and the further violence that it engenders. Although these essays are the only ones in the collection to address the Philomel story directly, many of the other essays concern works, such as Chaucer's *Troilus and Criseyde,* that allude to Philomel's rape, and our authors consider the various cultural meanings of the story as it recurs in Medieval and Early Modern texts.

Jane Burns's innovative essay, a development of her work in *Bodytalk* (1993), on the Old French version of the Philomel story, begins these studies because she clearly reveals the constitutive structural elements of rape under any patriarchal system. She demonstrates rape to be but one aspect of the sexual control of women's bodies, a control designed to legitimate male heirs, and one on a continuum of controls, including marriage. Burns makes comprehensible the seemingly inhuman and incomprehensible murder of Itys by his own mother Procne by showing that the killing of the heir was an appropriate revenge for women trapped in a marriage economy that reduced them to mere commodities. Burns's analysis initiates this volume's concern with the systemic functions of rape by pointing out the relationship between rape, marriage practices, and motherhood under patriarchy.

Studying the same Old French version of Philomel's story, the *Philomena*, Nancy Jones considers this tale's specific literary and cultural resonances for a twelfth-century audience in the light of recent debates about the status of women in medieval aristocratic households and the role of courtly literature in aestheticizing sexual violence. Jones historicizes the medieval adaptation's "anachronistic" treatment of the story of rape and revenge and its rhetorical exposure of women's vulnerability within a patrilineal family structure. She demonstrates that even at the linguistic level, the Old French tale encodes violence to women. The heroine's tapestry, she shows, becomes an ambiguous figure for the quasi-suppressed female voice and the civilizing power of the courtly text in French society.

Confronting the violence not only of the act of rape itself, but of the consequences of rape, Robin Bott studies the Philomel story in order to explore the cultural predilection—one that still remains—to punish the victim of rape by killing her. Her essay compares the Philomel story as rewritten in Shakespeare's *Titus Andronicus* with Livy's story of Virginia, killed by her father to prevent her rape, reinscribed as Chaucer's *Physician's Tale*. Bott makes it evident that rape, in both Chaucer's and Shakespeare's works and in the legal practices concerning rape specific to each culture, is viewed as a disease curable only by the killing of its victim, but distinguishes the medieval text's argument that a woman must be killed to prevent rape from the Early Modern text's argument that a woman must be killed after her rape. In Bott's argument, the real malady plaguing the patriarchal social body, however, is the homosocial power struggle between Virginius and Apius in the *Physician's Tale,* and between Titus and those vying for the control of Rome in *Titus Andronicus.* Both texts assert that a raped woman "should not survive her shame," a sentiment startlingly resonant with today's experiences of, for example, raped Muslim women in Bosnia who struggle to overcome their own sense of shame and personal culpability for their victimization by rape.[12] Underlying Bott's discussion is the recognition of rape as a political event and one deeply implicated in homosocial rivalry.

Karen Robertson's examination of the Philomel story as developed in *Titus Andronicus* also reveals the contours of patriarchal structures and the role women play within them in the Early Modern period. Moreover, she demonstrates how Shakespeare's treatment of the Philomel story discloses political issues specific to Shakespeare's day concerning justice and revenge. Robertson shows how Shakespeare reduces female agency and female alliances from the Ovidian source, and furthermore, explores how these alterations intersect with contemporary Early Modern anxieties about vengeance, more specifically female vengeance. In *Titus Andronicus,* she argues, Shakespeare conflates a variety of classical rape narratives, a process alluded to when Titus explicitly announces that his revenge for the rape of Lavinia outdoes that of Procne. The shift in the gender of the revenger foregrounds masculine injury in rape—rather than the suffering of women—and, by substituting a male for a female avenger of blood, doubly victimizes the woman whose agency in vengeance is excised. Placing this gender shift within the context of contemporary Elizabethan religious injunctions against anger for women and the revenge ethos articulated in the Bond of Association of 1584–85, Robertson considers the restrictions on female agency in the appropriation of Procne's revenge.

The violation of female consent inherent in the Philomel myth so often reinscribed by Medieval and Early Modern authors generates larger epistemological questions of human agency and, indeed, specifically codifies the nature of the female subject's ability to act as a self-determining agent. The implications of representations of rape for our understanding of Medieval and Early Modern constructions of female identity and agency are probed further in the next series of essays concerning law, consent, and subjectivity.

The potential of rape narratives to act as sites for epistemological inquiry is the subject of Anne Schotter's study of the little-known medieval Latin comedies. Her essay provides a perspective from within the establishment in her consideration of rape in twelfth-century Latin comedies, works produced by the university-trained clerical elite. Just as a number of the other essayists explore depictions of rape as loci of pressing contemporary cultural concerns, Schotter argues that in the medieval Latin comedy *Pamphilus,* representations of rape are not meant to reinscribe violence against women, but rather to reveal a medieval debate among men concerning the relations among choice, will, and the arts of persuasion.

The next two essays examine the canonical author Chaucer, a poet who was himself legally released from the charge of "raptus." Like Schotter who unveils contemporary issues beneath the surface representation of rape, Christopher Cannon revisits the biographical conundrum of the "Chaumpaigne release," in which Cecily Chaumpaigne excused Chaucer from culpability with respect to her "rape" (as it appears in the release that provides evidence of this historical event, "de raptu meo"). Cannon takes issue with the general presumption that any relation between the release and Chaucer's writing can be nothing more than speculation. Acknowledging that the document cannot tell us what happened between Chaucer and Chaumpaigne, Cannon argues that this enigmatic historical event provides a useful optic for understanding, first, the pervasive confusion about women's consent in the medieval law on sexual violence, and, second, Chaucer's incisive understanding of the dangers of such confusion as he explores it in his writing. The nexus between this important life-record and Chaucer's writing is not therefore biographical, but epistemological. Cannon begins his study with a consideration of the influence of the Ovidian Helen (in the *Heroides*) in the Middle Ages, and finds that unraveling the thread of meaning offered by Chaucer's representations of rape as well as by the legal documents related to his own rape case shows, as do the medieval Latin comedies discussed by Schotter, how continuous the act of rape is with larger philosophical issues fundamental to Western culture—consent, for example, or more broadly, free will.

In her essay on Chaucer's *Troilus and Criseyde,* Elizabeth Robertson reads the complicated character of Criseyde through the lens of representations of important classical "raped" heroines, Lucrece and Helen of Troy. Robertson explores further the fourteenth-century understanding of the degree to which women can exert free will as that understanding emerges in the conflict between the Church and State over the legitimacy of female consent, especially in clandestine marriages (cases of "raptus"). While Cannon focuses his attention on the fundamental ambiguity of secular legal comprehension of "raptus" and consent, Robertson, developing arguments first set forth by H. A. Kelly in 1975, recognizes how the theology of consent that underlies the formation of the law and that is made manifest in the ecclesiastical courts' assertions of the necessity of female consent to marriage, shapes medieval ideas of the female subject. Somewhat surprisingly, given the misogynistic clerical views of women circulating during the period, Church doctrine, Robertson shows, asserts the fundamental legitimacy of a woman as a subject by claiming the right of a woman to choose her own partner. Yet, this right conflicted with secular legal practices in which the father or lord had the ultimate power to control marriage choices. This cultural conflict becomes particularly acute in the fourteenth century in clandestine marriage cases. Such legal and doctrinal complexity is at the heart, says Robertson, of the celebrated indeterminacy of Chaucer's heroine, Criseyde. In Robertson's argument, Chaucer portrays Criseyde as a character under the threat of "raptus" in both of its medieval meanings—as forced coitus and abduction—thus exposing the framework of fourteenth-century legal debates between ecclesiastical and civil courts concerning the status of female consent under the law as it shapes female identity. This cultural framework crucially informs Chaucer's "modernization" of his literary inheritance of the two "rape" victims, Lucrece and Helen. Robertson contends that only through representing Criseyde as under the threat of rape may Chaucer draw together the elements of Criseyde's potential to be a self-determining subject.

In her study of Sir Phillip Sidney's late-sixteenth-century romance *Old Arcadia* (c. 1580), Amy Greenstadt also probes the slipperiness of the term "rape" in her description of a "rhetoric of ravishment" that she argues conditioned English Renaissance legal and literary descriptions of sexual violence. Like Robertson, she locates some of the ambiguity of rape in the role Church doctrine plays in the formulation of the law, but in her view that ambiguity emerges within theology itself in Augustine's conflicting gendered accounts of the relationship between pleasure and consent, on the one hand, and desire, intention, and signification, on the other. Greenstadt considers how "ravishment"—which in this period could describe either a state of ecstatic desire or a moment of sexual violation—suggested linguistic and rhetorical avenues of identification between the lustful male rapist and his female victim, even as it called attention to the radical distance separating their experiences. She shows how this text raises questions about the representability of desire both in the context of a trial for ravishment and in the interplay of sexual desire and violence that marks the romantic relationships between Sidney's characters. She further considers Sidney's critique of the law in which he associates the law with an oppressive rhetoric of ravishment, yet also dramatizes how inescapable such a rhetoric can become. Ultimately, says Greenstadt, Sidney looks for an escape from "ravishment" in the depiction of homoerotic love—a love in which the distinction between loving subject and beloved object appears to be obliterated.

The final two essays, by Susan Frye and Katherine Eggert, although exploring similar themes concerning female victimization, agency, and subjectivity, take a more focused look at the positionality of the author vis-à-vis his representations of rape. Since most works we consider in this volume are by major male canonical authors—Chaucer, the Gawain-poet, Shakespeare, Sidney, and Spenser—we must contemplate the assertion, made particularly by feminist readers, that male canonical authors unthinkingly reinscribe and therefore perpetuate violence against women in their representations of rape. Many of the above essays implicitly take issue with that assertion. The final pair of essays in the volume recapitulate and sharpen the conflicts for the reader produced by representations of rape by scrutinizing the question of the relationship between violence against women and the aesthetic of the text. These essays pick up the theme most explicitly articulated here by Greenstadt, but noted by other contributors, that male poets are drawn to rape narratives precisely because they identify with the rape victims. Frye and Eggert explore the implications of this observation for our understanding of male poetics itself.

Confronting the biography of the poet and his poetics directly, Susan Frye establishes the interconnection between Spenser's representations of rape and his own personal anxieties as subject to Queen Elizabeth. She argues that Book 3 of Spenser's *The Faerie Queene* conducts a literary/metaphoric rape of Queen Elizabeth I under the guise of the rape of Amoret, a figure for Elizabeth, watched by Britomart the cross-dressing female knight, who is herself representative of Elizabeth. Frye contends that Spenser tries to redefine *chastity* from Elizabeth's self-aggrandizing use of it as *virginity,* the source of her power, to the male-authorized definition of it as "purity from unlawful intercourse." Spenser encodes in the Amoret/Britomart episode the assertion of the rights of jurisdiction over women's bodies by men whether in marriage or rape. He usurps in his poem, modeled after court spectacles, Elizabeth's right to define women's chastity, and sets its parameters as determined by males instead. Watching the poet at work in his text, Frye closely attends to his diction of violence and to the queen as the metaphoric center of that violence in Book 3, suggesting that Spenser's preemption of Elizabeth's self-definition is his inscription of her vulnerability to men's definition and men's violence, resulting from his own displaced frustration at his lack of preferment by Elizabeth. The poet, his narrator, and his character Busirane seem to be conflated in the exaltation of male prerogative at this point in the poem. Spenser's goal in redefining chastity this way is to attempt to redefine the female body as possessible, whether in marriage or in rape. In Frye's argument, then, the canonical male author reinscribes violence against women through his representation of rape as part of his engagement with political concerns in the court.

Like Frye, Katherine Eggert examines the implications of rape narratives for Spenser's self-exploration. Contesting the notion that in *The Faerie Queene* the recurring phenomenon of women being sexually threatened constitutes the physical "stuff" of the poem, for which allegory attempts to provide theological, moral, or psychological tenors, Eggert argues, rather, that rape in *The Faerie Queene* is itself a metaphorical maneuver. Rape acts in the poem to distract the reader from what is truly physical in Spenser's work: the sensual, viscerally felt pleasure of reading poetry. *The Faerie*

Queene oscillates between two modes of poetic activity, which Eggert labels "rape" and "rapture." Here Eggert's argument explores further the ambiguity of the term "ravishment" raised earlier by Gravdal's book, and forwarded by Greenstadt. In a raping mode of poetics, poetry's sensual beauty is shunted aside in favor of an attempt to "know" what is at the center of feminine spaces (gardens, castles, etc.). In a rapturous mode, sensual poetry is allowed to suspend the reader's demands for certainty and plain knowledge. Thus, Frye and Eggert, at times contrasting in their views, further our understanding of the wide epistemological range of rape narratives.

Although the contours of sexual violence have altered surprisingly little over the past thousand years, rape is nevertheless a construct of a given community and serves each community in its own distinctive way. As literary scholars, we can only begin to unravel the particularity of rape by studying its meanings and functions in specific times and places, in specific works of art. Rape in the past structures rape in the present, and thus the contemporary reader and the Medieval and Early Modern artist are always intertwined. These essays promise to open up a discussion about the function of representations of rape in Medieval and Early Modern literature.

We have loosely conjoined these essays in order to highlight how a single narrative/poetic/artistic "event" can encapsulate multiple meanings and be approached from multiple critical perspectives. The collection is framed by the analyses of the aestheticization and reading of rape presented by Rose and Amsler, with Potkay providing a reading of a single medieval poem that uncovers such aestheticization; Jones adds a historically specific dimension to Burns's discussion of the Old French *Philomena;* Karen Robertson similarly historicizes the general issues Bott discusses in *Titus Andronicus;* Schotter, Cannon, Elizabeth Robertson, and Greenstadt explore different facets of Medieval and Early Modern concepts of consent as they shape discussions of free will and representations of both male and female subjectivity; Frye and Eggert offer sharply contrasting views of the meaning of rape for the poet's understanding of himself and his poetics. We learn from these essays that part of rape's ambiguity stems from its origins in a slippery legal term where "raptus" applies equally to forced coitus and abduction—abduction sometimes with the willing consent of the female victim. This ambiguity allows rape to become a locus of literary explorations of epistemological questions about the nature of consent and free will that apply often to men as well as women. Because "raptus" in these early periods rests upon a notion of the autonomy of the female subject, rape also becomes a focal point for literary studies of the nature of female self-determination, and thus studies of rape can further our understanding of the early periods' concepts of female subjectivity. We also learn that literary instances of rape often become the focal point for the male poet or artist's anxieties about his own passive helplessness, his "feminization" as an artist. Finally, we find that poetics and aesthetics are deeply enmeshed with violence against women in rape. We hope these essays will stimulate further treatments of this topic of such pressing concern not only to our perceptions of our literary-artistic inheritance, but also to our understanding of the present.

Notes

1. For Daphne's story, see Ovid, *Metamorphoses,* Book 1, trans. Mary M. Innes (New York: Penguin, 1976), pp. 41–43.
2. From "Holy Sonnet" no. 14 ("Batter my heart, three-personed God . . ."), ll. 12–14. *Norton Anthology of English Literature,* vol. 1, 4th ed. (New York: Norton, 1979), p. 1102.
3. Some of these tracts are anthologized in Alcuin Blamires, *Women Defamed and Women Defended: An Anthology of Medieval Texts* (Oxford: Clarendon Press, 1992). For an earlier discussion of such views of women, see R. Howard Bloch, *Medieval Misogyny and the Invention of Western Romantic Love* (Chicago: University of Chicago Press, 1991); see also *The Medieval Feminist Newsletter*'s response to earlier formulations of Bloch's ideas (Fall, 1988).
4. Catherine A. MacKinnon, *Toward a Feminist Theory of the State* (Cambridge, MA: Harvard University Press, 1989), p. 172.
5. See, for example, her *Lethal Love: Feminist Literary Readings of Biblical Love Stories,* (Bloomington: Indiana University Press, 1987) and her *Death and Dyssemetry: Death and Coherence in Judges.* (Chicago and London: The University of Chicago Press, 1988).
6. *Texts Of Terror: Literary-Feminist Readings Of Biblical Narratives* (Philadelphia: Fortress Press, 1984) and *God and the Rhetoric of Sexuality* (Philadelphia: Fortress Press, 1978).
7. In *Chaucer and Gower: Difference, Mutuality and Exchange,* ed. Robert F. Yeager, English Literary Studies Monograph Series 51 (Victoria, BC: University of Victoria, 1991), pp. 130–52. Reprinted in *Violence Against Women in Medieval Texts,* ed. Anna Roberts (Gainesville, FL: University of Florida Press, 1998), pp. 115–49.
8. Anna Roberts's collection *Violence Against Women in Medieval Texts* (see n. 7) appeared after the present volume had been substantially completed, and also considers aspects of this topic.
9. "Rereading Rape in Medieval Literature," *Partisan Review* 63, no. 2 (Spring, 1996): 280–91 and *Romantic Review* 88 (1997): 1–26.
10. Christine de Pizan in her *City of Ladies,* ed. and trans. Earl Jeffrey Richards (New York: Persea Books, 1982), pp. 160–63, in Book 2, 44.1ff., has Lady Rectitude refute the notion that women want to be raped, giving several examples, of whom Lucretia is one: "Rest assured, dear friend, chaste ladies who live honestly take absolutely no pleasure in being raped. Indeed, rape

is the greatest possible sorrow for them . . ." (161). Likewise, Marie de France's *Fables* recounts the particularly sinister rape of a female bear by a male fox ("The Fox and the Bear," Fable 70), and the author grimly notes in her *moralitas* at its end that even the wise and virtuous cannot escape the wiles of the wicked: "and it must always be this way," hoping perhaps that the heuristic force of witnessing the literary rape of the helpless bear, entangled in bushes by her fur (interestingly, her body is her trap) and mounted by the fox, will encourage her audience to keep it from "always" being "this way." See Harriet Spiegel, ed. and trans., *Marie de France: Fables* (Toronto: University of Toronto Press, 1987), p. 185; and Spiegel's "The Male Animal in the Fables of Marie de France," in *Medieval Masculinities: Regarding Men in the Middle Ages* (Minneapolis: University of Minnesota Press, 1994), pp. 111–26, esp. p. 116. Both Marie and Christine vehemently oppose eliding textual rape by finding it fun.

11. For recent collections of essays discussing the social construction of the body in the Middle Ages, see Linda Lomperis and Sarah Stanbury, *Feminist Approaches to the Body in Medieval Literature* (Philadelphia: University of Pennsylvania Press, 1993) and Sarah Kay and Miri Rubin, *Framing Medieval Bodies* (Manchester: Manchester University Press, 1994).

12. See *New York Review of Books*, "Bosnia: Questions About Rape," March 25, 1993, pp. 3–6.

PART I

READING AND TEACHING RAPE

CHAPTER 1

READING CHAUCER READING RAPE

Christine M. Rose

Rose explores Chaucer's uses of rape as a trope, where he displaces the focus on sexual violence against the female and replaces it with concern for contentions among men. Reading these rapes as both sexual violence and trope, however, enriches our interpretation of Chaucer's texts, enabling us to apprehend the dark societal issues surrounding rape beneath the dazzling aesthetic "pley" of the poetry.

> *And up he rist, and by the wenche he crepte.*
> *This wench lay uprighte and faste slepte,*
> *Til he so ny was, er she myghte espie,*
> *That it had been to late for to crie,*
> *And shortly for to seyn, they were aton.*
> *Now pley Aleyn, for I wol speke of John.*

—*Geoffrey Chaucer,*
The Reeve's Tale, *ll. 4193–97*[1]

> *. . . For women practicing feminist studies, readings of literary texts that focus on the metaphorization of women, readings that take no account of the existence of historical women in the Middle Ages, readings that distance the object of study—women—from the female observer/listener all tend to meet resistance, admittedly to varying degrees, in the body of the woman critic. . . . While theorizing the body, we also have to live with it.*

—*E. Jane Burns,* Bodytalk:
When Women Speak in
Old French Literature, *248–49*

Rape = Romp:
"And eek men shal nat maken ernest of game"
(Chaucer, The Miller's Tale, Prol. 3186)

Chaucer displays a disturbing propensity to inscribe rape in his narratives, yet often directs the readers *away* from reading rape to reading
not-rape. Or, his work demonstrates, as Nancy Jones notes, "the puzzling
way in which literary texts can open up new spaces then shut them
down."[2] Chaucer's audience discovers indeed that the rapes in his narratives are tropes for decidedly alternative purposes than highlighting violence to women. Troping (*trope*, from the Greek "turn") involves a turning
away from and displacement of the literal sense. The Chaucerian lines from
The Reeve's Tale above, and the quotation from E. Jane Burns that follows,
point to the complex response required of feminist readers and teachers of
Chaucer to instances of rape in the text. We are invited by the poetic narrator, as in *The Reeve's Tale,* to see sexual violence towards women as "pley."
Here, Chaucer's Reeve-narrator and the character of the student Aleyn
perform the rape of the miller's daughter Malyne as "pley," as "quyting"
[requiting] the miller for his social pretensions and his larceny of the students' cornmeal. The silent "wenche," "to late for to crie," is turned away
from and occluded by the male character's antic actions, the fabliau's
generic expectations, and the narrator's interpretation of "pley," as well as
by his brisk dispatch of the scene: "And shortly for to seyn, they were
aton." Nevertheless, here and in the ensuing rape of the miller's wife by
Aleyn's cohort John, as Burns might argue, lies the locus of the resistance
in the body of the female reader. Lived experience of gender makes the
feminist interpreter/reader conscious of the *legerdemain* the narrator is enacting in his depiction of the double rape scene. Depending upon whose
viewpoint one engages, there is a rape here as well as a romp. In the mas-
culinist/humanist manner of what Stephanie Jed has called "chaste thinking," this tale invites us to turn away from the visceral and to subordinate
the rape to another story of male interaction.[3] If, as Burns insists, while
theorizing and metaphorizing the body we have also to live with it, then
a woman might surely read in "ernest" simultaneously, and however con-
tradictorily, with the narrator's designation of the event as "pley." For the
purposes of this study, I might vary Chaucer the Pilgrim-narrator's
"ernest"/"game" desiderata for the *Canterbury Tales* collection from the
Miller's Prologue that opens this section, to make my point in this essay:
(wo)men *shal . . .* maken ernest of game. Women (and those who would
sympathize with their viewpoints) must read to recover the literal sense of
the trope; we cannot discount the visceral. The union of "ernest" and
"game" in the interpretation of rape may be an irreconcilable—or at least

ambivalent—one, but as contradictory as they seem, they must both be present in the readings we do.

The ironic interplay of the multiple facets of "ernest" and "game" surrounding the instances of rape in Chaucerian narrative can and should serve to demonstrate the elasticity of the poetry and its continuing appeal to interpreters of different eras, ideologies, and aesthetic agendas. I do not think that the historical Chaucer can be reincarnated as a proto-feminist just because he seems to provide us with instances where we ourselves recover unease, anxiety, and openings for feminist readings, although recent critics have eloquently argued for his awareness of the feminine perspective.[4] For example, Jill Mann maintains that Chaucer's project is to focus on the female and her "active" suffering as the measure of virtue, that a feminist reading of Chaucer "erases male/female role divisions" (Mann, 185); Carolyn Dinshaw says that he attempts to scrutinize the feminine Other in patriarchal society (Dinshaw, 10).[5] Both Mann and Dinshaw, whom I do not propose to package as having identical approaches, do, however, reduce the level of aesthetic "pley" to read Chaucer's poetry for what seem only serious agendas.

In *Geoffrey Chaucer* (1991), Jill Mann's tepid "feminism" is nevertheless to some extent compensated for by her brilliant, jewel-like close readings of Chaucer's works, especially on the Wife's tale and the tale of the Man of Law. Mann argues for Chaucer's encouraging the reader to see the woman character's perspective, and setting up "woman" and her "pitee" as the measure of men. Mann sees the Chaucerian project as one dedicated to placing "woman at the center instead of at the periphery, where she becomes the norm against which all human behavior is to be measured" (Mann, 3). While I am intrigued and in awe of how skillfully Mann marshals her argument, I cannot wholly agree with how she spins out this notion in many of the works of Chaucer and would argue that the ideals of Christianity, with its inherent doctrine of passivity, humility, and subservience to the will of a higher authority, is the model Chaucer uses to measure all humanity, not the female gender. That his women characters should approach this ideal closely should not surprise us, since women have been culturally inured to passivity and subservience, and thus do represent in Chaucer's work (when they are being most "feminine") the ideals Christians strive for. The work of Caroline Bynum and the writings of Julian of Norwich have shown us that Christ as a feminized hero is a commonplace of medieval discourse.[6]

But it is a tribute to the abundance of our responses to Chaucer's poetry—sometimes troubling ones—that theorizing, critiquing, and historicizing Chaucer-the-author within the Western antifeminist tradition in which he participates, and from which his work proceeds, does not diminish his art.

We cannot deny the fecundity of a poetry that keeps us so firmly locked in engagement with the social, moral, and aesthetic questions of the ages. That is, as a feminist, I do not want to belittle or ignore the presence of sexual violence in Chaucer's poetry, nor do I want to negate "game" for "ernest." We can apprehend both at once: "and shortly for to seyn, they were aton."

The "ernest" of this "game" in *The Reeve's Tale* that the two students "pley" may indeed, through the narrator's concluding directions for reading the tale, be interpreted as their town/gown revenge upon Sympkyn the miller:

> Thus is the proude millere wel ybete,
> And hath ylost the gryndynge of the whete,
> And payed for the soper everideel
> Of Aleyn and of John, that bette hym weel.
> His wyf is swyved, and his daughter als.
> Lo, swich it is a millere to be fals! (*The Reeve's Tale,* 4313–18)

Nevertheless, the revenge is achieved by objectifying the female bodies, and we thus simultaneously experience another kind of "ernest" reality here: a brutal rape takes place, and the act assumes a denial of female subjectivity. While this dark side of Chaucer's poetics is often ignored, acknowledgement of the rape here surely constitutes part of the richness that feminist readers can bring to the interpretation of his work. Sexual assault glimmers ominously just behind the rape-as-pley reading that the narrator's text provides.[7] The Reeve-narrator by his troping invites us to discount the visceral, to make the patriarchal hermeneutic decision to inhabit the metaphoric sense alone. Notwithstanding, we must both witness the "metaphorization of women" (Burns, above) and resist it by acknowledging the presence of rape and its significance(s) for the text and its readers. The significance may not be the same for both entities.

Carolyn Dinshaw shows a trope can be a "breaking apart of the 'proper' relation between word and thing," and how the ensuing possibilities for deceit are "obvious."[8] She also insists that we realize that a trope presents a disruption, a turning away, an alienation. Straight signification is avoided; meaning shifts from one locus to another—into an alien place. Of course, medieval readers, trained in allegorical interpretation, were no strangers to holding two ideas in mind at once and enjoying the richness of meaning this hermeneutical exercise afforded. We need to retain this reading model in examining rape and trope in Chaucer's works. The troping of rape, the shifting and shimmering between *figurative* rape in the narrative and the cognizance of *real* rape by the reader, can be a site of feminist readings of the Chaucerian texts.

This essay is an investigation of reading rape in some works of Geoffrey Chaucer, mainly from the *Canterbury Tales,* exploring what it might mean for the woman critic, reader, and teacher to forge a model of reading that reads rape; of what it might mean heuristically for us to teach rape when we teach Chaucer. Perhaps in a volume such as this one, with readers attuned to reading and theorizing rape, one might think such an essay gratuitous or covering ground feminists have already overrun.[9] But experience has shown me that colleagues and students still need to be made aware of the ubiquitous and unsettling presence of sexual violence in medieval texts. They don't want to see it. In addition, medievalist-feminists cannot stop engaging with texts that nevertheless demonstrate antipathy to women as characters and audiences. We must not overlook or read around the rapes as the poet, the narrator, or the text's generic expectations direct us. We must point out instances of gender violence, try to recover what they might mean for the poet and his society, and for us. We cannot rest complacent in masculinist readings, neither should we deny the troubling nature of the artist and his art, which recreates some of the norms of its own society— among them trivializing or displacing real rape. As Burns notes above, women critics and readers read with their real bodies, and come to a text with their own experiences of gender. Readers construct textual meaning, and female (or male) readers reading of literary rapes might indeed resist the directives of the author/narrator or other conventional interpretive clues to read rape as a trope.

Moreover, reading rape in Chaucer has been, in the experience and training of most female readers, reading *over* rape, or, reading *around* rape. Taught to read literature by men, as men (or male-authorized figures as surely my teachers were, in a Catholic women's college), women readers of literature have had to submerge their own reaction to rape in a work of literature to the traditional "male" reading of rape—and may in fact fail to react at all to the violence perpetrated on some female characters. We have become inured to what Missy Dehn Kubitscheck calls the oblique and symbolic treatment, the displacement of rape in Euro-American literature by white men.[10] This approach to reading patriarchally, in the experience of many female readers, is characterized by interpreting rape acts as vehicles for plot, as displacements, tropes, as the norm of the way men and women interact in literature (in real life, too?) and altogether to pass over or through the sexual/gender violence embedded in the text to, in the words of Geoffrey Hartman, a "higher" or "deeper" meaning.[11] Rape, whether in its medieval sense of "raptus"—assault, kidnapping, threats, actual forced sexual violation, or violence to the female by a powerful male—is glossed over by a dominant tradition of reading that has desired us to move on to what would be considered the more "important" aspects of a work of literature, often labeled the aesthetic or the political, the metaphoric "rape." Women, all of whom are potential or actual rape victims,[12] will surely attest that for them, the act of rape in a literary work might not be without its attendant problems in reading, especially when rape must often be read "like a man," counter to a woman's experience of rape as personal injury and humiliation.[13] We are asked to acknowledge or make sense of a "literary" use of rape—often a genre-determined, gross, male-bonding, humorously intended usage, or a political usage, a crime against property, a crime of class against class, of men against men. When rape is read, for instance, as a property issue—not that it is not a kind of property issue, but rather that in treating it as a trope the transgression is displaced—the critic turns away from the foundational element of the trope, violence against women, and fails to conceive how the parts of the trope-equation are related. As, for example in *The Reeve's Tale,* the equation *raping women = stealing corn from the students* presents us with a complex notion to unpack if we are to consider gender and violence in this context. I will return to *The Reeve's Tale* later to examine further those elided rapes.

So, in this essay I suggest that we consider collectively the many instances of rape and sexual violence in Chaucer's work. Moreover, I propose that we can read both the rape and its possible metaphoric meaning, privileging neither, in our appreciation of Chaucer's art, its darknesses, and its light. Before looking at specific instances in the poetry, I want to set forth some of the theoretical and practical considerations about reading rape that inform my reading of Chaucer: rape as it figures in medieval language and law, the ambiguous issue of rape in Chaucer's own life, as well as the notion of troping rape to displace its meaning onto another locus—that of male interaction. Even critics who acknowledge and write about rape in various Chaucerian narratives (Dinshaw, Crane, Hansen, Delany, Bloch, Saunders, etc.)[14] have not fully engaged the issue of how much rape lies in Chaucer's corpus, and no one has yet provided a catalog of the instances to survey the variety of ways in which rape is inscribed in Chaucerian texts, which I propose to do here. I offer in the last section of this essay primarily an overview of Chaucer's treatments of rape, no definitive or coherent unpacking of rape in these wonderful and perplexing tales. However, I want to put rape out there for scholars and readers to focus on, to stimulate further critical conversations about how rape functions in Chaucerian texts.

Doubtless, too, my essay responds to Evelyn Birge Vitz's acerbic attack on feminists reading rape, when she calls for tempering the scholarly handling of rape in literature. Vitz argues that "many feminists"—and she uses Katherine Gravdal as her whipping-girl—"take the view that literary depictions of rape should not distract attention from its ugly reality" (280).[15]

She contends that these "many feminists" require rape not ever to be laughed at, even though evidence from medieval literature demonstrates, she says, that all kinds of violence amused medieval audiences: "Why should the theme of rape alone have been exempt from laughter?" (281). She castigates "many feminists" for being "internally incoherent" in demanding that rape be acknowledged, and for finding rape scenes where none are apparent. Her article notes that rape fantasies seem to be psychologically universal, and that certainly some medieval women were entertained by this genre. Those tales she cites (Chrétien de Troyes's romances and some French pastourelles) are known to have been current in courts that had women as a significant part of their audience, or in fact, as major patrons of the arts (283). Tales of rape, says Vitz, eliminate the problematics of assent, and allowed medieval (and modern) women to act out sexually in their imagination without guilt or fear of real consequences (284). So why, she asks, do feminists take it all so seriously? Unfortunately, Vitz fails to acknowledge the categorical denial of rape as play by Marie de France and Christine de Pizan, well-known female medieval authors with aristocratic, courtly audiences, who both give short shrift to rapists in their fictive worlds.[16] Vitz's diatribe against Gravdal's work (however unfounded) and about "the indignation which so often suffuses scholarly discourse about the literary theme of rape" (291), does raise some serious points for us to ponder, mainly about bringing modern sensibilities to bear upon medieval works. She reminds me that my own endeavor is to try to talk about modern readers reading Chaucer and the way in which, however much we may understand the historical milieu and masculine sensibility that encodes rape as "pley," it is nevertheless important to take into account, while reading, the real rape that the trope displaces.

Rape = Romance:
Rape in Medieval Law and Language

Feminists propose that rape does not signal a breakdown of social organization, but rather maintains the social system in which it occurs as an aspect of patriarchal power, property rights, homosocial desire, and traffic in women.[17] As Levi-Strauss in *The Elementary Structures of Kinship* convincingly asserts, the exchange of women between men and groups of men provides the basis of social organizations.[18] A society based upon traffic in women is itself the basis of anthropologist Gayle Rubin's work on the genesis of the oppression and social subordination of women, where she explores "what would have to be changed in order to achieve a society without gender hierarchy."[19] Her "exegetical" reading of both Levi-Strauss and Freud convinces Rubin that women are not inherently oppressed, but

become oppressed in certain gender relationships constructed and pro-
mulgated by society (157). Rubin argues that the sexual relationships that
oppress women derive from the ancient requirement to tame women, to
deprive them of desire, in order that they not oppose their exchange between men, that they know their place in the exchange system, which is
in effect a rape culture. The system operates smoothly, says Rubin, if the
female has no desires of her own but responds to the desires of others
(men) about whom she should sleep with (182). In such a social system,
men are the beneficiaries of a social organization in which women are the
means of exchange; women do not own themselves to give themselves
away (175). Luce Irigaray, commenting on the system of the exchange of
women's bodies, remarks: "what if these 'commodities' refused to go to
market?"[20] Our readings must refuse to go to market.

Such a sexist culture as Levi-Strauss and Rubin describe existed in pre-
capitalist Europe throughout the Middle Ages, and it is more or less represented by Chaucer in his corpus.[21] Chaucer's *Shipman's Tale,* for example,
while not a rape-tale quite in the way that *The Reeve's Tale* and those tales
I discuss later (*The Wife of Bath's Tale, The Merchant's Tale, Melibee, The Man
of Law's Tale, The Physician's Tale, The Manciple's Tale, or The Franklin's Tale*) are,
expresses just such a commodification of women. The tale allows some uneasy space for a woman's manipulation of that commodification when the
wife gets "taken" by the friar both physically and financially, yet is able in
turn to hoodwink her husband into forgiving both transgressions against
his property rights by pleasuring him in bed. Medieval rape laws were conditioned by the legal view that women were the property of men.[22] The
linguistic signification of the tangled Latin legal term for rape, "*raptus,*"
demonstrated so well in the scholarly debate surrounding the
Chaumpaigne case against Chaucer for "raptus," which I will discuss in the
next section, proves itself as difficult to pin down as are the meanings of
the medieval representation of rape in literary discourse. "Raptus" can, and
was legally interpreted during certain periods to mean: forced coitus, sexual assault, abduction, assault on a woman. Its root "rapere" is ambiguously
defined by terms for carrying off: pluck, seize, drag off, abduct (a virgin).
The classical Latin sense connotes movement or transportation, appropriation, theft, coupled with speedy departure with the goods. But by 1155,
"*raptus*" had taken on a shift toward sexual meaning in which the abduction by violence was for the purposes of forced coitus.[23] The comparable
word to the Latin "raptus" in Old French, "ravir," spawned "ravissement"
and the English "ravish," and became used as a synonym for rape, or for the
spiritual action of a soul's being carried to heaven, transported by enthusiasm or bliss. Thus, "*raptus*" and its derivatives linguistically came to desig-
nate a state of emotional exaltation, and became associated in the Middle

Ages with the state of sexual pleasure. The slippage of meanings for this family of terms from theft to sexual ecstasy, from material to literary, from pain to pleasure (and we must remember the trilingual nature—Latin, French, English—of much of England during this period for any discussion of Chaucer) is in itself quite ravishing. The notions of a woman's attractiveness and a man's force in the act of raping become conflated into a state of bliss, and sexual violence is erased behind the troping, in what Gravdal calls "the romantization of ravishment" (15). The brutal warfare of feudalism and the blissful idolatry of the code of courtly love come neatly together in such a term, and form indeed the stuff of medieval courtly narrative, fabliaux, and even saint's lives, as Gravdal's work has demonstrated, and we see too inscribed in Chaucer's poetry.

Legally, the definition of "raptus" similarly blurs and shifts, but begins in early Christian Europe with the strictures against the abduction of women in order to effect forced marriages/forced coitus (modern rape). Marriage by abduction is its standard meaning. "Raptus" was a serious crime, a kind of theft, a violation of the authority of the male under whose jurisdiction the female victim resided. The stiff fines and penalties prescribed were in some measure a protection for women's bodies, but undoubtedly were more designed to protect the patriarchal family honor.[24] The corporate Church and ecclesiastical courts got into the picture when they took as their purview marriage law, legislating between contractual marriage arranged between the bride's father and the fiancé, versus marriage by abduction without knowledge of the bride's parents. The debate over these legalities persisted for centuries, but the focus was unfailingly *not* the protection of women from sexual violence, but the restoration of social order, the peaceful sharing out of women among men in arranged marriages that benefited the patrimony.[25] This is to say that both legal and literary texts and, I would argue, some Chaucer criticism regarding the Cecily Chaumpaigne matter of Chaucer's own "raptus" accusation, which I will discuss later, blur the distinctions between forced and voluntary sex, between love and assault.[26] "Raptus" could and sometimes did conclude in marriage; the victim might consent to marry the rapist. It is no wonder that rape is not viewed in the Middle Ages without conflict, and that perspectives on rape in medieval literary texts are fraught with ambiguity. We can't exactly define what rape is. Rape plots can be interpreted as *romantic narratives*. And it is no wonder that what I identify as Chaucer's "rape-tales" manifest anxious moments for readers alert to the trope of rape, where the narrative

> presents an event in such a way that it heightens figurative elements and manipulates the readers' ordinary response by suspending or interrupting that response in order to displace the reader's focus onto other formal or thematic

elements The mimesis of rape is made tolerable when the poet tropes it as moral, comic, heroic, spiritual, or erotic. (Gravdal, 13)

Psychologists and criminologists tell us that rape is not only a crime about sex; it is a crime about violence, aggression, power.

Men rape women out of aggressive motivation. That does not mean it's not sexually motivated. They find violence sexually arousing. The link is what is dangerous.[27]

This perspective can be useful for literary analysis, too, since rape is often a device used by Chaucer where our reading of the rape seems invited not to focus on a forced sexual act and a woman's pain, but rather on a male seizing of power, a reordering of social class relations, a disempowering of the victim (or her possessor), or an act of desecration of some institution the woman represents. And, the "link" between rape and its metaphoric equivalent is crucially interesting or "dangerous," because here we allow for a woman's lived experience to flicker between foreground and background in our readings.

Rape = Not-Rape:
The Historical Chaucer and Rape

Significantly, one of Chaucer's few uses of the word "rape," from the Middle English "rapen" (also used in the tale of the Canon's Yeoman and *Troilus,* IV, 596), in his works is a metaphoric one. In "Chaucer's Wordes unto Adam, His Owne Scriveyn," the poet excoriates his scribe for making mistakes in copying and misrepresenting on the manuscript page what the author had composed:

But after my makyng thow wryte more trewe;
So oft adaye I mot thy werk renewe,
It to correct and eke to rubbe and scrape,
And al is throrugh thy negligence and rape. (4–8)

In this short lyric, the text he composes is "raped" by the negligence of the scribe's miswriting his words, and rape here can be a figure for assault upon the female text with the "pen" of the scribe. A poet, when assuming the feminized position of openness to being acted violently upon, is as vulnerable to rape as a woman. Or, his property, the text, is violated by another man, reminiscent of the homosocial violations such as those in *The Reeve's Tale, The Physician's Tale, The Franklin's Tale, The Manciple's Tale* and *The Melibee,* as I argue further on in this essay.

In her introductory chapter of *Chaucer's Sexual Poetics,* discussing "Adam, His Owne Scriveyn," Carolyn Dinshaw convincingly analyzes the gendered and connected acts of rape, writing, and poetry-making, with the poet depicting the text as feminized and the author as performing "an act upon a body construed as feminine" (9).[28] Yet, as Dinshaw points out, the feminine position, that of the "raped" one, can also be seen to be occupied by Chaucer himself, as well as his text and his scribe:

> Whoever exerts control of signification, of language and the literary act, is associated with the masculine in patriarchal society—but that position can be seen to be occupied by both Chaucer and the scribe, and, in turn, the feminine is assumed as well by both characters. Adam, writer of a fallen letter, is associated with Eve (with his "long lokkes") and is feminized in relation to the "maker" Chaucer; but Chaucer, in turn, represents himself as the victim of scribal rape: his text, his work, his intent are violated by the pen of the scribe. . . . [I]t is such a positioning of himself as feminine, in fact, his extraordinary and difficult attempts to envision fully the place of the Other in patriarchal society—to imagine even the pleasures and pains of a woman's body, . . . that motivate, to a large extent, Chaucer's thematic concerns as well as the very forms and structures of his poetry. (10)

Dinshaw's argument points out the irony of the poet as raped and rapist, as assuming both masculine and feminine functions,[29] and she goes on to make the important distinction between *figurative* rapes and *real* rapes (11) or what Gayle Margherita has named "textual fantasy and material reality."[30]

> . . . it keeps in front of us the *difference* between literary activity and sexual violation. To equate reading with rape would be to underestimate drastically the transgressive reality of rape, on the one hand, and to slight the potentially positive value of literary interpretation on the other. (Dinshaw, 11)

What Dinshaw highlights here lies at the heart of this essay and is the model of feminist reading that seems to me most profitable: Readers attuned to Chaucer's use of rape must simultaneously hold *figurative* and *real* rape in their minds. It is the dialectic between the literary and the material that adds complexity to our response and power to the poetry and celebrates our own augmented powers as readers attuned to what the text includes and excludes. But this inscription-yet-elision of rape is central to the difficulties of understanding Chaucer's relation to rape. If we read and focus on rape where the text elides it, it is not to privilege the victimization of women, or to valorize it over other aspects of the tale, but to appreciate the significance of what is *there* in the text before us, and in the society that produced such documents.

Chaucer's repeated and multifaceted representation of rape as a major plot vehicle causes particular critical challenges and a certain unease, and this unease frequently evinces itself in the classroom when one begins to demonstrate to students how pervasive is the *topos* of rape and how various the questions it raises about Chaucer's work. Is Chaucer passively adopting a popular literary device and thereby acquiescing to the misogyny of his age, or, alternatively, is his investigation of rape an exploration and exposure of that misogyny? What audience, what socio-political values might Chaucer's treatment of this topic imply? Is rape treated with ambiguity by Chaucer because of private anxiety, because of personal history, or because of his ongoing poetic concern with doubleness of perspective, and finally with his failure to commit explicitly to a moral stance? Can we propose that Chaucer uses rape as a particular kind of border, a powerful literary event, a trope for his own literary transgressions? Is rape an act of "indifference," eliding the feminine and erasing gender difference, and really concerns men's relationships, as Dinshaw has argued?[31] Can we locate our own discomfiture with loving the art, but finding the artist's ideology unpalatable? Does literary genre determine textual representation of sexual violence?

On May 1, 1380, Geoffrey Chaucer was released from all legal consequences of his "raptus" of Cecily Chaumpaigne. Chaumpaigne signed a document releasing Geoffrey Chaucer from "actions of any kind either concerning my rape or any other matter."[32] This historical event has often been dismissed in the past as irrelevant to our understanding of Chaucer's work. Critics have balked at the possibility that Chaucer could have been involved in such a sordid episode as rape, and many have translated the elastic medieval legal term "raptus" as "abduction." Indeed, as Cannon, Kelly, Gravdal, and Hanawalt[33] have shown, the archaeology and praxis of this term presents a distinct hermeneutic problem for medievalists attempting to interpret not only this Chaucerian event, but any mentions of rape in medieval legal documents. Derek Pearsall's recent excursion on the Cecily Chaumpaigne business in *The Life of Geoffrey Chaucer* indicates that the accusation of "raptus" by Chaumpaigne, despite Pearsall's agreement that the charge referred to in the document was "indeed one of rape," likely represented an excuse to extort money from Chaucer.[34] Furthermore, the consensus among earlier critics has been that whether "*raptus*" meant forced intercourse or abduction, the accusation of Chaucer of real violence perpetrated upon a real female is so shrouded in mystery and ambiguity that it might just as well be ignored or dismissed. Gail Margherita accuses these "traditional Chaucerians" of rejecting the notion of Chaucer's actual sexual violence by their waffling about how hard rape is to prove, "because, legally speaking, it depends so much on attitude—that is, on particular configurations of intention on the rapist's part and consent, or lack thereof, on the victim's part."[35] Margherita cites a roster of famous Chaucerians (all male), D. S. Brewer, Donald Howard, John Gardner, who, like Pearsall, find the idea of Chaucer as a rapist "unimaginable."[36] It is ironic, though not unexpected, that those "traditional Chaucerians" who gloss over the author as not likely to have been a rapist would also fail to engage in any significant way with the implications of sexual violence in the texts of his works. But, however ambiguous and disregarded by Chaucer critics, rape—considered in its broadest sense, a violation—"*raptus*"—of the female by the male—plays a central role in Chaucerian narratives.

Meanwhile, it is impossible to avoid the suggestion of a connection between literary and actual historical violence against women. Texts have consequences, it is crucial to remember, as Jill Mann notes:

> . . . literature is not only produced, but it produces—that it is precisely in its imaginative engagement with the ideologies and myths of contemporary society that it can make a contribution to the formations of new social conditions. (xi)

Reading rape as not-rape, reading around the rape of Chaucer's female characters, can produce in male and female readers a climate of acceptance of rape, such as may have existed in fourteenth-century England, while the discourse that invalidates its violence on the body validates it as a trope.[37] A discourse that transmutes rape to metaphor has the potential to desensitize its audience to the ordinary response to rape that the bodies of the women readers might register, and to foster a system that legitimizes rape as the means of oppression, as the means to enforce and perpetuate male "maistrye" over women's bodies. Reading rape in Chaucer, then, can be a way to sensitize our students and to help effect social change at the level of the word. Perhaps I am naïve to think that if in some way we teach rape in texts where it is used as a trope—if we focus on the nexus between *literary* and *actual* rape embedded in the metaphor—that we might over time spawn a society that encourages fewer rapists, where rape is not a code for another agenda, where it is not a vehicle for oppression or mastery.[38] Our frequent inability to perceive the violence of rape is embedded not just in literary texts, but in law, social structure, and in the linguistic nature of the terminology used to describe medieval rape, in the fabric of language itself.

Rape = Revelation:
Reading Chaucer's Rape-tales

When one begins to tot up the representations of rape and sexual violence as a method of the control of women in Chaucer's works, it becomes clear

that his use of this plot vehicle is astonishingly prevalent and varied, including: the enforced marriage of the virginal Emelye in *The Knight's Tale,*
the attempted rape of Custance in *The Man of Law's Tale,* the bestial double rape of mother and daughter in *The Reeve's Tale* (mentioned above), the
virtual purchasing of a young wife by a hideous old man in *The Merchant's
Tale* (and the ensuing ugliness of the wedding night), the averted rape (at
the cost of her life) of Virginia in *The Physician's Tale,* the brutal assault on
Melibee's wife and daughter in *The Tale of Melibee,* the threat of the rape
of Dorigen in *The Franklin's Tale,* the murder of the adulterous woman in
The Manciple's Tale, the traffic in women that underlies *Troilus and Criseyde,*
the rapes of Lucrece and Philomel retold in *The Legend of Good Women,*
and, perhaps most memorably, the gratuitous rape of the peasant woman as
the motive for all the action in *The Wife of Bath's Tale.* Yet for all these instances of rape, I would argue that none of the tales (and few critical readings) takes significant account of rape's effect on a real woman as she
reads.[39] But we must grapple with Chaucer's choice of such a topic—a
most fearful matter for women in their real lives—as in some way informing his fiction and his poetics. I doubt we should deem the proliferation of
rapes in Chaucerian narratives a cornucopia of coincidence.

Critics regularly engage in examining Chaucer's attitude(s) towards
the power of women in his poetry.[40] The more I explore the alarming
occurrence of rape and violence against women in his works, the more
convinced I become that one of the solutions to the problem of
"woman" as Chaucer explored it *was* rape. In the works, where rape occurs or threatens, the women in question are in some sense "solved": they
are silenced, disempowered, put out of the way. The question of "What
do women want?" voiced in *The Wife of Bath's Tale* is answered in many
of Chaucer's works by: "They want too much; they are too hard to control; they may want male power." In Chaucer's fiction, rape (forced
coitus) or murder/violence (and I conflate the terms here as they were
conflated in the medieval "raptus") against women are vehicles his narrators use or report for keeping women characters in line.[41]

Chaucer inherited and was schooled in reading practices that read rape
allegorically or metaphorically. Yet, he often seems to step right up to the
problem of representing actual rape, but then displaces it, evincing some
tension about its depiction, a tension Corrine Saunders sees akin to the
Wife of Bath's being "born beneath both Venus and Mars."[42] Chaucer may
call the stereotypes of misogyny into question even while his works cannot entirely escape the influence of the dominant and pervasive view of
women as possessions, inferior, though dangerous. But, I think we must
tread carefully here. Representation of an act of rape by a male author does
not constitute valorization of that act or of patriarchal ideology, but may,

in fact, offer the possibility of subversion or critique.[43] At times Chaucer might provide a subversive, double, ambiguous, even androgynous perspective. He does seem to explore the female experience, as we see Dinshaw asserting in the quotation (above) on Chaucer's gendered language (10). He may be acknowledging female speech and desire even as he questions the misogynistic stance. Still, one cannot help finding in Chaucer's work a concomitant showcasing of women's victimization and silencing. Elizabeth Robertson, for example, while acknowledging the events in Chaucer's works as literal rapes, says that Chaucer, in the Ovidian tradition, utilizes rape for its power of transformation and for its ability to represent the strengths and limits of art as a force for social criticism.[44] Through his characters and narrators, particularly in *Canterbury Tales, Troilus,* and *The Legend of Good Women,* Chaucer rehearses much of the common stock of misogynistic lore that he inherited from classical and patristic sources, from Ovid to *The Romance of the Rose.* However, when Chaucer the male poet gives female characters speeches in which they discuss gender using the masculine discourse of misogyny, he displaces language and gender in a slippery manner. Such a displacement, to Irigaray and to Shoshona Felman, poses a question of agency and subjectivity. Felman's query "Who is speaking here?" reminds us of Irigaray's notion of the absence of a female-generated language, a lack that forces women to use the language of men. Irigaray argues that such a male discourse is transformed as it passes through the female body. The gender of the speaker does matter, then, when a male poet voices a female character's performance. Speeches of such characters as the Wife of Bath, the Shipman, the Merchant, Melibeus, and others, highlight the problem of what a deceitful and wicked creature "woman" is, and what is to be done about her. In the context of Chaucerian fiction, one of the things that is to be done about woman is to rape her. But it makes a difference when the words of misogyny are spoken by a woman character aping male discourse, quoting authorities that run counter to the lived experience of the female audience/readers and characters alike, as the Wife does in her Prologue.

Thus, for me, Chaucer uses rape in complicated ways. Because of the proliferation of rapes or near-rapes in his works, readers must both focus on rape, since it is so prevalent in his works, yet read around the rapes, inasmuch as the poetic constructs or genres and narrative directions do not point to the narratives being *about* rape at all. Rape acts as a figure for agendas other than sexual: property crimes, homosocial interaction, acts of war, or religious evil. Consequently, rape or gender violence in Chaucer's works can be cast as a transformative act, and, it might be argued, a way for the court poet to voice social criticism. But my point remains that even reading around the rape to find a further implication and meaning for the text, or perhaps to revel in the pleasure of the text, we cannot afford to forget the gender violence aestheticized and encoded in the trope.

In order to make more tangible some of the preceding remarks, I next delve into a selection of Chaucer's rape-tales, focusing on the moments of sexual violence and the troping that occludes it. I exclude the rapes of Lucrece and Philomel from further discussion in this catalog of rape-tales, since they do not present the same critical history of being read as not-rapes. The tales of Philomel and Lucrece that Chaucer inherited from his sources, and his redactions of the sources in *The Legend of Good Women*, sympathetically focus on the violated female "martirs," as he styles them. Because I am stressing in this essay those rapes elided, obfuscated, and troped, I want only to mention Lucrece and Philomel's stories as of course being about sexual violence to women, but set aside these pieces for another discussion. It does strike me, however, that the rape of Lucrece is linguistically elided by Chaucer, the actual act skipped over and merely alluded to (in *The Legend of Good Women*, 1818–25); and in Philomel's story, the punishment of the rapist Tereus (eating his own child cooked by Procne) is effaced from the tale by Chaucer in order to focus on the woe of the victim and her sister. So, Chaucer still uses rape as a locus for uneasiness with the text he reads and within the one he creates.[45]

The most egregious erasure of rape occurs in the tale the Wife of Bath tells. The knight, through raping the peasant maiden at the outset of the tale ("He saugh a mayde walkynge hym biforn, / Of which mayde anon, maugree hir heed, / By verray force, he rafte hire maydenhed" [886–88]) learns through the course of the tale about gentility and about a utopian social order in which class and gender do not determine dominance. The hag he is forced to marry lectures him on those fine points of ethics of which he seems ignorant: "Thanne am I gentil, whan that I bigynne / To lyven vertuously, and weyve synne" (1175–76). For the knight, rape becomes a transformative act: "Me lady and my love, and wyf so deere, / I put me in youre wise governance" (1230–31); he becomes willing to let the woman have mastery ("maistrye"). The hag herself, though, reflecting one sort of medieval perspective on rape, might be said to *misread* and deflect the rape of the peasant maid, as she addresses the knight-rapist on offenses against class, on lack of gentilesse, on poverty, not on gender violence, lack of consent, and the value of women's bodies. He learns a lesson about Christian ethics and class divisions, and what it might mean to be forced to have sex without desire (rape), not about the moral consequences of raping and violence. Of course, one might argue, the knight's transgression was simultaneously against the class *and* the gender of the peasant woman; he felt free to oppress her by any means or whim of his own upper-class male privilege. So, from this perspective, all is doubleness,

READING CHAUCER READING RAPE 37

and rape is not-rape, but rather a trope for schooling the knight in the "gentilesse" appropriate to his position. Too, he may have learned that he can (ab)use a woman's body—rape her—legally in marriage, rather than needing to force his pleasure by the roadside, as the hag's pressing him to pay his "marriage debt" might suggest.

In her recent discussion of the rape in the tale, Corrine Saunders argues convincingly for the detailed, technical legal realism that Chaucer incorporates into the Arthurian backdrop of the tale, which serves to accentuate the overlooking of the victim:

> The duality and changing history of the law of raptus, where real rape is often silenced, seems to underlie the Wife's—and indeed Chaucer's—treatment of rape and the silencing of the victim in the tale.[46]

Saunders sees romance triumphing over rape, but the tale remains "ambiguous" (130), achieving two ends simultaneously: exploring minutely the crime and the problem of rape and its legal confusions, while affirming patriarchal values:

> The tension created by these two interwoven strands of the tale reflects neatly the complexity of the fiction of the Wife of Bath herself, a figure who perceives clearly the problems of a patriarchal world yet ultimately revels within this world, alternatively angered and intrigued by the male overpowering of women which the crime of rape represents. (131)

Laurie Finke's argument similarly reveals the ways in which rape is elided, in another fine reading of the sexual violence in the Wife's tale, "that the primary function of the transformations that structure the Wife's tale is to mystify the sexual violence required as marriage is transformed to serve a money economy, not a land-based one."[47]

Perhaps an earlier reader of Chaucer was intrigued by the nullification of the rape, too. In 1700, John Dryden reworked the Wife's tale as "The Wife of Bath Her Tale," putting an illuminating spin on the sexual violence of the tale.[48] Where Chaucer's tale elides the raped maiden, who appears only as the impetus for the tale at its outset, Dryden's ravished peasant maiden in some ways permeates the tale in three telling additions to Chaucer's version. She is first depicted as horseflesh in the gaze of the knight before he rapes her:

> Soon on the girl he cast an amorous Eye,
> So strait she walk'd, and on her Pasterns high:
> If seeing her behind he lik'd her Pace,
> Now turning short he better lik'd her Face. (Dryden, ll. 51–54)

Chaucer's narrator ignores the violated damsel after the beginning of the action of the tale; we never see or hear of her again. In Dryden's rendition, after the rape, the hue and cry proceed with the weeping maiden to the court of Arthur, where her outraged virtue seemingly will get a fair hearing: "Mov'd by the Damsel's tears and common Cry, / He [Arthur] doomed the brutal Ravisher to die" (ll. 71–72). Nevertheless, the ladies of the court betray sisterhood and the maiden's cause by praying hard for mercy for the knight, and Dryden shows Geneura and her women "who thought it much a Man should die for Love"(l. 78), not wanting the knight to suffer chastisement. This alarming elision of the rape by the ladies of the court in front of the damsel and her community posse, and Dryden's emphasis on what Chaucer does not say (Chaucer's lines are: "that the queene and other ladyes mo / So long preyeden the kyng of grace / Til he his lyf hym graunted in the place" [895–96]) shows that the later poet works pointedly reading rape back into Chaucer's tale. Chaucer's ladies may recognize the wrong of rape, even as they want mercy for the knight, but they do not trope it as "love" as Dryden's courtiers ironically do. In front of the court, and ignoring the cries of the raped maiden, his ladies and queen "join'd in close Debate / (Covering their Kindness with dissembled Hate;) / If not to free him, to prolong his Fate" (11. 79–81). The betrayal of the peasant woman's violation and her right to the justice that the law in the poem stipulates (death) is exacerbated in Dryden's poem, where class solidarity and courtly good manners reign. The ladies don't think it such a terrible offense. Chaucer's tale hastily moves away from the rape and the court to the knight's adventures finding out what "wommen moost desiren."

Towards the end of the tale, Dryden's hag's lecture sharply recapitulates the rape of the maiden, and repudiates those who might have forgotten the reason for the whole adventure, including perhaps the knight. The damsel is seemingly brought onstage again. The hag in this rendition scolds the knight for his reluctance to engage in sexual congress with her, "When you my ravish'd Predecessor saw, / You were not then become this Man of Straw; / Had you been such, you might have scap'd the Law" (ll. 348–50), reminding us of how it all began, in male sexual selfishness and brutality, and putting a finger squarely on the narrative instability of this unresolved issue in Chaucer's poem, which his Wife and her hag abandon for other agendas, such as class pretensions and gentility in Christian terms. The hag's speech in Dryden's interestingly circular tale, however, draws attention to the knight's potential for sexual violence. The knight's punishment (and education) becomes reconnected with his crime. While Dryden's courtly ladies may trope the action of rape to "love," his tale emphasizes the two ways of reading rape (rape and not-rape), and uncomfortably forbids the veiled literary/figurative sense from triumphing completely, even though the tale ends as Chaucer's does, in the transformation of the hag and the blissful union of the two as a result of the hag/wife's genteel and masterful Boethian rhetoric. Dryden's version, bringing the assaulted maiden in from the margins of the tale, serves as an interesting reading of Chaucer, making it clear that the rape is central to the tale. This sexual violence and its reinscription and acceptance as simply the courtly way of life marks a crucial interpretation of Chaucer's text (and his own eighteenth-century milieu) by Dryden, even though the hag commodifies herself to this system at the end, and in fact becomes a member of that very court.

When Jill Mann reads Chaucer's tale, she construes the knight's punishment in the Wife's tale as "an educative process which will eradicate the male mentality that produced the crime," and she traces the knight's subsequent "feminization," even to the turnabout of a forced marriage, which Mann calls "a fantasy realization of rape-in-reverse."[49] I am not as sanguine about the fantasy of the reform of the rapist, and find that Chaucer's tale glosses over the rape to get to other issues that needed airing in the fictive society of the Wife's tale, and perhaps in his society as well.

In *The Reeve's Tale,* the rape epitomized in the quotation beginning this essay, rape is transformative too. Rape generates multiple transformations in the tale that then disturbingly eclipse the brutality of rape itself. There seems a level playing-field at the end; all characters' violence and trickery seem weighted equally, and rape is turned away from. Sympkyn the miller's dominance is transformed to subservience—the students' cleverness proves superior to his wiles and social pretensions. The daughter's marketability as a virgin is transformed; the wife, by being raped, becomes an adulteress, a shared woman, albeit initially unwilling. The tale, long recognized as an angry, ugly, and violent narrative performance, but read too as an amusing fabliau of male-fantasy and revenge by the Reeve upon the Miller of the *General Prologue,* enacts a double rape, of mother and daughter, by the two students, John and Aleyn, who come to have their meal ground at the avaricious miller Sympkyn's establishment. This rape is interpreted by the narrator in his concluding remarks as the students' "quyting" of the miller for his own greedy actions in skimming meal from his customer's sacks, rape for rapacity, in the passage quoted near the beginning of this essay ("Thus is the proude millere wel ybete," ff., ll. 4313–18). The stealing of the corn meal is commensurate in the narrative with the triple violence to the Miller: his paying for the supper of the clerks, being beaten, and the rapes of his wife and virgin daughter. Rape here is just one aspect of the revenge between men. No joy or music alleviate the grim sexual mayhem of this tale, unlike the happy eroticism characterizing another sexual union between a wife and an outsider in *The Miller's Tale,* which precedes it: "Ther was the revel and the melodye" (MT 3652). In this sexual assault/congress between the

students and the mother and daughter, there is no desire (except for material gain), no gazing (a feature of its closest analog). With a wonderful stroke
of poetic rightness, Chaucer sets the action of this part of the tale entirely
in the dark. As Derek Pearsall observes, "The story has been deliberately
emptied of that movement of affection, that tingling of sexual desire, that is
present in the closest analog . . . 'Le meunier et les ii clers.' . . . The coupling
is that of animals."[50] Additionally, a baby sleeps in a cradle in the center of
all the raping and beatings, so the further threat of violence to the child
hangs over the tale, yoked to the comic fabliau slapstick trappings.

Even so, there is an alarming absence of harm in the narrator's recounting of the rape. We note that the women are dispatched by the narrator—the daughter found "That it had been to late for to crie / And
shortly for to seyn, they were aton" (4196–97) and the mother: "And on
this good wyf he leith on soore / So mury a fit ne hadde she nat ful yoore;
/ He priketh harde and depe as he were mad . . ." (4230–33). Here rape is
not-rape again, transformed by its troping nature into fun for the men,
while the women are silent (and therefore content or at least complicit?).
The Reeve-narrator demonstrates indeed that rape is not the issue here; it
is the revenge that counts. Malyne the daughter even helps the clerks filch
a loaf her father made from the clerks' own stolen meal, and she wistfully
bids Aleyn adieu the morning after her defloration: "'And, goode lemman,
God thee save and kepe!' / And with that word almoost she gan to wepe"
(The Reeve's Tale, 4247–48).[51] The narrative voice of the Reeve betrays a
male-fantasy rape like that articulated in the old French lyric "La Clef
d'Amours": The act "pleases her greatly when someone takes her against
her will, regardless of how it comes about. A maiden suddenly ravished has
great joy, no matter what she says" (trans. Gravdal, 5). The victim enjoyed
it and is in love with her rapist, sad for him to leave. Rape narratives do
turn to romances! But, Chaucer's tale reveals the brutality of the romance,
a kind of tit-for-tat justice meted out by the students upon the miller. His
class pretensions, represented by his consciousness of his wife's claims to
some degree of gentility, and the advantageous marriage he aspires to effect in return for his daughter's virginity are both exploded through the
rapes by John and Aleyn. The students can't, of course, rape Sympkyn the
miller—and in any case that would not follow acceptable patriarchal literary revenge in the fabliau. Rape has become, in The Reeve's Tale, a crime
of property and class warfare—women, like corn, are property, and the
limits of the genre and tone allow us neither to focus on the women nor
the violence. The gaze is deflected from the suffering bodies of women to
the problems of men. Yet, rape remains rape, existing in what Gail
Margherita calls a "symbiotic relationship" (4) with the literary fantasy of
homosocial revenge.

The Merchant tells a different story of rape: the tale of January's (what to a modern reader is clearly) "rape" of May under the legal aegis of their marriage. The tale advances from a mock-romance to a kind of fabliau involving January's subsequent cuckolding and loss of mastery. Like *The Reeve's Tale*, *The Merchant's Tale* has at its heart a repulsive (but amusing) scene of rape. January's possessing of May after virtually purchasing her for his pleasure provides one of the most ghastly scenes of a wedding night in literature. In a finely balanced and tremendously memorable poetic passage, we witness January's distasteful aged lust and his subsequent ridiculous glory in his possession of the delectable May. Concomitantly, but in a darker key, we also behold May's docile acceptance of his abhorrent amorous advances and her mental distance from them. It is well worth quoting from the joyless bedroom scene:

And Januarie hath faste in armes take
His fresshe May, his paradys, his make.
He lulleth hire, he kisseth hire ful ofte;
With thikke brustles of his berd unsofte,
Lyk to the skyn of houndfyssh, sharp as brere—
For he was shave al newe in his manere—
He rubbeth hire aboute hir tendre face,
And seyde thus, "Allas! I moot trespace
To yow, my spouse, and yow greetly offende,
Er tyme come that I wil doun descende."
. . . .
Thus laboureth he til that the daye gan dawe;
And thanne he taketh a soppe in fyn claree,
And upright in his bed thanne sitteth he,
And after that he sang ful loude and cleere,
And kiste his wyf, and made wantown cheere.
He was al coltissh, ful of ragerye,
And ful of jargon as a flekked pye.
The slakke skyn aboute his nekke shaketh,
Whil that he sang, so chaunteth he and craketh.
But God woot what that May thoughte in hir herte,
Whan she hym saugh up sittynge in his sherte,
In his nyght-cappe, and with his nekke lene;
She preyseth nat his pleyyng worth a bene. (MerT 1820–54)

May says nothing, though she "preyseth nat his pleyyng worth a bene" (1854), and she later coolly proceeds to cuckold the blinded knight January with Damian the squire in a crude and seemingly pleasureless revenge demanded by the genre.[52]

And sodeynly anon this Damyan
Gan pullen up the smok, and in he throng. (2352–53)

The justice meted out to January by May through her adultery and deceptive words about his seeing falsely: "Ye han som glymsyng, and no parfit
sighte" (2383) is, in terms of the tale, fair reprisal for the unnatural act of an
old husband desiring a young wife, procuring her, and inflicting his horrible body upon her. Shimmering in the background as the vehicle for May's
giving the newly sighted January her glib and shrewish answer about her
treetop coitus with Damian, lies the goddess Proserpine, herself an abducted
rape-victim and now wife of Pluto her rapist, with whom she wrangles for
mastery over the ensuing scene of human cuckolding. When Pluto vows to
give January his sight back in order that he may gaze upon what offense to
his property rights May and Damian perpetrate, Proserpine gives May the
gift of confounding January with words, as if to compensate for her loss of
innocence and her lack of power over her state as chattel.

I again turn to Mann for a compelling reading of this tale, where she
argues that May's shrewishness comes as a "relief" (69) for the reader, but
I would insist, rather, that the narrator *solves* May by transforming her into
his available misogynistic stereotype of the shrew and turns our attention
away from the inscription of the rape. Yet this (dis)solving of May does not
come before we have glimpsed what it might mean for a young girl to
marry—even willingly—such a materialistic old man. Mann presents us
with an unsentimental, hard, jaded May, who has in a way taken us in with
her silence and passivity. She reads backwards from May's take-charge actions in the *hortus conclusus* to characterize her motives as selfish from the
earliest days of the marriage contract. Consequently, Mann says, when May
does speak and act it is with vulgarity (throwing her love-letter in the
privy) and selfishness and opportunism. Mann cautions us of the dangers
of our own responses on our first glimpse of May in the marriage-bed that
patronize her as a helpless victim when she can manage quite well, thank
you, without our sympathy (69).

There is a good deal that feels right about this interpretation, yet I cannot countenance reducing the scene quoted above. The coupling of January and May seems a supreme poetic instance of the disguise of rape as
romance and marriage as rape, with the double quality of the vision apparent in the doubleness of the responses of January and May, and of modern readers who do feel badly for May's predicament, but who might see
some possibilities in Mann's point too. Here Mann, like the male narrator
and those "traditional Chaucerians," mentioned earlier, uncomfortably
elides the evidence of rape that some readers of the tale do see, obviating
it for the more "important" matters in the tale, mainly the fabliau turn-

about ending, which the narrative emphasizes. The distinct comparison that the text invites between Proserpine and May as rape victims is exploded by Mann's reading them as ironic visions of two kinds of women, both of whom turn to opportunism and battle-of-the-sexes style rhetoric as a defense against male aggression. The tale, however, presents not only a story of come-uppance in the battle of the sexes and a turnabout between men of different social degree: The Merchant's tale is a story of traffic in powerless women, of rape encompassing and defining both heavenly and earthly relations between the sexes, and of marriage as legalized rape, inscribed in the heavens and enacted on earth.

The thwarted rape of Custance in *The Man of Law's Tale* results in her further identification as the ideal passive, faithful, and "feminized" Christian whom the Blessed Virgin Mary assists in her need, even while the narrator reasserts the power of the patriarchy in the end. In the tale, the attempted rape of Custance is couched in language suggesting that the false Christian steward attacks Custance, alone on her second rudderless boat voyage, intending to rape her, not because of her youth or beauty, but because of his antipathy to Christian virtue and his "foule lust of luxurie" (925):

> A theef, that hadde reneyed oure creance,
> Cam into ship allone, and seyde he sholde
> Hir lemman be, wher-so she wolde or nolde.
>
> Wo was this wrecched womman tho bigon;
> Hir child cride, and she cride pitously.
> But blisful Marie heelp hire right anon;
> For with hir struglyng wel and myghtily
> The theef fil over bord al sodeynly,
> And in the see he dreynte for vengeance;
> And thus hath Crist unwemmed kept Custance. (915–24)

Custance, an emblem of the Church or of Christian humility and its feminization in the tale, is assailed by a threat to her sinlessness, her Christianity, by the infidel. When she repulses him and remains "unwemmed" through the help of the Virgin Mary, the rapist is dispatched by heaven's aid, which tumbles him overboard. Chaucer uses the guise of sexual violence here allegorically to demonstrate temptation to sin assailing the Church or the faithful and offers an opportunity for his readers to see that sin punished on earth by the force of Custance's passive feminine faith (925–45). Notwithstanding, we should not forget that earlier in the tale Custance is given away by her father, despite her pleas to the contrary, to marry a stranger in a strange and infidel land, another act of patriarchal privilege over her desire, leading to her violation. While she escapes from rape in the scene quoted above, she is nevertheless handed from man to man. A tale of Christian piety is implicitly a tale of the exchange of women, with the potential for rape. After the death of her husband Alla, Custance finally returns to her father, in an odd echo of the tale's remote source in stories of incest, a topic that Chaucer's narrator pointedly eschews discussing.[53] One of Custance's most piteous speeches occurs at the end of her boating days when she begs her father the Emperor at their reunion please not to dispose of her against her will again:

> It am I, fader, that in the salte see
> Was put allone and dampned for to dye.
> Now goode fader, mercy I yow crye!
> Sende me namoore unto noon hethenesse,
> But thonketh my lord heere of his kyndenesse. (1109–13)

So, while *The Man of Law's Tale* can be, among other things, read as an exemplum of Christian piety, it presents also a tale of rape and the exercise of patriarchal privilege over the female body, as Custance complains: "Wommen are born to thraldom and penance, / And to been under mannes governance" (286–87).

Two other tales, those of the Physician and the Manciple, contain not rapes, but the murder of women, a variant of the violence of rape, connected to gender and to an overpowering male impulse to punish sexual acts offensive to male possessors' power. Both tales concern "raptus" and sexual control of women's bodies. Both tales solve the threat women's sexuality represents through murdering the women.

The honor of the knight Virginius in *The Physician's Tale,* for example, is sullied by the lust of the judge Apius for his daughter Virginia. This affront to patriarchy results in the father asserting his right over his daughter's body and killing her a virgin—with her consent to her own death couched as obedience to the father's will—rather than have her body taken forcibly by another man. Virginius chooses to murder his daughter over losing his property through the "rape" of another more powerful man. In this overt, even ridiculous, depiction of female children as property, the threat of rape transforms Virginia into a martyr for chastity, for male values and for obedience to them, and for her father's property rights. R. Howard Bloch, applying patristic texts about virginity to the events of the tale, argues compellingly that Virginia was raped the instant Apius gazed upon her, since that gaze constituted for the Church Fathers a figurative rape.[54] Thus, she "is deflowered from the moment she crosses paths with Apius. . . ." "The shame that Virginius offers to his daughter as an alternative to death has already occurred in the moment that Virginia is per-

ceived" (118). Furthermore, Bloch stresses that given the discourse surrounding virginity in the early and medieval Church, Chaucer too, is complicit in the despoliation of Virginia, since he "does to the characters
exactly what Apius, under the guise of fiction, does to Virginia. He deflowers at the very instant he depicts." Chaucer's excessive praise for her
violates the virgin (123–24).[55] And, tellingly, in a classic blame-the-victim
speech host Harry Bailly, after hearing the tale, laments "Hire beautee was
hire deth, I far wel sayn" [VI (C) 297)]. Multiple agents are involved in raping Virginia in this tale, a rape elided when male honor and fatherly ownership of a daughter's maidenhead take narrative precedence.

In *The Manciple's Tale,* the murder of Phebus's wife for cuckolding him
with a man of low degree signals what the narrator relates as the whole
point of the story: how the crow—here a figure for Woman, often associated in Chaucer's works with saying too much—because of its uncon-
trolled language, was deprived of its voice and splendid white plumage.
The crow can figure the poet, too, liable at any time to be deprived of his
voice for offending his patron or telling an unvarnished truth that others
do not wish to hear. And of course, as a cuckold, the Phoebus/poet character already is connected linguistically with birds. According to the narrator, the woman and the bird, both property of Phoebus in the tale, seek
to act according to their animal natures. The silent adulterous woman is
dispatched by Phoebus's arrow; the talkative captive bird is figuratively
raped—transformed into a dark squawking creature without words, cast
out into the darkness, but significantly, no longer caged. The man/god of
song and light has turned into a beast because of his rashness and violence.
The life of the tale, too, is transformed from talk, music, and light to silence, injury, deprivation, sorrow, and darkness, while through the male
narrator, his mother's complicated and otiose moralizing at the end focuses
on controlling speech, not on controlling women's sexuality or restraining
male violence. Yet Phoebus laments the death aloud, "O deer wyf! O
gemme of lustiheed! / That were to me so sad and eke so trewe" (274–75).
We cannot forget his brutal impulse, despite the narrator's garrulous displacement of it.

Displaced too, are some elements of Chaucer's Ovidian source (*Metamorphoses,* Bk. 2) an awareness of which complicates the reading of the tale
and its gender violence. In Ovid's story of Apollo and Coronis, it is the
raven's [*corvus*] plumage that changes from white to black.[56] Within the
raven's story is embedded the tale of the crow's [*cornix*] downfall, as she
tries to warn the raven not to tattle to Apollo of his Coronis's unfaithfulness. The crow, it seems, was expelled from its position as Minerva's attendant and demoted to a lower rank for rash speech. But, more important
regarding Chaucer's treatment of the tale, the crow was once a king's

daughter, pursued by Neptune who wished to ravish her. As she ran from her god-rapist, she prayed to Pallas and was metamorphosed into a crow, flying away to be Minerva's attendant, a virgin, spotless white within her black feathers. The raven, in Ovid's telling, scoffs at the crow's admonition against rash speech, and proceeds to inform Apollo of his lover's perfidy. As Apollo kills Coronis from sexual jealousy, with her dying breath she tells him she bears his child. The raven is thereafter cursed forever by Apollo with blackness for its officiousness. Chaucer's Manciple's treatment of this tale, in conflating the two birds, bears scrutiny, as the crow/rapable maiden is combined with the raven who won't take good advice about loose speech. Chaucer chooses the crow for his tattletale rather than Ovid's raven (Chaucer knows a lot about birds, as we have seen in *Parlement of Foules,* so we can't imagine he's at all confused about the species of the two black birds; nor are the terms confusing in Latin). What this choice does, for anyone knowing Ovid, is to highlight the crow *as* female victim, and carries with it the undertones of a tale of rape. In his economic and highly complex version of Ovid's story, Chaucer allows us to interpret the crow as a woman (despite the masculine pronouns assigned to the bird), rescued from rape only to be trapped in avian form, subsequently cast out into darkness, deprived of a voice because she/he cannot refrain from loose speech. Or, the crow can be the male court-poet, a feminized courtier, feminized because he must be silent about his true desires, liable to be handed around like a possession, a pet. The bird-switch from raven to crow in Chaucer's version suggests a background of misogyny, sexual predation, and violence, which is then reenacted in the tale when a woman appears to be violating her possessor's rights.[57]

The Tale of Melibee, too, depicts violence against women resembling that in the Physician's and Manciple's tales. Although Prudence and her daughter at the beginning of the tale are not raped (as in forced coitus), the "olde foes" of Melibeus "betten hys wyf, and wounded his doghter with fyve mortal woundes in fyve sondry places—/ this is to seyn in hir feet, in hire handes, in hir erys, in hir nose and in hire mouth—and leften hire for deed . . ." (l. 960 ff.). This violence must certainly qualify as a form of "raptus" under medieval rape law. The two women have become vehicles for his enemies' revenge against Melibeus, but, ironically, directly after the episode of physical violence inflicted on his women, Melibeus launches on his own misogynistic verbal abuse of womankind and their bad counsel, remonstrating with his wife Prudence: "Alle wommen been wikke, and noon good of hem alle" (1058–59).

The Franklin's Tale, for all its jocular narrator and delicate "demande d'amor" structure, has as its milieu the possible rape of Dorigen by the squire Aurelius—with her husband the knight Arveragus's consent to enforce the act. The tale turns on Dorigen's foolish agreement to become the lover of Aurelius in this tale, made in a rash and bantering promise, during a moment of courtly dalliance and despite her lack of desire for Aurelius and her intention to remain faithful to Arveragus. When her husband insists on the fulfillment of this vow so that he will not lose face in the courtly world of the poem, the rapable body of Dorigen presents a potent backdrop for the tale of male-male exchange. Dorigen's value as property is key to Arveragus's honor; and, no matter how the narrator seems to protest the equality of the two in marriage, it is Arveragus's loss of honor that plagues him, not the sexual violation of his wife. Emotionally, he cautions Dorigen:

> "I yow forbede, up peyne of deeth,
> That nevere, whil thee lasteth lyf ne breeth,
> To no wight tell thou of this aventure—
> As I may best, I wol my woe endure—
> Ne make no contenance of hevynesse,
> That folk of yow may demen harm or gesse." (*The Franklin's Tale*,
>   1480–86)

But, her awareness of her actual situation—possible rape—is lamented by Dorigen in an extended and rhetorically lavish complaint to Fortune, as she, alone and troubled, considers her situation (ll. 1355–1456). While some critics have found this lament otiose, or a digression, in fact the interruption of the poem with a catalogue of raped and rapable women represents Chaucer's acknowledgement of Dorigen's place in the system of traffic in women. She laments that she would rather die than suffer forced coitus, even to please her husband. She sees no way out of the problem the courtly world she lives in has created for women:

> But nathelees, yet have I levere to lese
> My lif than of my body to have a shame,
> Or knowe myselven fals, or lese my name
> And with my death I may be quyt, ywis. (1360–63)

Her knowledge and rehearsal of a long catalogue of actual and potential sexual violence to women underscores her understanding of what is at stake here: her rape. Her lament documents at length stories from the classics of women who commit suicide rather than submit to forcible sex (such as the daughters of Phidon—who drowned themselves escaping violation, or Hasdrubal's wife, etc.), women who commit suicide after being raped (like Lucrece), and a litany of famous faithful wives (including Penelope). However cordial the relationships among the men of the tale,

Dorigen, in sharp contrast to their civility, aligns herself with a cast of chaste characters/predecessors who are victims of real or attempted rape. Her admiration in the lament for faithful wives is particularly ironic in that being faithful to her own husband may entail his compelling her to sexual violation by another man. It is not the faithfulness (and chastity) of Penelope or Valeria, for example, but the standard of faithfulness to male desire for an untarnished public face to which she must sacrifice her body. The lament, nonetheless, focuses our attention on the body of Dorigen, and her desires.

These desires (not to be raped or traded away to Aurelius), alas, become swallowed up during the rest of the tale by the intricate interplay among the men so that each one of them might avoid the dishonor of backing down from the bargain of Aurelius's having sex with her. It is only after the men have worked out among themselves what to do about the violation of Arveragus's honor that the rape of Dorigen through Aurelius's falsehood and hired magic would represent, that Dorigen is restored to Arveragus, unraped. While it all seems to conclude happily, the tale's reader might be perplexed by the Franklin-narrator's question at its finish, "Which was the moost fre, as thynketh yow?" placing interpretive importance on the men's gentility in negotiating to avoid the exchange of a woman for sex, which would damage good-mannered relations between them.

The intended rape in *The Franklin's Tale* represents also an offense of class or "degre," since Aurelius, not yet a knight, transgresses by aspiring to the adulterous favors of the wife of a member of that higher class. Dorigen's forced assent to the squire's "earned" assault, we can be sure, would be most "genteel" in the terms of the tale. The magician, co-conspirator in the rape-plot reminds us of Pandarus in *Troilus* or the churl Claudius in *The Physician's Tale* as he engineers the assault on Dorigen's virtue. And like those men he is engaged in trafficking in women without regard for their desires in the matter. The magician here seems, in imitating the courtly (!) behavior of the other two, to have in fact raised himself somewhat in class. He is ironically their equal in masculine denial of female subjectivity. Resembling what Margaret Atwood calls "running-away-from-rape classics" such as *Clarissa Harlowe, Pamela,* and *Sir Charles Grandison,* the story the Franklin tells exposes the pretensions of social class. Yet, while in those three eighteenth-century novels, the picture of the English gentleman is a tarnished one (in *Grandison,* though, gentlemanly virtue does eventually triumph), in *The Franklin's Tale,* the Franklin-narrator sidetracks us from questions of judging a social class into judging the degree of virtue and good manners each man complicit in the latent rape has exhibited: the one who allows his wife to be used sexually by another man, the one who uses her, or the one who is remunerated to make it all happen. There is no question that each man *is* virtuous in terms of the tale. So the attempted rape becomes a test of male gentility and good manners, and the tale alarmingly stresses the similarity between the husband, the would-be rapist, and the manipulative magician—a similarity between "good" men and bad men that we find also in *The Manciple's Tale* and *Melibee* (and, I might argue, *The Reeve's Tale*). However absorbing the negotiations between the males who vie to possess Dorigen, the issue at hand is still sexual violence against women, coupled with Dorigen's forced silence about her own desires—to die rather than be raped—and submission to her husband's will—all of which the tale neatly elides in its insistence upon the notions of class and gentility of the participating males.

Several other female Chaucerian characters are not actually raped, but subjected to constraint because of their sexuality, such as the Wife of Bath records in her Prologue—although I would argue that such early marriage as she depicts "For, lordynges, sith I twelve yeer was of age . . ."(l. 4) might be construed as rape.[58] So, too, the wife in the *Shipman's Tale,* St. Cecelia of the *Second Nun's Tale,* and Criseyde (whose problematic position as rapable is argued elsewhere in this volume by E. Robertson), still represent the female position as that of pawn and object of male lust, susceptible to being traded away, taken against their will. Their rapes are possible, if not enacted. Like Emelye in *The Knight's Tale* and even the formel eagle in *The Parlement of Foules,* females who are disposed of to men without their desire are objectified in precisely the same way as are those women who are raped. Throughout Chaucer's corpus, and surely echoing his society, women are isolated, handed around from man to man, and male desire predominates, even where female desire/consent is acknowledged or discussed as in the Wife's prologue and tale, *Troilus and Criseyde,* and to some extent in *The Parlement of Foules.* Rape is regularly encoded by Chaucer as part of a larger system of the control of women's bodies.

Despite the foregoing evidence, and whatever his legal history, I want to argue, then, that Chaucer may not necessarily have been preoccupied with the actual act of rape when he created his literary rapes. His use of rape so often in his poetry is integral to the discourse of his own, and to some extent our, cultural inheritance; it objectifies and removes the woman as victim, focusing instead on the empowerment of men and rape as trope, changing it from violence to women to interactions between men. It consistently reveals women's status as property. While there may be good women—Chaucer's narrator can quote "auctorities" to prove this in *The Legend of Good Women*—most of his male characters distrust women for their slippery menacing nature. The long history of the discourse of misogyny itself—to which Chaucer was heir—threatens women with rape and the silencing of their voices; it dehumanizes them;

it gets control. Chaucer's works show us acts of male empowerment in many permutations, but his attitude towards women and sexual violence remains ambiguous. Reading rape in Chaucer is reading about class struggle, about the anxiety of the patriarchy regarding its power over women, about transformation, about the battle of the sexes, about the desire of the poet to write the truth—and, maybe, as Delany has posited, about one man's anxiety over his legal and marital status and his way of covertly articulating it. Perhaps fictional rape can have an opposite function of historical rape—forcing us to look critically at the power structure that informs it, and foregrounding the transgressions of patriarchal ideology.[59]

Notwithstanding, even though one can "read" rape in Chaucer's works in sensible male-authorized (literary) ways that make it not-rape, the words of Jane Marcus, writing about Virginia Woolf, need to be heeded:

> One lesson [in "A Society" by VW] is that if we allow male critics to universalize our stories—as Swinburne retold the myth of Procne and Philomela, and Geoffrey Hartman claims that reading the myth as the story of the artist and the truth rather than a sister's revenge for the rape of her sister is "higher" or "deeper" than the story of the power of sisterhood—we will be domesticated and subjugated into the loss of our own history.[60]

Marcus notes that Woolf herself in *Between the Acts* "tells us that 'what we must remember' is the rape; 'what we must forget' is the male rewriting of women's history" (62). By using what Dinshaw calls "patriarchal literary techniques" (81), the male-centered critical tradition appropriates the truth, the main event of the text (rape), and transforms rape stories into other kinds of events.

In the end, I cannot solve the question of why there is so much rape in Chaucer's corpus. His work seems at times informed by profound personal or societal uneasiness towards the female; possibly this unease becomes encoded in the act of rape. But we need not continue to read rape in literary terms as trope, as not-rape in order to approach Chaucerian texts. I believe we must read it and insist on its name. We can historicize it, "unveil" the relationship between romance and sexual violence.[61] Consider, as Chaucer has the Wife of Bath suggest, that if "wommen hadde writen stories" [III (D) 693], whether rape would have played the role of literary device, or would it have been written as the horror and degradation a woman experiences? (And we remember that Christine de Pizan and Marie de France spoke out most vehemently against forced sex in their fictive worlds.) We can keep in mind the words of Silver and Higgins in *Rape and Representation* that "Feminist modes of 'reading' rape and its cultural inscriptions help identify and demystify the multiple manifestations, displacements, and transformations of what amounts to an insidious cultural myth."[62]

Furthermore, we need to consider that, as Gravdal has demonstrated in her study of French texts, medieval writers were preoccupied with sexual violence. It was a highly politicized issue. Men in law courts and in the poetic texts such as Gravdal analyzes were aware of the criminal issues involved in rape. And such awareness informs the work of Chaucer himself who had his own brush with rape law, as Delany, Saunders, and others suggest. Medieval literary representations of rape were "neither simplistic, undifferentiated, nor thoughtless" (Gravdal, 142). Sylvana Tomeselli and Roy Porter note that:

> It may indeed be the case that in a world in which women are treated principally as means rather than ends, as objects rather than subjects, or in which they are primarily members of households deriving their status only through their membership of such social units rather than as individual political beings in their own right, men protected them from theft and violence, from abduction and rape, for reasons of their own self-interests. If this holds true we must be open to the possibility that such incentives might no longer hold good in a world in which the position of women is being radically changed. The relative modern silence, or if you wish the relative modern 'male' silence, on rape may point in this direction. . . . Only recently has the issue been brought back into public debate, and this is strictly owing to successful efforts by the feminism of the seventies and early eighties, a feminism which unlike its predecessors made rape the prime focus of its campaign.[63]

For her part, Gravdal asks, then, if rape, understood in the Middle Ages as a man's problem, has today been marginalized as a woman's issue? She contends that "certain ambiguous ways of discoursing on rape, forged in the Middle Ages, still function effectively (and invisibly) today" (2). And, a trope can act as a locus full of imaginative potential for discovery and expression; yet one can read it as having also the potential for violence or disruptiveness.[64] Chaucer's work may have vividly realized both of these potentials for his modern audience. Through his virtuosity in using rape as a trope, he exposes the truth of rape as a part of the ills of patriarchy. Still, subsequently he displaces and obliterates that truth by manipulating the direction of the narrative, and exhibiting for us that slippery vision of *real* rape just behind and informing the *fictional* representation. For me, Chaucer's own project is always to be "slydynge" in every way. As Pearsall states it, Chaucer remains, at the heart of his poetic enterprise, aloof, profoundly refusing social and moral commitment.[65]

If, as Irigaray suggests, women can appropriate and expose traditional patristically constructed discourse and thereby destabilize it by voicing it through the female body, where it becomes another text altogether, then perhaps we might thus follow her paradigm to become better, more subtle readers and teachers. By reading rape in its troped and "fictional," and therefore male-centered, mode, and simultaneously acknowledging and disengaging it from its metaphoric construct—to voice its existence as sexual violence in lived lives, we and our students can surely become more conscious readers and teachers, able to confront the darker side of the discourse that through its own figurative apparatus seeks to objectify women. We then can become the subjects of our own readings; we can voice the silent female in the text and subvert literary misogyny. Our ways of reading affect our ways of living. Feminisms need not be restrictive or reductive practices, ideology-driven, and somber. Rather, a feminist reading can be empowering and expansive. As another way of historicizing texts and reappropriating them, relating them to their contexts and readers, a feminist paradigm of reading and teaching represents a kind of double process, where woman as character/woman as reader is evoked, where both art and gender violence are acknowledged, where the indissoluble bonds of the metaphors in the texts they inhabit can be apprehended by the process of attempting to disentangle those bonds. To see rape as trope opens up new literary spaces, which we ultimately close again, metaphor intact, leaving them imbued with a richer if darker content. Chaucer's readers must ponder the problem of sexual violence in his work and what it meant for men, for medieval society, for the woman reader, or the victimized women characters. Our task remains to continue to explore the use of rape in Chaucer's art, and to call it by its name.*

Notes

1. Quotations from the works of Geoffrey Chaucer are from Larry D. Benson, ed., *The Riverside Chaucer* (Boston: Houghton-Mifflin, 1987), and will be cited by line numbers parenthetically in the text.

2. Nancy A. Jones, online review of E. Jane Burns, *Bodytalk: When Women Speak in Old French Literature* (Philadelphia: University of Pennsylvania Press, 1993) in *Bryn Mawr Medieval Review* (now *The Medieval Review*) 94.11.5, November 29, 1994.

3. Stephanie Jed, *Chaste Thinking: The Rape of Lucrece and the Birth of Humanism* (Bloomington: Indiana University Press, 1989).

4. Elaine Tuttle Hansen's introduction to *Chaucer and the Fictions of Gender* (Berkeley: University of California Press, 1994), discusses the use of "Feminist Chaucer," pp. 10–15, for example.

5. Carolyn Dinshaw, *Chaucer's Sexual Poetics* (Madison: University of Wisconsin Press, 1989); Jill Mann, *Geoffrey Chaucer* (Atlantic Highlands, NJ: Humanities Press, 1991).

6. See Caroline Walker Bynum, *Jesus as Mother: Studies in the Spirituality of the High Middle Ages* (Berkeley: University of California Press, 1982) and *The Shewings of Julian of Norwich,* ed. Georgia Ronan Crampton (Kalamazoo: TEAMS Medieval Institute Publications, 1993).

7. When students first read *The Reeve's Tale,* they typically are a generically driven fabliau audience, following the narrator's lead in moving to see the property issues in the woman = corn equation and the narrative rightness of the "quytyng" of Sympkyn the miller's greed. Nevertheless, once one directs them to the rapes embedded in the tale, they engage in the hermeneutic dimensions that this double awareness affords. They become better readers, in that the darkness of the tale is apparent to them, interrogating the text along the lines of historicism: what kind of a society engenders such a genre and orchestrates such a response? Aesthetic questions: how does Chaucer create such a narrator capable of such a slick trick (on us)? . . . , and so on. Not only do they evolve some sympathy with feminism, but also they suddenly comprehend the complexity of reading against the grain of the narrative's interpretational clues, the complexity of reading an ancient text with modern sensibilities, discovering the reading of women as character *and* as metaphor. They are generally impelled to discuss gender, sexual violence, and experience in this context, and they initiate fertile discussions on the nexus between the literary and the actual, which inform their subsequent readings of the rest of the *Canterbury Tales* and *Troilus.* See Karen Robertson's essay here on discussing rape in the classroom for some real pitfalls of this practice, one of which is the silencing of students and the privileging of pain to the detriment of aesthetic discussion of the work at hand. See also her piece "Discussing Rape in the Classroom," *Medieval Feminist Newsletter* 9 (Summer, 1990): 21–22.

8. Dinshaw, *Chaucer's Sexual Poetics,* p. 140.

9. See Anna Roberts's collection of essays for a recent addition to this discussion: *Violence Against Women in Medieval Texts* (Gainesville: University of Florida Press, 1998).

10. Missy Dehn Kubitscheck, "Subjugated Knowledge: Toward a Feminist Exploration of Rape in Afro-American Fiction," in *Studies in Black American Literature,* ed. Joe Weixlmann and Houston A. Baker, Jr., 3: 43–46; cited in Lynn Higgins and Brenda Silver, *Rape and Representation* (New York: Columbia University Press, 1991), p. 10.

11. Jane Marcus, "Liberty, Sorority, Misogyny," quoting Hartman, in *The Representation of Women in Fiction,* ed. Carolyn Heilbrun and Margaret Higonnet. Selected Papers from the English Institute, 1981, no. 7 (Baltimore: Johns Hopkins University Press, 1983), p. 97.

12. I do not exclude men as rape victims here, but rather for the parameters of my discussion will use the female as the "norm" of rape victims, the female sexual identity as a function, a body socially construed as feminine and therefore rapable; also, the rape victims I discuss are all female characters in Chaucer's work.

13. Jonathan Culler's "Reading as a Woman," in *On Deconstruction: Theory and Criticism After Structuralism* (Ithaca: Cornell University Press, 1982), pp. 43–64, and Susan Schibanoff's "Taking the Gold Out of Egypt: The Art of Reading as a Woman," in *Gender and Reading: Essays on Readers, Texts and Contexts,* ed. Elizabeth Flynn and Patrocinio P. Schweichart (Baltimore: Johns Hopkins University Press, 1986), pp. 83–106, provide useful ways to theorize gendered reading styles.

14. See Dinshaw's *Chaucer's Sexual Poetics;* Susan Crane, *Gender and Romance in Chaucer's* Canterbury Tales (Princeton: Princeton University Press, 1994); Elaine Tuttle Hansen, *Chaucer and the Fictions of Gender* (Berkeley: University of California Press, 1992); Sheila Delany, *The Naked Text: Chaucer's* Legend Of Good Women (Berkeley: University of California Press, 1994) and *Writing Woman: Women Writers and Women in Literature, Medieval to Modern.* (New York: Schocken Books, 1983); R. Howard Bloch, "Chaucer's Maiden's Head: the *Physician's Tale* and the Poetics of Virginity," *Representations* 28 (1989): 113–34; and Corrine J. Saunders, "Woman Displaced: Rape and Romance in Chaucer's *Wife of Bath's Tale,*" *Arthurian Literature* XII (1995): 115–31.

15. Evelyn Birge Vitz, "Rereading Rape in Medieval Literature," *Partisan Review* 63, no. 2 (Spring, 1996): 280–91, 280. She severely critiques Katherine Gravdal, *Ravishing Maidens: Writing Rape in Medieval French Literature and Law* (Philadelphia: University of Pennsylvania Press, 1991).

16. See Introduction, n. 10, and Mark Amsler's reading of one of Christine's works, in this volume. Many thanks to Harriet Spiegel for allowing me to read her work in manuscript on the work of Marie de France, "The Fox and the Bear: A Medieval Woman's Fable of Rape and its Transformations," and her essay "The Male Animal in the Fables of Marie de France," in *Medieval Masculinities: Regarding Men in the Middle Ages,* ed. Clare A. Lees (Minneapolis: University of Minnesota Press, 1994), pp. 111–26.

17. E. Robertson suggests this in her MLA paper (in manuscript) on *The Wife of Bath's Tale* (1990). See also the work of Catherine MacKinnon, esp. "Feminism, Marxism, Method, and the State: Toward Feminist Jurisprudence," *Signs* 8 (Summer, 1983): 635–58.

18. Claude Levi-Strauss, *The Elementary Structures of Kinship,* trans. James H. Bell, John R. von Sturmer, and Rodney Needham, rev. ed. (Boston: Beacon Press, 1969).

19. Gail Rubin, "The Traffic in Women: Notes on the 'Political Economy' of Sex.," in *Toward an Anthropology of Women,* ed. R. R. Reiter (New York: Monthly Review Press, 1975), p. 157.

20. *This Sex Which is Not One,* trans. Catherine Porter (Ithaca: Cornell University Press, 1985), p. 196.

21. Laurie Finke provides a convincing reading of the Wife of Bath's Prologue and Tale as evidence of the interplay of gender and emerging capitalism in "All is for to Selle: Breeding Capital in the Wife of Bath's Prologue and Tale." in *Geoffrey Chaucer: The Wife of Bath,* ed. Peter G. Beidler (Boston and New York: St. Martin's Press, 1996), pp. 171–88.

22. My discussion of rape language and law relies heavily on Gravdal's and Brundage's work: Katherine Gravdal, *Ravishing Maidens: Writing Rape in Medieval French Literature and Law* (Philadelphia: University of Pennsylvania Press, 1991) and James A. Brundage, *Law, Sex, and Christian Society in Medieval Europe* (Chicago: University of Chicago Press, 1987). See also Dinshaw, pp. 8–9, for the etymology of the ME "rapen." One would, of course need to study rape law in all sections of Europe to say anything absolutely true about rape in "the Middle Ages, " but English law is well served by Kelly's article and by Cannon's: Henry Ansgar Kelly, "Meanings and Uses of *Raptus* in Chaucer's Time," *Studies in the Age of Chaucer* 20 (1998): 101–66; Christopher Cannon, "*Raptus* in the Chaumpaigne Release and a Newly-Discovered Document Concerning the Life of Geoffrey Chaucer," *Speculum* 68 No.1 (Jan. 1993): 74–94. See also Cannon's essay in this volume.

23. Gravdal, *Ravishing Maidens,* p. 4.

24. Gravdal, p. 7.

25. Gravdal, p. 8. Under the jurist Gratian (*Decretum,* c. 1140), raptus as a crime consisted of four necessary elements: unlawful coitus, woman abducted from the house of her father, rape accomplished by violence, no previous marriage agreement negotiated between the woman and her ravisher (Gravdal, p. 8). This new legal interpretation underscores the patriarchal nature of rape law: The operative phrase is that the woman must be abducted from her father's house, and rape violates *his* rights, not his daughter's. Gratian also softened the punishment for rape, particularly for churchmen, who, if they were able to take sanctuary in a church, could get off with demotion rather than the death penalty. In England, from the time of the Statutes of Westminster II in 1285, rape was technically a felony and punishable by death or dismemberment, but in practice most rape cases were passed over to Church jurisdiction, where they were legislated as marriage cases and punished by fines or imprisonment. Sometimes they were treated as cases of trespass rather than felony. And, under the influence of Germanic law, in the thirteenth century, the ravisher, as penance for his crime, could marry the victim, if she consented; thus, raptus represents a vehicle for contracting a legal marriage to avoid warfare between families (10). Charges of rape might be erased if a pregnancy ensued, since according to accepted medieval notions of physiology, an act of will was required for the female seed to be emitted, and thus conception equaled willed enjoyment, not rape. For prevailing scientific and social notions of female biology, see Thomas Laqueur, *Making Sex: Body and Gender from the Greeks to Freud* (Cambridge, MA: Harvard University Press, 1990); Vern Bullough, "Medieval Medical and Scientific Views of Women," *Viator* 4 (1973): 485–501; and Elizabeth Robertson "Medieval Medical Views of Women and Female Spirituality in the *Ancrene Wisse* and Julian of Norwich's *Showings*" in *Feminist Approaches to the Body in Medieval Literature,* ed. Linda Lomperis and Sarah Stanbury (Philadelphia: University of Pennsylvania Press, 1993), pp. 142–67. What becomes increasingly clear in studying the

labyrinthine legal solutions is that forced coitus—rape in the modern sense—was not a crime in Church law, since Church law existed to codify marriage, not to protect individual women against violence. The "Church devoted vast pages to the codification of sexual behavior in canon law" but "it did not study, comment on, or codify simple rape" (Gravdal, 10).

26. Other essays in this volume provide ample evidence for this assertion (see E. Robertson, Greenstadt, and Cannon, for example), and see Kelly (above, n. 22). And, given the current news focus on celebrity rapes and gender violence, we are not far from that view today. A *New York Times* TV critic reviewing a 1990 television documentary on date rape, where, in the estimation of the men surveyed, forced sex was equated with good sex, notes that there seem to be "troubling" gendered responses to the definition of rape, with young college men far less likely to recognize themselves as rapists. When these young men "acknowledge that their achievement in bed involved a measure of force, they deny it was rape; a survey of male college students found that 80 percent of them described what the law might call rape as 'successful sex.'" See Walter Goodman, "Conflicting Attitudes About Rape on Campus," review of television program "Campus Rape: When No Means No," the *New York Times,* December 26, 1990. I am reminded of those Chaucerian critics (below, n. 34, 36) and who want to know more about Cecily Chaumpaigne's previous or later life (Howard), or allowed that it was logical for Chaucer to have had the odd romp with "a pretty and soft baker's daughter" (Gardner, 253), in classic blame-the-victim or boys-will-be-boys gendered attitudes towards Chaucer's accusation of *raptus.* See Gail Margherita "Some Thoughts on History, Epistemology, and Rape," *Medieval Feminist Newsletter,* no. 11 (Spring, 1991): 2–5.

27. Lucy Berliner, Director of Research, Harborview Medical Center, Seattle, WA, quoted in Thomas Shapley, "Those Who Prey On Kids," *Seattle Post-Intelligencer,* April 7, 1991: D-1.

28. Jane Chance also comments on the gendered/genital nature of the parchment and pen in this poem: "Chaucerian Irony in the Verse Epistles: 'Wordes Unto Adam,' 'Lenvoy a Scogan,' and 'Lenvoy a Bukton,'" *Papers on Language and Literature* 21 (1985): 115–28.

29. This concern seems, too, to be at the heart of the Manciple's tale of the poet Phebus as the maker and destroyer of music and language, as violator and violated. See also Dinshaw's article "Rivalry, Rape and Manhood: Gower and Chaucer," in *Chaucer and Gower: Difference, Mutuality, Exchange,* ed. R. F.Yeager, University of Victoria English Literary Studies Monograph Series 51 (Victoria, BC: University of Victoria Press, 1991), pp. 130–52, where she argues for rape as a homosocial issue between male poets.

30. Gayle Margherita. "Some Thoughts," p. 2.

31. Dinshaw implies this point in her discussion of rape in Chaucer's works. The wording of this paragraph derives from the editors' proposal for the 1990 Modern Language Association panel, "Chaucer and Rape," written

with the assistance of Carolyn Dinshaw, to whom we are grateful. Also, as a major source of Chaucerian material, Ovid's *Metamorphoses* is laden with rape-stories.

32. "Tam de raptu meo, tam [sic] de aliqua alia re vel causa." See Margherita and Cannon. The documents on this problematic legal case are accessible in *Chaucer Life Records,* ed. Martin Crow and Clair Olsen (Oxford: Oxford University Press, 1966). Cannon's discovery of a new document (*Speculum,* January 1993) and his discussion of the inflammatory nature of the language "de raptu meo" relating to the Chaumpaigne case adds fuel to the fire, but little categorically to clear up the mystery of the controversy of whether or not an actual rape took place.

33. Cannon, Kelly, Gravdal, op. cit.; Barbara Hanawalt, *"Of Good and Ill Repute:" Gender and Social Control in Medieval England.* (Oxford: Oxford University Press, 1998), esp. chapter 8, "Whose Story Was This? Rape Narratives in Medieval English Courts," pp. 124–41.

34. Pearsall, *The Life of Geoffrey Chaucer* (Oxford: Blackwell Publishers, 1992), p. 137: " . . . the temptation to offer an explanation is too strong to resist. The strongest likelihood, in my opinion, is that Cecily threatened to bring a charge of rape in order to force Chaucer into some compensatory settlement and that she then cooperated in the legal release. The actual offence for which she sought compensation is not necessarily the offence named in the charge that she used for leverage and did not press: there are many things that it might more probably have been than violent physical rape, including neglect and the betrayal of promises by the man, or some unilateral decision on his part to terminate an affair that he regarded as over but which the woman, in retrospect, regarded as a physical violation."

35. Margherita, "Some Thoughts," p. 2.

36. Margherita, p. 4, n. 4; she cites D. S. Brewer, *Chaucer,* 3rd. ed. (London: Longman, 1973), p. 40; her other "traditional" critics are John Gardner, *The Life and Times of Geoffrey Chaucer* (New York: Knopf, Random House, 1977) and Donald Howard, *Chaucer: His Life, His Works, His World* (New York: E. P. Dutton, 1987).

37. Kelly, Hanawalt, Cannon, op. cit., as well as Corrine J. Saunders, "Woman Displaced: Rape and Romance in Chaucer's *Wife of Bath's Tale,"* *Arthurian Literature* 12 (1995): 115–31, and John Marshall Carter, *Rape in Medieval England: An Historical and Sociological Study* (Lanham: University Press of America, 1985), have traced some aspects of the legal climate and rape law with which Chaucer may have been familiar.

38. See Jeri Laber on the rape of Bosnian and Serbian women in the *New York Review of Books,* "Bosnia: Questions About Rape," *New York Review of Books* (March 23, 1993): 3–6, where rape is immediately glossed as political action, and rape stories are interpreted in the context of her essay as shaped and manipulated by the tellers/victims for their own political ends "embroidering the facts for maximum effect" (4). The women are elided and the discourse of politics seems to be all, Laber reports.

39. The works of Carolyn Dinshaw, Sheila Delany, and Elaine Tuttle Hansen provide some of the early feminist models for reading rape and sexual violence in Chaucer.

40. It would be difficult for even a very long footnote exhaustively to mention the criticism collected around this topic, from Kittredge's "Marriage Group" theory to Donaldson's enchantment with Criseyde, to more recent discussions by Crane, Patterson, Mann, Fradenburg, and Delany, to name only the diverse ones immediately visible on my desk. Even on the Internet, Chaucernetters carry on a lively conversation about women in Chaucer from time to time.

41. Sheila Delany's insightful chapter of her *Writing Woman*, "Slaying Python: Marriage and Mysogyny in a Chaucerian Text," pp. 47–75, 202–7, is one of the first and certainly the foremost example of feminist criticism of Chaucer that highlights sexual violence in a tale whose narrative strategies are to displace it. Delany's discussion of the *Manciple's Tale* implies that Chaucer's own experience with his marriage and "profound ambivalence toward his wife and her distinguished lover-patron [John of Gaunt]" might have fueled some of the venom of the tale towards the adulterous wife. By extension, it could be argued that Chaucer replicated some personal agenda as he repeatedly depicted sexual violence in his works.

42. Saunders, "Woman Displaced," p. 131. See also Mark Amsler's essay in this volume for Chaucer's inheritance of medieval reading practices that displace rape and encode it as another thing, according to the interpreters' intentions for their work.

43. Elizabeth Robertson provided this valuable insight.

44. Elizabeth Robertson, "Rape in Chaucer," paper, unpub. draft of MLA 1990 presentation.

45. Sheila Delany in her superb *The Naked Text*, has written about these rapes in *The Legend of Good Women*. See also Regula Meyer Evitt (whose work came to my attention after this essay was completed) on *LGW*'s Philomel, as well as her discussion of the WBT: "Chaucer, Rape and the Poetic Power of Ventriloquism," in *Minding the Body: Women and Literature in the Middle Ages, 800–1500*, ed. Monica B. Potkay and Regula Evitt (New York: Twayne Publishers, 1997), pp. 139–65.

46. Saunders, "Woman Displaced," 118. Again, see Amsler's essay, this volume.

47. Laurie A. Finke, "'All is for to selle': Breeding Capital in the Wife of Bath's Prologue and Tale," in *Geoffrey Chaucer: The Wife of Bath*, ed. Peter G. Beidler (Boston and New York: St. Martin's Press, 1996), p. 180.

48. *Fables Ancient and Modern*, in *The Poems of John Dryden*, ed. James Kinsley, Vol. IV (Oxford: The Clarendon Press, 1958), pp. 1703–17.

49. Mann, *Geoffrey Chaucer*, p. 89.

50. Pearsall, *The Life of Geoffrey Chaucer*, pp. 256–57.

51. It is interesting that neither time does Malyne get to "crie": "it had been *to late* for to crie"; "*almoost* she gan wepe" [italics mine]. See also the essay by Pamela Bennett, "'And Shortely for to Seyn they were Aton:' Chaucer's

Deflection of Rape in the Reeve's and Franklin's Tales," *Women's Studies: An Interdisciplinary Journal* 22, no. 2C (1993): 145–62.

52. See Christine M. Rose, "Woman's 'Pryvete,' May and the Privy: Fissures in the Narrative Voice in the *Merchant's Tale, 1944–86*," *Chaucer Yearbook* 4 (Summer, 1997): 61–77, where I argue that the fabliau genre demands the dissolution of May from the sympathetic, silent bride abed with the old January into the glib and lusty type of the dangerous fabliau woman, and that the instability of the narrative at the point of this dissolution (ll. 1944–86) is the point at which the *fictional rape/real rape* distinction becomes most poignant, and where the narrator must turn away from a woman's experience and "solve" her by making her into a type character who "quyts" her rapist, and where both husband and wife look foolish. The narrative performer has to avert real rape and female pain and engage the stereotypes of misogynist fantasy to take control of the tale he tells. Material on *The Merchant's Tale* appearing here is adapted from that article.

53. Dinshaw, *Chaucer's Sexual Poetics,* chap. 3 "The Law of Man and Its 'Abhomynacions,'" pp. 88–112, provides a fascinating discussion of incest, which the Man of Law specifically insists he will not tell a tale about ("Of swiche cursed stories, I say fy!" MLT 80), and that in fact pervades his tale. See also my "Chaucer's *The Man of Law's Tale:* Teaching Through the Sources" 28.2 (Spring, 2001, *College Literature:* 155–177) for Chaucer's changes to the rape of Custance from his source, Nicholas Trevet's *Les Cronicles,* to make Custance a more passive victim.

54. R. Howard Bloch, "Chaucer's Maiden's Head: the *Physician's Tale* and the Poetics of Virginity," *Representations* 28 (1989): 113–34.

55. Linda Lomperis, in her essay "Unruly Bodies and Ruling Practices: Chaucer's *Physician's Tale* as a Socially Symbolic Act," in *Feminist Approaches to the Body in Medieval Literature,* ed. L. Lomperis and S. Stanbury (Philadelphia: University of Pennsylvania Press, 1993), pp. 21–37, provides an important discussion of the political role of the body in the PhysT.

56. Ovid, *Metamorphoses,* trans. Mary Innes (Harmondsworth: Penguin Books, 1976), pp. 64–67.

57. Gower uses the tale of Neptune and Cornix as his exemplum for robbery, with rape as theft of treasure. See Isabelle Mast, "Rape in John Gower's *Confessio Amantis* and Other Related Works," in *Young Medieval Women,* ed. Katherine Lewis, et al. (New York: St. Martin's Press, 1999), pp. 102–32. Mast sees this contemporary of Chaucer as portraying rape victims with some sympathy (121–23). For Gower's tale, see *The English Works of John Gower,* ed. G. C. Macaulay, *Early English Text Society,* no. 81, vol. II (Oxford: Oxford University Press, 1900, rpt. 1979), ll. 6204–11.

58. With the average age of menarche in the fourteenth century somewhere around 17, marriages of females at age 12, though perhaps common, seem distastefully like child abuse to us. That line of the Wife is tinged with pathos and the loss of a childhood. (Nevertheless, a student suggested to

me that it would be just like the Wife to lie about her age at her first marriage to make her fellow Pilgrims think she was younger than she actually
was!) Like Constance, May, Emelye, and even Griselde, the Wife acknowledges her part in the traffic in women that constituted her fictive (and historical) world.

59. E. Robertson, MLA paper, 1990.
60. Marcus, "Liberty, Sorority," p. 97
61. Margherita, "Some Thoughts," p. 2.
62. *Rape and Representation,* p. 2.
63. Sylvana Tomaselli and Roy Porter, *Rape: An Historical and Social Enquiry*
     (Oxford: Basil Blackwell, 1986), p. 5.
64. Dinshaw, *Chaucer's Sexual Poetics,* p. 141.
65. Pearsall, *The Life of Geoffrey Chaucer,* pp. 252, 266. Lee Patterson makes this
     argument in a similar vein, where he notes that he, as well as two essayists,
     Strohm and Wallace, in his *Literary Practice and Social Change in Britain,*
     1380–1530 (Berkeley: University of California Press, 1990) volume, sees
     Chaucer articulating an ideology, but eschewing "in any direct and explicit
     form, ideological statement. . . . Chaucerian politics are disingenuously
     and uncertainly apolitical" (10).
 *   Thanks are due to Elizabeth Robertson for her energy, rigorous intellect,
     and good will in the organization and presentation of the MLA and the
     Medieval Institute sessions on Chaucer and rape, her inestimable cooperation during the preparation of this volume, and especially for her helpful
     comments on this essay. Earlier versions of this work were presented at a
     Modern Language Association meeting, a Faculty Seminar at Portland
     State University, and at Simon Fraser University, the latter through the
     good offices of Sheila Delany, whose groundbreaking work has inspired so
     many of us to read and write about women in the Middle Ages. My gratitude to her, and to P.S.U. for its travel grants and computer support. Present and former colleagues in the English Department at Portland State,
     especially Peter Carafiol, Paul Giles, and Georgia Ronan Crampton, deserve kudos for their kindnesses as an audience for my work. And thanks
     to John C. Coldewey for his perceptive readings of this essay at every stage
     of its development.

CHAPTER 2

RAPE AND SILENCE:
OVID'S MYTHOGRAPHY
AND MEDIEVAL READERS

Mark Amsler

Medieval mythographers allegorized Ovid's rape narratives as stories
of cosmological creation or spiritual desire, or else they erased rape
altogether from their interpretations of *Metamorphoses*. However,
Christine de Pizan intertextually rewrote Daphne's assault as a disfig-
urement of the female body, while Chaucer's "Legend of Philomela"
problematizes affective reading in texts about sexual violence.

> *"well interruption is addition*
> *read and follow"*
>
> —*Lyn Hejinian*, Writing Is an Aid to Memory

Thinking about representations of sexual violence in Medieval and
Early Modern texts, we will always return to Ovid's writings, to how
they might have been read and reread by medieval audiences and writers,
to how we read them being read. Ovid has already partially preempted us
by writing *Remedia amores* as a self-ironic rebuttal to his earlier texts on
love and sex. But medieval readers of Ovid interpreted and revised Ovid
within other hermeneutic codes—cosmological, allegorical, ethical, historical, courtly. In this essay, I explore how medieval readers of Ovid's mythographic rape narratives often elided or erased the rape itself (the letter of

the text and the literal body) by interpreting sexual violence as an allegory
of creation or spirituality, or as a moral *exemplum* in which gender and sexual behaviors are subordinated to other sociopolitical codes. Constructing
readings framed primarily by categories of ethical or spiritual *utilitas*, official commentaries and mythographies participated in later medieval discourses about rape and sexuality in various ways: by downplaying legal
questions of rape, by silencing sexual violence (in the textual letter and the
literal body) or by decoding rape narratives as *integumenta* structured around
gendered binaries of virtue and vice. However, some later medieval readings and rewritings of Ovidian rape narratives (by Chaucer, Gower, Christine de Pizan) challenged many of these mythographers' assumptions about
reading for pleasure or moral edification. Chaucer and Christine de Pizan
often implicitly rehearse Ovid's self-conscious, destabilizing inscriptions of
multiple subject positions within narratives that unpack *in different ways* the
gendered semiosis of how we read and write rape.

Ovid's writings are filled with erotic scenarios, myths of rape, forced
sex, attempted rape, seduction, and kidnapping, not to mention cannibalism, bestiality, and species transformations, almost always perpetrated by
male figures. Furthermore, Ovid's narrative voices present readers with
multiple subject positions, ironic undercutting, self-conscious textual parody, and cross-gender representations. With these narrative instabilities,
Ovid's texts occupied an uncertain place in the medieval canon.

Ovid's erotic and exile writings—*Amores, Ars amatoria, Remedia amores,
Fasti, Heroides*—provided medieval readers and writers with a rich archive
of narratives, vocabularies, themes, and literary conventions. As medieval
scholars have long noted, the language of courtly love, real or imagined, is
permeated with Ovidian tropes. In addition, the *Metamorphoses* was the
base or hypotext for medieval versions of myths and stories. "Ovidianism"
and "anti-Ovidianism" threaded through the literary-cultural domain,
from Juvenal's rejection of Ovid's foolish stories to the *Antiovidianus* and
medieval critics of the *Roman de la rose*, from Chrétien de Troyes, Jean de
Meun, and troubadour poets to Chaucer, Gower, and Christine de Pizan.

Although some grammarians, such as Aimeric (eleventh century), considered Ovid as one of the nine golden *auctores*,[1] many other grammarians and
writers regarded Ovid's texts as the sites of dangerous reading, writing, and
desire, especially for young readers. Conrad of Hirsau in his *Dialogus super auctores* (twelfth century) rejected Ovid's erotic writings and *Metamorphoses* from
the grammatical canon and only tolerated Ovid's *Ex Ponto* and *Fasti*. Alexander Nequam in his *Sacerdos ad altare accessurus* (twelfth century) described the
typical Latin literacy curriculum (Donatus, Priscian, Theodulus, Cato, Virgil,
Horace, Old and New Testaments), but waffled on Ovid: "Placuit tamen viris
autenticis carmina amatoria . . . subducenda esse a manibus adolescentium"

[Nonetheless, some men of authority hold that (Ovid's) love poetry should be kept from the hands of adolescent boys].[2] Specifically, Nequam omits the *Metamorphoses* and recommends the *Remedia amores* to counter Ovid's more pernicious writings. Earlier, Guibert de Nogent in his *Monodiae* (c. 1108) condemned his own desire to rival Ovid and "pastoral poets" and his "striving to achieve an amorous charm" in his manner "of arranging images and in well-crafted letters." Guibert writes that reading Ovid inspired him to produce "lascivious . . . poetic expressions," texts that then prompted his "immodest stirrings of the flesh."[3] Dangerous writing produces silence, censorship, or dangerous reading and responses, which in turn produce more dangerous writing. Medieval grammarians' proscriptions of Ovid's writing were caught up in repetitions of desire and guilt.

While rigorists like Conrad of Hirsau proposed that the *Metamorphoses* be removed from the list of acceptable pagan writers, many Christian commentators and official readers appropriated or assimilated Ovid's narratives within a set of moral, authoritative, and useful [*utilitas*] interpretive procedures. As Jean Seznec, D. C. Allen, J. B. Allen, and others have shown, Ovid's stories of rape, attempted rape, and kidnapping were read and interpreted not only as adventurous, fantastic narratives but just as often as *exempla,* coded texts requiring contextualizing interpretation, especially learned exegesis, to make clear the stories' moral messages for Christian readers.[4] Ovid's texts presented medieval audiences with the experience of reading for profit and reading for pleasure, and with the problem of determining the advantages and dangers of reading.

Official readers of Ovid—commentators, allegorists, and glossators—produced interpretive frames for medieval audiences. Sometimes these frames were explicitly displayed on the page, as text + gloss + allegory; other times, the reading frames were implicitly embedded within a mythographic discourse or attached as prefaces [*accessus*]. But outside this grammatical discourse of guided reading, medieval Latin and vernacular writers rehearsed Ovid's narratives without overt allegorical gloss or mythographic hermeneutics, leaving readers and listeners to interpret the intertextual relation between the medieval text and Ovid's underlying narrative.

Romance, Mythography, And Law

Ovid's narratives of rape and sexual violence were framed differently in later medieval romances, fabliaux, courtly allegories, and pastourelle from the ways they were contextualized in mythographic texts.[5] As many critics have noted, Chrétien de Troyes's romances draw extensively from Ovid's texts to construct a new language of romance, sexuality, and love. Chrétien's heroes and heroines speak versions of Ovidian discourse to express their desires, anxieties, sexual imaginings, and everyday relationships. Within Chrétien's Ovidian discourse, rape is positioned as a moral countersign, where female consent is crucial for "good" sexual and romantic relationships. Cliges and Fenice (*Cliges*) and Yvain and Laudine (at least before she banishes the knight, in *Yvain*) are paradigms of consensual romance lovers in what George Duby called the "ecclesiastical model of marriage." Cliges and Fenice are also represented as having a "clandestine marriage," since Fenice never consents to her marriage with Alis nor has sexual intercourse with him.[6] Yvain's loyalty to Laudine is tested more than once as he abstains from other sexual or romantic relationships, despite having won several battles, often against knights or giants who are themselves depicted as rapists, would-be rapists, and sexual violators. In Chrétien's *Lancelot,* the already complex relationship between Arthur, Guinevere, and Lancelot is further complicated by the depiction of Guinevere and Lancelot as consensual lovers. Lancelot's loyalty to Guinevere and (because of her) to women in general is tested more than once by titillating rape narratives in which Lancelot refrains from dominating a woman sexually even though the situation presents itself and he himself is shown capable of doing so. Within the romance scenario of consensual sex, rape narratives represent contained, sensational, titillating narratives of female trauma that nevertheless are supposed to help us as readers distinguish between "good men" and "bad men." (Chrétien de Troyes himself is supposed to have composed a version of Ovid's story of the rape of Philomela, a story we will return to later). Simply put, in romance discourse (unlike pastourelle), good knights don't sexually violate women.

Unlike most romance representations of rape and sexual violence, medieval mythographers and commentators interpreted Ovid's narratives in *Metamorphoses* by reframing the narratives as:

1. fictionalized representations of natural processes or physical processes or in some cases historical persons (euhemerism);
2. allegories of moral traits or cognitive processes;
3. allegories of spiritual or Christian truths revealed more fully in Scripture.

All these ways of reading and appropriating classical myth were already well known in the ancient and early Medieval worlds.[7] Jesus established one strand of allegorical reading by representing himself as the "fulfillment of the scriptures." Early Christianity appropriated mythographic commentary strategies from the Stoics and early Jewish exegetes and applied them to Christian readings of scripture. Christian commentators, to varying degrees, also applied grammatical and hermeneutic methods of exegesis and allegorizing to classical texts as refutations of the "rigorist" argument that sought to discredit pagan or scandalous texts in favor of the new received Christian truth. By the twelfth century, allegorical interpretations of Ovid and other classical writers (especially Virgil, Lucan, Martianus Capella), together with grammatical and etymological glosses on classical texts, were established within the grammar curriculum and increasingly became part of learned mythographic writing and the preacher's and writer's archive of *exempla*. Classical myths were read as "cloaked" ancient writing [*integumentum*] concealing moral or cosmological truths beneath the textual letter.

Textual commentaries and *accessus ad auctores* (prefaces to canonical authors) established the basis for reading classical texts as part of an ethical or moral program. Conrad of Hirsau omitted Ovid's scandalous *Metamorphoses* from his curriculum, but other grammarians, employing an authorial mode of interpretation, read Ovid's mythographic and erotic writings in relation to the poet's life, from his career as a controversial erotic poet to his exile by Caesar for obscure reasons to his attempts to secure a pardon.[8] Later medieval commentators often approached classical texts by posing six interpretive questions, derived from Aristotle's *Categories:* Who is the author [*auctor*]? What is the subject [*materia*]? What is the author's intention [*intentio*]? What is the utility of the text [*utilitas*]? What is the title [*titulus*]? To what part of philosophy does the text belong [*cui parti philosophie suponatur liber iste*]? What are the causes [*causae*] of the text (based on Aristotle's four causes: *efficiens, materialis, formalis, finalis*)? These *accessus* questions formed the basis for an ethical inquiry into the pagan text that compensated for teachers' and grammarians' anxiety about the young readers holding or hearing Ovid's writings. A late medieval commentator on the *Ars amatoria* (Cod. Paris 7998, dated 1305) wrote that "Ethice sponitur liber iste quia loquitur de moribus iuvenum et puellarum, quos introducit in hac arte" (Ghisalberti 45) [The book (*Ars amatoria*) pertains to ethics because it speaks of the behavior of young boys and girls, whom it introduces into that art]. Another fourteenth-century commentary on the *Metamorphoses* (Cod. Ambrosiana N. 254 sup.) specifically identified Ovid as an "ethical poet," playing on the writer's name: "vel dictus est Naso per similitudinem, quia sicut canis venaticus odore nasi feras percipit et sequitur, sic Ovidius odore et discrecione nasi sui bonas percipiebat sententias" (Ghisalberti 53) ["... or he is called 'Naso' as a simile, because just as a hunting dog senses wild animals with his nose and follows them, so Ovid perceived good moral instruction by the suggestion and discernment of his nose" (see Horace's *Satires,* e.g., 1.2, for the association of *naso* with scorn or satire)]. The Codex Ambrosiana commentator distinguishes two uses [*utilitates*] for the *Metamorphoses* on the axes of textual production and reception. Ovid writes the poem to redeem himself in Caesar's eyes and

compensate for his earlier erotic works. Readers [*legentium*] discover in the
Metamorphoses what comes of wicked behavior ["quid de pravis moribus
acciderit"] and learn how to avoid vices and beast-like sin ["a viciis et a
belvina turpitudine abstineamus"]. These later medieval commentators
read the narratives within an ethical frame to legitimize Ovid as an advanced canonical writer whose writing addresses both the natural world
and ethics ["Epithicus et phisicus est actor iste"; Ghisalberti 54).

Some commentators on the *Metamorphoses* focus more directly on narrative mutations and ethical reading. A fourteenth-century reader of the
Metamorphoses (Cod. Paris 8253) used Aristotle's categories to elaborate an
ethical commentary on the text:

> Causa efficiens est illud a quo res agitur sicut est ipse deus, quia est causa ef-
> ficiens cuiuslibet rerum. Causa materialis est illud de quo res agitur sicut
> sunt ligna et lapides que sunt causa materialis domus. Causa formalis est illud
> quod in esse rei, sicuti divinitas in deo, humanitas in homine. Causa finalis
> est illud propter quod res agitur sicuti bonitas quia propter bonitatem et, ut
> ad bonum finem deveniant, omnia procreantur. (Ghisalberti 51)

> [The efficient cause is that by which something is brought into being, such
> as God himself, because he is the efficient cause of everything. The material
> cause is that from which something is brought into being, such as wood and
> stones, which are the material cause of the house. The formal cause is that
> which inheres in something, such as the divinity in God, the humanity in a
> person. The final cause is that because of which something is brought into
> being, such as goodness, because on account of goodness everything is cre-
> ated, so that people come to a good end.]

Then the commentator, adapting scholastic analyses of being, classified the
mutationes represented in *Metamorphoses: mutatio naturalis* (earth to water, air
to fire), *mutatio spiritualis* (Agave goes insane, Orestes becomes mad after
killing his mother), *mutatio moralis* (Lycaon is punished by being turned
into a wolf), *magica mutatio* (Circe turns Odysseus's men into pigs), *mutatio
de corpore in corpus* (Io becomes a cow), *mutatio de re inanimata in rem ani-
matam* (Deucalion's stones become people), *mutatio de re animata in ani-
matam* (Actaeon is turned into a deer), *mutatio de re animata in inanimatam*
(a serpent trying to devour Orpheus becomes a stone), *mutatio de re inanimata in rem inanimatam* (Philemon's house becomes a temple). Arnulf of
Orleans, in his influential *Allegoriae super Ovidii Metamorphosin* (eleventh
century), linked Ovid's *materia* to three kinds of transformation (natural,
magical, spiritual) and then read the physical transformations in *Metamorphoses* as literal metaphors for spiritual change. These changes, he wrote,
bring "proper" Christian readers back to God and call on readers to avoid

vice and follow virtuous reason (Ghisalberti 18). The commentators primarily interpret Ovid's bestial transformations as signs of characters' failing or punishment.

Some scholars have sharply distinguished between early medieval and later medieval commentaries on Ovid's *Metamorphoses,* but the differences are not so clear. Tenth- and eleventh-century grammatical glosses on Ovid and Ovid-based mythographies formed the hypotext from which later medieval moralizing readings of Ovid's *Metamorphoses* derived. The *Vulgate Commentary* (c. 1250) collects earlier marginal or interlinear grammatical and lexical glosses on the *Metamorphoses.* The First and Second Vatican Mythographers, most likely writing in the tenth century,[9] emphasize genealogies, euhemerist or historical fables, and cosmology in Ovid's mythic narratives and transmit earlier mythographies by Fulgentius and Lactantius to the later Middle Ages. Then starting in the late eleventh century, moralized commentaries on Ovid's *Metamorphoses* became more popular. The ethical use [*utilitas*] of texts became commentators' principal concern. Arnulf of Orleans's influential *Allegoriae super Ovidii Metamorphosin* (eleventh century) was followed by an explosion of moralizing commentaries in the fourteenth century: especially the *Ovide moralisé* in vernacular verse (prose version, fifteenth century) and the Latin allegorizing mythographies of John of Garland, Thomas Waleys, John Ridewall, and most important, Petrus Berchorius (Pierre Bersuire, d. 1362). Berchorius's prose *Ovidius moralizatus* (often attributed to Waleys in the fifteenth and sixteenth centuries) made up Book Fifteen of his encyclopedic *Reductorium morale.* The first chapter, *De formis figurisque deorum,* circulated independently in the later Middle Ages and Early Modern era. These allegorical readings of *Metamorphoses* were part of a broader mythographic discourse, centered in the twelfth century around the School of Chartres, which continued to influence literary and learned uses of myth through the sixteenth century. Allegorical and moralizing readings of texts were considered advanced literate strategies, not for beginning readers. While Horace's *Satires* were read more literally as ethical texts, Ovid's *Metamorphoses* presented an archive of symbolic and metaphoric texts requiring hyperliterate and interpretive attention to remain part of an ethical reading program.[10] Medieval anxieties about the effects of reading were operating fully with Ovid's texts, more so than for any other classical text in the canon.

To frame a text for profitable reading [*utilitas*], medieval commentators did not require that an interpretation should recapitulate a classical author's intention or pagan historical context (the letter, *littera*). Commentaries and mythographies appropriated Ovid's rape stories for cosmological, euhemeristic, or moral purposes, or in some cases simply omitted the rape narratives altogether. In other words, the mythographers tried to make Ovid's texts instructive, rather than pleasurable for readers, either by reading rape as a signifier of other behaviors with other, frequently gendered, meanings (male cosmological creativity) or by rewriting Ovid and erasing rape narratives altogether from the mythographic landscape.

Despite their interest in ethical reading, later medieval commentaries on Ovid's narratives (unlike other medieval texts such as pastourelle and beast fables) do not engage much with the important shifts in legal discourses about *raptus* taking place at the time. In twelfth- to fourteenth-century secular and canon law, *raptus*, "clandestine marriage," and sex crimes were redefined in ways that sometimes favored female consent and legal recourse, but sometimes reduced the criminality of raping women (other than virgins) and placed a greater burden of proof on the rapist's accuser. In England, for example, both Glanvill (twelfth century) and Bracton (thirteenth century) defined *raptus* as "forced coitus." But Westminster I (Parliamentary statute, 1275) identified *raptus* as either "ravishment" or forcible kidnapping, with or without the woman's consent, while Westminster II (Parliamentary statue, 1285) restricted *raptus* to kidnapping and forced coitus without a woman's consent, "neither before or after." During this same period, *raptus* was changed from a capital crime that broke the king's peace to a felony with a lesser punishment.[11]

Moral commentary and mythographic discourse operated with little reference to such changes in later medieval legal discourse. Rather, the vocabulary mythographers and allegorizers used to describe sexual violence is replete with different kinds of ambiguities. *Raptus* (n.) and *ravere* (v.) occur often in Ovid's *Metamorphoses*. While medieval commentators used these and related Latin and vernacular words, semantically related words do not necessarily replicate the base word's meaning. The French legal term for rape, *efforcier*, foregrounds the criterion of force or violence in Roman legal definitions. But does OF *ravir* always carry the same connotation? Does MedLat *rapina* refer to rape as well as pillaging or destruction of property? Both the *OED* and the *MED* list Gower's "Tale of Tereus" (aka "The Tale of Philomela") as one of the earliest appearances of *raviner* (1393), with the primary meaning of "greed or violent seizure of goods." Given the context, a story about rape, does this first appearance of *raviner* also connote rape or fierce hunger/desire (ME *ravinous*)? Does the Middle English *ravysch* refer to kidnapping or rape, or both? Which of these semantic fields overlap, identifying the woman as someone else's property and therefore subject to pillaging?

Although some of these ambiguities are unresolvable, in what follows I will explore how medieval mythographers read Ovid in this social context of changing definitions of rape, especially in retellings and moralizations of the narratives of Callisto, Pluto and Proserpina, Daphne and Apollo, and

Philomela and Tereus. Juxtaposing mythographic accounts with those in Christine de Pizan's *L'Épître Othéa à Hector* and Chaucer's version of the story of Philomela in *The Legend of Good Women,* we will see how medieval writings and rewritings of Ovid's rape narratives constitute a textual field of erasures and supplements.

Moralized Ovid

As we noted earlier, the *accessus* and commentaries on *Metamorphoses* provided medieval audiences with different ways of reading Ovid's transformation narratives. Moral allegorizations of the *Metamorphoses* read off textual meanings independent of the writer's intention or historical circumstances. Physical mutations were read as metaphors of natural, moral, magical, or spiritual change. Narratives of moral transformation, which might seem ready signifiers for ethical readings, nonetheless complicated mythographic commentaries on rape. For example, many commentators singled out Lycaon and his daughter Callisto as humans transformed into animals for their crimes.[12] But Ovid's stories are not parallel with respect to the characters' culpability. The tyrannical Lycaon questions Jupiter's authority and is punished by being turned into a wolf. However, Callisto is raped by Jupiter (in the shape of Diana in order to embrace her), then turned into a bear by the vengeful Juno after Callisto gives birth to a son, Arcas (*Meta.* 2.468–69). Ovid's narrative foregrounds Callisto's wariness of men and same-sex desire as well as Juno's humiliation at her husband's sex crime and eagerness to cover her shame by punishing the rape victim.

Medieval commentaries and mythographies reiterate and expand on Ovid's different narrative contexts for why father and daughter are changed into beasts, but the moral discourse is not always restricted to rape. The thirteenth-century *Vulgate Commentary* revises Ovid's narrative and annotates Lycaon as a king who changes "de benigno in raptorem" [from a generous (or favorable) character into a plunderer (and rapist?)]. An interlinear gloss on *Metamorphoses* 1.144 associates Lycaon with "rebus per rapinam adquisitis" [acquisition of things through plunder].[13] Lycaon's transformation into a wolf is interpreted as an appropriate punishment for his tyranny and rapacious avarice. The words "raptor" and "rapina" in the *Vulgate Commentary* denote greedy acquisition and seizure of property, which may or may not include sexual oppression.

Earlier, the First and Second Vatican Mythographers (tenth century) describe how Lycaon was punished for his arrogance towards the gods, whereas Callisto, whom Jupiter overpowered [*viciasset*] and raped, was banished by Diana and punished by the jealous Juno.[14] In both Ovid's and the mythographers' accounts, the young Callisto is drawn to Diana and her circle of women, but then raped by a deceptive Jupiter. Both Ovid and the mythographers describe her further humiliation and punishment by two female gods (Diana and Juno) because she had sex with a male god, even though against her will, and because she got pregnant, thus making the rape public. According to the first two Vatican Mythographers, Callisto, the victim, bears the blame for bringing "male pollution" into Diana's circle and for "showing" the rape to gods and humans. By contrast, the mythographers are silent about Jupiter's responsibility.

Unlike moral commentators, other commentators interpreted Ovid's rape narratives as fictional representations of natural processes or cosmological creation. In commentary after commentary, Ovid's narratives of forced sex and rape were read off as representations of divine creation.[15] For example, Proserpina's kidnapping and forced marriage (*raptus*) to Pluto were frequently interpreted as an allegory of natural forces. Early mythographers such as Fulgentius (sixth century) refer to Proserpina's marriage as an allegory of vegetative growth.[16] The First Vatican Mythographer interpreted Pluto's kidnapping (*raptus*) of Proserpina as an explanation of the origin of the seasons or as a representation of the lunar cycle: "Quod ideo fingiatur quia Proserpina ipsa est et Luna que toto anno sex mensibus crescit, sex deficit, scilicet per singulos menses quindenis diebus ut crescens apud superos et deficiens apud inferos videatur"[17] [This is written thus because Proserpina herself is the moon, which grows six months of the year and decreases six months of the year. Plainly, she/the moon appears in each month for fifteen days as though growing and (for fifteen days) as though decreasing]. Commentators often etymologized the kidnapped young woman's name as a key to a natural exegesis. For example, the *Vulgate Commentary* marginally glosses Persephone (*Meta.* 10.15–16) as: "*Persephone* id est pergens sine sono. Cum maiore enim strepitu movetur sol quam luna que intelligitur per Proserpinam"[18] [*Persephone,* that is, "going forward without sound." The sun changes its countenance with a greater commotion than the moon, as is comprehended through the figure of Proserpina]. Other commentators, following Fulgentius, gloss Proserpina as the image of a seed growing silently into a plant, an agricultural reading motivated by the etymological interpretation of *Proserpina* as signifying "[crops] creeping through the earth with root."[19]

These naturalizing commentaries on Proserpina's *raptus* [kidnapping] displace the letter and the literal in Ovid's story (and also in Claudian's influential rehearsal of the story, *De raptu Proserpinae* [fifth century]). The mythographers overwrite the pathos of the abducted young Proserpina and Ceres's tearful search for her lost child with a cosmological allegory of agricultural cycles and planetary motion. They also suppress Ovid's ambivalence towards Pluto's actions. In *Metamorphoses,* Venus's desire that the

god of the underworld and Ceres's daughter should fall in love is coun-
tered by the nymph Cyane's reply to Pluto, "You cannot be the son-in-law
of Ceres, if she does not wish it. You should have asked for the girl, instead
of snatching her away [*Non rapienda fuit*]" (*Meta.* 5.414–16). Ovid's narrative intratextually links this structural ambivalence, expressed through two
different female voices, with the later story of Orpheus (*Meta.* 10.27–31).
Pleading for his kidnapped Eurydice, Orpheus asks Pluto and Proserpina
to release his wife as a reminder of their own love: " . . . I imagine that he
[Love] is familiar to you also and, if there is any truth in the story of that
rape [*rapina*] long ago, then you yourselves were brought together by
Love." The *Vulgate Commentary,* unlike many others, explicitly notes the
tension between *amor* and *rapina* in Orpheus's speech and directs the reader
to recall an earlier passage from the poem: "*amor.* Ad hoc respicit quod dixit
supra Iupiter excusando Plutonem de raptu dicens: Non hoc iniuria factum, verum amor est"[20] [*amor.* On this passage, refer back to what Ovid
said above about Jupiter, excusing Pluto from rape, saying, "If no harm was
done, it is certainly love"]. The commentator connects Ovid's textual utterance (no harm, no rape), in the voice of Jupiter, with his own description of Jupiter's narrative motive (to excuse Pluto of rape).

But other moral commentaries omit Proserpina's kidnapping altogether. They interpret Proserpina simply as Pluto's counterpart, queen of
the underworld or, in John Ridewall's (fourteenth century) unironized
"Orphean" reading of infernal marriage, as the depiction of "joy" or "fe-
licity."[21] Women's relationships with men and male gods, real and imagined, stand for the human condition vis-à-vis gods. Ridewall's
interpretation of Proserpina as a figure of marital joy silences her kidnapping, rape, and the pain they cause: "Tercia vero pars beatitudinis, scilicet
eternitas tencionis, figuratur per suum tercium nomen, scilicet Proserpinam. Dicitur enim Proserpina a procul serpendo; et convenit tencioni
beatifice, cuius est perpetuo permanere" [The third part of beauty, namely,
eternity of desire, is figuratively represented by its third name, namely,
Proserpina. Indeed, she is called *Proserpina* from *creeping far,* and this is appropriate to beautiful desire, in which she is to remain forever]. Ridewall
also interprets Proserpina as "poetic joy" and "delight in cithar,"[22] as does
the *Vulgate Commentary,* based on Orpheus's musical performance for the
underworld audience: Proserpina (*pergens sine sono* [going forward/passing
over without sound]) is a fitting ruler for the underworld, filled with *silen-
cia* because the gods lack the "instrumenta corpora ad loquendum"[23] [bod-
ily instruments/organs for speaking].

Berchorius's (fourteenth century) influential moralization of Ovid's
Metamorphoses (*Reductorium morale,* Book 15) incorporated materials from
Ridewall's commentary as well as from the *Ovide moralisé.* Like earlier

mythographers, Berchorius erases Proserpina's kidnapping/rape, and reads the narrative according to the semiotic grid of Christian virtues and vices, *in malo* and *in bono*. Producing alternative readings of Ovidian narratives and figures, Berchorius's commentary recasts narrative events as *exempla* of moral behavior and attributes to a character multiple positive and negative meanings. In the Prologue to *De formis figurisque deorum* (in *Reductorium morale*), Berchorius explains how advanced Christian readers should allegorically interpret Ovid's *Metamorphoses*. Properly read, Ovid's narratives are *fabulae* ("enigmatibus et poematibus") that affirm scriptural truth, teach morals, and reveal how both classical fables and sacred scripture teach "natural" or "historical" truth through fictions: "Sic etenim Sacra Scriptura in pluribus passibus videtur fecisse, ubi ad alicius veritatis ostensionem fabulas noscitur confecisse . . . Simili modo fecerunt poete qui in principio fabulas finxerunt, quia s. per huius[modi] figmenta semper aliqua[m] veritatem intelligere voluerunt . . ."[24] [Thus sacred scripture seems to have been written on many levels, whereby it is known that fables can be composed for the representation of another truth. . . . The poets who originally constructed fables did the same, because they always wanted (people) to understand some truth by means of this kind of imaginary representations (*figmenta*)]. For Berchorius, fables' falseness, their fictionality, nonetheless "may be forced to serve the truth," especially because not all fables can be understood literally. The textual letter cannot be trusted or taken at face value. Figures interpreted *in bono* and *in malo* reproduce the pagan text as a plural text, meaning-full. Berchorius argues that poetic art properly transforms truths into fables, fictions, and enigmas, multiple layers ["multis modis"] of encoding and textual meaning that the reader must attend to in several ways, "s. litteraliter, naturaliter, historialiter, spiritualiter" (fol. 1vb = Engels 5) [namely, literally, naturally, historically, spiritually]. However, Berchorius's allegorical interpretation ultimately reduces rather than produces multiple meanings. In his commentary, the pagan text signifies repeatedly the same set of moral meanings or Christian referents (e.g., Devil-Christ, Virgin Mary, tyrant-good ruler). Berchorius's mythography reveals the mono-logic of many medieval allegorists, and assimilates the ambivalences in Ovid's text into a singular Christian moral interpretation, buttressed by correspondences between Ovid's narratives and scripture.

Berchorius's allegorical reading of Pluto and Proserpina illustrates this mono-logic. Allegorically, Pluto *in malo* is a figure of the devil ["ymaginem . . . dyaboli"] or an example of "malus & austerus princeps vel eciam prelatus cum sua uxore terribili i. cum domina avaricia vel rapina" [an evil and harsh ruler, or indeed a prelate, with his terrible wife, that is, with Lady Avarice or Pillaging]. Proserpina *in malo* is his sordid consort who co-rules in hell and whose "evil suggestions" [*malis suggestionibus*] are followed by all there (fol. 9rb = Engels 43). Surprisingly, Proserpina *in malo* is interpreted as an attribute of a male figure, "domina avaricia vel rapina," making the kidnapped bride take on the allegorical meaning of violent seizure and oppression. The lexical collocation of *rapina* [plunder, robbery, pillaging, violent seizure] with Proserpina, even as an allegorical attribute of Pluto, shifts her textual representation from kidnap victim to controlling influence, from kidnapped woman [*rapta*] to *uxor* to *domina*. The phonetic (or graphic) similarity between her proper name and the vice deforms "Proserpina" into the allegorical signified she encodes, "pro rapina." Berchorius's Proserpina *in malo* becomes a signifier of the very actions to which the Ovidian female character was subjected.

In his master allegorization, Berchorius can also interpret the Pluto and Proserpina story as a positive example for Christian audiences. Fabulously, Pluto *in bono* signifies "virum iustum" [just man], "pro eo quod terribilia vincit & eis principatur" [because he overcomes awful/hellish things and governs them] or a type of Christ because he rules in hell. Going one step further, Berchorius reads Proserpina *in bono* as signifying the Virgin Mary, "coniugatus per amorem & dilectionem" (fol. 10rb = Engels 48–49) [joined to him (Christ) by means of love and worthiness]. In the allegory, Proserpina's status as a married woman consistently positions her as an attribute of a male figure, silencing her abduction, flattening the ambivalences in Ovid's narrative, even erasing the naturalistic interpretations of the narrative we find in other commentaries on *Metamorphoses*.

Although Berchorius's readings almost entirely erase *raptus* as sexual violence, at least as explicitly narrated, *rapina* and *rapere* permeate his versions and interpretations of Ovid's narratives. Berchorius's multiple interpretations often divide along social lines. *In bono* readings usually refer to ecclesiastics, while *in malo* readings often refer to secular aristocrats, rulers, and overbearing prelates. As the "ymago" of the devil, Pluto *in malo* manifests himself in different monsters: Cerberus (avarice), Furies (concupiscence), Fates (cruelty), and Harpies ("rapina"; fol. 9rb = Engels 43–44). The Furies signify excessive material desire: "Sicut patet quia concupiscencia diviciarum cogitat usuras, rapinas, etc." (fol. 9va = Engels 44) [As is evident because desire for riches calls to mind usury, pillaging, etc.]. Like Proserpina, wife of Pluto and figure of *rapina,* the Harpies attack others (e.g., "rapere & acquirere sicut aves" [seize and acquire as birds do]). Consequently, rapacious persons are textually transformed, literally and metaphorically, into greedy beasts or birds. In fact, the literal and the metaphorical are sometimes hard to differentiate in Berchorius's mythography. Following Fulgentius (*Mitologiae,* fifth century), Berchorius imagines the rapacious Harpies with talons "quia pro certo ad proprium lucrum ambiunt & aliquid rapere & extorquere nituntur et circa hoc continue meditantur," or more explicitly, "Harpie i. malorum ministrorum rapacitas" (fol. 9vb–10ra = Engels 46–47) [because truly they grab wealth for themselves and endeavor to pillage/rape and extort others and continually plan for this action . . . Harpie, that is, the greed of evil underlings]. Allegorical discourse shapes ideas and concepts in the physical.

Earlier, we noted how fourteenth-century English parliamentary legislation established harsher penalties for raping a virgin than a married or sexually active woman. But following earlier allegorists (e.g., Fulgentius), Berchorius also reads the Harpies as an image of virginity *in malo,* that is, *rapina,* in a striking semantic interpretation supported by Scriptural language: "Rapina significatur per Harpias que s. v[irg]ines dicuntur pro eo, secundum Fulgencium, quod omnis rapina sterilitatem & paupertatem comitatur; quia ut communiter illi qui libenter rapiunt aliena, virgines i. steriles & pauperes, inveniuntur. Prov. XI: Alii rapiunt non sua & semper in egestate sunt" (fol. 9va = Engels 44) [Rapine/pillaging is signified by the Harpies, who are called virgins because, following Fulgentius, rapine accompanies sterility and poverty, and because commonly those who freely pillage/rape others, become virgins, that is, sterile, poor ones. Proverbs 11: They pillage/rape others, not themselves, yet they are always lacking]. Here, virginity *in malo* (feminized in the image of Harpies) signifies moral as well as physical lack. A perverse and dangerous feminine. Rather than raping virgins, Harpies greedily pillage others but remain virgins, that is, without profit to themselves. In his *Confessio Amantis* (Book 5, on Avarice or *ravine*), Gower's Genius similarly interprets virginity *in malo* as feminized lack, unfruitfulness, and punishment for greed.

Within the domain of *rapina,* Berchorius's allegorization of Pluto and Proserpina consistently emphasizes social and economic oppression. There are "tres species rapinarum . . . videl. publice per tyrannos, occulte per usurarios, fraudulenter per exactores & ballivos" (fol. 9va = Engels 44) [three types of rapine . . . namely, public [rapine] perpetrated by tyrants, secret [rapine] perpetrated by usurers, and fraudulent [rapine] (extortion?) perpetrated by tax collectors and bailiffs]. *Rapinae* signify a powerful ruler's moral or political faults or social oppressions, read imaginatively and intertextually (*Daniel* 7) as bestial acts ("Unde rapina est iste bestia . . ."; fol. 9va = Engels 44–45). This semiotic whirlwind of allegorical associations dismembers Ovid's narrative and assimilates the pagan text to an allegory of political virtue and medieval Christian critiques of ruthless governance and seizure of property. At the same time, Proserpina's kidnapping and later medieval prescriptions about raping virgins are written out of the allegorization. In Berchorius's commentary, Ovid's narrative of the rape of Proserpina contains a set of figurative signs cloaking an underlying economic and political story in the masculine world.

In Berchorius's *Reductorium morale,* rulers like Pluto or Jupiter are interpreted as both positive and negative examples of masculinity. Jupiter signifies alternately a "bonus prelatus," "malus prelatus & princeps," or "malus princeps." Jupiter *in bono* represents "a good man and a great ecclesiastic or prelate" [*virum bonum & maxime bonum ecclesiasticum vel prelatum*], while Jupiter *in malo* signifies " . . . a proud or indeed any evil or violent/shameful ruler [*superbus vel eciam quilibet malus dominus vel protervus*] because like those evil gods, princes and tyrants have a ram's head for having persecuted others for a long time [*caput arietis dure alios percuciendo*]" (fol. 3vb–4ra = Engels 12–14). Berchorius, like Bernard Silvestris and other commentators, regards bestial transformation as metaphoric, a sign of a character's punishment or moral change.

Like his readings of Pluto and Proserpina, Berchorius's interpretations of Jupiter—serial rapist and serial sign—are permeated with the language of *rapina.* As the figure of a bad prince or king, Jupiter violently attacks innocents, servants, and the weak because of his crushing pride in his own power (" . . . violenterque rapiunt per seviciem" [violently pillages/rapes on account of his maliciousness]). As an image of a prideful (*superba*) yet legitimate tyrant, Berchorius's Jupiter holds the "virga" of temporal jurisdiction and carries lightning bolts of cruelty and rapaciousness ("fulmina rapine & crudelitatis"; fol. 4ra = Engels 14). Berchorius's Jupiter tramples on Giants (great and holy men), while Jupiter's eagles are "cruel bailiffs" [*crudeles ballivos*] who "rape young boys" [*que rapiunt pueros*], that is, "oppress the innocent [*innocentes afficiunt*], seize their servants, and advance themselves in the courts [*curiis*] and other offices" (fol. 4ra = Engels 14). *Rapina* and *rapere* describe tyrants' violence against others and excessive desire for material goods (avarice), perhaps, but not clearly, including rape. In this allegorization, Berchorius's collocation of eagles ["aquilas"] with the phrase "rapiunt pueros" echoes Jupiter's passion for Ganymede in *Metamorphoses:* "Wishing to turn himself into a bird, he nonetheless scorned to change into any except that which can carry his thunderbolts [i.e., eagle]. Then without delay, beating the air on borrowed feathers, he snatched away the shepherd of Ilium, who even now mixes the winecups, and supplies Jove with nectar, to the annoyance of Juno" (*Meta.* 10.157–58). We can turn intertextuality on its head and reread Berchorius's allegorical reading against Ovid's earlier story of Jupiter and Ganymede. In the *rapina* code, the Christian allegorist submerges sexual violence within a more general account of social violence and tyrannical oppression, especially by powerful lords. Berchorius's embedded glosses on "pueros" as "simplices" and "innocentes" suggest how Christian allegorists (unlike writers of saints' lives) generalized virginity as a moral or spiritual state, *in malo* or *in bono,* and specifically silenced the sexual crimes connoted by "rapere/rapiunt." In

Berchorius commentary, rape is read as a sign of something else. Ganymede stands for not divine creation but male rulers' social and economic injustice. The masculine "pueros" stand for all victims of oppression. As our rumination on medieval mythography has shown, such eliding interpretations of Ovid's rape narratives distance the letter of the feminine from the official text and depend on a hermeneutic in which male figures are read as symbols of power, narrative control, or divinity, while women or boys are objects of desire or dangerous attractions.

Daphne and Apollo

In the fourteenth century, the massive French *Ovide moralisé* in octosyllabic verse (prose version, fifteenth century) was a key source for many moralizations of Ovid's narratives, including those by Berchorius and Christine de Pizan. Like Berchorius, the writer (or writers) of the *Ovide moralisé* retold the mythic narratives, provided allegorical and moral interpretations for Christian readers, and linked the pagan stories with biblical accounts of the creation of the world, the rule of the giants, the Tower of Babel, and the giants as rebel angels in Heaven.[25] For Christine de Pizan and other writers, the manuscripts of the *Ovide moralisé* presented a vernacular archive of classical narratives and an index of official moral reading. Chaucer's knowledge of the text is less certain, although he was clearly aware of later medieval moralizations of Ovid's *Metamorphoses.*[26]

Unlike Berchorius and other allegorizers, the writer of the *Ovide moralisé* represents many of the sexual conflicts in Ovid's narratives in a direct narrative style. Comparing Ovid's narrative of Apollo's attempted rape of Daphne (*Meta.* 1.452–567) with the allegorizations of the narrative in the *Ovide moralisé* and Christine de Pizan's *Épîstre,* we can see how different commentators negotiated problems of gendered representation and moral signification in texts about rape and sexual violence. In particular, we shall see how Daphne's problematic transformation—she loses her humanness to avoid being raped—was often refigured as a representation of men's public voices or writing.

In Ovid's text, Apollo and Cupid argue, and Cupid one-ups Apollo by piercing him with an arrow that arouses desire in him (*Meta.* 1.557–64). Then Cupid pierces Daphne with another arrow that puts love to flight, just to spite Apollo. Daphne, emulating Diana and "fleeing the very word 'lover'" [*fugit altera nomen amantis* (1.474)], defies her father's wish that she marry. The reference to Diana suggests that *amans* refers to 'male lover,' although at this point in Ovid's narrative Daphne is resisting the idea of hetero-romance rather than its reality. The narrator, however, describes the gap between desire and effect: "her very loveliness prevented her from being what she desired, and her beauty defeated her own wishes." Apollo, struck by Cupid's arrow of desire, sees Daphne and becomes completely enthralled with her beauty. First, he woos her by presenting his credentials as a worthy lover: son of Jupiter, founder of medicine, creator of music. But Daphne runs away, and as the wind stirs her clothes, Apollo becomes even more aroused by the sight of her body. Finally, as Daphne's strength wanes and Apollo gains on her, the woman prays to the river god Peneus: "'If you rivers really have divine powers, do something, and by transformation destroy this beauty which makes me please all too well'" ["'Fer, pater,' inquit, 'opem si flumina numen habeiis; / Qua nimium placui, mutando perde figuram'"] (*Meta.* 1.545–46/47). Both the narrator and Daphne suggest that her beauty makes her vulnerable, so she comes to disdain her *figura* (body, shape, image—*Figura* is also the grammatical term for orthography). Publicly, Daphne is willing to disfigure herself in order to avoid both marriage and rape. Then, just as Apollo reaches her, the river god answers Daphne's prayer and turns her into a laurel tree. Apollo embraces the laurel as if it were Daphne's body, saying, "'Since you cannot be my bride [*coniunx*], surely you will at least be my tree [*arbor*].'" In a parody of Roman imperial, heroic verse, Apollo proclaims the laurel sacred to him forever and prophesies, with a fictional character's accurate foresight, that the laurel will adorn Caesar Augustus's doorways and will be the imperial symbol of triumph and victory. But the narrator destabilizes this triumphal ending with a final twist of subjective ambiguity: "the laurel tree inclined her new-made branches, and seemed to nod her leafy top, as if it were a head, in consent" [" . . . factis modo laurea ramis / Annuit utque caput visa est agitasse cacumen"; *Meta.* 1.566–67].

In many ways, Ovid's narrative is a paradigmatic story of attempted rape, although it is sometimes read as an attempted seduction. It all depends on whether Daphne, or her narrative descendents, consent to their Apollos's desires. Many tropes of medieval courtly love rehearse Ovid's narrative of Daphne and Apollo: love at first sight, irresistible love, female hesitation (in Daphne's case, sheer flight), a male suitor pursuing against all odds, the problematic role of female beauty in the seduction or rape narrative, an ambiguous resolution suggesting not only female consent but also Apollo's problematic eagerness to read natural "tree" behavior as an intentional linguistic sign. Ovid's syntax—"seemed to nod . . . as if it were a head"—and substitution of "the laurel tree" for Daphne as the subject of the sentence point to the gap between Daphne's new mutated (mute) being and Apollo's interpretation of the tree's behavior. Also, Apollo's rivalry with Cupid suggests how Ovid ironizes romantic narratives and posits a homosocial motivation for Apollo's heated desire for Daphne. That Apollo fails in his quest for Daphne, first when he woos her verbally, then when he chases her physically, differentiates him from Jupiter, whose shape-changing and forceful modes of seduction or rape are more successful. But in Ovid's narrative, Apollo gets the last, if ironized, word, when he in mock-Homeric style links himself with Daphne and the laurel for all eternity. Apollo's over-the-top, ironized voice reimagines Daphne as the unlikely origin of an imperial symbol—Ovidian undercutting of Augustan mythmaking. Although Apollo embraces the now treeified Daphne, the narrative continues to separate Daphne's voice from how her story will be told and read (unlike the female crow who tells her own story of transformation to avoid Neptune's rape; *Meta.* 2.569–88). As a victim of attempted rape, Daphne loses narrative control over her own experience. Finally, the transformation of Daphne's soft skin into bark, branches, and leaves, the same skin that had excited Apollo as he chased her, suggests the alienating, disfiguring self-loathing, she experiences as she escapes from the potential rapist.

Some medieval allegorizations of Ovid's narrative all but erase Daphne from the narrative and focus instead on Apollo's connection with the laurel.[27] But the *Ovide moralisé* rehearses Ovid's narrative in some detail and then gives an elaborate allegorical interpretation of the story (*OM,* I.2737–3064, 3065–260). The narrative follows Ovid's text fairly closely, but transposes the characters into the vocabulary of vernacular romance, incorporating sections from Chrétien de Troyes's version. Phoebus argues with Cupid about whose arrows are more powerful. Phoebus pleads with Daphne (referred to as "Belle fille," "la pucele," and "chiere amie") to marry him, but she refuses, wishing to remain unwed in order to protect her maidenhood ("vuel garder mon pucelage"; *OM,* I.2838, 2856, 2907, 2857–58). Like a medieval courtly lover, Phoebus is completely in love with Daphne and praises her beauty in a courtly blazon of dismemberment (arms, eyes, hair, mouth, etc.). Then, as in Ovid's narrative, Phoebus presents Daphne with his credentials as a potential lover/husband (founder of music and medicine, son of Jupiter, wise and powerful), but Daphne will not consent, so she flees. As he pursues her, Apollo is even more aroused by the glimpses he gets of her body as the wind stirs her clothes. But Daphne races on, despite her fatigue, because she does not wish to lose her virginity ("Com cele qui pas n'atalente / De perdre sa virginité"; *OM,* I.2992–93). As she is about to be caught by Apollo, Daphne pleads to Peneus to save her from sin ("a perdicion"; I.3024), an ambiguous utterance that echoes Ovid's narrative in which Daphne feels she is partially to blame for her attempted rape. Daphne is then turned into the laurel tree, which Apollo takes as his sacred ornament, prophesying that the laurel will be a sign of nobility, love, and glory for all those who are victorious (*OM,* I.3044–51).

This vernacular retelling of the Daphne and Apollo narrative is close in many ways to Ovid's Latin version, but it omits the narrator's consistent irony and streamlines the psychological narrative. Nonetheless, a moralized Ovidian narrative is not a *texta nuda*. It is a guided reading. Along with the classical narrative recoded as courtly (e.g., *honneur, pucelage, chevalrie, d'a-complir son plesir*), the writer of the *Ovide moralisé* also presents several different readings of Phoebus's attempted rape of Daphne—multiple readings of the pagan text, naturalist, historical, and moral readings. The second, historical reading explicitly engages with the question of rape. *Naturaliter*, the narrative can be read as a geographical allegory to explain how the river Peneus and the sun nourish the laurel tree (*OM*, I.3065–74). Quickly turning to an "Autre sentence," the commentator interprets the story *historialiter* as how a young woman, daughter of a great family ("un damoi-sele / . . . / Riche et de grant nobilité") wants to defend her virginity ("Sans violer son pucelage"; *OM*, I.3077, 3079, 3081). She flees a young suitor who wants to *force* her, seize her virginity ("la cuida forçoier / Et tolir li son pucelage"; I.3092–93), and *deflower* her ("Et malgré sien la des-florast . . . Ains que cil l'eüst desfloree"; I.3098, 3101). Whereupon the woman dies at the foot of a laurel tree. In the historical allegory, Daphne becomes an emblem of chastity. Unlike other allegorical and mythographic texts, the writer of the *Ovide moralisé* explicitly reads the letter of Ovid's story as attempted rape. Daphne's desire to remain a virgin is foregrounded in the aristocratic vocabulary of *honneur* and *pucelage*. Apollo's desire for Daphne is directly represented by the legal term for forced sex [*(e)forçoier*] and by the narrative pun on *desflorier*, connoting sexual violence and setting the stage in the vernacular for Daphne's *floral* escape from Apollo. *His-torialiter*, Daphne's desire to remain chaste is represented in the *Ovide moralisé* as an escape from both marriage and attempted rape.

After these *naturaliter* and *historialiter* readings, the writer of the *Ovide moralisé* turns to what he (or she?) refers to as a different "Autre sentence profitable"; *OM*, I.3110), an interpretation *moraliter*. Daphne's physical coldness, noted by the river god, signifies her virginity, while her perfect virginity is represented by her transformation into a tree, motionless and nonfruitbearing. Once again, Daphne's sterility is ambiguously coupled with her figural purity and narrative fate (to avoid being raped). This "moral" interpretation draws on textual features not found implicitly or explicitly in Ovid's narrative. Yet, as in Ovid's text, the *Ovide moralisé* de-picts the beautiful, desirable Daphne as choosing to disfigure herself in order to escape rape. Apollo is glossed as the god of wisdom, following the *Integumenta* (perhaps a reference to John of Garland on pagan belief; *OM*, I.3126), while his desire for Daphne is renamed in the moral allegory as wisdom's desire for purity and spiritual virginity that transcends the body.

In this vernacular interpretation, Apollo's sexual arousal and desire are reread positively as the desire for spiritual transcendence. Just as Daphne's body is transformed literally into a tree that Apollo ultimately can embrace and claim for himself, so Daphne's actions are assimilated by the moralizing commentator into a signifying system in which the masculine Apollo is the agent while the feminine Daphne remains the object of desire and, significantly, mute. Despite the *Ovide moralisé* writer's direct engagement with the story as an attempted rape, the goal of Christian allegory is to read the rape scenario otherly, as a narrative of transcendent desire. Ovid's "wise" Apollo, who interprets the laurel tree's ambiguous motion as signifying consent, becomes in the "authoritative" *Ovide moralisé* the masculine soul desiring Daphne, the fleeing woman, the object of the soul's desire for purity and salvation.

With this reading *spiritualiter* in place, it is not a stretch for the allegorist in the *Ovide moralisé* to move to Christology. Daphne is interpreted/glossed [*gloser*] as the Virgin Mary ("Cele glorieuse Pucele"; *OM*, I.3216–17), cherished by all who stand in the "light" of spiritual understanding. Apollo (light) is crowned with laurel, that is, with Daphne herself in the image of the Virgin, just as God/Christ is enclosed within the body of his mother (see *OM*, I.3221–36). The Christological allegory of Apollo as Christ is customary among Christian mythographers, and Apollo's signification controls the allegorical code. In the allegory *historialiter*, Apollo's desire signified a young male aristocrat's desire to deflower the maiden, and Daphne is figure of chastity and moral purity resisting a rapist. But in the allegory *moraliter* and *spiritualiter*, Apollo's desire is transformed into something spiritually pure, while Daphne must again submit to a masculine interpretive moral discourse that reads rape in other terms controlled by masculine desire.

Christine de Pisan clearly read the *Ovide moralisé* as she worked on her own mythography, *Épistre d'Othéa la déesse à Hector* (c. 1400; English translation by Stephen Scrope c. 1440). The text, composed as advice for a young prince, was one of Christine's most popular works. Christine closely supervised the production of the *Épistre*—text, gloss, allegory, and manuscript illustrations.[28] Like other mythographic writing (e.g., Fulgentius's *Mitologiae*, Gower's *Confessio Amantis*), Christine organized the *Épistre* with a fictional frame narrative: the wise and prudent Minerva/Othea writes to Hector during the Trojan War to instruct him in proper heroic behavior. Within the framing genre of female advice literature, Christine weaves a polylogic mythographic text from a trio of narrative and interpretive discourses, each associated with the female voice/writing of Minerva. The Christian glossator/commentator redescribes classical narratives as examples of "droite chevalerie," "parfaicte chevalerie," and "l'esperit chevalereux" (*Épistre*, Prologue; 201.135 and 139, 202.149). The society foregrounded by Christine's mythography is masculine, Christian, and aristocratic.

Like the *Ovide moralisé*, Christine's mythography repeats classical narratives in the vernacular and follows each brief narrative "Texte" with a "Glose" and an "Allegorie." Whereas the *Ovide moralisé* writer renders Ovidian narratives in elaborate, complex ways, Christine's Textes only briefly allude to mythological or historical narratives. The Glose in prose somewhat expands the verse narrative and interprets each episode with a classical moral teaching to illustrate proper chivalric attitudes. The Allegorie elaborates the spiritual implications of the narrative with citations from Scripture and Christian *auctores*. In the Prologue, Minerva says that her stories are *exempla:* "Je leur lis leçons en chayere / Qui les fait monter jusqu'au cieulx" (*Epístre*, Prologue; 198.57–58) [I read/teach to them lessons in charity, so they can climb to heaven]. The allegorist identifies the audience as Christians without restriction to men or women (*Epístre*, Prologue; 199.82), but the advice focuses almost entirely on male knighthood. While medieval mythographies recontextualize pagan myths and narratives for Christian audiences, the *Epístre* juxtaposes the ancient world and Trojan war with Christian and chivalric readings of Ovid's narratives. The allegorist's voice is figured as the female Minerva, but fifteenth-century male knighthood emerges from ancient heroic ideals.

In *Epístre*, the fiction of the wise woman counselor suggests that the allegorization of Ovid's narratives might address the stories' sexual politics differently than other mythographies do. And, to some extent, Christine's text does alter how rape narratives are represented. Christine de Pizan's role in restructuring women's textual and public voices in the later Middle Ages is well known. So, too, is her explicit criticism of rape narratives and masculinist ideologies of women's rape fantasies. Diane Wolfthal has argued that Christine de Pizan "disrupts the traditional rape script, first by refusing to imagine women as victims of sexual violence and then by visualizing them as forceful avengers."[29] Responding to the story of Lucrece and the misrepresentations of women's desires by male writers, Christine wrote in her *Cité des dames:* " . . . chaste ladies who live honestly take absolutely no pleasure in being raped. Indeed rape is the greatest possible sorrow for them" [*douleur sur toutes autre*].[30]

However, Christine treats rape narratives differently in her mythographic *Epístre* from the way she contextualizes rape narratives in her later *Cité des dames*. In the *Cité*, Lucretia and the Galatian queen occupy a central place in the catalogue of violated females. But replaying its Ovidian hypotext, the *Epístre* gestures toward many of the rape narratives (kidnapping, attempted kidnapping, as well as sexual violence) from *Metamorphoses,* including Proserpina/Pluto (3), Aurora (44), Ganymede (53), Orpheus/Eurydice (70), and

Daphne/Apollo (87). In addition, the Trojan frame narrative and Minerva's advice to Hector take Helen's abduction as a key narrative and interpretive thread in the text. Repeatedly, the French text refers to women or men who are forced (*efforcier;* e.g., Eurydice; *Épístre;* 297.11; Ganymede; 274.2 and 10) or kidnapped (*ravir;* e.g., Helen, "que en Grece raviroit Helayne . . . ou Paris ravi Helayne" [294.7–9]; Proserpina, "que Pluto ot ravi" [240.8]). The narrator introduces the Latin *rapina* in the allegory for the story of Aurora (44), citing Psalm 61 [62] ("Nolite sperare in iniquitate, rapinas nolite concupiscere" [Don't trust in extortion; don't put your hope in pillaging]) to counsel the reader to avoid covetousness (*rapina* = avarice), signified by Aurora's weeping for her lost son (*Épístre* 44; 262.29–34). Whereas in Berchorius's allegorizations, *rapina* usually signifies seizure of property rather than a sexual crime, in Christine de Pisan's mythography, *rapina* and *raptus,* along with *efforcier,* signify both property crimes and crimes against person, sexual crimes.

Editors and critics have long noted Christine's use of the verse *Ovide moralisé* to compose her own mythography, but the *Épístre*'s text, gloss, and allegory of the Daphne and Apollo story depart from earlier mythographies in significant ways. As Wolfthal notes, Christine's visual and verbal representations of women resist depicting them as rape victims, but not entirely, as we shall see. Christine's text departs from earlier mythographic discourse in other ways as well. For one thing, the glossing and allegorizing in *Épístre* are much more concerned with chivalric codes of male knighthood than with the conflicts between male and usually female characters. Second, and surprisingly, Daphne is almost entirely absent from Christine's *verbal* allegorization of the Ovidian narrative. However, some manuscript illustrations for the text depict Daphne not with the traditional iconography of the raped woman (grabbed by a man), but treeified, her head laurel branches, her skin scarred as bark, a grotesque figure, a disfigured body, in a parody of the medieval female nude. The mutated Daphne, faceless and mute.

The Glose multiplies the textual letter: "Plusieurs entendemens peut avoir la fable" (87; 323.20–21) [The fable can have many meanings], historical as well as moral. The moral gloss interprets the rape as a representation of the knight's worthy pursuit of "une dame." The word phonetically close to Christine's French form for Daphne, "Damné," a born lady (323.7 and 22). The male knight's pursuit of Damné is legitimated in terms of his struggle to receive the laurel, that is, "en signe de victoire que il ot eue de ses amours soubz le laurier; et peut estre aussi le laurier pris pour or, qui signiffie noblece" (323.25–27) [as a sign of the victory which he had over his love beneath the laurel. And perhaps also, the laurel is taken for gold, which signifies nobility]. In the moral Glose, Christine rewrites Daphne's attempted rape as a chivalric allegory of a male knight's *successful* pursuit of a woman, or glory.

So much for reading *moraliter*. Turning back to Christine's first interpretation, her historical reading is striking for what it does *not* say. According to the glossator, the story of Daphne and Apollo might represent *historialiter* how "un poissant homme" [a powerful man], after much wooing, finally "attaigni a sa voulenté" (323.21–24) [accomplished his desire] with his lady under a laurel tree. (Christine uses the same phrase in a more explicitly sexual sense in the story of Pygmalion: "En la parfin tant la pria et tant se tint pres que la pucelle l'ama a sa voulenté et l'eut a mariage"; 235.33–35). In her Daphne story, Christine substitutes the contextually more ambiguous "accomplished his desire" for the sexually explicit and legally inscribed *efforcier*, as in the *Ovide moralisé*, to describe what went on under the laurel tree. Surprisingly, Christine again focuses narrowly on the male lover's point of view, unlike Ovid or the *Ovide moralisé* writer, and as a result her gloss erases Daphne's motives and actions even from the historical level of the text. In both the historical and the moral interpretations, Christine's mythography uses Ovidian narrative to exemplify the knight's romantic or chivalric quest. At the same time, Christine's language and textual erasure open up the narrative to multiple interpretations of Daphne's motives. Could the lady signified by "Damné" have consented to the knight's pleas? Christine's rereading and rewriting of Ovid's narrative leaves ambiguous the question of Daphne's consent. Finally, although *attaigni a sa voulenté* might be sexually more discreet, the glossator's meaning, sexual rather than just chivalric, is underscored by the fact that Anthony Babyngton, unlike Scrope, prudishly omitted lines 21–24 of the French text from his late fifteenth-century English translation.

In the Allegorie attached to the Texte and Glose, the allegorist erases Daphne altogether, and instead emphasizes the good knight's quest: "se le bon esperit veult victoire glorieuse avoir, il lui couvient perseverence qui le menra a la victoire de paradis dont les joyes sont infinies" (324.36–39) [if the good soul wants to have a glorious victory, he must have perseverance, which will lead him to victory in paradise, whose joys are infinite]. The allegory in Christine's text is decidedly aristocratic, unlike the more clerical interpretation of the story in Berchorius' *Reductorium morale*. For Berchorius, the story shows how the laurel *in bono* is sacred to Apollo and signifies wise men of right learning ("sani ingenii") or the image of the poet or light or truth or knowledge or "virum iustum," "qui bene interpretatur exterminans pro eo quod iste in se exterminat omne mal(i)um" (*Reductorium*, fol. 4vb, 5rb–5va = Engels 18, 21) [the just man . . . who is understood well as banishing (a banisher?) because he rids himself of all evil]. *In malo*, the laurel signifies "la[s]civos iuvenes & mulieres" (fol. 5ra = Engels 19) [lecherous

young men and women]. Both Berchorius and Christine read the myth *historialiter*, with the implication of a literal meaning. But unlike Christine's
successful male lover, Berchorius's Apollo *in malo* suggests dangerous sexuality in young men and women. Berchorius's elaborate moralization marks
by contrast how much Christine de Pizan's mythographic readings focus on
male aristocratic codes and the promotion of "l'esperit chevaleureux."
Berchorius's allegorization says nothing about Daphne, whereas Christine's
allegorization at least renders Daphne as a narrative goal or object of desire.

In Ovid's narrative, Daphne resists an unwanted male lover by becoming disfigured and giving up control of her voice. But in Christine's text,
the verbal and pictorial versions of the myth stage an ambiguous dialogue.
The glossator imagines the story as a representation of a male knight's *successful* wooing or seduction of his lady. The allegorist, continuing the text's
masculine orientation, interprets Apollo as the masculine soul, persistently
pursuing heavenly glory, despite the difficulties of the world, signified by
Daphne. In the allegory, the female figure stands in for the world, linking
the romance hero's pursuit of the object of his sexual desire with the hero's
spiritual quest for salvation. Daphne's disfiguring resistance is silenced in
the text. But in some manuscript illuminations for *Épístre,* Daphne is depicted as a grotesque female figure without a head, tongue, or voice. At the
same time, this mute and mutated Daphne is beyond Apollo's grasp.
Nonetheless, in at least one manuscript (Paris, BN, MS fr. 606, fol. 40v),
Apollo might still have the last word, as he is depicted plucking Daphne's
leaves, gathering pieces of her treeified body into his self-decorating
crown, the symbol of (whose?) poetic achievement.

In the final section (100) of the text, the allegorist cites Hugh of St. Victor's *Didascalicon* on the nature of discourse. The message is more important than the messenger: "il ne considere point qui c'est parle mais que
c'est que il dit" (341.40–42) [the reader (should) not pay attention to who
is speaking but to what is said]. Readers should attend to the utterance, not
the utterer, content rather than authority or individual voices. As we have
learned from Ovid's narrative of Daphne and Apollo, female utterances and
gestures can be disregarded by desiring men or read according to what
men desire to know. The allegorizing mythographies we have considered
show us how authoritative interpretive discourse can disregard or silence
parts of the text or generalize characters (Daphne) into walking concepts
or male heroes' goals, depriving them of voice, autonomy, or textual subjectivity. Christine de Pizan's mythography in some ways rewrites Ovid's
narratives and those of earlier mythographers, especially with respect to
depictions of women in distress. In the Daphne and Apollo story, Christine's historical gloss multiplies the signification of the woman in the textual field: object of the knight's desire, feminine symbol of chivalric goals,

a woman who may have consented to the knight's romantic suit. Christine de Pizan's rewriting of the story reminds us that authoritative mythographic discourses, which silence narratives of rape or transform them into other utterances, do not belong only to male interpreters and readers.

The Voices of Daphne and Philomela

Chaucer, Christine de Pizan's near contemporary, was equally at home with medieval mythography. Scholars have reconstructed Chaucer's knowledge of Ovid's erotic writings and mythography, as well as of Ovidian texts and mythographies such as Berchorius's *Reductorium morale* (and perhaps the *Ovide moralisé*). Chaucer of course translated at least part of the *Roman de la rose*. The story of Daphne and Apollo appears only twice in Chaucer's writings: in the description of Diana's temple in the *Knight's Tale*[31] and in *Troilus and Criseyde,* Book III, when Troilus anxiously waits to come to Criseyde's bedroom. Chaucer's allusion in *Troilus* is especially suggestive about medieval readings of Ovid because of its textual collocations. Troilus prays to a number of gods—and all seven planets!—to strengthen him as he waits for Pandarus to give him the go-ahead to approach his beloved. In one stanza, Troilus invokes Jupiter, Apollo, and Mars, all three in their narrative roles as dominant males: raping Europa, attempting to capture Daphne, and symbolizing male warrior action and covered with a "blody cope" (*TC,* III.722–28). Two of the three are specifically rapists, one successful, one not. Troilus's emphasis on sexually dominant males differs markedly from the moral-allegorical interpretations of Jupiter's rape of Europa in the *Ovide moralisé,* where Jupiter's transformation into a bull and assault on Europa are re-signed as an allegory of Christ coming to earth to save humanity (*OM,* II.4937–5138). The allegorist of the *Ovide moralisé* specifically narrates the story as a rape narrative ("ravir"; II.5063, 5101, etc.), which makes the Christological allegory all the more a "strong" or mastering reading. In addition, Troilus's description of Mars as another "action male" contrasts with medieval mythographic readings (for example, Fulgentius) of Mars and Venus as a representation of public male virtue (Mars) lured or seduced from proper masculine duties by private female pleasure or luxury (Venus).[32] Like Christine de Pizan's allegory, Troilus's use of the Daphne and Apollo narrative contextualizes the Ovidian narrative primarily from the point of view of the male pursuer and potential rapist's experience.

One of Chaucer's most deliberate uses of Ovidian rape narrative is his retelling of Philomela's rape in *Legend of Good Women* (2228–393). A vivid version of the narrative, probably by Chrétien de Troyes, was incorporated into the *Ovide moralisé,* with graphic illustrations of Tereus's mutilation of

Philomela. Mythographers often included the story in their texts, as does Gower in *Confessio Amantis,* Book 5 (as one of Genius's *exempla* of avarice, *rapina,* and male infidelity). But the gruesome story does not appear in Christine's *Épístre,* even though Ovid's narrative includes a female revenge plot. Rather than allegorizing the story, Chaucer's version is set within a collection of stories (much like Ovid's *Heroides*) about virtuous yet wronged women, stories written by the male poet as penance for what queen Alceste describes in his dream vision as the derogatory ways the poet has portrayed female characters in earlier texts (especially Criseyde). Chaucer's fictionalized writer in *Legend of Good Women* is modeled on the *accessus* biographies of Ovid, in which Ovid is said to write the *Heroides* and other texts to redeem himself in Augustus's eyes. Whereas many of the mythographic commentaries either depicted women as rape victims or erased rape altogether from the narratives, Chaucer's narrative, like Ovid's, specifically represents Philomela as a raped and mutilated woman. But unlike Ovid's, Chrétien's, and Gower's versions, Chaucer's text cuts off the final portion of the narrative in which Philomela and her sister Procne get their revenge on Tereus. Chaucer's mutilation of Ovid's text problematizes the reading of rape and the reading of women's writing.

Ovid's narrative graphically depicts not only a violent rape and mutilation but also a dionysiac revenge plot in which the mother Procne and her violated sister brutally kill the boy Itys and serve him up as dinner to his father. Philomela, covered with blood, holds the boy's head in front of his horrified father. Enraged at the loss of his patrimony, Tereus chases the women, but they are all magically transformed into birds, one (not clearly identified in Ovid's text) bearing the "traces of the murder" in her bloody feathers. Although Tereus had cut out Philomela's tongue to prevent her from reporting his crime, the woman manages to weave a text with purple thread and write ("Purpureasque notas" [*Meta.* 6.577], where "nota" signifies a letter) the story of her rape and mutilation. Tereus's cruel attempt to silence Philomela does not prevent her from producing a written narrative. When Procne reads the text, she falls silent, a reading response suggesting her empathy with her sister's muteness. Procne is unable to speak because she cannot adequately represent her rage in language: "when she sought for words, she could find none bitter enough" (*Meta.* 6.584–85). While in this essay I have considered separately the narratives of Daphne/Apollo and Tereus/Philomela, Ovid links the rapes together by repeating the language of Apollo's desire for Daphne in Tereus's more bluntly represented lust for Philomela.[33] Ovid reiterates sexual violence as a frenzy in his mythological narratives.

Some medieval mythographies and *accessus* to classical texts harshly condemn Philomela's and her sister's revenge on Tereus at least as much as they condemn the rapist himself. Bernard of Utrecht, in his commentary on Theodulus's *Eclogue,* reads Philomela as an example of an evil woman, despite her having been raped and mutilated. The commentary downplays the rape itself and focuses instead on the fact that the mother and aunt kill Itys. The commentary then extends this interpretation by reading the transformations of Tereus, Procne, and Philomela into birds as a sign of their alienation from human society on account of their crimes.[34] In other words, the sisters' revenge, which uses Tereus's patrilineal capital against him (emphasized in Ovid's text when Procne notes the resemblance between the boy and his father), is equated with the rape itself. While Tereus violates the taboo of incest, the sisters violate the taboo of cannibalism and, I would add, the code of femininity. Tereus's rape and the sisters' bloody revenge are depicted as equally heinous crimes.

The first two Vatican Mythographers often interpret classical stories, of rape and other events, as representations of divine creative processes or natural generative processes. But they also implicitly condemn illicit sex and rape among gods and humans by delineating genealogies, patrilineal chains, in which the offspring of rapes repeat the errors of the parent(s) or continue to suffer for their *father's* crimes.[35] Jupiter's rape of Leda initiates a chain of abducted and revengeful women, some of whom get back at their fathers in violent ways (Clytemnestra; Helen, daughter of Leda, is herself abducted).[36] In the First Vatican Mythographer's genealogy, Philomela's rape plagues succeeding marriages and generations: "Philomela married Tereus and gave birth to Itys, Procrin, and Orithia. Procrin had Cephalus, who was engendered by Aeolus. Boreas raped [*rapuit*] Orithia and begat from her Zetus and Calain." Rape continues to infect Pandion's lineage, as much because of his daughters' violent, taboo-violating revenge as because of Tereus's sexual violence and mutilation of Philomela. In this respect, the First Vatican Mythographer's vocabulary for sexual crime is at odds with the theme of infected genealogy. Tereus *abducts* [*"abducit"*] the young woman [*"puellam"*], then *conquers* or *successfully attacks* her [*"viciavit"*].[37] In this story, the mythographer does not use the verb *rapere* or the noun *raptus,* preferring the more legal, but less sexual, *abducere,* and the neutral *rem.* However, the mythographer does indicate that Tereus uses force [*viciare*] against Philomela. Also, the mythographer heightens the pathos of Philomela's mutilation by altering her purple letters (*notae* in Ovid) into "veste cruore" [a bloody tapestry/cloth], but this change obscures Philomela's status as a writer. For the First Vatican Mythographer, rape in ancient narratives is ambiguous: allegorical signs of natural processes and divine creativity, but also generative acts that call forth violent repetition. Rape begets rape and bloody disaster, and historicizes human history as a tragic repetition of violence. According to the mythographer, the Thebans' foundational crimes

are fratricide and self-destruction, whereas the Trojans' foundational crimes
are rape and betrayal of kin.[38]

Chaucer's narrative of Philomela's rape moves provocatively against the
grain of mythographic allegorizations. As a truncated—mutilated, mutated,
transformed—text, Chaucer's narrative erases the bloody revenge that many
mythographic commentators emphasized to condemn Procne and
Philomela as bad women, and which Ovid's narrative exploited as an out-
break of dionysiac payback and feminine rage. More important, the narrator,
rather than silently passing over his elision, explicitly gestures towards the
textual truncation: "The remenaunt is no charge for to telle, / For this is al
and som . . ." (LGW 2383–84). In one respect, the textual manipulation (a
cutting off and silencing, thematically similar to Tereus's mutilation of
Philomela) makes the story more appropriate as a "legend" in a collection of
narratives about wronged, virtuous women. But the textual elision also
opens up the question of sexuality and reading in the narrative, and the question of how women's writing is read. Chaucer's textual erasure works to protect Philomela and Procne from the authoritative mythographic discourse
that condemns the two, especially Procne, as vengeful, bad women who
transgress their natural, feminine, maternal natures and commit infanticide
and cannibalism. However, the textual mutilation problematizes the relationship between the male author/narrator and the rapist. The narrator repeats Tereus's attempt to silence part of a woman's story, but this time for
supposedly "good" reasons. Whether Alceste would agree is not clear.

Chaucer's legend of Philomela foregrounds a theme of Ovid's narrative
not attended to by most medieval mythographies: writing and reading, in
particular, the writing and reading of rape narratives. The text specifically
identifies the mute Philomela as a literate, aristocratic woman who with
great effort tells her own awful story:

> She coude eek rede and wel ynow endyte,
> But with a penne coude she nat wryte,
> But lettres can she weve to and fro,
> So that, by that the yer was al ago,
> She hadde ywoven in a stamyn large
> How that she was brought from Athenis in a barge,
> And in a cave how that she was brought;
> And al the thing that Tereus hath wrought,
> She waf it wel, and wrot the storye above,
> How she was served for hire systers love. (LGW 2356–65)

Many mythographers mentioned that Philomela wove her story in a tapestry or cloth. But like Ovid, Chaucer's narrator says that Philomela embroi-

ders letters (Ovid's *notae*). Chaucer's text is also ambiguous about the kind
of text Philomela weaves. For an interesting medieval example of a text
woven by a woman, see Yephimia's (d. after 1405) silk burial pall containing
a panegyric for Prince Lazar made with silver letters.[39] Does Philomela
write her story in words above, or does she create an illustrated text? Does
her embroidered cloth contain a pictorial representation of her rape with a
text written above it ("She waf it wel, and wrot the storye above"), or does
the narrator mean that the text she wove into the cloth was the text we
have just read? Does *above* refer to the text she makes or the one we read?
The reference to Progne's reading—"And whan that Progne hath this thing
beholde" (*LGW* 2373)—does not disambiguate the earlier line. Either way,
Philomela is the first writer of the story that Ovid and then Chaucer repeat, but the point is made more forcefully with respect to Philomela's writing and Chaucer's text if we adopt the second reading of *above*. Philomela
is represented as the first writer of her story, and Progne as the first reader.
Chaucer's version, which reproduces Philomela's—that is, the raped
woman's story without the revenge plot—gives greater prominence to the
original mythological female textual community.

Progne's response to Philomela's writing prompts us to consider the
multiplicity of textual effects. When she reads the unglossed text composed
by Philomela, Progne becomes mute, "for sorwe and ek for rage" (*LGW*
2374). Recalling Ovid's version, Progne's voiceless response to Philomela's
text empathetically identifies Progne with her violated and lacerated sister.
Later, when she discovers her sister "Wepynge in the castel, here alone"
(*LGW* 2378), Philomela vocalizes the emotional distress for both of them:
"Allas! The wo, the compleynt, and the mone / That Progne upon hire
doumbe syster maketh!" (*LGW* 2379–80). The reference to *compleynt*
echoes Ovid's description of Philomela's writing as a *carmen,* and then supplements Progne's role as a reader with that of being a possible writer of
Philomela's story, someone who produces an emotional poetic response to
the rape, parallel with her sister's narrativization of her rape and woe. A
mute woman's rape narrative begets another woman's vocalized complaint,
orally expressing in the present moment women's sorrow and rage ("for
sorwe and ek for rage") for the violence Philomela has suffered. But, unlike the mute Philomela's writing, the vocal Progne's oral *compleynt* paradoxically goes unrecorded, unlettered, unliteral. Her *compleynt* is only
described, not inscribed. In the genealogy of medieval mythographies, few
women characters have been granted the opportunity or the power to tell
their own stories. Philomela's female literacy gives her a public mode of
expression by which she can make known the crimes she has suffered and
who's responsible. The first reading of the story, by a woman, gives rise to
an affective, oral response, but not the last word.

Chaucer's "Legend of Philomela" foregrounds the multiple readings of rape narratives. Philomela's writing of her own story is specifically framed by the narrator, who inscribes his reading responses to the story at the beginning and the end of the text. In a startling supplement to the Ovidian narrative, Chaucer's text opens with two narrating-time utterances. The narrator's first question, "Whi sufferest thow that Tereus was bore . . . ?" (*LGW* 2234), is directed at God/Jupiter and situates Tereus the rapist within the larger ethical question of why evil exists in the world and within the *accessus* interpretive discourse that foregrounds the ethical *utilitas* of reading. The second narrating-time utterance foregrounds possible effects of reading rape narratives:

> And, as to me, so grisely was his dede
> That, whan that I his foule storye rede,
> Myne eyen wexe foule and sore also.
> Yit last the venym of so long ago,
> That it enfecteth hym that wol beholde
> The storye of Tereus, of which I tolde. (*LGW* 2238–43)

This metanarrative addition to the Ovidian text opens the story with a masculine gesture and unsettles the later representation of Philomela as the first author of her story. The narrator inscribes himself as a male reader linked with Tereus, the rapist, and worries about how reading rape might "enfecteth" him as the letters inject him with images of narrative "venym" through his eyes. Whereas the female reader Progne is associated with Philomela and her sorrow, the male reader inscribed in the text is associated with Tereus and his crime. The narrator's initial concern about knowing or repeating Tereus's crimes is echoed in the narrator's later mutilation of the Ovidian text. The narrator represents his reading of Ovid or an Ovidian text as infectious, poisoning rather than pleasurable, unlike Guibert de Nogent and others for whom Ovid is the archetypal erotic read. Or are they so different? Chaucer's narrator omits the ethical context that Guibert and others provide for their moralized accounts of reading: the pleasure of reading Ovid's narrative is itself the poison, the vice, the corrupting image that they both desire and fear. But for the narrator of the "Legend of Philomela," the danger of reading lies within the problem of reading and identification: How can the story of Tereus be replaced in the reader's mental imagination with the story of Philomela; that is, how can the story be recontextualized and narrated or read from the raped woman's rather than rapist's point of view? The textual mutilator, inverting Tereus's action, severs the story from the mythographers and from masculine authoritative moral discourse, which reads female behaviors and women's bodies as signs of luxury, danger, and lust. But unlike Gower's Genius, Chaucer's narrator presents the severed text as a rumination on rewriting one's stories and on representing and reading sexual violence.

The narrator's second inscribed response occurs at the end narrative. After Progne's initial reading of Philomela's text and vocal response, the narrator cuts off the end of the Ovidian text—"The remenaunt is no charge for to telle, / For this is al and som," then adds a moral:

> Ye may be war of men, if that yow liste,
> For al be it that he wol nat, for shame,
> Don as Tereus, to lese his name,
> Ne serve yow as a morderour or a knave,
> Ful lytel while shal ye trewe hym have—
> That wol I seyn, al were he now my brother—
> But it so be that he may have non other. (*LGW* 2387–93)

Like Philomela's bloody, lacerated bit of tongue in Ovid's narrative, the gendered moral, separated from the text, comes creeping back across the floor in the narrator's interpretive gloss. The narrator moralizes the text, Philomela's text, not as a mythography, erasing or assimilating rape to masculine Christian allegorizing, but as an *exemplum,* an object lesson in male infidelity in love. The pronoun of address "yow" seems gendered and directed towards women in the (reading?) audience.

Unlike other guided readings, Chaucer's glossing narrator is casual about his lesson: Beware of men *if you want* or *if you listen* ("liste"). The ambiguity of the verb is crucial here. *Liste,* listen: The male Tereus is specifically redescribed in the gloss as violent ("a morderour or a knave") and inherently untrustworthy. The narrator's second response to Philomela's story replaces his first, not because he has avoided becoming Tereus nor because he has avoided the infection that the narrative of Tereus's actions might produce in him, but because he acknowledges that Tereus, beneath the violent rapist behavior, is a more fitting image of men than he initially cared to admit: "For al be it that he wol nat, for shame, / Don as Tereus, to lese his name, / Ne serve yow as a morderour or a knave. . . ." *Liste,* want: If women readers want to understand Tereus as an *exemplum* of infidelity and untrustworthiness, and not just an example of violent male domination, they can do so, and no one can stop them. Not the mythographers, not the allegorizers, not the narrator.

Rape narratives in the later Middle Ages provide a principal textual loci for the fear of poetic affect. Readers interpret them variously as cautionary tales for women, moral or Christian allegories, erotic imaginings for men, infectious violent narratives. Medieval authoritative commentary, allegorizing, and glossing, by male writers and at least one female writer, sought to contextualize such narratives in order to maintain Ovid's canonical position in the grammatical curriculum, to read rape metonymically as signifying something other than itself, to erase rape altogether from some classical narratives, or to subordinate rape within a broader interpretive scheme designed to produce "profitable" readings of potentially scandalous texts. Ovid's rape narratives were the objects of some of the strongest mastering allegorical readings in the later Middle Ages. Within later medieval reading practices, Ovid's texts, not only the erotic texts but also his mythography, constituted a problem for official literacy. Grammarians, commentators, and mythographers sought to appropriate Ovid's narratives for "proper" reading, and so keep readers from the luxurious pleasures that Guibert of Nogent and others described as their guilty reading experiences with Ovid's erotic writings. Reading for pleasure was figured as immodest stirrings of desire and sexual thoughts, whereas ethical reading was represented as useful reading and an appropriate mastering of canonical classical texts. But ethical or useful readings for women may not coincide with ethical readings for men. Reading without gloss was dangerous, so readers were thought to need guidance, authoritative commentary, ethical interpretations with proper, sanctioned "utilitates." However, as ethical discourses, official mythographies and allegorizations seldom considered how women's texts and stories might be read differently from men's, especially with respect to rape. Christine de Pizan's verbal and visual depictions of rape narratives in her *Épître Othéa* stand as an ambivalent rewriting of Ovidian narratives, reenforcing a male aristocratic viewpoint as the allegorical center of her readings even as she resists representing women as rape victims. The complexity of reading differently is a point Chaucer makes more than once in his fictions, with Philomela, with Progne, with Alisoun of Bath.

Chaucer's "Legend of Philomela" inscribes textual mutilation as rewriting and reaffirms a woman writer's story as the origin of a rape narrative. The text also inscribes Progne as a female reader, the first reader of Philomela's story, but dampens her revenge against her husband by representing her response not as bloody violence but as an oral, affective, and empathetic response to her sister's sorrow. Finally, the last narrator (after Philomela and Ovid) of the legend inscribes his own reading responses to the story, acknowledging Tereus as a possible exemplum of male untrustworthiness and again bracketing the Ovidian narrative's sexual and dionysiac violence.

The pseudo-hagiographic discourse of the "Legend of Philomela" problematizes Ovid's authority within medieval mythographic discourses and mutes or erases women's revenge for their rape and sexual violation. In Chaucer's text, the sisters' grief is juxtaposed with the narrator's caution against men's unfaithfulness, a gendered moral that creates some friction against the narrator's description of his own reading responses. Reading effects are complex and ambiguous. The "Legend of Philomela" mutilates Ovid's narrative of Philomela in order to separate women from the mythographers' misogynist moralizing. Christine de Pizan ambiguously represents Daphne as the silenced, disfigured, allegorical object of male knighthood. Later medieval mythographers repeatedly moralize or allegorize rape and sexual violence as signifiers of authorized cosmological or ethical or spiritual meanings. Reading the pagan text as plural, mythographic allegory seeks to separate women's voices from their own stories, while Chaucer and Christine de Pizan, in different ways, regender narratives of rape and refocus our reading on the myths we readers make.

Notes

1. Aimeric, *Ars lectoria,* ed. H. J. Reijnders, in *Vivarium* 9 (1971): 119–37; 10 (1972): 41–101, 124–76.

2. Conrad of Hirsau, *Dialogus super auctores,* ed. R. B. C. Huygens (Leiden: Brill, 1970); Alexander Nequam, *Sacerdos ad altare accessurus* (in *Corrogationes Promethei,* MS Oxford, Bod. Lib., Bodley 550), cited in Tony Hunt, *Teaching and Learning in Thirteenth-Century England,* 3 vols. (Cambridge: Cambridge University Press, 1991), I:270. For a useful typology of grammatical glosses on Ovid's texts in the Middle Ages, see Ralph Hexter, *Ovid and Medieval Schooling: Studies in Medieval School Commentaries on Ovid's Ars amatoria, Epistulae ex Ponto, and Epistulae heroidum* (Munich: Arbeo-Gesellschaft, 1986).

3. Guibert de Nogent, *Monodiae,* trans. Paul J. Archambault (University Park: Penn State University Press, 1996), I:17.

4. Jean Seznec, *The Survival of the Pagan Gods: The Mythological Tradition and Its Place In Renaissance Humanism and Art,* trans. Barbara Sessions (Princeton: Princeton University Press, 1953); Don Cameron Allen, *Mysteriously Meant: The Rediscovery of Pagan Symbolism and Allegorical Interpretation in the Renaissance* (Baltimore: The Johns Hopkins University Press, 1970); Judson B. Allen, *Friar as Critic: Literary Attitudes in the Later Middle Ages* (Nashville: Vanderbilt University Press, 1971), esp. pp. 3–28, 59–60, and *The Ethical Poetic of the Later Middle Ages: A decorum of convenient distinction* (Toronto: University of Toronto Press, 1982), esp. pp. 3–116.

5. Kathryn Gravdal, *Ravishing Maidens: Writing Rape in Medieval French Literature and Law* (Philadelphia: University of Pennsylvania Press, 1991) and *Vilain and Courtois: Transgressive Parody in French Literature of the Twelfth and Thirteenth Centuries* (Lincoln: University of Nebraska Press, 1989).

6. Georges Duby, *Medieval Marriage: Two Models From Twelfth-Century France,* trans. Elborg Forster (Baltimore: Johns Hopkins University Press, 1978), pp. 1–22.

7. E. R. Curtius, *European Literature and the Latin Middle Ages,* trans. Willard Trask (Princeton: Princeton University Press, 1953), pp. 36–61, 203–13, 436–67; Seznec, *Survival of the Pagan Gods* pp. 11–17, 37, 51, 84–109; Jane Chance, *Medieval Mythography: From Roman North Africa to the School of Chartres, A.D. 433–1177* (Gainesville: University Press of Florida, 1994), pp. 18–64.

8. Fausto Ghisalberti, "Medieval Biographies of Ovid," *Journal of the Warburg and Courtauld Institutes,* 9 (1946): 10–59. Hereafter cited in the text.

9. *"Vulgate Commentary"* on *Ovid's Metamorphoses,* ed. Frank Coulson (Toronto: Pontifical Institute of Mediaeval Studies, 1991), pp. 6–7. The first two Vatican mythographers are now identified as most likely Irish scholars writing in the tenth century. On the problems of identifying the two mythographers, see *Mythographi Vaticani I et II,* ed. Peter Kulcsár, CCSL 91C (Turnholt: Brepols, 1987), p. v; Chance, pp. 162, 164; *Mythographi Vaticani I et II,* ed. Nevio Zorzetti and trans. Jacques Berlioz (Paris: Belles Lettres, 1995), pp. xi–xii.

10. See Martin Irvine, *The Making of Textual Culture: 'Grammatica' and Literary Theory, 350 to 1100 AD* (Cambridge: Cambridge University Press, 1994); Suzanne Reynolds, *Medieval Reading: Grammar, Rhetoric, and the Classical Text* (Cambridge: Cambridge University Press, 1996); John Dagenais, *The Ethics of Reading in Manuscript Culture: Glossing the "Libro de buen amor"* (Princeton: Princeton University Press, 1994), pp. 3–79.

11. For summaries of the changes in medieval secular and ecclesiastical law regarding sex crimes, see James Brundage, "Rape and Marriage in the Medieval Canon Law," *Revue de droit canonique* 28 (1978): 62–75; Brundage, *Law, Sex, and Christian Society in Medieval Europe* (Chicago: University of Chicago Press, 1987), pp. 47–48, 209–10, 311–13, 469–72, 530–33; John Marshall Carter, *Rape in Medieval England* (Lanham, MD: University Press of America, 1985), pp. 35–37; Christopher Cannon, *"Raptus* in the Chaumpaigne Release and a Newly Discovered Document Concerning the Life of Geoffrey Chaucer," *Speculum,* 68 (1993): 74–94; Gravdal, *Ravishing Maidens,* pp. 6–11, 122–40.

12. Ovid, *Metamorphoses,* 2.401–40, 466–505, in *Les Metamorphoses,* ed. and trans. Georges Lafaye, 3 vols. (Paris: Belles Lettres, 1966). Hereafter cited in the text.

13. Coulson, pp. 27, 112–13.

14. On Lycaon, see: First Vatican Mythographer, 17 (CCSL 91C:8); Second Vatican Mythographer, 76 and 78 (CCSL 91C:153–55).

15. See Chance, pp. 183–89.

16. Fulgentius, *Mitologiae* 1.10, in *Opera,* ed. Rudolph Helm (Stuttgart: B. G. Teubner, 1970).

17. On Proserpina as Luna and her rape as an agricultural allegory, see: First Vatican Mythographer, 7 (CCSL 91C:5). See also: Remigius of Auxerre (ninth century), *Commentum in Martianum Capellam,* ed. Cora Lutz, 2 vols. (Leiden: E. J. Brill, 1962, 1965), I.36.4 (I:133), VII.369.1 (II:185); Bernard

of Utrecht, *Commentum in Theodulum (1076–1099),* ed. R. B. C. Huygens (Spoleto: Centro Italiano di Studi sull'Alto Medioevo, 1977), 3:95–109; Bernard Silvestris (twelfth century), *Commentary on Martianus Capella's 'De nuptii⸱ Philologiae et Mercurii'* attributed to *Bernardus Silvestris,* ed. Haijo Jan Westra (Toronto: Pontifical Institute of Mediaeval Studies, 1986), 5.630–32, 5.682–90; *The Berlin Commentary on Martianus Capella's "De nuptiis Philologiae er Mercurii"* (late twelfth–early thirteenth century), ed. Haijo Jan Westra, assisted by Christine Vester, 2 vols. (Leiden: E. J. Brill, 1994), I:57–58; Petrus Berchorius (fourteenth century), *Reductorium morale, Book 15: Ovidius moralizatus: De formis figurisque deorum,* ed. Joseph Engels (Utrecht: Instituut voor Laat Latijn der Rijksuniversiteit, 1966), fol. 6vb (= pp. 28–29).

18. Coulson, pp. 121.

19. Fulgentius, *Mitologiae* 1.10; cf. Remigius of Auxerre, *Commentum in Martianum Capellam,* I.36.4 (Lutz I:133).

20. Coulson, pp. 129.

21. John Ridewall, *Fulgentius Metaforalis,* ed. Hans Liebeschütz (Leipzig and Berlin: B. G. Teubner, 1926), c. 6 (= pp. 106–7).

22. Ridewall, pp. 107–8.

23. Coulson, p. 127.

24. Berchorius, *Reductorium morale,* fol. 1va (= Engels p. 1). Hereafter cited in the text.

25. *"Ovide moralisé." Poème du commencement du quatorzième siècle publié d'après tour les manuscrits connus,* ed. C. de Boer, 5 vols. (Amsterdam: Nord-Hollandsche Uitgevers- Maatschappij, 1915–36), I.71–453 (Creation), I.1065–1184 (giants and Tower of Babel), I.1185–1202 (giants and rebellion in Heaven). Hereafter cited in the text.

26. Helen Cooper, "Chaucer and Ovid: A Question of Authority," in *Ovid Renewed,* ed. C. A. Martindale (Cambridge: Cambridge University Press, 1988), pp. 71–81, argues that Chaucer most likely did not know the *Ovide moralisé* and learned his Ovid elsewhere, probably from the *Roman de la rose* and Berchorius. Michael Calabrese, *Chaucer's Ovidian Arts of Love* (Gainesville: University of Florida Press, 1994), pp. 11–32, cogently examines how Chaucer and other later medieval writers read Ovid through the interpretive frame of the *accessus ad auctores* rather than from the *Ovide moralisé.* John Fyler, *Chaucer and Ovid* (New Haven, CT: Yale University Press, 1979), pp. 1–22, believes that Chaucer read his Ovid "straight."

27. For example, Fulgentius, *Mitologiae,* 1.14.

28. For Christine's use of the *Ovide moralisé,* see Gabriella Parussa, in *Epistre Othéa,* ed. Gabriella Parussa (Geneva: Librairie Droz, 1999), pp. 32–36; Sandra L. Hindman, *Christine de Pizan's "Epistre Othéa": Painting and Politics at the Court of Charles VI* (Toronto: Pontifical Institute of Mediaeval Studies, 1986), p. 93. For Christine's supervision of the manuscripts of the text, see Hindman pp. 63–77, 92, 98; Millard Meiss, *French Painting in the Time of Jean of Berry: The Limbourgs and Their Contemporaries,* 2 vols. (New

York: Braziller, 1974), I.8–15. Christine's text is hereafter cited in the text from Parussa's edition.

29. Diane Wolfthal, "'Douleur sur toutes autres': Revisualizing the Rape Script in the *Epistre Othea* and the *Cité des dames*," in *Christine de Pizan and the Categories of Difference,* ed. Marilynn Desmond (Minneapolis and London: University of Minnesota Press, 1998), pp. 41–70 (see p. 42).

30. *Le Trésor de la cité des dames,* II.44; trans. Earl Jeffrey Richards (New York: Persea, 1982), pp. 160–63.

31. *Knight's Tale,* in *The Riverside Chaucer,* ed. Larry Benson, 3rd ed. (Boston: Houghton Mifflin, 1987), I.2062, 2064. Hereafter, Chaucer's writings are cited in the text, by work and line numbers.

32. Fulgentius, *Mitologiae,* 2.7. For examples of how Abelard and Chaucer reinterpret mythographic and allegorical readings of the Venus and Mars myth, see my "Mad Lovers and Other Hooked Fish: Chaucer's *Complaint of Mars,*" *Allegorica* 4 (1979): 301–14, and "Genre and Code in Abelard's *Historia calamitatum,*" *Assays,* 1 (1981): 35–50. See also Martin Irvine, "Heloise and the Gendering the Literate Subject," in *Criticism and Dissent in the Middle Ages,* ed. Rita Copeland (Cambridge: Cambridge University Press, 1996), pp. 87–114.

33. *Meta.* 1.492–96, 6.451–54; cf. G. A. Jacobson, "Apollo and Tereus: Parallel Motifs in Ovid's *Metamorphoses,*" *CJ,* 80 (1984): 45–52.

34. Bernard of Utrecht, *Commentum in Theodulum (1076–1099),* 3.895–904

35. First Vatican Mythographer, 201 and 228 (CCSL 91C:79–81, 90); cf. Chance, p. 199.

36. See Fulgentius, *Mitologiae,* 2.14; Second Vatican Mythographer, 155–56 (CCSL 91C:217–18); Bernard Silvestris, *Commentary on Martianus Capella's "De nuptiis Philologiae et Mercurii,"* 10.470–73; cf. Chance, p. 477.

37. First Vatican Mythographer, 4, 201, 228 (CCSL 91C:4, 79–81, 90).

38. Cf. Chance, pp. 189–91.

39. See Carolyne Larrington, *Women and Writing in Medieval Europe: A Sourcebook* (London and NY: Routledge, 1995), pp. 250–51.

CHAPTER 3

THE VIOLENCE OF COURTLY EXEGESIS
IN *SIR GAWAIN AND THE GREEN KNIGHT*

Monica Brzezinski Potkay

> *Sir Gawain and the Green Knight* exposes courtly discourse's potential
> for sexual violence, attributes that violence to a hermeneutic that
> imagines reading as rape, and responds to linguistic violence by de-
> claring its own textual integrity. The poem warns that those who vi-
> olate texts or women will themselves be violated.

> *The significance of rape to romance is not often discussed. . . . What has rarely been
> said is that rape (either attempted rape or the defeat of a rapist) constitutes one of the
> episodic units used in the construction of a romance. Sexual violence is built into the
> very premise of Arthurian romance. It is a genre that by its definition must create the
> threat of rape.*
>
> —Kathryn Gravdal, Ravishing Maidens:
> Writing Rape in Medieval French Literature and Law, *43*.

M ust romances create the threat of rape? Perhaps not; yet even a cur-
sory survey of the genre will show that a surprising number of medieval romances feature instances of *raptus*—defined in the medieval sense
as either sexual violence or the forced abduction of a woman. Kathryn
Gravdal, in her provocative study, persuades that the representation of rape
is intrinsic to the aesthetics and chivalric ideology of the works of Chrétien
de Troyes, the most influential and imitated of romancers.[1] Dietmar Rieger
details the frequency with which medieval French romances and other

courtly genres depict rape.[2] And just a glance at my office bookshelf reveals that a startling number of English romances and Breton lais feature ravishment. In the Auchinleck manuscript alone, among other instances of *raptus*, the King of the Fairies abducts *Sir Orfeo*'s Heurodis, and a princess lost in the woods conceives *Sir Degaré* when violated by a knight who then blithely bids her "Hav god dai!"[3] Rape may not be necessary to romance, but it does seem a well-established topos of the genre. If rape is a generic commonplace, it is hardly surprising that that crown jewel of medieval English romance, *Sir Gawain and the Green Knight*, should be concerned with rape. The Lady who attempts to seduce the title character from fidelity to his knightly code casually—almost comically—brings up the threat of rape twice.

Yet, as I will argue here, rape is no passing topic in *Sir Gawain* but central to its very fabric. For *Gawain* uses the theme of rape as a trope for its own poetics, which it presents as a version of the traditional poetics of the courtly romance. The poem is a notoriously self-reflexive work, playfully yet seriously inviting readers to ponder the ways in which it both participates in and subverts all sorts of literary conventions. And it implicates rape as part of those compositional and interpretive rules. *Sir Gawain* sees ravishment in the courteous language that constitutes the romance and other courtly genres. The poem shows that courtesy, the language of seduction, can all too easily slide into a language of compulsion that at least threatens the use of physical force against women.

Sir Gawain attributes the violently compelling aspect of courtliness to that discourse's tendency to elide the literal meaning of words, to—in medieval exegetical terminology—sever the letter of language from its spirit. The exegetical tradition did sometimes view the separation of letter from spirit as a violent act. Metaphors of force are especially common when biblical exegetes discuss the interpretation of secular discourse, specifically the attempt of a reader to extract a Christian or moral truth from a nonreligious work. Carolyn Dinshaw, in *Chaucer's Sexual Poetics*, draws our attention to the frequency with which patristic and medieval authorities imagined this sort of reading against the grain as the act of a masculine reader who masters, and even rapes, a text identified with the female body.[4] Dinshaw focuses on the analogy as elaborated by St. Jerome, who offers his metaphor of the beautiful captive woman in his Letter 70, an *apologia* for reading and quoting from pagan writers. Jerome's model of how to split letter from spirit will be central to my argument about *Sir Gawain*, and I will therefore discuss it in some detail before proceeding to my reading of the poem.

Jerome borrows the captive woman from Deuteronomy 21: 10–13, which prescribes what an Israelite warrior must do if he wishes to marry a gentile woman taken captive in battle—a woman, that is, who is the victim of *raptus:* the woman must "shave her hair, and pare her nails, And shall put off the raiment" in which she was taken.[5] Jerome reads the desire of the warrior for a foreign bride as a figure for his own desire for the secular text, rhetorically eloquent yet dangerously and carnally mortal, from which he wishes to derive a Christian moral:

> Is it surprising that I, too, admiring the grace of her eloquence and the beauty of her members, should desire to make that secular wisdom which is my captive and my handmaid into an Israelite matron? Or that, when all that is dead in her—whether this be idolatry, pleasure, error, or lust—has been cut away or shaved off, I should couple with her most pure body to beget servants for the Lord of Sabaoth?[6]

For Jerome, the Christian who desires to "couple with" the secular text must follow the example of the Israelite warrior. He, too, must deprive his bride of her hair and clothing, that is, of precisely those external feminine beauties that he finds alluring—in the text's case, Dinshaw argues, its literal level, often figured in exegesis by a veil that must be removed to reveal a "naked" truth beneath. Such a stripping away of the letter renders the text harmless to its reader, who is now safe from entrapment by its feminine and carnal snares as he embraces the spiritual truth within.

As I hope to show in the following pages, the author of *Sir Gawain* is aware of the hermeneutic that imagines reading as rape. The poet, however, spotlights this model in order to critique it, and he performs that critique through its female characters, depicted in the text as accomplished readers. Both the Lady and Morgan la Fee reject Jerome's assumption that the textual woman can (or should!) be stripped, for they reject its underlying hermeneutic, which assumes that a text's spirit can be split from its letter, a moral detached from an integral text. The text of *Sir Gawain,* too, rejects the assumption of its binary nature, and accordingly presents itself as integrated, its spirit and letter inseparable and indistinguishable. The poem effects this critique of Jerome's model by standing it on its head: in *Sir Gawain* we see a knight who not only fails in his attempt to strip the secular text of romance of its carnality, to detach courtly rhetoric's "grace of eloquence" from eroticism, but who also is himself handled as if he were a text, a captive and unwilling object of desire for two female readers. Gawain's captivity, however, does more than function as a symbol of what can happen to a text when it's willfully, even forcefully, misread. As a victim of erotically tinged compulsion, Gawain suffers a fate that brings the violence of rape home to the poem's male audience. Gawain is not, of course, literally raped; but he is subjected to an experience that, like rape, destroys his physical and psychic integrity. We will see, too, that Gawain is less a victim of women than of his own courtly discourse, whose force is brought home, visited on its point of origin. *Sir Gawain and the Green Knight*'s seduction scenes, then, are presented as just one battle in the war between men and women—a war of cyclical violence that, the poem suggests, is only fueled by the superficially polite, actually violent discourse of courtliness.

Ravishing the Letter: Jerome's Hermeneutic and the Practice of Courtesy

Sir Gawain and the Green Knight does not at first look like a story that questions its own hermeneutic tradition or that tradition's complicity with rape.[7] Rather, as I hope to show in this first section, it appears to participate in the poetics of rape that Jerome espoused (though this participation, like so much else in the poem, is only a misleading appearance). Gawain, the poem's hero, its representative of chivalry, is a Jerome-like rhetorician who aims to safely embrace a dangerous femininity by stripping it of an ensnaring and mortal covering of desire. Like Jerome, Gawain hopes to accomplish his aims by using a secular discourse known for its eloquence—in the knight's case, the courtly idiom he uses in skirmishing with the Lady.

Sir Gawain and the Green Knight claims that it has accomplished precisely what Jerome advised Christian readers to do, read a secular and even pagan text so as to produce Christian wisdom: the poem claims to reinterpret the well-known saga of the fall of pagan Troy into a Christian exemplum about Gawain's fall. This claim first appears in the poem's opening stanza, which employs the familiar topos of the *translatio imperii* [passage of empire] from Troy to Rome to Britain. Here the story so familiar from Virgil (whom Jerome's writings quote so frequently) of "Ennias þe athel" [Aeneas the noble] becomes a story concerning "þis Bretayn" (lines 5, 20).[8] As the narrator makes clear in the poem's last stanza, a mirror to this first one, his notion of *translatio* is not just a historical but also a literary one—a *translatio studii* [passage of learning] wherein the "Brutus bokez" chronicling the coming of Aeneas' descendent Brutus to Britain (2523) are succeeded by the Arthurian "best boke of romaunce" (2521), which in turn engenders *Sir Gawain,* an explicitly Christian tale that ends with an appeal to him "þat bere þe croun of þorne" (2530).

Sir Gawain thus has the same goal as Jerome, the rendering of a pagan tale into a Christian one. Its titular character, Sir Gawain himself, has a similar Hieronymian project. He aims to be the sort of rhetorician who can safely traffic with women by stripping them of their ensnaring and mortal covering of desire even while enjoying their beauty and eloquence. The knight follows Jerome's program for rapacious reading at first quite literally: he scorns the veiled woman, image of the secular and deadly letter, in order to enjoy on his own terms a nearly naked one, whom he views—despite her repeated efforts to voice her overtly sexual desire—as chaste matron.

We see Gawain conforming to Jerome's model of reading when he first meets the Lady and Morgan at Hautdesert. The garb of the two women indicates that they respectively symbolize moralizing spirit and fatal letter (but only provisionally—the poem actually complicates the women's identities and confounds their symbolism of textual components). Their appearance together illustrates the necessary presence of both elements in a text. The descriptions of the two women in this scene emphasize the Lady's relative nakedness, resembling the condition of the captive bride who most doff her raiment, and Morgan's concealment under garments. The Lady has "Hir brest and her bry3t þrote bare displayed" (955), and the narrator keeps drawing our attention to her bare flesh: the Lady is "þe fayrest in felle [skin], of flesche and of lyre [literally *cheek,* but with pun on *flesh*] (941). Later the hostess arrives in Gawain's bedroom, once "Wyth chynne and cheke ful swete, / Boþe quite [white] and red in blande [blended]" (1204–5), another time with "Hir þryuen [fair] face and hir þrote þrowen al naked, / Hir brest bare bifore, and bihide eke" (1740–41).

In contrast, Morgan's flesh is invisible, so swathed is she in veils as the meaning of a text is held to be hidden by its *involucrum* [wrapping] of the literal level. This grand dame looks less like a body than a collage of garments:

þat oþer with a gorger [wimple] watz gered ouer þe swyre [throat]
Chymbled [wrapped] ouer hir blake chyn with chalkquyte vayles
Hir frount folden in sylk, enfoubled ayquere [muffled everywhere],
Toreted and treleted [edged and meshed] with tryflez aboute
þat no3t bare of þat burde [woman] bot þe blake bro3es
þe tweyne y3en and þe nase, þe naked lyppez. (957–62)

Morgan's cloaking codes her as a Hieronymian figure of the secular text, and her age—she is "an auncian hit semed" (948)—as symbolic of its deadliness. Jerome noted that "all that is dead" in his captive bride must be removed; and Andrew and Waldron, in their edition of the poem, suggest that Morgan's description as decrepitly aged recalls the lyric tradition of the "Signs of Death," a symbol of carnal mortality.[9] As a symbol of the veiling deadly letter, Morgan must be stripped away to permit Gawain to embrace the naked Lady chastely.

And Gawain does strip Morgan away. Faced with the two women, Gawain attempts to separate the clothed from the naked, the letter from the spirit. Like his patristic role model, Gawain clearly prefers the stripped woman. He gives Morgan only token respect. After this introductory scene, the fairy is briefly mentioned in the three feasting scenes that end each day's activities, but she virtually disappears from Gawain's consciousness until the Green Knight reveals her, at the end of the poem, as the instigator of Gawain's predicament; in the words of Sheila Fisher, Gawain is guilty of "leaving Morgan aside."[10] Gawain reserves his real interest for the Lady. After politely bowing to the old lady—"þe alder he haylses [greets], heldande [bowing] ful lowe"—he gives a lustier greeting to her "[m]ore lykkerwys [tasty]" companion: "þe loueloker he lappez a lyttel in armez, / He kysses hir comlyly" (968, 972–74). Gawain regularly attends upon both women at Hautdesert, but he takes special pleasure in the company of the Lady. And she pleases him precisely with those virtues that Jerome found delightful in his literary maid—"the grace of her eloquence and the beauty of her members." Gawain understandably enjoys the Lady because her members are beautiful. The Lady pleases not just Gawain's eye but his ear, too; the couple "lanced wordes gode," producing "merþe," "blis," and "wynne [joy]" in the knight (1763–66). The Lady delights Gawain with the beauty both of her *cors* [body] and of her discourse.

Gawain considers this aesthetic appreciation of his hostess innocent enough (although the poem, as I will argue later, does not) because he has no intention of consummating a sexual alliance with her, no matter how often or how overtly she invites him. Like Jerome, who defends his appreciation of the beauties of secular rhetoric, he seeks a pure and not a prurient coupling, a meeting of minds and not of bodies. Gawain is indeed horrified at the thought of physically possessing the Lady, as such possession would constitute sin. One of the passages that gives us insight into Gawain's thoughts tells us that "He cared for his cortaysye, lest craþayn [rude] he were, / And more for his meschef ʒif he schulde make synne" (1773–74). The knight's game is one of brinksmanship where he can be titillated by the Lady's visual and verbal charms but unsullied by the temptations they offer. Gawain takes pleasure in the Lady's come-ons even while repulsing them. In a word, he flirts.

This stance, where Gawain enjoys the Lady while taking care she does not enjoy him too much, is part and parcel of his Hieronymian project. Jerome confessed that he "desire[s] [*cupio*] the captive woman but that he must "cut away" her "pleasure" and "lust" [*voluptatis, libidinum*] to possess her. Just as Jerome attempted to use language to protect himself from the sexual allure of the text to which he was attracted, Gawain utilizes rhetoric to guard himself against the powerful desire of the woman who tempts him. Gawain, however, does not use the biblical semantics that the Church Father did. Rather, he attempts the desexing of the Lady through a verbal mode that has the same aims: Gawain uses courtly language—a discourse that, as R. Howard Bloch argues, like the Christian asceticism Jerome advocates distrusts the female body and seeks to repress its desires.[11] A man speaking in the courtly mode may pretend to enkindle a woman's love, but his real agenda, as Bloch and other feminist critics say, is to voice *his* desires while ignoring or eliding those of his "beloved."[12]

Courtliness represses *feminine* desire, and in *Sir Gawain* the knight employs his trademark courtesy precisely to counter the Lady's overtures.[13] In the scene where he strips Morgan away, we are assured that such behavior is chivalrous: while addressing the ladies, "kny3tly he melez [speaks]" (974). In every consequent meeting with the Lady, his courtliness seeks to deny her sexual desire by transmuting it into social convention and chaste kissing: a physical temptation becomes a mind-game. Gawain, like Jerome, tries to reconcile Christianity and a secular, though dangerous, rhetoric. He tries to strip courtesy of its sexuality, to use the very language of love as a shield against eros, as Jerome thought to defeat paganism through pagan authors. The narrator notes Gawain's courteous defense against the Lady's sexual aggression:

> þus hym frayned þat fre, and fondet hym ofte, . . .
> [Thus that noble lady inquired and tested him often]
> Bot he defended hym so fayr þat no faut semed,
> Ne non euel on nawþer halue. (1549, 1551–52)

And another time he comments that "þe kny3t with speches skere [pure], / Answered to vche a [every] cace" (1261–62). Gawain hopes that courtliness can effect his chastity: three times the poem links Gawain's courteous language to *clannes*—a virtue that may not strictly equal sexual virtue but which surely includes it (653, 1013, 1298).

But if Gawain wants to use courtly discourse to protect his chastity, he has chosen a dubious weapon. As Joseph E. Gallagher puts it in his study of the inherent eroticism of Gawain's speech, this is "a paradoxical and absurd method of preserving his purity."[14] For despite the frequency with which the poem describes Gawain as practicing a "clene cortays carp [speech] closed fro fylþe" (1013), more often it admits that courtesy is practically synonymous with male desire. Bloch reminds us that courtliness is how men demand that their desires be fulfilled, and *Sir Gawain* keeps reminding its knight that his language bespeaks what he himself would repulse. When Gawain arrives at Hautdesert, he is celebrated by its inhabitants as one skilled in "þe teccheles [faultless] terms of talkyng noble," and they term this noble speech "luf-talkyng" (917, 927). The Lady also keeps reminding Gawain that courtesy is almost by definition talk of love. She requests that he, "þat ar so cortays," teach her "sum tokenez of trweluf craftes"—provide her with a letter that signifies authentic desire (1525,1527). It is richly ironic that Gawain uses a discourse intrinsically linked to male desire to shield his chastity, an irony not lost on the poem. Just after revealing, in the words I've quoted above, that Gawain strives to avoid adultery with the Lady, the poem informs us that he tries to effect abstinence through the playfulness of love talk!: "With luf-laȝyng a lyt he layd hym bysyde / Alle þe spechez of spe-cialté þat sprange of her mouthe" (1777–78). No wonder Gawain feels caught between courtesy and virtue—chaste innocence demands that he abandon an idiom that can voice only desire.

If courtesy speaks male desire, sometimes that desire may be over-whelming, and perhaps even violent. Let us remember that Jerome's model of reading does far more to its metaphorical captive than simply frustrate her desires. It rapes her—it subordinates her desires to those of the "male" reader. A similar threat of ravishment bedevils the seeming chastity of the courtly language that Gawain uses, as the Lady's conversation shows. She draws our attention to sexual violence and identifies it as a potential corol-lary of courtly discourse. The Lady twice alludes to rape, suggesting once that Gawain, as befits a courteous knight, could rape her if he liked, and once that she is constrained by the rules of courtly behavior to submit to such violence.

The Lady explicitly brings up the topic of sexual violence during the second of the three seduction scenes where she apparently attempts to talk Gawain into committing some sexual impropriety. She begins this partic-ular conversation with the knight by soliciting a kiss in a non-direct fash-ion: she chides him that he hasn't remembered her "lesson" of the previous day, that a knight "þat cortaysy vses" (1491) will claim a kiss whenever a woman appears likely to bestow one. Gawain demurs, excusing himself from the implied invitation to kiss the Lady by saying that his claim might be objected to, putting him in the wrong for having demanded a kiss in the first place: "If I were werned [refused], I were wrang, iwysse [indeed], ȝif I profered" (1495). The knight's response is couched in highly polite language, with all of its subjunctive verbs and hypothetical clauses, and its refusal to name the hostess or indeed any woman.

The Lady, in answering Gawain's demurral, speaks just as politely as he does:

"Ma fay," quoþ þe meré wyf, "ȝe may not be werned,
ȝe ar stif innoghe to constrayne with strenkþe, ȝif yow lykez,
ȝif any were so vilanous þat yow devaye [deny] wolde." (1495–97)

Her lines here are phrased just as courteously as Gawain's, just as subjunc-tive and hypothetical. This courtesy, however, accords badly with her meaning: that Gawain, if he pleases, can take from any woman who refuses his advances a kiss—and by implication whatever else he wishes, for as Dinshaw points out, in medieval thought passionate kisses almost always lead to other things.[15] The rhetorical elegance of her speech softens but does not conceal the violent message.

The Lady's careful choice of words, in fact, rather than deflecting attention away from the brutality of the message, actually works to show that courtesy dictates that any woman must submit, willingly or unwillingly, to Gawain's desires. As John Burrow points out, the Lady uses "a quite subtle sophistry, which can be stated in the following syllogistic form: Anyone who refuses you is a villein . . . ; *but* it is legitimate to use force on a villein (*teste* Andreas Capellanus and others); *therefore* it is legitimate for you to use force on anyone who refuses you." Burrow refers us to the section of Andreas's *De Amore* that concerns the love of peasants.[16] There Andreas advises that, might one of his readers unfortunately fall in love with *villeins,* he should "be careful to puff them up with lots of praise and then . . . do not hesitate to take what you seek and to embrace them by force [*violento*]."[17] I would add that the Lady's lines imply still another syllogism: Since only a peasant would deny Gawain, any woman who wishes to be courteous would not deny him in the first place. Therefore, Gawain need not fear refusal from any woman: ladies will submit to him and he can rape any woman who's not a lady.

The Lady again links the practice of courtly language with sexual violence, although this time more implicitly, in the first seduction scene. Here the Lady expresses a wish that Gawain entertain her "with tale" and with "your daynté wordez" (1235, 1253). Yet her speech suggests that the knight's words encode not only courtesy but the threat of violence, too. This suggestion occurs in what might be the most discussed lines of the Lady's speeches:

"ʒe ar welcum to my cors,
Yowre awen won to wale,
Me behouez of fyne force
Your seruaunt be, and schale." (1237–40)

The first two lines have received much critical attention because of the studied ambiguity of the Lady's offer of *my cors,* its treading the line between sexual solicitation and conventional hospitality.[18] On the one hand, the Lady seems to be blatantly offering herself to Gawain, giving him free access to her body—in French, her *cors.* Take me!, the Lady seems to be saying, and the sexual implication is underlined by the context of her preceding lines, where she informs Gawain that the two of them, protected by a locked door, are quite alone—her husband and men are away, the other guests and her ladies asleep in their beds (1230–33). On the other hand, the Lady's words can be interpreted as innocuously conventional, an almost ritual offer of hospitality, since *my cors* could simply mean "my self." So the Tolkien-Gordon/Davis edition of the poem says in its notes to these lines, which translate the first line of this wheel as "I am glad to have you here" (pp. 108–9 n. 1237). Of course, as most commentators of these frequently analyzed scenes point out, the line is both forthright *and* courteous: it conflates the sexual and hospitable meanings; it means both things at the same time.

A similar politic ambiguity inhabits the last two lines of the Lady's wheel. Here, however, the sexual subtext moves from an implied invitation to a suggestion that the Lady must give in to Gawain's desires, that it is necessary that she be raped. The Lady states that she is behooved *of fyne force* to be Gawain's servant. The italicized phrase is, like the Lady's earlier *cors,* an idiom borrowed from French, and it means "by absolute necessity."[19] Thus, these two lines, as Tolkien-Gordon/Davis comment, can be read as a social pleasantry, "It behooves me of necessity to be your servant, and I shall be" (p. 109 n. 1238–40). David Mills, in his perceptive analysis of the seduction scenes, similarly notes that "As hostess, the Lady must be Gawain's *seruaunt,* and *of fyne force* would refer to the social duties imposed upon her by her lord which she must fulfill." Yet Mills also notes that *of fyne force,* especially in conjunction with the emphatic *schale,* conveys an "idea of compulsion," and in the context of Gawain's bedroom the Lady's lines carry "an assertion of sexual service by implication."[20] Mills's argument—one with which I agree, and a point to which I will return below—is that it is Gawain who is being constrained to sexual service here. Yet we should note that the Lady speaks of herself being compelled—"*Me* behouez of fyne force."

One thing to which she may be compelled is rape. *Force*—although a word with a broad range of meanings and connotations—as both verb and noun is one of the usual Middle English words for sexual violation: *Cursor Mundi* tells us, concerning the sexually criminal antedeluvians, that "Wimmen þai forced a-mang þaim," and presents a lecher confessing that he "forced sum woman with nede, / And maþens [maidens] reft þair maþenhede."[21] Chaucer has Tereus, in *The Legend of Good Women,* take Philomena "by force," and the rapist-knight in *The Wife of Bath's Tale* deflowers his victim "by verray [real] force."[22] *Force* can carry a similar meaning in medieval French: among the many instances of courtly rape that Dietmar Rieger documents, we find that in the chanson de geste *Chevalerie Ogier* a group of Saracens "En un boscel . . . vorent force fere" [in a wood want to work *force*] on an English princess, and in Chrétien de Troyes's *Perceval,* the

misogynist Orguelleus de la Lande claims that a woman wishes to be overcome "a force" [by force].[23]

The Lady's speeches in general mix English with French idioms (*ma fay,
cors, fyne force*), and in both languages she chooses words that vacillate between civilized conventionality and blunter sexual references. The English
"Yowre awen won to wale" can be taken innocuously ("'to choose your
own course [of action],' 'do as you like,'" is how Tolkien-Gordon/Davies
puts it, p. 109, n. 1237), or given a more erotic charge—"to take your own
delight," is how Mills renders it; "to take your own pleasure" is the translation of the Andrew and Waldron edition.[24] With the latter sexual sense,
the line may translate one of various French periphrases for rape: "*faire sa
volonté* (to do as one will), *faire son plaisir* (to take one's pleasure), or *faire son
buen* (to do as one sees fit)," as Gravdal lists them.[25] It is certainly not clear
that the Lady is referring to sexual violence in this dense wheel; but any
blunt mention of sexual violence would discord with both her habit of refined suggestiveness and the restrained decorum of courtly discourse generally. But rape is a possible reference for what the Lady is behooved to
here, given all of the sexual innuendo in her speech, especially its bringing
attention to her *cors*. The Lady makes it clear, overall, that courtesy demands she fulfill Gawain's desires.

The phrase *of fyne force* may derive from a French idiom, but in English it seems curious to use the adjective *fyne,* as the Lady does, to modify *force*. This oxymoronic phrase, used within a contextualizing
discussion of courtesy, recalls the more well-known French term *fin
amors*. If the Lady is talking about rape, it would appear to be a courtly
one. What makes ravishment *fine* in *Sir Gawain* is that it is effected
through language: it is the courtly idiom itself that comes to compel
women to submit to men's desires. The Lady, as I've just shown, in the
two speeches where she alludes to rape, introduces the topic within a discussion of courtesy in general and of courtly language specifically. On
the first morning, the wheel with the phrase *of fyne force* and all its accompanying linguistic markers of compulsion comes after the bob that
reports the Lady's expectation that Gawain will provide her "with tale"
(1236). On the second morning, the notion that Gawain's strength gives
him the ability to take what he wants is part of the Lady's lesson on how
"vche a knyȝt þat cortaysy vses" acts (1491).

In both scenes, the Lady, by linking courteous language with sexual
compulsion, agrees with other medieval texts that the blandishments of *fin
amours* are designed to achieve the repression of the feminine, to fulfill male
satisfaction that ignores its object's desire. If words fail, perhaps force may
do. Andreas Capellanus wrote that peasant women were acceptable victims
of physical force, but the process of their ravishment begins with flattery:

"be careful to puff them up with lots of praise, and then . . . do not hesi-tate to take what you seek and to embrace them by force;" elsewhere *De amore* notes that talk can be just as compelling as physical violence: Andreas as narrator tells us that, once wooing a nun, "we spoke so well on the art, not being ignorant of the art of soliciting nuns, that we forced [coegimus] her to assent to our desire."[26] Another *ars amoris,* Rieger reports, shows that "the courtly norm does not only not exclude rape . . . but on the contrary can provoke it": in the early-thirteenth-century didactic work *Commens d'Amours,* a lover "when he saw that, neither by asking nor begging nor by any fair word which he knew how to say to her, would he obtain mercy," he rapes her; she consequently sleeps with him willingly.[27] Seduction slides into rape in these texts, as it did in *Sir Gawain* when the Lady's notorious invitation to her *cors* turns out less to be an offer than an obligation.

It makes sense that *Sir Gawain* should find that the discourse of cour-tesy can be so forceful, for the poem finds language in general to be effi-cacious: the Green Knight appears in response to and as an incarnation of Arthur's request for "an vncouþe tale" (93), and Gawain, it seems, speaks Bertilak's castle into being when he beseeches Mary "in his prayere" to send him safe harborage and the palace then appears "Pyched on a prayere [with pun on *prairie*]" (759, 768). The speech-acts in the poem, however, can be hostile, even violent, as when Camelot takes fright at the Green Knight's rudely spoken challenge, a challenge that erases the court's rep-utation for supremacy: "Now is þe reuel and þe renoun of þe Rounde Table / Ouerwalt [overthrown] wyth a worde of on [one] wyȝes [per-son's] speche" (313–14). The language of Arthur's court that Gawain speaks is no less violent than that of the uncourtly Green Knight, for all of its elegant surface. Courtesy only veils ravishment; we have the iron fist in a velvet glove.

Gawain, however, though reputedly a master practitioner of the courtly arts, and though conscious of his attempt to separate the eloquence of courtesy from the mortal carnality of its letter, seems completely unaware of the violence implied by his polite words. When the Lady tells him that he is "stif" enough to constrain a woman (1496), Gawain quite rightly de-clares that rape is not his intention: "Bot þrete [compulsion, force] is vn-þryuande [ignoble] in þede [country] þer I lende [dwell], / And vche gift þat is geuen not with good wylle" (1499–1500). But wordsmith that he is, Gawain can never master courtesy to bring it fully into conformity with his intentions; it will always go its own way. Still he insists on sticking to his slippery politeness: he "dalt with hir al in daynté [courteously], how-se-euer þe dede turned / towrast [twisted away]" (1662–63). And events do take on a terrible twist, as Gawain is confronted with the very erotic violence he would deny.

The Failure of Jerome's Raptus:
The Integrity of the Letter and Spirit

Gawain's innocence about language is destined for a fall. He soon finds out that he cannot control desire, female or his own, with a courtly version of Jerome's literary rape. For the saint's theory of reading, his semiotics, is inherently flawed. It cannot stamp out desire; it cannot achieve what it set out to accomplish, the severing of a chaste wisdom of the text from its alluring fleshy veil. Any attempt to possess the naked spirit of a text is unrealistic, since readers can appropriate texts only through their letter. In reading, "it is natural to man to attain to intellectual truths through sensible objects, because all our knowledge originates from sense," writes Aquinas in the *Summa Theologica*'s discussion of biblical metaphor.[28] Without the sensible letter, there can be no perception of spiritual truth.

Sir Gawain insists on this necessary link between letter and spirit. Although the poem seems at times to participate in Jerome's letter-phobic hermeneutic of rape, it offers in the description of Gawain's shield an altogether different notion of the poetics by which it is written. For the shield may be said to stand for the text of the poem—its device, the pentangle of *trawþe* in which each of the five "lyne[s] vmbelappez [wraps around] and loukez in oþer" (628) mirrors the narrator's description of his story as told "With lel [loyal] letteres loken" (35).[29] Certainly the knottiness of the pentangle mirrors the highly complex and interwoven plot/s of the poem. And the shield bespeaks an integrated text, its two inseparable faces representing the spirit and the letter that can not be severed from each other.

The pentangle and the shield on which it appears have often been discussed as symbolic of integrity, wholeness, the interdependence of virtues, particularly of the interrelatedness of physical and spiritual ideals.[30] The pentangle insists that all of Gawain's 25 enumerated virtues are interconnected: "vchone halched [embraced] in oþer" (659); and these virtues include those of the body—"fayled neuer þe freke [man] in his fyue fyngres" (641)—and those of the soul—"all his afyance [faith] vpon folde [earth] was in þe fyue woundez / þat Cryst kaȝt on þe croys" (642–43). So intertwined are flesh and spirit, even in the few lines I've just quoted, that it is almost impossible to distinguish one cleanly from the other: Gawain's spiritual faith is founded in the flesh of Christ, his five wounds. Such interlocking of soul and body is natural to a Christianity whose central belief is that God took on human flesh in a hypostatic union of divine and mortal elements.

The Incarnate God is also the Word made Flesh in Mary's womb (John 1: 14, "verbum caro factum est") on the Christmas Day celebrated among the other revels at Hautdesert, "þat tyme / þat Dryȝtyn [the Lord] for oure

destiné watz borne" (995–96). The well-known Johanine formula should
alert us to the possibility that the pentangle's linking together Gawain's
spirit and flesh with the flesh of Christ and of his mother Mary—for one
of Gawain's set of five virtues is derived from "þe fyue joyez / þat þe hende
[courteous] heuen-quene had of hir chylde" (646–47)—is intended to link
together the textual letter and the spirit that so often are represented in exegesis by the figures of the body and soul. The pentangle is notoriously a
self-conscious symbol of a symbol, a sign that means a sign. It is "a syngne"
set up "in bytoknyng," a sign set up to mean (625, 626). Normally we
might then associate the pentangle *qua* sign with the flesh that so often
represents the sensible letter of a text. Jerome's figure of the captive
woman, however, reconfigures the soul/body metaphor in seemingly paradoxical ways: for Jerome, it is the naked body of the captive woman that
represents the pure spirit of the text, and her clothing, hair, and nails, onto
which are displaced the carnal attributes of mortality ("all that is dead"),
"pleasure," and "lust," which represent the textual letter. Gawain's shield,
like other sections of the poem, seems to echo Jerome's textile model of
the sign, since the pentangle is described as if it were a cloth. Its lines "vm-
bellapez" each other in the way Gawain's clothes wrap him—Bertilak at
one point grabs him by a fold of his garment, "by þe lappe" (936)—and
"A lace lapped aboute" the Green Knight's ax. The pentangle is most famously "þe endeles knot" (630), but so too is the woven green girdle a
knot, "Knit vpon [the Lady's] kyrtel [tunic]"(1831). The pentangle isn't literally a piece of cloth, but the poem's descriptions of artwork confuse the
attributes of painting and of clothwork. The pentangle is "depaynt"
[painted] on the shield, and Gawain's helmet is similarly with a "brode
sylkyn borde [band] . . . paynted"—embroidered with birds and loveknots
(610–11).

   If the pentangle then stands in for the veil of Jerome's model of reading, the pure body of his bride is symbolized by the figure of Mary, most
pure, wise, and intact virgin, who inhabits the other side of Gawain's shield.
She is "In þe inore half of his schelde" (649) or inside the pentangle in the
way that the bride's body is inside her clothes. Yet, which side of the shield,
in or out, is Mary on? She is also on the outside of the shield, firmly knit
into the pentangle, as Geraldine Heng has detailed: the narrator, in the
process of explaining the pentangle's significance, enumerates the fourth of
its five fives as Mary's "fyue joyez." This prompts him to mention that "At
þis cause þe knyȝt comlyche hade / In þe inore half of his schelde hir
ymage depaynted" (645–49), before going on to complete his pentad of
fives.[31] Mary is thus on both sides of the shield—but so too are her five
joys, from which Gawain takes strength each time "quen he blusched
[looked]" at her image on the inside (650). If "vchone [is] halched in oþer,"

then Mary's five joys carry with them all of Gawain's other virtues onto her side of the shield. We, like the narrator, cannot be certain where one face of the shield stops and the other begins. Its two halves can be visually distinguished, but not otherwise separated. The image of the shield thus insists, as *Sir Gawain* repeatedly does, that there are no clear binary distinctions in what merely looks like a dualistic world.[32] And it specifically insists on the complex interdependence of spirit and letter, the unity of both in an integrated textuality.

In a world where letter and spirit cannot be separated, Jerome's model of translation clearly does not work: the veiled women that is the secular text refuses to be transformed into a stripped yet chaste Christian matron, just as the Lady of Hautdesert refuses to be separated from Morgan, who is her other side. The women possess a joint identity and joint agency, as *Sir Gawain*'s initial description of them makes clear. Firstly, it describes them entering holding hands: "An oþer lady [Morgan] hir lad bi þe lyft honde" (947). Then the description continues by intertwining their characteristics, knotting them together as the image of Mary is knit into the pentangle:

> . . . þat watz alder þen ho [she], an auncian hit semed,
> And heȝly honowred with haþeles [knights] aboute.
> Bot vnlyke on to loke þo ladyes were,
> For if þe ȝonge watz ȝep [fresh], ȝolȝe [yellow] watz þat oþer;
> Riche red on þat on rayled [were set] ayquere [everywhere],
> Rugh ronkled [wrinkled] chekez þat oþer on rolled;
> Kerchofes of þat on, wyth mony cler perlez, . . .
> þat oþer wyth a gorger watz gered ouer þe swyre [throat]. (948–54, 957)

The rhetoric of comparison/contrast here ("the one, the other") weaves together the descriptions of the two women into a single complex passage; one cannot think of one without thinking of the other. The description at its end undoes all of the contrasts, the differences it first drew between the women. For Morgan possesses under her clothing the same, if more unsightly, flesh that demarcates the Lady: "Hir [Morgan's] body watz schort and þik, / Hir buttokez balȝ [bulging] and brode" (966–67). Some of her flesh cannot be neatly distinguished from garments: her "Rugh ronkled chekez" "rolled" on her like the "Riche red" robes of the Lady (952–53). And not all of her flesh is swathed. Noteworthy in her appearance are "þe naked lyppez" (962), which predict the "lyppez smal laȝande [laughing]" (1207) with which the near-naked Lady later seduces Gawain with both words and kisses. After this introduction, the two women always appear together in the banqueting scenes, acting in concert—and usually to seize

Gawain for their own amusement: "þay tan [take] hym [Gawain] bytwene hem [them]" (977); "Watz neuer freke [man] fayrer fonge [seized] / Bitwene two so dyngne [worthy] dame" (1315–16); "þe lede [man] with þe ladyez layked [played] alle day" (1560). Of course the Lady appears alone in the seduction scenes. But in his desire to enjoy the Lady, Gawain fails to observe her link to Morgan. Only at the end of the poem does he recognize that he has failed to separate the veiled woman from the stripped one. He acknowledges, perhaps by instinct, that both "my honoured la- dyez, / . . . þus hor [their] knyȝt with hor kest [their trick] han koyntly [skillfully] bigyled" (2412–13)—*before* Bercilak reveals Morgan's authorship of the plot to test one of Arthur's knights. Gawain recognizes at last that the women have always acted with one intent—the veiled Morgan creates the plot that motivates the stripped Lady's behavior. Both women are two personae of the same feminine will, two sides, you might say, of the same shield.[33]

Gawain learns at last that the ugly hag he thought he could discard like the deadly carnal letter is not discardable. Indeed, when he looks beneath the finely woven nets that make up the plot in which he is trapped, he finds lurking not a chaste and submissive captive but the very willful Mor- gan who engineered the plot to trap him. As the author of the narrative in *Sir Gawain,* Morgan indeed confounds the differences between letter and spirit, for she unites the ensnaring desire that Jerome struggles to remove from his captive with the wisdom he wishes to retain in his Christian bride. She is a woman who refuses to be stripped, and whose female de- sire will not be denied.

The Ravisher Ravished:
Gawain's New Letter

Yet, *Sir Gawain and the Green Knight* does more than demonstrate that Jerome's model of reading is an inadequate one. The poem also shows that the model can backfire: for not only will Christians who read like Jerome have small chance of safely extracting wisdom from the letter of secular texts, but also they are very likely to be captured by the texts they read. Similarly, men who seek to bend women to their will run the risk of be- coming tamed by the very women they seek to dominate.

Jerome was obviously aware of the perils of splitting the letter from the spirit according to his model. His Letter 57 warns that the Christian war- rior *cum* reader who does not master the ensnaring letter will be mastered by it. The translator Hilary of Poitier, he notes, luckily escaped the temp- tation to "[bind] himself to the drowsiness of the letter or [fetter] himself by the stale literalism of inadequate culture." Instead, Hilary successfully "led away captive into his own tongue the meaning of his originals."[34] But Jerome himself was not as lucky as Hilary. As the famous dream of his Letter 22 to Eustochium details, his lifetime of reading Cicero failed to baptize the orator but instead resulted in Jerome becoming an apostate, a Ciceronian. Undergoing a different sort of ravishment—he is "raptus in spiritu" [ravished in the spirit]—Jerome's soul is stripped of his body, his flesh already "so wasted . . . that scarcely anything was left of me but skin and bone." He is dragged before Christ, who charges him, "Thou art a follower of Cicero and not of Christ." Chastened, Jerome vows that he would never "again read the works of the Gentiles," for secular rhetoric cannot be reconciled with Christian morality: "How can Horace go with the psalter, Virgil with the gospels, Cicero with the apostle?" The Christian ascetic must eschew female flesh not only when it is literal but metaphoric as well; he should embrace neither women nor "worldly books."[35]

If a reader as flesh-denying as Jerome cannot ravish secular rhetoric without becoming beguiled by the desiring carnal letter, who can? Hardly anyone, as *Sir Gawain and the Green Knight* shows. The poem depicts the perils of ravishing women, human or textual, in the misogynist outburst Gawain delivers after his fall. Here Gawain provides as an apology for his fall a brief and conventional catalogue of women's crimes against Old Testament men; if these biblical heroes were taken in by women, surely he should not be ashamed that he, too, was deceived: "þaȝ I be now bigyled, / me þink me burde [it seems to me I should] be excused" (2427–28). The knight specifically notes four biblical forerunners who were fooled by women:

" . . . watz Adam in erde [earth] with one bygyled,
And Salamon with fele sere [very many], and Samson eftsonez [too]
Dalyda dalt hym hys wyrde [fate]—and Dauyth þerafter
Watz blended with Barsabe, þat much bale þoled [trouble endured]."
(2416–19)

Three of the four male victims listed here are men who tried to do literally what Jerome instructed, marry a woman from an enemy people: Sampson first sought a Philistine wife before becoming besotted with Delilah (Judges 14–16); David desired Bathsheba, a Hittite woman (2 Samuel 11); and Solomon loved his "fele sere" [very many] foreign wives (3 Kings 11: 1). What Gawain emphasizes, however, is not the Israelite males' capture of their brides, but rather their undoing by the women. Of these three cases, the wise Solomon's is the most central to the poem, since it associates Gawain with Solomon twice—once here, and once in the description of Gawain's shield, whose pentangle "is a syngne þat Salamon set sumquyle / In bytoknyng of trawþe [fidelity, truth]" (625–26). (And Solomon, we should note, is cited by Jerome in Letter 70.2 as preceding him in advocating the study of Gentile texts.) Solomon's eventual fate, however, is not a happy one. He is a failed spousal conqueror: not even having attempted to convert his wives into good Israelite matrons, he is convinced by them to become an idolater. The biblical book of 3 Kings blames Solomon's apostasy on his failure to observe the Law's warning that any attempt to traffic with enemy women will always be self-defeating. The text narrates, "But King Solomon loved many strange women . . . of the nations concerning which the Lord said unto the children of Israel, 'Ye shall not go in to them, neither shall they come in unto you'" (3 Kgs. 11: 1–2). This verse quotes Deuteronomy 7: 1–4 (a text alluded to in the Sampson story as well, at Judges 14: 3), which directly contradicts the verse that Jerome used as the basis for his model of reading. This text sternly warns against marriage with Israel's enemies, predicting that the captors will become the captives, victims of a fall, "for surely [foreign women] will turn away your heart after their gods."

The moral of the story then, for anyone who puts down *Sir Gawain* and picks up the Bible to check its letter, is not the one that Gawain comes away with (and the same moral that Jerome himself derives from these narratives), that women are inherently evil and men blameless.[36] Rather, an interpretation of the stories better in keeping with the letter and the spirit of these texts is that men who fall because of women deserve to, because of their own foolishness and lust. Certainly the book of 2 Samuel doesn't blame Bathsheba for beguiling David; instead, it presents God, through the prophet Nathan, castigating David's sin of taking her (2 Samuel 12: 1–14). As Robert Holcot put it in a passage that echoes Jerome's warning against dealing with clothed women as well as Gawain's misogynist speech:[37]

It is said in Ecclesiasticus 9, . . ."Turn away thy face from a woman dressed up, and gaze not upon another's beauty." These women . . . [are] "a temptation to the souls of men, and a snare to the feet of the unwise." For in this mousetrap David was caught, and this idol also seduced the wisdom of Solomon to the worship of idols as we read in 3 Kings 12 [: 11]. These idols are to be fled, and not sought out through curiosity, for as the letter says [Wisdom 14: 12], "the beginning of fornication is the devising of idols." For it is impossible for a curious and lascivious man associating with these idols not to be corrupted by them; indeed, a man, diligently seeking out and considering in his thought the beauty of women so that he makes idols for himself, necessarily prepares for his own fall.

Gawain is wrong when he excuses himself and his biblical forebears, for, as Holcot makes clear, not all men who deal with women are duped. Rather,

Holcot says, that end is reserved for fools who lust after women in the first place: beautiful women are "a snare to the feet of the unwise" for the "curious and lascivious man . . . diligently seeking out" women. Men ensnared by women are only getting what they deserve. What goes around comes around.

Like his royal Israelite patron, then, and like Jerome, Gawain becomes the victim of his own attempts to embrace strange women, albeit chastely. His plan to defuse feminine desire backfires and he, the captor, is captured. Gawain, rather than being a masterful interpreter, becomes a text stripped and interpreted by two female readers. For Morgan and the Lady acting in concert turn the tables on Gawain. They ravish him using a modification of the Hieronymian strategy he himself had used and in doing so expose the violence undergirding it. The ladies, additionally, are more successful in their project than Gawain was, because they have a more sophisticated notion of semiotics. The women recognize, and correct, two problems inherent in Jerome's hermeneutics. First, whereas Jerome thought a reader might grasp the sapiential spirit of the text alone, the ladies realize that reading can only be accomplished through the letter, ideas apprehended through some sensible sign. Second, Jerome erred when he assumed that a text could somehow be interpreted against the grain to provide a contradictory meaning, via a sort of perverse conversion: just as the Gentile bride can become an Israelite matron, the fundamentally pagan letter can render up a Christian spirit. The ladies suffer no such delusions. They realize that the task of writers and readers, rhetoricians and interpreters, is to recognize the integrity of the sign, the sure (if not always unproblematic) fit between letter and spirit, signifier and signified. They thereupon improve Jerome's model of reading. When they "read" Gawain they do strip him of his letter, as Jerome counseled. But then they proceed to give him a new letter, one that better, more truthfully accords with his spirit. This new token declares that he has been, all along, not the flesh-denying Christian knight he pretends to be but a creature of the very desire he denied.

In stealing Gawain's hermeneutic weapon and using it against him, the ladies do no more than what Jerome advised his readers—though with a twist. In Letter 70, Jerome introduces the instructions for stripping the beautiful captive as a prooftext for his argument that Christians ought to use quotations from secular texts to defend their faith, should turn the tables on their heathen opponents by using their own writers against them. As he metaphorically put it, the Christian is "to wrench the sword of the enemy out of his hand and with his own blade to cut off the head of the arrogant Goliath." The ladies adapt Jerome's advice to their own ends by stealing Gawain's hermeneutic sword in order to defeat his misogynist hermeneutic. In essence, they appropriate the kinds of reading strategies that men like Gawain use to read women and modify them to read a man.[38]

The poem acknowledges that Morgan consciously practices this sort of literary revenge. Bertilak tells us that her power derives from her "koyntyse of clergye" (2447), her skill in the sort of learning normally restricted to males and sometimes used by them to oppose women; as the Wife of Bath comments with only a bit of exaggeration, "no womman of no clerk is praysed" (*Canterbury Tales* III: 706). Morgan appropriates *clergye* and employs it to dominate men—including Gawain. As Bertilak notes, the potent arts Morgan has learned from a male teacher, Merlin, now make proud men "ful tame" (2455).

Morgan devises the plot, but the Lady does most of the work by reversing the dynamic of Gawain's own courtly rhetoric. As readers of the seduction scenes almost uniformly comment, the Lady in these scenes reverses the gender roles of the ordinary courtly scenario: she employs the rhetoric usually used by the male lover as she addresses a Gawain who occupies the feminine position. The Lady aggressively woos, Gawain gingerly resists. The Lady, however, doesn't just mimic a conventionally male courtesy, but enacts the compelling force obscured by its elegant surface. For example, I earlier addressed the Lady's speech in which she spoke of compulsion: "Me behouez of fyne force / Your seruaunt be, and schale" (1239–40). The context of these lines, as I argued, draws our attention to the way courtly language compels women to serve male desire. But the lines also echo some earlier words of Gawain's. The knight had just greeted the Lady's opening feints in their battle of words with his courtly demurral that he must do what she says, "for me behouez nede [necessity]" (1216). Gawain does not actually mean this; his intention is at variance with the words he speaks here. Indeed, he speaks these words in an attempt to get out of bed—which is clearly what the Lady doesn't want. He speaks an empty if elegant letter in order to be politely contrary. But the Lady, by employing her integrated version of courtly rhetoric, will come to show Gawain that words mean what they say: if he says he's behooved, well then, she'll behoove him. And she indeed does. In the third seduction scene, as the sexual tensions come to their climax, the narrator tells us, "For þat prynces of pris [worth] depresed [pressed] hym so þikke [relentlessly] / . . . þat nede hym bihoued"—to choose whether to accept or reject the Lady's advances (1770–71). What behooves Gawain, in actuality, is the literal meaning of his own words, which the Lady takes at face value. Although the Lady says, on the second morning, that Gawain may force a kiss from a woman, the effect of her words is to compel a kiss from Gawain—but only because Gawain counters her frank suggestion with the courtly formula that "I am at your comaundement" to kiss when she pleases (1501). So she commands him. As Myra Stokes details in her analysis of the bedroom scenes, what Gawain confronts in these scenes is "the insidious pressure of language."[39]

The Lady compels Gawain to her desire by literalizing courtliness's usual metaphors, making these figures' tenors conform to their vehicles. The Lady, basically, makes words mean what they seem to say. As Stokes points out, the bedroom scenes are replete with a number of military metaphors, completely conventional in character, which make the point that debate in general, and courtly dialogue in particular, entail the same sorts of conflict and antagonism as war.[40] The Lady takes these battle metaphors at their word and enacts them by programmatically following Jerome's model of ravishment—the captive bride, after all, is one of the spoils of battle—although she reverses the gender roles. Under her attack, Gawain is no longer the warrior who desires a captive bride but a captive knight dominated by a woman. The first seduction scene makes Gawain's capture explicit. The Lady's first action is to take Gawain prisoner: "Now ar 3e tan as-tyt! [taken at once]," she gloats on entering his room for the first time, "I schal bynde yow in your bedde" (1210–11). And Gawain meekly acknowledges that he is her "prysoun" (1219).

With the assistance of other residents of Hautdesert, the Lady continues to enact Jerome's model by stripping Gawain. His divestiture is begun immediately upon his entering Hautdesert. No sooner through the door, he begins to remove his arms and armor (including the shield with its pentangle), which is taken away by waiting hands: "Quen he hef vp his helme, þer hi3ed [hastened] innoughe / For to hent [take] hit at his honde, þe hende [elegant one] to seruen; / His bronde [sword] and his blasoun [insignia] boþe þay token" (826–28). Once in his chamber, Gawain is further "despoyled . . . of his bruny [breastplate] and of his bry3t wedez [clothes]" (860–61). In the seduction scenes, Gawain, stripped again of his clothing, lies naked in bed as the Lady seeks to reach his inner self, "His mode [spirit] to remwe [change]" (1475).

Gawain's nakedness is, in keeping with the Ladies' notion of the integral sign, both literal and symbolic. He is stripped not only of his armor, but also of everything that armor and shield symbolize: his public identity as Christian knight. For when the pentangle represents the letter, it is Gawain's letter, as Gawain *is* the pentangle knight: the knot "acordez to þis kny3t" (631). The pentangle at face value signifies a complex of chivalric virtues that Gawain, by displaying it on his shield, claims to possess. Above all he claims to be the knight of truth, "tulk [hero] of tale most trwe" (638). But the knight doesn't deserve to carry the pentangle as his device, as his lying courtliness attests. He loses the pentangle almost the instant that he enters Hautdesert, because the ladies there see the pentangle as a false token of identity, a faithless letter that does not name the real Gawain and therefore must be detached from him.

Gawain's false letter, however, is not all the ladies desire to detach. Jerome's program for reading, let us remember, consisted not only of stripping his foreign bride but also of having "all that is dead in her . . . cut away or shaved off." So, too, do the ladies of Hautdesert cut away the excessive portions of Gawain. They do not shave his head, as Jerome's model dictates (a model, by the way, literally followed by Delilah at Judges 16: 19). Instead, they reveal that model's latent violence (which is furthermore emphasized by the courtly scenes being embedded in the hunts that feature the flaying and dismemberment of animals) by symbolically performing the action for which shearing is a gentler displacement: they enact Gawain's beheading. The context of Letter 70 makes clear that the barbering and disrobing of the captive bride are displacements of decapitation: just before introducing the captive woman, Jerome offers a more violent figure for the masterful Christian reader as a warrior who can "wrench the sword of the enemy out of his hand and with his own blade to cut off the head of the arrogant Goliath."[41] To decapitate and to shear are equally valid figures for interpretation construed as stripping a text of its mortal letter.

The Green Knight, acting as Morgan's agent (2456), threatens this decapitation, an act so annihilating that even its amelioration into a nick in the neck destroys Gawain's integrity—as rape destroys a woman's. Gawain's imminent beheading is a symbolic rape, a revelation of and repayment for his courtesy's complicity with the violent compulsion of women. Beheading, after all, is the verbally logical punishment for the rape committed in *The Wife of Bath's Tale:* because the knight there "By verray force . . . rafte hire maydenhed," he "sholde han lost his heed" (*CT* III.887, 92). The example of this Chaucerian tale is apposite here, since Gawain is the protagonist in some of the analogues to this story, "The Marriage of Sir Gawain" and "The Wedding of Sir Gawain and Dame Ragnell." Gawain's losing his head would be a fit repayment for the maidenheads the knighthood he represents has taken by courteous force. This repayment constitutes a kind of exchange just as equal as any of the bargains Gawain makes with the Green Knight.

But while the women enact a rapelike ritual on Gawain, we must remember that in *Sir Gawain* rape also functions as a metaphor for interpretation. Thus, the ladies' behavior, while motivated by a desire to reveal the violence against women underlying courtly behavior, also has an aspect that is literary; their project is a textual one. The bookish nature of their actions reveals itself in the second seduction scene, where the Lady uses a self-consciously literary vocabulary in discussing knighthood. She lectures Gawain that "þe lel layk [loyal play] of luf" should serve as "þe lettrure [letters] of armes; / For to telle of þis teuelyng [effort] of þis trwe kny3tez, / Hit [i.e., love] is þe tytelet token [entitling sign] and tyxt of her werkkez"

(1513–15). But the Lady is not merely pursuing a learned interest in sign theory. She is obviously talking about life as well as art, comparing the "real" Gawain to knights she has read about in romances. Her using a literary vocabulary to manipulate Gawain reveals that for her chivalry is a matter of textuality, a verbal artifact, but an institution that is a part of the real, material world as well. By applying her discussion of bookish chivalry to the body of the knight before her, by conflating the institution of chivalry with the Gawain before her, she indicates that she, unlike Jerome, will not separate the abstract meaning of a text from the flesh that incarnates it.[42] She believes that knights *are* texts, and Gawain in particular is a text she wants to know by heart.

The Lady's literary vocabulary here thus demonstrates that she has not just followed Jerome's hermeneutic but substantially improved it. For she realizes, as Jerome does not, that texts require letters if they are to be read. Jerome spoke of taking a text and stripping it of its letter in order to detach it from its dangerous pagan culture. But such stripping would result in a disembodied idea that, *pace* Jerome, cannot be embraced. Even Christian writers must produce a letter for spiritual wisdom, since surely even the most pure-hearted Christian cannot grasp a wisdom that is naked. After all, Christ, Wisdom himself, had to take on a letter, the fleshy veil of the human body, in order to be intelligible to men. As Boccacio put it, using a common metaphor, in the Incarnation God is "clothed in the flesh."[43] And, as biblical commentators frequently note, Christ was given this fleshly integument by Mary. Composition then, writing words, is essentially conception and birth, and is therefore a feminine activity. The Lady, as a woman, understands the spirit's need for the letter, and so takes Jerome's hermeneutic a step further. She not only strips Gawain of a letter he doesn't deserve but reclothes him with a new letter that more truthfully reveals his spirit: the letter of a love that is hardly *caritas*.

The Lady states, in the literary speech I have just quoted, that if knighthood is a text, then its letter and sign, its "lettrure" and "token," should be love-play, "þe lel layk of luf." Here she insists that the eroticism that Gawain denies is the most faithful sign of knightly courtesy. And this is the letter she imposes on Gawain: in essence, she names him as the courtly lover whose desire he sought to deny. If Jerome wished to strip his captive of the letter of desire, the Lady wishes to imprint that letter on Gawain. The Lady bestows this new letter on Gawain at the moment in the third seduction scene when she persuades him to accept the green girdle. The girdle is a fitting symbol of the veiling letter, since it, of course, is a piece of cloth, a "wede," which the Lady wove herself (2359–60). This letter establishes Gawain's identity as lover—the girdle is after all a love token, a "luf lace" (1874, 2438) and a "drurye" [love token] that he wears as his new garment:

"dressed he his drurye double hym aboute" (1033). So attired, Gawain becomes identified as the Lady's lover; thus Bertilak associates the girdle with
"the wowyng of my wyf," and Gawain himself vows he will wear it as a
reminder of the desires of the body—"þe faut and þe fayntyse [frailty] of
þe flesche crabbed [perverse]" (2361, 2435).

The moment when Gawain accepts the girdle and, with it, the carnal
desire it represents should remind us that the knight has simply received
his come-uppance in the poem, that this is a fall of Gawain's own making.
Gawain accepts the girdle as the culmination of his antifeminist diatribe:
"'Bot your gordle . . . / þis wyl I welde wyth guod wylle'" follows hard on
the heels of "'þaȝ I be now bigyled / Me þink me burde be excused'"
(2427–30). As I argued earlier, in this speech Gawain undermines himself,
for the misogynist interpretation of scriptural texts he offers can easily be
dismissed as misreading by appealing to the letter of the Bible, as Holcot
does: "for as the letter says," Holcot notes in quoting the books of Ecclesiasticus and Wisdom. Holcot's more literal reading of scripture arrives at
the conclusion that only foolish, lascivious men will be trapped by women,
and the language of Gawain's speech along with the image of the girdle
suggest that the poet who created Gawain knew Holcot's reading or one
like it. Beautiful women are "a snare to the feet of the unwise," and girdle,
after all, as a *lace* is also a "snare." Then, too, the knight acknowledges he
has been "a fole" [fool; 2414]—and that the biblical heroes he cites "'were
biwyled [beguiled] / With wymmen þat þay *vsed*'" (2425–26, emphasis
added). The poem shows us that Gawain has used women—if only through
a courtly rhetoric whose power he does not recognize. If Gawain used
women, then it is poetic justice that he is used by them.

But *Sir Gawain* delineates the dynamics of the women's revenge not to
advocate the *lex talionis* for either women or men. Rather, it wishes to expose the cyclic violence inhering in courtesy, wherein men assault women,
women respond in kind, and men defend themselves with renewed offense—Gawain's misogyny, if anything, is only augmented by the women's
actions in the poem; his screed occurs after his handling by the women.
The romance offers, as Sheila Fisher says, a cautionary lesson to its male
readers. But that lesson may not necessarily be as Fisher understands it, that
men beware women and maintain their hierarchical domination of them.
Rather, *Sir Gawain* can teach that men should acknowledge and beware
the violence concealed in their own behavior, for that violence can be
turned against them. The rapist can easily become raped.

Sir Gawain is as interested in textual as in sexual politics, and it seeks to
protect not just its readers against violence, but its own letter. It exposes
the essentially destructive, and self-destructive, nature of any hermeneutic
that envisions reading as an act of rape. Readers who rape texts, it cautions,

will end up raped by texts (just as men who ravish women will be be-headed); like Jerome, that is, they will be converted to beliefs and practices they abhor. In order to protect both its readers and itself, *Sir Gawain* seeks to disassociate itself from the letter-disdaining poetics of rape. The poem declares itself to be a tale whose hermeneutic depends on the power of the integral letter: it is, as the narrator tells us, a narrative told through the faithful medium of the letter, a story "[w]ith lel letteres loken" (35). The reader must respect its integrity and receive the story's proffered letter along with its concealed spirit, as Gawain's two ladies would teach us.[44]

Notes

1. Kathryn Gravdal, *Ravishing Maidens: Writing Rape in Medieval French Litera-ture and Law* (Philadelphia: University of Pennsylvania Press, 1991), pp. 42–71.

2. Dietmar Rieger, "Le motif du viol dans la littérature de la France médié-vale entre norme courtoise et réalité courtoise," *Cahiers de civilisation médiévale* 31 (1988): 241–67.

3. *Sir Degaré*, line 132, ed. Anne Laskaya and Eve Salisbury, in *The Middle En-glish Breton Lays* (Kalamazoo, MI: Medieval Institute Publications, 1995), which also includes *Sir Orfeo*.

4. Carolyn Dinshaw, *Chaucer's Sexual Poetics* (Madison: University of Wiscon-sin Press, 1989), pp. 2–25. On the exegetical tradition, see Henri de Lubac, *Medieval Exegesis,* vol. 1, trans. Mark Sebanc (Grand Rapids, MI: Eerdmans, 1998), pp. 211–24. I am indebted to Dinshaw for the captive woman, but do not agree that Jerome wishes to deprive the text of "its stylistic . . . blan-dishments" (p. 24). Jerome seeks to preserve pagan wisdom *and* eloquence even while stripping off erotic carnality. My understanding of exegetical carnal and spiritual readings of gendered violence is informed by Shari Horner, "The Violence of Exegesis: Reading the Bodies of Ælfric's Female Saints," in *Violence against Women in Medieval Texts,* ed. Anna Roberts (Gainesville: University Press of Florida, 1998), pp. 22–43.

5. Biblical quotations are from the Douai-Rheims version (1899; rpt. Rock-ford, IL: Tan, 1971).

6. Letter 70.2; CSEL 54, 1: 702; translation mine, based on that of W. H. Fre-mantle, *Jerome: Letters and Select Works,* Nicene and Post-Nicene Fathers 6 (1893): 149.

7. At least two critics have argued that the poem and/or its critics repress fe-male desire. Sheila Fisher, "Taken Men and Token Women in *Sir Gawain and the Green Knight,*" in *Seeking the Woman in Late Medieval and Renaissance Writings: Essays in Feminist Contextual Criticism,* ed. Sheila Fisher and Janet E. Halley (Knoxville: University of Tennessee Press, 1989), pp. 71–105; and "Leaving Morgan Aside: Women, History, and Revisionism in *Sir Gawain and the Green Knight,*" in *The Passing of Arthur: New Essays in Arthurian Tra-dition,* ed. Christopher Baswell and William Sharpe (New York: Garland,

1988), pp. 129–51. Geraldine Heng, "Feminine Knots and the Other *Sir Gawain and the Green Knight,*" *PMLA* 106 (1991): 500–514.

8. All quotations are from *Sir Gawain and the Green Knight,* ed. J. R. R. Tolkien and E. V. Gordon. 2nd ed. rev. Norman Davis (Oxford: Oxford University Press, 1967). Bracketed translations are my own, informed by this edition's glossary and the studies cited below.

9. Malcolm Andrew and Ronald Waldron, *The Poems of the Pearl Manuscript* (Berkeley: University of California Press, 1982), p. 243, n. to ll. 943–69.

10. Fisher, "Leaving Morgan Aside."

11. R. Howard Bloch, *Medieval Misogyny and the Invention of Western Romantic Love* (Chicago: University of Chicago Press, 1991), especially pp. 113–65.

12. E. Jane Burns and Roberta L. Krueger, eds., *Courtly Ideology and Woman's Place in Medieval French Literature, Romance Notes* 25 (1985); Joan Ferrante, *Woman as Image in Medieval Literature from the Twelfth Century to Dante* (New York: Columbia University Press, 1975).

13. David Mills, "An Analysis of the Temptation Scenes in *Sir Gawain and the Green Knight,*" *Journal of English and Germanic Philology* 67 (1968): 612–30; and Ad Putter, Sir Gawain and the Green Knight *and French Arthurian Romance* (Oxford: Oxford University Press, 1995), pp.117–39.

14. Joseph E. Gallagher, "'Trawþe' and 'Luf-Talking' in *Sir Gawain and the Green Knight,*" *Neuphilologische Mitteilungen* 78 (1977): 365.

15. Carolyn Dinshaw, "A Kiss is Just a Kiss: Heterosexuality and its Consolations in *Sir Gawain and the Green Knight,*" *Diacritics* 24 (1994): 210–11.

16. J. A. Burrow, *A Reading of* Sir Gawain and the Green Knight (London: Routledge & Kegan Paul, 1965), p. 91. Gravdal provides a survey of texts dealing with the rape of peasants in *Ravishing Maidens,* pp. 104–21.

17. Andreas Capellanus, *The Art of Courtly Love* 1.11, trans. John Jay Parry (New York: W. W. Norton, 1969), p. 150. Latin text *De Amore,* ed. Graziano Ruffini (Milan: Guanda, 1980).

18. The history of commentary is neatly summarized by Arthur Lindley, "Lady Bertilak's *cors: Sir Gawain and the Green Knight,* 1237," *Notes & Queries* 42 (1995): 23–24.

19. *Oxford English Dictionary,* 2nd ed., electronic version, *fine* A.I.3.

20. Mills, "An Analysis," 615, 616–17.

21. *Cursor Mundi,* ed. Richard Morris, 3 vols. EETS o.s. 57, 59, 62, 66, 68, 99, 101 (London: Kegan Paul, 1874, 1893), lines 1577 and 28483–84.

22. Geoffrey Chaucer, *Legend of Good Women,* line 2324; *Wife of Bath's Tale,* line 888; ed. John H. Fisher, *The Complete Poetry and Prose of Geoffrey Chaucer* (New York: Holt, Rinehart and Winston, 1977).

23. *La Chevalerie d'Ogier de Danemarche,* ed. Mario Eusebi (Milan:Varese, 1963), line 11198; Chrétien de Troyes, *Der Percevalroman,* ed. Alfons Hilka (Halle, 1932), line 3875. Both quoted by Rieger, "Le motif du viol," pages 250, 255.

24. Mills, "An Analysis," p. 616, n. 8; Andrew and Waldron, *The Poems,* p. 253, n. 1237f.

25. Gravdal, *Ravishing Maidens,* p. 3.

26. Andreas Capellanus, *Art of Courtly Love* 1.8, p. 143; Latin, *De Amore,* p. 142.

27. "[L]a norme courtoise n'*exclut* pas seulement le viol . . . mais qu'au contraire, cette même norme peut également le *provoquer* en tant qu'expédient à l'aporie de l'amour courtois. . . . [D]ans un exemple du *Commens d'Amours,* . . . l'amant Lernesius, 'quant il vit que par requerre ne par proier ne par nul bel mot qu'il li seüst dire, il ne porroit merchi avoir,' viole son amante, Diphile." Rieger, "Le motif du viol," p. 260.

28. *Summa Theologica* 1.1.9; trans. Fathers of the English Dominican Province, 5 vols. (1948; rpt. Westminster, MD: Christian Classics, 1981), 1: 6.

29. Ralph Hanna III, "Unlocking What's Locked: Gawain's Green Girdle," *Viator* 14 (1983): 289–302, rejects the pentangle as an icon for the poem's textuality because its meaning is "clear and exemplary (if not locked to the point of rigidity)"; p. 290. But the pentangle, as any survey of the criticism shows, is indeed a slippery sign.

30. Of many discussions, my reading of the pentangle owes most to Burrow, *A Reading,* pp. 41–51; Roger Lass, "'Man's Heaven': The Symbolism of Gawain's Shield," *Medieval Studies* 28 (1966): 354–60, for whom the shield represents the necessary relationship between flesh and spirit; and Florence Newman, "Sir Gawain and the Semiotics of Truth," *Medieval Perspectives* 4–5 (1989–90): 125–39, who reads the shield as symbolizing "perfect coherence between external appearance and internal reality" (p. 134).

31. Heng, "Feminine Knots," p. 504.

32. Lawrence Besserman, "The Idea of the Green Knight," *English Literary History* 53 (1986): 219–39; John M. Ganim, "Disorientation, Style, and Consciousness in *SGGK,*" *PMLA* 91 (1976): 376–84.

33. Mother Angela Carson, "Morgain la Fee as the Principle of Unity in *GGK,*" *Modern Language Quarterly* 23 (1962): 3–16, first argued the joint identity of the ladies as aspects of Morgan. For a list of other discussions of the characters' doubling, see Heng, "Feminine Knots," p. 503.

34. Hilary's literary activities are not the ones Jerome defends in Letter 70; Hilary was translating biblical exegesis from Greek to Latin, not extracting spirituality from pagan authors. But underlying Jerome's discussion here are the same military metaphor and the same letter-phobic hermeneutic as in his commentary on the captive woman.

35. Jerome, Letter 22.30; CSEL 54, pp. 189–90; Fremantle, pp. 35–36.

36. Gawain's listing of Adam, Samson, David, and Solomon is, of course, a misogynist commonplace, but one whose most authoritative occurrence was in the writings of Jerome. See Letter 22.12 (Fremantle, p. 26) and *Against Jovinian* I.23–24 (Fremantle, pp. 363–64).

37. Robert Holcot, *Commentary on the Book of Wisdom,* quoted by D. W. Robertson, Jr., *Preface to Chaucer* (Princeton, NJ: Princeton University Press, 1963), p. 99.

38. In her "Getting Medieval: *Pulp Fiction,* Gawain, Foucault," in *The Book and the Body,* ed. Dolores Warwick Frese and Katherine O'Brien O'Keeffe

(Notre Dame, IN: University of Notre Dame Press, 1997), p. 152, Carolyn Dinshaw suggests that the poem contains a "deeply buried plot, profound and hidden, in which Gawain is a pawn—between women." Dinshaw's idea of why the women manipulate Gawain differs from mine, though we agree on the violence of what they do to Gawain. Her idea of buried plots of same-sex desire certainly complicates the question of who is raping whom in the poem—as does the inclusion of the Green Knight/Bertilak in the women's plot as either author or collaborator. I owe this last perception to Brad Sisk.

39. For Myra Stokes, "*Sir Gawain and the Green Knight:* Fitt III as Debate," *Nottingham Studies* 25 (1981): 36, language specifically has the power to "debase and trivialize the values [Gawain] stands for."

40. Stokes, "Fitt III," pp. 42–43.

41. Letter 70.2; CSEL 54: 702; Fremantle, p. 149.

42. Geraldine Heng discusses the corporeality of the Lady's speech in a stimulating analysis, "A Woman Wants: The Lady, *Gawain,* and the Forms of Seduction," *Yale Journal of Criticism* 5 (1992): 108–10; she also spotlights the girdle as a means by which the Lady imprints desire on Gawain; "Feminine Knots," pp. 506–9.

43. Boccaccio, *Genealogy of the Pagan Gods* 15.9, trans. Charles Osgood as *Boccaccio on Poetry* (Indianapolis: Bobbs-Merrill, 1956), p. 125.

44. My thanks for helpful and supportive comments on previous versions of this essay go to several anonymous readers, Ross Arthur, Paula Blank, Chris Bongie, Theresa Coletti, Lee Patterson, Adam Potkay, Brad Sisk, Peter Wiggins, and especially the editors.

PART II

THE PHILOMEL LEGACY

CHAPTER 4

RAPING MEN:
WHAT'S MOTHERHOOD GOT TO DO WITH IT?

E. Jane Burns

> This essay draws on the Old French *Philomena* to understand how the abusive effects of sexual violence against women are positioned within and cushioned by larger cultural narratives of beauty, allurement, and love and, less predictably, within traditions of marriage and motherhood.

A s a cultural phenomenon, rape stands disturbingly at a crucial nexus of the historical and mythic dimensions of Western society, providing, on the one hand, a daunting material record of sexual violence against women[1] and offering, on the other, a compelling icon of how women's bodies have been constructed as alluring, provocative, and necessarily violable.[2] In Catharine MacKinnon's formulation, rape both actualizes and symbolizes the cultural disempowerment of women in the Western world.[3] If women are sexually assaulted because they are women, it is not, as MacKinnon explains, individually or at random, but "because of their membership in a group *defined by gender*" ("Reflections," 379, my emphasis). To be treated like a woman in this sense does not derive from "any universal essence or homogeneous generic or ideal type" but results from a "diverse material reality of social meanings and practices . . ." ("Reflections," 378).

This essay investigates how some of those social meanings and practices, which might seem at first tangential to the physical act of raping women, contribute substantially to the phenomenon of rape. It seeks to understand how the abusive effects of sexual violence against women are positioned within and cushioned by larger cultural narratives of beauty, allurement, and love and, less predictably, within traditions of marriage and mother-hood. The existence of rape has come to feel inevitable to many of us partly because of the alarmingly high figures that record sexual attack as frequent and commonplace. But equally important, the high incidence of rape in the United States has perhaps not typically met with an immedi-ate and unflinching resolve to eliminate it because the cultural narratives we have heard from childhood tend to make rape familiar. Accounts of rape in literature, fairytales, folklore, classical myth, and the visual arts through the ages remind us brutally that sexual violence against women is not only a violation of individual rights but a systemic feature of our cul-tural heritage. Incessantly restaged and played out, rape seems ever to grow and spread in our cultural unconscious rather than being itself forcefully attacked and eradicated.

Indeed, women who live in a culture that constructs rape as a pre-dictable response to seductive female anatomy tend at times to internalize that message and begin to act it out through gestures that come to be con-sidered, ironically, "typically female," as Susan Griffin has explained:

> These gestures seem so commonplace among women—we draw the win-dow shades before undressing, pull a cloth quickly over the middle of our bodies, cross our arms over our breasts. Thus we imagine we protect men from themselves. The very existence of our bodies then, our own gestures say, is provocation to violence; our bodies become *things* which we must hide. How does one move about the world in this body which has the power to invoke malevolence against oneself? (Griffin, 76)

At the opposite extreme, some women have returned the violence of rape with violence of their own devising, as the following ritual performed by the Portland Women's Nightwatch in 1978 attests:

> My name is Inez Garcia. I killed the man who held me down while his friends raped me. I spent 19 months in prison, my case was three years in the courts. I was found not guilty (California). . . .
>
> My name is Virginia Tierce. I shot the man who raped me. I was found guilty of manslaughter. I was granted a retrial. I was acquitted.[4]

These women's violent responses offer one way, many would contend a desperate and untenable way, of fighting against the cultural myths that re-duce women's bodies to rapable objects. They warn forcefully that the fe-male body that "has the power to invoke malevolence against itself" can also strike back with equal violence, reminding us hauntingly that raped women can be as brutal as their attackers.

RAPING MEN   129

But neither path, whether uncomfortably embracing the cultural stereotypes of alluring femininity or furiously and violently rejecting them, will effectively reduce the threat or incidence of rape. If what we seek is to make a safer place for women in the social sphere so that we can "move about the world" without feeling compelled to cover up the body that we are told incites desire and provokes attack, we will have to move beyond the physical gestures of fighting back, however justified and understandable those gestures may now seem. We will have to try instead, at some imagined point in the future, to rewrite the very cultural definitions that use female beauty and the alluring woman's body to authorize rape.[5] But how can this be done?

The question is posed in a complex and thoughtful way by one of Western literature's most violent tales of rape and revenge: the story of the ancient Philomel and her sister Procne. Most readers are familiar with Ovid's brief recounting of the myth in the *Metamorphoses*.[6] But I want to concentrate on a twelfth-century rewriting of Ovid's tale in the anonymous Old French *Philomena*,[7] not because it provides a workable solution to the serious and pressing problem of rape. It does not. But the Old French tale, which follows the basic Ovidian plot closely, includes lengthy narrative additions that focus in particular on provocative female responses to rape. This medieval recasting of the Ovidian myth reveals how thoroughly rape is imbricated within narrative plots of virginal beauty that progress seamlessly from attraction, love, and passion to seduction, abduction, and violation. It shows further how rape can be safeguarded by cultural narratives of the supportive wife and the protective mother, even though they too are also often victimized by the rapist's attack. But by foregrounding issues of women's knowledge, skill, and talents within an economy of women's collective work, this medieval recasting of Ovid's tale also substantially rewrites the myths of virginal beauty and maternal love. Emphasis here falls on working women who join forces to change the path of myth, calling into question cultural stereotypes of the beautiful maiden and nurturing mother. Could we begin to do the same? Could we no longer repeat and reinscribe the timeworn tales of rape and ravishment but begin to rethink and then further rewrite the founding cultural narratives that have made rape part of our collective history?[8]

The tale of Philomena, in both antique and medieval versions, is shockingly brutal. The innocent virgin Philomena is carried off, with her father's consent, by her sister's husband, Tereus, who savagely rapes Philomena and, to keep her from revealing his crime, cuts out her tongue. The revenge plot follows in which Philomena "writes" the tale of her violation, the French account tells us, into a tapestry that she sends to her sister, Progne (in the Old French spelling), the ravisher's wife. The two sisters then join forces to kill not Tereus, but his innocent young son, whose body they chop into bits and serve to the unsuspecting ravisher as a delicious meal.

If in the Ovidian tale Philomel's weaving "threatens to retrieve from obscurity," as Patricia Joplin has explained, "all that her culture defines as outside the bounds of allowable discourse, whether sexual, spiritual or literary,"[9] the woven *cortine* in the Old French story does this and more. The medieval Philomena's clothwork not only redefines the terms of female expression through speech and writing, it also recasts the standard function attributed to the beautiful body in courtly romance: the body that typically incites love and passion that can so easily turn to rape.[10] Outlining an economy of seeing and knowing based on women's work that is defined in terms of gesture rather than speech, Philomena's tapestry offers a concerted challenge to the male gaze that constructs female beauty throughout the romance, displacing the beauty fashioned by Tereus's eyes to a beautiful pictorial message crafted by Philomena's hands.

To understand how this transformation occurs, we need to read the story depicted in Philomena's tapestry against the story emblematized in her sister Progne's brutal infanticide. To do so will be to practice what Nancy Miller, in another context, has called reading for the underread.[11] The tendency among readers of the Ovidian Philomel at least has been to privilege the liberating and peaceful artistry of this heroine over the male-inspired violence and brutality of her sister.[12] Indeed it is difficult to accept Procne's savage decapitation of her own son, whose body parts she subsequently cooks and serves to the unsuspecting Tereus, or to understand this act as anything but a hopeless repetition of the mutilation and dismemberment earlier visited upon Philomena.

And yet the Old French version of Ovid's tale encourages us at every turn to read these women's stories as two parallel accounts of seduction, abduction, and silencing: one of a beautiful virgin, the other a nurturing mother. We are moved by the interaction of these female protagonists to ask how rape and motherhood are related, and how each intersects with cultural expectations of female beauty. More specifically, in terms of narrative outcome, we are encouraged to ponder how infanticide on Progne's part might compensate for the rape of her lovely virgin sister. Although it is true, as Jane Marcus points out for the Ovidian version of the tale, that Philomena plays the creator/writer to her sister's role as reader—receiver of the fateful message (79), there is also an important way in which both women, especially in the French text, can be seen as writers who recast standard narrative plots. They do so not with words—written or oral—but by using their hands to draw portraits that must be seen in order to be read. Philomena's tapestry retells the story of erotic beauty that typically features a seductive virgin who guarantees male pleasure. Progne's barbaric

meal recasts the narrative of unfaltering maternal love that focuses traditionally on the mother who guarantees male patrimony and the husband's
legal right to possess offspring. Together these two heroines' gestures ask:
what if women fought back against rape in a different way, by recasting the
very cultural narratives that construct the woman's body as beautiful, available, and violable? What might the alternative narrative plot look like?

Beauty and Knowledge

Philomena appears in the Old French tale as a classic medieval beauty possessing all the requisite attributes of the typically gorgeous heroine in
courtly romance.[13] Her beautiful body and bright face are accompanied by
shiny golden hair; a smooth white forehead; clear, wide-set eyes; well-
formed eyebrows; a long straight nose; a pink and white complexion; a
smiling mouth with full, slightly red lips; sweet breath; small white teeth
closely set; a chin, neck, throat, and chest whiter than ermine; two small
breasts like apples, thin long white hands; thin thighs and slightly curving
hips. But to the standardized medieval catalogue of fetishized female body
parts, the Old French text appends a listing of things that this heroine
knows how to do. Initially, we hear only of a beautiful body carefully fashioned by the text's narrator[14] along with God and Nature, who function
as parallel creators of the heroine's beauty.[15] The opening description is
governed tellingly by a repeated use of the verb *avoir,* which constructs
Philomena as an alluring object of desire who *has* a smooth white forehead, a lady who *has* a high long straight nose or *has* small close set teeth,
"Le front *ot* blanc et plain sanz fronce. . . . Le nes *ot* haut et lonc et
droit, . . . Danz *ot* petiz, serrez et blans" (vv. 145, 149, 158). The standard
usage of the verb *avoir* suggests to the attentive listener not that Philomena
has these qualities herself, but that she "has" them in the eye of the be-
holder. Indeed, Philomena's beauty derives, in this instance, from Tereus's
gaze as he observes her stately entrance into the room.

The subsequent catalogue of extraordinary beauty that the ravisher's
sight constructs, focuses in typical medieval fashion on the heroine's head
and face: 16 out of 21 lines (vv. 143–58) are devoted to these uppermost
body parts. Most significantly, however, special attention is paid within this
portrait to the heroine's mouth, which receives nearly half of those 16 lines:

Boche riant, levres grossettes
Et un petitet vermeillettes
Plus que samiz vermaus an grainne,
Et plus soef oloit s'alainne
Que pimanz ne basmes d'ancans;

Danz ot petiz, serrez et blans. (vv. 153–58)

> [A smiling mouth, plump lips / And a little red. / Redder than red silk cloth.
> / And her breath smelled sweeter / than spice and incense. / She had small
> white teeth, close together.]

Philomena's other attributes are allotted only an average of one or two
lines apiece. This heroine's mouth is, interestingly, an alluring, erotic, and
seductive mouth, a smiling mouth with plump reddish lips that evoke the
other erotic female lips unmentioned here except as they appear eu-
phemistically as *le sorplus* (v. 165), meaning generally "all the rest" and more
specifically the unspeakable "female genitalia." Philomena's teeth are typically small: delicate and not menacing (v. 158). But, most important, her
tongue, which is necessary for speech, is absent. This is the beautiful body
that speaks the language of seduction without speaking at all,[16] a body
whose beauty allures, even compels, Tereus to fall hopelessly, helplessly in
love with it.

In its utter silence and systematic fragmentation into fetishized body
parts, this beautifully constructed body differs little from the body of the
heroine subjected to rape a few scenes later. There, Tereus's uncontestable
power as subject of the action is rendered most clearly in the reduction of
the female object of desire to its smallest and most objectified linguistic
unit. The desired woman becomes no more than the direct object pronoun, "la":

> Car cil totes voies l'assaut,
> Si l'esforce tant et justise
> Que tot a force l'a conquise
> Et trestot son buen an a fet. (836–39)

> [He attacks her immediately. / He so forces and overpowers her / that he
> conquers her by force. / And he takes his pleasure from her.]

There is no Beauty here. Only body remains as a haunting echo of the
more subtle reduction of woman to body parts charted in the preceding
glorified image of femininity. We can see in both instances how fragmentation of female anatomy and its inscription in cultural narratives of beauty
subtly reinforce rape.

A crucial feature of this speechless body is that it lacks not only a
tongue to articulate thoughts but even a brain to conceive them. We are
reminded repeatedly of Philomena's naive ignorance. She suspected nothing of Tereus's ulterior motive:

Cele ne set que ce puet estre
Ne ne se puet aparcevoir
Que cil la vueille decevoir. (vv. 746–48)

[She does not know what this might mean. She cannot imagine that he wants to trick her.]

She cannot conceive of Tereus's plot:

Mout cuidoit bien estre seure
D'aler bien et de revenir.
Et comant poïst ç'avenir
Que s'apansast de la mervoille
Que li tiranz li aparoille? (vv. 678–82)

[She thought she would be safe / in going and returning. How could she have imagined the incredible incident that the tyrant was preparing for her?]

She later laments her inability to perceive his ruse:

Ha, lasse, por quoi ne conui
La feintise et la traïson? (vv. 826–27)[17]

[Alas, why didn't I recognize / his dissembling and betrayal?]

The second half of Philomena's portrait offers an altogether different image of the heroine's reputed beauty as repetition of the verb *avoir* gives way to phrases dominated instead by *savoir*. Two pivotal lines make the transition:

Avuec la grant biaute qu'ele *ot*
Sot quanque doit savoir pucele. (vv. 170–71)

[Along with the great beauty she possessed / she knew everything a young woman should know.]

Philomena's beauty is rivaled only by her knowledge [*sagesse*], we are told, "Ne fu pas mains sage que bele" [She was no less wise than beautiful], in a second portrait that grants to the quintessentially beautiful heroine a subjectivity missing from the earlier account:

Plus sot de joie et de deport
Qu'Apoloines ne que Tristanz,

Plus an sot voire voir dis tanz.
Des tables sot et des eschas,
Del vieil jeu et del "sis et as,"
De la bufe et de la hamee.
Por son deduit estoit amee
Et requise de hauz barons.
D'espreviers sot et de faucons
Et del jantil et del lanier;
Bien sot feire un faucon muiier
Et un ostor et un tercuel. (vv. 174–85)

[She knew more about games and pleasures—ten times more—than Apollonius or Tristan. She knew how to play chess, backgammon, and the old six
and ace game. She knew the slap and trap game too. Because of her delight
in games she was loved and sought after by noble lords. She knew about
sparrowhawks and falcons, gentles and lanners. She knew how to moult a
falcon, a goshawk or a tercel.]

Here and in the following 19 lines (vv. 186–204), the silent and statuesque
female body comes to life. Philomena knows more about joy and amusement than Apollonius and Tristan, acclaimed in the twelfth and thirteenth
centuries as accomplished performers and musicians. Her skill at games—
she knows dice, chess, backgammon—is matched by a specialized knowledge of hawking and hunting. Along with these, she has unparalleled talents
of weaving and working cloth, "Avuec c'iert si bone ovriere / D'ovrer une
porpre vermoille / Qu'an tot le mont n'ot sa paroille" [In addition, she was
such an accomplished weaver/embroiderer that no one in the world could
equal her at weaving/embroidering red cloth] (vv. 188–90).

So skilled is Philomena at weaving, moreover, that in addition to creating the complicated patterns of figured silk, she can depict Hellequin's
troop. That is to say, she can make cloth talk:

Un diaspre ou un baudequin
Nes la mesniee Hellequin
Seust ele an un drap portreire. (vv. 191–93)

[On patterned or rich silk she knew how to depict in cloth even Hellequin's
followers.]

This harlequin's troop was thought in the Middle Ages to be a band of suffering souls who, under the guidance of Hellequin, wandered through the
night making a hideous racket. To portray them fully would require images
and sounds, to relay voice through weaving or to make cloth speak much

in the way Philomena uses the famed tapestry later in the tale to convey her own speech. We also learn from this portrait that Philomena's knowledge of the authors and grammar enables her to write verse and prose. She knows how to play the psaltery, the lyre, the mandolin, and the violin, and can reproduce any sound or note on the medieval stringed instrument called the *viol*.

More than simply imputing agency to the beautiful body of the preceding portrait, this long list of talents rewrites the earlier account by shifting the previous focus on the woman's face, as a surrogate for female genitalia, to another emblematic body part: the hands.[18] What is implied by the repeated invocation of *savoir* to describe Philomena's gameplaying, hawking, writing, and music playing is the activity of able hands that carry out these tasks. Hands entirely different in their role and function from the "thin white delicate hands" of the first portrait, immobile hands, which seemed, in their studied immobility to be incapable of action.

The list of activities that Philomena *knows* how to carry out ends, significantly, with a reference to her accomplished speech: so well (knowledgeably) does she speak that she could run a school merely by teaching the art of speaking or dialectic:[19]

Et tant sot sagement parler
Que solemant de sa parole
Seust ele tenir escole. (vv. 202–4)

[And she knew how to speak so well / that she could teach from her speech alone.]

Speaking, one might think initially, differs from the other activities comprising Philomena's *sagesse* in that it does not require use of the hands. And yet that is the very point of this tale in one respect at least: that one can speak with the hands to produce images in weaving as one might also produce sounds in music, gestures in hawking, words in writing, all of which could substitute for meaningful speech and voice. The point is especially cogent for female protagonists so often constructed in the standard portrait of medieval beauty as the artistic product of male hands. If in Chrétien's *Yvain*, Laudine's great beauty comes from the hand of God, "Don fust si grant biaute venue? / Ja la fist *Dex, de sa main* nue" [Where did such great beauty come from? God made it with his own hands] (vv. 1501–2), Blancheflor emerges in the *Perceval* as a double of Pygmalion's well-crafted statue:

Le front ot haut et blanc et plain
Come s'il fust *ovrez a main,*

Et que de *main d'ome* ovrez fust
De pierre ou d'yvoire ou de fust. (vv. 1815–18)

[She had a high, white, smooth forehead / As if worked by hand, / the way a man's hand fashions stone or ivory or wood.]

If Philomena is fashioned by Nature's touch and the narrator's words, she also writes and tells her own story in a tapestry made by hand.

In a very subtle way, Philomena's talent at speaking through pictures, which is cast in the second portrait as an uncanny ability to weave or work costly red silk like no one else (vv. 189–90), is itself woven into the initial portrait of her silent face. In a tellingly unusual line, used to describe this heroine's slightly reddish lips, those very lips that will soon be unable to send any message, we learn that they are redder than cloth. They are redder even than scarlet samite dyed expensively with cochineal:

Boche riant, levres grossettes
Et un petitet vermeillettes
Plus que samiz vermauz an grainne. (vv. 153–55)

[Smiling mouth, plump lips / and slightly reddish / redder than silk cloth.]

This allusion to colored cloth announces very early in the tale how the heroine's lovely lips might later be replaced by skilled hands that tell a woven story, much as the reference to her portraying Hellequin's troops implies an uncanny skill at speaking without words.

The Politics of the Male Gaze

If this message regarding Philomena's exceptional gifts is given to us, the reader/listener, from the outset of the tale, its import remains well-hidden from Tereus who imagines confidently that depriving Philomena of her tongue will effectively prevent her from recounting her tale. That Tereus sees only the lovely and powerless Philomena constructed by the catalogue of her beauty is made especially clear when the lengthy indexing of all the heroine's features comes to an end and she advances to embrace her father and Tereus. For a brief moment the accomplished Philomena endowed with knowledge dissolves into thin air as the beautified disembodied face of the earlier portrait emerges to represent her. "Vermoille" now refers only to the heroine's complexion and "samit" to the silk cloth enveloping her eroticized body:

La pucele vint a son pere
Qui la face ot vermoille et clere;

An un samit estoit laciee
Et Tereus l'a anbraciee,
Sa la salue et beise ansanble.
Si granz biautez son cuer li anble
Et sa tres bele contenance. (vv. 205–11)

[The young girl came to her father, / her light skin blushing. She was laced
in silk / And Tereus embraced her. / He greeted her and they kissed. / Her
great beauty and beautiful looks stole his heart.]

The "tres bele contenance" that Tereus sees and kisses has none of the attributes so carefully laid out in the preceding description of Philomena's
sagesse. Unlike the earlier account, this portrait of Philomena's beauty results as much from Tereus's longing gaze as from the narrator's creative
words. In typical medieval fashion, Tereus's attraction to Philomena derives
from visual observation:

Mes Tereus ne se deduit
An nul servise qu'an li face
S'au jant cors non et an la face
De la pucele regarder. (vv. 596–99)

[Tereus takes no pleasure in anything they do for him. He derives pleasure
only from looking at the beautiful body and face of the young woman.]

His all-consuming look replaces even the consumption of food and drink:

A grant mervoille la regarde
Qu'a nule autre rien n'est pansis.
Au mangier ont longuemant sis
Et mout li pleisoit a seoir,
Plus por la pucele veoir
Que por boivre ne por mangier. (vv. 608–13)

[He looks at her in wonder thinking of nothing else. They sat a long time
while eating and it pleased him to sit there more in order to look at the
young woman than to eat or drink.]

Similar sentiments are expressed by Philomena's father Pandion. When
Philomena is about to leave for Thrace, her father begs her to return
promptly because seeing her brings him such great pleasure, "Car tant sui
liez quant je te voi / Et tant ai de joie et de bien" [I am so delighted when
I see you. / It gives me such joy and well-being] (vv. 692–93).[20] The sexual

connotations of this remark, well hidden behind the pose of a concerned parent, become more obvious in another passage where Pandion explains his reluctance to let his daughter depart. It is the way Philomena serves him, he says, that pleases him so much, the way she waits on him day and night, putting on his shoes and dressing him, "Que ma fille me garde et sert / Et nuit et jor et soir et main; . . . Ma douce fille m'a tant chier / Qu'ele me chauce, ele me vest, / Et son servise tant me plest" [My daughter takes care of me and serves me / night and day, evening and morning . . . My sweet daughter holds me so dear / that she dresses me and puts on my shoes. Her service pleases me so] (vv. 370–71, 374–76). In effect, both men, despite their diverse characterizations as treacherous tyrant and loving father, want to have Philomena in their company so they can watch her as she pleases and serves them. That is what makes her beautiful in their eyes.

Denise Riley has taught us how "the body becomes visible as a body and as a female body only under some particular gaze," a historicized gaze specific in time and place.[21] Tereus's gaze is that of the medieval lover conditioned by that particular brand of Ovidian passion that typically makes the suitor ill, crazy, and speechless, reducing him to utter helplessness. Love in this formulation reverses the standard male/female relation by making women into warriors who hunt their male prey. Tereus thus falls victim to a love that attacks him, "Qu'Amors a vers lui prise guerre" [Love made war on him] (v. 238), a love that temporarily vanquishes and destroys the most valiant of men, "Folie? Mes Amors, ce cuit, / Cele qui tot vaint et destruit" [Was it madness? No, Love, I think, who vanquishes and destroys all] (vv. 393–94).

In a curious reversal of gender roles, love is shown here to empower women with the amorous equivalent of the military might generally reserved for medieval knights. The suitors themselves become concomitantly more womanlike, losing their strength, their wits, and often their rational speech. As Tereus falls prey to Philomena's alluring body, emotion overtakes his intellect, "Sa folie son savoir vaint," forcing him to adopt behaviors appropriate to the stereotypical female.[22] In a desperate attempt to gain possession of his "beloved," Tereus lies, cajoles, begs, and pleads, "Tant a li fel tiranz luitie / Par fiancier et par jurer / Et par proiier et par plorer / Qu'il espleita si con li plot" [The treacherous tyrant had battled so long, promising, swearing, begging, and crying, manipulating in every way he could] (vv. 548–51). Having fallen under the spell of love, this powerful monarch falls apart emotionally, sobbing uncontrollably at his initial inability to satisfy his desire.

When we hear in Tereus's case that it is specifically the sight of woman, the very woman his gaze constructs, that supposedly robs the male subject of the control and mastery that typically accompany his *savoir,* the claim rings false. "Knowing" for Tereus as for the ogling Pandion, means controlling the female body through the desiring look they cast upon it, freezing it as an object of their gaze much as the medieval narrator does in his standard portrait of feminine beauty. When we are told that even the tongues of Plato, Homer, and Cato, men "de grant savoir," would not have been able to narrate the "granz biaute" of Philomena, our credulity wanes further. The woman's *granz biaute* is precisely what fills the pages of ancient and medieval accounts of female protagonists. It is woman's *savoir* in all the complexity suggested by this narrator's second portrait of Philomena that typically escapes the pen or voice of the knowledgeable male creator whose gaze reads the body alone, much as Tereus reads only beauty.

The Economy of Women's Work

Atypically, the Old French *Philomena* offers, against the politics of the male gaze on female beauty, an alternate economy of seeing and knowing cast in terms of women's work. Sight more than speech connects the female protagonists throughout this tale but it is a sight moving between women that restructures the abuse of power enshrined in the classic male gaze. Progne's initial request to Tereus articulates a desire not only to visit but specifically to see her sister, "De Philomena sa seror / Ot talant que veoir l'alast" [She wanted to go see / Philomena her sister] (vv. 52–53). Tereus denies this request in two lines that exploit the homophony between the Old French *voie* referring to the path one travels and *voie* meaning sight:

Et si il li deffant la voie
Tant qu'ele sa seror ne voie. (vv. 61–62)

[And he forbid her passage (the path) / to see her sister.]

The sisters work throughout the narrative to establish and pursue that *voie* that will enable them to see each other again. Progne's disappointment at not seeing Philomena when Tereus returns from Athens, "Car tot maintenant qu'ele vit / Son seignor et sa compaignie / Et de sa seror ne vit mie" [Now she saw / her husband and his retinue / but she did not see her sister] (vv. 890–92), echoes in Philomena's melancholic gaze at the distant city where Progne lives in ignorance of her sister's fate, "Antre les bois et la riviere / Vit la cite ou sa suer iere / Si comance a plorer mout fort" [Between the woods and the stream / she saw the city where her sister was. / She began to sob heavily] (vv. 1167–69).[23] Prevented from travelling the path [*voie*] to Progne's home, Philomena sends the tapestry via her female guardian who in turn passes it to her daughter: "Mes el ne set mie par cui / Se sa mestre n'anprant la voie / Ou se sa fille n'i anvoie" [But she does not know via whom (to send the tapestry) unless her mistress shows her the way or unless the mistress's daughter takes it] (vv. 1140–42). Contact between the sisters is reestablished initially when Progne sees the visual images woven by her ravished sister and through this woman's work learns of Tereus's mutilating deed [*uevre*], "Si li a la cortine oferte, / Et la reïne l'a overte, / Si la regarde et conut l'uevre" [She gave the queen the woven curtain / and she opened it and learned of the deed / the handiwork / what had occurred] (vv. 1235–37). But Progne must then visually follow the sight of the female messenger, stealthily, along the path leading back to Philomena's prison hut, "Cele s'on va et cest apres, / Ne de trop loing ne de trop pres, / Si qu'onques n'an pert la veüe" [She (the messenger) left and the queen followed, / not too close nor too far behind / so that she would not lose sight of her] (vv. 1241–43). Tracing this visual thread made by the woman's body moving through the forest, Progne weaves her way back to the sight of a lost sister in partial imitation of Philomena's own woven thread sent forth for Progne to see and read.[24] Thus do the two meanings of the Old French *voie*—signifying both "path" and "sight"—conjoin to produce a homophonic echo and semantic restructuring of the third meaning that the same sound in another spelling (*voix*) could evoke: that of "voice."

Threads of weaving and sight connect all the female protagonists in this tale that refigures woman's speech. Different from Ovid's heroine, the Old French Philomena has not fashioned her tapestry alone. The *vilainne* stationed in the forest hideaway to prevent Philomena's escape is an accomplished weaver as is her daughter in residence:

> Car filer et tistre savoit
> Et une soe fille avoit
> Qu'ele aprenoit a son mestier. (vv. 871–73)

> [She knew how to spin and weave and she had a daughter to whom she taught her craft.]

Though in ignorance of the tapestry's message, both women help to create and transmit the meaningful cloth. In addition to providing colored thread and other supplies, the old woman weaves a pattern into one of the tapestry's corners or borders:

> La vieille ne li contredist
> Mes mout volantiers li eida
> Et trestot quanqu'ele cuida
> Qui a tel uevre convenist
> Porchacier et querre li fist.
> Trestot li quist son aparoil,

Tant que fil inde et fil vermoil
Et jaune et vert a plante ot,
Mes ele ne conut ne ne sot
Rien de quanque cele tissoit;
Mes l'uevre li abelissoit
Qui mout estoit a feire gries,
Car tissu ot a l'un des chies
Que Philomena l'avoit feite. (vv. 1108–21)

[The old woman did not impede her but gladly helped her. She sought out
and tracked down everything she thought would be appropriate to such a
work. Soon Philomena asked to use the loom and attached to it blue, red,
yellow, and green threads. The woman knew or understood nothing of what
Philomena was weaving. Yet she made the piece more attractive/added to
the work, with some difficulty, by weaving one of the edges that Philomena
had prepared.]

Just as they work together on this joint project that will "talk" to Progne
in the absence of words, these female protagonists "speak" to each other in
visual gestures, Philomena making signs that the old woman reads effort-
lessly without ever misunderstanding:

La cortine qu'ele ot tissue
Prist, puis est arriere venue
La ou sa mestre l'atandoit
Qui toz ses signes antandoit
Que ja n'i mespreïst de rien,
Ainz l'antandoit pres d'aussi bien
Con s'ele li deïst de boche. (vv. 1185-ll91)[25]

[She took the tapestry she had woven and came to her mistress who understood all her signals without mistaking anything about them. The woman
understood her as well as if she spoke from the mouth.]

This collaborative woman's work substantially redefines the intersection
of knowledge and sight that constructs the medieval portrait of female
beauty under a desiring male gaze. At issue ultimately is the challenge posed
by this community of women to systems of male knowledge that lead to
possession and control of women's bodies. The tapestry's visual depiction of
Tereus's actions designed for Progne's eyes to read, reverses the terms of this
cultural equation, making the lascivious male viewer into the silent object
of a female gaze. Progne *sees* how he crosses the sea to arrive in Athens,
brings Philomena to Trace, rapes her, cuts out her tongue, and imprisons her
in the secluded hut (vv. 1122–33). She sees the action without having to

hear Tereus speak. Significantly, the woven surrogate for Philomena's words contains no representation of Tereus's imposing voice.

But the woman's gaze in this scenario does not simply mimic the imprisoning look of the empowered male observer who created Philomena's beauty in his own eyes. In place of Tereus's one-way look that constructs his subjectivity in opposition to the object of desire, the female gaze circulates between women as a means of communication, carrying messages back and forth in a motion that resembles instead the passage of thread between two poles of the weaver's loom. As the *vilaine* reads Philomena's gestures, so, too, Progne then reads the images in her sister's tapestry and later follows with her eyes the path of the *vilaine's* daughter moving back through the forest to establish final contact with the sister whose voice has been cut off from her.

Yet Philomena's tapestry does not only make the silent woman speak. It also transfers the terms of embodiment and beauty from the lovely woman to her newly found woven "speech," allowing Philomena to write the body instead of being the body.[26] As an example of work done with woman's hands, hands that extend out from the female body to make contact with other women, this tapestry emblematizes a kind of woman's narrative that comes not solely from the voice, which in the traditional male formulation proceeds from the mind and thought, but through the hands. The product of this women's "speech" (not unlike the meal Progne will cook shortly) is here embodied to a greater degree than the voice ever could be as this woman's story takes on a distinctly material form. The very definition of the woman's body has thus shifted significantly from an objectified erotic body without voice to an embodied narrative that speaks to another woman, though without sound or words.

Women's knowledge defined here as the knowledge of weaving cloth possessed jointly by Philomena, the old woman, and her daughter, implies agency and cognition in terms very different from those structuring the masterful, speaking subject that Tereus represents.[27] Tereus fails utterly to perceive the existence of this alternate form of knowledge. After taking drastic precautions to conceal his crime: isolating his captive in a secluded forest and cutting out her tongue, this tyrant foolishly selects, according to the narrator, a female guard who knows how to weave:

> Mes Tereus folie fist
> Qui avuec Philomena mist
> Por la garder une vilainne
> Qui vivoit de sa propre painne,
> Car filer et tistre savoit. (vv. 867–71)

[But Tereus made a foolish mistake when he chose as Philomena's guardian a peasant woman who made her living by spinning and weaving.]

The very presence of this skilled woman and her apprentice daughter call forth from the beautifully embodied heroine a crucial knowledge—depicted in the earlier portrait of her own *savoir*—that Tereus previously failed to see. When Tereus mutilates Philomena's tongue so that she will not be able to "conter a home" [tell any man/anyone] the shame and attack she has suffered, "Et por ce que cele ne puisse / conter a home qu'ele truisse / Ceste honte ne cest reproche" [So that she would not be able to tell any man/anyone that she might find about this shame and this attack] (vv. 847–49), he does not imagine she might tell the tale to women through an economy of seeing and knowing so radically different from his. He cannot conceive that her handiwork might respond to or correct his master *oeuvre*. But that is precisely what takes place as Philomena puts her own *savoir* to work.[28]

The Revenge Plot

Commentators on both Ovidian and Old French versions of the Philomena story have generally found the narrative of Progne more problematic than that of her sister.[29] Certainly it is more complex. To Philomena's single, peaceful, and constructive action of weaving cloth, Progne performs two violent and destructive deeds: decapitating her son and cooking parts of his chopped up body into a stew while roasting the rest. Cooking, no less a traditionally woman's craft than weaving, seems here to have been caught up in a cycle of male violence that only mimics and prolongs the damage of Tereus's initial crime. This perception results in part because Philomena's woven tale circulates unproblematically within a female economy, passing from the ravaged heroine to her guardian and the guardian's daughter to arrive finally at the distanced sister without ever confronting or engaging the eyes of the male ravisher. Progne's response to the rape, by contrast, reenters the patriarchal world by addressing Tereus directly.

But, in so doing, Progne's actions in the Old French tale reveal the impossibility of their own professed goal of avenging a rape. What can women do to men, they seem to ask, that would parallel the savage violation of rape? Murder of the rapist would be repayment in kind for murder of the female victim. But that is not what Tereus has done to Philomena. It is in this sense that Progne's response to Tereus's *oeuvre*, however bloody and violent it may be, can never function neatly, unproblematically, in the cycle of male violence that demands equal retribution for crimes committed, requiring an eye for an eye, a tooth for a tooth, one human body for another. The part of Philomena's body that has been violated in rape has no equivalent in the male anatomy. Or does it?

I want to suggest here that Progne's actions of mutilation and cooking can be read as a continuation of the narrative begun in Philomena's tapestry. If Progne functions first as a reader of her sister's text, she can also be seen as writing a text of her own, or rather composing a visual sequel to the images she saw in Philomena's woven story. In fact, the sisters work together here to forge a new narrative plot, much as the *vilaine* and her daughter helped earlier to make and circulate the tapestry. In so doing, they begin to address the systemic culture of rape that surrounds and defines them. In helping Philomena to rewrite the suppressed story of her rape along with the fictions of courtly love and beauty that accompany it, Progne also rewrites her own gruesome past: the tale of her marriage to Tereus and the motherhood that followed it. Taken together the stories woven by Philomena and Progne rework two myths of female nature: that of the beloved beauty which conditions Tereus's classic line to Philomena, "sachiez bien, / Que je vos aim" [Know this: that I love you] (vv. 766–67) and the tale of the loving mother emblematized in the narrator's comment, "Que mere ne doit son anfant / Ne ocire ne desmanbrer" [A mother should not kill or dismember her child] (vv. 1318–19).

Seduction and Food

Progne's careful words inviting Tereus to partake of the fateful stew she has prepared from his son's body read, curiously, as a seduction scene. Suggesting that he come without companions so that the two of them can be alone together when she "serves him completely," Progne holds out the promise of something akin to the erotic pleasure Tereus sought from Philomena:

> Au roi qui de rien ne se gueite
> Vient, si li prie et le semont
> Que de la rien an tot le mont
> Qu'ele cuide que il plus aint
> Vaingne mangier et si n'amaint
> Ne conpaingnon ne escuiier,
> Mes que li ne doie enuiier
> Car ja n'i avra que aus deus:
> Ele iert sole et il iert seus
> Et ele del tot servira. (vv. 1342–51)

[She comes to the king who suspects nothing. She begs and implores him to come and eat the thing that she believes him to love most in all the world. She implores that he not bring along any companion or squire. He needn't worry; there will be no one there but the two of them. She will be alone and he will be alone/safe. She will serve him completely.]

Progne's allusions to an intimate setting, "There would only be the two of them, she alone and he alone" (vv. 1349–51) echo hauntingly the isolation of Tereus and Philomena in the rape scene:

> Et quant il sont leanz andui,
> Seul antre la pucele et lui,
> Que nus ne les voit ne ne ot. (vv. 741–43)

[And when they are both there alone, the young woman and him, such that no one can see or hear them.]

Indeed, before raping Philomena, Tereus attempted a fake seduction similar to the one that Progne stages here by promising a different kind of secret liaison:

> Bele, fet il, or sachiez bien
> Que je vos aim et si vos pri
> Que de moi façoiz vostre ami,
> Et ceste chose soit celee
> Se vos volez qu'ele et duree. (vv. 766–70)

[Beautiful one, he said, know that I love you and thus ask you make me your lover. It will be a secret if you want it to last.]

But why the use of food and its gory preparation in Progne's recasting of the ill-fated love story? As Progne replays the scene of Philomena's seduction and violation, she switches the roles of its key participants so that Tereus no longer occupies the subject position. She substitutes for the forceful assault that formerly guaranteed this tyrant's pleasure in raping Philomena (vv. 836–39) the pleasure that Tereus expects to derive from eating. But Progne's rewriting of the rape scene reverses the gendered roles of its key participants so that Tereus no longer occupies the subject position. His "pleasure" is now no longer his. Throughout the revenge sequence, emphasis falls ironically on the delight Tereus will have in consuming the camouflaged meal. He will be eating the thing he loves most in all the world, Progne assures him ("Que de la rien an tot le mont / Qu'ele cuide que il plus aint / Vaingne mangier . . . ," vv. 1344–46). The erotic overtones of her claim that Tereus will eat this meal with pleasure, "Que vos mangeroiz a deduit" [You will eat with pleasure] (v. 1364), echo in the narrator's description of the scene, "Progne l'an mainne et si l'assiet / Mout pleisammant et a grant eise / Por ce que li mangiers li pleise" [Progne leads him and seats him, pleasantly and comfortably, so that the meal will please him] (vv. 1372–74).

When we come to the moment where Tereus savagely cuts the flesh on his plate and puts it in his mouth, we realize how feeding the tyrant this gruesome meal aptly reverses the terms of the original rape. As retribution for Tereus having forced his body into Philomena's, Progne here forces another body into Tereus's open mouth. And as with the rape of Philomena, the putative pleasure is attributed to him alone.[30] The appropriateness of feeding as retribution for rape is further reinforced when we remember how Tereus himself was said previously to feed off the pleasurable sight of Philomena rather than partaking of the banquet offered at Pandion's palace:

> Au mangier ont longuemant sis
> Et mout li pleisoit a seoir,
> Plus por la pucele veoir
> Que por boivre ne por mangier. (vv. 610–13)[31]

[They remained seated and ate for a long time. It pleased him to sit there, moreso in order to watch the young woman than to eat or drink.]

Now Progne feeds Tereus, but not according to his desire or pleasure.

But why involve the innocent son Itys in this gruesome plot of mutilation and perverse meal planning? Through subtle word play on *norreture* (meaning food and feeding) and *issir* (meaning to come out of, issue from) the narrator tells us how Tereus's mutilation of Philomena's tongue follows from the rape just as one evil deed generates another to feed and nourish itself:

> Voir dist qui dist: 'Toz jorz atret
> Li uns maus l'autre et sel norrist.' (vv. 840–41)

[He speaks the truth who says: One evil attracts another and feeds off of it.]

The result of this process is a "male norreture" that issues forth as a kind of deformed offspring:

> Et male norreture an ist,
> Si male come issir an doit. (vv. 842–43)

[Evil/male nourishment/offspring is born of this, as bad/male as can come from it.]

What Progne engineers in her cooking of Itys's innocent flesh is an apt transformation of this "male norreture" into a "norreture male." The mutilated mouth that emerges as the bad offspring of Tereus's having raped Philomena is matched appropriately by a literal offspring made monstrous through mutilation. At this juncture, Progne's rewriting of the plot of the lovely virgin turns tellingly to recast the cultural narrative of the loving wife and mother.

Progne's Marriage to Tereus or
The Abduction and Silencing of the Second Sister

When Progne discovers her ravaged sister in the forest hideaway, a woman abducted, raped, silenced, and forcefully kept from seeing her family, the distraught sister's first words allude curiously not to Philomena's plight but to her own marriage to Tereus:

> Suer, dist ele, venez vos an,
> Car trop avez ci sejorne.
> Tant mar veïstes ajorne
> Le jor que li fel m'esposa . . . (vv. 1270–73)

[Sister, she said, come away, you have stayed here too long. Cursed is the day you saw the sunrise when the traitor married me.]

Indeed, the Old French *Philomena* itself begins with an account of Tereus and Progne's marriage that makes reference to Itys's unfortunate end, then detours into the Philomena story only after promising to return to Itys: "Ithis ot non. Ce fu diaus granz / Qu'il ne vesqui plus longuemant. / Je vos dirai assez comant / De lui avint a la parclose, / Mes ainz vos dirai autre chose" [His name is Itis. It was tragic that he did not live longer. I will tell you what happened to him at the end of my tale. But first I will speak of something else] (vv. 44–48). Philomena's rape stands as a subsidiary part, a detour to "something else" within the companion story of Progne's marriage and her son Ithis from which it draws its meaning.

And, in fact, Progne's liaison with Tereus parallels Philomena's brutal encounter with the ravisher more fully than one might initially suspect. Traded in a marriage deal struck between Pandion and Tereus, Progne was given away by her father (Cele fu a mari *donee*, v. 6) and carried off by her husband (S'an *mena* Tereus sa fame, v. 33), much as Philomena is later bartered away temporarily by Pandion, "Que sa fille li a *bailliee*" [He gave him his daughter] (v. 673) and led off as a virgin ripe for ravishing, "La pucele que il an *mainne*" [the maiden that he led away with him] (v. 717).[32] Whether Progne was raped either before or during her marriage to Tereus, we have no direct evidence. That he used force against her, to counter her wishes, however, is made explicit by Tereus himself when he explains to Philomena why Progne did not accompany him on the sea voyage to Athens:

Se je li leissasse venir
Ele fust ca a vos venue,
Mes je l'ai de la retenue
Tot a force contre son cuer. (vv. 252–55)

[If I had let her come, she would have come here to see you. But I restrained
(retained) her, forcefully, against her wishes.]

The line describing how Tereus prevented Progne from traveling to her sis-
ter, much as he later restrains Philomena from leaving the forest hut, reit-
erates the very terms used in the rape scene. "Tot a force contre son cuer"
[Forcefully against her wishes] (v. 255) prepares tellingly for the subsequent
"Que tot a force l'a conquise" [forcefully he overcame her] as Tereus rapes
Philomena against her "heart" to please himself (v. 839).

Both women are thus subjected to the ravisher's imposing force. And
although Tereus does not literally cut out Progne's tongue, he does effectively eliminate her speech in a crucial scene at the outset of the tale.
When Tereus comes to Athens in Progne's place, he serves as her messenger. Speaking for her, ostensibly on her behalf, he also speaks in her place,
substituting his words for hers in a way that effectively silences the female
voice that had wanted to communicate directly with her sister (v. 108).[33]
Although Tereus voices the same request that Progne would have made,
the simple presence of his male body critically deforms the female voice
it represents:

La pucele antre ses braz prant
Et si li dist: "Ma douce amie,
Vostre suer vos salue et prie
Que vos veigniez deduire o li." (vv. 242–45)

[He takes the maiden in his arms and says, "Sweet one, your sister sends
greetings and begs you to come enjoy yourself with her."]

Delivering Progne's purely verbal message with a physical embrace that
echoes the designs of his own carnal desire for Philomena, Tereus effectively transforms the expression of friendship between sisters into a more
sinister message between ravisher and victim. "Deduire" in Old French
carries the dual meaning of enjoying oneself in the company of others and
enjoying oneself sexually. Progne's words suggest the first meaning—that
the sisters will enjoy each other's company—while Tereus's delivery implies the second—that he will amuse himself, taking pleasure in Philomena. Speaking ostensibly for Progne, Tereus makes her voice speak only for
him as if she, like Philomena, had no voice at all.

Progne remains significantly different from Philomena, however, to the extent that she exerts no seductive influence over Tereus. Nowhere in the tale do we hear of Tereus taking pleasure in Progne's body or beauty. His gaze never rests on her physiognomy, which goes unnoticed, unmentioned altogether. Neither does Progne profess any interest in him. When Tereus returns empty handed from Athens and approaches his wife, it is she who looks at him, remarks the absence of Philomena and without a word of greeting for her husband expresses concern for her sister alone:

Car tot maintenant qu'ele vit
Son seignor et sa compaignie
Et de sa seror ne vit mie
Qu'ele cuidoit mout conjoïr
Ne li plot rien nule a oïr
Ne de respondre ne li chaut,
Ne "Bien veingniez," ne "Deus vos saut."
Ainz demande come esfreee
Quant il l'orent tuit saluee:
"Ou est ma suer? Por quoi ne vient?" (vv. 890–99)

[Now she sees her husband and his retinue but she does not see her sister whom she had planned to greet joyously. Nothing she hears can please her and she takes no interest in speaking, not even to say "welcome back" or "thank God." Rather she asks, as if in distress, after they all greet her, "Where is my sister? Why hasn't she come?"]

The lavish kisses exchanged between Tereus and Pandion (vv. 93–95, 711–12) and the ravisher's deceptively delicate hugging and kissing of Philomena (v. 749) find no equivalent expression of affection between Tereus and his wife. Rather, as Progne herself explains, the thing Tereus "loves best in all the world" is his son, Itys (vv. 1345–46). The virgin bride that Progne once was serves now only as a procreative vessel to produce the cherished male heir. As the imprisoned Philomena guarantees the tyrant's sexual pleasure, his wife, restrained at home, secures his legal patrimony.

A Murderer or a Mother?

That women who kill their children are rare in literature as in life makes Progne's decapitation and murder of her own son both shocking and powerful. For recent examples of similar maternal violence, one has only to recall Toni Morrison's compelling novel *Beloved*, based on the plight of nameless escaped slave women in the American South known to have murdered their own children, or Adrienne Rich's reference in *Of Woman*

Born to the suburban housewife, Joanne Michulski, who decapitated and chopped up the bodies of her two youngest children in 1974.[34] Both narratives make us wonder what could push mothers, the quintessential givers of life, traditional nourishers of children and families—whether in the womb, through breast milk, or later cooking—to kill? A slave woman's bloody attempt to prevent her children from returning to slavery constituted, in Morrison's reading of it, a savage indictment of racial oppression. Joanne Michulski's crime, in Rich's narrative, stands as a woman's angry response to the clean-cut and quiet but still devastating oppression sometimes endured by the suburban housewife. But why protest oppressive institutions by killing one's own children? What is the relation between motherhood and infanticide that Morrison's slave mother, Joanne Michulski, and the Old French Progne play out on different historical stages and in significantly different ways?

For Progne, the killing of Itys (made frequently to rhyme with *fils* in this tale) redirects the murderous gaze that led to Philomena's rape from the beautiful and innocent female body onto an equally beautiful and innocent male heir. Indeed, it is precisely when Progne, previously at a loss to know how to avenge her ravished sister[35] *sees* her son approach, that the murder plot comes to mind. The child's beauty, reminiscent of Philomena's own attractiveness, helps spark the thought:

Atant ses fiz devant li vint
Qui biaus estoit a desmesure
Si l'amena mesavanture
Qui li estoit a avenir.
La mere voit son fil venir. (vv. 1292–96)

[Her son, who was exceedingly handsome, came to her. Thus did he bring forth the misfortune that he would suffer. The mother saw her son approach.]

As the loving mother fondles her son "Si con la tenoit acolee / Li petiz anfes par chierte," [As she held her young son tightly and lovingly] (vv. 1328–29) in an echo of Tereus's earlier gentle hugging of Philomena "doucement l'acole et baise" (v. 749), she lays plans for the action that will turn the tables on Tereus in a most unexpected way, provoking him to echo Progne's own previous question to him, "ou est ma suer?" [Where is my sister?] with his stupefyingly naïve and fateful, "ou est Itis?" [Where is Itys?] (v. 1381).

But Progne's decapitation of her own son also rewrites the story of her marriage to Tereus, her role as the faceless procreator of heirs that will only repeat their fathers' savage ways.[36] The killing of Itys in this sense would put an end—albeit violent—to the cycle of brutality and vilification that hallmarks Tereus's relations to women, a cycle that Progne has been made to participate in, to foster and further by producing, from her own body, one such future male. By killing Itys, Progne can extricate herself from an unwitting collusion in producing ravishers of women and she can also effectively stop the cycle of abuse. Tereus has no other children; he can produce no future legitimate heir alone. This is perhaps the most cogent point made by Progne's murder of their son.

When considered from this perspective we can see how Progne's act, cast as a message to her savage husband, might read less as a mother's senselessly brutal infanticide than a move on the part of a complicitous procreator to take back the child she gave in birth. It is almost as if, in killing Itys, Progne unravels the threads of time, reversing the course of past events to return to a moment before the birth of her child, a moment perhaps even before her marriage, a time when she, like Philomena, was an innocent *pucele*. In undoing the story of the abduction and imprisonment that lead her to help perpetuate a tyrant's family line, Progne reveals both to the ever-blind Tereus, and to the shocked reader as well, the plot of the underread. What we as readers tend to miss by focusing our sympathy and interest on the violated Philomena and her ingenious handiwork is the more hidden narrative of the "loving" mother who has herself also been mutilated to the extent that her sexuality, her desire, her subjectivity, and her role in reproduction have been summarily effaced behind the label "mother." Progne's rash action flies in the face of the convention that asserts that it is "right and natural for all human beings . . . : that a mother not kill or dismember her child" [Si con requiert droiz et nature / De tote humainne creature . . . : Que mere ne doit son anfant / Ne ocire ne desmanbrer] (vv. 1315–16, 1318–19). Her violent response reveals how what is here termed natural for mothers reflects female sentiment less than it mirrors cultural values that construct what women should feel.

As an answer to Philomena's rape and to her own subjugation in marriage to the ravisher Tereus, Progne's decapitation of Itys corrects this misprision, stating without words that whereas women may not be able to control what enters the vagina by force, they can more readily control what is produced from that vagina in the form of children. To assert that women are life-givers alone, denying them the ability to also take life away, is to wrest from them the full force and potency of the subjectivity attendant to the life-giving process. If Philomena's tapestry conveys to Progne the message that she is not indeed dead, not finally silenced, not ultimately powerless, that is to say that she refuses the verbal and sexual subjugation imposed by Tereus, that she is in short, NOT HIS, Progne's meal of human flesh sends Tereus a parallel message: that his child is NOT HIS alone, but also a product of the woman's body that thinks and feels and acts in ways that defy the marital and maternal subjugation that tend to view her as HIS vessel for procreation.

It is true that in killing her son, Progne also kills part of herself, and this heroine fully acknowledges the tragedy of such an act: that Itys does not deserve death and that death at the hand of the mother is an especially bitter one, "Morir t'estuet de mort amere / a mere" [You must die a bitter death / death from the mother's hand] (v. 1301). But in killing Tereus's son, Progne also kills the fetishized phallus, redefining the child as hers to both produce and destroy. Thus does she remind Tereus, in an especially poignant way, of woman's power to create human flesh. As the two sisters work together, mixing with their hands the parts of Itys's body into a palatable stew: "Puis ont la char apareilliee / Antr'eles deus mout bien et tost" [Then they prepared the flesh, working together well and quickly] (vv. 1334–35), they prepare to make of Tereus a body, pregnant with child, but one that he cannot deliver into life. When Progne explains finally, in response to Tereus's insistent "ou est Itis?" (vv. 1380) that he carries the child within him though it is not whole, "Dedanz toi as ce que tu quiers, / Mes n'i est mie toz antiers. / Partie an as dedanz ton cors / Et partie an as par defors" [You carry everything you want inside you, but it is not whole. You have part of it inside your body and part outside], she implicitly contrasts Tereus's vile state with that of a mother who carries a whole future being within her.

It is significant that Tereus does not fully understand these words, just as he earlier fails to perceive the hidden meaning in Progne's invitation to eat, "Mes cil ne puet aparcevoir / De quel mangier ele li prie" [But he does not understand which meals she alludes to] (vv. 1366–67). It is only when his gaze falls on the more tangible image of his son's severed head, tossed in his face by Philomena as a silent reminder of her silenced voice, that Tereus finally knows that he has been tricked:

> Si li a tote ansanglantee
> La teste an mi le vis gitee.
> Tereus voit qu'il est traïz. (vv. 1411–13)

[She threw the thoroughly bloody head in his face. Tereus then saw that he had been betrayed.]

It is at this point, when looking at the visual image of his son's mutilated body, an image prepared by Progne's savagely sculpting hands, that Tereus falls silent. In a twisted mimicry of the silence that previously held him spellbound and speechless when gazing on Philomena's parceled body, he now cannot say a word:

S'estut une piece esbaïz
Qu'il ne se mut ne ne dist mot. (vv. 1414–15)

[He remained stunned a while, not moving or saying a word.]

The tables have turned, the revenge is complete. Not so much because
Tereus has shed the role of victimizer to become the victim, but because
the sisters' joint work has redefined the terms of Tereus's sight. The effect of
Progne and Philomena's plot is to refocus the male gaze, transferring it from
the female body beautified through metaphorical dismemberment to the
male body literally dismembered. Rather than constructing the image he
views, the ravisher is now forced to read a message sent to him by another,
by two women who use their hands to communicate in images rather than
words. Much as Progne earlier read the silent message that was encoded visually in Philomena's tapestry, Tereus now reads the visual representation of
his son's death and his own helplessness in restoring the dismembered body
to life. Women's work in this context forces Tereus to see that no matter
how hard he looks at the decapitated head of his innocent son, his eyes cannot recreate what only the woman's body can produce: the male issue
needed to inherit his kingdom. He cannot play Pygmalion with his son.

In taking away her child's life, Progne also significantly gives life to another, to Philomena, substituting for the natural birth of a male heir the
metaphorical rebirth of a sister she has believed to be dead.[37] The verb *issir*
figures prominently throughout this tale, first marking Philomena's appearance before Tereus as she emerges [*issir*] from an adjoining room to be
"born" into her beautiful static pose in the lengthy portrait that constructs
her femininity: "Atant est d'une chanbre issue / Philomena eschevelee"
[Philomena, disheveled, came out of a room] (vv. 124–25). In the revenge
scene, immediately following Progne's explanation that Tereus holds his
son captive within his own body (vv. 1403–6), Philomena again emerges
unexpectedly from an adjoining room, this time holding the bloody head
that makes Tereus realize his tragic inability to give birth to the child
within him: "Philomena qui s'iert reposte / An une chanbre iluec decoste
/ S'an issi fors a tot la teste" [Philomena, who had been waiting in an ad-
jacent room, came out of the room with the head] (vv. 1407–9). If Tereus
created the first Philomena with his desiring gaze, this second "birth" of
the heroine results from Progne's concerted efforts to free her sister from
the confines of the *maison gastee,* the womb-like prison where the ravisher
enclosed his captive, denying her nothing but the ability to leave [*issir*]:

Ne ja ne li fust contredite
Nule chose granz ne petite

Fors l'issue de la meison. (vv. 1151–53)

[Nothing was denied her, great or small, except passage out of the house.]

As Tereus's prior imprisonment of Philomena is now revisited upon him in the form of an offspring made captive, Progne gives the male child back to Tereus, putting it literally inside his body, and gives birth instead to a female, restoring life to a "murdered" sister.

One haunting detail of the seduction scene leading up to Tereus's fateful meal makes especially clear how the murder of Itys provides a thorough rewriting—not just of Philomena's rape—but of the more pervasive medieval formulation of the heroine's constructed beauty. Amid the details of Progne's careful preparations for the feast—her guiding Tereus to the table and seating him comfortably for a pleasurable meal (vv. 1372–74)—a single, unexpected line referring to the "beautiful white tablecloth" spread out beneath the tyrant's dinner by the mother/murderer carries us back instantly to the initial portrait of Philomena's beauty. There, the virgin's forehead, teeth, chin, neck, throat, and chest were all as white as her beautifully static hands; all stilled, killed into a picture of virginal loveliness. The *biaute* established in this image resonated most tellingly in Tereus's direct address to the innocent virgin just before he raped and imprisoned her. Professing his passion, he calls her not "Philomena" but more anonymously "Bele," the Beauty he will devour in the name of love, "Bele, fet il, or sachiez bien / Que je vos aim et si vos pri / Que de moi façoiz vostre ami" [Beauty, he said, know that I love you and thus I implore you to make me your lover] (vv. 766–68).

In the dinner scene, the beauty and whiteness of the eroticized female body are transferred to a tablecloth spread out by woman's hands as part of the act of serving food (a cloth perhaps even woven by a woman):

Cele li a la table mise
Et la nape fu bele et blanche. (vv. 1376–77)

[She set the table. The tablecloth was beautiful and white.]

Although tablesetting is not one of the skills attributed to Philomena in the initial portrait of her *savoir,* it is something that the women in this narrative know how to do. The tablecloth detail emblematizes how the woman's body has shifted in the course of this tale from being beautiful to being knowledgeable in a way that redefines the very terms of *biaute* and *sagesse.* Throughout this gory chronicle of rape, mutilation, decapitation, and murder, the lovely and silent Philomena is depicted initially as *bele* and only secondarily as *sage:* "Avuec la grant biaute qu'ele ot / Sot quanque doit savoir pucele" [Along with the great beauty she possessed, she knew how to do everything a young woman should] (vv. 170–71). But in the final scene Philomena speaks on behalf of every *pucele* whom she defines first as *sage* and then *cortoise* (v. 1461). Speaking here not as a woman but as a nightingale who "sings as sweetly as she knows how" [chante au plus *doucemant* qu'el set] (v. 1466, my emphasis), Philomena uses a partially restored voice to recast Tereus's prior deceptively sweet seduction of her, "*doucemant* l'acole et beise" [Sweetly/gently he hugs and kisses her] (v. 749, my emphasis). Her song, composed of a single word, evokes murder in all the complex ramifications this tale has shown it to possess.[38] Singing the sweet song of killing, "oci, oci" [killed, killed] (v. 1467), she reminds us how women have worked with their hands throughout this tale to speak in unconventional ways, thereby "killing" off conventions that oppress them. Itys has been killed, it is true; Itys, the son of Progne, but also Itys heir to his father's brutal violation of virgins and wives. But what else has come to an end? The unwilling complicity of a mother in propagating and fostering such offspring, Tereus's empowered gaze on Philomena's body, the innocence of the naïve virgin who knows nothing of rape and deceit, cultural narratives of passionate love and feminine beauty, cultural constructions of marriage, maternal love, and paternal protection. What survives is a realignment of the patrilineal configurations that traditionally linked father to son, wife to husband, and father to daughter into an alternative bonding between women. Sisters join together with a mother not their own and with that mother's daughter by using language based on sight not sound. Their newly defined "voice" issues from a female body that includes the maternal body, the nurturing body, the life-giving and life-destroying body, the silent body that speaks through movement, gesture, and the activities of women's work.

That is the beauty of this female body. Collapsing the dichotomy that typically holds beauty apart from knowledge, these women's bodies know, know how to do things, extraordinary things, like speaking without words. Their hands can talk.

Beauty, thus recast as a result of women's collective work, does not incite "love" or provoke violation, but issues a strong warning against it. Unquestioned maternal love thus reconfigured certainly does not suggest that mothers should take the Old French *Philomena* as a model for action and begin to kill their children. That would be absurd. But I do think this text asks a probing hypothetical question that helps push the limits of our understanding of rape and its potential link to the cultural narratives of virginity, love, beauty, marriage, paternity, and motherhood. For in killing Itys, Philomena and Progne are probing towards the roots of a larger, systemic problem involving patriarchal definition and control of the female body. Their disturbingly violent gestures ask, in different ways, what would have to be destroyed in order for rape to cease? Could we imagine a scenario in which women work together to change embedded definitions of the female body, whether as provocative and violable or maternally giving, rewriting the stories that we live out, most often unwittingly, from day to day? These violent and creative women ask, in effect, whether we have enough imagination to take this haunting story seriously and continue refashioning the cultural narrative of rape until it disappears.

Notes

1. Susan Brownmiller first argued years ago that rape is not a sexual crime but a violent weapon of political oppression, a conscious process of intimidation by which men keep women in a state of fear, *Against Our Will: Men, Women and Rape* (New York: Simon and Schuster, 1975). More recently, feminist critics have articulated the historically specific conditions of that violence as it differs, for example, from Euro-American to African American women. See Carla Freccero's opening remarks in "Rape's Disfiguring Figures: Marguerite de Navarre's *Heptameron* Day 1:10," *Rape and Representation,* ed. Lynn Higgins and Brenda Silver (New York: Columbia University Press, 1991), pp. 227–47.

2. See, for example, Catharine MacKinnon's argument that "rape focuses more centrally on what men define as sexuality than on women's experience of our sexual being, hence its violation," *Feminism Unmodified* (Cambridge, MA: Harvard University Press, 1987), p. 87; and her "Feminism, Marxism, Method and the State: Toward Feminist Jurisprudence," *Signs: Journal of Women in Culture and Society* 8, 4 (1983): 635–58; along with Susan Griffin, *Rape: The Politics of Consciousness* (New York: Harper & Row, 1979), p. 76.

3. Sexual violation symbolizes and actualizes women's subordinate social status to men, "Reflections on Sex Equality Under the Law," *American Feminist Thought at Century's End: A Reader,* ed. Linda Kauffman (Cambridge: Basil Blackwell, 1993), p. 379.

4. Portland Women's Night Watch 2nd Annual Flashlight March to stop Violence Against Women and Children, August 25, 1978; cited by Griffin, p. 123.

5. I draw a distinction here between existing legal statutes prohibiting rape and the coexistent cultural codes that convey its inevitability. See especially MacKinnon, "Law actively engages in sex inequality by apparently prohibiting abuses it largely permits, like rape" ("Reflections," p. 378).

6. Ovid, *Metamorphoses,* trans. Rolfe Humphries (Bloomington: Indiana University Press, 1968).

7. Chrétien de Troyes, *Philomena,* ed. C. de Boer (Paris: Editions Paul Geuthner, 1909). For an English translation, see *Three Ovidian Tales of Love,* ed. and trans. Raymond J. Cormier (New York: Garland, 1986).

8. This essay first appeared in *Bodytalk: When Women Speak in Old French Literature* (Philadelphia: University of Pennsylvania Press, 1993) as a setpiece for rethinking a related mythic scenario, perhaps best exemplified by the Ovidian tale of Pygmalion's ivory statue in which the masterful male artist constructs an idealized feminine beauty as physically embodied but speechless, pp. 109–50.

9. For an incisive feminist reading of rape in Ovid's "Philomel and Procne" and related myths, see Patricia Klindienst Joplin, "The Voice of the Shuttle is Ours," *Stanford Literary Review* 1, 1 (Spring 1984): 25–53, esp. 43. Other literary accounts of rape and lingual mutilation are found in Shakespeare's *Titus Andronicus,* where Lavinia is raped, her tongue cut out, and her arms cut off to prevent her from writing, though she writes using a stick in her teeth. See Jane Marcus, "Still Practice, A/Wrested Alphabet: Toward a Feminist Aesthetic," *Feminist Issues in Literary Scholarship,* ed. Shari Benstock (Bloomington: Indiana University Press, 1987), pp. 80–81. On Shakespeare's *Lucrece,* see Stephanie Jed, *Chaste Thinking* (Bloomington: Indiana University Press, 1989); and Coppelia Kahn, "*Lucrece,* The Sexual Politics of Subjectivity," in *Rape and Representation,* pp. 141–59. Nancy K. Miller gives a feminist reading of women weavers Ariadne and Arachne in "Arachnologies: The Woman, the Text and the Critic," *The Poetics of Gender,* ed. Nancy K. Miller (New York: Columbia University Press, 1980), pp. 270–95. On Penelope, see Peggy Kamuf, "Penelope at Work," *Signature Pieces: On the Institution of Authorship* (Ithaca, NY: Cornell University Press, 1988), pp. 145–73; and Carolyn Heilbrun in *Hamlet's Mother* (New York: Columbia University Press, 1990), pp. 103–11. On Helen and Philomena, see Christine Froula, "The Daughter's Seduction: Sexual Violence and Literary History," *Signs* (Summer 1986): 621–44.

10. For a cogent analysis of this phenomenon in a range of medieval French texts, see Kathryn Gravdal, *Ravishing Maidens: Writing Rape in Medieval French Literature and Law* (Philadelphia: University of Pennsylvania Press, 1991); and her carefully argued "Chrétien de Troyes, Gratian, and the Medieval Romance of Sexual Violence," *Signs* 17, 3 (1992): 558–85. For recent feminist analyses that highlight, in different ways, how rape offers a complex nexus for literary and historical issues confronted by medievalists in particular, see Carolyn Dinshaw, *Chaucer's Sexual Poetics* (Madison: University of Wisconsin Press, 1989), pp. 3–27; Anne Howland Schotter, "Rhetoric vs. Rape in the Medieval Latin *Pamphilus,*" in manuscript; Gayle Margherita, "Some Thoughts on History, Epistemology and Rape," *Medieval Feminist Newsletter* 11 (Spring 1991): 2–5.

11. "Arachnologies," p. 274.

12. See especially Joplin, "The Voice of the Shuttle is Ours," pp. 45–52.

13. Considered by some to be the first work of the master of twelfth-century French romance, Chrétien de Troyes, *Philomena* has been contested by others, largely on linguistic grounds, as not belonging to Chrétien's corpus. For a concise summary of the arguments on both sides and an analysis of

proverbial expressions within the *Philomena* that lends credence to the
view that Chrétien composed the work, see Elisabeth Schulze-Busacker,
"Philomena: Une Revision de l'attribution de l'oeuvre," *Romania* 107
(1986): 459–85.

14. The narrator's voice is especially obvious in the following lines: "Philomena
eschevelee / Ne sanbloit pas nonain velee, / Car granz mervoille iert a *re-
treire* / Son jant cors et son cler vieire" [The disheveled Philomena did not
appear as a veiled nun. Her beautiful body and light face were wonders to
describe] (vv. 125–29); "Se je apres ces trois i fail / Et j'i metrai tot mon tra-
vail. / Desqu'anpris l'ai n'an quier recroire:/ Plus dirai qu'on ne porroit
croire" [Though I, like these other three writers, might fail (in describing
her), I will work hard at it. Until I have undertaken it, I do not plan to give
up. I will say more than one might believe possible] (vv. 135–38).

15. "Tel l'ot Deus feite que Nature / Mien esciant i fausist bien / S'ele i vo-
sist comancier rien" [God had fashioned her such that Nature, it seems to
me, would do wrong if she attempted to add anything] (vv. 142–44); "Car
Nature s'an fu penee / Plus que de nule autre rien nee, / Si ot tot mis
quanqu'ele pot" [Nature worked harder on her than on any other creature.
She put all she had into this] (vv. 167–69). For Nature's role in fashioning
Enide, see vv. 430–32 of Chrétien de Troyes's *Erec et Enide,* ed. Mario
Roques (Paris: Champion, 1976). For God's efforts in creating Soredamors
see Chrétien's *Cliges,* ed. Mario Roques (Paris: Champion, 1957), v. 800
and, on Nature's role, vv. 820–21.

16. In "Shakespeare's *Will:* The Temporality of Rape," *Representations* 20 (fall
1987): 35, Joel Fineman highlights Shakespeare's reference to the beautiful
female body that speaks like an orator who seduces but without noting the
extent to which this body's "voice" results from male fantasy and desire.

17. Philomena's ignorance places her in a very different category from the
women of Susan Brownmiller's *Against Our Will: Men, Women and Rape*
(New York: Simon and Schuster, 1975), which sees rape as a strategy of
keeping women in a perpetual state of fear. As the perfectly innocent virgin, Philomena has neither will nor fear.

18. The portraits are evenly balanced in terms of space: 30 lines for beauty (vv.
140–70) and 35 for knowledge (vv. 170–205).

19. Jean Frappier, *Chrétien de Troyes, l'homme et l'oeuvre* (Paris: Hatier-Boivins,
1957), p. 69. Cf. Frappier's example of dialectic in Philomena's query about
women's words.

20. See also vv. 363–66 where Pandions explains that nothing pleases him
more than Philomena, that all his pleasures are in his daughter, that he lives
by her alone and has no other sustenance: "Mes or n'ai mes rien qui me
pleise; / An ma fille sont tuit mi eise, / Par li vif je tant solemant, / Car n'ai
autre sostenement" [I have nothing else that pleases me now. All my joys
are in my daughter. I live by her alone for I have no other sustenance].

21. Denise Riley, *Am I That Name? Feminism and the Category of "Woman" in
History* (Minneapolis: University of Minnesota Press, 1988), p. 106.

22. "Love" as the source of the trouble is cast as a female since the Old French "Amors" is a feminine noun. She is not "sage" and does not act "wisely" when carrying out her will, "D'on n'est ele pas sage.- / -Si est. Mes ele a tel corage / Qu'il ne li chaut de nul savoir, / Quant sa volante puet avoir" [Thus is she not wise.- Yes she is. But she has such courage/will that wisdom makes no difference to her when she can have her way] (vv. 421–24). The narrator tells us that Tereus would have been sage to avoid this liaison (vv. 449–51). Succumbing to it, he is reduced to the braying and shouting of love's victims (v. 400), becoming quintessentially womanlike as he suffers, temporarily, a complete loss of speech, "Tote a perdue la parole" [He completely lost his speech] (v. 390). It is also significant in retrospect that when Philomena refuses to speak to her father on Tereus's behalf, she explains that Tereus should have enough power and *savoir* to get what he wants (vv. 280–86).

23. See also v. 1194.

24. The passage provides a distinct counterpoint to Ariadne's thread that guided Tereus into the labyrinth and out again. For a revealing analysis of how this text exploits the semantic resonances suggested by the heroine's name, Philomena, *fil, fille, fils, mener*, see Nancy Jones, "The Daughter's Text and the Thread of Lineage in the Old French *Philomena*," in this volume.

25. Ovid tells us only that Philomena "Gave it [her tapestry] to one old woman, with signs and gestures / To take it to the queen, so it was taken," v. 148.

26. This is in fact the major tenet of the widely misunderstood phenomenon of *ecriture feminine*. See *Bodytalk*, pp. 7–9.

27. That Progne cooks instead of weaving to tell her story and how that activity relates to women's work in weaving will be discussed below.

28. "Quant ele ot *s'ovraigne* finee / Tel come ele la *sot ovrer*" [When she had finished her work, as she knew how to do it] (vv. 1134–35, my emphasis).

29. For an especially cogent reading of the Old French *Philomena* in terms of its feudal context, see Nancy Jones, "The Daughter's Text."

30. After the initial rape, we remember, Tereus returned regularly to the forest hideaway to "take his pleasure": "Qu'a force tot ses buens feisoit / de li cil qui l'avoit traie" [Forcefully, he who had betrayed her repeatedly took his pleasure from her] (vv. 1068–69).

31. Pandions, too, is said to have been nourished by his virginal daughter, v. 366.

32. The introduction to the Philomena provided by the *Ovide Moralisé* in which the text is preserved, explains how Pandions gave Progne to Tereus in payment for having saved his lands from invasion by barbarians (vv. 8–20).

33. Progne later explains how Tereus's intervention specifically prevented the sisters from speaking with each other (vv. 1274–75).

34. Toni Morrison, *Beloved;* Adrienne Rich, *Of Woman Born: Motherhood as Experience and Institution* (New York: W. W. Norton, 1976), pp. 24, 256–57.

35. "Ne vangier ne vos sai ne puis / Del felon qui ce vos a fet" [I do not know how to avenge you against the traitor who did this to you] (vv. 1288–89).
36. Itys is said to resemble Tereus on many occasions.
37. Cf. Progne's mourning and burial of her sister, though in the absence of a body, v. 1056.
38. This birdsong harks back to the raucous bird noises that furnished bad omens during Tereus and Progne's wedding ceremony, vv. 15–36.

CHAPTER 5

THE DAUGHTER'S TEXT AND THE THREAD OF
LINEAGE IN THE OLD FRENCH *PHILOMENA*

Nancy A. Jones

> This essay shows how the Old French *Philomena* reveals debates about
> the status of women in medieval aristocratic households and the role
> courtly literature plays in aestheticizing sexual violence.

T he Philomela-Procne myth persists through the Western tradition as a
disturbing narrative in which sexual violence and revenge intermin-
gle with aesthetic self-consciousness. In Ovid's treatment the myth takes
on a specifically self-conscious literary quality. Philomela's tapestry functions in the *Metamorphoses* as the symbol for art's resistance to a barbaric
and destructive world that would dismember and silence the self. More recently, feminist interpretations view the myth as an emblem of women's
victimization and resistance within literary history.[1] Perhaps more than any
other Western myth, Philomela's story articulates the link between sexual
violence, the silencing of women's voices, and the alternative discourse
women fashion in weaving and embroidery.[2] Western literary aesthetics
have also privileged the arts of weaving and embroidery as emblems for
narrative art and textuality itself. This essay traces the uneasy merger of
these themes in a twelfth-century French adaptation of Ovid known as the
Philomena.[3] Since 1884, when Gaston Paris discovered it embedded within
the *Ovide Moralisé,* the debate over the *Philomena*'s authorship has obscured
the intrinsic interest of the text itself. Paris and later scholars identified the
1,468-line verse adaptation as none other than the early work mentioned
by Chrétien de Troyes in the prologue to *Cligés* under the title of *La
Muance de la hupe et de l'aronde et del rossignol.*[4] This essay will not attempt

to argue whether or not the *Philomena* is one of Chrétien's early works. Instead, I seek to identify the appeal of the Philomela redaction to a twelfth-century audience by examining its courtly elements and the techniques of adaptation employed to translate the myth into a cautionary tale of family disaster. The tale, I shall show, not only rewrites the story to embed its characters firmly within a specifically courtly milieu, but it also reveals the violence that underlies the courtly world. It becomes then a commentary on the decadence of contemporary feudal society and on the fragility and brutality of the patrilocal exogamous aristocratic marriage practices that form the foundation of such a society. Furthermore, in its evocation of an alternative culture of women in its portrait of a place akin to a small-scale textile workshop in which women earn their own living and in which class distinctions between women dissolve, the work carves out a space for women's art (both textile and textual) that counters the violence of feudal society—especially its violence towards women enacted in rape. The potential of this female artistic realm to act as a critique of feudal marriage and inheritance practices is subtly conveyed, I shall show, through the text's wordplay, especially on *fil, fil(z)*, and *Phil* (from the name Philomena.)

A twelfth-century writer might be drawn to the gruesome tale of rape, mutilation, and infanticide for several reasons. The nightingale, as the traditional symbol of love and poetry, had associations with tragic, thwarted passion. Ovid's text offered the Old French writer an opportunity to treat this popular theme and to retell an exotic tale of transformation. The *Philomena*, like the longer *romans d'antiquité*, reflects the twelfth-century vogue for vernacular adaptations of classical narratives. Like similar adaptations, however, the *Philomena* not only exhibits revived interest in the Latin *auctores:* it also represents the new confident self-consciousness of literary culture in France. The highly rhetorical *descriptio* of Philomena (ll. 124–204) shows a courtly writer using a classical character to create a flattering microportrait of courtly society. The heroine's beauty and refined accomplishments (greatly amplified from the Latin source) clearly reflect the ideals of a courtly audience. Such epideictic display is conventional in twelfth-century romance. So is the adaptor's expanded treatment of *Amor.*

Like other courtly narratives of the period, the *Philomena* exploits Ovidian love psychology. The writer draws repeatedly upon Ovid's amatory writings to apostrophize and analyze Tereus's illicit passion for Philomena. In the *Metamorphoses,* the narration of their initial meeting illustrates how a visual stimulus (i.e., a beautiful woman richly clad) can incite hot passion:

> ecce venit magno dives Philomela paratu
> divitior forma; quales audire solemus

Naidas et Dryadas mediis incedere silvis,
si modo des illis cultus similesque paratus.
non secus exarsit conspecta virgine Tereus,
quam si quis canis ignem subponat aristis
aut frondem positasque cremet faenilibus herbas. (VI, 451–57)[5]

[Behold Philomela comes, richly clad, and richer still in her beauty, just as we
are wont to hear of the nymphs and dryads walking among the woods if only
you should give them similar refinements and garb. Not otherwise did Tereus
blaze forth at the sight of the girl than if one should place fire beneath dry,
whitened ears of grain or should burn foliage or hay stored in its barn.]

The Old French version retains the simile of kindled hay, but precedes it
with a long disquisition on *Amor* characteristic of twelfth-century *Ovidiana:*

Sa granz biautez son cuer li anble
Et sa tres bele contenance;
Pechiez le met an esperance
De mauvestié et de folie;
Amors vilainement le lie.
Vilainement?—Voire, sanz faille.
De vilenie se travaille,
Quant il son cuer viaut atorner
A la seror sa fame amer.
. . . .
Qui porroit Amors contrester
Que trestot son voloir ne face?
Mal issi Tereus de Trace
Por aler Philomena querre,
Qu'Amors a vers lui prise guerre,
S'est angigniez et mal bailliz,
Qu'au cuer li est li feus sailliz
Qui de legier art et esprant. (210–18; 234–41)

[Her great beauty and lovely face seize his heart. Sin leads him to hope for
foul and foolish things; Love basely binds him. Basely? Yes, indeed. It strives
at villainy when it wants to turn his heart to love his wife's sister. . . . Who
could oppose Love which would ever do its will? In an evil hour did Tereus
leave Thrace in order to seek Philomena, for Love has declared war upon
him, and he has been tricked and mistreated; for the flame which burns and
catches easily has jumped up into his heart.]

The narrator adds an even longer speech on the nature of Love
(392–444) in describing Tereus's silent frustration. The passage shows the

writer eager to display his mastery of Ovidian love lore. He parades all
the clichés about the power of Love: Love is a mighty, yet unjust lord to
his vassals (393–420); Love is a deceitful master who promises much but
gives little (425–30); Love is a fire fed by the lover's sighs and complaints
(439–42); and Love is a wound whose medicine only deepens the disease
(443–44).

To the swift and suggestive narrative of the *Metamorphoses,* the Old
French writer has added the lore and voice of the *magister amoris* of the
Amores and the *Ars Amatoria.* A character like Tereus would especially appeal to the adaptor's interest in the (sometimes perverse) psychology of
love.[6] And yet are we correct in privileging the psychological dimensions
of *Amor?* Let us compare the two other surviving Ovidian tales translated
and adapted into Old French during this period, *Piramus et Tisbé* and *Nar-
cisus et Danae.*[7] Both narratives end in a Liebestod: the respective heroines,
Tisbé and Danae, choose to die in a last embrace with the body of their
beloved.[8] The narrator's approving tone indicates that these deaths are
beautiful testimony to the power of Love (*Amor*). In the *Philomena* however, Love leaves a bloody trail of rape, mutilation, and child murder. Where
the narrator of *Piramus et Tisbé* pays tribute to Love in his closing line,
"How great was their loyal love" [Con lor leal amor fu granz], the narrator of the *Philomena* makes no reference to *Amor* in his epilogue. In fact,
the narrator had earlier turned away from the term *Amor* in his explanation of Tereus's behavior:

> . . . amors ne doit nus ce clamer.—
> Amors?—Non voir.—Et quoi?—Outrage,
> Desleauté et forsenage,
> Car, s'au voir cuit bien assener,
> N'est pas amors de forsener. (482–86)

> [No one should call this love. Love?—No indeed.—Then what?—Outrage,
> disloyalty and madness, for if one intends to aim at truth, it is not love to go
> mad.]

The terms "outrage," "desleauté," and "forsenage" mark a new authorial
stance. They shift the moral onus away from Tereus's passion to his plot
against Philomena. This plot, we are told, is inspired by the Devil (462–70).
Here the writer's real focus comes into view: this is a story of treachery
and excess rather than an analysis of love.[9] And, indeed, recent work by
Kathryn Gravdal and E. Jane Burns on the *Philomena* has brought about an
essential shift in the way we read this text by emphasizing the centrality of
rape in the Old French version.[10] I want to extend their analyses of rape

in this text by exploring the ways in which representations of rape act as a critique of contemporary twelfth-century society.

Henceforth, the narrator refers to Tereus as a "fel" [felon], a "desleal" (711), and a "traitor." As a virtual "thief" [*lerre*] (750), he is the opposite of the feudal ideal. Later, Philomena's furious denunciation of her attacker brings the characterization of Tereus as felon to its rhetorical climax:

Ha, fet ele, "fel de put'eire,
Fel enuieus, que viaus tu feire?
Fel mauves, fel desmesurez,
Fel traitres, fel parjurez,
Fel cuiverz, fel de pute loi,
Fel, don ne plevis tu au roi
Que tu enor me porteroies
Et que a lui me ramanroies
Sainne et heitiee an mon pais?" (807–15)

[Ha, she says, "low-born traitor, loathsome traitor, what do you want to do? Evil traitor, outrageous traitor, treacherous traitor, perfidious traitor, wretched traitor, traitor of dirty morals; traitor did you not pledge to the king that you would act honorably toward me and that you would bring me back safe and sound to him and my country?"]

The narrator's epilogue echoes her rebuke. After telling how Tereus, Philomena, and Progne were transformed into birds, the narrator lashes out at the villain's real-life counterparts, the "felons and the perjurers" who slander and betray young ladies:

Ancore, qui crerroit son los,
Seroient a honte trestuit
Li desleal mort et destruit
Et li felon et li parjure
Et cil qui de joie n'ont cure
Et tuit cil qui font mesprison
Et felenie et traison
Vers pucele sage et cortoise . . . (1454–61)

[Again, he who would believe the nightingale's reputation would be disgraced: the disloyal, the traitors, the perjurers, and those who have no care for joy, and all those who commit outrage, felony and treason toward a wise and courteous maiden will be killed and destroyed . . .]

This outburst is no conventional courtly denunciation of "false lovers" as it later becomes in courtly lyric.[11] The tone here recalls the punitive response to rapists in Arthurian narratives. In such texts the exemplars of chivalry (Arthur, Lancelot, Gawain, Bohort) fight to defend or avenge beautiful maidens. These episodes, Antoinette Saly suggests, may stem from a mythic taboo associated with Celtic fertility cults in which the forces of fertility are personified as fairies who guard magic springs.[12] Philomena's violation by Tereus does not, however, form part of a mythic cycle of loss and redemption. Following Ovid, the *Philomena* depicts a world devoid of heroic or chivalric values. Its narrative *matière*, moreover, involves much more violent transgressions than do the adulterous tales of Lancelot and Guinevere and Tristan and Iseut.

The literary currency of the story about a daughter's rape may be partially explained as the influence of another Latin text, Claudian's *De Raptu Proserpinae*, which was an equally popular school text in twelfth-century France.[13] The parallel is an intriguing one, for this text relates the rape of a vulnerable daughter who is forcibly carried off by the gruesome Lord of the Underworld. Many details in this text, in particular the role of treachery and outrage, the daughter's weaving, and the emphasis on the powerful bond between Proserpina and Ceres, suggest that the author of the *Philomena* drew upon it in adapting his Ovidian source (Progne and Ceres, for example, have some interesting similarities).

In closing his story, the narrator uses the image of Philomena's transformed state to reiterate the sense of outrage. The narrator's gloss reveals how much Tereus's treachery and Progne's revenge overwhelm any courtly moralizing:

> Car tant l'an grieve et tant l'an poise
> Que, quant il vient au prin d'este,
> Que tot liver avant passe
> Por les mauves qu'ele tant het
> Chante au plus doucemant qu'el set
> Par be boschage: "Oci! Oci!"
> De Philomena leirai ci. (1462–68)

[For it grieves and burdens the bird so much that when early summer arrives, she sings ever so softly through the woods for those whom she so hates "Oci! Oci!" I will leave off about Philomena here.]

The bird's springtime call conveys the maiden's (suppressed) hatred for evil men. The woman's grief, uttered in the deceptively soft tones of the bird, is disturbingly ambiguous. Its characteristically soft call cannot completely disguise (or rather, contain) a lingering violent impulse. The second meaning is conveyed on the aural level of the signifier. As several readers have noted, the words "Oci! Oci!" appear in a number of Old French texts as an onomatopoeia of the nightingale's plaintive cry and as the imperative form of the verb *occir,* "Kill! Kill!," a battle cry that seems more suitable to the *chanson de geste.*[14]

The narrator's closing denunciation of all "felons" and "liars" (terms associated with legal accusation) forms an indirect address to his audience. His rebuke of Tereus's behavior thus extends to certain elements in the author-narrator's feudal society and flies in the face of his previous accolades to Love. He sounds not unlike that moralizing scourge of courtly society, the troubadour Marcabru, who frequently denounces the decadence of the secular courtly society around him in his verse. In one sense, the tale would then be a framed as negative moral exemplum, although in a different form from the schematic moral allegory appended to it in the *Ovide Moralisé,* in that rather than providing an allegorical interpretation focused on the body as does the moralized text, this version comments directly on twelfth-century society.[15]

Yet, the exotic setting and the courtly psychology of *Amor* together might serve as a kind of screen behind which the author conceals the link between *Amor* and domestic violence. Presented within the doubly fictionalizing discourse of courtly manners and fable, the grim topics of rape and infanticide remain safely distanced from a contemporary audience, much as the exotic barbarian Thracian setting had undoubtedly served this purpose for Ovid's Greco-Roman audience.[16] In other words, the pagan myth here functions as a "cover story" that simultaneously displays and masks the tensions felt within high feudal society around the ambiguous position of women, who are seen both as innocent targets of sexual violence and as distrustful plotters. Through the myth the author can also highlight elements of family structure crucial to the functioning of the patrilineal kinship system within feudal society, particularly the sexual economy of patrilocal exogamous cultures, wherein daughters are exchanged between men and live under the dominion of either father or husband. In Ovid's work, the Athenian king Pandion gives his eldest daughter Procne to the Thracian king Tereus in exchange for military aid. The Old French text adapts this exchange to the perspective of feudal society. Apparently naïve anachronisms, like the feudal and courtly epithets for the major characters, are part of this attempt to naturalize the narrative. These anachronisms superficially resemble those found in the *romans d'antiquité.* For instance, Pandion, king of Athens, is described as "possanz et larges et cortois" (2). To a twelfth-century audience, however, he would appear as a weak feudal lord. Pandion's court, for all of its splendor (detailed at length by the Old French writer), lacks any male authority. Ovid emphasizes the old king's character flaws. To a medieval audience, however, Pandion's weakness is most evident in his lack of a male heir. Without a son, his second daughter is one daughter too many.[17] Pandion worsens the problem by doting on his younger daughter instead of designating a male heir. The danger of such a family situation would be clear to a medieval audience.[18] Not only is the lineage thus jeopardized, but within the structural economy of the feudal household, such an undefended daughter is intrinsically vulnerable to *raptus*—violent abduction by a man covetous of her inheritance. Philomena has no brothers to defend her honor, and no legitimate suitor in sight.

Philomena's vulnerability is also sexual in nature and corresponds to that of noble daughters in historical situations described by historian Georges Duby.[19] In reviewing contemporary chronicle literature, Duby notes how daughters often became pawns in the violent struggles between lords over lands and castles. He tells how the young countess of Namur, "betrothed" at an early age and sent to grow up in the bridegroom's household, was apparently forgotten when the match fell through. One might also add the example of Alix of France, the long-suffering betrothed of Richard the Lionhearted. The Capetian princess was said to have been spurned by Richard who believed that she had become his father's concubine during the long period when she was the king's ward in his household in England. Such a woman becomes the "surplus" daughter of the castle; her body is of no value to the patrimony, and consequently, Duby speculates, she becomes the sexual chattel of the men of the household, and her name disappears from the record. Within a society conditioned to expect sexual promiscuity on the part of women and to tolerate it on the part of males, Philomena's family status would signal her sexual vulnerability. The power struggle between Pandion and Tereus is also intelligible in feudal terms. As a politically and culturally inferior vassal to Pandion, the latter's marriage to Progne illustrates the practice of hypergamy among the French aristocracy. He resembles the young men of the lower nobility who sought to increase their wealth and status by marrying a socially superior heiress. But later, as a married *senior*, his succumbing to *Amor* is especially shameful.

Duby's study has demonstrated how the paradoxical medieval attitude towards women in twelfth-century France was in fact accommodated by the evolving marriage practices of the eleventh and twelfth centuries. As the Church and the aristocratic laity gradually coordinated their control over the institution of marriage, the increasing recognition of women's vulnerability to male violence could coexist alongside the persistent distrust and fear of women as deceitful beings apt to plot against their husbands. Both attitudes appear in the writings of eleventh- and twelfth-century ecclesiastes, jurists, and romance writers. Churchmen of this period inveighed against the violent abduction of women (probably heiresses carried off by property-hungry knights) and in other moments preached contempt for and mistrust of women and female sexuality. Likewise, men of the nobility acted to exercise control over female sexuality by sequestering wives and daughters within the castle's women's quarters or in a nearby convent. For entertainment these same clan leaders listened to stories emphasizing the adulterous tendencies of wives.

Significantly, the conflict between the Church and the nobility over cases of abduction and wife repudiation did not concern women's welfare. Rather, it concerned the ultimate control over the social institution of marriage and, hence, the distribution of property. While the Church acted to protect widows and repudiated wives under the doctrine of the *Pax Dei,* it left men the right to dispose of the women, children, and animals of their households as they saw fit. In other words, the father or husband's authority took precedence over an individual woman's right to appeal on her own behalf to public justice, whether secular or ecclesiastic. What happened to a woman in the household was considered a private matter.

To the contemporary audience, the Philomela-myth's revenge episode would evoke malaise about the supposed treachery of wives. The frequent repudiation of wives within feudal society and the frequent accusations of adultery and witchcraft, Duby argues, are symptomatic of a male social psyche that is deeply fearful of women.[20] The projection of blood guilt onto the women at the end of the myth would appeal to such a mentality, and their revenge plot would confirm the deeply ingrained misogyny of clan patriarchs and ecclesiastical authorities.[21] Progne's murder and dismemberment of her son Itys is the fictional fulfillment of the worst fears on the part of a feudal patrimony's male guardians. Reaction to Tereus's brutal silencing of Philomena after the rape (he cuts off her tongue) is more difficult to gauge. The sexual violation of a virgin was considered by medieval society (and many others) to be a crime against her family, rather than against the woman herself. Because it was considered the sacred vessel of family honor and the functional vessel necessary to the patrimony, a daughter's body was family property (especially if she were an heiress) and had to be guarded against foreign pollution. Rape by an outsider is a treacherous act punishable by loss of limb or life; as a crime against the family honor, it could set in motion the law of vengeance, although actual pursuit and punishment of rapists depended entirely on the will and power of the woman's male kinsfolk. The ambiguous laws concerning rape, and indeed the equivocal definition of rape in the customaries, help to explain the Old French writer's efforts to present his heroine as the paragon of feminine courtliness and virtue, while Tereus appears from the first as a "roi felon."[22]

By itself, however, a woman's word was insufficient proof of violation. Her accusation had to be supported by male kinsfolk in order to gain public credence; otherwise she could be considered guilty of fornication.

Without powerful male kinsmen, she was effectively deprived of the major form of legal accusation, known as the "hue and cry."[23] Tereus's crime has particular significance when considering medieval attitudes towards rape and the principle of the hue and cry. Customary law seems to have reserved the hue and cry [le clameur de haro], to the betrayed male. Upon discovering the adulterous couple *in flagrante delicto,* the husband's legal and family duty was to raise the hue and cry and slay them both on the spot.[24]

Viewed from this perspective, Philomena's mutilation symbolizes the social and legal predicament facing the victimized daughter of a feudal household if she lacks powerful male kinsmen. Such a woman has little legal power to accuse her rapist. The author of the *Philomena,* however, is not concerned with criticizing the customary law that deprives the woman of the right to vengeance if she lacks male kinsfolk. He seems to take the patriarchal viewpoint in which the murder of Itys represents the degradation of clan warfare into female "*deablie*" (1330). The mother, ordinarily the nurturing guardian of the sacred lineage, here incarnated by the child Itys, now becomes instead the agent of its destruction. In dismembering and decapitating her son (O.F. nom. *fiz*/obj. *fil*), Progne literally cuts the thread [*fil*] of the lineage. The rape plot, then, is not so much a mirror of social reality as a frame through which an audience could view from a distance its shared anxieties about the destructive potential of sexuality and female power upon the lineage. The *Philomena* articulates in narrative form what R. Howard Bloch calls "the poetics of disruption."[25]

The Threads of Kinship

The tapestry episode represents the text's most remarkable amplification of its Ovidian source. As in Ovid, mute Philomena weaves a tapestry version of the events and sends it to her sister Progne who secretly liberates her. After telling of Tereus's return to Procne and his lies about her sister's death, Ovid returns to Philomela:

> Signa deus bis sex lustraverat anno.
> quid faciat Philomela? fugam custodia claudit,
> structa rigent solido stabulorum moenia saxo;
> os mutum facti caret indice. grande doloris
> ingenium est, miserisque venit sollertia rebus.
> stamina barbarica suspendit callida tela
> purpureasque notas filis intexuit albis,
> indicium sceleris, perfectaque tradidit uni,
> utque ferat dominae, gestu rogat; illa rogata
> pertulit ad Procnen: nescit quid tradat in illis. (VI, 571–80)

[Twice six times the god had traversed the constellations in the year. What could Philomela do? Her imprisonment closes off flight, (and) the walls of the stable are firm, built with solid stone; her silent mouth lacks the accuser of the deed. There is great cleverness in grief and energy comes to wretched circumstances. She hung the warp on the barbarian loom and wove crimson letters on the white threads as evidence of the crime, and she handed the finished work to her single companion, and with a gesture asked that she carry it to her mistress; the woman, having been asked, carried it to Procne: she is ignorant of what she hands over/betrays in these things.]

The Old French writer turns this ten-line passage into a more fully dramatized, 178-line episode. In an interesting form of *translatio,* he adapts the circumstances of Philomela's imprisonment in the Thracian countryside into twelfth-century terms. Philomena has not one guardian, as in Ovid, but two. The shadowy "servant" of the Latin text becomes a more individualized figure: we learn that Philomena has been left with a *vilainne* and her daughter. The new details about this household provide ironic foreshadowing:

> Mes Tereus folie fist
> Qui avuec Philomena mist
> Por la garder une vilainne,
> Qui vivoit de sa propre painne,
> Car filer et tistre savoit
> Et une soe fille avoit
> Qu'ele aprenoit a son mestier. (867–73)

[But Tereus committed folly to have put Philomena under the guard of a peasant woman who lived from her own effort, for she knew how to spin and weave and she had a daughter to whom she was teaching her trade.]

The Old French writer, however, has other intentions besides foreshadowing in mind. By turning Ovid's servant figure into a full-fledged weaver-artisan, he imaginatively picks up the thematic thread incarnated in Philomena herself. Indeed, Philomena's name evokes the idea of weaving, for *mener le fil* means "to guide the thread," and Philomena is s/he who has guided the thread [*fil/a mene*]. Finally, the doubling of the lone female servant into a mother-daughter household reinforces the idea that the tapestry scheme takes shape within an all-female zone of domestic apprenticeship, a figurative no man's land. Tereus's folly, the narrator intimates, is his failure to appreciate the danger of leaving women to themselves.

Tereus also overlooks the fact that he leaves someone he believes to be helpless in the company of a woman who "lived from her own labor" [*vivoit de sa propre painne*]. The Old French version suggests that a kind of female solidarity develops between the aristocratic heroine and her peasant prison guardians. They have no male provider and she has no male champion. Thus by dint of her own "need" [besoings] (1090), Philomena weaves a tapestry, and becomes a figurative *fille* of the *vilainne*. Although the old woman obeys the *letter* of Tereus's command to keep Philomena shut up inside the house, her spirit of motherly concern leads her unwittingly to provide the means of the girl's escape. First, she supplies the heroine with thread [*fil*]; later she offers her daughter's [sa *fille*] delivery service. Furthermore, whereas Ovid's Philomela begins weaving spontaneously on the "barbarian loom" that she sees against a wall, the medieval Philomena arrives at the idea of the tapestry-message only gradually, as a result of helping the *vilainne* and her daughter spin thread. The text conveys Philomena's perceptual breakthrough. Having seen the *vilainne* simply as a prison-guard, she now sees that the women provide her with the means of escape:

> Einsi mout longuemant estut
> Tant qu'an la fin se porpansa,
> Si con besoingns li anseigna,
> Qu'an la meison avoit filé,
> Que mout an avoient file
> Antre la vieillete et sa fille,
> Ne ne li falloit (une ostille)
> A feire une cortine ovree . . . (1088–95)

[Thus she remained there for a long time until at last she reflected, as necessity taught her, that she had spun thread in the house and that between them the old woman and her daughter had spun a good deal, nor did she lack any tool to make an embroidered coverlet.]

In the Old French interpolation, tutelage eventually takes the place of surveillance. Philomena's prison virtually becomes a small-scale textile workshop, a gynaeceum, in which women earn their own living. The setting corresponds to the textile workrooms of twelfth-century Champagne, where women serfs spun thread, worked silk, and wove cloth.[26] Such workrooms are thought by some to have inspired the Serves de Pesme episode in *Yvain*. The parallel is noteworthy, not to prove that Chrétien de Troyes wrote the *Philomena* but to show the double role of women textile workers in each text. They appear as both exploited members of the peasantry and damsels in distress.[27] Here, of course, no knight errant will appear to liberate the hapless Philomena. Instead, the myth provides the writer with an opportunity to develop an analogy between Philomena's tapestry and his own text. Both tapestry and text are products of courtly *savoir-faire*, but they have potentially dangerous effects.

The telling link between weaving, embroidery, and literary authorship emerges early in the narrative. In the remarkable 75-line description of Philomena (124–204), much elaborated from the Ovidian original, the narrator praises his heroine at equal length for her beauty and her accomplishments. The portrait is highly conventional, based on well-established models of feminine beauty and accomplishment.[28] Philomena is a lady who has mastered all the courtly pastimes (board games, falconry, hunting). Furthermore, she excels at letters, cloth-working, music, and dialectic! These descriptive details turn out to be foreshadowing, of course, but the non-Ovidian talent for embroidery deserves particular comment:

> Avuec c'iert si bone ovriere
> D'ovrer une porpre vermoille
> Qu'an tot le mont n'ot sa paroille.
> Un diaspre ou un baudequin
> Nes la mesniee Hellequin
> Seust ele an un drap portreire. (188–93)

[Besides, she was such a fine needleworker at adorning a fine purple cloth that in all the world she had no equal. She would know how to draw arabesque on silk or a brocade or even Harlequin's troop on a cloth.]

Thus, the Old French writer even improves on Ovid by introducing Philomena's prodigious skill at needlework before the tapestry episode. He gives a specific detail about her high technical skill, mentioning, to quote Alice Colby-Hall, "an extraordinarily difficult pattern, the *mesniee Hellequin* 'Harlequin's troop', which he probably conceived of as a band of souls in purgatory who, when driven about in the night, were visible because of the fiery envelope or phosphorescent glow surrounding their bodies."[29] Such colorful details may serve merely to rationalize the myth. Yet, if "Harlequin's troop" is, as Colby-Hall asserts, "one of the many examples of the Christianized version of the Wild Host," then the image also alludes to the transformed states of Tereus, Progne, and Philomena. Their bird forms locked in eternal flight and pursuit suggest sin's abasing effect and its infernal or purgatorial punishment. In any case, the Harlequin image implies not only technical difficulty, but also the embroidery's connection with violence.

The old woman's naïve assistance enables Philomena to weave (or embroider) a pictorial account of Tereus's treachery and the location of her prison.[30] Again, the Old French text elaborates freely upon its Latin source and heightens our sense of Philomena's craftsmanship:

La vieille ne li contredist,
Mes mout volantiers li eida
Et trestot quanqu'ele cuida
Qui a tel uevre covenist
Porchacier et querre li fist.
Trestot li quist son aparoil,
Tant que fil inde et fil vermoil
Et jaune et vert a plante ot,
Mes el ne conut ne ne sot
Rien de quanque cele tissoit;
Mes l'uevre li abelissoit
Qui mout estoit a feire gries,
Car tissu ot a l'un des chies
Que Philomena l'avoit feite;
Apres i fu la nes portreite
Ou Tereus la mer passa
Quant querre a Athenes l'ala,
Et puis comant il se contint
An Athenes quant il i vint,
Et comant il l'an amena,
Et puis comant il l'esforça,
Et comant il l'avoit leissiee
Quant la langue li ot tranchiee.
Tot ot escrit an la cortine,
Et la meison et la gaudine
Ou ele estoit anprisonee. (1108–33)

[The old woman did not oppose her, but rather helped her gladly, and goes
to seek everything that she thinks necessary to such work. She quickly
sought her equipment for her, until she had plenty of purple, scarlet, yellow
and green thread; but she didn't recognize or understand anything that
Philomena wove; yet the work was pleasing to her because it was grievously
difficult to do. For on one end Philomena had woven what had been done
to her. Next there was portrayed the ship on which Tereus crossed the sea
when he went seeking her in Athens, and then how he behaved when he
came to Athens, and how he carried her off, and how he raped her, and how
he had abandoned her when he had cut off her tongue. She had written
everything on the coverlet, including the house and the forest where she was
imprisoned.]

The passage makes explicit the Ovidian metaphor of weaving as a kind of
writing (and writing as a substitute for speech): "Tot ot escrit an la cortine" (1131). The narrator summarizes the tapestry's pictorial contents in a
way that suggests the sort of courtroom accusation that Philomena cannot
make in person. Her skill at "portraying" figures in embroidery now evokes

a secondary meaning of the Old French verb *portreire,* that is, to bring to justice, or accuse. The tapestry thus represents the female victim Philomena's form of hue and cry.

While effectively replacing the audible voice of legal accusation, the tapestry also represents the thorny nature of textuality for a twelfth-century audience. The text suggests that the translation of a story into writing is difficult for both writer and reader. Philomena's embroidery is a sad, painful process ["mout estoit a feire gries"] (1119). The line recalls the romance's initial description of the heroine. Here, Natura *creatrix* and *poeta artifex* toil to create and recreate Philomena's wondrous beauty.[31] Both embroidery and writing are forms of artistic production that require slow, laborious effort. This dignifies them: such humble patience and diligence are unknown to hot-blooded felons such as Tereus.[32] From this perspective, the tapestry represents the writer's toil in the service of a worthy goal. The subsequent responses to the tapestry (first by the peasant women and then by Progne) comment upon the nature of reading. The embroidered tapestry represents the idea of a craft (writing) that can be practiced and interpreted on two levels. It is of course crucial to the plot that that Philomena's guardian(s) do not comprehend the meaning of her tapestry. The Old French writer, however, develops the theme of literacy somewhat further than does Ovid. His peasant woman is an active, if insufficient, interpreter. While the old woman doesn't understand anything of what Philomena is embroidering, she finds it pleasing to look at (1116–18). Later, she interprets Philomena's desire to send the tapestry to the queen (expressed through gestures) as that of an artist seeking reward from a patron (1197–1205).

Philomena's artistic prowess consists in her ability to create an artifact that is not only beautiful, but also carries a partially hidden meaning. Wrought out of many diverse elements and delivered by an uncomprehending messenger, the tapestry is the perfect emblem for the written text whose decoding demands both literacy and refinement. As a partially comprehended narrative, the tapestry may also stand as a metaphor for pagan myth in general. It stands for the "cover plot" of exotic, artful fable used by the writer in order to expose the sexual violence endemic to his society. The work also develops a homology between disrupted language and disrupted family ties. The obsession with the lineage in the recurrent play on the first syllable of the heroine's name confuses the semantic differences between the homophones *fille, fil(z),* and *fil.* And this linguistic destabilization is acted out in the plot, where the surplus, unwanted *fille* kills the necessary *fils* and thereby cuts the *fil* of Tereus's house. This disruption of familial and social boundaries and hierarchies coincides with the linguistic confusion and produces the effect of surplus, which the moralizing epilogue cannot quite contain.

Lineage is also at issue in the play on the term "fille" [daughter] and the
"Phil" in the heroine's own name, which underscores her relationship to
the tale's other victim, Itys, himself the *fiz* or *fil*. Both are offspring who
become the innocent objects of violent mutilation. The Old French writer
goes further than Ovid in emphasizing their complementarity. In both versions, Philomena appears from hiding to throw the severed head of Itys at
the horrified Tereus. But in the Old French version, she herself had received it from the mad Progne, who had cut it off "out of devilry and
pride" (1330–33). The added detail suggests a primitive form of retribution. The boy's severed head may represent Philomena's own lost "piece,"
that is, her broken hymen and her tongue (the head being a displaced
metaphor for the genitals and connected by metonymy to the power of
speech).[33] And yet the retribution is not complete until Philomena brings
the head "back" to its body (now in Tereus's stomach), thus restoring Itys's
identity, disguised by dismemberment and cooking. Furthermore, the narration aurally intimates a shared identity between Philomena the beloved
daughter (of Pandion) and Itys the beloved son (of Tereus). While Ovid
loads the scene with rhetorical paradoxes to underscore the terrible perversion of human nature that child murder and cannibalism represent, the
Old French writer offers what seems to be a prosaic expansion of the
dense Latin text. As in other instances, the gratuitous quality of such added
dialogue should not blind us to the text's more subtle effects. Here, the expanded dialogue between Progne and Tereus contains echoes of earlier
scenes involving the "fille," Philomena. By playing on the noun *"fil/z"*
[son] and the verb *a/mener* ['to bring forth'], the Old French writer suggests an overlapping of the two triangles, Progne-Philomena-Tereus and
Progne-Tereus-Itys. Having been invited by Progne to a tête-à-tête dinner, Tereus insists on the presence of Itys:

> Cil li respont que il ira
> Mes que ses *fiz* Itis i iert;
> Ja plus conpaingnie n'i quiert
> Fors que lui et li et son *fil*. (1352–55; my italics)

[He responds that he will come, but that his son Itys should also come; he
would seek no other company than that of his son.]

A few lines later, when the narrator reports Tereus's second request in indirect discourse, he echoes the heroine's name:

> Lors l'an va aporter un haste
> Et cil tote voie la haste,

Que qu'il mange et que qu'il taille,
Que son *fil amener* li aille.
"Dame," fet il, "mal me tenez
Covant quant Itis n'*amenez* . . . (1389–94; my italics)

[Then she goes to bring in a roast and the whole time as he eats and carves, he presses her to go bring in his son to him. "Lady," he says, "You hardly keep your promise to bring in Itys to me."]

In another link between Philomena and Itys, Tereus asks, as he unknowingly eats the child's flesh, "Dame, ou est Itys?" (1381), echoing Progne's own question to him upon his return from Athens: "Ou est ma suer?" (899). Thus, beneath the immediate irony of Tereus's horrible mistake, lies a second irony that a *fille* now replaces the *fil(z)*. At her sister's cue, Philomena, not Itys, bursts forth on the scene:

Philomena. qui s'iert reposte
An une chanbre iluec decoste,
S'an issi fors a tot la teste. (1407–8; my italics)

[Philomena, who stands in an adjoining chamber, comes out with the head.]

The passage contains a second symmetry: instead of bringing forth [O.F. *mener*] her son, Progne has brought forth the daughter. Figuratively, she has substituted a daughter (Pandion's) for Tereus's son, thereby replicating in Tereus's house the patrilinear weakness of Pandion's. The narrator's pronouncement of the heroine's name at the beginning of this passage not only caps the symmetry of the revenge, but implies a more complex meaning beneath the combined components of her name. Not only does "Phil" evoke *fil(z)* and *fille,* but when taken together with the second half of the name, "mena," the name "Philomena" encapsulates an action: it aurally evokes not only the two victims in the story, but what happens to them. Both daughter and son have been led off—*mené(e)*—to their doom. Given the fascination of this period with etymologies, one might press the implications of Philomena's name still further. "Phil" recalls the Greek *philia* signifying "love," and thus stands in opposition to the epithet hurled repeatedly at Tereus, "fel."[34] Philomena's story revolves around other characters' love for this "daughter" and their desire to carry her off. The very sounds of her name in the verse contain her story.

The verb *mener* virtually guides the plot. Events are set in motion when her sister asks to have her brought [*amener*] to Thrace. Twice we hear Progne's request to her husband, and twice we hear Tereus repeat it in Athens:

Et si il li deffant la voie
Tant qu'ele sa seror ne voie,
Don li prie ele qu'il l'aut querre,
Si *l'amaint* an la soe terre
. . . .
Au departir Progné li prie
Que sa seror tost li *amaint.*
. . . .
Tant me dist, ains ne le cela,
Quant je de li le congie pris
Que ses sire ne ses amis
Ja mes a nul jor ne seroie
Se sa seror ne li *menoie* . . . (61–64; 74–75; 264–68; my italics)

[And if he forbids her the journey so that she can see her sister, then she asks
that he go fetch her and bring her back to her land. . . . At his departure
Progné asks him to bring her sister back to her soon. . . ."For so she said to
me, and didn't hide it, when I took leave of her that I wouldn't be her lord
or her sweetheart for one more day if I didn't bring her sister back to her."]

Later, Tereus makes his plea to the king, linking Progne's requests to his
own plea to take Philomena back with him ["Tant que je avuec moi *l'an
maigne*"] (334; my emphasis). Meanwhile, Tereus himself wants to carry
off Philomena in a different sense. Obsessed with her beauty and charm,
he fantasizes about taking her by force if he can't win her by love, or else
'carrying her off' secretly at night ["Ou par nuit *mener* an amblee"] (467;
my italics).

The ensuing contest between Tereus and Pandion over Philomena turns
on the conditions attached to her removal from the patriarchal household.
The Old French writer uses the pledge scene between Tereus and Pandion
to repeat the verb:

Biaus sire, car la me bailliez
Par tel covant qu'einçois quinzainne
La vos *ramanrai* liee et sainne . . . (534–36)

["Noble sire, do turn her over to me, on the pledge that in two weeks I will
bring her back to you happy and well."]

Pandion, moved to pity, agrees to accept his pledges: "you shall take my
daughter off tomorrow" [*an manras* ma fille demain] (561), provided that
Tereus "bring her back" on time [Et *ramenez* jusqu'a cort terme]. The king
dwells on the words "fille" and "ramener" still further:

Ja mi oel ne seront sanz lerme
Ne mes cuers liez por rien qu'avaingne
Jusque ma fille a moi revaingne.
Se m'amor volez retenir
Don pansez del tost revenir
Et de ma *fille ramener.* (566–71; my italics)

[My eyes will never be dry, nor my heart happy over any event until my daughter comes back to me. If you wish to keep my love, then think of coming back soon and bringing back my daughter.]

Tereus replies:

"Non ferai je," dist Tereus,
"Sire, ja mes n'an parlez plus,
Car plus m'iert tart qu'a vos assez
Que de ça soie repassez
Et que je l'aie *ramenee.*" (575–79)

["I won't, sire," said Tereus, "now speak no more of it, for the later it will be for me it will be for you, and the more delayed I will be from bringing her back."]

The verb *mener* allows the narrator to exploit the many ironies in this farewell scene. The next day, Tereus "leads" Philomena and company down to the waiting ships ["Au port *l'an mainne* Tereus"] (684), escorted by Pandion and his court. Pandion repeatedly asks his "fille" to return soon, kisses her, and asks her to pledge a quick return, and turns back to her "mil foiz." The narrator adds that soon Pandion would badly deliver the maiden whom he "leads forth" [*que il an mainne*] (717). The irony of the scene becomes ever clearer, when Pandion's copious weeping unwittingly anticipates the disaster:

Mes de tot ce ne panse il,
Et s'est ja mout pres de peril
Et de corroz *Philomena.*
Car sole *menee l'an a*
An une soe meison gaste
Cil, qui sa desverie haste. (727–32; my italics)

[But he did not imagine all this, and yet Philomena is already very close to peril and grief, for he whose madness drives him now carries her off alone to a deserted hut.]

Philomena, in other words, is being "led off" to grief [*corroz*]. This passage
recalls another meaning of the verb *mener:* to "lead forth" a woman is also
to wed her. The passage thus suggests that Philomena's being led forth by
Tereus is a degraded version of Progne's own marriage, in which Pandion
had shown as little care:

> Quant les noces furent finees,
> *S'an mena* Tereus sa fame
> An Trace come haute dame. (32–34; my italics)

> [When the wedding was over Tereus carried his wife back to Thrace like a
> noble lady.]

When Tereus reveals his true intentions, Philomena realizes that she has
been "forcibly led" [*demenee*] to "great shame" [*a tel honte*] (806). This most
negative meaning of *mener* is fulfilled at the very end of the story, when the
enraged Tereus jumps up to pursue the fleeing women:

> Ainz s'an fuient, et cil les chace.
> Qui del ocire les menace,
> Si con ses mautalanz l'aporte
> Jusqu'a l'issue d'une porte
> Les a chaciees et *menees*. (1437–41; my italics)

> [Thus they both flee, and he chases them and threatens to kill them as his evil
> rage transports him. He has chased and threatened them up to a doorway.]

As we have seen, *mener* has a spectrum of related yet distinct meanings.
In the course of the story, the meaning of the verb extends from the neutral sense of bringing or leading someone off, to that of violently attack-
ing them. Here, at the end of the tale, the play of meanings around the verb
mener reaches its climax. Tereus's final human act is unambiguously violent.
The verb *mener* [*menees*] has become an expression of pure aggression.
Thus, while the transformation of Tereus, Progne, and Philomena into
birds signifies the utter loss of humanity on the level of plot, the progressive semantic shifts represent a similar return to a more primitive state.
From an etymological perspective, the Old French text offers a gradual
revelation of the verb's ominous core meaning, "to threaten or to drive
forth," that lies beneath its more general meaning.

Because the tapestry retells the story in veiled form, it is an emblem for
narrative art. As a gendered art-form, however, the tapestry resists such a
neat allegorical interpretation. As we have shown, the play on *fille, fil,* and
Phil marks the tapestry/text as female. Although Ovid and his tradition al-

ready genders the art of embroidery as female, the feminizing principle is much more visible in the verbal play of the Old French text. As Burns and others have noted, the tapestry reunites the sisters by being passed through a series of female hands as fibers and threads pass through their hands in the cloth-making process. Within the plot (both the author's and Philomena's), the tapestry metaphorically serves to "re-member" the mutilated daughter by telling her story. Likewise, Progne's revenge plot implies that the daughter's tapestry/text may provoke reciprocal violence and cut off the lineage. Rape in this text thus entwines deeply with aristocratic marriage practices, a concept revealed in this work's linkage of the threads of tapestry with the threads of kinship, lineage, and inheritance.

Ultimately, the play between the signifiers evoked by Philomena's name and the multiple meanings of her weaving suggest that the tapestry is a metaphor for the *Philomena* itself, signifying the text's potentially destabilizing effect upon its listeners. This adaptation of an Ovidian tale, while displaying many elements of courtly taste, tests the limits of the courtly appropriation of myth, for it suggests that savage, disruptive violence lies within the closest family ties, within the most beautiful and accomplished heroine, and within writing itself.

Notes

1. Thus, Patricia Klindienst Joplin argues against a universalizing reading and readings that mystify the myth's sexual violence. She asserts that Philomela the weaver/artist must first be recognized as female, and then as human. Cf. "The Voice of the Shuttle is Ours," *Stanford Literature Review* 1 (Spring, 1984): 26. For a wide-ranging feminist critique of historical and literary representations of rape, see the collection, *Representing Rape,* ed. Brenda Silver and Lynn Higgins (New York: Columbia University Press, 1991).

2. Textile metaphors for voice and writing have become the hypertrope of feminist criticism. For two recent discussions of the figuration of the woman writer and reader as spinner, weaver, or embroideress, see: Nancy K. Miller, "Arachnologies: The Woman, the Text, and the Critic," in *The Poetics of Gender,* ed. Nancy K. Miller (New York: Columbia University Press, 1980), pp. 270–95; and Christine Froula, "The Daughter's Seduction Sexual Violence and Literary History," in *Daughters and Fathers,* ed. Lynda F. Boose and Betty S. Flowers (Baltimore: Johns Hopkins University Press, 1989), pp. 111–35. Also see: Ann S. Bergren, "Language and the Female in Early Greek Thought," *Arethusa* 16 (1983) 1, 2: 69–95 and "Helen's Web: Time and Tableau in the *Iliad."* *Helios* n.s. 7, 1 (1980): 19–34, and Rozika Parker, *The Subversive Stitch: Embroidery and the Making of the Feminine* (London: Women's Press, 1986).

3. All quotations have been taken from the edition by C. De Boer, *Philomena: Conte Raconté d'après Ovide* (Paris: P. Geuther, 1909). De Boer explains that

the shift in the spelling of the heroine's name from the original Greek form "Philomela," meaning "nightingale" to the form found in the romance is a result of the dissimulation of the vowels *1* and *n* and of the confusion between the original form and the Greek proper name "Philumena" meaning "she who is loved," associated with the virgin martyr of this name. The author of the Old French *Philomena* would have found the heroine's name already spelled with an 'n' in the Latin manuscripts of Ovid copied in France (pp. 97 and 123).

4. Paris's article, "Chrétien Legouais et autres traducteurs ou imitateurs de Ovide," *Histoire Littéraire de France* 29 (1885): 455–517, first attributed the interpolated text to Chrétien, and De Boer (1909) produces lengthy arguments to support this attribution in the introduction to his edition (pp. icxx). A general bibliography on the ensuing debate about authorship appears in Raymond J. Cormier, ed. and trans., *Three Ovidian Tales of Love,* Garland Library of Medieval Literature 26 (New York: Garland Press, 1986), pp. 193–98. More recently, Elizabeth Schultze-Busaker has argued in favor of the attribution, based on the links she sees between the use of proverbs in the *Philomena* and other works by Chrétien. See "*Philomena:* une revision de l'attribution de l'oeuvre." *Romania* 107 (1988): 459–85.

5. *Metamorphoseon Libri I-XV,* ed. B.A. van Proosdij et al. (Leiden: Brill, 1982).

6. Of the Ovidian tales, Per Nykrog writes: "Like the Lavinia episode (in the *Eneas*), they are set in the framework of a striking individual biography, and . . . , the main concern is neither political nor military, but psychological—dealing with the feelings that lead to dramatic, tragic, or rare events, rather than with those events themselves. The focus is on subjective personal experience—characteristically rendered in the form of lengthy interior monologues—more than on objective conduct." Cf. "The Rise of Literary Fiction," in *Renaissance and Renewal in the Twelfth Century,* ed. Robert L. Benson and Giles Constable (Cambridge, MA: Harvard University Press, 1982), p. 599.

7. *Piramus et Tisbé,* ed. F. Branciforti, Biblioteca dell' "Archivum Romanicum," 57 (Florence: L. S. Olschki, 1959). *Narcisse,* ed. Martine Thiry-Stassin and Madeleine Tyssens (Paris, 1976). Translations appear in Cormier, *Three Ovidian Tales of Love.*

8. Cil est mors et cele est pasmee.
   Diex, quele amor est ci finee!
   La pucele s'est acesmee,
   A ses deus mains a pris l'espee,
   Parmi le piz, souz la mamele
   Sen referest ia demoisele.
   D'ambe parz raie li sans fors,
   Le cors acole et si l'embrace,
   Baise les iex, baise la face,
   Baise la bouche par grant cure,
   Tant corn sens et vie li dure.

Tant con li dure sens et vie
Se demoustre veraie arnie.
Ici fenist des deus amanz,
Con lor leal amor fu granz. (917–32)

Li valles muert, l'ame s'en vait.
La pucele plus pres se trait;
Vers soi le trait par tel aïr,
Du cors se fait lame partir.
C'a fait Amor[s] qui la souprise.
Andui sont mort en itel guise.
Or s'i gardent tuit autre amant
Qu'il ne muirent en itel sanblant! (995–1002)

9. The *Philomena* cannot easily be assimilated to the model used to describe the chivalric romances of Chrétien de Troyes. It is difficult to accept Edith Joyce Benkov's interpretation of the *Philomena*. She argues that the poem "must be read as the first of Chrétien's *romans à thèse*," the "thèse" being a critique of the adultery plots then in vogue. "*Philomena*: Chrétien de Troyes's Reinterpretation of the Ovidian Myth," *Classical and Modern Literature* 3 (1983): 209. Adultery and seduction hardly seem to be the issue in the Philomena story. The primary theme is sexual violence, not sexual transgression: this is a story of brutal rape, incest, and murder. Its erotic triangle consists not of an uncle, nephew, and bride, as in the Tristan and Arthurian legends, but a degraded one between husband, wife, and sister, brought forcibly into being by the man's treachery and rape.

10. See *Ravishing Maidens: Reading Rape in Medieval French Literature and Law* (Philadelphia: University of Pennsylvania Press, 1991) and *Bodytalk* (Philadelphia: University of Pennsylvania Press, 1993). Also see Burns's essay in this volume.

11. Wendy Pfeffer, *The Change of Philomel* (New York: Peter Lang, 1985), p. 136.

12. "La demoiselle 'esforciée' dans le roman arthurien" in *Amour, mariage, et transgressions au moyenâge,* ed. Danielle Buschinger and André Crépin (Goppingen: Kümmerle, 1984), pp. 215–24.

13. For information on the twelfth-century manuscripts of the work, see Claire Gruzebier's edition of the text (Oxford: Clarendon Press, 1993).

14. On the Old French and Middle English instances of the call of the nightingale as "Oci" or "Ocy," see Otto Glauning, *Lydgate's Minor Poetry: The Two Nightingale Poems* (Millwood, NY: Kraus Reprint, 1987), pp. 35–38; F. J. F. Raby, "Philomena praevia temporis amoeni," *Mélanges Joseph de Ghellinck* (Gembboux: Ducubot, 1951), vol. 2, pp. 435–48; and Pfeffer, op. cit., pp. 39–41 and 134–40. Pfeffer discusses the nightingale's cry of "Oci! Oci" in two songs by the thirteenth-century trouvère, Guillaurne be Vinier, "Li louseignoles avrillouz" and "Mout a mon cuer esjoi." According to Pfeffer, Guillaume le Vinier "appears to be the first to put an imitation of the bird

song into lyric poetry" (136). She follows Guillaume's editor, Philippe Mé-
nard, in citing the Old French *Philomena* (which she ascribes to Chrétien de
Troyes) as Guillaume's source. She interprets the romance's epilogue, quoted
above, as a cautionary discourse on how not to love.

15. In the *Ovide Moralisé,* the moralizing gloss designates the following scheme:
Tereus is to be understood as the Body, Progné as the Soul, and Philomena
as False Love (lines 35–73 of excerpt, rpt. in De Boer, pp. 142–43).

16. Charles Segal, "La tela di Filomela e i piaceri del testo: il mito di Tereo nelle
Metamorfosi," in *Ovidio e la poesia del mito* (Venice: Marsilio editori, 1991),
pp. 190–91.

17. My assumption of a lineage-minded audience is based on the rich historical literature on the evolution of kinship relations in medieval France that
has followed upon the work of Marc Bloch. On the rise of patrilinear succession in eleventh-century France, see Georges Duby, "Lineage, Nobility,
and Knighthood: The Mâconnais in the Twelfth Century," in *The Chivalrous Society,* trans. Cynthia Postan (Berkeley: University of California Press,
1980), pp. 59–80. Duby has since elaborated upon the social consequences
of the agnatic lineage on aristocratic society in numerous other articles and
books, most recently "Aristocratic Households of Feudal France" in *A History of Private Life: Revelations of the Medieval World* ed. Georges Duby (Cambridge, MA: Harvard University Press, 1988), pp. 35–85. Kinship relations
and women's experiences within the family are discussed in the same section by Dominique Barthélemy, pp. 85–155. Much has been written about
twelfth-century genealogical literature—chronicles, epics, and romances—
with its interest in the rise, decline and fall of great lineages. Barthélemy
asserts the interpretive value of literary sources for the reconstruction of
life in secular aristocratic households (p. 93).

Duby's work on the status of women in aristocratic families in North-
ern France is controversial. American historians working on inheritance
patterns in regions other than the Mâconnais have questioned the general
validity of his conclusions about the ubiquity of primogeniture and patrilineal family structure in the twelfth century. See the critiques by David
Herlihy, *Medieval Households* (Cambridge, MA: Harvard University Press),
pp. 79–111; Theodore Evergates, "Nobles and Knights in Twelfth-Century
France," in *Cultures of Power: Lordship, Status, and Process in Twelfth-Century
Europe,* ed. Thomas N. Bisson (Philadelphia: University of Pennsylvania
Press, 1995), pp. 17–28; and Amy Livingstone, "Kith and Kin: Kinship and
Family Structure of the Nobility of Eleventh- and Twelfth-Century Blois-
Chartres." *French Historical Studies* 20 (1997): 419–58. His studies have been
criticized more broadly on ideological and methodological grounds by
feminist historians as exemplified by the papers delivered by Amy Livingstone, Linda F. Mitchell, Sharon Farmer, and Constance Bouchard in a session entitled "The Legacy of Georges Duby: Family, Marriage and
Women," organized by Professor Livingstone at the Thirty-Third International Congress on Medieval Studies at the University of Western Michi-

gan, May 8, 1998. While much of the criticism of Duby's work is justified, and he may have paid insufficient attention to the voices of women in a variety of historical sources, there remains strong evidence that patrilineal kinship patterns, however intermittently applied, did lessen women's rights and visibility within the aristocratic family. Livingstone herself notes that in times of diminishing fortunes, aristocratic families were less likely to practice collateral kinship.

18. While citing evidence for daughters' rights to inherit and control property during the High Middle Ages, Jo Ann McNamara and Suzanne Wemple concur with Duby that with the rise of patrilineage in the eleventh and twelfth centuries, "the daughters of the nobility suffered a severe diminuation of their rights." "The Power of Women Through the Family," in *Women and Power in the Middle Ages,* ed. Mary Erler and Maryanne Kowaleski (Athens: University of Georgia Press, 1988), p. 96.

19. *Le chevalier. la femme, et le prêtre* (Paris: Hachette, 1981), p. 273. See also Duby's remarks about the domestic promiscuity rampant within aristocratic households and the double standards applied to men's and women's sexual conduct, especially when the "adulteress" (should we not add "or rape victim"?) in question was a hindrance to the patrimony. Cf. "Aristocratic Households," pp. 80–82.

20. This mentality surfaces in accounts of Philip Augustus's repudiation of Ingeborg of Denmark after spending the night with her following their wedding in 1194. Accounts sympathetic to the king's cause state that she had "bewitched" him.

21. Cf. Duby, "Aristocratic Households," pp. 77–80, and Barthélemy, op. cit., pp. 138–40.

22. For a recent study of rape in medieval France that details customary law, see Gravdal, 1991.

23. For an interesting narrative analogy in which an innocent vulnerable child has its tongue cut off by a cruel knight after the child inadvertently witnesses an illicit sexual encounter with a married lady, see *Miracles de Notre-Dame de Chartres,* ed. Pierre Kunstmann (Ottawa: University of Ottawa Press, 1973).

24. R. Howard Bloch, *Medieval French Literature and Law* (Berkeley: University of California Press, 1977), pp. 53–57.

25. Many elements in my reading of this text parallel the anthropological approach to Old French literature outlined by R. Howard Bloch in *Etymologies and Genealogies: A Literary Anthropology of the French Middle Ages* (Chicago: University of Chicago Press, 1983). Bloch uses the term "poetics of disruption" to represent the lyric project of the troubadour Marcabru, whose songs, he argues, show an obsession with the "deleterious effects of adulterous desire" upon the lineage, and his sense of his own role, *qua* poet, as "a defiler of language" (p. 111).

26. M. Natalis Rondot, *L'industrie de la soie en France* (Lyon: Imprimerie Mougin-Rusand, 1894); Charles Foulon "Les Serves du Chateau du Pesme

Aventure," *Mélanges offerts à Rita Lejeune* (Gembloux: J. Duculot, 1969), II, p. 1004. For a more comprehensive study of the medieval women's work-room, see David Herlihy, *Opera muliebria: Women and Work in Medieval Europe* (Philadelphia: Temple University Press, 1990), pp. 75–102. According to his survey of this medieval institution, this female labor force consisted primarily of slaves, half-free tributaries, and free women condemned for crimes. The workshops were also associated with "slavery, imprisonment, and illicit sex" (84–85). Herlihy notes that the typical textile workroom contained between 10 and 40 women, far fewer than the 300 girl workers found in Chrétien's story.

27. Of this scene, Eugene Vance writes: "(I)t does not take a Marxist eye to discern that the economic message of the Château de Pesme Aventure is a thinly veiled criticism of the exploitation of labor in a nascent textile industry lying just to the west of Champagne in Flanders. . . . Chrétien and his powerful patron were quite capable, it seems, not only of revindicating certain commercial values in the dominant discourses of their time (those of the clergy and the knights) but, just as importantly, of calling for limits in the exploitation of the *laboratores* by a rapacious new middle class." "Chrétien's *Yvain* and the Ideologies of Change and Exchange," in *Images of Power: Medieval History/Discourse/Literature, Yale French Studies* 70 (1986): 59. A woman weaver appears as the subject of one of the tales in the early thirteenth-century collection edited by Pierre Kunstmann, *Miracles de Notre-Dame de Chartres* (Ottawa: University of Ottawa, 1973), VI.

28. For an analysis of this passage, see Alice M. Colby-Hall, *The Portrait in Twelfth-Century Literature* (Geneva: Librarie Droz, 1965), pp. 123–38.

29. Colby-Hall, p. 136.

30. In Ovid's text, Philomela weaves her story in scarlet thread on white cloth [*purpureasque notas filis intexuit albis*] (VI, 577). The medieval version stresses the richness of the tapestry. The old woman, upon seeing Philomena's intent to weave, supplies her with an abundant variety of thread: "Trestot li quist son aparoil, / Tant que fil inde et fil vermoil / Et jaune et vert a planté ot . . ." (1113–15) and Philomena produces a magnificent, brilliantly colored artifact.

31. Tant par fu bien fet li sorplus
    Que tant bele rien ne vit nus,
    Car Nature s'an fu penee
    Plus que de nule autre rien nee,
    S'i ot tot mis quanqu'ele pot. (165–69)
    Don ne doi je pas honte avoir
    Se je apres ces trois i fail,
    Et j'i metrai tot mon travail. (134–36)

32. The moral superiority of these two arts is implied in the prolonged scenes at the court of Athens where Tereus slyly cajoles Philomena to intercede with Pandion and plead his cause for him. She rebukes what she thinks is

sloth and cowardliness on his part with a dictum about the rightful way to
gain what one desires:

Cil qui viaut la chose avoir,
Sil a tant proesce et savoir,
Del avoir se painne et travaille,
Et s'il avient que il i faille
N'espleiter ne puisse par lui,
Lors doit feire proiier autrui. (281–85)

33. For a somewhat different reading of this scene, see the perceptive commentary by Burns.
34. See note 3 above.

CHAPTER 6

"O, KEEP ME FROM THEIR
WORSE THAN KILLING LUST":
IDEOLOGIES OF RAPE AND MUTILATION
IN CHAUCER'S *PHYSICIAN'S TALE* AND
SHAKESPEARE'S *TITUS ANDRONICUS*

Robin L. Bott

> Looking at the metaphor of rape as disease as it occurs in Chaucer
> and Shakespeare, Bott argues that such stories adversely shape societal
> beliefs about rape and the female body.

The telling and retelling of the sensational tale of Virginius and Virginia
in the literature of Medieval and Early Modern England indicates this
society's concern with the social and political consequences of sexual access to women. Recorded first by the Roman historian Livy, the story of
Virginius and Virginia is a tale of political intrigue intertwined with an additional tale of threatened rape and subsequent murder. Apius, a corrupt
judge, desires Virginia, the chaste daughter of Virginius, who murders his
daughter to counter Apius's plot to obtain her. When Apius tries to punish Virginius, the Roman people rise up and overthrow Apius, who commits suicide.[1] This version of the story provides the text of Chaucer's
Physician's Tale and other medieval works. By the sixteenth century, however, there are two versions of the Virginius and Virginia story, Livy's version in which Virginius kills his daughter before she is defiled, and an
alternate version, in which Virginius murders Virginia after she is raped.[2]
Medieval and Early Modern accounts of this story are almost always told

as an exemplum of evil government; the moral is that men who use their authority for evil purposes are always punished.[3] In these redactions of the tale, however, as the Virginiuses who have helped to restore a righteous reign step to the forefront, the Virginias who have endured unspeakable harms fade into the background. Their suffering is minimized and refigured as a small part of the larger political drama centered around the homicidal clashes of powerful men.

This essay refocuses attention on the women in these retellings to uncover the ideological implications of the violent acts performed upon their bodies. The Virginius and Virginia story in both Chaucer's *Physician's Tale* and Shakespeare's *Titus Andronicus* underscores the jeopardy to social order encoded in unauthorized sexual access to women's bodies. This jeopardy can be seen as a metaphorical disease threatening the health of the Roman state. The fact that Chaucer chooses to have his story told by a physician suggests that medical ideas of remedies and cures are being brought into the arena of this story. Implicit in Chaucer in a tale told by a physician, the metaphor of disease becomes explicit in Shakespeare's *Titus Andronicus*. In these two works, enemies attack fathers through their rapable daughters to expose these fathers and their patriarchal society to potential contagion that is abated only by the destruction of the woman. Such destruction of the female body reveals an attitude towards these raped women analogous to attitudes towards disease or diseased tissue—the damaged body part must be excised in order to prevent further harm to the whole. In this formulation, the female subject is reduced to the status of a mutilated body part or some dangerously contaminated flesh that may infect the father, making the destruction of the raped woman not only permissible, but also highly desirable.

Within both texts, women belong to and are disposed of by fathers who show more concern for personal honor than their daughters' lives. Thanks to gendered re-readings of culture and literature, the idea that women function as objects of exchange between men is now commonplace among scholars.[4] Fathers, aristocratic ones in particular, give daughters to friends and enemies in order to enlarge estates, gain political power, or otherwise profit in some social, financial, or political manner. Commercial and sexual realms are thus conflated when the successful bonding for profit between men hinges upon the chastity of the woman being exchanged. During the Medieval and Early Modern periods, not only were many women, particularly aristocratic women, treated by their menfolk like property with real social and economic value, but that value was also determined by their sexual roles. These women in both periods were assigned to rungs on a hierarchical ladder based upon sexual access; they were classified in descending order as maid, widow, or wife.[5] The absence of any other classification of woman in medieval instructional manuals such as *Hali Meithhad* implies that sexual roles, not vocational ones, identified women within the patriarchal social system.[6] Originally a spiritual categorization, this hierarchy also held social significance in both periods. Indeed, Shakespeare employs this classification in *Measure for Measure,* when the jilted Mariana comes forth to accuse Angelo of fornicating with her sans marriage.[7] Before hearing her story, the Duke asks Mariana if she is a maid, a widow, or a wife. She answers in the negative to each question. In an ideologically telling moment, the Duke then replies to Mariana, "Why, you are nothing then: neither maid, widow, nor wife?"[8] Lucio then further emphasizes Mariana's liminal position by claiming that "she may be a punk; for many of them are neither maid, widow, nor wife."[9] He provides an additional category for fallen women who are not accorded a place in the sexual hierarchy. This group includes whores, adulteresses, and other "loose" women who are unclaimed by any father, husband, or family. Dishonored through unlawful sexual contact, Mariana seeks to be reinscribed back into the hierarchy of sexual access as a wife now that she is no longer a maid. To avoid being cast out, Mariana must make herself valuable to society by repairing her reputation.[10] She must ensure that she becomes a wife; otherwise she will remain a whore, because, as Eve Sedgwick argues, "to identify *as* must always include multiple processes of identification *with*. It also involves identification *as against.*"[11] Angelo's sexual access to Mariana outside of marriage has rendered her a whore; in order for her to be identified *as* a wife, she must now be identified *with* other wives and *against* other whores. Angelo must therefore marry her and retroactively correct the wrong, making it right. Thus, social identifications based upon sexual access institutionalize the necessity to control such access to women.

Only within the hierarchy of sexual access can women serve the patriarchy as valuable objects of exchange. Since lineage, legitimacy, inheritance, and social order depend upon who has access to a woman's womb, female bodies need constant protection against depreciation and depredation. Any trespass, such as rape, "inevitably threatens the values of the patrilineal society and necessitates a breakdown of its value systems and laws."[12] This perceived threat manifests itself in the rape laws of Medieval and Early Modern England. In the medieval period, the legal discourse of the law defined rape as a crime against male property. Kathryn Gravdal maintains that medieval law "was concerned primarily with the protection of the father's rights, not those of his daughter."[13] Consequently, any crime against the female body "became a crime against the male estate."[14] From an economic view or, as Patricia Cholakian states, "from the male perspective," the raped woman "became 'damaged goods,' a potential carrier of alien seed who could no longer be exchanged for political or economic gain."[15] By placing a price tag on a woman's womb, rape law reflected and contributed to social views of women as property. However, the commercial metaphor fails to explain satisfactorily why in the *Physician's Tale* and *Titus Andronicus,* Virginius and Titus kill their daughters. The answer lies in looking at women's bodies in relation to the larger body of society.

While the commercial metaphor explains *how* Virginius and Titus can murder their daughters (as property, these women can be disposed of as their fathers see fit), the analogy of the physical body and its relation to the social body helps to explain *why* murder is the outcome. As is well known, it was common during the Medieval and Early Modern periods to compare the workings of society or government to the workings of a physical body. Similarly, the machinations of society were linked metaphorically to the operations of the literal body.[16] Regarding the literal body in the Middle Ages, Linda Lomperis and Sarah Stanbury argue that the political function "of making the body intelligible—indeed, of establishing its literal existence—demands that one regard it as a politically charged discursive construct, a representational space traversed in various ways by socially based power relations."[17] Not only does the literal body represent the figurative body and vice versa in politically significant ways, but, as Peggy McCracken maintains, the physical body may also be used to symbolize anxieties and tensions about social stability, or it may be used to contain those anxieties.[18] It seems that in Chaucer's tale and Shakespeare's play, horrific dismemberings of the physical bodies of women perform both functions—to symbolize and contain anxieties about social stability. Acts of violence against the physical body represent the decimation of the larger political body; but these acts are also a means of containment in the fight to reestablish social order.

Indeed, women are more than objects of value, they are "members" of society: literal individuals among a group of individuals as well as figuratively interconnected parts of a whole. If we examine attitudes about raped women in light of their role as members of the larger body of society, we can better understand why Virginia in the *Physician's Tale* and Lavinia in *Titus Andronicus* are killed. In both texts, the economic model fails to explain why destruction is the only remedy for raped women, because rape does more than damage goods, it pollutes them. As Carolyn Williams argues:

> [The raped woman's] physical condition determines her status. She is a contaminant to her entire family; if she cannot be married to her ravisher, she must be segregated from former contacts. In ancient Rome, such pollution—whether incurred by rape or adultery—could be removed only by death.[19]

From this perspective, the raped woman is more than devalued property, she is a "contaminant" to her entire family, and her rape is a "pollution." Within a physical body, such contamination or pollution can be the result of disease. Social attitudes towards disease are similar to those associated with contamination or pollution: disease is threatening to society and must be contained or, if possible, eradicated. Likewise, diseased tissue in a body must be cured or removed to prevent the spread of disease to the rest of the body. The disease analogy explains more satisfactorily why segregation seems desirable: the literal rape infects the woman and that infection figuratively threatens the health and safety of her family and other "contacts." Thus, when Virginius and Titus murder their daughters, they behave like a literal body warding off infection in itself, or like a surgeon amputating a diseased limb. As literal and figurative "members" of society, raped women in both tales are more than damaged goods, they are diseased tissue to be removed from the larger body of society in order to prevent the spread of infection.

Both Chaucer and Shakespeare preserve and improve upon the classical Roman solution for rape in their retellings of the Virginius and Virginia story by incorporating within their works the metaphor of disease. This metaphor is implicit in Chaucer's story when told by the Physician and then more explicit in Shakespeare. From the beginning of his tale, the Physician links the overall health of the state to the responsibility of parents and other adults to protect the innocence and moral well-being of children. In his prologue to the tale, the Physician discusses at length the importance of proper adult supervision of children, and he claims that "Of all tresons sovereyn pestilence / Is whan a wight bitrayseth innocence."[20] According to the OED, some of the definitions of "treson" current in Chaucer's day included "the action of betraying a trust," a "breach of faith," and a "treacherous action." In addition, high treason was a subject's violation of "his allegiance to his sovereign or to the state," while petty treason was considered "the murder of one to whom the murderer owes allegiance." Both public and private as well as political and personal types of betrayal are connoted in the word "treson." Likewise "sovereyn," while in this case means "supreme" or "greatest," also connotes a supremacy of rank. The Physician does not emphasize "pestilence" with "supreme" or "greatest," but with the adjective "sovereyn," again adding a political flavor to his phrasing. As for the word "pestilence," the OED provides several meanings, all current during Chaucer's time, including (1) "any fatal epidemic disease, affecting man or beast, and destroying many victims," (2) "the bubonic plague," (3) "that which is morally pestilent or pernicious; moral plague or mischief, evil conduct, wickedness," (4) "that which is fatal to the public peace or well-being," and (5) "a cause of trouble or injury." Hence, "pestilence" was not only literal disease, but it was also moral wickedness, a cause of injury, and fatal to many victims as well as to public peace or well-being. Before he even begins his story, the Physician sets the tone for the tale: that an adult's betrayal of a child's innocence will occur, and such an act will constitute a breach of faith and a violation of allegiance so grievous that this moral plague is likened to a supremely fatal epidemic disease that can jeopardize the well-being of an entire state. From the outset, Chaucer through his choice of a Physician-narrator and the Physician's richly connotative choice of words, invites a medical reading of Livy's tale of political corruption. A problem within the tale arises, however, when Virginius mislocates the source of disease in his daughter's body rather than in his failure and Apius's failure to protect Virginia's innocence.

If we use the body metaphor to discuss raped women as diseased members plaguing the social body, then the two methods of healing the body can be described as preventative and curative. In the *Physician's Tale,* Chaucer follows Livy and chooses the preventative approach: Virginius kills his daughter before she is raped, thereby separating the potentially diseased member from the social body *before* it is infected. After Apius's false judgement on Virginia, Virginius returns home to tell his daughter that "Ther been two weyes, outher deeth or shame, / That thou most suffre" (ll. 214–15). The two offered solutions betray his anxieties and, by extension, his patriarchal society's anxieties about raped women: that they should not be allowed to remain within the fellowship of the system. For Virginius, there is no middle road between death and shame as he chooses death for his daughter, saying, "Take thou thy deeth, for this is my sentence" (l. 224). Virginia, understandably, pleads with her father, "Goode fader, shal I dye? / Is ther no grace, is ther no remedye?" (ll. 234–35). Here, in the storyteller's voice of the Physician, the idea of remedy has particular resonance. The *OED* demonstrates that both definitions of "remedye," as (1) a cure for disease and (2) an alternative, were current in the Middle Ages. Hence, Chaucer has the Physician narrate Virginia asking for an alternative "remedye" or "cure" for her condition that does not include death or shame. In other words, Virginia asks for a second opinion. Virginius rejects Virginia's request, denying her any other alternative but death. After allowing her a space of time to mourn her virginity, Virginius cuts off Virginia's head and takes it to Apius. Virginius chooses death over shame for his daughter to prevent her from becoming his "laste wo" (l. 221) by being forced "in lecherie to lyven" (l. 206) with Apius. Significantly, Virginius's planned murder of Virginia, his announcement of it and his execution of it at home, is original to Chaucer.[21] By retelling the Virginius story and embellishing it with the father's premeditation of murder, the physician does his part to reflect and perpetuate social views of women as disposable property.

When Virginius tells his daughter that there are only two ways, death or shame, that she must suffer, and then chooses death for her, he robs her of any agency to find a suitable alternative for herself. The ideological message encoded in his decision is that Virginia is an object, a possession of her father with no right to her own body. Even more chilling is that Chaucer, through his Physician, has Virginia assert her absorption of the ideological view of herself as property when she validates her father's claim to her body by consenting to his plan: "'Yif me my deeth, er that I have a shame; / Dooth with youre child youre wyl'" (ll. 249–50). In addition, commercial and sexual worlds merge when Virginius calls Virginia his "'gemme of chastitee'" (l. 223): not only is she an object of value, but that value is determined by her sexual purity. More than a precious jewel, though, Virginia is a valuable part of Virginius's anatomy. Even her name signifies that she is a part of the whole that is her father—again, the body and member analogy. With the threat of rape, more is at stake than a possession's lost value; the possessor's social well-being or honor is in jeopardy. Virginius cannot merely discard his soon-to-be tarnished gem because Virginia is more integrally connected to him than that. In order to preserve his own honor, Virginius must remove his appendage, Virginia, from further contact with himself. Driven by his own anxieties over the threat of rape and not the occurrence of it, Virginius tells Virginia: "For love, and nat for hate, thou most be deed; / My pitous hand moot smyten thyn heed." (ll. 225–26). Certainly Virginius kills Virginia out of love, but for love of whom? Virginius chooses between his own survival and that of his appendage, his "deere doghter myn" (l. 237). By destroying Virginia, whom Virginius acknowledges as the "endere of my lyf" (l. 218), he preventatively cures himself of the possible infection that his daughter's defilement and subsequent shame would have brought him, ending her life before she can end his.

However, the real malady infecting the patriarchal social body is the homosocial power struggle between Virginius and Apius. As Lomperis argues:

> Male homosocial relations, in short, are dominant right to the end of the tale. The maid's own body, her own sexuality, becomes in this instance little more than the space across which these power relations move.[22]

Virginia's body is merely one of the locations where that struggle takes place. Destroying her body alleviates but does not cure the real infection, patriarchal rivalry manifested through rape. Her body is just one "battlefield, a parade ground for the victor's trooping of the colors."[23] Another battle site is in the courtroom where Apius manipulates the law and awards custody of Virginia to his friend, who in turn will hand her over to Apius. Vanquished by Apius and the law, Virginius finds that he "Moste by force his deere doghter yiven / Unto the juge, in lecherie to lyven" (ll. 205–6). Unable to wage war against Apius in the courts, Virginius the "worthy knyght" (l. 202) retreats to yet another battle site: he moves to surer ground, his home, and counterattacks Apius. At home, Virginius overrides Apius's judgement with a verdict of his own, telling Virginia, "'Take thou thy deeth, for this is *my* sentence'" (l. 224, my emphasis). Using the same legal rhetoric of sentencing as Apius, he asserts the superiority of his own laws and judgements.

In this contest of wit and wills, Virginius succeeds against Apius. By murdering his daughter, Virginius overturns Apius's recent courtroom victory, and he reclaims control over the situation and over the flesh of his flesh. Taking his daughter's maiden head for himself, Virginius successfully denies Apius access to her other maidenhead. The beheading of Virginia powerfully confirms the absolute control Virginius demands and exercises over the body of his daughter. Furthermore, his public presentation of Virginia's severed head to Apius not only vanquishes Apius through its blatant disregard of his judgement, but it also establishes Virginius as the final victor in the fight for Virginia's body. While murdering Virginia before she is defiled may preserve her reputation, more importantly, her death safeguards Virginius's own honor and shows Apius that despite his corrupt judgement, Virginius is still master of his own body and the product of that body.

Chaucer and his Physician-narrator forget about Virginia's suffering as her murder fades into the background of the larger political drama of this tale. The people of Rome are silently indifferent to Virginia's plight: no one comes forward at the beginning to counter Apius's false judgement, no one intervenes to save Virginia from Apius or Virginius, and no one mentions her death at the end. Instead, the focus of Chaucer's tale centers on the cleansing of evil government and the reestablishment of political order. Only after Apius threatens to punish Virginius for his act does anyone intervene to save Virginius (l. 260). Other elements of contagion are eliminated from the body of Rome: the corrupt people of Apius's party are hanged and the false claimant Claudius is exiled. However, Virginia remains an unmourned and unmentioned casualty of this political pruning. The complete lack of concern over Virginia's death at the end of the *Physician's Tale* sends a disturbing message that female suffering is inconsequential compared to the reestablishment of righteous government—an act that really boils down to one powerful male defeating another.

From the beginning of the tale, the message that parents ultimately control the destinies of children is clear. The Physician-narrator holds parents and other adults employed to care for children accountable for their moral well-being. He further claims that any betrayal of a child's innocence is the worst type of treason: "Of all tresons sovereyn pestilence / Is whan a wight

bitrayseth innocence" (ll. 91–92). The medical, moral, and political connotations present in his language link the physical health of individuals to the
political well-being of the state. Obviously Apius's evil conduct is a pestilence, making him guilty of treason against Virginia, but Virginius's murder
of his daughter, one to whom he owes allegiance, also makes him guilty of
treason. He betrays Virginia and her innocence, allowing his daughter no
other "remedy" or cure but death. By murdering his daughter, Virginius
purchases his honor with her blood. The words "sovereyn pestilence" or
supreme wickedness also connote disease, suggesting that Apius's and Virginius's acts of betrayal are a cause of contagion within society. Their personal betrayal of Virginia as contagion also takes on a political significance
with the word "treson." Not only do their characters commit treason, but
Chaucer and his Physician-narrator also betray Virginia's innocence by
retelling a tale of violence against women for public consumption.
Chaucer even "improves" upon the horrific details of the original
source—Virginius's premeditation of Virginia's murder, his announcement
of it, and his execution of it at home are original to the *Physician's Tale*.[24]
Not even Chaucer breaks away from his society's attitudes about sexual
pollution of women; instead, he perpetuates them. Although his Physician
promisingly begins his tale by identifying adult betrayal of innocence as a
cause of societal disease, in his execution of the tale the "sovereyn pestilence" becomes Virginia herself, rather than the treason committed against
her. Her death reinforces the notion that part of the cure for such "pestilence," or "that which is fatal to the public peace or well-being," must involve the destruction of the female body.

In the Early Modern period, Shakespeare incorporates this tale of violence into his wildly popular revenge tragedy, *Titus Andronicus*
(1593–94). Numerous references to Rome as a body infected and mutilated suggest a link between certain medical practices and notions of disease and the moral and political machinations of society. Shakespeare
adopts the alternate version of the Virginius and Virginia story current
during the Renaissance in which the father kills his daughter *after* she has
been raped. This curative approach—the diseased appendage is removed
after it is infected—demonstrates the theory that radical surgery performed on infected members helps to heal the sickened body of Rome.
As subtext—Titus refers to the Virginius and Virginia tale right before he
kills Lavinia in act 5, scene 3—the tale informs the larger issue of the play:
the effect of the growth and spread of a type of "sovereyn pestilence" or
political corruption in the body of Rome. Shakespeare's references
throughout the play to Rome as an unhealthy body invite a comparison
between the political and social causes of Rome's malaise and a disease
plaguing a physical body. This disease manifests itself as sexual violence

and adulterous fornication. For instance, Lucius offers the two instances of sexual transgression, the rape of Lavinia and the adultery of Tamora, as the reasons for Rome's "civil wound,"[25] suggesting that unauthorized sexual access to women creates lesions on the body of society. In *Titus Andronicus,* the outside invaders responsible for bringing this injury and attendant disease into the body of Rome are the Goth queen Tamora, her sons Demetrius and Chiron, and the Moor, Aaron. Metaphorically, these foreign others seem to function as disease-bearing agents who lacerate the body of Rome and infect it.

As a political body, however, Rome is already weakened from the internal strife of fighting factions in the government. From the outset Rome is "headless" (I, i, 186), a decapitated body in search of a new emperor to head it. The headless body of Rome is severed further into three parts: those who want Saturninus for emperor, those who side with Bassianus, and those who favor Titus. In addition to the question of succession, Saturninus's appropriation of Lavinia in the opening scene, Bassianus's reappropriation of her, the resulting quarrel between Titus and his sons, Saturninus's freeing of the Goths, and his hasty marriage to Tamora all signal the chaotic state of Rome's social system. The unhealthy body of Rome is a primed and easy target, ready for destructive foreign bodies to invade and infect it. Titus, who has left the body of Rome to conquer the Goths, is responsible for bringing these sources of contagion back to his society. When Titus returns to Rome with Tamora of the Goths and her Moorish lover, Aaron, in tow, he in effect looses upon the body of Rome two foreign organisms whose sole desire is to destroy their host/conqueror.

In order to succeed at their task, Tamora and Aaron plot to destroy the most powerful parts of Rome's body, Saturninus and Titus Andronicus, through illicit sexual acts. Like Claudius, who poisons his brother King Hamlet, and then takes his wife, Aaron will ruin Rome through his adulterous relationship with Tamora, the new emperor's bride. He will:

> wanton with this queen,
> This goddess, this Semiramis, this nymph,
> This siren that will charm Rome's Saturnine,
> And see his shipwreck and his commonweal's. (*Titus,* II, i, 21–24)

Aaron explicitly links adultery to social and political ruin. Like the leprous liquor used on old Hamlet that enters his ear and poisons his body from the head downwards, Aaron's unlawful sexual relationship with Tamora will be the bane of Saturninus and Rome, spreading pestilence downwards from the ruling head of Rome through its entire social and political body. Although Tamora consents to sexual relations with Aaron, the effect politically is the same as rape in that their fornication wounds the wronged husband. As Williams argues, "cuckolding is a sexual act performed by one man upon another. . . . The cuckold's dishonour is an 'unfelt sore' . . . until he is enlightened."[26] In other words, Aaron's sexual plundering of Tamora in effect rapes Saturninus. However, Tamora is now "incorporate in Rome" (I, i, 460) or part of the body of Rome, sharing the position of head with Saturninus. When Aaron "does" Tamora, he also undoes Rome, since the queen's political role, according to McCracken, is "entirely located in her physical body: the major duty of her office is to produce heirs in order to guarantee succession and political and social stability."[27] Consequently, not only does Aaron harm Saturninus himself by polluting the Emperor's legitimate line of succession, but he also jeopardizes the stability of the social body.

Just as Aaron seeks to ruin Saturninus through sexually contaminating Tamora, so he plots Titus's destruction by having Chiron and Demetrius rape Lavinia. Plotting the rape of Lavinia poses no moral dilemma for Aaron, Chiron, and Demetrius because they have already objectified her. She is likened to a little bit of water stolen from a miller, a slice pilfered from a cut loaf, and a doe struck down and poached from her keeper (II, i, 85–94). Lavinia's chastity becomes nothing more than a piece of a whole to be stolen from her owner. Her humanity vanishes as Aaron ceases to talk about her as a human being but as a "dainty doe." Using a hunting metaphor, he admonishes the boys to "Single you thither then this dainty doe, / And strike her home by force" (II, i, 117–18.). Significantly, they will attack Lavinia during the royal hunt scheduled for the next morning. Against the backdrop of the royal hunt, Lavinia becomes an animal fit for poaching, a royal prize to be stolen from her royal owner. She is objectified further as treasure when Aaron finalizes the plot for her rape: "There speak, and strike, brave boys, and take your turns, / There serve your lust, shadowed from heaven's eye, / And revel in Lavinia's treasury" (II, i, 129–31). Once more the sexual and the commercial realms commingle, as sex with Lavinia becomes a material plundering of her coffers. From the outset, Lavinia herself means nothing to her attackers; instead, she is merely a means to several ends. She is used to satisfy sexual lust, to cuckold her husband, and, most importantly, to gain revenge on Titus Andronicus.

Again, sexual trespass, in this case violent rape, becomes instrumental in Tamora's plot to destroy Titus. Defenseless in the woods with Tamora and her sons, knowing that she is about to be raped, Lavinia realizes that, like Virginia, there are only two options available to her, either death or shame. She desperately begs Tamora for death:

> O, keep me from their worse than killing lust,
> And tumble me into some loathsome pit,

Where never man's eye may behold my body:
Do this, and be a charitable murderer. (II, iii, 175–78)

Lavinia understands her function as a chaste woman in the patriarchy and comprehends the damaging effects of rape to herself and her society. She voices the ideological tenet that rape is a fate worse than death, and murder an act of mercy. Tamora, who also knows the social consequences of rape, refuses to grant her request. Not a "charitable murderer," Tamora wants Lavinia to suffer this "worse than killing lust," because the shame of rape will hurt Titus worse than merely killing her. As in the *Physician's Tale,* death before shame seems like a blessing, one that Lavinia, unlike Virginia, cannot claim. Realizing that her fate is inevitable, Lavinia asks that her body be destroyed and hidden that no "man's eye may behold" it; instead, Tamora sees to it that Lavinia survives her shame so that she may in turn infect her father with it.

Lavinia's pain fades into the background as her rape and mutilation become one instance in a series of wounds inflicted upon Titus's social and political body. Indeed, Titus views Lavinia's violation as an attack upon himself: "It was my dear, and he that wounded her / Hath hurt me more than had he kill'd me dead" (III, i, 91–92). His words confirm the chilling success of Tamora and Aaron's plot. While he echoes Lavinia's earlier assertion that rape is a "worse than killing lust," to Titus it is an act that has harmed himself, not his daughter, more than death itself. Tamora and Aaron systematically continue to mutilate the social and political "body" of Titus Andronicus, which includes his martial reputation, the valor of his sons, and the purity of his daughter. Just as Titus's dismembering of Alarbus in the opening scene symbolized and punctuated his destruction of the Goth nation, so the literal dismemberings of his hand, his sons' heads, and Lavinia's hands and tongue are an emblematic amputation of body parts vital to Titus's social and political strength. The loss of his hand signifies the loss of his military career, the wrongful execution of his sons for Bassianus's murder signifies the loss of Titus's honor, and the mutilation of Lavinia signifies the devaluing of his property. Through the act of rape, Chiron and Demetrius become conquering soldiers. According to Brownmiller, rape by a conquering soldier "destroys all remaining illusions of power and property for men of the defeated side."[28] Like vandals who destroy the value of an owner's property, Chiron and Demetrius rob Titus of the patriarchal bargaining power that comes with possession of a stainless daughter. Lavinia's rape symbolically castrates Titus of his ability to create a socially advantageous bond through marriage and denies him the possibility of legitimate heirs.

The damage to Titus is more than social and emotional, however; it is also politicized as treason against Rome. From the beginning of the play,

Shakespeare's characters speak of rape, both as abduction and as sexual violence, as an act of treason. When Bassianus calls upon a prior claim to Lavinia and carries her away from Saturninus, both Saturninus and Titus—who has just "given" Lavinia to the new emperor in token of his fealty—decry Bassianus and the Andronici sons who support him as traitors. Saturninus threatens Bassianus: "Traitor, if Rome have law, or we have power, / Thou and thy faction shall repent this rape" (I, i, 403–4). In this case, rape as abduction becomes treason and a crime against Saturninus and Rome. Similarly, at the end of the play, Titus labels rape as sexual violence an act of treason. Just as Saturninus represents the body of Rome, so Titus, from the Roman people's perspective, also represents the body of Rome. Titus therefore views Lavinia's rape as a crime against himself and Rome. No ordinary woman, Lavinia is "Rome's rich ornament" (I, i, 52), an object of value and desire not only of her family, but also of Rome. Like Virginia, Lavinia's name carries some symbolic significance. Lavinia was the name of Aeneas's last wife and daughter of King Latinus, who was considered the mother of the Roman people. The name itself is the feminine form of Latinus, which derives from Latium, the area surrounding and including ancient Rome. So, connoted in Lavinia's name is the origin and identity of Rome itself. Crimes against her body are not only crimes against Titus's body, they are crimes against the body of Rome. Titus highlights this political significance before he kills his daughter's attackers, explaining the importance of her chastity and the severity of their deed:

> Both her sweet hands, her tongue, and that more dear
> Than hands or tongue, her spotless chastity,
> Inhuman traitors, you constrain'd and forc'd. (V, ii, 175–77)

By labeling his daughter's attackers "Inhuman traitors," Titus constructs Lavinia's rape as an act of treason, punishable by death, and thus justifies the vengeance he takes on Chiron and Demetrius. This capital offense against Titus and Rome, the staining of Lavinia's "spotless chastity," has caused the "unrecuring" or incurable "wound" (III, i, 90) that Marcus speaks of—a wound that can only be removed from the social body with Lavinia's murder at the end of the play. Again, rape described as an incurable wound suggests a metaphorical link between sexual violence and disease.

Rape in this play also serves as a political message of conquest etched on Lavinia's body, sent from one rival to another. Raped and mutilated, her body becomes a slate on which Tamora and her sons scrawl a message of victory to Titus. At first, however, this message of rape and victory located on Lavinia's body is indecipherable to Titus and the Andronici. Of course, Lavinia's hewn off hands and tongue cause Titus's brother, Marcus, to exclaim:

> But sure some Tereus hath deflow'red thee,
> And lest thou shouldst detect [him], cut thy tongue.
> Ah, now thou turn'st away thy face for shame! (II, iv, 26–28)

But despite this obvious comparison to the rape of Philomela and Lavinia's visible reaction to it, neither Marcus nor Titus draw the conclusion that Lavinia has indeed been raped. In fact, for much of the action after this scene, Titus cannot read correctly the signs carved upon Lavinia's body. He constantly asks her to give him a sign, but cannot read what is already there. Two acts elapse before Lavinia shows the Andronici that she was raped by pointing out to them the tale of Philomela in a storybook. Only then does Titus remark:

> This is the tragic tale of Philomel,
> And treats of Tereus' treason and his rape—
> And rape, I fear, was root of thy annoy. (IV, i, 47–49)

However, still a little confused, Titus again asks Lavinia for signs. By this point in the play, Shakespeare pushes the convention of dramatic irony beyond comfortable limits. The Andronici's inability to discover Lavinia's rape draws out for the audience the pain of her situation. Their ineptitude transforms Lavinia into a grotesque spectacle, a caricature of her violated self. Her family should have recognized sooner what the audience has known for most of the play. Indeed, as Gail Kern Paster argues, the "precise and wholly conventional metonymic replacement of mouth for vagina," and "the blood flowing from Lavinia's mutilated mouth," which "stands for the vaginal wound that cannot be staged or represented," would have been immediately recognizable to sixteenth-century audiences.[29] However, the characters do not seem to get it.

This bizarre staging of Lavinia's situation is an example of how Shakespeare, like Chaucer, "improves" upon his source material: Demetrius and Chiron do Tereus one better by cutting off Lavinia's hands (Tereus only cuts out Philomela's tongue), and then Shakespeare has Lavinia, mutilated and bleeding, paraded around the stage for the next two acts while Titus, constantly referring to her mouth and hands, asks her to speak to him or hold something for him—tasks that Lavinia cannot do. What possible purpose could such a dramatic milking serve? I suggest two intentions: to reinscribe the dominance of patriarchal modes of communication, and to further humiliate Lavinia by staging a reenactment of her rape. The drama

of Lavinia's seemingly inadequate sign system highlights the male characters' urge to control communication. Unable to speak her own bodily
condition, Lavinia must rely upon physical signs and her family's ability to
read them. Yet, despite all of their talk of reading Lavinia's signs, the Andronici cannot diagnose her condition correctly. If Lavinia is indeed the
Andronici's "map of woe, that thus dost talk in signs" (III, ii, 12), then the
Andronici are terrible navigators. Not until Marcus shows Lavinia how to
communicate by writing in the sand with a stick can she explain her situation to her father and the rest of her family. Unable to read the signs
written upon her female body, Titus must have Lavinia employ a phallic
staff to create signs in a language he can understand. This scene thus underscores Lavinia's dependency upon the patriarchy and the language of
the patriarchy. Incapable of communicating adequately with her family,
Lavinia requires "a male voice to signify her bodily condition."[30] The
male voice takes the form of the phallic staff bestowed upon Lavinia by a
male patriarch.

The act of communicating with the staff symbolizes the patriarchal social system's role in defining rape; ultimately, it is this system that speaks for
the violated woman and interprets her condition. Conversely, Marion
Wynne-Davies asserts that Lavinia assumes a position of power when she:

> consumes the masculine signifier, whether pen or phallus, and takes over the
> textual discourses, thereby castrating the source of male power.[31]

While some readings like this one and Karen Robertson's (in this volume)
support the argument that there is a signaling of women's power with writing in this scene, that power is still given to Lavinia, and only temporarily,
by the patriarchy. Despite whatever redeeming notions of female empowerment some critics may look for within Lavinia's victimization, in this
scene Lavinia is clearly at the mercy of the patriarchal system: because her
own signs are indiscernible to the men, they must provide her with their
own means of communication by teaching her how to write with the stick,
and she is only comprehensible to them while using this medium. Her
voice, entirely constructed through her menfolk's agency, is not her own.
Lavinia is not empowered with the staff, creating, as Wynne-Davies suggests,
a "liberated female language."[32] Instead, using a tool of the patriarchy to
scratch out a message in its own sign system, she affirms her dependence
upon patriarchal authority to make meaning. While Wynne-Davies correctly states that the source of male power has been castrated, it is Tamora
and Aaron, not Lavinia, who have done this. Indeed, through her rape and
mutilation, Lavinia's chastity—a source of male power for the Andronici—
is a source of male power castrated from Titus. From this perspective,

Lavinia has not consumed the masculine signifier, she *is* the masculine signifier, and, as such, she has suffered a mortal wound.

This scene not only affirms patriarchal power by establishing the supremacy of a male-engineered system of communication, but it also forces Lavinia to restage for public gaze the private details of her rape. This brings up another weakness in the argument that Lavinia empowers herself by consuming "the masculine signifier." As cited above, Paster correctly identifies the symbolism of staff for penis, mouth for vagina, and blood from the mouth as blood from the raped vagina. If so, when has a penis, real or figurative, inserted uninvited into a vagina, real or figurative, ever signified strength and power for the woman? Consuming the masculine signifier is an act of penetration, and an act of penetration empowers the penetrator, not the one penetrated. We see a representation of the unrepresentable when Lavinia takes the staff into her bleeding mouth and writes her testimony in the sand. By swallowing the phallus, Lavinia is made to reenact her rape symbolically for her family and for the audience. And although Lavinia testifies for herself, her father and uncle control the manner in which she presents her narrative. As Lynn A. Higgins and Brenda R. Silver rightly assert, "who gets to tell the story and whose story counts as 'truth' determine the definition of what rape *is*."[33] Ultimately this authority comes from the patriarchy—its control over "truth" and its definition of rape determines the fate of raped women. Indeed, Lavinia typifies many raped women in court who must retell the details of their violation, an experience that often makes victims feel as if they are being raped all over again. The spectacle of Lavinia writing with the staff dramatizes her attack visually, while her words force her to relive her rape. Whether in court or in the woods, experiencing rape and reporting it feels the same; in either case, the woman is victimized, once by her attacker(s) and again by the ones appointed to protect her. If Chaucer betrays Virginia by ignoring her suffering, then Shakespeare moves in the opposite direction and betrays Lavinia by exploiting her pain.

Finally able to decipher Lavinia's situation, Titus retaliates and defeats his daughter's attackers. His revenge symbolically neutralizes the spreading pestilence in his body and in the body of Rome. Chiron, Demetrius, Tamora, and Aaron, the foreign invaders plaguing Rome, are finally destroyed; but so is Lavinia. Titus determines that the foreign attack upon Lavinia, her rape or "unrecuring wound" can only be cured through radical surgery. At a banquet for Saturninus and Tamora given at his home, Titus asks the Emperor:

> Was it well done of rash Virginius
> To slay his daughter with his own right hand,
> Because she was enforc'd, stain'd, and deflow'r'd? (V, iii, 36–38)

Saturninus replies that Virginius was correct:

> Because the girl should not survive her shame,
> And by her presence still renew his sorrows. (V, iii, 41–42)

Although Titus calls Virginius "rash," Saturninus, the supreme patriarch of Rome, validates his act as "well done." According to Saturninus, Virginia needed to die, not because of her rape, but because of the resulting shame visited upon her father. Again, the focus shifts away from the wronged woman as patriarchal authority reinscribes rape as a crime against men. Titus agrees heartily with Saturninus and strikes down Lavinia in front of his shocked dinner guests:

> Die, die, Lavinia, and thy shame with thee,
> And with thy shame thy father's sorrow die! (V, iii, 46–47)

As the highest ranking male representatives of the patriarchy, Titus and Saturninus, like Virginius, also pass judgement upon Lavinia's condition. They define her rape as shameful, and while she lives, that shame will infect Titus. According to both men, only death can cure Titus of this contagion. When Titus purges Rome of its "sovereyn pestilence," not only does he destroy the infectious Goth organisms, but he also excises the infected tissue that is Lavinia. Since, in her father's mind, her contamination cannot be parted from her body, Lavinia must be entirely destroyed to ensure its containment. By killing Lavinia, Titus sacrifices a member for the good of the whole body, thus saving himself and his country from further infection.

Both the *Physician's Tale* and *Titus Andronicus* affirm the patriarchy's absolute power over women. The fact that both Virginia and Lavinia are murdered at home demonstrates how the patriarchal social body polices and politicizes all spaces, public and private. Lomperis argues that when Chaucer sets Virginia's murder in the home, he "politicizes the domestic space" and, in effect, affirms Virginius's "status as a powerful ruler."[34] The same is true of Titus. Not only are the women in these societies disposable objects, they also have no space to call their own. As Catharine MacKinnon asserts:

> Privacy is everything women as women have never been allowed to be or have; at the same time the private is everything women have been equated with and defined in terms of *men's* ability to have.[35]

When Titus and Virginius kill their daughters at home, they demonstrate to their audiences the full range of their authority. Besides upholding the patriarchy's ownership of all spaces, the executions at home signify the merging of private and political worlds.

If all spaces are politicized, then all actions occurring within those spaces have political significance. In both stories, rape plotted in a court-room or executed in a secluded wood is more than an act of violence against an individual woman; it is a threat to public safety and likened to treason. In the *Physician's Tale,* when Apius's political corruption connects with his sexual desire, his threatened rape of Virginia becomes a plot sig-nifying political intrigue and corrupt government. The political and pri-vate spheres likewise combine in *Titus Andronicus,* as several references to rape as treason identify sexual violation as a significant political danger. This ideological construction exists in Edward I's laws on rape; its presence in literary and legal texts reflects Medieval and Early Modern society's per-ceptions of rape and its public danger. Indeed, Coppélia Kahn maintains that these texts exist "interactively, reciprocally, with the social world in which the poet [Shakespeare] lived."[36] A. Robin Bowers adds that "these two areas of private rape and public rapine were widely discussed in Re-naissance society."[37] Bowers further argues that:

> Shakespeare chose and developed his stories of rape in *Lucrece* and *Titus An-*
> *dronicus* to draw attention both to the private, personal insult and injury of
> rape, and also to the public social repercussions which inevitably followed
> from such a destructive act.[38]

The ideological messages thus encoded in the *Physician's Tale* and *Titus An-dronicus* are detrimental to the futures of raped women. Metonymically, the attack upon a particular part of a woman's anatomy affects her whole body and soul, just as an attack upon members of a society threaten the well-being of the entire social body. Such attitudes towards rape resemble sim-ilar attitudes towards disease and diseased tissue. Raped women, like diseased tissue, must be cut off from the body of society in order to pre-serve its health and halt the spread of infection.

Not only are raped or rapable women in both works viewed as a men-ace to patriarchal stability, but eliminating them becomes a means of at-taining social and political reform. According to Stephanie H. Jed, rape often leads to revolution: "from the earliest historiographic records, some 'erotic' offense . . . is always required in order to justify the overthrow of tyrants."[39] In the *Physician's Tale,* Chaucer depicts the tyrant Apius as over-thrown only after the threatened rape and subsequent murder of Virginia becomes public. The result of his downfall is that others of his conscience are hanged and the city returns to social and political health (ll. 260–76). Similarly, in *Titus Andronicus,* it is only after the discovery of Lavinia's rape that the Andronici rise up in revolt against Saturninus and swear to expel the disease-bearing agents, the Goths, as Brutus did the Tarquins (IV, i, 87–94). As part of the revolution, the new emperor Lucius acts much like a surgeon, cutting away the foreign invaders from the body of Rome in order to "heal Rome's harms" (V, iii, 148). Then the Andronici promise the people that through righteous rule they will knit together "These broken limbs again into one body" (V, iii, 72). The act of healing Rome's body thus becomes the symbol of political reform. As a catalyst, then, "rape authorizes revenge; revenge comprises revolution; revolution establishes legitimate government."[40] In this light, not only is rape a political crime with political consequences, it also helps to bring about social change. However, while rape may authorize revenge and then revolution, the problem is that such positive change occurs at the cost of women. Clearly in both works, men, not women, seem to be the only beneficiaries of such types of political reform.

The telling and retelling of such stories of bodies raped, mutilated, and destroyed adversely shapes beliefs about rape, sexual access, and the role of women's bodies within the body of society. When raped bodies are treated like diseased tissue that can spread contagion to other family members and the general population, when raped women must be "segregated from former contacts" by death, then the true evil of rape is misunderstood. Exploring how raped women are treated like diseased tissue shows us that they are not really diseased at all, that rape is a symptom of a more deadly affliction, homosocial rivalry. The bodies of women, used to create bonds between men, can also be used as conduits through which men can harm other men. They vanquish each other by raping their enemy's women, damaging them, infecting them, and rendering them useless and even dangerous to their possessors. When a rival uses it as a weapon to vanquish his opponent, rape can incapacitate the patriarchal social system by causing an infection in the foe's appendage—a type of Medieval and Early Modern germ warfare. In this kind of conflict, not only is the tragedy of the raped woman overlooked, but attention is refocused upon her male owner as the true rape victim. Moreover, as a preventative or curative measure applied to rape, the murder of raped or potentially rapable women avoids curing the real disease; it only treats a symptom. While the raped body as diseased tissue analogy explains why Virginia and Lavinia are murdered, it in no way justifies their deaths. At this point the metaphor begins to break down when we realize that human beings are not appendages, bodily members, or disposable pieces of a whole. Nor is it always right to overlook individual humanity in favor of the general good. The better solution to the problem of jealous aggression lies not in the host cutting off his appendage, but in abstinence from unsafe political intercourse.

Unfortunately, the conduit receives blame too often for the currents running through her. Rape, too often essentialized into her being, always implicates her in the act when the result of rape is shame.[41] As Brown-miller asserts, husbands and fathers of raped women "place a major burden of blame for the awful event" on them because "the hallowed rights of property have been abused, and the property herself is held culpable."[42] However, like homosocial rivalry, social constructions of rape and shame are responsible for the instability of the patriarchy, not the women who are the victims of these ideological constructions. Indeed, this ideology has no foundation in the letter of secular or religious law. The punishment for rape has never included killing the victim. Rape law in England was based in part on that of the ancient Hebrews; their religious law on rape found in Deuteronomy is clear regarding sexual violation. The punishment for rape prescribed there is death for the *rapist:*

> But unto the damsel thou shalt do nothing; *there is* in the damsel no sin *worthy* of death: for as when a man riseth against his neighbour, and slayeth him, even so *is* this matter.[43]

Neither secular nor religious laws say anything about punishing the victim because the raped woman has committed no sin worthy of death.[44]

The destruction of female bodies in texts sends negative messages to audiences concerning rape. Fearful and condemnatory attitudes about rape present in the *Physician's Tale* and *Titus Andronicus* help to shape the identities of men and women within patriarchal society. My purpose has not been to praise or vilify Chaucer and Shakespeare as feminists or misogynists, but to explore how the literary transmission of misogynist messages in their texts contributes to views of women and their roles in society. Significantly, the telling and retelling of the Virginius and Virginia story, from the time of the Romans to the Medieval and Early Modern periods and beyond, has perpetuated the belief that rape is a fate worse than death. Perhaps a new alternative to this story needs to be told, a new cure found, one that deals with the disease of rivalry rather than the symptom of rape, one that incorporates the stated truth that "there is in the damsel no sin worthy of death," one that allows the wronged daughter to survive her father's shame.

Notes

1. Livy, *Livy,* ed. and trans. B. O. Foster et al., vol. 3 (London: Loeb, 1919–59), pp. 44–50, 56–58.
2. In David Bevington, ed., *The Complete Works of Shakespeare,* 4th ed. (New York: HarperCollins, 1992) p. 974, Bevington maintains that both versions

detailing Virginia's murder before and after her rape were current in the
Early Modern period. Besides the *Physician's Tale,* medieval versions of the
story are found in Boccaccio's *De claribus mulieribus,* Gower's *Confessio
Amantis,* and *The Roman de la Rose.* Early modern versions of the tale in-
clude John Webster's and/or John Heywood's *Appius and Virginia* (pub.
1654) and a later 1709 play of the same name by John Dennis. J. C.
Maxwell, in Maxwell, J. C., ed., *Titus Andronicus* (London: Routledge,
1987), p. 119, cites examples of the alternative version, including George
Chapman's *Alphonsus, Emperor of Germany* (no date given), and Ludowicke
Lloyd's *The Pilgrimage of Princes* (1573) and *The Consent of Time* (1590).

3. Larry Benson, ed., *The Riverside Chaucer,* 3rd ed. (Boston: Houghton Mif-
    flin, 1987), p. 902.
4. For further reading on this subject, see Gayle Rubin, "The Traffic of
    Women: Notes on the 'Political Economy' of Sex," in *Toward an Anthropol-
    ogy of Women,* ed. Rayna R. Reiter (New York: Monthly Review Press,
    1975), pp. 157–210. For arguments about the role of women in homoso-
    cial bonding, see Eve Kosofsky Sedgwick, *Between Men: English Literature
    and Male Homosocial Desire* (New York: Columbia University Press, 1985),
    and *Epistemology of the Closet* (Berkeley: University of California Press,
    1990).
5. In *Hali Meithhad,* in *Medieval English Prose for Women,* ed. Bella Millet and
    Jocelyn Wogan-Browne (Oxford: Clarendon, 1990), pp. 2–43, the narrator
    discusses the pros and cons of each role. Spiritual value is placed upon each
    position, with the maid most blessed because of her virginity, the widow
    second most blessed because, although she is not a virgin, she is now liv-
    ing a chaste life, and the wife third most blessed because she is living
    chastely within the bounds of marriage. Although in the Church virginity
    has top priority in the Middle Ages while marriage gets more of the focus
    during the Early Modern period, this hierarchy of sexual access is com-
    mon to both periods.
6. While being a nun or a prostitute was arguably a vocation, these occupa-
    tions were strongly associated with sexual identity.
7. This is a fine literary example of how a woman uses the existing rape laws
    to her advantage. Mariana, deserted by Angelo before their wedding, sex-
    ually consummates their betrothal in the famous bed-trick, and then
    comes forward to force Angelo legally into honoring her retroactively with
    marriage.
8. William Shakespeare, *Measure for Measure,* in *The Riverside Shakespeare,* ed.
    G. Blakemore Evans et al. (Boston: Houghton Mifflin, 1974),V, i, 177–78.
9. Shakespeare, *Measure for Measure,* V, i, 179–80.
10. In Patricia Frances Cholakian, *Rape and Writing in the* Heptameron *of Mar-
    guerite of Navarre* (Carbondale: Southern Illinois University Press, 1991), p.
    13, Cholakian argues that during the Early Modern period, "a woman's
    honor could signify her reputation, what was known about her chastity in
    public, that is, what she was *worth* in the eyes of society."

11. Eve Kosofsky Sedgwick, *Epistemology of the Closet* (Berkeley: University of California Press, 1990), p. 61.

12. Marion Wynne-Davies, "'The Swallowing Womb': Consumed and Consuming Women in *Titus Andronicus*," in *The Matter of Difference: Materialist Feminist Criticism of Shakespeare,* ed. Valerie Wayne (Ithaca, NY: Cornell University Press, 1991), p. 133.

13. Kathryn Gravdal, *Ravishing Maidens: Writing Rape in Medieval French Literature and Law* (Philadelphia: University of Pennsylvania Press, 1991), pp. 8–9.

14. Susan Brownmiller, *Against Our Will: Men, Women and Rape* (New York: Simon and Schuster, 1975), pp. 17–18. Punishments for rapists in Medieval and Early Modern England included death, marrying him to his victim, and/or paying remuneration to the victim's father or husband. For rehearsals of the rape laws that illuminate Chaucer's and Shakespeare's days, see Henry Ansgar Kelly, "Meanings and Uses of *Raptus* in Chaucer's Time," *Studies in the Age of Chaucer* 20 (1998): 101–66; Christopher Cannon (this volume), and Kathryn Gravdal.

15. Cholakian, *Rape and Writing,* p. 13.

16. The perceived interrelationship of the physical body and the social or political body manifests itself, for example, in the notion of Queen Elizabeth's two bodies. She was herself possessed of a body, but she was also identified as the body of England. Crimes against England were crimes against the queen and, conversely, crimes against her body were crimes against England.

17. Linda Lomperis and Sarah Stanbury, "Introduction: Feminist Theory and Medieval 'Body Politics,'" in *Feminist Approaches to the Body in Medieval Literature,* ed. Linda Lomperis and Sarah Stanbury (Philadelphia: University of Pennsylvania Press, 1993), p. ix.

18. Peggy McCracken, "The Body Politic and the Queen's Adulterous Body in French Romance," in *Feminist Approaches to the Body in Medieval Literature,* ed. Linda Lomperis and Sarah Stanbury (Philadelphia: University of Pennsylvania Press, 1993), pp. 46, 50.

19. Carolyn D. Williams, "'Silence, Like a Lucrece Knife': Shakespeare and the Meanings of Rape," *Yearbook of English Studies* 23 (1993): 94–95.

20. Geoffrey Chaucer, *The Physician's Tale,* in *The Riverside Chaucer,* ed. Larry D. Benson, 3rd ed. (Boston: Houghton Mifflin, 1987), lines 91–92. Further citations to this tale will be noted in the text by line numbers.

21. Benson, *Riverside,* p. 903.

22. Linda Lomperis, "Unruly Bodies and Ruling Practices: Chaucer's *Physician's Tale* as Socially Symbolic Act," in *Feminist Approaches to the Body in Medieval Literature,* ed. Linda Lomperis and Sarah Stanbury (Philadelphia: University of Pennsylvania Press, 1993), p. 29.

23. Brownmiller, *Against Our Will,* p. 38.

24. Benson, *Riverside,* p. 903.

25. William Shakespeare, *Titus Andronicus,* in *The Riverside Shakespeare,* ed. G. Blakemore Evans et al. (Boston: Houghton Mifflin, 1974), V, iii, 87. Further references to this play will be noted in the text by Act, scene and line numbers.

26. Williams, "Silence," p. 108.
27. McCracken, "Body Politic," p. 38.
28. Brownmiller, *Against Our Will,* p. 38.
29. Gail Kern Paster, *The Body Embarrassed: Drama and Disciplines of Shame in Early Modern England* (Ithaca, NY: Cornell University Press, 1993), p. 98.
30. Paster, *Body Embarrassed,* p. 106.
31. Wynne-Davies, "Swallowing Womb," p. 147.
32. Wynne-Davies, "Swallowing Womb," p. 147.
33. Lynn A. Higgins and Brenda R. Silver, "Introduction: Rereading Rape," in *Rape and Representation,* ed. Lynn A. Higgins and Brenda R. Silver (New York: Columbia University Press, 1991), p. 1.
34. Lomperis, "Unruly Bodies," p. 30.
35. Catharine A. MacKinnon, "Feminism, Marxism, Method, and the State: Toward Feminist Jurisprudence," *Signs* 8 (1983): 656–57.
36. Coppélia Kahn, "*Lucrece:* The Sexual Politics of Subjectivity," in *Rape and Representation,* ed. Lynn A. Higgins and Brenda R. Silver (New York: Columbia University Press, 1991), p. 143.
37. A. Robin Bowers, "Emblem and Rape in Shakespeare's *Lucrece* and *Titus Andronicus,*" *Studies in Iconography* 10 (1984–86): 79.
38. Bowers, "Emblem," p. 82.
39. Stephanie H. Jed, *Chaste Thinking: The Rape of Lucretia and the Birth of Humanism* (Bloomington: Indiana University Press, 1989), p. 3.
40. Kahn, "Sexual Politics," p. 141.
41. It is frightening to know that such views plague us still. In certain societies today the rape of a woman and its attendant shame is enough justification for her male relatives to kill her. On October 7, 1999, *The Seattle Times* reported that three women in Jordan were killed by fathers and brothers for bringing shame to their families. In Jordan, "honor crimes"—the beating and killing of women who are perceived to have shamed their families—is a widespread practice. Women can be punished for as little as talking to a man or dating, and rape is seen as a serious disgrace. According to the article, "punishment is widely accepted by citizens and the state as an honorable tradition."
42. Brownmiller, *Against Our Will,* p. 40.
43. Deut. 22: 26.
44. Although in practice women were often put in prison for false appeals, there still was no law on the books making it illegal to be the victim of a rape. Raping was illegal; *being raped* was not a crime.

CHAPTER 7

RAPE AND THE APPROPRIATION OF PROGNE'S REVENGE IN SHAKESPEARE'S *TITUS ANDRONICUS,* OR "WHO COOKS THE THYESTEAN BANQUET?"

Karen Robertson

The essay explores how the appropriation of Progne's vengeance by Titus recapitulates prohibitions against anger for women articulated in contemporary legal and religious documents and limits feminine subjectivity in reaction to rape.

Titus Andronicus centers on the family of Titus, a Roman general who disastrously refuses to accept the mantle of rule on his return from the conquest of the Goths and sparks the animosity of the new emperor, Saturninus, as well as the Goth queen, Tamora, whose son he sacrifices. Vengeance is visited on him through the execution of two sons falsely accused of murder, the amputation of his hand through a trick, and most spectacularly, the rape and mutilation of his daughter, Lavinia. Lavinia, seized in Act I, wed, raped, and mutilated in Act II, is presented as a spectacle of extreme suffering who outdoes her classical antecedents, Philomel, Lucrece, and Virginia. The emendations from the two primary sources in Ovid and Livy are signaled as piquant variations to surprise the audience.[1] Like Lucrece, she is the virtuous wife whose rape exposes the sexual licence that contaminates the ruling family and precipitates their overthrow. Like Virginia, she has a father who removes the pollution of her rape by killing her. Yet, she becomes a Philomel with a difference, for not only is her tongue, like Philomel's, cut out to prevent testimony against her rapists,

but she suffers the further mutilation of the loss of her hands so that she
will be incapable of weaving a cloth that reveals her rape.

In refashioning the classical story for the Elizabethan stage, Shakespeare
deliberately signals changes in the source. When Titus boasts: "For worse
than Philomel you used my daughter/And worse than Progne I will be revenged" (V.ii.194–95), the line not only points towards the gender shift of
the revenger, but also insists on the father's superiority in revenge. Shakespeare's emendations intensify the isolation of the rape victim, for the
raped woman is not only stripped of her sister, but a female antagonist who
incites the rape is deliberately added to the story. When the angry sister
Progne is excised, feminine indignation at rape and agency in its punishment is muted. Vengeance becomes the responsibility of the male avenger
of blood. This extreme gendering of anger and revenge reinforces Tudor
homiletic prohibitions of anger for women and Elizabethan conceptualizations of revenge in legal documents to contribute to the production of
a representational norm, the masculine gendering of vengeance in Tudor
and Stuart tragedy.

Analysis of Shakespeare's use of his sources has concentrated for the
most part on identification of source texts and a debate over the relative
influences of Ovid and Seneca on the play.[2] Jonathan Bate, pointing to the
overlapping configuration of the two central rape narratives of Philomel
and Lucrece, rightly describes Shakespeare's use of sources in *Titus* as
"composed out of series of precedents in the dramatic repertoire of the period and a series of patterns in Shakespeare's reading of the classics."[3] Yet
simple identification of the narrative and dramatic sources of the play can
recapitulate a process of erasure common to humanist practice then and
now, the elision of the gendered meaning of stories. In conflating two popular humanist narratives from Livy—Lucrece and Virginia—which feature
vengeance against a tyrant by outraged male kin with the Ovidian story of
vengeance by two sisters, Shakespeare produces a Tudor configuration of
masculine agency and feminine objectification. The changes in the well-
known school text, with the elimination of Progne's revenge for her sister,
a story that had been performed on the English stage in Latin at Oxford
in 1566, and the appropriation of her revenge by a male revenger of blood
all emphasize rape as a wound to the patriline.[4] Shakespeare creates a dramatic novelty when Lavinia, stripped of the tools and audience available to
Philomel—hands, a loom, and a sister—manages to communicate the fact
of her rape to her father. The dazzling display of the literary screens the excision of women's anger at sexual violation. Philomel without hands and
without a sister to read her story becomes a startlingly mutilated figure.

While it is possible to describe the relationship of play and sources as
simply the sewing together of two different stories—Virginius appliquéd

into the plot of Philomel—the cutout figures have meaning and leave significant traces in the Elizabethan play. As Jane Burns's reading of the Old French romance of Philomena makes clear, in both romance and Ovidian source, there is a narrative balance between the work of Philomena's hands weaving her tapestry and the work of Progne's hands cutting up her son. "In helping Philomena to rewrite the suppressed story of her rape along with the fictions of courtly love and beauty that accompany it, Progne also rewrites her own gruesome past: the tale of her marriage to Tereus and the motherhood that followed it" (133). In Burns's analysis, the sisters repudiate patriarchal positionings of women through the answering of one sister's story of rape by the second sister's story of maternal infanticide.[5] Shakespeare's reworking of the story places a narrative of marital violation and betrayal within a larger critique of the failures of state systems of justice, yet the shadow of Progne marks the text.[6]

The transformation of the gender of the revenger and his antagonist in *Titus Andronicus* shifts the narrative of rape from a violation of a woman's body punished by women through sacrifice of the products of their bodies to a violation of masculine property laws punished violently by men. The excision of Progne as agent of vengeance for her sister's rape substitutes the aristocratic male subject for the betrayed wife. The absence of the angry wife is then redoubled by her metamorphosis into criminal eater at the cannibal banquet. Shakespeare's emphasis on the exchange of the daughter between men through the mutation of the two central female characters from loyal sisters into antagonists could be used to illustrate Levi-Strauss's structural analysis of all societies in which he sees women used as tokens to bind men together and in which reciprocity among women is unimaginable.[7] To explore this extreme expression of Elizabethan patriarchalism that not only violently excludes the figure of Progne from agency in the execution of revenge but insists on feminine culpability for sexual crimes, this essay situates the Shakespearean transformations of the classical sources in the context of Protestant homilies on anger, conceptualizations of revenge in contemporary Elizabethan legal documents, and the gendering of vengeance in Tudor revenge plays. These texts repudiate the expression of anger for women, a repudiation resolved in the play by the heroic appropriation of vengeance by the male revenger of blood.[8]

Yet, it is reductive simply to condemn the transformations between source and play, since remnants of the older plot not only remain but are deliberately acknowledged as absences. Lavinia's use of a copy of Ovid's *Metamorphoses* marks a complicated moment in the construction of feminine subjectivity, for the absent Progne, seemingly excised from the text to proscribe women's expressions of anger, is made most prominent in a scene when a woman reads a book and writes. Thus, the cultural prohibitions over expressions of feminine anger reinscribed in the play occur at a moment that dramatically enacts the entrance of women into written culture. This moment when Lavinia searches for her literary analogue offers an opportunity for a feminist reading of what Jane Burns calls the "underread" (142). Although the scene overtly records the erasure of Progne, the infanticidal mother is replaced with a new figure, the woman writer, who despite alienation from other women and traditional feminine modes of representation, moves towards participation in public realms through literacy and the book. The mutilated figure of Lavinia, reconstituted not as weaver but as monstrous writer of words read only by a male audience, signals a potential for women's participation in written culture, though that participation has been slow.[9] As modern feminist readers, we can begin to read the underread.

Source analysis that ignores the change in the gender of the revenger takes as a norm the agency of the male and the objectification of the daughter, a norm whose meanings can become invisible. The invisible dynamics of traditional humanist practice came home to me in an incident that happened during a class on *Titus Andronicus* over a decade ago. As prelude to a discussion of the appropriation of Progne's revenge, I began with a summary of the sources of *Titus*. My detached recapitulation of three classical rape narratives as reshaped for the Elizabethan stage produced an outburst among twentieth-century American students. In one of those extraordinary classes that crack open insight, at the next class meeting the students challenged me for my failure to understand that the summary of those stories was a verbal blow to the women in class that awakened memories of pain. To my distress at least one-fifth of the students in the class admitted that they had been raped, a statistic that took me aback. Unwittingly, my prelude to a discussion of Shakespeare's gendering of vengeance had produced exactly the effect I wished to examine. The students had felt silenced and they felt that I, their Women's Studies teacher, had appropriated their suffering for academic purposes. Their intervention into the sequence of storytelling has deepened my understanding of the ideological function of tales of rape.

Their anger made me realize that detachment, developed in my work on Jacobean revenge tragedy and mimicking the aloofness of my training, was an inadequate stance towards material that had for some students a deeply personal resonance. Certainly, my familiarity with the violence of past texts had led me to forget the potential shock for those reading for the first time.[10] To the students, in providing a cool summary, I seemed to have no empathy for their suffering. During our subsequent discussion, one student, after describing her rape, said that rape was worse than having your hands cut off and tongue cut out, a claim from personal experience that inhibited all subsequent discussion. The single male student in the class said afterwards that he dared not comment that he regarded her statement as a reiteration of traditional attitudes towards rape that consider the female body as a chaste vessel, irrevocably damaged by rape.[11]

The incident encapsulates the problems of what Stephanie Jed calls "chaste thinking," a process by which a story circulates in culture positioned in limited ways, purified and cut off from some associations.[12] Jed analyzes the humanist positioning of the story of the rape of Lucrece as foundational to the story of republican liberty, a celebration of liberty that occludes the material suffering of the female body. My summary of the sources of *Titus* inadvertently mimicked the humanist versions of the rape by cutting my recital off from any overt acknowledgement of the pain and suffering implicit in such stories and their possible resonance for women in the class. When the students, insisting that the sixteenth-century text be understood from the position of their twentieth-century experience of sexual violence, creatively violated the traditional boundaries of the classroom, the inclusion of experience so deeply painful actually led to another kind of silencing. The pain of the survivors, and the empathy and perhaps fear before that pain felt by other students, produced an absolute barrier to discussion. Perhaps such silence is a necessary beginning to discussion of violations that leave such intimate scars, though I see a danger in the silences that can occur in classroom discussions that draw on the authority of experience.[13] Had we been able to ask questions of one another, we might have been able to elicit understandings of the representation of rape blocked at that time by the students' outrage. The questions that I could not ask then lie at the core of my analysis now and guide my consideration of the gendering of anger and the restrictions it imposes on female victims of rape. How can women's anger at rape usefully interrupt the smooth ideological structures that have defined rape for thousands of years? What stories of rape can usefully be told without a reinscription of traditional hierarchies of power? How can we discuss the social mechanisms at work in a representation of rape without reinforcing victimization and enjoining silence on women? How can we distinguish a literary trope from a physical act? Why is women's anger over representation considered illegitimate? This essay focuses not on the specific act of rape itself, but on the possible responses to rape and the ways in which women's responses are appropriated and contained by dominant interpretive structures.

To begin, what does it mean when Titus boasts "worse than Progne I will be revenged"? The boast guides us to recognize that the narrative balance that Burns uncovers in the Old French tale has been distorted by a variety of changes in *Titus,* all of which are deliberately marked as superior emendations. Titus's vengeance has been precipitated by a more extreme mutilation of the rape victim who has lost not only her tongue but her hands. As a number of critics have observed, this change, too, is marked as a superior emendation of the source, with the words "craftier," "worse," and "better," as in the observation by her uncle that Lavinia has been subjected to a rapist "craftier" than Tereus, for he has acted to prevent the weaving of a tapestry: "And he hath cut those pretty fingers off, / That could have better sewed than Philomel" (II.iii.41–43). Uncovering in what way Titus's revenge is "worse" reveals at first simply numerical superiority in murder. Progne serves one child in a pie; Titus serves two. Yet when Tamora, the avenging mother, becomes the antagonist rather than ally of the rape victim, and the mother becomes the cannibal eater, the shift breaks the logical connection in Ovid between rape and infanticide. Transforming the mother into the cannibal, Shakespeare demonizes maternal anger.[14] Choosing to erase the conflict between maternal and sororal love endured by Progne, Shakespeare isolates women within patriarchal families and transforms Ovid's representation of the sororal bonds between women. When a mute female provides a text read by the male avenger of blood, one version of outrage is produced—a violation of the male bloodline and masculine property. When the mute female produces a text read and interpreted by her sister, a different community of anger is produced.[15]

Progne's alliance with her sister is central to the Ovidian tale, though that alliance is brought into view only after Progne has been given in marriage to cement a peace treaty between her father Pandion and Tereus.[16] In Arthur Golding's 1567 translation of Ovid, after several years of marriage, Progne, eager to see her sister, sends her husband to fetch Philomel, saying "the highest great good turne / That can be, if you bring to passe I may my sister see" (p. 50). Tereus lusts after his sister-in-law and instead of delivering her to the palace takes her to a moated grange where he rapes her. The first word Philomel says after the rape is her sister's name. Her lament leads Tereus to cut out her tongue. Returning to his home, Tereus falsely claims to his wife that Philomel has died on the voyage, a report that provokes "piteous tears" from Progne. Imprisoned at the grange, Philomel weaves the story of her rape into a tapestry of cloth that she manages to send to her sister. Most striking evidence of sororal empathic connection is Progne's ability to read the woven tale correctly.[17] Progne rescues her sister and returns with her to the palace. While Progne ruminates about revenge on her husband, their son Itys walks in, precipitating a comparison between the claims of the sister and the son. Cognatic alliance competes with loyalty and service to the male agnates.

> She turned to hir sisters face from *Itys,* and behelde
> Now t'one, now t'other earnestly and said, why tattles he,

And she sittes dumbe bereft of tongue? as well why calles not she
Me sister, as this boy doth call me mother? Seest thou not
Thou daughter of *Pandion* what a husband thou has got?
Thou growest wholy out of kinde. (Golding, 56–57)

The question "why calles not she me sister?" materializes the conflicting
claims of natal bonds and marital links. Marriage requires the muting of
the claims of cognates, the silence of the sister. For Progne, stimulated by
that silence, the blood link between sisters proves more powerful than the
link between mother and son; the operations of patriarchal marriage (the
daughter given in marriage to the visiting suitor) have failed to transform
the affines created through the marriage bond into those she recognizes as
kin. Progne chastises herself for her failure to maintain connection to her
natal family: "Thou growest wholy out of kinde." Maternal affection submits before the bonds of her natal family. Anger, first directed at the rapist,
with threats to fire the palace, cut out his tongue, or castrate him, transmutes into an attack on the entire agnatic line. Through the son, she will
punish the father. The father's inability to control his lust is punished by
the ingestion and reincorporation of his child in a pie. When Tereus realizes what he has eaten, he pursues his wife and her sister until they are all
transformed into birds.

Whatever the significance of this story for a Roman audience, when
Shakespeare rewrites it for performance by Pembroke's men, feminine
anger and sororal alliance are overtly erased.[18] In *Titus,* the complicated
figure of Progne, the angry woman willing to sacrifice her own son for
vengeance for the rape and mutilation of her sister, is split between Titus
and Tamora. Titus appropriates Progne's position as reader of the rape victim's story and the patriarchal father thus effects the revenge. No female
character debates the complex loyalties that pull her between her natal and
marital families. An angry and vengeful mother does have a part in the
play—Tamora's revenge for the death of her son Alarbus is the engine of
the plot—yet the mother is set in opposition to the rape victim, for it is
she who urges the rape. A woman's willingness to encourage rape shocks
Lavinia into silence. The Goth mother becomes a figure of uncontrollable
feminine anger, so monstrous that her dead body itself must be cast out of
the state.[19] The substitution of an evil mother for the rapist father as cannibal eater in the banquet that concludes the play not only separates feminine anger from feminine victimization in rape but also doubly visits
punishments for rape on women's bodies. In the story of Philomel, the
rapist is punished by being forced to eat the body of his son, a punishment
that conflates rape with unlawful eating; the male body out of control
manifests its disorder through cannibalism. As Burns observes about

Philomena, "We realize how feeding the tyrant this chilling meal aptly reverses the terms of the original rape. As retribution for Tereus having
forced his body into Philomena's, Progne here forces another body into
Tereus's open mouth." "At this juncture Progne's rewriting of the plot of
the lovely virgin turns tellingly to recast the myth of the loving mother."[20]
In *Titus,* the cannibal feast is prepared not for the rapists, but for their
mother, Tamora, who devours her own sons in a pie. Thus, the violent in-
trusion into the body of Lavinia is punished by a horrific ingestion, not by
the rapists themselves, but by their mother. This extreme version of Elizabethan patriarchy foregrounds feminine culpability for violation, making
women both victims and criminal agents of rape. The conflation between
the womb and stomach of the monstrous mother produces a common
misogynist analogy between the devouring womb and tomb of the earth
and leaves the rape victim doubly isolated, both in her loss of alliance with
a sister who joins in directly punishing the male rapist and in the elision
of the punishment of the rapists themselves. While the rapists are indeed
killed in Titus and ground into a pie, the culminating punishment is reserved for Tamora, their mother, suggesting ultimate feminine culpability
for sexual crimes.

In this play, a clear gender binarism is established. Masculine anger is
mobilized to cast the culpable female out of the state. This play, which presented to the London public the spectacle of masculine vengeance with a
male rather than female cooks, is one of the early examples of Tudor and
Stuart revenge plays,[21] which feature masculine execution of justice and
the erasure or marginalization of feminine agents and feminine anger.[22]
The revenge plays of the sixteenth century, in their considerations of issues
of justice and the state, form one element in the ideological process of state
formation in the late Tudor and early Stuart period, as the state centralized
control over the execution of justice, particularly control over private
blood feuds.[23] Jean Howard's modification of Louis Althusser, observing
that it is "only partly useful to think of theater as an ideological state apparatus, that is an institution for the discursive, non-violent control of social subjects in the interests of the ruling segments of society" provides an
important reminder, but representations of revenge do tend to follow prescriptions that restrict justified revenge to authorized males and demonize
feminine vengeance.[24] Frequently in these plays, women are excluded
from participation in the activities of just vengeance and become reposi-
tories of monstrous illegitimate cruelty that must be cast out of the state.
Shakespeare's Tamora prefigures the monstrous feminine of later plays, the
figure of horror that justifies masculine control of state systems. Construction of subjectivity and political agency demonstrated by participation in
the execution of justice are allied processes—for women no legitimate

agency or psychological coherence can be imagined by the male authors of the plays, though female audience members may respond against the moral grain of the text.[25] The violence represented on stage as suitable or approved for women is self-cancellation—or agency expressed through death.[26] Such exclusions of the female characters from the operations of justice anticipate their exclusion from conceptualizations of the citizen in enlightenment thought. Curiously, vengefulness or vindictiveness begins to be seen in the later seventeenth century as a particular aspect of the feminine psyche—an assumption that follows the successful control of the blood feud and appropriation of the blood feud by state agencies of justice in the late sixteenth and early seventeenth century.[27]

The play participates in the ideological exclusion of women and lower-class males from the execution of justice, a process speeded by the Tudor bureaucratic centralization of justice. In the classical story, the women are the agents of punishment. Fredson Bowers, in his study of Elizabethan revenge tragedy, points out that while in Anglo-Saxon codes of *wergeld* [man payment] and execution of justice, women might participate as witnesses or members of tribal groups, the Tudor state was in the process of shifting from an earlier Anglo-Norman judicial method in which injured parties, including widows, were required to seek justice by bringing an appeal to a method of indictment by the king.[28] Such centralization removed women from active participation in the seeking of justice and, although Elizabeth I was nominal chief justicer of the state, justice was administered by her male judges. This shift of the gender of the revenger has profound implications for the status of anger as an emotion suitable for and available to women. The appropriation of Progne's vengeance by Titus rejects the dramatization of feminine alliance and feminine anger in defense of that alliance and participates in the Tudor ideological suppression of the anger of inferiors. The changes in the source echo and mark Tudor prohibitions against feminine anger and participation in the operations of justice clearly articulated in the homiletic injunctions against anger and in the absence of women's participation in the Bond of Association, a major loyalty oath and pact for vengeance. The exclusion of women from participation in the Bond, an extraordinary oath that legitimized the blood feud as an instrument of public policy in 1584–85, is anticipated by the clear proscriptions against anger for women in the homilies, the sermons prepared and authorized by the Anglican hierarchy for weekly reading in English churches. The melding of state and religious power for the control of inferiors marks the homilies, particularly in the homily against strife and contention: "The holy apostle S. Peter commaundeth servauntes to be obedient to their masters, not onely if they be good and gentle, but also if they be evil and froward, affirmyng that the vocation and callyng of Gods people is to bee

pacient and of the sufferyng syde."[29] In the homily on obedience, Christ's
meekness is counseled as a model in response to the question: "If I be evil
reviled, shal I stand stil like a goose, or a foole, with my finger in my
mouth? Shall I be such an ydiot and diserde to suffre every man to speake
upon me what thei list, to rayle what they liste, to spew out al their venyme
agaynst me at their pleasaures? . . . For the true strength and manlines is to
overcome wrath, and to despice injury and other mennes folishnes."[30]
Obedience to superior powers, with an exception for orders contrary to
god's law, is absolutely enjoined: "[w]e maye not in any wyse resist violently or rebell against rulers, or make any insurrection, sedicion or tu-
multes, either by force of armes or other waies, against the anoynted of the
Lord or any of his appointed officers. But we must in suche case paciently
suffre all wronges and injuries, referryng the judgement of oure cause
onely to God."[31] The homiletic prescriptions are engaged in a reconcep-
tualization of true manliness and the restraint of masculine wrath, prescribing for subordinate males the meekness and patience long enjoined to
wives. The story of Griselda, disseminated in a variety of humanist texts,
exemplifies the appropriate patience of a wife.[32] The status of anger for
women was further complicated by the Protestant reevaluation of marriage that in acknowledging the equality of male and female souls required
the reiteration in sermons and conduct books of prescriptions for control
of anger in women. A characteristic example is William Whately's marriage
sermon, *A bride-bush* (London, 1623):

> The whole duty of a wife is referred to two heads. The first is, to acknowl-
> edge her inferiority: the next, to carry herself as inferior. First then the wife's
> judgment must be convinced, that she is not her husband's equal, yea, that
> her husband is her better by far; else there can be no contentment, either in
> her heart, or in her house. If she stand upon terms of equality, much more
> of being better than he is, the very root of good carriage is withered, and
> the fountain thereof dried up. Out of place, out of peace. And woe to these
> miserable aspiring shoulders, that content not themselves to take their room
> next below the head.[33]

In imagining the new body constructed through the marriage ceremony,
Whately makes the husband the head, and the wife the envious shoulders—an image that embeds a potential for rebellion in that envious body
part. These English homilies and sermons admit and attempt to deflect the
particular pains felt by the inferior, through the use of comic figures—the
goose with a finger in his mouth, the envious shoulders. A comparison between the two tropes shows that the wrongs and injuries imagined for the
inferior male in the homily visits only the indignity of a childish posture

but does not impinge on the bodily integrity of the individual, while the Whately sermon actually decapitates the wife, reducing her to her shoulders. Speech is reserved to superior males, who are granted the option of judicious reprimand if their words "Proceeded not of anger, rancor, or malice, or appetite of vengeance, but of a fervent desire to bryng them to the true knowledge of God and from ungodly livyng, by an earnest and sharpe objugacion and chidyng."[34] Such comic mutilations and injunctions to silence fail to address the ruptures of bodily and psychic integrity endured by those assaulted in rape.[35]

Tudor prescriptive literature does admit the existence of the emotion of anger in inferiors while insisting on its transformation into meekness in an obvious mobilization of Christian theology for political control. Modern philosophical analyses of anger offer insight into the structure of emotions that point towards the link between emotion and political systems. E. V. Spelman, in an analysis of the epistemology of anger, argues that anger is an emotion that is composed of an element of rational judgement as well as physiological reaction.[36] Such an analysis offers insight into the persistent proscription of anger for women and other subordinates. Class and gender hierarchies require the repression of anger by subordinates because the presumption of judgement embedded in the emotion impinges on a central prerogative reserved to social superiors. The occluded text in these prescriptions is the judgement implicit in the anger of inferiors.

The prohibition of the expression of anger by women as well as male inferiors both marks and reinforces a process that excludes them from participation in public life, while anger and judgement remain the prerogative of the subject—a prerogative confined to a narrow class of males. The prohibition on anger marks an exclusion from the expression of public judgement, an exclusion from agency, and a confinement to a narrow and canceled realm—without subjectivity, without public authority.[37] The restriction of anger to a narrow band of males in the social hierarchy anticipates and ensures various forms of political exclusion.

The homiletic prescriptions attempt to set the general parameters for the behavior of individuals in the society, with particular limits on the expression of anger by inferiors. The Bond of Association is a singular political document that actively enjoined on its signatories violent anger and the execution of blood revenge. Those invited to participate in the bond are separated from the ordinary ranks of Christian society. Constructed by William Cecil as a preventive against the assassination of Elizabeth I and the succession of the Catholic claimant, Mary Queen of Scots, the oath joins Englishmen in a band of revengers who would pursue the assassins, Mary herself, and her heir. The bond is remarkable for the extremity of its language and its production by the cautious Cecil indicates the gravity of

English governmental anxiety over an assassination attempt. The oath bound those who joined to swear to kill anyone who attempted to harm the queen:

> We "do hereby vow and promise by the Majesty of Almighty God, that with our whole Powers, Bodies, Lives and Goods, and with our Children and Servants" we will obey Elizabeth and "with our joint and particular forces during our lives, pursue and ofend, as well by force or arms, as by all other means of Revenge, all manner of persons, of whatsoever state they shall be, and their abbeters, that shall tend to the harm of her Majesty's Royal Person, and will never desist from all manner of forcible pursuit against such persons, to the utter extermination of them, their counsellors, aiders and abettors."[38]

The language both echoes and inverts the terms of the "Homily on Obedience." The Bond's "as well by force of arms as well by all other means" reverses the homiletic prohibition of rebellion, "either by force of armes or other waies." The peaceful and orderly hierarchy of the homily dissolves into the incitation to "utter extermination" of those who harmed or even counseled harm to Elizabeth. The oath invites the imaginative construction of unusual revenge devices; pursuit will encompass not simply force of arms, but "by all other means of Revenge." The oath imposes a remarkable barrier to the peaceful inheritance of Mary Queen of Scots and her son with its promise that all loyal subjects of Elizabeth who had sworn the oath would refuse to submit to any that "have, may or pretend title to come to this crown by the untimely death of her Majesty" and would "act the utmost revenge upon them, that by any means we do or any of us can devise and do, or cause to be devised and done for their utter overthrow and extirpation." While the imaginative construction of "all other means of revenge" was not pursued by English gentlemen in general, the invitation is amply fulfilled in the revenge devices imagined on the popular stage in the next decades.

Women, with one notable exception, were precluded from participation in this demonstration of loyalty and design for defense. No woman's signature is recorded on the bond,[39] though in a remarkably disingenuous move, Mary Queen of Scots, the individual against whom the entire edifice was constructed, did offer to sign. Her offer was refused and it was under provisions of the Act for the Queen's Safety that Mary was executed for her consent to the Babington Conspiracy against Elizabeth I. Of great interest is the exclusion of women from participation in the bond. Although the hierarchy of England signed this oath, from Privy Council, to Church, to gentlemen of the counties, when William Cecil organized the blood feud as an instrument of state policy, a sexual division of labor was clearly demarcated. Although women who served in the Privy Chamber did enter the Queen's service and were actually urged in a pamphlet in 1584 by Catholic rebels to act as Judith and take revenge on the wicked tyrant, Elizabeth standing for Holofernes, women did not participate in this masculine exercise of public fealty and promise of aggressive protection of the queen.[40] While the language of the bond projects the construction of extraordinary devices of revenge, participation in such devices does not seem to include female members of the household, except possibly under the direction of the master of the household. A violent attack on the integrity of the body of the state was to be punished by male justicers.

Such a gender division organizes the distribution of justified revenge in *Titus Andronicus*. The gender transformations of the Ovidian source serve to set the justified avenger of blood, Titus, against a range of outlaw figures, most notably the monstrous Tamora. Tamora's disguise as Revenge sets the Roman father against the Goth mother—paternal Roman law unmasks and vanquishes the false face of Revenge, to expose the maw of devouring mother. While both the Roman father and the Goth mother seem remarkably inimical to the survival of their children, only one is given triumphant legitimacy. Titus's body is given honorable burial, while in the last lines of the play, Tamora's body is cast out. "But throw her forth to beasts and birds to prey. / Her life was beastly and devoid of pity; / And being dead let birds on her take pity" (V.iii.198–200). This fantasia of paternity is made even more pointed by the transformation of the villain Moor, Aaron, whose desire to protect his newborn son leads to a remarkable character transformation in which he is moved to speak the truth and reveal his own villainy.[41] In contrast to such celebrations of paternity, Tamora, although in the first scene allowed to plead pitifully for the life of her son Alarbus, is soon revealed in an aside as malevolent and hostile to Roman law. Through these shifts that emphasize paternity and repudiate maternal and sororal alliances, Shakespeare changes his source to construct a more satisfactory story for his contemporary audience. The end of the play offers the image of patriarchal triumph, in which Rome has lost or cast out the bodies of women.

The absence of Progne and the fracturing of the feminine alliance of the source asserts the justice of masculine anger and effaces that of women. In a play that seems to elaborate horror—in one notable moment, the raped and mutilated daughter holds a chopped-off hand in her tongueless mouth and the mutilated father, who has just chopped off his hand, grieves over the decapitated heads of his sons—the discreet effacement of the revenge of Progne is remarkable. The public theater audience may view the monstrous, but feminine agency in the pursuit of vengeance

ranks as unsuitable fare. The union of two sisters who take vengeance on
the tyrant husband for the most intimate violation of the sister's body
does not seem fitting for representation on the public theater stage, yet reminders of that earlier narrative surface in the text.

Those reminders of the earlier narrative demonstrate that feminine initiative in blood feuds lies entirely outside the law. Feminine violence has
been appropriated by the masculine representative of law, Titus. The antagonism between Tamora and Lavinia denies the possibility of alliance between women. Tamora, the queen whose sexuality is entirely in her own
possession—the absence of any husband is notable; her sons, Demetrius
and Chiron produced by some form of parthenogenesis—attempts revenge with violence that is named monstrous and bestial. Lavinia, the virtuous patriarchal daughter whose sexuality is entirely in the possession of
males, submits to, assists, and dies by the hand of her father.[42]

Yet, the play does not produce a seamless ideological construction, and
indeed points towards the absences cut from the text. The reading scene of
Act IV, by making overt the suppression of the Ovidian story of feminine
alliance and vengeance with its insistence on the absence of Progne, evokes
alternative possibilities. When Lavinia uses a copy of Ovid's *Metamorphoses*
to lead, painfully slowly, her uncle and her father to recognition of her
rape, Progne's absence becomes pointed. The scene, by marking a shift in
feminine production from cloth to use of a book, presents in little the
problem of women's place in interpretive communities.[43] The "tedious
sampler" (II.iv.39) gives way to a written text and provides an image of the
long struggle of women to find their voices within and against the patriarchal canon.

The adult male figures in the scene remain remarkably obtuse to the
possibilities of feminine power. Lucius, the schoolboy not yet fully trained
in humanist reading practices, reads old texts in less constrained ways than
his grandfather and great-uncle and finds terror in them. The scene opens
with a submerged echo of the flight of Itys from the rage of his mother
and Philomel, as Lucius desperately flees from his aunt, Lavinia. The
schoolboy's alertness to the possibilities narrated in stories is not shared by
Marcus and Titus. Confident in their assessment of the patriarchal daughter, they assure him that she would not harm a child. "She loves thee, boy,
too well to do thee harm" (IV.ii.6). The boy's response—"Ay, when my father was in Rome she did"—marks his assertion that the loyalties of
women may be checked by the presence of the father, and suggests that
Roman order can only be sustained by the presence of the father. Lucius
directs his grandfather's attention to the potential in women for destructive anger by reminding him of the story of Hecuba, who took revenge by
gouging out the eyes of Polymestor and then killing his sons. "I have read

that Hecuba of Troy / Ran mad for sorrow" (IV.ii.20–21).[44] Yet, Lucius is sufficiently schooled in Roman assumptions to insist that Hecuba's rage was madness, while still perceiving in women a potential for harm, a perception unavailable to his father and grandfather. When Marcus sees Lavinia toss the *Metamorphoses* with her stumps, he sentimentalizes her activity: "For love of her that's gone / Perhaps she culled it from the rest" (IV.ii.43–44). For Marcus, Lavinia's reading selection indicates a pious affection for a dead sister-in-law, covering over the sinister hint of another absent sister by sentimentalizing feminine connections.

Finally, with an obtuseness tilting toward the comic, Titus notices the narrative that Lavinia has so agonizingly presented, and then summarizes the story in ways that he finds pertinent. "This is the tragic tale of Philomel, / And treats of Tereus' treason and his rape" (IV.i.47–48) presents a truncated summary of the Ovidian narrative in which Progne remains unnamed. As Lavinia reads the story of feminine alliance and anger, searching perhaps for the sister who can read her signs aright, Titus translates the story of rape and feminine vengeance into that of Lucrece, whose suicide after rape precipitates the fall of the first Roman emperors. This translation shifts attention from the body of the woman to the actions of the revengers of blood, a shift quite common in visual representations of the rape of Lucrece, in which the body of the dead women is shunted to one side of the picture frame and the band of revengers become central.[45] In the final act, Titus will construct the common trope of Lucrece in which masculine responsibilities and actions in the foundation of the state are raised on the passive body of a suffering woman. Nevertheless, this reading scene deliberately marks the shift from the Ovidian story. As Lavinia continues to look at the book, Marcus's observation "See, brother, see, note how she quotes the leaves," draws our attention to the story to suggest that Titus's summary of the story may be inadequate.

Of central significance is the change in Lavinia's method for the revelation of her rape. Lavinia uses the tools of literacy, a book and writing, rather than Philomel's traditional weaving in cloth. Although the image of the woman writer presented on the stage is a monstrous one, the tongueless, handless woman reassembles an organ capable of communication. Lavinia's writing practice clearly images Woman as Lack, and severe restrictions are placed on the narrative she can write.[46] She writes in Latin, the tongue of the educated male, and she writes a word that will activate a system of punishment performed by males. She can name rape only in Latin—*stuprum*—just as in the forest she could not speak the word.[47]

Despite the mutilated horror of this female figure, she succeeds in communication, however limited, and moments in the scene hint at feminine resistance to masculine appropriation. Marcus suggests a very clumsy method for writing by guiding a staff with his mouth and feet, a method that Lavinia changes: "She takes the staff in her mouth and guides it with her stumps and writes" (IV.i.76).[48] These small elements in the reading scene hint at feminine resistance to masculine appropriation and provide elements available for later readers. Sororal pity and grief and rage central to the Ovidian story cannot yet be spoken, because this version of rape insists on the mutilated agency of women.

To her onstage interpreters, Lavinia can be understood when she takes up their tools and constructs herself in their image of the feminine. They allow her to become an instrument in the process of vengeance, but only a subordinate. While men may perform the task of vengeance directly, feminine hands can only testify to assault, seek male protection, and perhaps bear a basin in the stumps. At this moment, Progne is erased, as the story of Lucrece prevails. The uneasy oscillation in the play of narratives of vengeance between a rape avenged by a woman, by domestic means, through the killing of her child, and a rape avenged by a male, against a tyrant, here tilts to the public community of male avengers. Stories of masculine action take priority over stories of feminine anger. The woman's words, written in the sand, are accepted as they fit into a masculine order. Having given evidence, Lavinia withdraws from central stage. She takes a subordinate role, returns veiled, to be displayed by her father as motive for his revenge, fitted into his play. However, the submerged Ovidian story of feminine alliance in anger does surface in the penultimate scene, when Titus prepares his grim banquet and cheerfully tells Chiron and Demetrius that they are to become their mother's supper. "For worse than Philomel you used my daughter / And worse than Progne I will be revenged" (V.ii.95–96). Titus's boast unites the Senecan topos of excess in vengeance while pointing to the act of appropriation that has taken place.

In this scene, masculine responsibility for vengeance is affirmed, while feminine agency in revenge is demonized. Throughout the scene, audience tension builds through fear that Titus has failed to penetrate Tamora's disguise as Revenge. His discernment of her disguise and his threats to her in asides pull the audience into complicity with him against the false feminine revenger. Whatever modicum of sympathy Tamora may have earned at the beginning of the play she forfeits by her cruel encouragement of rape. In the last lines of the play, her death unmourned, she returns to the kingdom of beasts. "But throw her forth to beasts and birds of prey. Her life was beastly and devoid of pity / And being dead let birds on her take pity" (V.iii.198–200). These final lines align the homiletic prescriptions and prohibitions about anger to legitimize the actions of the male avenger of blood.

The gendering of emotions stands as a central didactic process in the final moments of the play. The woman without pity is categorized as bestial, a tiger, one whose body cannot be contained within the state. Lavinia has defined the appropriate arena for feminine emotion, when in Act III she trains Titus in the empathic use of tears, moving him from grandiose ambitions to cover the earth with water to participation in a community of mourners, amplifying his authority as suffering and empathic father, moved to revenge by grief. These final lines reiterate the gendered division of emotional labor that the play constructs. Titus, who has taken a notable vengeance, receives honorable burial in the family monument.

In transforming the Ovidian narrative, Shakespeare shifts rape from the realm of feminine suffering and anger to one of patriarchal responsibility. When Progne is excised from the text, the meaning of rape changes. In turning attention to the male avenger of the blood, the play shifts away from focus on the suffering body of the female and towards the damage to the patriarchal family and the dismembering of paternal authority over the body of the daughter. The female experience of pain transforms not to anger but to a trope. The rape of a woman is a demonstration of tyranny, which must be punished for its damage to the property of its citizens. Any potential for the imagination of political agency for women possibly figured in the Ovidian text in Progne's anger has been appropriated in the play for the male avenger of blood.

The potential agency of the female victim becomes further limited by the mutilation of her hands, which denies her the possibility of communication with a female audience through the medium of fabric. The separation of Lavinia from the traditional medium of fabric anticipates changes in the production of cloth and the growth of the cloth industry that removed women from their traditional responsibilities for cloth production, though presumably women continued to spin fiber into thread.[49] Lavinia's inability to form an alliance with any other woman is made explicit in the rape scene, when she begs pity from Tamora, who repudiates her. Yet, despite the excesses of mutilation and silencing, Lavinia does manage to communicate the name of her rapists. Her agency in the reading scene marks the painful movement of individual women into authorship and participation in exercises of literacy.[50]

While the overt narrative in Titus reiterates a patriarchal story about the exchange of women, the necessary silencing of feminine anger, and the appropriation of justice by males, within the text lie fragments of another story, in which two women ally in anger against the rapist. The mutilated agency of Lavinia as reader and writer describes the painful movement of women as writers and readers of stories. The incident of pedagogic failure with which I began this essay has opened a method for teaching the text that offers agency to those students who may find themselves momentarily frozen through identification with a mutilated victim.

Instead of reinscription of victimization, source analysis, when introduced as a quest, can offer agency to the readers who may find in Lavinia's search for the absent Progne, revenger of her sister's wrongs, an anticipation of twentieth- and twenty-first-century feminist challenges to patriarchal understandings and positionings of rape.

Notes

1. The story of the rape of Philomel by her brother-in-law, Tereus, and the subsequent revenge by her sister Progne from Book VI of Ovid's *Metamorphoses* had been translated into English by Arthur Golding in 1567. Sylvan Barnet, editor for the Signet edition of *Titus Andronicus* (New York: New American Library, 1963), points towards Golding's translation as an influence, noting that the spelling of the title of Ovid's text, "'tis Ovid's Metamorphosis" (IV.i.42) repeats Golding's spelling of the title in his translation of Ovid (London, 1567). Tarquin's rape of Lucrece, originally told by Livy in his history of Rome (Book I), was a well known humanist trope and had already served as the subject of Shakespeare's poem, *The Rape of Lucrece*. Another story from Livy, of Virginia and her noble Roman father Virginius, provides a further analogue for the vengeance of a father for rape. Two versions of that story were in circulation in Elizabethan England. In Livy's History (Book III), Virginia's father kills her after her rape. In the hybrid morality *Appius and Virginia* (c. 1559–68), her father preserves her chastity by killing her before rape. Livy's version is cited in *Alphonsus, Emperor of Germany* (1594) as precedent for a father's murder of his daughter after she is tricked into sexual intercourse (Act IV, scene iii.). For discussion of the analogues, see J. C. Maxwell, ed., *Titus Andronicus*, Arden Shakespeare 2nd series (London: Methuen, 1968), pp. xxvii–xxxii. For sources, see Geoffrey Bullough, *Narrative and Dramatic Sources of Shakespeare* (New York: Columbia University Press, 1966), Vol. 6, pp. 3–79. Quotations from Livy are from *The Romane Historie written by T. Livius of Padua*, translated by Philemon Holland (London, 1600), Book 1.

   I would like to thank my sister Elizabeth Robertson for her sensitive and incisive comments throughout the long gestation of this work. My thanks also to Jim Brain, Mita Choudhury, Carole Levin, and Paul Russell for their help.

2. Edward Ravenscroft's earlier dismissal of the play in 1687, "'tis the most incorrect and undigested piece of all his Works; it seems rather a heap of Rubbish then a Structure" expresses the attitudes that produced doubt over authorship. More recently, critics have engaged in an ongoing debate over classical influences on the play. Eugene Waith's influential essay arguing for Ovidian rather than Senecan influence, "The Metamorphosis of Violence in *Titus Andronicus*," *Shakespeare Survey* 10 (1957): 39–49, draws on the earlier work of Howard Baker, *Introduction to Tragedy: A Study in the Development of Form in Gorboduc, The Spanish Tragedy, and Titus Andronicus*

(Baton Rouge: Louisiana State University Press, 1939), pp. 121–53. Albert Tricomi resituates the play as Shakespeare's "witty competition with [both] Ovid and Seneca" in "The Aesthetics of Mutilation in *Titus Andronicus,*" *Shakespeare Survey* 27 (1974): 11–19. Grace Starry West, *Going by the Book: Classical Allusions in Shakespeare's* Titus Andronicus (Chapel Hill: University of North Carolina, 1982), pp. 62–77, reads the play as an analysis of the failures of humanist education. Maurice Hunt in "Compelling Art in *Titus Andronicus,*" *Studies in English Literature* 28 (1988): 197–218, traces misreadings of the Ovidian story by characters remarkably alert to classical texts, though he fails to comment on the shift in the gender of the revenger. For a magisterial summary of the Ovidian tradition and the critique of humanism that produces only cannier criminal minds educated by their classical reading, see Jonathan Bate, *Shakespeare and Ovid* (Oxford: Clarendon Press, 1993), pp. 100–117.

3. Bate, ed., *Titus Andronicus,* Arden Shakespeare, 3rd Series (London: Routledge, 1995), p. 90. Unless otherwise noted, all quotations from *Titus Andronicus* are taken from this edition.

4. Alfred Harbage and Samuel Schoenbaum, *Annals of English Drama* (Philadelphia: University of Pennsylvania Press, 1964), pp. 38–39 record James Calfhill's adaptation of a Corraro play, *Progne,* produced at Christ Church, Oxford, on September 5, 1566.

5. See E. Jane Burns, *Bodytalk: When Women Speak in Old French Literature* (Philadelphia: University of Pennsylvania Press, 1993), pp. 115–50, for a rich analysis of the Philomela story.

6. For an early feminist discussion of the Ovidian influence, see Nancy L. Paxton, "Daughters of Lucrece: Shakespeare's Response to Ovid in *Titus Andronicus,*" *Classical Models in Literature,* ed. Warren Anderson, Walter Dietze, and Zoran Konstantinovic (Innsbruck: Inst. für Sprachwissenschaft der Univ. Innsbruck, 1981), pp. 217–24. Paxton distinguishes the violence of Lavinia's rape from interpretations that collapse it with other forms of symbolic and emotional violence in the play. For feminist examination of the meaning of rape in the Lucrece poem, see Coppélia Kahn, "The Rape of Lucrece in Shakespeare's Lucrece," *Shakespeare Studies* 9 (1976): 45–72. See also Kahn's "Lucrece: The Sexual Politics of Subjectivity," *Rape and Representation,* ed. Lynn A. Higgins and Brenda R. Silver (New York: Columbia University Press, 1991), pp. 141–59, for discussion of the scopic economy of rape and the construction of masculine subjectivity. Her work on Lucrece has paralleled my examination of Lavinia.

7. For a feminist rereading of Levi-Strauss's *The Elementary Structures of Kinship,* see Judith Butler, *Gender Trouble: Feminism and the Subversion of Identity* (New York: Routledge, 1990), pp. 40–41. See also Butler on Gayle Rubin's important, early feminist essay on Levi-Strauss, "The Traffic in Women: Notes on the 'Political Economy' of Sex," *Toward an Anthropology of Women,* ed. Rayna R. Reiter (New York: Monthly Review Press, 1975), cited and discussed by Butler, pp. 72–77.

8. See Gwynne Kennedy's recent book, *Just Anger: Representing Women's Anger in Early Modern England* (Carbondale: Southern Illinois Press, 2000).

9. In Chaucer's version of the Philomel story in *The Legend of Good Women,* Philomel weaves actual letters into her tapestry that Progne reads. The story ends with the sisters' grief and does not tell the story of their revenge.

10. While the class was taught in the English department, it provided credit for women's studies majors and had drawn a wide range of non-English majors. As a practice, I now introduce material about rape with an acknowledgement of its potential for pain to some members of the class.

11. The class had only one male student. For an earlier discussion of this incident, see my essay, "Discussing Rape in the Classroom," *Medieval Feminist Newsletter* 9 (1990): 21–22. This example of the silencing produced in the classroom by the recourse to experience is one example of the problems raised by Diana Fuss in "Essentialism in the Classroom," *Essentially Speaking: Feminism, Nature, and Difference* (New York: Routledge, 1989), pp. 113–19. I recently introduced the topic in another class with a careful acknowledgement of its painful meaning for some members of the class. Benjamin J. Kohl, my co-teacher and a Renaissance historian, observed that while for most students whom we teach, the horrors of history—starvation, pillage, death or dismemberment in war, and slavery—are remote, rape has an immediate resonance for women who discover a personal connection that transforms their relationship to representations of past suffering. For the most part, male students have not experienced rape, though they can make an empathic connection. Feminine superiority in the experience of suffering can then make male students feel defensive. One further layer: In the spring of 1996, a queer student pointed out that my presumption of the significance of rape for women reinscribes traditional gender categories. After his comment, male students in the class sheepishly affirmed that while they had agreed that they tended not to fear rape in daily life, they were apprehensive about rape should they go to jail. While I think it is important that we acknowledge that men can be raped and that the shame and silencing after such an experience may actually be greater than that for women because of homophobia and the assault on heterosexual male identity, classical stories are engaged in the construction of heterosexual binarisms in which women are the primary victims of rape. I am grateful to Damien Keane for his comments on the complicated position of male students during such discussions in class. Similar silences may be produced for students of color when historical narratives of racist violence violate the boundaries of academic space and isolate them as witnesses with a particular connection to those past experiences. See bell hooks, "Representing Whiteness in the Black Imagination," *Cultural Studies,* ed. Lawrence Grossberg, Cary Nelson, and Paula Treichler (New York: Routledge, 1992), pp. 338–46.

12. Stephanie Jed's complex argument in *Chaste Thinking: The Rape of Lucretia and the Birth of Humanism* (Bloomington: Indiana University Press, 1989) challenges the humanist interpretation of the story of Lucrece's rape as a

narrative of freedom by examining and interrupting the rhetorical and material means by which the story of Lucretia circulates.

13. That such problems can occur in introductory Women's Studies classes has
led to a conservative denigration of their value. I by no means intend to
urge a return to a traditional separation between experience and intellect,
but am suggesting the difficulties in creating a shared intellectual community, in which pain is open to question and discussion as well as empathy.
Such classroom silences seem induced in part because the political understandings of the phrase, "the personal is political," have been coopted by a
therapeutic use of narrative for personal recovery. See Wendy Kaminer, *I'm
Dysfunctional, You're Dysfunctional: The Recovery Movement and Other Self-
Help Fashions* (Reading, MA: Addison-Wesley, 1992), on the depoliticiza-
tion of feminist consciousness-raising techniques in the recovery
movement. Painful histories were recounted in consciousness-raising
groups for purposes of understanding and political analysis, not individual
therapy. See Joan Scott on the foundational use of experience, "Experience," in *Feminists Theorize the Political,* ed. Judith Butler and Joan W. Scott
(New York: Routledge, 1992), pp. 22–40. For a discussion of the place of
"experience" within contemporary theories of knowledge, see Sneja
Gunew, "Feminist Knowledge: Critique and Construct" in *Feminist Knowledge: Critique and Construct,* ed. Sneja Gunew (London: Routledge, 1990),
pp. 13–25. The continuing controversy over appropriate feminist discussions of rape erupted in England in the summer of 1998, when Fay Wel-
don was severely castigated in the press when she suggested that rape was
not the worst injury that women could endure.

14. For a psychoanalytic study of maternality in Shakespeare's later plays, see
Janet Adelman, *Suffocating Mothers: Fantasies of Maternal Origin in Shakespeare's Plays, Hamlet to The Tempest* (New York: Routledge, 1992) and for a
cultural study of the demonic mother, see Deborah Willis, *Malevolent Nurture: Witch-Hunting and Maternal Power in Early Modern England* (Ithaca, NY:
Cornell University Press, 1995).

15. My understanding of the meaning of the story of Philomel is grounded in
Jane Marcus's "Still Practice, A/Wrested Alphabet: Toward a Feminist Aesthetic" in *Art and Anger* (Miami, OH: Ohio State University Press, 1988),
pp. 215–49, and Patricia Klindienst Joplin's "The Voice of the Shuttle is
Ours," in *Rape and Representation,* ed. Lynn A. Higgins and Brenda R. Silver, pp. 34–64. My reading of Lavinia has been deepened by the sensitive
analysis of the meaning of the suffering woman by Cynthia Marshall in "'I
can interpret all her martyr'd signs': *Titus Andronicus,* Feminism, and the
Limits of Interpretation," in *Sexuality and Politics in Renaissance Drama,* ed.
Carole Levin and Karen Robertson (Lewiston, NY: Edwin Mellen Press,
1991), pp. 193–211. Her psychoanalytic approach differs from my placement of the play within Elizabethan juridical arguments over vengeance.

16. Pandion's war with Tereus and subsequent offer of the daughter as token
to cement peace in the feud is a device central to classical and medieval

revenge narratives. The story of Progne and Philomel is unusual because
it foregrounds the conflict of the wife and grants her agency in demonstrating her loyalty to her natal family. All quotations from Ovid are taken
from Arthur Golding's English translation, *Metamorphosis* (London, 1567)
as cited in Bullough, pp. 49–58.

17. Jane Marcus, in "Still Practice, A/Wrested Alphabet" is eloquent on the
empathic process required for reading her sister's story, p. 217. In the recent
production by the Royal Shakespeare Company, *Tales from Ovid,* Progne
carefully reads the cloth banners that depict the rape through a sequence
of stick figures.

18. Ovid's critique may perhaps signal the difficulty of transforming barbarians
into Romans. For a study of Ovid, see Joseph B. Solodow, *The World of
Ovid's Metamorphoses* (Chapel Hill: University of North Carolina Press,
1988). I am grateful to Molly Levine and Margaret Fusco for directing me
to this work. For two recent feminist analyses of the *Metamorphoses,* see
Genevieve Lively, "Reading Resistance in Ovid's *Metamorphose,*" pp.
197–213 and Alison Keith, "Versions of Epic Masculinity in Ovid's *Metamorphoses,*" pp. 214–39 in *Ovidian Transformations: Essays on Ovid's Metamorphoses and Its Reception,* ed. Philip Hardie, Alessandro Barchiesi, and
Stephen Hinds (Cambridge: Cambridge Philological Society, 1999). For a
study of Ovid in the Renaissance, see Lynn Enterline, "Petrarch Reading
(Himself Reading) Ovid," in *Desire in the Renaissance: Psychoanalysis and Literature,* ed. Valeria Finucci and Regina Schwartz (Princeton, NJ: Princeton
University Press), pp. 120–46.

19. See Catherine Belsey's argument in *Subject of Tragedy* (London: Methuen,
1985), particularly on murderous women, pp. 129–48.

20. Burns, pp. 135, 137.

21. *Titus Andronicus* was sufficiently popular to be used by Ben Jonson in
Bartholomew Fair in 1614 as an example of a hopelessly old-fashioned play:
"He that will sweare, Ieronimo, or Andronicus are the best play, yet, shall
pass unexcepted at here, as a man whose judgement shews it is constant,
and hath stood still, these five and twenty, or thirty years," ed. G. R. Hibbard (New York: Norton, New Mermaids, 1981), Introduction, 103–6.

22. Despite Hunt's engaging alertness to the Ovidian misreadings, his argument rests on an assumption of the tilting of Titus from sympathetic
avenger to a "scourge worthy of ruin" (206), a critical commonplace that
I dispute. For less moralized readings of the status of the avenger of blood,
see S. F. Johnson, "The Spanish Tragedy or Babylon Revisited," *Essays on
Shakespeare and Elizabethan Drama in Honor of Hardin Craig,* ed. Richard
Hosley (Columbia, MO: University of Missouri Press, 1962), pp. 29–32.

23. One example of state control over the private blood feud can be seen in
the reduction of the number of acts of violence by aristocrats between
1580 and 1639, Lawrence Stone, *Crisis of the Aristocracy* (Oxford: Clarendon Press, 1965), Appendix XV, p.770. See also attempts to control duel-
ing. For the foundational discussion of the relationship between revenge

plays and the state, see Fredson Bowers, *Elizabethan Revenge Tragedy* (Princeton, NJ: Princeton University Press, 1940). See also Ronald Broude, "Four Forms of Justice in *Titus Andronicus*," *Journal of English and Germanic Philology* 78 (1979): 494–507. Jonathan Dollimore in *Radical Tragedy: Religion, Ideology and Power in the Drama of Shakespeare and His Contemporaries* (Brighton: Harvester, 1984) draws on J. W. Lever, *The Tragedy of State,* 1971 (rpt. London: Methuen, 1987), to initiate his important antifoundationalist reading of late Elizabethan and Jacobean tragedy.

24. Jean E. Howard, *The Stage and Social Struggle in Early Modern England* (London: Routledge, 1994), p. 14. Despite the exclusion of women from justified vengeance, some female members of the Jacobean audience may have derived new understandings for feminine agency from the concomitant representation of revenging women as monstrous Furie. Such possibilities seem opened more by Jacobean revenge tragedies than by the Elizabethan *Titus.*

25. The exclusion of women from bands of revengers can be contrasted with the transformation of the foolish courtier, Balurdo, in John Marston's *Antonio's Revenge,* into a sensate man capable of judging and punishing the tyrant. See Karen Robertson, "*Antonio's Revenge:* The Tyrant, the Stoic and the Passionate Man," *Medieval and Renaissance Drama in England IV,* ed. Paul Werstine (New York: AMS Press, 1989), pp. 92–106.

26. Livy's story of Lucrece emphasizes her vigorous agency in suicide. Significantly, she constructs her death as necessary for the disciplining of other women. "And never shall there by example of Lucretia, any unhonest woman or wanton callot live a day: and thus having said, with a knife which she had close hidden under her clothes, shee stabbed her selfe to the heart, and sinking downe forward, fell upon the floore readie to yield up the ghost." *The Romane Historie,* Book 1, p. 41.

27. The *OED* citation of Byron's line from *Don Juan* (CXXIV) "Sweet is revenge—especially to women" (1818) marks and participates in that ideological construction.

28. Bowers, pp. 5–8.

29. "An Exhortacion concernyng Good Ordre and Obedience to Rulers and Magistrates," *Certayne Sermons or Homelies (1547) and A Homily against Disobedience and Wilful Rebellion (1570): A Critical Edition,* ed. Ronald B. Bond (Toronto: University of Toronto Press, 1987), p. 164.

30. "An Homelie agaynst Contencion and Braulynge," *Certayne Sermons,* p.195.

31. "An Exhortacion concernyng Good Ordre and Obedience to Rulers and Magistrates," *Certayne Sermons,* p. 166.

32. Griselda's story appeared at the end of the *Decameron* and so pleased Erasmus that he retold it in Latin. See Maureen Quilligan, *The Allegory of Female Authority: Christine de Pizan's Cité des Dames* (Ithaca: Cornell University Press, 1991), p. 165. Chaucer retold it in the *Clerk's Tale* in the *Canterbury Tales.*

33. William Whately, *A Bride-bush* (London, 1623). I am grateful to Gwynne Kennedy who first drew my attention to this text.

34. *Certayne Sermons,* p. 199.

35. Modern testimony of rape survivors suggests that the experience of rape produces permanent trauma, testimony affirmed by the claim of the student who said that rape was worse than having your hands cut off and tongue cut out. See Nancy V. Raine, whose discussion of the impact of the anniversary of the day on which she was raped in a *New York Times* "Hers" column (October 2, 1994) and her subsequent book, *After Silence: Rape and My Journey Back* (New York: Crown, 1998) makes clear the absolute transformation of her world after rape and the damage inflicted by silence. For discussion of the effects of trauma, see Judith Lewis Herman, *Trauma and Recovery* (New York: Basic Books, 1992). I am grateful to Damien Keane for drawing my attention to this reference.

36. Elizabeth V. Spelman, "Anger and Insubordination" in *Women, Knowledge, and Reality: Explorations in Feminist Philosophy,* ed. Ann Garry and Marilyn Pearsall (Boston: Unwin Hyman, 1989), pp. 263–73.

37. My understanding of the distinction between power and authority is taken from Michelle Rosaldo's "A Theoretical Overview," in Rosaldo and Louise Lamphere's *Women, Culture, and Society* (Stanford: Stanford University Press, 1976). She quotes M. G. Smith: "Authority is, in the abstract, the right to make a particular decision and to command obedience. . . . Power . . . is the ability to act effectively on persons or things, to make or secure favourable decisions which are not of right allocated to the individuals or their roles" *Government in Zazau* (London, pp. 18–19), cited by Rosaldo, note 2, p. 21.

38. The Bond, three paragraphs long, is reproduced in E. M. Tenison, *Elizabethan England* V, Appendix B, pp. 206–7.

39. David Cressy, in *Literacy and the Social Order* (Cambridge: Cambridge University Press, 1980), notes that two women householders signed an instrument of association in 1642, but does not note women's names in the 1584 bond.

40. James Anthony Froude, *History of England from the Fall of Wolsey to the Defeat of the Spanish Armada,* Part 6 (1862–90; rpt. New York: AMS Press, 1969), XII, p. 13.

41. A Lacanian reading of the opposition between Titus and Tamora could see the subordination of the mother-child dyad before the law of the father, as the alliance of the tiger dam and her cubs gives way before the Roman father, with all approval vested in the father.

42. The Longleat manuscript depicts Lavinia holding a bowl in her stumps to catch the blood of her rapists to be added to the pie.

43. The reading scene is discussed by Mary Lamb in *Gender and Authorship in the Sidney Circle,* as well as by Hunt and Marshall. For a rich discussion of Deborah Warner's production and RSC policies towards women in general, see Joyce Green Macdonald, "Women and Theatrical Authority: Deborah

Warner's *Titus Andronicus,*" in *Differences in Women's Revisions of Shakespeare,* ed. Marianne Novy (Urbana: University of Illinois Press) pp. 185–205.

44. Grace Starry West observes that Titus's revenge also subsumes the vengeance of Hecuba for the death of Polydorus, recounted in Euripides' *Hecuba.*

45. See Ian Donaldson's valuable study of that process in *The Rapes of Lucretia: A Myth and Its Transformations* (Oxford: Clarendon, 1982).

46. The painful writing of the mutilated woman provides an image of the humanist monster, the woman writer, and suggests anxieties over authorship in the late Tudor period. See Lamb and Susan Frye's essay on Spenser in this volume.

47. See Diana Moses for analysis of the changing conception of the term *stuprum* in Roman law, "Livy's Lucretia and the Validity of Coerced Consent in Roman Law," in *Consent and Coercion to Sex and Marriage in Ancient and Medieval Societies,* ed. Angeliki E. Laiou (Washington, DC: Dumbarton Oaks, 1993), pp. 39–81. The archaic term described defilement or pollution. Augustan meanings began to include a condemnation of the "victim," the persons being used, although the term does not necessarily signal coercion. Non-consent was indicated by the qualification *per vim.* T. E., in his explication of Roman law in *The Lawe's Resolution of Women's Rights* (London, 1632), attempted to confine coerced sexual intercourse to the term *stuprum* and reserve *raptus* for forcible abduction, a verbal distinction that is dramatized in the play in Lavinia's abduction in Act I and her subsequent rape in Act II.

48. Cynthia Marshall perceptively comments on Lavinia's transformation of Marcus's instruction, a difference in the stage directions not noted by Hunt, and a significant resistance by the female character to male instruction.

49. On women and cloth production in general, see Elizabeth Wayland Barber, *Women's Work: The First 20,000 Years* (New York: Norton, 1994). For women in Early Modern cloth production, see Judith Bennett, "Medieval Women, Modern Women: Across The Great Divide," in *Culture and History 1350–1699: Essays on English Communities, Identities and Writing,* ed. David Aers (London: Harvester Wheatsheaf, 1992), pp. 147–75 and Merry Wiesner, *Women and Gender in Early Modern Europe* (Cambridge: Cambridge University Press, 1993), pp. 97–100.

50. Mary Ellen Lamb, *Gender and Authorship in the Sidney Circle* (Madison: University of Wisconsin Press, 1990), pp. 194–228, places Philomel as revenger within the context of female authorship. For a recent study of the problems of female authorship more generally, see Wendy Wall, "Dancing in a Net: The Problems of Female Authorship" *Imprint of Gender: Authorship and Publication in the English Renaissance* (Ithaca, NY: Cornell University Press, 1993), pp. 279–347.

PART III

LAW, CONSENT, SUBJECTIVITY

CHAPTER 8

RAPE IN THE MEDIEVAL LATIN COMEDIES

Anne Howland Schotter

> The twelfth-century Latin "comedies" simultaneously condone rape
> (reflecting the school culture in which they were used to teach the
> trivium to young boys) and condemn it (reflecting the new concern
> for consent among canon lawyers).

The interest in rape in the lives of medieval authors, as well as in medieval literature itself, has grown in recent years. Christopher Cannon has explored the exact nature of the charge of *raptus* from which
Geoffrey Chaucer was released, and its implication for the treatment of
rape in his poetry.[1] Kathryn Gravdal, in *Ravishing Maidens: Writing Rape in
Medieval French Literature and Law,* has argued that in the genres of pastourelle and beast fable, rape is often tolerated, if not actually relished.[2]
Few, however, have noticed that another medieval genre, the little known
medieval Latin works referred to variously as "comedies," "elegiac comedies," and "Latin comic tales," often use rape as either a plot device or a
subtext, generally to condone or euphemize it.[3]

Most of the medieval Latin comedies were written by clerics in north-
ern France during the twelfth-century revival of classical learning as rhetorical exercises for adolescent males learning the trivium.[4] While there is no
consensus as to what their exact genre was or whether they were enacted
dramatically, it is agreed that the comedies are short narratives in Latin elegiac verse with a plain style and a happy ending.[5] Their plots involve a
clever intrigue, often a sexual one in which a husband is duped by either
another man or his own wife. Generically they have often been compared
to the Latin and vernacular fabliaux, which they resemble in presenting
women as lustful, whether sexually aggressive or merely compliant.[6] Most

of the comedies that deal with rape justify it implicitly with assumption that it is women's true desire; these include *Geta, Alda, De Tribus Puellis,* and *De Nuncio Sagaci.* One, however, *Pamphilus,* complicates the misogynistic attitude by attending to the woman's feelings and by including her voice.

These two attitudes in the comedies show the influence of opposing strands of thought in the twelfth century. The first view, that women want to be raped, had long been held in the Middle Ages, while the second, that women, as well as men, desired and deserved a choice in partners, was much newer, being debated at the time by theologians and canon lawyers. The first attitude was actually inculcated in the medieval schoolroom, where both the pedagogical practices and the curriculum itself had the effect of normalizing violence. Rita Copeland has written that the "countless images of the medieval school room and . . . the iconography of Lady Grammar herself, often depicted with flagellum in hand" remind us that "the teaching of grammar is inextricably linked in ancient and medieval imagination with violence to the body."[7] Furthermore, as Marjorie Curry Woods has pointed out in her insightful article "Rape and the Pedagogical Rhetoric of Sexual Violence," rape was an actual plot device in many school texts. She suggests that given their regular experience with corporal punishment, young students in the process of forming masculine identities would have been led to identify with both the victims and the perpetrators of rape in such texts.[8] Although, as will be seen below, I believe that *Pamphilus* presents the woman's situation with more sympathy than Woods acknowledges, her argument is persuasive for most of the other medieval Latin comedies.

The second attitude towards rape in the comedies was influenced by theories propounded in the twelfth century by Gratian and other canon lawyers and implemented by Pope Alexander III—that consent won by persuasion rather than force was essential to forming a good marriage.[9] Such theories supported a couple's freedom from parental intervention in choosing spouses, and while showing more interest in marriage than in rape, indicated a climate in clerical circles in which sexual violence was coming under criticism. Even in practice, James Brundage has argued, rape was becoming less widespread among aristocratic men as a means of gaining wives:

> Suitors wishing to win the hand of a lady whose parents opposed their wooing were beginning to find more subtle ways of securing their goal. Where such a suitor a century earlier might have abducted the woman and pressed his suit by force and intimidation, early twelfth-century males seem to have been more inclined to resort to charm, blandishments, and acts of valor to win over the lady's heart. Ravishment was giving way to seduction as the preferred method of capturing an heiress against her family's wishes.[10]

Historians and literary critics alike have linked this new emphasis on consent to the rise of "courtly love" in twelfth-century literature. R. Howard Bloch, for instance, notes that romances stressing the power to choose appeared at precisely the moment that such choice was becoming possible.[11]

The authors of the comedies explored this tension between the defense of rape and the promotion of consent. In doing so they turned to classical texts that shared similar concerns, among them the Roman comedies of Plautus and Terence, which often recount sexual intrigues, explore the relation between deception, coercion, and the will, and finally, explicitly condone rape. With their insistently happy endings in which boy gets girl, such plays reveal remarkably little concern with the woman's will, and far more with the competition between men—clever lovers and possessive husbands or fathers—over women as sexual property.

A classical source more influential than either Plautus or Terence and far more complex, was Ovid, who both described subtle erotic persuasion, and explicitly recommended rape. In the *Metamorphoses,* he includes tales of mythological rape and seduction, showing Jupiter transforming himself into a bull or a shower of gold in order to "ravish" mortal maidens.[12] Although he aesthetically distances these acts, he also gives attention to the woman's feelings. In his amatory poetry, however, Ovid addresses the issue of rape more literally, apparently justifying it with the claim that women secretly want it. In the didactic *Ars Amatoria,* for instance, the speaker, though he insists on the importance of eloquence in seduction, advises the lover to use force when the time is right:

uim licet appelles: grata est uis ista puellis;
quod iuuat, invitae saepe dedisse uolunt.
quaecumque est Veneris subita uiolata rapina,
gaudet, et inprobitas muneris instar habet.
at quae, cum posset cogi, non tacta recessit,
ut simulet uultu gaudia, tristis erit.[13]

[Force is all right to employ, and women like you to use it;
What they enjoy they pretend they were unwilling to give.
One who is overcome, and suddenly, forcefully taken,
Welcomes the wanton assault, takes it as proof of her charm.
But if you let her go untouched when you could have compelled her,
Though she pretends to be glad, she will be gloomy at heart.[14]]

Ovid is the primary source of the medieval Latin comedies, and their authors found his representations of rape, whether empathetic or cynical, of great importance. *Geta, Alda,* and *De Tribus Puellis,* whose plots involve seduction, deception, or even female sexual initiative, all allude to either the mythological rapes described in the *Metamorphoses* or to the advice in the *Ars Amatoria*. While the last comedies to be considered both focus on literal rape, one, *De Nuncio Sagaci,* does so simplistically, supporting the cynical advice given in Ovid's amatory poetry, while the other, *Pamphilus,* does so with more subtlety, showing, by the woman's strong protests, that she has not given her consent. The strong and eloquent voice that she is given marks this poem as an unusual departure from the medieval Latin comedies, one that looks forward to the portrayal of female voice in vernacular romance.

Most of the comedies that deal with sexual violence justify it by assuming women's innate lustfulness, and therefore their consent. Vitalis of Blois, for instance, in his *Geta,*[15] an adaptation of Plautus' *Amphitryon,* makes it clear that Jupiter's impersonation of Amphitryon to make love to his wife, Alcmena, meets with her satisfaction. Rather than a rape, he presents the act as a mythological "ravishing" in the Ovidian manner, and applauds Alcmena's cleverness in explaining the situation to her jealous husband. The poem ends happily with the married couple's embrace. Similarly, the *Alda*[16] of William of Blois assumes that the woman's consent is automatic, and in this case applauds a male lover's cleverness in deceiving another man. The woman's father has locked up his innocent daughter Alda in order to shield her from all contact with men, but her would-be lover Pyrrhus gains access to her chamber by disguising himself as her best friend, his own sister. As they caress each other, Alda is greatly intrigued by the surprising "tail" that gives such pleasure, and regrets that her friend has failed to purchase a bigger one at the marketplace. Despite Alda's enthusiasm, however, the poem's explicit allusions to Ovid's recommendation of rape in the *Ars Amatoria* suggest an element of sexual coercion. For, as Alison Elliott has pointed out, the lines "Sumpta satis Pyrrhus post oscula cetera sumit. / Defloratus abit uirginitatis honor" (*Alda* l. 465; "After Pyrrhus / has taken enough kisses, he takes all the rest—/ he enjoys her virginity's flower"[17]) echo Ovid's scornful advice to the timid lover, "oscula qui sumpsit, si not et cetera sumit, / haec quoque, quae data sunt, perdere dignus erit" ("Once you have taken a kiss, the other things surely will follow, / Or, if they don't, you should lose all you have taken before").[18] The poet asserts that Alda was pleased by the act, and with the couple's marriage, provides a happy ending: "Acta placent, culpaque sua laudatur uterque, / Et deceptoris sponsa fit Alda sui" (ll. 565–66).

With their cynical view of rape and seduction, *Geta* and *Alda* certainly fit the model of school texts for adolescent males described by Woods. The anonymous comedy *De tribus Puellis*[19] fits that model as well, but also includes the woman's expression of her desires in such a way as to suggest the influence of the contemporary theological interest in consent. Since the woman has neither husband nor father to constrain her, she is a free agent, and the poem is able to focus on the lovers' reciprocal testing of each other. Here the many allusions to Ovid's mythological treatment of rape are used ironically, often to point to the woman's playful coercion of her lover. The poem opens with a contest reminiscent of the judgement of Paris, as three beautiful young women ask the male speaker to decide who is the most skillful singer. The first maiden sings of Jupiter's battle with giants, and the second of Paris' love for Helen, but it is the third maiden who prevails, with a song of divine rape, telling of Jupiter's "tender amorous smiles, and how he sported with his fair Europa" (ll. 89–90; "Ipsa Iovem, teneros risus cantabat amorum, / Qualiter Europam luserat ipse suam"). This detail is most likely adapted from Ovid's account of Arachne's weaving contest with Minerva (*Met.* 6.103–8), but rather than using it, as Arachne did, to expose the adulteries of the gods, the maiden uses it to seduce the speaker.

The allusions to Ovidian rapes take on a slightly sinister tone, after the speaker awards the third maiden the prize, and says that she herself is what he desires. For he takes on the guise of the Ovidian sensualist when he couches his request to "enjoy" her virginity ("Da michi, queso, tua virginitate frui" [l. 142]) in language that echoes Daphne's prayer to her father, the river god, to *save* her from being raped by Apollo, in the *Metamorphoses*: "'da mihi perpetua, genitor carissime,' dixit, / 'virginitate frui!'" (1. 486–87; "Dearest father, permit me to enjoy [perpetual] virginity").[20]

The middle of the poem returns to the theme of gender reversal, using Ovid's rape imagery to convey female desire. When the maiden agrees to grant his request that very night, she adopts the humorous conceit of a woman forcing a man against his will, saying, "Miror si tria, nox et amor et pulchra puella, / Non poterunt unum retinere virum" (ll. 179–80; I marvel if we three,—night, love, and a beautiful girl—/ If we three cannot restrain a single man). Although the speaker is in fact more than consenting, the poet seems to be exploring a world turned upside down, in which women rape men. Furthermore, the exquisitely painted images on the bed to which she leads him after a sumptuous meal suggest such a reversal:

> Hunc manus artificis mira sculptaverat arte;
> Namque deos illic pinxerat atque deas.
> Iupiter hic stabat ridens fallensque puellas;
> Has cigni specie decipit, has aquile.
> Hunc in tam variis habuit pictura figuris,
> Vt vix ullus eum crederet esse deum. (ll. 229–34)

> [An artist's hands had carved that bed with wondrous skill,
> And on it had painted the gods with their ladies.

Jupiter was there, laughing, deceiving virgins;
some he deceived disguised as a swan, others as an eagle.
Indeed, the artist had painted the god in so many shapes
that one found it hard to believe his divinity.]

Though these are conventional mythological portrayals of rape, their presence on the maiden's bed suggests, like the song with which she won the speaker's love, she is in control.

The speaker reveals that he feels vulnerable to sexual constraint by his reaction to the painting of Vulcan catching Mars and Venus in his net on the bed (ll. 235–38):

Nec non pertimui ne nos comprendere vellet,
Tam bene picture finxerat auctor eum.
Cumque satis risi, risit quoque nostra puella,
Sed magis hic risus conveniebat ei. (ll. 239–42)

[Indeed, I feared that he wanted to catch us too,
so realistically had the painter portrayed him.
and when I had laughed at my fear, my lady
laughed too, but the laughter became her far better than me.]

For all the speaker's expressed nervousness, however, the comedy really has a conventional Ovidian seduction plot, in the manner of the other school texts. After an extended description of the maiden's exquisite body, there is the obligatory happy ending, as the speaker coyly refuses to narrate the pleasures that both enjoyed (ll. 297–300). Thus, De Tribus Puellis ultimately depends for its wit on the social reality that it inverts: the fact that it is men who rape women.

The last two comedies to be considered, De Nuncio Sagaci and Pamphilus, also exhibit the tension between the school-boy attitude toward rape and a more mature understanding of consent. De Nuncio Sagaci[21] is the more simplistic of the two, like De Tribus Puellis, using Ovid's mythological rape imagery, but doing so to justify rape. While soliciting Cupid's help in seducing a young woman, the speaker boasts that he is so attractive that even the most reluctant of mortal maidens and goddesses would have pursued *him:*

Nam mea forma placens ad amorem traxerat omnes.
Ecce puellarum sequitur me turba tuarum.
Daphnis et Europa, Phillide Deianira:
Profuga cessat Yo; me uult cum Pallade Iuno;
Telis succincta sequitur lasciua Diana . . . (ll. 15–19)

[For my pleasing face would have led all of them to love.
Look, a crowd of your maidens follows me.
Daphne and Europa, Phyllis and Deinira:
Fleeing Io stops in her tracks; Pallas and Juno desire me.
Diana, now lustful, girded with weapons, follows me.]

The irony of his being pursued by the goddesses of wisdom, marriage, and chastity is furthered by his addition of mortal women who are actual or potential rape victims: Daphne, Europa, and Io, as well as Proserpina, whom he mentions soon afterwards. In contrast to *De Tribus Puellis,* the poem reverses the sex roles within the Ovidian *exempla,* with the effect not of exploring female sexual initiative, but rather of expressing male sexual fantasies.

The literal subject of *De Nuncio Sagaci* ("Concerning the Clever Messenger") is acquaintance rape. Its plot is worth recounting, as it bears a close and somewhat vexed relationship to *Pamphilus,* as either a clumsy source or a clumsy adaptation.[22] Though its disjointed action, gaps in motivation, and apparent contradictions, together with the fragmentary nature of its manuscripts, make it hard to follow, the plot can be summed up simply: boy rapes girl, girl admits her folly, and parents accept their marriage. The poem is part dramatic monologue (by the male speaker) and part dialogue (by the speaker and either Cupid or the messenger), but gives very little voice to the girl. When, after the rape, she begins to cry, the messenger silences her. After some confusion in the narrative, her parents arrive and accuse the messenger of seducing their daughter, but are mollified by the outcome of the couple's marriage.

Pamphilus,[23] though it comes out of the same schoolroom tradition and shares many of the plot elements of *De Nuncio Sagaci,* deploys them in such a way as to question the Ovidian assumption that women want to be raped. When the hero tells Venus of his love for a young girl, Galathea, the goddess advises him to court her with eloquence, but to be ready to use force. Frustrated by the girl's clever parrying of his seduction rhetoric, Pamphilus hires a go-between, an Old Woman, who arranges a rendezvous and then leaves the couple alone. When just as Galathea seems on the point of yielding, Pamphilus rapes her, she is outraged and protests eloquently. Upon returning, the Old Woman feigns ignorance of what has happened, declares that the couple will get married and live happily ever after, and demands her payment. Though full of echoes of Ovid's amatory poetry, the poem has none of his mythological machinery except for Venus, and is notable for its literal description of rape. In many ways it resembles Terence's *Hecyra* (whose rapist hero is also named Pamphilus) in dealing with ordinary mortals rather than gods or goddesses.

The most unusual aspect of the poem is the articulate protest that the heroine makes while being raped:

> Pamphile, tolle manus! . . . te frustra nempe fatigas!
> Nil ualet ille labor! quod petis esse nequit! . . .
> Pamphile tolle manus! . . . male nunc offendis amicam! . . .
> Iamque redibit anus: Pamphile tolle manus! . . .
> Heu michi! quam paruas habet omnis femina uires! . . .
> Quam leuiter nostras uincis utrasque manus! . . .
> Pamphile! nostra tuo cum pectore pectora ledis! . . .
> Quid me sic tractas? est scelus atque nephas! . . .
> Desine! . . . clamabo! . . . quid agis! male detegor a te! . . .
> Perfida, me miseram, quando redibit anus?
> Surge! precor! . . . nostras audit vicinia lites! . . .
> Que tibi me credit non bene fecit anus! . . .
> . . . .
> Hujus uictor eris facti, licet ipsa relucter,
> Sed tamen inter nos rumpitur omnis amor![24] (ll. 681–89, 695–96)

> [Pamphilus, take away your hands! You are exhausting yourself in vain!
> This action is useless! What you seek cannot be!
> Pamphilus, take your hands away! You are badly offending your friend!
> Already the old woman is returning! Pamphilus, take away your hands!
> Alas, how little strength a woman has;
> How easily you conquer my hands!
> Pamphilus, you're hurting my breasts with your breast.
> Why are you treating me this way? It is a crime and an unspeakable act!
> Stop! I'll cry out! What are you doing? It is wrong to undress me!
> Wretched me, when will that treacherous old woman come back?
> Get up, I beg you. The neighbors will hear our quarrel!
> That old woman did wrong to trust me to you.
> . . . .
> You're the victor in this matter, although I resisted,
> but all love between us is destroyed.]

Such attention to the woman's experience strongly violates the conventions of the medieval Latin comedies, which, as we have seen, generally euphemize rape. Alison Elliott in *Seven Medieval Latin Comedies* argues, I think persuasively, that the focus on Galathea's outrage challenges Ovid's claim that women want to be raped.[25] Nevertheless, most earlier scholars, including F. J. E. Raby, in *Secular Latin Poetry* and Wilfred Blumenthal, in his exhaustive study of *Pamphilus,* refer to the poem's main action as a "seduction."[26] Even more recent scholars have seen Galathea as consenting. Ian Thompson and Louis Perraud, in the introduction to their translation

Ten Latin School Texts of the Later Middle Ages, deny that she is the "guileless virgin imagined by Elliott," whose interpretation they see as "influenced by feminist theory," and therefore dependent on "values foreign to the literary imperatives of the medieval period."[27] To support their assertion that Galathea is compliant, they point to the ease with which the girl in *De Nuncio Sagaci* is convinced that she should rejoice in her defloration.[28] In doing so, however, they overlook the fact that Galathea differs from that girl precisely in her refusal to be so convinced. Her anticipation of the long-term consequences of what happened to her shows deep understanding of her loss:

> Sed modo quid faciam? fugiam captiua per orbem?
> Hostia iure michi claudet uterque parens.
> Meciar hac illac oculis uigilantibus orbem,
> Leta tamen misere spes michi nulla uenit. (765–68)

> [But now, what am I to do?
> Am I to flee through the world, already caught?
> My parents will be right to close the door on me.
> I shall wander the earth, searching,
> But nowhere shall I find happiness,
> Poor betrayed wretch that I am.]

Thus, despite the Old Woman's statement that Galathea and Pamphilus will get married, the reader is left with Galathea's own statement of despair.

More recently, Marjorie Woods has also questioned the sympathetic reading of Galathea, but for reasons other than Thompson and Perraud's. She opens her analysis of medieval school texts that focus on rape with a quotation from Galathea's protest in *Pamphilus,* along with ones from Ovid's recommendation of rape in the *Ars Amatoria* and Statius' description of the rape of Deidamia in the *Achilleid.*[29] While she does not deny that Galathea has been raped, she argues that her response is a rhetorical construct reflecting the context of the medieval schoolroom, rather than a realistic representation.[30] For this reason, she takes issue with Elliott's reading, as well as with my own in an earlier article, that Galathea as a character stands out by virtue of her strong voice.[31] Woods sees the medieval school tradition as "a site of anxiety about control in two directions: those who control the boy and those whom he might be able to control."[32] Consequently, she argues, adolescent male students could have taken on the role of the female rape victim, as well as of the male perpetrator, and would have been as likely to identify with Pamphilus as with Galathea. Thus, Woods, like Thompson and Perraud, regards a sympathetic reaction to Galathea's role as ahistorical.

I would argue, however, that there are historically valid reasons, and not just modern ones, for reading Galathea's protests realistically. The reception of *Pamphilus* would not have been determined entirely by the tastes of adolescent boys in the schoolroom, but could also have been influenced by the belief of more mature clerics in the importance of consent. Twelfth-century canon lawyers and theologians might have easily read the poem as an *exemplum* of a marriage precipitated by rape, which, according to Michael Sheehan, they did not regard as a marriage at all.[33] In *Pamphilus*, there is even greater tension between the school boy approval of rape and the clerical emphasis on consent than we saw in *De Tribus Puellis*. *Pamphilus* thus stands apart from most other medieval Latin comedies, with their affinities with the misogynistic genres of ancient Roman comedy and medieval fabliau. With a heroine who is innocent rather than lustful and scheming, and who furthermore speaks out forcefully to protest her violation, it seems closer to medieval genres that give more prominence to the female voice, such as woman's song and saint's life.[34]

The five works we have examined—*Geta, Alda, De Tribus Puellis, De Nuncio Sagaci* and *Pamphilus*—all use rape as either imagery or subject matter. Why, we may ask, is rape such an important theme in these works? I have suggested that as an extreme example of coercion, rape is particularly well suited to dramatize the questions of will and consent that concerned twelfth-century clerics, as canon lawyers began to write about freedom in choosing a marriage partner. Such concerns, which are implicitly reflected in the portrayal of courtship in twelfth-century romance, are graphically addressed in the portrayal of rape in the comedies. The surprising popularity of Ovid among twelfth-century clerics, newly pledged to celibacy, is perhaps due to his exploration of all these themes: the importance of consent in love, the rhetorical strategies to achieve it, and the use of force if these should fail. Neither the canon lawyers, nor Ovid, nor most of the authors of the comedies were, of course, as concerned about the freedom of the women's consent as the men's. In *Pamphilus*, however, we are left with a woman speaking out, eloquently asserting that she did not consent, and refusing to allow us to aestheticize the act of rape.

Notes

1. Christopher Cannon, "*Raptus* in the Chaumpaigne Release and a Newly Discovered Document Concerning the Life of Geoffrey Chaucer," *Speculum* 68 (1993): 74–94; see also Henry Ansgar Kelly, "Meanings and Uses of *Raptus* in Chaucer's Time," *Studies in the Age of Chaucer* 20 (1998): 101–65.
2. Gravdal (Philadelphia: University of Pennsylvania Press, 1991). Further treatments have been by Dietmar Rieger, "Le motif du viol dans la littéra-

ture de la France médiévale entre norme courtoise et réalité courtoise," *Cahiers de Civilisation Médiévale* 31 (1988): 241–67; and Robert J. Blanch, "'Al was this land fulfild of fayerye':The Thematic Employment of Force, Willfulness, and Legal Conventions in Chaucer's *Wife of Bath's Tale,*" *Studia Neophilologica* 57 (1985): 41–51.

3. F. J. E. Raby, *A History of Secular Latin Poetry in the Middle Ages,* vol. 2 (Oxford: Clarendon Press, 1957), p. 54. For further definition of comedies, see Tony Hunt, "Chrétien and the *Comediae,*" *Mediaeval Studies* 40 (1978): 122–24.

4. See Peter Dronke, "A Note on *Pamphilus,*" *Journal of the Warburg and Courtauld Institutes* 42 (1979): 226.

5. See n. 3, above. The most comprehensive edition of the poems in the Latin original is by Gustave Cohen, *La "comédie" latine en France au XIIe siècle,* 2 vols. (Paris: Société d'Edition "Les Belles Lettres," 1931), and a convenient English translation is Alison Goddard Elliott, *Seven Medieval Latin Comedies* (New York: Garland, 1984).

6. Cohen (p. xli) sees an attitude like that of the fabliau in the misogynistic portrayal of unfaithful wives *(Geta)* or young girls who are hesitating (in *Pamphilus* and *De Nuncio Sagaci*) or forward *(De Tribus Puellis)*; see also Elliott (p. xvi). For recent work on the misogyny of the fabliaux, see E. Jane Burns, "Knowing Women: Female Orifices in Old French Farce and Fabliaux," *Exemplaria* 4 (1992): 81–104.

7. Copeland, "Introduction: Dissenting Critical Practices," *Criticism and Dissent in the Middle Ages,* ed. Rita Copeland (Cambridge: Cambridge University Press, 1996), p. 6.

8. Woods, in Copeland, ed., *Criticism and Dissent,* pp. 73–74.

9. See John Noonan, "The Power to Choose," *Viator* 4 (1973): 418–34; Charles Donahue, Jr., "The Canon Law on the Foundation of Marriage and Social Practice in the Later Middle Ages," *Journal of Family History* 8 (1983): 144–58; Michael M. Sheehan, "The Choice of Marriage Partners in the Middle Ages," *Studies in Medieval and Renaissance History,* n. s. I (1978): 1–33; rpt. in Michael M. Sheehan, *Marriage, Family and Law in Medieval Europe: Collected Studies,* ed. James K. Farge (Toronto: University of Toronto Press, 1996), pp. 87–117; and James Brundage, *Law, Sex, and Society in Medieval Europe* (Chicago: University of Chicago Press, 1987).

10. Brundage, p. 210.

11. Bloch, *Medieval Misogyny and the Invention of Western Romantic Love* (Chicago: University of Chicago Press, 1991), pp. 184–85. Feminist historians as well have pointed out this connection; see Penny Schein Gold, *The Lady and the Virgin: Image, Attitude, and Experience in Twelfth-Century France* (Chicago: University of Chicago Press, 1985), pp. 147–48, and Gloria K. Fiero, ed. and trans. with Wendy Pfeffer and Mathé Allain, *Three Medieval Views of Women* (New Haven, CT:Yale University Press, 1989), p. 33.

12. See Leo Curran, "Rape and Rape Victims in the *Metamorphoses,*" *Arethusa* 11 (1978): 213–41; Patricia Klindienst Joplin, "The Voice of the Shuttle is

Ours," *Stanford Literature Review* 1 (1984): 25–53; Julie Hemker, "Rape and the Founding of Rome," *Helios* 12 (1985): 41–47; and Leslie Cahoon, "Raping the Rose: Jean de Meun's Reading of Ovid's *Amores,*" *Classical and Modern Literature* 6 (1986): 261–85. I have argued that Ovid's account of Tereus's rape and mutilation of Philomela in the *Metamorphoses* was an influence on *Pamphilus,* in "The Transformation of Ovid in the Twelfth-Century *Pamphilus,*" in *Desiring Discourse: The Literature of Love, Ovid Through Chaucer,* ed. Cynthia Gravlee and James J. Paxson (London: Associated University Presses, 1998), pp. 72–86.

13. Ovid, *Ars Amatoria* I. 673–78, in *Amores, Faciei Femineae, Ars Amatoria, Remedia, Amoris,* ed. E. J. Kenney (Oxford: Clarendon Press, 1961). Woods cites this passage as an example of the prominence of rape in school texts in the Middle Ages (pp. 56–58).

14. Ovid, *The Art of Love,* trans. Rolfe Humphries (Bloomington: Indiana University Press, 1955), p. 126.

15. Ed. Keith Bate, *Three Latin Comedies* (Toronto: Pontifical Institute of Medieval Studies, 1976), pp. 13–34; trans. Elliott, pp. 26–49.

16. Ed. Marcel Winzweiler, in Cohen I, pp. 107–51; trans. Elliott, pp. 104–25.

17. Trans. Elliott. Unless otherwise indicated, subsequent citations to English translations of the comedies will be to this text.

18. *Ars Amatoria* I. 669–70, trans. Humphries, p. 126; cited by Elliott, p. 125, n. 9.

19. Ed. Paul Maury, in Cohen II, pp. 225–42; trans. Elliott, pp. 147–58.

20. Ed. Frank Justus Miller; 2nd ed. rev. by G. P. Goold, Loeb Classical Library (Cambridge: Harvard University Press, 1977), 9.283–334 (my translation); connection pointed out by Elliott, p. xlviii.

21. Ed. Alphonse Dain, in Cohen II, pp. 103–56.

22. For different opinions on the relationship between the two poems, see Stefano Pittaluga, ed., "Pamphilus" (*Commedie latine del XII e XIII secolo,* ed. Ferruccio Bertini [Genova: Instituto di Filologia classica e medievale, 1980], Introduction, p. 14), and Wilfrid Blumenthal ("Untersuchungen zur pseudo-ovidianischen Kömodie *Pamphilus,*" *Mittellateinishes Jahrbuch* 11 [1976]: pp. 272–74). Peter Dronke argues that *De Nuncio Sagaci* was written in 1080, before *Pamphilus,* also at Tegernsee in southwest Germany (p. 230).

23. Ed. Eugène Évesque, in Cohen II, pp. 167–233, as well as by Pittaluga (see n. 22, above, pp. 13–137); Bate, pp. 61–89; and Franz G. Becker (*Pamphilus. Prolegomena zum Pamphilus [de amore] und kritische Textausgabe Beihefte zum Mittellateinischen Jahrbuch* [9 Ratingen] 1972). English translations are available by Elliott (pp. 1–25), Thomas Jay Garbaty ("*Pamphilus, De Amore:* An Introduction and Translation," *Chaucer Review* 2 [1967]: 108–34), and Ian Thompson and Louis Perraud (*Ten Latin School Texts of the Later Middle Ages: Translated Selections* [Lewiston, NY: Edwin Mellen Press, 1990], pp. 158–91).

24. This and subsequent citations will be to Évesque's edition.

25. Elliott, pp. xxviii–xxxii.

26. Raby, p. 67, and Blumenthal, p. 232. This is in contrast to Gustave Cohen, general editor of the comedies, who notes that despite the fact that most comedies depict women as willing or sexually aggressive, *Alda, De Nuncio Sagaci,* and *Pamphilus* show them as innocent victims, subjected to a "conquête parfois brutale et violente" designed to force them to consent to marriage (pp. xxxviii–xxxix).

27. Thomson and Perraud, p. 159.

28. Thomson and Perraud, p. 160.

29. Woods, pp. 56–57.

30. Woods, p. 60.

31. Woods, p. 58; she cites Elliott, p. xxix; and Anne Howland Schotter, "Rhetoric versus Rape in the Medieval Latin *Pamphilus,*" *Philological Quarterly* 71 (1992): 243–60.

32. Woods, p. 69.

33. Sheehan, p. 91.

34. See John F. Plummer, *Vox Feminae: Studies in Medieval Woman's Song* (Kalamazoo, MI: Medieval Institute Publications, 1981), and Gravdal, "Camouflaging Rape: The Rhetoric of Sexual Violence in the Medieval Pastourelle," *Romanic Review* 76 (1985): 360–73. On the resistance to rape in female saints' lives, see Gravdal, *Ravishing,* pp. 21–41 and Maureen Quilligan, "The Name of the Author: Self-Representation in Christine de Pizan's *Livre de la cité des dames,*" *Exemplaria* 4 (1992): 217–23.

CHAPTER 9

CHAUCER AND RAPE:
UNCERTAINTY'S CERTAINTIES

Christopher Cannon

The role Geoffrey Chaucer played in the "raptus" of Cecily Chaumpaigne can be specified, not through any history of terminology but, as this essay argues, through consideration of the grounds on which a particular act of sex can be described as nonconsensual, both now and in the Middle Ages.

Rape is a brutal crime and implies a degree of depravity which should make us cautious in fixing such a charge. There is really no evidence for it. That he seduced Cecilia we may well believe; that she was angry with him, and still more with herself, is extremely probable. She may have honestly thought that because it all happened against her better judgement, that therefore it was without her consent. Her scandalized family would naturally treat that as an irrebuttable presumption. But there is nothing to suggest that Cecilia could have convicted Chaucer of felony.

—*T. F. T. Plucknett (1948)*[1]

Gone are the days when conjoining Chaucer's name to the crime of rape seemed repugnant even to those scholars who would address its possibility. In place of Plucknett's insistence that the gravity of such a crime converts uncertain guilt into certain innocence—where the documents that raise the issue provide "no evidence"—we now have Carolyn Dinshaw's demonstration that the conjunction makes us better readers: as it "invites us to consider causal relationships between gendered representation and actual social relations between men and women," we may acknowledge that there are "real rapes" as well as "fictional rapes" and thereby learn to see what is and is not "figurative" in Chaucer's "sexual poetics."[2] That on May 4, 1380 Cecily Chaumpaigne had enrolled in Chancery a document that released Chaucer of "all manner of actions such as they relate to my rape or any other thing or cause" ["omnimodas acciones tam de raptu meo tam de aliqua alia re vel causa"] is a fact that few now would try to put by: it is, as Dinshaw also says, "perhaps the one biographical fact everyone remembers about Chaucer."[3] And the resilience of that memory, we have also learned to recognize, is not simply due to the gravity of the released crime. As Jill Mann has shown, the subject is one that Chaucer does not himself shrink from: throughout his writing "rape remains a constant touchstone for determining justice between the sexes."[4]

But, if we have arrived at a stage where considering Chaucer and rape together no longer seems dangerous, if we are even able to make that consideration critically enabling, we are not yet at a stage where the Chaumpaigne release seems able to teach us anything more than we are willing to presume. Clearer understanding of the role rape may play in Chaucer's poetics has not been born in any clearer understanding of what precisely the Chaumpaigne release refers to, largely because the release is so parsimonious of description while the language and procedure of medieval English law are so frequently ambiguous as they pertain to "*raptus.*" Although I have argued elsewhere that this word must refer to forced coitus in the Chaumpaigne release, central to that earlier argument was the claim that mention of a '*raptus*' in fourteenth-century law was itself an attempt to achieve clarity in the face of a legal tradition that had become hopelessly confused about the naming of sexual violence and its punishment.[5] That confusion will always make it possible to say that "raptus" *might* have been used to describe an "abduction" in the Chaumpaigne release, as has been said in the past, although, I think, not because the term has always had wide reference in Latin (as past claims for "ambiguity" have maintained), but because, first, a legal document in the fourteenth century as well as now is necessarily an instrument at some remove from "what happened" and, second, because sexual violence is itself a crime where "what happened," the very act that might constitute the crime, can be variously defined even by those who have identical "facts" in hand.[6] The first point is clear enough even to the casuist Plucknett: although he is certainly wrong to suppose that uncertainties about the Chaumpaigne release's historical witness are themselves necessarily absolving, he is certainly right that even if *raptus* refers to "rape" in that release (which he believes) this does not demonstrate that Chaucer raped Cecily Chaumpaigne. Plucknett gets at the second point, too, when he explains how different parties in a rape case can position the act in question on different sides of the line that marks crime: the "irrebut-table presumption" of Cecily and her "scandalized family" is a presumption that Plucknett, taking Chaucer's part, is perfectly willing to rebut. But the relation of this second point to the first—whether an event that Chaumpaigne would call "rape" and Chaucer would call something else is or is not rape, either to fourteenth-century courts or to us—is an issue that has not been explored. What definition will we use for rape, in other words, when we ask what *raptus* means? What does the Chaumpaigne release re-ally say if the *raptus* it refers to is an act that, according to the vigorously de-fended affective states of both those involved in it, is *at once* rape and not rape? What does the Chaumpaigne release teach *us* if that act is one that we would now call "rape" (because, say, Chaumpaigne felt it was but Chaucer did not) but that fourteenth-century law was entirely happy to throw into a category it understood as "abduction?"

This essay claims that, while many questions about the Chaumpaigne release will never be answered, answers are available for the questions I have just posed: its implication, therefore, is that we are wrong to assume that the release's witness allows us only to reconstruct possibilities and "be-yond that, all is speculation."[7] We have not yet been fully schooled by this document, I will suggest, because our worry that we will be wrongly cer-tain has prevented us from realizing that uncertainty is itself something we may be certain about. The fault in our method of inquiry relates directly to its object here, since definitions of rape necessarily occupy the gray area we have refused to define: we mistake what this crime *is* when we insist that it has only occurred under conditions of absolute agreement between accuser and defendant or when it has been named and punished by the law. The improvement of our understanding is given an imperative, more-over, in the ways that Chaucer's writing shows *him* to have defined such grayness with precisely the situational and philosophical specificity we have lacked. It may not constitute proof of the biographical relevance of either the Chaumpaigne release or of rape to describe the great imagina-tive and intellectual energy Chaucer devoted to such definition in his po-etry and prose. But it should be relevant that Chaucer understood rape better than we have done in our scrutiny of the Chaumpaigne release, that he answers questions we have not as yet really posed. As I will argue in what follows, understanding the Chaumpaigne release and reading Chaucer ought to be identical endeavors precisely because a more careful definition of the conditions that make an act rape shows Chaucer know-ing those conditions and carefully delineating them for us.

Since, as I have suggested, any definition of rape we discover in four-teenth-century law is necessarily subject to revaluation according to modern definitions, it will be well to make clear from the start what such modern definitions are themselves both certain and uncertain about. "Rape defined" in the modern criminal code turns at every junction on "consent" and the "victim's will."[8] The principle matter of this definition is the set of conditions or rules by which an "act of sexual intercourse" can be judged to have been accomplished without consent, against the victim's will: the specificities of these rules go, in every case, to the *circumstances* that would indicate nonconsent at the moment of an act. Where an act of sexual intercourse occurs and there is mental disorder, developmental or physical disability, force or violence, fear of bodily injury either immediately or as threatened for the future, unconsciousness of the nature of the act, intoxication or anaesthetization, or an artificially induced belief that the person committing the act is the person's spouse, then consent is deemed not to have been given and the act is judged to be "rape."

The modern law's strength is, therefore, the extent to which it determines consent on the basis of clear rules, but the mode of that determination is also this law's most serious weaknesses: while the copiousness of conditions specified makes rape detectable and prosecutable in an extraordinarily wide variety of modern circumstances, acts inevitably occur for which no rule has as yet been devised. Rules about conditions inevitably leave some conditions out; the law can therefore not be certain about consent to acts committed under those conditions; and the law necessarily renders such uncertainty legally equivalent to consent (insofar as the acts then in question are excluded from criminal punishment). Indeed, as Susan Estrich has shown, what might appear to be relatively small gaps in these rules can still render most acts of forced coitus undefinable as "rape": until relatively recently, the modern law required nonconsent to be manifest in some corroborating physical evidence of "resistance" (that is, by the visible harm of bruises and torn clothing), and so it could not define as nonconsensual acts of sex that had themselves been forced, but which were not accompanied by evidence of violence of some *other* kind.[9] It is true that the rigor of these rules has recently been dramatically increased, particularly as they now specify conditions that allow for nonconsent within marriage (making spousal rape prosecutable).[10] But even the newest rules still ignore some conditions: where, for example, mental or physical disability or intoxication bars the giving of consent or unconsciousness of the nature of the act precludes agreement to sex, it is still maintained that, for such an act to be "rape," that disability or that unconsciousness must be *known* to the perpetrator.[11] And the conviction that assures that some limitations will always remain in the modern law (that some rapes will go "undefined" and therefore unpunished) is clearly set out in that law's most careful definition of "consent":

In prosecutions under Section 261 ["rape defined"] . . . in which consent is at issue, "consent" shall be defined to mean positive cooperation in act or attitude pursuant to an exercise of free will. The person must act freely and voluntarily and have knowledge of the nature of the act or transaction involved.[12]

Our law is simply unwilling to make judgements about the status of an interior faculty (as both this section and the section on "rape defined" name this faculty, it is the "will") unless that faculty can be transformed into an activity (so the "free will" is "exercise[d]" and "consent" takes the form of "positive cooperation"). In its need to externalize the inner territory that is the acknowledged site of its investigations, in other words, the modern law ensures definitional failure: if "cooperation" must be indicated by "act," then any conflicting "attitude" (a concomitant reluctance of the "will") may itself be hidden *by means of* a cooperative act. Where certainty about consensual states is necessary for an act to be defined as rape and conditions of consent cannot be rendered certain, there must be acts that are rape that remain unknown to the law—and therefore unpunished by it—because the law's own definitions make it impossible to know what they are.

If such severe definitional problems remain for modern understandings, we should hardly be surprised to find that definitions of rape in the English Middle Ages were troubled. But what makes the lens of modern problems particularly apposite for understanding earlier confusions is the extent to which, even in the context of different legal and social circumstances, they can be analyzed by exactly the terms I have just used. The codes in question here—that is, those with most direct relevance to the legal circumstance of the Chaumpaigne release—are the notoriously difficult Chapter 13 of Westminster I (1275), the equally difficult Chapter 34 of Westminster II (1285), and the so-called Statute of Rapes (1382).[13] There are, indeed, a host of problems yet to be solved in relating the language of these statutes to the complex court procedures that arose in their name, but fundamental to these problems is, again, the determination of nonconsent as a means to defining the acts these laws would punish.[14] The first phrases of Chapter 13 in Westminster I make this clear in themselves for they have the king prohibiting "that none do ravish nor take away by force any maiden within age, *neither by her own consent,* nor without" ["le rey defent qe nul ne ravie ne prenge a force damoysele dedenz age, ne par son gre ne saun son gre"].[15] It is not surprising to find that "by force" ["a force"] comes and goes in the manuscript tradition of this statute since, when present, the phrase proposes a circumstance in which force is required to accomplish a "ravishment" although the victim *agrees* in the first place.[16] On the other hand, the presence of the phrase only intensifies that odd proposal, since, even without it, we have a statute prohibiting *consensual* "ravishment"—whatever that might be. Although, as J. B. Post has noted, Westminster II seems to have returned to the matter of Westminster I to clear up language that "was considered wholly inadequate," definitions grow no clearer there.[17] Chapter 34 of Westminster II prohibits "ravishment" where a woman "did not consent, neither before nor after" ["ou ele ne se est assentue ne avaunt ne apres"] but, also, where that "ravishment" occurs "with force, although [a woman] consent *after*" ["a force, tut seit ke ele se assente apres"].[18] In the first clause we find a newly rigorous attention to consent, in which a victim's nonconsent actually creates the wrong; in the second clause, however, the law uses this attention to imagine, yet again, circumstances in which a woman would consent to something that it still thinks might appropriately be called "ravishment" (because it here disallows her from withdrawing her consent). Time has become an issue in this statute, it is clear, because it remains possible to conceive of a woman as still in some measure responsible for her own ravishment. What would motivate such imaginings in both Westminster I and II finally becomes clear if we look to the next clauses in Chapter 34 of Westminster II, which, first, describe the suit required when "women [are] carried away with the goods of their husbands" ["de mulieribus abductis cum bonis viri"] and, second, describe how a woman may be punished for her own ravishment:

> if a wife willingly leave her husband and go away and continue with her advouterer, she shall be barred forever of action to demand her dower that she ought to have of her husband's lands, if she be convict thereupon, except that her husband willingly, and without coercion of the Church, reconcile her and suffer her to dwell with him; in which case she shall be restored to her action.[19]

The Westminster statutes try to determine the status of a woman's consent *not* because they are interested in *non*consent and the prohibition of acts accomplished under this condition, but because they are worried that a woman's consent has the power to accomplish acts—in particular, to threaten her husband's financial interest in the act that is *marriage*. Lest we wonder how unmarried women might fit into this logic, we need only look at Chapter 35 of Westminster II, which concerns "children, males and females, whose marriage belongeth to another" where the "ravisher" has "no right in the marriage."[20] It is therefore clear that, in Westminster I, consent can be given when a ravishment occurs "by force" in Westminster I, because ravishment is not generally committed against the person ravished but against those, either husband or guardian, who have an interest in the marriage; the "force" in question, therefore, is exerted against that husband or that guardian.[21] What confirms this logic and testifies to its strength in the later decades of the fourteenth century is the more explicit effort in the Statute of Rapes (1382) to include those persons who have been ravished in its definition of the *perpetrators* of this wrong. Under prohibitory scrutiny in this statute are not only "ravishers" ["raptores"] but the women who "after such rape do consent to such ravishers" ["post huiusmodi raptum huiusmodi raptoribus consenserint"]; such women are dispossessed of "all inheritance, dower, or joint feoffment" ["omnem hereditatem, dotem, sive conjunctum feoffamentum"], and, what is more, in such cases the statute actually transfers "the suit to pursue" ["sectam prosequendi"], in the event of the act (now called *raptus*), to the husband, fathers, or next of blood of the person ravished.[22] A woman's consent in this statute is no longer examined for conditions that will make a *"raptor"* culpable—to determine in what cases she is the victim of a wrong—but in order to determine *her* culpability in the accomplished act and to make her, finally, one of the perpetrators of her own *raptus*.

Particularly as they worry about an *enabling* consent on the part of women, what all these statutes seem most concerned with is the act that we (and the women in question) might call "elopement" or "marriage choice" but which the law calls "ravishment" and seems to imagine as a kind of "seizing" in order to prohibit it; forced coitus is not the medieval law's concern.[23] I have argued elsewhere that such an emphasis in the statutes must be understood in relation to the case law contemporaneous with it, for, in the latter, the language and logic of the statutes was often ignored, and explicit definitions of *raptus* as forced coitus were often set out.[24] But it is, in fact, the definitional method employed in medieval statutes and not the intention behind them that commands our attention, for "consent" is, in this sense, also the overwhelming concern of the older law. To compare the role of consent in medieval and modern definitions of rape (or "ravishment" or *raptus*) is also to see, however, that, while both laws are fundamentally concerned with this condition, the modern code is so concerned in order to make consent the single condition determining the criminality of the act, whereas the Westminster statutes and the Statute of Rapes are so concerned in order to make the victim's consent *irrelevant* to that act: the medieval statutes define "ravishment" or *raptus* as punishable acts even when the "victim" consents to them. Most pertinent to any attempt to understand the Chaumpaigne release in terms of medieval statutes then is the way that medieval definitions disregard—and therefore inevitably render uncertain—precisely the condition that our own definitions of rape require us to be certain about.

We might try to mitigate such a drastic definitional difference by looking at "what happened" in individual medieval cases, by applying our own

definitions of crime to acts regardless of the names the medieval law gives
them. The problem with such an investigation, of course, is that any record
we have of such acts is itself everywhere infected by those very rubrics for
determining "consent" that ignore precisely the information we require:
where "consent *after*" is of most interest in such records, and where a victim's "consent" is adjudged a problem (and might therefore be unreported
or hidden), how will we find out what *we* need to know? A more profitable method, I think, is to explore the different kinds of definitional
judgement the medieval statutes and our own must make of a single hypothetical act: applying the logic of both rubrics to even an imagined scenario should help us to see how differing rubrics for consent's relevance
will affect the crucial designation (is the act rape, or is it not?). A scenario
imagined in literature offers us as good a site as any for such a definitional
experiment, and, if we choose, say, the *raptus* of Helen of Troy, we find a
useful exchange in Ovid's *Heroides,* in the imagined letters of Helen and
Paris, where the nature of the act and the consensual state that preceded it
are precisely the matters under discussion.[25] Paris's letter, which begins this
exchange, makes the issue explicit when he enjoins Helen not to fear the
raptus he plans ("nec tu rapta time," XVI, 341). And he clearly defines the
acts that he would fit under this designation when he recalls Helen's previous *raptus* by Theseus and Pirithous and, in that recollection, describes
what he would have done had he been the *raptor:*

> vel mihi virginitas esset libata, vel illud
> quod poterat salva virginitate rapi. (XVI, 161–62)

> [Either your virgin flower I should have plucked, or taken what could be
> stolen without hurt to your virgin state.]

Paris promises Helen marriage (she will be "nupta," XVI, 370 and "coniunx," XVI, 374), but he does not see marriage as necessarily distinct from
conquest either, since, as his bride, Helen will still be his "prize in a mighty
contest" ("pretium magni certaminis," XVI, 263). Helen's reply to Paris is
even more interesting, however, for she focuses at length on the status and
evolution of her own consent. She begins by making clear that she is af-
fronted by Paris's suggestion that a previous instance of *raptus* should make
her seem to be generally rapable:

> an, quia vim nobis Neptunius attulit heros,
> rapta semel videor bis quoque digna rapi? (XVII, 21–22)

> [Because the Neptunian hero employed violence with me, can it be that,
> stolen once, I seem fit to be stolen, too, a second time?]

Her main line of defense stresses her nonconsent in the previous act, which, she says, she should not be reproached with precisely because, as a *raptus,* it was against her will:

crimen erat nostrum, si delenita fuissem;
cum sim rapta, meum quid nisi nolle fuit? (XVII, 23–24)

[The blame were mine, had I been lured away; but seized, as I was, what could I do, more than refuse my will?]

The change in what Helen says she wants over the course of this letter, from allowing that Paris's offer might be attractive ("a woman might well wish to submit to your embrace" ["potestque/velle sub amplexus ire puella tuos," XVII, 93–94]) to admitting her own desire ("Grant, nonetheless, that I desire to become your bride at Troy" ["ut tamen optarim fieri tua Troica coniunx," XVII, 109–10]), to anticipating her capitulation ("I perchance . . . [shall] yield in tardy surrender" ["aut ego . . . fortasse . . . dabo cunctatas tempore victa manus," XVII, 259–60]) might be understood to lend Ovid's representation of consent the kind of titillating humor we do not much enjoy anymore: even Helen's claims of guiltlessness in the earlier *raptus* are progressively impugned by her steady progress towards consenting to this one. But, however we read Ovid's tone, what may very much interest us in the subtlety of these letters is the way both consent and nonconsent are made inherent to the accomplishment of this act of *raptus:* were Helen to withhold her consent, it is suggested, the *raptus* would not happen, but even when she *does* consent, as it is clear she will, the act will not be categorized by her choice, but, still, *as a raptus.* Indeed, when we finally find Helen capitulating to Paris's persuasion in her letter, she imagines herself agreeing to an act that she still imagines as a "surrender" to conquest (she will be "victa," XVII, 260).

By way of analyzing what this complicated set of conditions might mean to either the modern or medieval law we may turn at this point to Chaucer whose thinking about these issues, I have said, can instruct our own, and who, in addition, takes up the *raptus* of Helen of Troy at precisely the point any law must encounter it: that is, *after* the act. I do not refer here to the "teeris of Eleyne" mentioned in the Introduction to *The Man of Law's Tale* (II, 70), although it is Chaucer's location of those "teeris" in "Ovide['s] Episteles" (II, 54–55) that, if there be any doubt, makes clear Chaucer knew the passages just examined.[26] More interesting for the definitional investigation in progress here is the ex post facto portrayal of Helen in *Troilus and Criseyde,* where there is no doubt that both the grounds of the war and the grounds of Helen's presence in Troy

is a "ravishment": the narrator tells us in the poem's first few lines that
Greeks have laid their siege "the ravysshyng to wreken of Eleyne" (1.62),
and, when Pandarus instructs Troilus to "Go ravysshe" Criseyde much
later (4.530), Troilus points out that "this town hath al this werre / For
ravysshyng of wommen" (4.547–48). It is of equal interest then, that,
within such a frame, we actually meet Helen and, also, that, when we do,
she is just one member of the big, happy, Parisian family:

> The morwen com, and neighen gan the tyme
> Of meeltid, that the faire queene Eleyne
> Shoop hire to ben, an houre after the prime,
> With Deiphebus, to whom she nolde feyne;
> But as his suster, homly, soth to seyne,
> She come to dyner in hire pleyne entente. (2.1555–60)

Helen, now indeed Paris's "wif" (1.678), exhibits nothing but enjoyment of
her status as (in Pandarus's words) "lady queene Eleyne" (2.1714). Helen's
regal and domestic comfort here, her placidity, might simply be taken at face
value, but the "ravysshyng" that is their stated predicate also makes the exhibition of these qualities ostentatious, shocking evidence really of the "consent after" that the medieval law would notice on the way to discounting it.
It is just here, moreover, as he notices an acquiescence that would transform
"ravysshyng" into marriage choice *and* continues to call that choice
"ravysshyng," that Chaucer follows both the interest of the medieval law and
its judgement ("consent after" still equals "ravishment"). It is in the shock of
the juxtaposition, however, that he also registers the conditions of such consent that the modern law would depend upon for its own claim that such
an act was rape. To better see how this complex double movement is present in *Troilus and Criseyde* it is worth glossing Helen's depicted acquiescence
there with a worry Ovid shows her having before her *raptus:*

> quis mihi, si laedar, Phrygiis succurret in oris?
> unde petam fratres, unde parentis opem? (XVII, 227–28)

> [Who will succour me on Phrygian shores if I meet with harm? Where shall
> I look for brothers, where for a father's aid?]

Chaucer cannot allow Helen to voice such worries given the comfort he
envisions for her, but he can envision them for Criseyde, since, on Phrygian
shores, she is in precisely the condition Helen was in before her *raptus:*

> Now hadde Calkas left in this meschaunce,
> Al unwist of this false and wikked dede,

His doughter, which that was in great penaunce,
For of hire lif she was ful sore in drede,
As she that nyste what was best to rede;
For bothe a widewe was she and allone,
Of any frend to whom she dorste hir mone. (1.92–98)

The extent to which Criseyde's choices are themselves glosses on Helen's (and, for that matter, Helen's are a gloss on Criseyde's) is an interesting issue that I will turn to below, but it is enough to note here that Chaucer also frames our witness of Helen's comfort in a Trojan "brother's aid" with acknowledgement that having one's protectors on the other side of the siege is a proper source of petrifying fear ("of hire *lif* she was ful sore in drede"). By modern definition, of course, "fear of . . . bodily injury" or a "threatening to retaliate in the future against the victim" establishes non-consent and makes an act rape,[27] but we do not even need to point the issue to this extent to realize that what Chaucer is giving us, alongside the definition of "ravysshyng" current in the medieval law, is the means *we* need to realize what that definition leaves out.[28] Once she has been ravished, Helen's resistance would not merely have been useless but would likely constitute a positive harm to her, and in that circumstance how can *we* equate "consent after" with "consent?" If medieval definitions of an act of "ravishment" can imagine (as Chaucer daringly does here) a woman *happily* married to her *raptor*, what Chaucer helps us to see is how such definitions ignore precisely those conditions of consent that make such an act wrong. The terms of Chaucer's portrayal, in other words, invite us to wonder about all the acts of sex between Paris and Helen from the "ravysshyng" up until the "meeltid" at Deiphebus's house. If that sex is now consensual (as Helen is Paris's "wif"), *when* did it become consensual, and what were the precise conditions of Helen's consent at the moment of *raptus*? Moreover, if the act of that *raptus* was itself "merely" abduction, and sex, when it followed, was indeed consensual, how can we admit that consent since, after the abduction, Helen has been placed in conditions of "force" and "fear" that make her will *un*free?

Chaucer understands what modern rubrics will only intensify and confirm, which is that, while the act of Helen's *raptus* might be categorized as a "ravysshyng," "mere" abduction, the conditions that must govern any consent given subsequent to that abduction make such consent equivalent to nonconsent: as Chaucer implies, and we may safely say, Helen of *Troy* is Helen raped. It is in this harsh light, moreover, that we may find all attempts to wonder whether Chaumpaigne released Chaucer from *either* rape or abduction, forced coitus or consensual sex, deeply misguided. To be sure, there was a forum in the medieval law that was deeply concerned with investigating and protecting the freedom of a woman's consent. As Gratian had it, "no woman should be coupled to anyone except by her free will,"[29] and the canon law on marriage was everywhere alive to the ways "force" and "fear" could make the will unfree: it did declare that "a marriage contracted under duress could be subsequently dissolved,"[30] and that "where [consent] was wanting, there was no marriage."[31] In the forum of the criminal law, however, such insights about the potential for coercion to qualify consent did not operate: that legal thinking, accepting on the one side that a woman such as Helen was, first, as in Ovid, "a lawful wife" ("legitima nupta," XVII, 4) and, second, as in Chaucer, the "wif" of another, could not have cared less about the consensual states that intervened between these two "marriages." Interested above all in protecting the interests of the Menelauses of its world, the medieval English law on *raptus* and "ravishment" lumped together nonconsent before and consent before and gathered consent after together with these, prohibiting *as a single wrong* categories of act that we would call, on the one hand, marriage choice, and, on the other hand, rape. The raped woman in medieval England did have an option beside the law set down by the statutes we have examined: she could employ an older form of appeal that allowed her to come into court and assert, above all else, that she had not consented to an act of sexual intercourse (that it was "contra voluntatem suam"); where these cases appear in court records contemporaneous with the Chaumpaigne release they call that act *raptus*.[32] But, in the context of the statutes, knowing that such acts fit the modern definition of rape does not help us know what most acts of *raptus* mentioned in contemporaneous documents were simply because consensual states are *not* specified there. All the medieval law makes certain to us is that we cannot know precisely what we need to know to categorize most of its mentions of *raptus*. Where the extended portrait of affective states that Ovid and Chaucer give us for Helen is wanting—which is, according to its concerns, in nearly *every* case in the medieval law—all we know for certain is that we are uncertain. It is in this sense that saying the Chaumpaigne release does not prove Chaucer was a rapist does not measure our current, even temporary, ignorance, but our knowledge: the document is not incomplete evidence for judging between two different crimes ("rape" or "abduction") but complete evidence of the medieval law's commitment to joining those crimes so thoroughly that modern rubrics will never distinguish them.

As I have been suggesting, Chaucer knew this—if not by the rubric of the modern law, then at least in the terms of the uncertainty that would have surrounded the Chaumpaigne release as implacably in the fourteenth century as it does now. But we do not only see this as Chaucer raises questions about consent's determination in the case of Helen's "ravysshyng."

The large significance of the Chaumpaigne release and our need to understand its witness is most strenuously proved by the extent to which an exploration of the conditions of consent that may attend acts of sexual intercourse finally becomes, in Chaucer's thinking, a consideration of the conditions of consent that attend *all* human acts. It is, in fact, the exploration of this much larger penumbra that was Chaucer's means for investigating the crucial distinction between an act and the names that might be given it, a distinction we too must make in order to read the Chaumpaigne release aright. Less central to this exploration, then, are those acts of forced coitus in Chaucer's writing where consent's conditions are clear and indisputable by any rubric (i.e., the rapes in the *Legend of Philomela,* the *Legend of Lucrece,* and the *Wife of Bath's Tale*). Central to it, however, is the consideration of consensual states where the nature of the act ("what happened") is either indeterminate or varying according to those states.

Acts that we would call rape still matter, but, according to the terms of Chaucer's investigation, we must expect his observations to be most acute when he does *not* call an act "rape." A useful paradigm here is the representation of acts of sex at the conclusion of *The Reeve's Tale.* There is, first, the simplest form of such nonconsent when Aleyn sneaks into bed with Malyn:

> This wenche lay uprighte and faste slepte,
> Til he so ny was, er she myghte espie,
> That it had been to late for to crie,
> And shortly for to seyn, they were aton. (I, 4194–97)

There is, second, a more complicated kind of nonconsent when the miller's wife thinks she is getting into bed with her husband but is tricked into having sex with John:[33]

> Withinne a while this John the clerk up leep,
> And on this goode wyf he leith on soore.
> So myrie a fit ne hadde she nat ful yoore;
> He priketh harde and depe as he were mad. (I, 4228–31)

In Malyn's case what is most significant to the representation is the way that clear nonconsent before the act ("it had been to late for to crie") quickly becomes consent after: once she is "aton" with Aleyn (a phrase that conflates both physical and affective acquiescence) he becomes, in her own words, her "deere lemman" (I, 4240). But in both these cases what is significant is the way this tale details the conditions that govern these acts of sex but then knows nothing more at its conclusion than that those acts were accomplished: that the miller's "wyf is swyved, and his doghter als" (I,

4317). That these acts are *not* rapes by this tale's measure are judgements that we may fold back into the Reeve's "ire" (I, 3862), the violence of a vengeful poetics whose aim is the "bleryng of a proud milleres ye" (I, 3865) or the "cherles termes" of fabliau (I, 3917), but we may not, I think, attach these judgements to Chaucer. As relevant to the tale's final ignorance of the conditions of consent that might define a particular kind of "swyving" here are the fact that we, as readers, are made to know all that we need to know about those conditions to call this "swyving" rape. Most important for the concerns addressed here, then, is the way that Chaucer's representation of these acts goes straight down the line of the rubrics of the medieval statutes (Symkyn's belief that a wrong has been done to Malyn because her "lynage" has been "disparage[d]" [I, 4271–72] despite her "consent after" is the logic of a medieval law obsessed with marriage rights), but also investigates consent sufficiently to satisfy definitions of rape (like our own) that care about a woman's nonconsent.[34]

The *Reeve's Tale* is, however, only a small example of how attentive Chaucer can be to the conditions that the modern law cares about, and it is to *Troilus and Criseyde* that we must look to see Chaucer understanding, not just the relevance of consent's certainties, but the crucial nature of its uncertainty, here, in fact, in all the complexity that still troubles the modern law. At issue in this respect is not the determination of Helen's consent in her "ravysshyng" but of Criseyde's in whatever we will call the act that consummates her relations with Troilus. The difficulty is pointed by the way we are everywhere given careful detail about Criseyde's consensual states, *even as* Criseyde is haunted by what Louise Fradenburg has called the "specter of rape."[35] Such haunting is sufficient to make the story of Troilus's "wooing" equally well a story about the difficulties Criseyde must have in acceding to his blandishments in circumstances where even her agreement is compelled by a variety of forces. Relevant here are descriptions of Criseyde's physical vulnerability in Troy (as Pandarus introduces her to Deiphebus she is one "which that some men wolden don oppressioun / And wrongfully han hire possessioun," (2.1418–19), Troilus's relative strength (as Criseyde fears it, that her refusal would lead to his "dispit" and her "worse plit" (2.711–12), Pandarus's extensive trickery in manipulating Criseyde into Troilus's bed, as well as the extensive imagery of rape that immediately surrounds the consummation scene (songs of nightingales, dreams of violent bodily invasion).[36] But the conditions barring Criseyde's freedom are nowhere more clear than when she must be free if sex with Troilus is not to be coerced and the act of sex is not to be rape:

> This Troilus in armes gan hire streyne,
> And seyde, "O swete, as evere mot I gon,

Now be ye kaught; now is ther but we tweyne!
Now yeldeth yow for other bote is non!"
To that Criseyde answerde thus anon,
"Ne hadde I er now, my swete herte deere,
Ben yolde, ywis, I were now nought here!" (3.1205–11)

The indications of force in the instant (Troilus "gan hire streyne," Criseyde "kaught" without "other bot") as well as the terms of Criseyde's consent make clear that her "yielding" can no longer be simple agreement under conditions where a decision has already been embodied in a set of compulsions, where a "no" would be a meaningless gesture towards an act whose accomplishment is already foreclosed. And yet the claim made by the complex tracing of these conditions is not, I think, that this *is* rape, but that we must *wonder* if it is, even as we are encouraged to decide it is not. Fradenburg suggests that "we cannot 'decide' whether Criseyde has consented or not, whether she has been raped or not,"[37] but the opposite judgement has been made by Jill Mann in an equally compelling argument.[38] Crucial to Mann's case is the sensitivity to Criseyde's predicament that Chaucer has Troilus show: so worried is he, in fact, that he swoons and thereby relinquishes his own "will" at the very moment that this will really is about to coerce Criseyde.[39] As the "specter of rape" proposes this crime for our consideration, the careful handling of consent in this scene keeps the crime just beyond our judgement; we *may* accept Criseyde's "yielding" as consensual even as that consent is qualified to the very edge of freedom. But it is also in this double movement that we can see Chaucer acutely aware of the definitional requirements for rape that preoccupy us—as, that is, the definition of the act here is not made to turn on consent given or denied, but on the conditions of the consent, on the constraints and qualifications that interact with agreement. The material of the scene, in other words, is that vast gray area between consent and nonconsent that the medieval law had created, but its interest is to identify the fine line between rape and not rape that the modern law sees consent making. Chaucer's aim is, with infinite care, to place Troilus and Criseyde on neither side but just *on* that line.

At the same time, we may notice that, even if rape is shaded away from definitional possibility in the consummation scene, it is not finally dismissed from consideration in this poem. The crime returns by name still later as Pandarus denies that it will have any relevance on relations between Troilus and Criseyde ("It is not rape, in my dome, ne no vice, / Hire to withholden that ye love moost," 4.596–97). And, insofar as this poem raises the threat of rape in this earlier scene by defining the crime as a function of constrained consent, we may also observe that the crime *occurs*, according to the poem's definition, when Criseyde finally *is* "in the snare" of the Greeks (5.748), really caught now in Diomede's "net" (5.775), again "allone" and in "nede / Of frendes help" (5.1026–27), coerced by circumstance with no protector as sensitive as Troilus to protect her from compulsion. Of the act of sex between Diomede and Criseyde this poem presumes, it says that Criseyde "falsed" Troilus (5.1053), but, where it also makes all the constraints on Criseyde's decision so clear, where it describes Diomede's consolation as an act that "*refte*" Criseyde "of al hire peyne" (5.1036), it also makes clear that the act that constitutes this falseness is forced. The poem's analysis gives us the material to know, in other words, that just as certain conditions will make being "kaught" and "streyne[d]" no act of rape, other acts, differently named, *are* rape nonetheless. If we focus, for example, on the extended anatomy of Criseyde's "slydyng of corage" (5.825), we may also recall that there are two characters in this poem notable for such "slydyng," and, furthermore, that we have already seen how the first of these slidings is called "ravysshyng." Criseyde's will changes as a direct result of what is called her "chaungynge" (4.231) for Antenor as she does not initially agree to it but, as the poem puts it, she is "yielded" by the Trojans to the Greeks (4.347). If Helen's "ravysshyng" is a rape by modern measure, what then can the act resulting from Criseyde's unwilled exchange otherwise be? Since, in the former case we are only urged to ask the questions that would result in this classification and never given the classification itself, it is irrelevant by this poem's logic that Criseyde's rape is not so named. Indeed, the anatomy this poem offers of rape's definition emphatically proposes that an act accomplished under the conditions of "force" and "fear" that make it rape may well be described by other emotional languages, languages that would figure the crime, instead, as the giving of a "herte" (5.1050), or, even, as a "betrayal." If it should seem preposterous that "rape defined" could ever be so outrageously named, we need only pause to consider (as I think this poem asks us to) what word the Greeks can have been using at this point to characterize Helen's acquiescence in *her* "ravysshyng."

The truly general importance of Chaucer's thinking about the definitional problems posed by the Chaumpaigne release is best approached, however, through a much more simple connection between the matter of the release and the matter of Chaucer's writing. Indeed, it is so simple to suggest that the "lyf . . . of Seynt Cecile" (*The Legend of Good Women,* 426) was meant to count as some kind of pious reparation for wrong done to Cecily Chaumpaigne that the connection has hardly ever been proposed.[40] Still, the date of the poem's original composition may be made to work,[41] and, that aside, we know the poem was again in Chaucer's mind as it became the *Second Nun's Tale* during composition of the *Canterbury Tales.* That a *poem* could have even been thought reparatory had Chaucer raped Cecily

Chaumpaigne might itself cause us to wonder whether Chaucer understood anything about the terrifying realities of *raptus* when he wrote this
"life." And yet, it is precisely the generality of the poem's investigation of
the conditions of consent that shows its understanding of what is at stake in
the release to be complicated indeed. If we look to the poem's detail, for
example, we may note that the first thing Cecilia must overcome is the sexual compulsions imposed by marriage: she must live in "pure chaastnesse of
virginitee" (VIII, 88) by protecting herself from the "touche" of "vileynye"
(VIII, 156) that is, in this case, the touch of her husband. In its detailing of
the kind of force that even the sanctioned act of marriage might represent,
this poem also investigates the more general forms of unfreedom that a lack
of concern for consent's conditions produced in the medieval period. But
it is, in particular, the language Chaucer uses to describe what Cecilia
achieves that connects the analysis of this poem to a more general investigation of consent in much of Chaucer's other writing. When Valerian finally
agrees to leave her "body clene" (VIII, 225) he also acknowledges that she
is as undefiled in attitude as in act, that her "will" has been the instrument
of her resistance, that it is her "*thoght*" above all that is "unwemmed" (VIII,
225). For Chaucer, "unwemmed" is the condition of a woman whose consent is uncoerced: he uses it to describe a Mary whose "maidenhede" is also
preserved, "unwemmed," in marriage (*ABC* 91), and, also, to describe a
Constance who divine intervention has just saved from rape ("And thus
hath Crist unwemmed kept Custance," II, 924). But, for Chaucer, this word
also connotes the general conditions of *any* person whose will remains free:
in the *Boece*, in particular, the "arbitrie" of such a person is also said to be
"hool and unwemmed" (2.pr.4.21).[42]

To see how a consideration of the human will in Chaucer's writings
might bear upon consideration of the problems entailed in understanding
the *raptus* mentioned in the Chaumpaigne release, it will be helpful to
make a brief and preparatory detour through the *quaestio* in Thomas
Aquinas's *Summa Theologiae*, in which *raptus* and the "will" are carefully examined together.[43] *Raptus* in this context is probably best translated as
"rapture," for what Aquinas is puzzling over here is Paul's claim that he
knows "a man in Christ who was caught up to the third heaven" ("Scio
hominem in Christo . . . raptum usque ad tertium coelum," 2 Corinthians
12:2), and what he wants to analyze is how, by *raptus,* a man may be "raised
to divine things" ("ad divina elevetur," 2a2ae.175.1). Even if this *raptus* is
not forced sex, Aquinas remains much alive to the way force must be part
of an act so described:

> Raptus violentiam quandam importat . . . Violentum autem dicitur cuius
> principium est extra, nil conferente eo quod vim patitur. (2a2ae.175.1)

> [Rapture does imply a certain violence . . . Violence . . . is done when the
> principle is external and the sufferer confers nothing to it.]

And in a nuanced analysis that may remind us of the analysis of "consent"
in the modern law, Aquinas also explores ways that, under pressure of such
violence, what we regard as "free" about the "will" depends entirely on
how we involve that will in our definition of the act itself:

> Ad ea quae excedunt liberi arbitrii facultatem, necesse est quod homo
> quadam fortiori operatione elevetur: quae quidem quantum ad aliquid
> potest dici coactio, si scilicet attendatur modus operationis, non autem si at-
> tendatur terminus operationis, in quem natura hominis et eius intentio or-
> dinatur. (a2ae.175.1)

> [For what exceeds the capacities of the free-will, a man needs to be uplifted
> by a more powerful source of action. This source might be termed coercive if
> we consider the mode of action, not so however if we consider the term of
> the action, namely the end to which man's nature and tendency is ordered.]

Focus on the act itself, Aquinas says, and you will find violence, but focus
on the end toward which that violence is directed and you will find
"order." Aquinas can finally dismiss the coerciveness of violence in this *raptus* because its end is God—"divine love causes ecstasy" ["divinus amor
facit extasim"] (2a2ae.175,2)—at the same time, however, he shows how
the exigencies of *any* "order" may be made to justify a "certain violence,"
how the higher claims of a "term of action" [*terminus operationis*] can redefine the state of freedom that is ostensibly its "mode" [*modus operationis*].
Such a description is itself a gloss on the logic of the medieval English law,
for that law ignores a woman's will at the moment of an act of "ravishment" or *raptus* in favor of the higher order of marriage, which it understands as a "right" of fathers and husbands. But the gloss is even more
general than this, since Aquinas also helps us to see that *raptus* in any period (or by any name) may be investigated not only by considering the
state of the will (its "consent," simply put) but the nature of the order that
could define the violent compulsion of that will as "freedom." The conditions that make an act *raptus,* Aquinas teaches, may be described apart from
definitions of crime, as a pure consideration of the will and the scheme and
method by which that will may be said to be "free."
    That Chaucer considered this issue in just such schematic terms hardly
needs to be pointed out for it is well known that the main concern of
Books 4 and 5 of the *Boece* is the freedom and constraint of the "will." Still,
it is probably worth noting for the purposes of the connections I want to
stress here that, in the *Boece,* the "unmoevable purveaunce," which "con-

streyneth the fortunes and the dedes of men by a bond of causes nat able to ben unbownde" (4.pr.6.153–59) has as one of its forms of constraint a kind of "ravishment":

> This atempraunce norysscheth and bryngeth forth ale thinges that brethith lif in this world; and thilke same attempraunce, ravysschynge, hideth and bynymeth, and drencheth undir the laste deth, alle thinges iborn. (4.m6.34–39)[44]

The dreamer's extensive worries about what freedom the "will" *can* have in the context of such constraint are, at least here, pointed directly at the category of act whose relation to the will occupies us. In this light, what we find when we examine how "philosophy" can find "any liberte of fre wille in this ordre of causes" (5.pr.2.3–4), is an order that, again, dismisses the nonconsent that "ravishment" would seem to propose, defining the "will" as "free" *even in such cases*. And the dreamer learns to understand such constraint in terms that exactly parallel the effect constraint is shown to have on Criseyde's character: as "the destinal cheyne constrenith the moevynges of the *corages* of men" (5.pr.2.5–7, emphasis mine) so do Trojan movings constrain the "corage" of Criseyde. The dreamer is made to agree that "corage" is rightly constrained in this way—that "corages" *necessarily* "slide"—because Lady Philosophy shows that what is called force by the "resoun of mankynde" is *not* force when named in "the symplicite of the devyne prescience (5.pr.4.9–15). Philosophy's claim—that the "will" in such cases is "free"—is of course Aquinas's claim, but this position becomes directly relevant to Chaucer's consideration of consent in marriage as it is couched in the language I have also said Chaucer uses to describe such a woman:

> And syn that thise thinges ben thus . . . thanne is ther fredom of arbitrie, that duelleth *hool and unwemmed* to mortal men; ne the lawes ne purposen nat wikkedly medes and peynes to the willynges of men that ben unbownden and quyt of alle necessite; and God, byholdere and forwytere of alle thingis, duelleth above, and the present eternite of his sighte renneth alwey with the diverse qualite of our dedes, dispensynge and ordeynynge medes to gode men and tormentz to wikkide men. (5.pr.6.286–98, emphasis mine)

The insight is also deepened here, for rather than claiming that a "term of action" or an "ordre of causes" such as marriage does *not* constitute compulsion, what we learn is that this higher order *may* compel by a "certain violence" and the "mode of action" is still "free." Put the medieval law that enforces marriage "rights" in the place of the "devyne prescience" and you will be able to define as consensual ("free") even the marriage that begins in rape. By this same definitional insight, of course, put the *modern* rape law in the place of that "devyne prescience" and you will also be able to define many medieval marriages as rape. Chaucer, I would also suggest, offers just such judgements when, in his poetry, he unsettles Philosophy's neat scheme and puts personal agents in the crucial position of the "devyne prescience." When Theseus, for example, stands in for God and imposes order at the end of the *Knight's Tale,* marrying Emelye to Palemoun without even consulting Emelye's wishes, we are made to see Theseus defining her "arbitrie" as "unwemmed" even as we are also made to see that this will is compelled. When Griselde's will is made everywhere to cleave to Walter's as if he were God ("But as ye wole youreself, right so wol I," IV, 361) we are also made to see how this general yielding results in a series of acts to which Griselde ostensibly consents but to which the terms of her marriage bar any other response. It is in these instances (as well as many others) that we may say that Chaucer is concerned with considering the issues at stake in understanding the Chaumpaigne release to precisely the extent that his poetry is Boethian—that is, to a very great extent indeed.

Less stressed in the *Boece* but emphatically explored in Chaucer's Boethian poetry are the implications to the quotidian world of the claim that an act is only ascertainable as it is referred to the order that defines (ignores or credits) the conditions of consent that allow it to happen: such a claim suggests that, as that order alters—as say rubrics of the modern law are substituted for the rubrics of the medieval law—the *act itself* will change. Where that act might be rape, Chaucer also shows his awareness of this possibility by exploring the conditions of consent so fully that we may see how what is not rape by the medieval law may still be rape by our own definition. Moreover, as we come to understand the medieval law in light of Chaucer's incisive diagnosis of definitional possibility, we also learn to see how the "order" of that law guarantees that we will never have the means to know whether Chaumpaigne's *raptus* was her rape. And it is here—as he shows us this—that Chaucer also establishes his relation to this *raptus.* What we do not know and cannot know about the act the Chaumpaigne release names as *raptus* is what Chaucer knew was not and could not be known about any such act in circumstances that routinely co-opted or ignored a woman's consent. It is the uncertainty of such consent in the fourteenth century that is also all we may count as our own certainty in determining what the Chaumpaigne release "really means." But, as I have been arguing, this does not convert all we may say about the release into "speculation." If we do not know what act prompted the Chaumpaigne release we do know precisely why and precisely how the medieval law carefully put our particular uncertainty in place.*

Notes

* Elizabeth Scala and Elizabeth Robertson created the different, but simultaneous, opportunities that occasioned this piece, and I thank them for these invitations as well as for their helpful responses to my earliest attempts. I would also like to thank all my interlocutors at the University of Texas at Austin, and, for careful and extremely useful readings, Jessica Brantley, Juliet Fleming, H. A. Kelly, Jill Mann, and James Simpson.

1. T. F. T. Plucknett, "Chaucer's Escapade," *The Law Quarterly Review* 64 (1948): 35. This epigraph has more than incidental status in framing an exploration of Chaumpaigne release. With the exception of the first sentence I quote, these words are also repeated for their authority in the standard source for the Chaumpaigne release, the *Chaucer Life-Records,* ed. Martin M. Crow and Clair C. Olson (Oxford: Clarendon Press, 1966) p. 343 (for the release) and pp. 345–46 (for Plucknett's words).

2. Carolyn Dinshaw, *Chaucer's Sexual Poetics* (Madison: University of Wisconsin Press, 1989), p. 11.

3. Dinshaw, *Sexual Poetics,* p. 10.

4. Jill Mann, *Geoffrey Chaucer* (Hemel Hempstead: Harvester Wheatsheaf, 1991), p. 45.

5. See my "Raptus in the Chaumpaigne Release and a Newly Discovered Document Concerning the Life of Geoffrey Chaucer," *Speculum* 68 (1993): 74–94 (esp. 76–89).

6. For a survey of the various positions that have been adopted on the meaning of *raptus* in the Chaumpaigne release, see, again, my "Raptus in the Chaumpaigne Release," p. 75 and p. 75, nn. 5–7. To these may be added the more recent remarks of Derek Pearsall: "Quite commonly in legal documents of the time, *raptus* means 'abduction'" (*The Life of Geoffrey Chaucer: A Critical Biography* [Oxford: Blackwell, 1992], p. 135). For exploration of other fourteenth-century legal records that mention *raptus,* see Henry Ansgar Kelly, "Meanings and Uses of *Raptus* in Chaucer's Time," *Studies in the Age of Chaucer* 20 (1998): 101–65. Kelly attempts to reconstruct the events that lead to the use of this term, and he finds evidence that those events were sometimes more like abduction than rape. His evidence certainly extends the gray area in the record, particularly as it relates to one case (Yeuelcombe/Mann), which I have relied upon to argue that *raptus* means rape in the legal milieu in which the Chaumpaigne release was drafted. In contrast, Kelly's important deepening of our knowledge of legal language should be read against my exploration here of the problems involved in either believing or understanding what that legal language "means." If *raptus* may "mean 'abduction'" then what does "*abduction*" mean? For my discussion of the Yeuelcombe/Mann case as well as the beginnings of my claim that the "persistent gray area" in legal records must be related to the "complex continuum of behavior" that constitutes acts of "abduction" and "rape," see my "Raptus in the Chaumpaigne Release," pp. 86–89.

7. Pearsall provides an admirable reconstruction of this kind in the *Life of Geoffrey Chaucer* and nearly ends with the phrase I quote here, which he calls the "safest conclusion" in a case for which "there is not enough evidence to come to a conclusion." On the other hand, Pearsall does not forebear speculation, some of which usefully defines the uncertainties in question ("the actual offense . . . is not necessarily the offense named in the charge"), but some of which obscures what "violent physical rape" might be as it suggests that problems would be ameliorated if this were a case of "violent physical passion." See *Life of Geoffrey Chaucer,* pp. 135–38.

8. I will take the code of the state of California as paradigmatic of the "modern" here, because it is progressive (and so its definitional failures are the more interesting and significant) and lengthy (providing substantial text for the detailed analysis I undertake). The issues I will take up in relation to this American code are also raised in modern English provisions (in particular, the crucial relation between sexual violence and "consent"), but these issues are less easy to ventilate because the detail of English provisions is spread so much more diffusely through the case law. The framework for this law is set out, however, by Section 1 of the Sexual Offences Act of 1956 (as amended by Section 142 of the Criminal Justice and Public Order Act of 1994): "(1) It is an offence for a man to rape a woman or another man. (2) A man commits rape if—(a) he has sexual intercourse with a person (whether vaginal or anal) who at the time of the intercourse does not consent to it; and (b) at the time he knows that the person does not consent to the intercourse or is reckless as to whether that person consents to it. (3) A man also commits rape if he induces a married woman to have sexual intercourse with him by impersonating her husband." For the text of the California Code, see California Penal Code, sec. 261 in *West's Annotated California Codes* (St. Paul, MN: West Publishing, 1954-), vol. 48: 50–51. Here and subsequently I cite the version of the code in the "Cumulative Pocket Part" for this volume of *West's Annotated California Codes.* For the text of the English law see Alan Reed and Peter Seago, *Criminal Law* (London: Sweet and Maxwell, 1999), p. 387. I am grateful to my colleague, Adrian Briggs, for guidance on points relating to the English law.

9. See Susan Estrich, *Real Rape* (Cambridge, MA: Harvard University Press, 1987), pp. 29–56.

10. On "rape of spouse," see California Penal Code, sec. 262 in *West's Annotated California Codes* 48 (supplement). For the addition of this definition by statute in 1979, see the 1988 volumes of *West's Annotated California Codes,* 48: 160–61. The English law, it should be noted, does not take the possibility of spousal rape into explicit account (for it only makes the "impersonation" of a spouse unlawful), although a decision in the House of Lords in 1992 has made prosecution of spousal rape possible under the Sexual Offences Act. See Reed and Seago, *Criminal Law,* p. 388 and nn. 95 and 98.

11. See California Penal Code, sec. 261 (subsections "1," "3," and "4"), in *West's Codes,* 48 (supplement).

12. California Penal Code, sec. 261.6, in *West's Codes,* 48 (supplement).

13. The "Statute of Rapes" follows the Chaumpaigne release, of course, but its proximity in time gives it relevance. For text and translations of these statutes, see *The Statutes of the Realm,* 12 vols. (London, 1810–28; rpt. 1963), 1: 29 (Westminster I, Chapter 13), 1: 87–88 (Westminster II, Chapters 34–35) and 2: 27 ("Statute of Rapes"). I have been aided greatly in my research on these statutes by Henry Ansgar Kelly's "Statutes of Rapes and Alleged Ravishers of Wives: A Context for the Charges Against Thomas Malory, Knight," *Viator* 28 (1997): 361–419.

14. For crucial examinations of the procedural ramifications of these statutes, see two articles by J. B. Post: "Ravishment of Women and the Statutes of Westminster," in *Legal Records and the Historian,* ed. J. H. Baker (London: Royal Historical Society, 1978), pp. 150–64 and "Sir Thomas West and the Statute of Rapes, 1382," *Bulletin of the Institute of Historical Research* 53 (1980): 24–30. See also Sue Sheridan Walker, "Punishing Convicted Ravishers: Statutory Strictures and Actual Practice in Thirteenth and Fourteenth-Century England," *Journal of Medieval History* 13 (1987): 237–50.

15. *Statutes,* 1: 29. The chapter further prohibits this for "any wife or maiden of full age, nor any other woman against her will [ne dame ne damoisele de age, ne autre femme maugre seon]."

16. For an edition of this chapter of Westminster I that leaves "a force" out, see the appendix to Post, "Ravishment of Women," pp. 162–63. For the salient differences between the edition of this chapter in the *Statutes of the Realm* and Post, I rely upon Kelly, "Statutes of Rapes," pp. 364–66.

17. Post, "Ravishment of Women," p. 156.

18. *Statutes,* 1: 87 (emphasis mine).

19. "Uxor, si sponte reliquerit virum suum et abierit et moretur cum adultero suo, amittat imperpetuum accionem petendi dotem suam que ei competere posset de tenura viri, si super hoc convincatur, nisi vir suus sponte, et absque cohercione ecclesiastica, eam reconciliet et secum cohabitari permittat; in quo casu restituatur ei accio" (*Statutes,* 1: 87).

20. "De pueris, sive masculis sive femellis, quorum maritagium ad aliquem pertineat, raptis et abductis, si ille qui rapuerit, non habens jus in maritagium . . ." (*Statutes,* 1: 88).

21. See H. A. Kelly, "Statutes of Rapes," p. 366.

22. *Statutes,* 2: 27.

23. Kelly, "Statutes of Rapes," pp. 380–81.

24. See my "*Raptus* in the Chaumpaigne Release," esp. pp. 84–89.

25. In what follows I take both letters and their translations from the Loeb edition: Ovid, *Heroides and Amores,* trans. Grant Showerman, rev. ed. G. P. Goold (Cambridge, MA: Harvard University Press, 1977). Quotations hereafter will be cited by epistle number (XVI: "Paris to Helen"; XVII, "Helen to Paris") and line number in my text.

26. Quotations from Chaucer here and throughout will be taken from *The Riverside Chaucer,* ed. Larry D. Benson, 3rd. ed. (Boston: Houghton Mifflin, 1987). All subsequent citations will be by line number in my text.

27. California Penal Code, sec. 261 (subsections "2" and "6") in *West's Annotated California Codes,* 48 (supplement).

28. It should be emphasized that Chaucer alone is responsible for the subtle portrayal of Helen I have traced here; he is not absorbing these distinctions from Boccaccio's *Filostrato:* the key stanza I quote in this paragraph on Helen's domestic comfort (2.1555–60) has no direct parallel in Boccaccio's poem. See the *en face* comparison in Geoffrey Chaucer, *Troilus and Criseyde,* ed. B. A. Windeatt (London: Longman, 1984).

29. "Nisi libera voluntate nulla est copulanda alicui." Gratian, *Decretum in Corpus iuris* canonici, ed. E. Friedberg (Leipzig: Bernhard Tauchnitz, 1879–81), dictum post c. 4, cited and trans. in John T. Noonan, Jr., "Power to Choose," *Viator* 4 (1983): 422 and 422 n. 6.

30. R. H. Helmholz, *Marriage Litigation in Medieval England* (Cambridge: Cambridge University Press, 1974), p. 90. On force and fear as impediments to consent in marriage generally, see that volume, pp. 90–94, 178–81, and 220–28.

31. Noonan, "Power to Choose," p. 425.

32. These are the cases and legal forms I connect to the Chaumpaigne release in *"Raptus* in the Chaumpaigne Release."

33. That the wife remains certain that she has had sex with her husband both during and after is made clear when the fight between Aleyn and Symkyn breaks out and Symkyn falls on the wife: her cries show that she believes this person is someone *else* ("Awak Symond! The feend is on me falle," I, 4288) and that it is the clerks, arisen from *their* bed, who are fighting ("Help Symkyn, for the false clerkes fighte!" I, 4291).

34. In the instance of Malyn, a modern judgement of rape would be easy by legal standards of "force," but even the more complex nonconsent of the wife is expressly covered in the California code covering acts of spousal rape ("where a person submits under the belief that the person committing the act is [her] spouse"). See California Penal Code, Sec. 621 (subsection, "5") in *West's Annotated California Codes* 48 (supplement).

35. Louise O. Fradenburg, "'Our owen wo to drynke': Loss, Gender, and Chivalry in *Troilus and Criseyde"* in *Chaucer's* Troilus and Criseyde, *"Subgit to alle Poesye": Essays in Criticism,* ed. R. A. Shoaf (Binghamton, NY: Medieval Renaissance Texts and Studies, 1992), pp. 88–106 (for the phrase, see p. 99).

36. Fradenburg carefully traces these images and their ramifications in "'Our owen wo to drynke,'" pp. 98–101.

37. Fradenburg, "'Our owen wo to drynke,'" p. 100.

38. Jill Mann, "Troilus' Swoon," *Chaucer Review* 14 (1980): 319–35. In this article, Mann shows how the "developing relationship between Troilus and Criseyde is conceived and described in terms of power" so that "the shifts

and transformations in the way each of them either exerts or refuses to exert power over the other lead to the achievement of a mature and complex relationship on which the consummation can be fittingly based" (p. 320).

39. On this crucial relation between the swoon and the consummation, see Mann, "Troilus' Swoon," pp. 325–30.

40. To my knowledge, this connection has only been proposed once, by George H. Cowling in *Chaucer* (New York: E. P. Dutton, 1927), p. xviii, cited in P. R. Watts, "The Strange Case of Geoffrey Chaucer and Cecilia Chaumpaigne," *The Law Quarterly Review* 63 (1947): 491–515.

41. The uncontroversial chronology offered by Larry D. Benson in "The Canon and Chronology of Chaucer's Works" (*The Riverside Chaucer,* pp. xxvi–xxix) places the "lyf" between "1372–80" and, within this group, notes that its date is "possibly later" (p. xxix).

42. In addition to the instances I cite here, Chaucer also uses this word on one other occasion in the *Second Nun's Tale* (as Cecilia prays to preserve her chastity in marriage [VIII, 137]). See Larry D. Benson, *A Glossarial Concordance to the Riverside Chaucer* (New York: Garland, 1993), s.v. "unwemmed adj."

43. St. Thomas Aquinas, *Summa Theologiae,* vol. 45 "Prophecy and Other Charisms (2a2ae.171–78)," ed. and trans. Roland Potter (New York: Mc-Graw-Hill Book Company, 1970), 2a2ae.175, 1 (pp. 94–117). Hereafter, all quotations and translations from the *Summa* will be taken from this edition and cited in my text. I have made a few silent alterations in the translation for the sake of clarity.

44. Chaucer is not here inventing this image but discovering it, for the figuration is already present in Boethius's Latin: "Haec temperies alit ac profert, / quicquid vitam spirat in orbe; / eadem *rapiens* condit et aufert / obitu mergens orta supremo." *Philosophiae Consolationis Libri Quinque,* ed. Karl Büchner (Heidelberg: Carl Winter, 1977), IV.m.vi.30–33 (emphasis mine).

CHAPTER 10

PUBLIC BODIES AND PSYCHIC DOMAINS: RAPE, CONSENT, AND FEMALE SUBJECTIVITY IN GEOFFREY CHAUCER'S *TROILUS AND CRISEYDE*

Elizabeth Robertson

Using two classical literary heroines as models, the essay explores how rape, in its various historical meanings, shapes the indeterminate subjectivity of Geoffrey Chaucer's Criseyde.

> *"Now be ye kaught; now is there but we tweyne!*
> *Now yeldeth yow, for other bote is ther non!"* . . .
>
> *"Ne hadde I er now, my swete herte deere,*
> *Ben yolde, ywis, I were now nought heere!"*
>
> —*Geoffrey Chaucer*, Troilus and Criseyde *(Book III, 1207–8; 1210–11)*

In Book IV of Geoffrey Chaucer's fourteenth-century poem *Troilus and Criseyde*, Pandarus and Troilus debate whether or not Troilus should "rape" Criseyde, using the word "rape" for nearly the first time in English literature. As Henry Ansgar Kelly and Christopher Cannon have shown, this discussion, as it unfolds, captures the ambiguous meanings of rape in the legal language of fourteenth-century England where rape (as it appears in medieval legal terminology in various forms of *rapire* in Latin or in its Old French forms) can refer to various events including abduction, forced coitus, or both.[1] Although a host of critics (as various as John Fleming,

Carolyn Dinshaw, David Aers, Jill Mann, and Louise Fradenburg) have established the significance of at least the threat of rape in the poem, what has yet to be explored fully are the ways in which the cultural formations determining how rape was understood in fourteenth-century England are foundational to the elusive and ambiguous character for which Criseyde is famous.[2]

In this study of the role rape plays in the formation of Criseyde's character, I explore how female subjectivity emerges even under severe restraint, that is, even when a woman is subjected to rape. Despite the overwhelming impulse in early cultures for men to treat women, especially those of higher social status, as prized objects to be guarded, fought over, and exchanged, women, because they can never completely become objects, either willingly or unwillingly, resist such classification. That is, as Judith Butler puts it, "'Subjection' signifies the process of becoming subordinated to power as well as the process of becoming a subject" and "the subject emerges both as an *effect* of a prior power and as the *condition of possibility* for a radically conditioned form of agency."[3] In Classical, Medieval, and Early Modern societies, rape or "raptus" had two meanings: forced coitus and abduction, usually for the purposes of marriage. Forced coitus clearly denies a woman agency and choice; abduction, however, under most circumstances also denies a woman agency and choice, but surprisingly, especially in the Middle Ages, abduction for the purposes of marriage might involve a woman's expression of her own choices. Indeed, in some circumstances, abduction cases might be among the few occasions in medieval culture where female consent and agency are affirmed in the public domain.

Before turning to Criseyde, I shall consider two paradigmatic literary models of women who endure such acts, the classical figures of Lucrece and Helen of Troy. These two figures demonstrate the ways in which the female subject is paradoxically (in a Hegelian sense) both determined by these acts and resistant to that determination. Their legends disclose how female subjectivity emerges under constraint when a woman is subjected to forced coitus, or to abduction, and thus can help us understand Criseyde who is subject to both forms of rape. In the case of Lucrece, the female subject internalizes the culture's view of her as the valued, and then violated, property of her husband; death by suicide after rape becomes her only available choice of response within the logic of her society. Her status as a speaking subject with choices—a status granted in only a few versions of her story, most fully in a late form of this paradigm in Shakespeare's "Rape of Lucrece"—conflicts with the objectification she struggles to absorb. Helen, a woman who suffers rape as abduction when Paris seizes her from her husband, is, however, a more intricate model, because the various versions of her story cloud the degree to which she consented to her abduction. During at least the Classical to the Early Modern periods, this very obscurity of choice highlights the right to choose as a defining principle of female subjectivity.

Analysis of Chaucer's Criseyde within the context of these two paradigmatic models brings into sharper focus the enigmatic and paradoxical status of Criseyde as a choosing subject. The question of choice that underpins the stories of Lucrece and Helen becomes all the more charged in Christian cultures in part because of a paradigm shift about rape first articulated by Augustine who, in a discussion of the Lucrece story, condemned the act of suicide as an appropriate response to rape. His analysis of Lucrece's rape and his rejection of suicide as an appropriate response to it depends on his assumption of the autonomy of the female soul. This assumption also underlies Church doctrine and ecclesiastical law governing the necessity of choice in marriage. That women were granted choice in doctrine and could assert that choice in law troubles a system (especially a feudal system) that identifies women primarily as commodities on the marriage market. The ambiguities that reside in cultural assumptions of female identity that both deny and affirm the right of the female subject to choose are particularly at the fore in fourteenth-century England when feudal assumptions about female choice in marriage (that she has no choice) clash with ecclesiastical assumptions (that she does have choice). Chaucer's Criseyde, I shall show, fully articulates the complexities of the female subject in Western culture always already subject to the objectification that underlies rape and, furthermore, crystallizes the particular ways those ambiguities emerge in fourteenth-century secular and ecclesiastical conflicts over definitions of rape.

The Victim of Rape as Sexual Assault: Lucrece

Lucrece, an upper-class woman who is sexually violated against her will, represents the archetypal literary rape victim. In brief, following Livy, the story tells of the Roman, Collatinus, whose boast of his wife, Lucrece's, chastity stirs his cousin, Sextus Tarquinius, son of the ruling tyrannical king, to test that chastity. Incited to lust by her chaste beauty, Tarquin rapes her. Suffused with shame after her rape, Lucrece kills herself and her death becomes the motivation for the Romans to overthrow the "barbarian" Tarquins and to replace rulership by kings with government by consuls.

As Stephanie Jed has so ably demonstrated, the story of Lucrece illustrates how societies from the Ancient to the Early Modern periods view the nature of the female subject who has been raped.[4] Lucrece's story reveals rape as an act that profoundly discloses how culture objectifies women whose choices and desires are subordinated to, if not irrelevant to, those of both the rapist and her husband. Not only must Lucrece's desires perfectly reflect those of her husband, but also the integrity of her body must stand for the integrity of his household, the city, and the "state," however that larger social organization is understood from period to period. According to this logic, violating a woman violates her husband, the city, and the state as well. Furthermore, rape becomes the rationale for territorial aggression not by the victim, but by those who feel their property— the rape victim—has been violated.[5]

This model rests on a notion, reinforced by secular and in certain cases by canonical law throughout the early periods, that women are nothing but the property of men, commodities whose subjectivities are circumscribed by the three roles traditionally available to them: as virgins, married women, and widows. Peter Stallybrass reminds us that "the conceptualization of woman as land or possession has, of course, a long history. The commandments catalog wife, maid, ox, and ass side by side as a form of masculine acquisition of slaves, cattle, and other belongings."[6] The view of women as property facilitates what Gayle Rubin has described as "the traffic in women," social practices controlling female sexuality and reproduction that undergird patriarchal social structures.[7] Rubin was referring to marriage practices, but I would extend her analysis to include other forms of the control of the female body ranging from chastity to marriage to rape. All these controls are rigidly prescribed by rules, regulations, and ideologies produced by those other than the female subject, and all elicit female compliance.

After a woman has been raped, her status as property—now damaged property—is reasserted. Historically, the law made this status clear by the fact that women throughout the Ancient and Medieval periods typically did not seek redress for rape; rather, men sought reparation for the damage done to their property by the rapist. The award for damages a man received varied depending on the class and circumstances of the raped woman; for example, a raped housemaid would command less compensation than a raped aristocratic wife. A 1383 English Statute of the Realm, for example, states that a woman who has been ravished who consents to that ravishment afterwards loses all rights of inheritance and dower.[8]

As damaged goods, a raped woman no longer holds a fixed position in society. Because her unstable position has the potential to unsettle her very definition as an object, society often seeks to restabilize and rigidify the meaning of a woman who has been raped either by having her killed or by isolating her from the community through shame. Dying forecloses a woman's ability to redefine the social meaning of her rape, leaving the choice to define the meaning of rape only to others—and in early accounts of a rape victim's story (either literary or biblical), a rape victim usually died either by her own hand or by the hands of others. Social systems that depend on the exchange of women as commodified objects will be best supported if the raped woman internalizes views of herself as damaged goods and, thus, being overcome with shame, isolates herself from the community, most effectively by suicide.[9] If the victim does not choose suicide, she may be killed by her relatives as was the unfortunate victim of rape in *Judges*. Lucrece is just one of numerous literary representations and historical examples of the raped woman's death either by murder or suicide.

In choosing suicide in response to her rape, Lucrece implicitly recognizes the potential danger of her unstable identity. In Livy's account, Lucrece only becomes a speaking subject after rape and she only speaks twice.[10] She first asserts her noncompliance to the act of rape: "ceterum corpus est tantum violatum, animus insons" ["all the rest of my body has been violated; my soul is guiltless"], but claims only her death will bear witness to this "mors testis erit" ["death will be the witness."][11] Her observers urge her to acknowledge that "mentem peccare, non corpus" ["It is the mind that sins, not the body"] and "unde consilium afuerit, culpam abesse" ["where resolution has been absent, there has been no guilt"]. Lucrece concludes, however, "ego me etsi peccato absolvo, supplicio non libero; nec ulla deinde inpudica Lucretiae exemplo vivet" ["I myself absolve myself from sin, but I am not free from punishment; nor in any way shall henceforth an unchaste woman live by the example of Lucrece"].

This debate encapsulates a problem that troubles understandings of rape to the present day: how can the degree of female consent to coitus be assessed; how can what is private and inner be brought into the public arena? Because consent is described here by Lucrece as an act of the "mens" or the "animus," it is difficult to assess publicly. What is crucial here in this early account and in later versions of the story is the assumption that the rape victim does have a mind, or a soul. Even at this moment of extreme subordination and objectification, her subjectivity is at least granted. While her body may be the public possession of her husband, her mind and soul remain her own. Livy's Lucrece, however, cannot fully accept that.

Lucrece's liminal position as a raped woman suggests a paradox: the very event, rape, that defines a woman as an object, reveals her to be a subject, for just after rape, a woman's subjectivity is released from the social constraints that determine not only her value or worth as property, but also her identity. This places her in the unusual position of being able to define herself. Therefore, she has the potential to articulate a position that can actually counter patriarchal structures. Lucrece rejects that potential; she assumes that because she no longer has a clearly defined identity, others will define her as unchaste. Because patriarchal societies have afforded women no other identity outside of their sexual roles, that momentarily released subjectivity can find no positive social place. Representations of rape, such as the story of Lucrece, can thus reveal not only the subjectivity denied by rape, an act that defines women as objects, but also the potential subjectivity released by rape, when women no longer function as objects.

I would like to turn briefly to a version of the Lucrece legend that postdates Chaucer, Shakespeare's "Rape of Lucrece," because it illustrates precisely the ways in which Lucrece's subjectivity emerges both in spite of and because of constraint, and thus can help us understand the problematics of female subjectivity when revealed by rape that I find so crucial to our understanding of Chaucer's Criseyde.[12] Unusually full in its representation of Lucrece's response to her rape, Shakespeare's version exposes the processes by which the female subject comes to internalize prescriptions that demand the erasure of her subjectivity by suicide, an act that terminates choice. Furthermore, Shakespeare's Lucrece measures her conservative choices against the experiences of the other paradigmatic figure of rape, Helen, one who declines to choose suicide, thus illustrating their crucial similarities and differences.

After Lucrece is raped, she struggles to accept a view of herself as the damaged property of Collatinus. As she assesses her newly forming identity, however, she occupies, for a time, an unstable position. Shakespeare presents her first response as lament. The narrator speaks of her as a "lamenting Philomel" (1079), and she calls "Come, Philomel, that sing'st of ravishment, / Make thy sad grove in my disheveled hair" (1128–29). She can, however, identify only with the lament of Philomel, never considering Philomel's revenge as possible for herself. In order to fulfill her patriarchally prescribed role as a supporter of, rather than a potential challenge to, patriarchy, she must introject society's prescriptions. Lucrece considers the possibility of escaping social definitions of her as damaged goods by longing to hide herself forever in the night. Overcome with shame, she does not find in darkness a possibility of a counter world, but only a cover, which she finally rejects. She cannot engage the utopian possibilities that come into being because of rape.

Lucrece turns to meditate instead on a piece of art through which she assesses her possible new identities: "At last she calls to mind where hangs a piece / Of skillful painting, made for Priam's Troy, / Before the which is drawn the power of Greece, / For Helen's rape the city to destroy" (1366–69). As Lucrece continues musing on this painting, she shifts her gaze away from Helen, the woman who would appear to be her most obvious mirror, and towards Hecuba:

To this well-painted piece is Lucrece come,
To find a face where all distress is stelled.

Many she sees where cares have carved some,
But none where all distress and dolor dwelled,
Till she despairing Hecuba beheld,
Staring on Priam's wounds with her old eyes,
Which bleeding under Pyrrhus' proud foot lies (1443–49).

Surprisingly, it is on Hecuba that she focuses her attention, rather than on the woman in her own situation—the raped/abducted Helen. Contradicting her initial identification with Helen, and merging with Hecuba, Lucrece now condemns Helen, labeling her a whore rather than a victim of rape: "Show me the strumpet that began this stir / That with my nails her beauty I may tear" (1471–72). While in this line she blames Helen as a whore, thus implying that Helen acts on her own desires, further on Lucrece shifts her focus again and criticizes Paris for his lust: "The heat of lust, fond Paris, did incur / This load of wrath that burning Troy doth bear. / Thy eye kindled the fire that burneth here" (1473–75). While Lucrece grants Helen enough agency to be at fault, she ultimately grants full agency only to Paris. Lucrece further blames Paris for articulating desires that are not consonant with those of the public. She asks, "Why should the private pleasure of some one / Become the public plague of many moe" (1478–79). Lucrece cannot imagine a private realm for a woman; and although she grants a private realm for a man, she disapproves of one not fully consonant with the public sphere.

It may seem startling at first that Lucrece should identify with Hecuba rather than Helen, but this identification can be understood if we view rape as part of a larger system of sexual controls including marriage. Like Hecuba, herself once a rape victim who had been married to Priam as a war prize, Lucrece embodies the invaded city. Hecuba is the prop of the patriarch—the now dead Priam—and her role, like that of so many women in war, is to grieve. Helen, when seen as a victim, as a piece of property stolen from Menelaus, also represents a woman with whom Lucrece can identify, as she does early on in her contemplation of the painting. But because Lucrece grants Helen a flicker of agency as a woman who might be complicit with Paris in the pursuit of "private pleasures," she must then reject Helen and name her only as a whore. Lucrece internalizes the woe that Collatinus will feel upon learning that his most prized possession has become a valueless object. Like Hecuba, she grieves the damage done to the patriarch, a grief that emerges primarily from the denial of her own subjectivity. As Collatinus's damaged goods, Lucrece feels the need to remove herself from the system before she can act on her own. Death becomes her only choice.

Why must Shakespeare's Lucrece reject identifying with Helen? While Helen can at times represent a voiceless counter in a game played by men, she can additionally be understood as a figure with desires and choices of her own. But Lucrece refuses to accept Helen as a legitimately desiring subject. The legendary Helen is a socially unstable figure, marked not only by her potentially treacherous relationships with both Greek and Trojan men, but also by her own emergent subjectivity, which, as we shall see, only glimmers in Homer and Virgil, but perhaps becomes more fully realized in Ovid. When we turn to Criseyde, we will see how she eludes identification as a Lucrece despite her representation as one who, like Lucrece, is defined primarily in terms of her relationships to men, whose body is aligned with a city, and who is placed under the threat of rape, if not actually raped, due to the machinations of homosocially bonded men (Collatinus and Tarquin; Pandarus and Troilus). Yet, Criseyde is finally more of a Helen than a Lucrece.

The Victim of Abduction: Helen

As the other exemplar of a rape victim in literature, Helen complicates our understanding of how early cultures perceived the rape victim, first and foremost, because Helen does not follow the cultural dictate that demands suicide after rape; instead, she is a survivor, and survival problematizes her identity.[13] And, like that of Lucrece, studying the characterization of Helen of Troy, will aid in our interpretation of Chaucer's Criseyde. Second, the kind of rape to which Helen is subjected is unclear. She is abducted, seized, and carried away, and she is perhaps also subjected to forced coitus. In some versions, her agency is entirely eclipsed by the fact that she simply exists as Paris's prize for calling Aphrodite the most beautiful of goddesses. Furthermore, the degree to which she acquiesced to her own abduction is difficult to assess; some versions, those in which the Gods' desires take prominence, remain silent about her motivations; other versions represent her as conflicted in her desires. Paradoxically, the more complicit she is in her "raptus," the more she emerges as a subject. Helen fascinates us in part because her own desires, unlike Lucrece's, are neither consonant with those of her husband nor with the civic entity with which she is identified (at times with Greece; at times with Troy); finally her desires are elusive. Importantly, however, all versions represent her, like Criseyde, as both an object of the desires of others and as a desiring subject herself.

Classical sources afford us only glimpses of Helen, but these fragments offer provocative details that stimulate questions about the degree to which the literary Helen can be described as a desiring subject whose choices have meaning in the public arena. The Helen of Book III of Homer's *The Iliad* casts doubts on the moral vision created as the motivation for war, for she herself is portrayed as allied with *both* Menelaus and Paris. The narrative confirms Helen's status as property as Paris and Menelaus fight over who will possess her. It is unclear with whom Helen allies herself, for when told of this contest, Helen, inspired by the Gods, remembers her husband fondly, feeling γλυκὺν ἵμερον ["sweet longing"] (III, 139) for him, yet she had apparently agreed to follow Paris.[14] When speaking to Priam, Helen expresses her ambivalence about her abduction. Responding to Priam's denial of blame, she declares: ὡς ὄφελεν θάνατός μοι ἀδεῖν κακός, ὁππότε δεῦρο υἱέι σῷ ἑπόμην, θάλαμον γνωτούς τε λιποῦσα: ["I wish bitter death had been what I wanted when I came hither / following your son, forsaking my chamber and my brothers"] (III, 173–74). Here, as a speaking subject, Helen articulates her rejection of Lucrece's response to rape, suicide. Although Helen's rage suggests her to be a victim of abduction against her will, it at the same time also suggests some agency on her part: she herself follows Paris; she herself forsakes her chamber. But this recognition of her own potential autonomy leads only to her self-condemnation as she describes herself as a slut, κυνώπιδός (III, 180).[15] Nonetheless, the representation of Helen as a desiring subject with conflicting wishes complicates her status as an object and passive instigator of war. She internalizes the culture's identification of the raped woman as damaged goods; but she also demonstrates an incipient and fiercely independent subjectivity.

The degree to which she is subject not to the culture's dictates, but to the desires of the Gods complicates our understanding of the classical Helen's agency in *The Iliad.* Priam asserts that the Gods, not Helen, deserve to be blamed (III, 164–65). Helen herself complains against the Gods' manipulations (III, 399–400) and when Aphrodite commands her to go to Paris, she strongly resists. She expresses rage at the system that has made her subject to rape, but Aphrodite refuses to allow her to resist Paris in bed. Her resistance to the system that produced rape is thus naturalized, here and in *The Aeneid,* by its displacement onto the realm of the Gods, and Helen's potentially resisting subjectivity is thus obliterated. Our final Homeric vision of Helen occurs at Hector's funeral where she eulogizes one she should have hated as her most bitter enemy as her only friend. Helen behaves not unlike Criseyde here in her dependence on individuals from the enemy camp for protection.

The brief glimpse of Helen in Book Four of *The Odyssey* makes her inner life and motivations even more obscure than they seem in *The Iliad,* thus reinforcing the traditional Helen's position as a rape victim with a divided identity. Restored to Menelaus, she appears to be happy as a gracious, generous, and well-attended queen. Yet, as one who had endured rape and been the motivation for a brutal war, she seems oddly untouched by pain. She also possesses extraordinary powers, among them the ability to see through disguises: she is the first to recognize Odysseus at this meeting, and as she reminisces about the war, she recalls that she recognized, but did not betray Odysseus, when he entered the Trojan camp in disguise as a spy. She claims to have been glad of his arrival: αὐτὰρ ἐμὸν κῆρ χαῖρ', ἐπεὶ ἤδη μοι κραδίη τέτραπτο νεέσθαι ἂψ οἰκόνδ', ἄτην δὲ μετέστενον, ἣν Ἀφροδίτη δῶχ', ὅτε μ' ἤγαγε κεῖσε φίλης ἀπὸ πατρίδος αἴης, παῖδά τ' ἐμὴν νοσφισσαμένην θάλαμόν τε πόσιν τε ["but my soul was glad, for already my heart was changed by now and was for going back / home again, and I grieved for the madness that Aphrodite / bestowed when she led me there away from my own dear country, / forsaking my own daughter, my bedchamber and my husband"] (IV. 260–63).[16] The language is double here attributing agency for Helen's betrayal of her husband simultaneously to Aphrodite and to Helen herself. She claims her heart had changed, but it is not clear in what manner.

Menelaus's recollection of Helen further deepens the ambiguity of Helen's subjectivity. When the Trojan horse is pulled into the city, Menelaus tells us, Helen suspects a Greek trick and, speaks to each Greek in the voice of his wife; all but Odysseus long to leave the Trojan horse. Here Helen clearly acts as an agent of the Trojans; yet this story praises her special knowledge of the Greeks. It is difficult to ascertain whose side Helen is on; perhaps the rape victim ultimately has no side. This utopian position, one also occupied by Lucrece, affords the rape victim surprising potential as a subject, a potential more fully realized by Helen, who refuses death. The scene also delineates Helen as something of a sorceress as she mixes herbs of forgetfulness into her guests' drinks. Her herbal knowledge and her powers of ventriloquism reinforce the mystery of Helen and suggest that women with private desires and thoughts are dangerously Other.

In the Roman formulation of the Greek legend, Helen is most notable for her marginality. In the *Aeneid,* Virgil describes her literally as a liminal figure, and Aeneas recalls, "cum limina Vestae / servantem et tacitam secreta in sede latentem / Tyndarida aspicio" (II. 567–69) ["I saw / Lurking beyond the doorsill of the Vesta, / In hiding, silent, in that place reserved / The daughter of Tyndareus"] (II. 743–44).[17] With fear as her primary characteristic, she is: "illa sibi infestos eversa ob Pergama Teucros / et Danaum poenam et deserti coniugis iras / praemetuens" (II. 571–73) ["terrified of the Trojans' hate / For the city overthrown, terrified too / Of Danaan vengeance, her abandoned husband's / Anger"] (II. 748–51). This fear marks her divided subjectivity as one complicit with two societies, and, thus, with no identity. Wanting to kill her, Aeneas particularly condemns her for having articulated her own desires, feeling "subit ira cadentem / ulcisci patriam et sceleratas sumere poenas" (II. 575–76) ["A passion to avenge my fallen town / And punish Helen's whorishness"] (II. 754–56).

His passion is acceptable; hers is not. Aeneas's murderous desire complicates the alliance of cities and women's bodies so often articulated in acts of rape; here, the fallen town of Troy is associated with (though not identified with) the wantonly open body of Helen, portrayed as complicit with the common body of a whore. Yet Venus intervenes at this point, reminding Aeneas not to blame Helen, but rather to blame the Gods, those who represent the superstructure of the system.

These Virgilian and Homeric sources present a complex picture of Helen's textual status as rape victim. On the one hand, these narratives repeatedly represent her as the cause of war; on the other hand, they represent her as a desiring subject who counters her objectification in the war game. In one version of the Helen legend, Euripides's *Helen,* Helen is not even present in Troy. This play thus reveals the irrelevance of the female subject as source of martial conflict; only as an object— preferably dead as Lucrece—can she act fully as a clear motivator of war; as desiring subject, she remains elsewhere. And in Homer, Helen both is and is not "elsewhere." She comprises a complex of subject identities: the cause of fighting, a speaking subject autonomous and challenging, and to the Trojan patriarchs (*Iliad* III) undamaged, a woman of unsurpassed beauty.

In a work well known to Chaucer, the *Heroides,* Ovid most fully develops the ambiguity of Helen's consent to her abduction.[18] He offers a reading of Homer in which he grants Helen agency and complicity only faintly suggested in Homer. Ovid presents a letter written by Helen to Paris in response to his letter begging her to submit to his desire for her. Helen firmly rejects his seduction at first, and like Lucrece, criticizes him for violating his friend's home: "ausus es hospitii temerati, advena, sacris / legitimam nuptae sollicitare fidem!" (XVII, l. 3–4) ["You, an alien, have broken the sacred law / of hospitality so that you might trifle with a lawful wife's faithfulness"] (p. 167). Like Criseyde, Helen's dominant concern throughout her letter is her reputation; at first she asserts that her reputation will not be sullied; towards the end of the letter, she poses the possibility of an affair with Paris as long as it remains secret. Her contradictory desires are captured in thoughts such as the following: "ferrea sim, si non hoc ego pectus amem. / ferrea, crede mihi, non sum; sed amare repugno / illum, quem fieri vix puto posse meum" (XVII, l. 136–38) ["If I did not love a heart like yours, / I would be made of iron; but iron I am not, / believe me, though I resist loving / one I have decided can hardly be mine"] (p. 171). This musing is followed immediately by, "sum rudis ad Veneris furtum, nullaque fidelem—di mihi sunt testes— lusimus arte virum" (XVII, l. 141–42) ["I am not skilled at stealing love and never—/ I call the gods as my witnesses—/ have I cleverly played with my husband's trust"] (p. 171). Wavering, she declares "et libet et timeo, nec adhuc exacta voluntas / est satis; in dubio pectora nostra labant." (XVII, l. 177–78) ["I am torn between desire and proper fear, / I have not decided, I waver"] (p. 173). She wishes that she might not have to be an agent enacting and thus responsible for her own desires when she writes "quod male persuades, utinam bene cogere posses!" (XVII, l. 185) ["I wish you could compel me with honour / To do what you have so vilely invited"] (p. 173). She concludes, "dabo cunctatas tempora victa manus. / Quod petis" (XVII, l. 260–261) ["worn out by time / I will yield and surrender to you"] (pp.175–76).

As one of the few extended soliloquies by an intended rape victim, Ovid's treatment of the Helen legend epitomizes the ambiguity of Helen's desires as a subject. Undoubtedly, this particular treatment profoundly influenced Chaucer's presentation of a similarly wavering heroine fraught with anxiety about her safety, her reputation, and her lover's faithfulness and similarly unsure of her own desires. In his portrait of Criseyde, however, Chaucer develops and complicates the potential subjectivity of the Helen figure.

Even though most early Western cultural representations of rape share the basic structural features illuminated by the models of Helen and Lucrece, these features are articulated differently depending on the historical circumstances of any given moment. Criseyde, like both Lucrece and Helen in that she is threatened with both sexual assault and abduction, nonetheless resists the identification of her body both with her husband or potential husbands and with the city of Troy itself, and refuses to accept her status as an object. This more complex subject, one developed from the repressed subjectivity of the Lucrece paradigm and the potential subjectivity of the Helen paradigm, emerges, I shall argue, from Chaucer's response to a fourteenth-century cultural legitimization of the female subject not yet fully articulated in the classical world. Although Helen as a divided subject with conflicting desires more directly resembles Chaucer's Criseyde, and indeed most probably influenced Chaucer's portrayal, certainly both Helen and Criseyde's subjectivities struggle to emerge under the cloud of the definitive model of what they are supposed to be as rape victims—Lucrece, that is, willing to die rather than be seen as desiring subjects. Criseyde could enact Lucrece's story as a victim of the unwanted sexual advances of a ruler; she could be a Helen, one abducted by her lover. As a widow whose father is a traitor, Criseyde's ability to play either role presents complications. Criseyde's subjectivity, we shall see, emerges under the constraint of both kinds of rape, forced coitus and abduction, but it is her identity as one whose consent matters that ultimately both defines and condemns her.

Rape and the Divided Subject:
Criseyde

The discussion in Book IV of *Troilus and Criseyde* in which Pandarus and Troilus debate whether or not Troilus should rape Criseyde captures the various ways rape functions in Chaucer's fourteenth-century poem. The debate begins when Pandarus suggests that Troilus "ravysshe" Criseyde, arguing that she herself would agree to it.[19] Initially, Troilus rejects this possibility because he fears the consequences of ravishment: "First, syn thow woost this town hath al this werre / For ravysshyng of wommen so by myght, / It sholde nought be suffred me to erre."[20] Here Troilus implicitly accepts the cultural assumption underlying rape that characterizes women as property. Because Menelaus's property has been violated, Paris's property, the city of Troy, must be violated.

In his reluctance to ravish Criseyde in this first passage, Troilus does not necessarily refuse to objectify Criseyde; he simply chooses not to participate in the homosocial competition of which rape is a part. Indeed, Troilus's acceptance of Criseyde's status as an object rather than a subject is implied by his next comment, since he sees her exchange with Antenor as essential for the security of Troy: "I sholde han also blame of every wight, / My fadres graunt if that I so withstoode, / Syn she is chaunged for the townes goode" (Book IV, 550–53). In his first objection, Troilus refuses to instigate war by improperly possessing another man's object (Calchas's property) suggesting his refusal to participate in a system that objectifies women, yet, in his second comment, he legitimates her status as an object—not his, but that of Troy—in his willingness to allow her to be exchanged for the sake of the safety of the city.

Some of Troilus's confusion might be attributed to the ambiguity of Criseyde's status: just whose property is she? As a widow, she has a certain degree of autonomy, but future alliances (her marriage) should be controlled first by her father and then by her lord. Because Criseyde's father has betrayed Troy, however, Criseyde's identity as a possession to be controlled by men has been destabilized, for she is at once allied with two civic entities—Greece, through Calchas, and Troy, through Priam.

Pandarus, however, urges him to abduct Criseyde despite Troilus's fears of public condemnation, claiming that such an action would not be a rape because "It is no rape, in my dom, ne no vice / Hire to witholden that ye love moost" (Book IV, 596–97). Here, in this early literary use of the word "rape" in English, Pandarus articulates the complexity of the various legal Latin terms for rape including "raptus."[21] While Pandarus here means that Troilus should abduct Criseyde rather than sexually assault her, the discussion as it develops captures the ambiguity of the word in terms of female consent. As Kelly and others have argued, rape, as it appears in various forms of *rapire* in the fourteenth century, can refer to a wide variety of events including sexual assault, abduction for the purposes of marriage without the consent of the abductee, abduction for the purpose of marriage with the consent of the abductee, and abduction for the purposes of marriage with the later consent of the abductee. All of these events were considered crimes, although whether or not they were named felonies or trespasses, or tried in the king's courts or the ecclesiastical courts, depended on how the act was described.[22]

As the argument proceeds, Troilus again rejects Pandarus's advice that Troilus ravish Criseyde, but this time he raises the issue of Criseyde's agency: "'for no cas, it is nat myn entente, / At shorte wordes, though I deyen sholde, / To ravysshe hire, but if hireself it wolde'" (Book IV, 635–37). Pandarus expresses surprise that Troilus has not consulted her desires, "'But telle me thanne, hastow hire wil assayed?'" (Book IV, 639). When Troilus answers in the negative, Pandarus says, "'Whereof artow,' . . . 'thanne amayed, / That nost nat that she wol ben yvele appayed / To ravysshe hire, syn thow hast nought ben there'" (Book IV, 641–43). Pandarus then suggests that he arrange a meeting so that Troilus can inquire about "hire entente" (Book IV, 657). The possibility of abduction discussed in these passages foregrounds the question of Criseyde's agency and keeps her from being completely identified with the city. Both Troilus and Pandarus here agree that Criseyde has the right to make up her own mind about the fate of her body. The irony of this whole exchange, as Pandarus finally recognizes, is that this discussion should not be taking place between two men, but rather between Troilus and Criseyde. That Chaucer turns next to a meeting between Troilus and Criseyde alone suggests that mutual love exists outside of the system of homosocial desire that bonds Pandarus and Troilus, and perhaps Trojan society at large.

Pandarus's and Troilus's acknowledgement of the necessity and desirability of seeking Criseyde's consent to her potential rape captures the complexity of the status of the female subject under the law particularly contested in fourteenth-century law courts. As in earlier periods, fourteenth-century secular rape and marriage law are intertwined, bound together by a view of women as property. Because rape was first and foremost a property crime rather than a crime against persons, there was a fine line between rape as forced coitus and rape as abduction; both were described by various forms of the verb *rapire* and both were viewed as violations of the proprietorship of the lord. The ambiguous definitions of rape explain the difficulty critics have experienced in trying to determine exactly what charge was invoked when in 1380 Cecily Chaumpaigne released Geoffrey Chaucer from "all manner of actions as they relate to my rape or any other thing or cause" ["omnimodas acciones tam de raptu meo tam de aliqua re vel causa"].[23]

The assumptions underlying these secular laws, however, become challenged by a conflicting ideology and legal practice emerging from the Church. The Church's doctrine of mutual consent, developed in twelfth-century theological commentaries and further refined in canon law, destabilizes the assumption that women are objects by assuming the legitimacy of women as subjects who have the right to consent to the fate of their bodies in marriage. This doctrinal legitimacy, only at times asserted, comes to the fore in thirteenth-century England when it is upheld, as has been shown by legal historians, by the ecclesiastical courts in clandestine marriage cases.[24]

In clandestine marriage, often closely related to "raptus" as abduction, a man and a woman could declare their vows against the desires of the family and the feudal lord and have their vows deemed valid by the Church. Crucial to the survival of a clandestine marriage in the courts was each partner's acknowledgment of his or her desire to marry. Although women were often pressured to deny their declaration of promises beginning with "I choose" or "I wish," if these declarations were affirmed by the individuals, the marriage would be validated by the ecclesiastical courts. The first-person affirmations of volition in the court records of these cases provide unusual evidence of one arena in which women's desires had social force.

In the fourteenth century, however, the feudal courts reacted against the rights granted to the individual by the ecclesiastical courts in the case of clandestine marriage and reasserted the feudal notion of rape and marriage as property issues controlled by the feudal lord. In order to assert the rights of the feudal lord, charges of rape were often brought against participants involved in clandestine marriage. The fact that a high percentage of the cases in the remaining records in both the Ely and Rochester registers are clandestine marriage cases suggests both the prevalence of these marriages and late medieval anxiety about them.[25]

Some time ago, H. A. Kelly suggested the importance of clandestine marriage to a study of Chaucer's *Troilus and Criseyde*, and his arguments deserve reconsideration here.[26] Kelly claims that clandestine marriage deeply influences the representations of relationships between men and women in fourteenth-century literature in general and Chaucer's representation of the relationship of Troilus and Criseyde in particular. He carefully demonstrates the origins of the justifications for clandestine marriage in the decretals of Gratian and Gregory, and goes on to trace its prevalence in extant fourteenth-century court records. Using this evidence to argue for the morality of the relationship of Troilus and Criseyde, he suggests that if they were not in fact legally married, their relationship would be considered a marriage if it ever fell under the scrutiny of a bishop's or archdeacon's court. Kelly argues that Chaucer, although deliberately obscuring the status of their relationship, treats the lovers as if they were married.

Kelly further suggests that Chaucer obscures the lovers' marital status simply because the plot requires that they not be married at the time of the exchange. I would argue, rather, that a marriage between the two lovers would lessen the complexity of the status of the female subject; an official marriage between Criseyde and Troilus would ensure her containment within a recognized social structure, and thus render her agency less problematic. By keeping her unmarried to Troilus, Chaucer draws our attention to the culture's anxiety about the legitimacy of female desire, an anxiety that also underlies clandestine marriage cases. Thus, I agree with Kelly (and Jill Mann) that mutuality is at issue in this poem, but mutuality assumes a legitimate female subject, a precondition not self-evident in fourteenth-century social practice.[27]

While Kelly explores legal and ecclesiastical precedent for the efficacy of a doctrine of mutual love in the Middle Ages, my interests lie in what these documents reveal about the period's conception of the female subject. Conflicting theological discussions about female identity, most of which stress female inferiority, but some of which argue for female autonomy shape these clandestine marriage cases. In most theological commentaries (for example, on Genesis) a woman's role as silent and obedient handmaid to the leader, the head, Adam, works hand-in-hand with secular practices that deny women autonomy.[28] A number of theological commentaries, however, validate the autonomy of women. This is especially true of those commentaries stressing the legitimacy of female consent to marriage.

Underlying the doctrine of consent is the assumption that women have souls and consequently are subjects. That assumption lies behind one of the few theological works to consider the issue of rape directly, Augustine's discussion of the rape of Lucrece in his *City of God*. Perhaps most significant in this context are Augustine's arguments against female suicide after rape. In his discussion of Lucrece, Augustine states that a person consists of both body and soul, with the will controlling the body: "Sit igitur in primis positum atque firmatum virtutem, qua recte vivitur, ab animi sede membris corporis imperare sanctumque corpus usu fieri sanctae voluntatis, qua inconcussa ac stabili permanente, quidquid alius de corpore vel in corpore fecerit quod sine peccato proprio non valeat evitari praeter culpam esse patientis" (Chapter XVI, p. 74) ["Virtue, the condition of right living, holds command over the parts of the body from her throne in the mind, and that the consecrated body is the instrument of the consecrated will; and if that will continues unshaken and steadfast, whatever anyone else does with the body or to the body, provided that it cannot be avoided without committing sin, involves no blame to the sufferer"].[29] Summarizing the conclusions he has reached concerning Lucrece, Augustine writes: "An forte huic perspicuae rationi, qua dicimus corpore oppresso nequaquam proposito castitatis ulla in malum consensione mutato illius tantum esse flagitium, qui opprimens concubuerit, non illius, quae oppressa concumbenti mulla voluntate consenserit" (Chapter XIX, p. 82) ["We have given clear reason for our assertion that when physical violation has involved no change in the intention of chastity by any consent to the wrong, then the guilt attaches only to the ravisher"].[30] In his consideration of the degree to which Lucrece committed a crime, Augustine concludes that she was innocent as a victim of rape, but guilty of murder in committing suicide. While Augustine recognizes the appropriateness of shame for an act that he believes by necessity involves carnal satisfaction, he nonetheless concludes that suicide does not provide an acceptable response to that condition of shame. Augustine's argument fails to resolve all the difficulties raised by the problematic status of the rape victim and in fact partially reinscribes shame as an appropriate response to rape.[31] Nonetheless, Augustine grants a woman some agency and subjectivity, and privileges the fact of her consent or resistance over the fate of her body. What is implicit in Livy's version of the legend—that Lucrece has a mind or a soul that allows her to make her own choices—finds theological justification in Augustine.

Female autonomy—at least in terms of the existence, legitimacy, and integrity of the female soul—was also assumed in a number of medieval Christian commentaries on marriage, especially those that underlie ecclesiastical legal assertions of the legitimacy of female consent in marriage. Based on the same argument upon which Augustine bases his validation of female consent in his discussion of rape—the integrity of the female soul—medieval theologians insist upon female consent in marriage. While this theological position, set forth in decretals from Gratian onwards, was virtually ignored in most feudal aristocratic marriage practices, nonetheless, a marriage shown to have been contracted by mutual consent was held to be valid by the ecclesiastical courts—whatever the desires of the father or lord—because of the justification found in this theological tradition.

It is not clear what motivations underlie this validation; perhaps the Church intervened in clandestine marriage cases to assert its authority over the Crown or because of its own interest in the property transfers that occur during marriage; nonetheless, the Church's ideas about marriage include a concept of mutuality that, while not explicitly allowing for female independence in marriage, at the very least presupposes the autonomy of women.[32]

One reason why the status of female consent might be particularly at issue in late medieval England is that the post-plague economy destabilized the association of a woman's body with property. In England, when land became more available after the plague, the urgency to acquire and control land transfers through opportune aristocratic marriages was lessened. As Michael Sheehan summarizes: "beginning about 1300 in some areas, directions to widows to marry tend to disappear from the rolls of the manorial court. It is obvious that late in the fourteenth century the diminishing demand for land lessened the likelihood that she would be required to marry against her preference or to give up her property; but there is a strong possibility that the earlier appearance of this freedom found at least a partial cause in the more refined view of the widow's needs and rights of which canon law was the vehicle."[33] Clearly, changes in land ownership and refinements in canon law about widows' property rights contribute to the complexity of Criseyde's self-examination of her "freedom" as a widow. In addition, because the Crown might be less interested in the land transfer of a particular marriage, the Church might be more effective in asserting its controls over marriage in cases of clandestine marriage.

Chaucer's *Troilus and Criseyde,* a poem concerned with the efficacy of female subjectivity under constraint, responds to and reshapes this complex tension in the fourteenth century between the acknowledgement of individual desire granted in the ecclesiastical courts and the denial of subjectivity and agency in aristocratic feudal practices regarding rape, abduction, and marriage. At the heart of Chaucer's representation of Criseyde as a woman subject to rape is the vexed question of the potential status of her consent to these events. Fradenburg points out that Chaucer highlights this potential for consent by adding it to his Boccaccian source: "It is well-known that Chaucer in effect brought out Criseyde's consent as a *problem,* whereas in Boccaccio she is more straightforward. . . . Criseyde's story [is] partly that of the feminine chivalric subject, a subject produced *for* consent."[34] The fact that consent is a vexed issue in other arenas of fourteenth-century culture only sharpens Chaucer's representation of a heroine so defined by the issue of consent.

Various kinds of rape permeate *Troilus and Criseyde.* Helen's rape, or abduction, instigates the war against Troy. Throughout the work, Criseyde is threatened with rape as forced coitus, first from Troilus, and then from Diomedes. Before she is given over to the Greeks, Troilus considers the possibility of "ravishing" Criseyde. Criseyde fears that she will be raped if she attempts to escape from the Greeks. Finally, the Trojans deliver her— against her will—to the Greeks in an act that shares with rape the medieval view of a woman as property. In the opening summary of the Trojan War, the narrator emphasizes the centrality of rape as an instigator of the war:

Yt is wel wist how that the Grekes stronge
In armes with a thousand shippes wente
Assegeden, neigh ten yer er they stente,
And in diverse wise and oon entente,
The ravysshyng to wreken of Eleyne,
By Paris don, they wroughten al hir peyne (Book I, 57–63).

The "oon entente," singular intention, of the war lies in avenging the rape of Helen. That rape has inspired the siege is further articulated by Diomedes, who warns Criseyde that because of the Greek invasion of Troy, "men shul drede, unto the worldes ende, / From hennesforth to ravysshen any queene" (Book V, 894–95). Chaucer's version of the Troy story underlines one of Helen's subject identities as rape victim and thus as instigator of war. The ways in which female subjectivity complicates such an equation are explored not through the character of Helen, but rather through the character of Criseyde, who, as we shall see, refuses to play her expected role in war. In this concluding part of my essay, I consider the various ways the poem presents Criseyde as both subjected to and resistant to rape.

In keeping with the paradigm of the woman under the threat of rape, Chaucer repeatedly compares Criseyde's body to a city under attack, Troy; throughout the first half of Book I and II of *Troilus and Criseyde,* Troilus's seduction of Criseyde is described as if she were under siege and runs parallel with descriptions of the progress of the Trojan war. It is unclear, however, to which civic entity she belongs. Because Criseyde is a widow abandoned by her father, it is not evident who holds her as property. Unlike Helen or Lucrece, Criseyde is not identified with a ruling patriarch. Furthermore, her status as a widow allows her a degree of relative independence not available to married heroines such as Lucrece and Helen. In Book II, Criseyde revels in the relative freedom she experiences as a widow and hesitates to entertain thoughts of a new lover who might compromise that status. She values her own position as she proclaims, "I am myn owene womman, wel at ese—I thank it God—as after myn estat" (Book II, 750–51). Criseyde's status as a widow forms a crucial factor in her relative autonomy as a subject. Marriage, because of the doctrine of "unity of person" or, as later described, "coverture," in which women lose much of their identity as legal persons upon marriage, would severely restrict that legal autonomy.[35]

The class distinction between Helen and Criseyde further problematizes Criseyde's relationship to the city. Unlike Helen, a queen and thus a prized possession of the ruling classes of Greece, Criseyde enjoys neither the protection, the social obligations, nor the status that royalty affords. In addition, as a traitor's daughter, her own loyalties to the city are suspect from the beginning. Like many women objectified by culture as counters in alliances between men, her value depends on her ability to act as a possible peaceweaver; her waiting woman says of her trade "I hope ywis, that she / Shal bryngen us the pees on every syde" (Book IV, 692–93).

But not only Criseyde's status enables her to upset the traditional equation of rape and civic contestation. More importantly, Criseyde's agency, self-determination, and articulation of her own desires resist the Trojan patriarchy's system of rape. We saw some glimpses of representations of female desire in the classical sources for the character of Helen, but there Helen's identity finally reflects the gods' desires alone. Because Chaucer obscures the classical naturalizing power of the gods, the potential for individual agency opens up. The gender theme of Chaucer's poem fluctuates between denying female desire through rape ambiguously represented, and validating female agency.

This agency is problematic for Criseyde as she considers her situation. We have seen that Shakespeare's Lucrece uses the Troy story as a guide for sorting out her own choices and options. As such she "reads" or interprets the Troy painting. Throughout *Troilus and Criseyde,* although most thoroughly in Book II, we see Criseyde's thought processes as she "reads" her situation. She sorts through the possible consequences of an alliance with Troilus, carefully assessing the advantages and disadvantages of such an alliance to her status as a widow. Among the matter that Criseyde reads is rape. In Book II, we see her pondering *The Romance of Thebes,* a work that clearly delineates women's function in war as either bereaved war-bride or war prize. Further on in Book II, Antigone's song celebrating love inspires a critical response in Criseyde, as she first questions the origin of the song before contemplating how its message might have meaning for her. A good literary critic, she asks first "Who made this song" (878) and then "is ther swych blisse among / Thise loveres, as they konne faire endite?" (885–86). Criseyde, not unlike her soothsaying father, Calchas, interprets events and tries to assess her own place in relationship to them. Her severely circumscribed roles and what she knows of her position as a woman in war make ʰer (like Virgil's Helen) legitimately fearful, as David Aers has so thorᵒughly demonstrated.[36] She recognizes a woman's role in the face of such knowledge: "we wrecched wommen nothing konne, / Whan us is wo, but wepe and sitte and thinke; / Oure wrecche is this, oure owen wo to drynke" (Book II, 782–85).[37] Struggling to counter this predetermined role, Criseyde tries to find for herself a more efficacious one.

Most notably, Criseyde rejects her prescribed role as the object of male desire. Critics as different as John Fleming and Carolyn Dinshaw have discussed Book II's strong focus on rape as a threatening subtext, which the opening of the book hints at when the narrator alludes to Procne's song that awakens Pandarus:

> The swalowe Proigne, with a sorowful lay,
> Whan morwen com, gan make hir weymentynge
> Why she forshapen was; . . .
> Til she so neigh hym made hir cheterynge
> How Tereus gan forth hire suster take,
> That with the noyse of hir he gan awake. (Book II, 64–70)

Indeed, Chaucer adds to Boccaccio a variety of Ovidian references, many of them to Jove's escapades, that reinforce the text's interest in rape.[38] While in Book II Chaucer asserts the machinery of the rape plot as it is set in motion, he at the same time grants Criseyde an autonomy that counters that plot as it follows the inner workings of Criseyde's mind as she considers Pandarus's and Troilus's propositions.

Throughout Book II, Criseyde contends with a plot she only partially ascertains. She recognizes how carefully she must tread given Troilus's potential to seize her at will:

> Ek wel woot I my kinges sone is he,
> And sith he hath to see me swich delit
> If I wolde outreliche his sighte flee
> Peraunter he myghte have me in despit
> Thorugh whicch I myghte stonde in worse plit. (Book II, 708–11)

Although Criseyde cannot completely prevent the rape plot—she may only be able to redefine it—her awareness of her vulnerable situation and her repeated articulation of her agency and subjectivity trouble the system that describes her as property.

Whether or not Troilus rapes Criseyde remains a matter for debate. The scene in which Troilus finally embraces Criseyde captures both the threat of rape and Criseyde's potential agency. Described as a lark caught by a hawk, Troilus says "Now be ye kaught; now is ther but we tweyne! / Now yeldeth yow, for other bote is ther non!" Criseyde replies, "Ne hadde I er now, my swete herte deere, / Ben yolde, ywis, I were now nought heere!" (Book III, 1207–8; 1211–13). Mann argues that although rape is threatened, it is averted. She explains Troilus's swoon in Book III as a pivotal event that alters the power differential between Troilus and Criseyde, thus allowing them the possibility of mutual love.[39] She is right that rape is averted and that by swooning, Troilus releases his power over Criseyde, thus allowing them the possibility of forging a new, more equitable, relationship. The success of that relationship demands that Troilus cease viewing Criseyde as an object, one to be competed for by men. Furthermore, the acknowledgment of that subjectivity seems a prerequisite for the experience of mutual love.

Mann has urged us to recognize the importance of the scene in Book III where Criseyde declares her repugnance for jealousy, a scene I would like to draw attention to in slightly different ways than Mann does. Early in Book II, Criseyde expresses her hatred of jealousy:

> I am myn owene womman, wel at ese,
> I thank it God, as after myn estat,
> Right yong, and stonde unteyd in lusty leese,
> Withouten jalousie or swich debat:
> Shal noon housbonde seyn to me 'chek mat!"
> For either they ben ful of jalousie
> Or maisterfull, or loven novelrie. (II, 750–56)

In these lines, jealousy springs naturally from marriage, a practice that fundamentally describes a woman as a possession. Criseyde's outburst against Troilus's supposed jealousy in Book III reasserts her rejection of the social system that attempts to limit or control her. As Mann writes,

> We are alerted to this dangerous implication [that Troilus wishes to assert his control over Criseyde] by Criseyde's long and passionate outburst against jealousy when she finally sees Troilus (III, 1009–43), and her vehement denial that jealousy is a mark of love—an outburst which shows that the "process" of courtship has in no way made this manifestation of masculine possessiveness less repugnant to her. Pandarus is clearly relying on the traditional view that 'jalousie is love' (III, 1024) in order to use this story as a stimulus towards the consummation. But he completely fails to understand, on the one hand, Criseyde's sensitivity to the threat of "thralldom" and, on the other, how remote from Troilus's nature is any tendency towards such possessiveness. So, far from being necessary to bring about the consummation, Pandarus's story very nearly destroys the whole love affair.[40]

While Mann's argument here depends upon the psychological, locating Criseyde's and Troilus's rejection of jealousy in character (Criseyde's sensitivity to constraint; Troilus's nature), I want to identify the social structures that shape a given psyche at a given time. Criseyde's resistance is surely not idiosyncratic, but rather systemic; that is, as a widow, she has found out how constraining the system of marriage and even "love" can be. Where Mann focuses on characters as constellations of affects (jealousy, sensitivity, possessiveness), I contend that these inner states are formations of powerful social contingencies. Avoiding the thralldom inherent to the system requires that both Troilus and Criseyde make delicate and complex maneuvers, as Mann has shown in her analysis of the "process" of power negotiations that take place between the couple in Book III. By forging a love based on respect and exchange rather than a relationship determined by the exchange of property, the two are able to establish a mutual love, the affirmation of which in Book III celebrates effective independent subjectivity in both Troilus and Criseyde.

Yet, such mutuality cannot last long unless it is supported by the society as a whole. The threat of rape recurs when Criseyde, still not her own woman (despite her previous proclamations of being so), is traded against her will for Antenor. Hector initially rejects the view of Criseyde as property: "We usen here no wommen for to selle," (Book IV, 182), but the people overrule his opinion and insist on her exchange. That Criseyde herself, for a moment, internalizes the status granted her as lifeless property, is suggested by her swoon of Book IV. When Troilus and Criseyde meet to discuss their fate, Criseyde cries

'O Jove, I deye, and mercy I beseche!
Help Troilus!' And threwithal hire face
Upon his brest she leyde and loste speche—
Hire woful spirit from his propre place,
Right with the word, alwey o pont to pace.
And thus she lith with hewes pale and grene,
That whilom fressh and fairest was to sene. (Book IV, 1149–55)

This swoon, as important in its delineation of the power dynamics between Troilus and Criseyde as Troilus's earlier swoon, marks a change in their relationship. For until this point, Troilus and Criseyde had determined their actions by mutual exchange and negotiation; after this point, Criseyde takes matters solely into her own hands. Criseyde seems to recognize the inefficacy of their mutual love in the face of a culture that cannot fully acknowledge such mutuality.

As noted above, Troilus grants Criseyde the right to determine her own fate by leaving the decision about a possible "rape" to her. Book V dramatizes the tragic results of her choices. One might argue, as Carolyn Dinshaw does, that by agreeing to be the object of a trade, Criseyde finally capitulates to the patriarchal marriage market she has wrangled with throughout the poem. And indeed, Criseyde's definition as an object of male desire and a subject defined only in relationship to male protectors does not change. Yet, I prefer, unlike Dinshaw, to allow the text more ambiguity on the matter of Criseyde's potential personhood. Although Criseyde's actions in giving her brooch and, says Chaucer, "perhaps" her heart to Diomedes suggest that she has transferred her affection from Troilus to Diomedes, her circumstances, as Aers has demonstrated, also signal her fear and vulnerability; she herself expresses her fear of rape at the hands of the enemy should she try to escape the Greek camp: "lo, this drede I moost of alle—/ If in the hondes of som wrecche I falle, / I nam but lost" (Book V, 704–5).[41] And surely she is not invulnerable to Diomedes's repeated confident warnings about the impending destruction of the Trojans. We know of her final thoughts only through her last letter, one that stresses her sense of her inadequacy as a writer and the constraint she feels in her present circumstances. In her letter she asserts only that she wishes and intends to return to Troilus but that she cannot at the moment and is too afraid to be able to explain why. She declares, "Come I wole; but yet in swich disjoynte / I stonde as now that what yer or what day / That this shal be, that kan I naught apoynte" (V.1618–20). Shortly afterwards, Troilus observes that Criseyde has presumably given to Diomedes the brooch Troilus had given her. The disjunction between what we know of her actions and her words simply reasserts the fact that Criseyde has an autonomous subjectivity of her own, however constrained and determined by patriarchal structures, a subjectivity that even Chaucer cannot know or control. The poet represents this "otherness" in the gaps between words and actions, and even in the disjointed and unclear time sequences in this part of the poem. I would agree with Dinshaw, however, that the subjectivity Criseyde possesses offers her little efficacy.

Book V shows the tragic plight of an emergent female subject who is granted no social role outside of a sexual one. Criseyde refuses to be allied with a man, and therefore has no social identity. Widows and single women, as Sharon Farmer, Ruth Mazo Karras, and Judith Bennett have argued, trouble a social system that reduces women to objects.[42] Because Criseyde's control of property as a widow has been shattered by the Trojan War, even her position as a widow is destabilized and consequently her social role remains ineffable. She does survive the Trojan War but, as a kind of female Aeneas, her translation from Troy to a new civilization can only be partial since she does not carry with her the full citizenship that Aeneas does. This partial transfer might be said to reflect Chaucer's own role as a translator of a classical legend—as one bringing the story of Troy to London, or as some in the fourteenth century argued it should be renamed, Troienovant.

Geoffrey Chaucer's *Troilus and Criseyde* provides a particularly complex poetic exploration of the troubled status of female consent in late medieval England and of the ways in which the controversies over consent engaged in his poem can comment upon and destabilize patriarchal structures, even those as fundamental as marriage. In the ancient texts of Helen and Lucrece considered here, we can see how basic marriage practices—Rubin's traffic in women—are unsettled by the female subject's degree of acquiescence or resistance to that system; but these texts displace the potential play of the female subject by naturalizing it, that is, by removing the question of female agency and choice, and attributing agency only to the Gods. In the Early Modern period, female agency and choice become central to Shakespeare's endeavor in his poem; but the potential for choice is shut down. We might attribute the closing down of options here to the Reformation's shift in marriage practices, where the Church no longer holds the authority it once had in relationship to the Crown, making the ecclesiastical concept and regulation of the companionate ideal of marriage even more vexed than it appears to be in the late medieval conflict between the Church and the Crown over clandestine marriage.[43] In this period in medieval England, female bodies, especially those of aristocratic women, are publicly marked, but their souls are private; this private sphere, however, only receives irregular legitimization in the public realm. In the fourteenth century, the ecclesiastical courts' inconsistent assertion of the legitimacy of female consent in cases of rape assumes that medieval women were relatively autonomous subjects, yet that legitimacy was neither uniformly asserted nor did it confer upon women fully articulated citizenship; each incident of Geoffrey Chaucer's poem that reveals Criseyde's character—her intelligence, her manipulativeness, her treachery, her vulnerability—emerges from this particular cultural moment and reveals the tragedy of such a restrictive social formation.[44]

Notes

1. See Christopher Cannon's study in this volume as well as his earlier discussion of the meanings of the term "raptus," in his "*Raptus* in the Chaumpaigne Release and a Newly Discovered Document Concerning the Life of Geoffrey Chaucer," *Speculum* 68 (1993): 74–94. Cannon argues forcefully that *raptus* can only mean forced coitus in fourteenth-century England, though he acknowledges that other forms of *rapire* carry the ambiguous meaning of abduction or forced coitus or both; furthermore, he reminds us that abduction also usually involved a degree of force. Henry Ansgar Kelly, in "Meanings and Uses of *Raptus* in Chaucer's Time," *Studies in the Age of Chaucer* 20 (1998): 101–66, argues that Cannon is right about the probable meaning of *raptus* in this particular situation, but that the word has a wider variety of meanings in the period. I will use *raptus* in its double meaning in this essay even if it may have a narrower definition at times.

2. See John Fleming, "Deiphoebus Betrayed: Virgilian Decorum, Chaucerian Feminism" *Chaucer Review* 21, no. 2 (1986): 182–99; Carolyn Dinshaw, *Chaucer's Sexual Poetics* (Madison: University of Wisconsin Press, 1989), pp. 28–64; David Aers, "Criseyde: Woman in Medieval Society" (1979), in *Critical Essays in Chaucer's Troilus and Criseyde and His Major Early Poems*, ed.

C. David Benson (Toronto: University of Toronto Press, 1991), pp. 128–48; Jill Mann, "Troilus' Swoon," (1980) in Benson, 149–63; Louise Fradenburg, "'Our owen wo to drynke': Loss, Gender and Chivalry in *Troilus and Criseyde*," in *Chaucer's Troilus and Criseyde, "Subgit to alle Poesye:" Essays in Criticism,* ed. R. A. Shoaf (Binghamton, NY: Medieval and Renaissance Texts and Studies, 1992), pp. 88–106.

3. Judith Butler, *The Psychic Life of Power: Theories in Subjection* (Stanford: Stanford University Press, 1997), p. 2; pp. 14–15.

4. Stephanie H. Jed, *Chaste Thinking: The Rape of Lucretia and the Birth of Humanism* (Bloomington: University of Indiana Press, 1989).

5. Mieke Bal analyzes the *Book of Judges* to show how patriarchy co-opts the meaning of the violated woman's body for its own militaristic purposes. The body of the Levite's concubine is cut into 12 pieces, which then become the motivation of the Israelite assault on the Benjamites. See Mieke Bal, *Death and Dyssymmetry: The Politics of Coherence in the Book of Judges* (Chicago and London: The University of Chicago Press, 1988).

6. Peter Stallybrass, "Patriarchal Territories: The Body Enclosed," in *Rewriting the Renaissance: The Discourses of Sexual Difference in Early Modern Europe,* ed. Margaret Ferguson, Maureen Quilligan, and Nancy J. Vickers (Chicago and London: University of Chicago Press, 1986) p. 127.

7. See Gayle Rubin, "The Traffic in Women: Notes on the 'Political Economy of Sex,'" in *Toward an Anthropology of Women,* ed. Rayna R. Reiter (New York and London: Monthly Review Press, 1975), pp. 157–210. This review is a response to Levi-Strauss's *The Elementary Structure of Kinship.* For a recent excellent discussion of both of these, see Dinshaw, 56–64.

8. See *The Statutes at Large, of England and of Great Britain: From Magna Carta to the Union of the Kingdoms of Great Britain and Ireland* (London: George Eyre and Andrew Strahan Printers, 1811), Anno 6 Richard II. Statute 1. Chapter 6, p. 442.

9. While most contemporary cultures no longer validate murder or suicide as an appropriate fate for the rape victim, they nonetheless still attempt to isolate the rape victim from the community or encourage the rape victim to isolate herself. Such a response is overwhelmingly evident in the recent experience of the raped Muslim women of Bosnia who have isolated themselves from their families and are suicidal.

10. Although Ovid in the *Fasti* generally follows Livy closely, in his version, Lucrece speaks at length before her rape in chastising the wives who play while their husbands are at war, and is almost silent afterwards. Indeed, she resists speaking at all stating: "eloquar infelix dedecus ipsa meum" ["Must I myself, unhappy one, utter my own disgrace"] (l. 826) and simply concludes "veniam vos datis, ipsa nego" ["the pardon you give, I refuse"] (l. 830). See *Publii Ovidii Nasonis: Fastorum Libri Sex, The Fasti of Ovid Volume I,* edited and translated by Sir James George Frazer (London: Macmillan, 1929), pp. 99–109.

11. B. O. Foster, ed. and trans., *Livy: In Fourteen Volumes: I, Books I and II* (Cambridge, MA: Harvard University Press, 1947). The Latin text is taken from page 202 of his edition. Translations are my own.

12. Barbara Baines has also written about Shakespeare's Lucrece from the point of view of rape law. Her argument suffers from her lack of awareness that medieval law sometimes valorizes female consent in rape cases. She misses the fact that views like Augustine's, which stress the autonomy of the female soul, actually did have an effect on the law, on canon law, that is. See Barbara J. Baines, "Effacing Rape in Early Modern Representation" *ELH* 65 (1998): 69–98. For an essay that discusses a number of Shakespeare's rape victims including Lucrece within the context of Renaissance rape law, see Carolyn D. Williams, "'Silence, like a Lucrece knife': Shakespeare and the Meanings of Rape," *Yearbook of English Studies* 23 (1993): 93–110. See also Nancy J. Vickers, "This Heraldry in Lucrece' face" in *The Female Body in Western Culture,* ed. S. R. Suleiman (Cambridge, MA: Harvard University Press, 1986), pp. 209–22.

13. Fradenburg discusses the difficulties Criseyde poses for the reader as a survivor in a culture that valorizes heroic sacrifice. She writes, "Does *Troilus and Criseyde,* while displaying with extraordinary fullness the aristocratic power to recuperate loss for the practice of violence, ask us at the same time to deheroize suffering and to grant 'mere' survival, not a mirroring heroic privilege, but more simply the depth of our desire for it, and the ultimately political power of the possibility of that survival, as ideology and as practice, might go unpunished? Does Criseyde become the bearer of a valued ability to mourn in a way that makes a future, permits survival, without celebrating renunciation and legitimating violence? . . . And what might be the relation between the feminization of suffering in *Troilus and Criseyde* and heroic constancy in *The Legend of Good Women,* on the one hand, and, on the other, of Chaucer's own need to survive the vagaries of a political career?" See p. 95.

14. The Greek text is taken from Hans Rupe's Heimeran edition. The translation is by Richard Lattimore, *The Iliad of Homer* (Chicago: University of Chicago Press, 1951). Line numbers are the same in each text and they will be given in parentheses in the body of my text. I have chosen to provide published poetic translations for texts other than Livy, rather than provide my own, because to my mind these translations capture the richness and ambiguities of the originals. Of course, these translations are interpretations and by providing the originals, I leave it to the reader to decipher the degree of ambiguity about female agency revealed in each passage.

15. The Greek has many connotations such as "dogfaced," "shameless," or "carrion eater." It seems to carry within it both Helen's perceived sexual wantonness and her culpability in causing the deaths of many. I am grateful to Ernst Fredricksmeyer for discussing the Greek passages with me.

16. The Greek text is taken from Anton Weihar's Heimeran edition. The translation is by Richard Lattimore, *The Odyssey of Homer* (New York: Harper

Collins, 1965). Line numbers are the same in each text and will be given
in the body of the essay.

17. R. D. Williams, ed. *The Aeneid of Virgil: Books 1–6* (London: Macmillan,
1972). The Latin text is taken from this edition and line numbers are given
in the body of my text.

18. Grant Showerman, ed. and trans. *Ovid: Heroides and Amores* (Cambridge,
MA: Harvard University Press, 1914). The Latin text is taken from this edi-
tion and page numbers are given within the body of my text. Letter XVII,
"Helen to Paris," in Ovid's *Heroides,* trans. Harold Isbell (London: Penguin
Books, 1990). All quotations from this letter are taken from this edition and
page numbers will be given in parentheses in the body of my text.

19. Kelly also discusses these passages in "The Meanings of *Raptus,*" pp. 118–29.

20. Geoffrey Chaucer, *Troilus and Criseyde* in *The Riverside Chaucer,* ed. Larry
Benson et al. (Boston: Houghton Mifflin, 1987), Book IV, 547–49. All further quotations from this poem will be taken from this edition and book
and line numbers will be cited within parentheses in the body of the text.

21. As Kelly points out, the word does not always appear as rape in the manuscripts; in some versions it appears as "shame." However, "rape" is a plau-
sible reading of the manuscripts because the Boccaccian source uses
"rapir." Windeatt suggests that alternatives, "rape" or "shame" may indicate
Chaucer's translation process. See Kelly's discussion in "Meanings of *Raptus,*" pp. 119–20, as well as Barry Windeatt, ed. *Geoffrey Chaucer: Troilus and
Criseyde: A New Edition of the Book of Troy* (London and New York: Longman, 1984), p. 384.

22. Cannon has argued that in its noun form *raptus* in the fourteenth century
can only mean forced sexual coitus, but he also points out how clouded
study of medieval rape in the court records can be precisely because cases
that refer to forced sexual coitus are often difficult to distinguish from cases
that refer to abduction alone. See Cannon in his *Speculum* essay and Kelly's
response in *Studies in the Age of Chaucer.*

23. Cannon has argued persuasively that *raptus* in this context must refer to
sexual coitus. Nonetheless the various usages of the term in the courts, as
Kelly has shown, have made it difficult for critics until Cannon to assess
the nature of the release. As Kelly reminds us, the likelihood that the word
here refers to sexual coitus does not convict Chaucer of rape; it only tells
us that Chaucer was released from a charge of forced sexual coitus.
Nonetheless, Cannon's argument has considerably advanced our understanding of this obscure event in Chaucer's biography. See Cannon in
Speculum and Kelly in *Studies in the Age of Chaucer.*

24. For preliminary discussions of the importance of the debates about clandestine marriage in this period, see R. H. Helmholz, *Marriage Litigation in Medieval England* (Cambridge: Cambridge University Press, 1974); H. A. Kelly,
Love and Marriage in the Age of Chaucer (Ithaca, NY: Cornell University Press,
1975); J. B. Post, "Ravishment of Women and the Statutes of Westminster" in
Legal Records and the Historian, ed. J. H. Baker (London: Royal Historical So-

ciety, 1978), pp. 150–64; Charles Donahue, "The Canon Law on the Formation of Marriage and Social Practice in the Later Middle Ages," *Journal of
Family History* (1983) 8:144–58; Michael Sheehan, *Marriage, Family, and Law
in Medieval Europe* (Toronto: University of Toronto Press, 1996). For a discussion of the complexity of these issues in fourteenth-century England, see
Christopher Cannon, "*Raptus* in the Chaumpaigne Release."

25. Kelly's book includes an excellent summary of the ecclesiastical precepts
that concern marriage, *Love and Marriage,* pp. 163–66.

26. See Kelly, *Love and Marriage.*

27. Jill Mann also celebrates mutual love as a theme in the poem in her essay
"Troilus' Swoon."

28. For examples of these contradictory views of women see *Woman Defamed
and Woman Defended: An Anthology of Medieval Texts,* ed. Alcuin Blamires
(Oxford: Oxford University Press, 1992). For a general summary of commentaries on women, see my chapter "Medieval Views of Female Spirituality," in *Early English Devotional Prose and the Female Audience* (Knoxville:
University of Tennessee Press, 1990). For a summary of positive theological views on marriage, see Kelly's book, *Love and Marriage.*

29. St. Augustine, *Concerning the City of God: Against the Pagans,* trans. Henry
Bettenson (London: Penguin Books, 1972), Book I, Chapter 16, p. 26.

30. Ibid., Book I, Chapter 19, p. 28.

31. See Amy Greenstadt's fuller discussion of the complexities of Augustine's
argument in this volume.

32. For some evidence of the Church's views on marital mutuality as shown
in pastoral handbooks, see Rüdiger Schnell, "The Discourse of Marriage
in the Middle Ages," *Speculum* 73, no. 3 (July, 1998): 771–86.

33. Michael Sheehan, "Canon Law and English Institutions: Some Notes on
Current Research" in *Marriage, Family and Law,* p. 36.

34. Fradenburg, "Our owen wo to drynke," p. 103.

35. For a discussion of the ways in which the legal principle of coverture
shaped female subjectivity in late medieval England, see Elizabeth Fowler,
"Civil Death and the Maiden: Agency and the Conditions of Contract in
Piers Plowman," *Speculum* 70 (1995): 760–92. For a discussion of "coverture" as a doctrine that becomes finalized only after the Middle Ages and
that underestimates the complexity of the legal rights women did in fact
enjoy in the Middle Ages, see Christopher Cannon "The Rights of Medieval English Women: Crime and the Issue of Representation," in *Medieval
Crime and Social Control,* ed. David Wallace and Barbara Hanawalt (Minneapolis: University of Minnesota Press, 1999), pp. 156–85.

36. Aers, "Criseyde," pp. 128–48.

37. See Fradenburg's discussion of this line in terms of her argument about the
"heroization" of suffering in this poem.

38. I am grateful to Julia Boffey for pointing out to me the plethora of Ovidian references that have been added to Boccaccio. See, for example, Book
III, 722–35.

39. Mann, "Troilus' Swoon," pp. 149–63.

40. Mann, "Troilus' Swoon," p. 155.

41. Aers, "Criseyde," pp. 128–48.

42. All three of these historians have announced forthcoming work on this topic and have presented the beginnings of their research in panels and lectures in recent years in such meetings as the International Congress on Medieval Studies. See also Judith Butler and Amy M. Froide, eds., *Single Women in the European Past, 1250–1800*. (Philadelphia: University of Pennsylvania Press, 1999).

43. For an overview of Renaissance debates about marriage, see Valerie Wayne's introduction to her edition of Edmund Tilney's *The Flower of Friendship: A Renaissance Dialogue Contesting Marriage* (Ithaca, NY: Cornell University Press, 1992).

44. My thanks to Mark Amsler, Katherine Eggert, Bruce Holsinger, Judith Kellogg, Karen Palmer, Jana Matthews, Catherine McKenna, Gerda Norvig, Teresa Nugent, Christine Rose and James Simpson for their helpful editorial advice. I am especially grateful to Karen Robertson and Jeffrey Robinson who read numerous drafts of the essay and to Christopher Cannon for a careful and perspicacious reading.

CHAPTER 11

"RAPT FROM HIMSELF":
RAPE AND THE POETICS OF
CORPOREALITY IN SIDNEY'S *OLD ARCADIA*

Amy Greenstadt

> Focusing on the *Old Arcadia* and *Apology for Poetry*, this essay links
> Sidney's notions of authorship to his exploration of the legal and aes-
> thetic meanings of "ravishment."

In a scene in the original version of Sir Philip Sidney's *Arcadia* (c. 1580),
the romance's hero, Pyrocles, comes to the bed chamber of his lover
Philoclea, intending to convince her to elope with him. As he approaches
her door he is, the narrator tells us, "rapt from himself with the excessive
forefeeling of his near coming contentment." A few lines later, we learn
that such "rapture" works by "ravishing" the senses "from the free use of
their own function" in an action that is at once "forcible" and "charming."[1]
The words "rapt" and "ravishing," derived from the Latin *raptus,* meaning
"violently carried away," by the later Middle Ages were used to describe a
psychological state in which the individual was transported by an emotional experience. Renaissance culture identified female beauty as a primary agent of such rapture, a ravishing power that seduced men's senses
and overturned their higher mental faculties of reason and will.[2] The
"rapt" Pyrocles seems to be under the sway of such enthralling effects of
the feminine, as his "excessive forefeeling" of sexual consummation with
Philoclea robs him of the "free use" of his own "function[s]."
   In Sidney's day, these ravishing effects were ascribed not only to women,
but also to works of verbal art. In his *The Arte of English Poesie* (1589), for example, George Puttenham described the power of well-constructed poetic

phrases: "The eare is no lesse ravished with their currant tune, than the mind
is with their sententiousnes." [3] Similarly, Thomas Wilson argued in *The Arte
of Rhetorique* (1553) that a skillful orator could "ravish" and "draw" members
of his audience so that they would be "forced even to yelde in that, whiche
most standeth againste their will." [4] Wilson's phrasing suggests the connection
between this aesthetic meaning of "ravishment" and its use in English law,
where it was a synonym for "rape" (a word also derived from *raptus*), or the
"carnal knowledge of a woman's body against her will." Both aesthetic
beauty and male sexual violence were therefore conceived as forces that invaded the body of another individual through superseding or contradicting
his or her will. The above episode from Sidney's original *Arcadia* (now
known as the *Old Arcadia*), emphasizes the connection between these two
forms of ravishment. Although the "rapt" Pyrocles goes on to engage Philoclea in a sexual act that the narrator assures us is consensual, in the morning
he is hauled off by the authorities in Arcadia and charged with "ravishment,"
or attempting to "prevail against [Philoclea's] chastity" by "violence" and
"force" (328). The love scene itself foreshadows this outcome when the narrator compares Philoclea to "a solitary nightingale," linking her to the similarly named rape victim Philomela. Later, Pyrocles's trial for rape ironically
reprises the romantic language of the earlier episode when the judge describes Philoclea as "ravished from herself" in an echo of Pyrocles's being
"rapt from himself."

By inviting a comparison between an aesthetic experience and an immoral sexual act, it may seem as if Sidney casts doubt upon the entire enterprise of literary creation. Indeed, many writers criticized the poetic arts
as agents of ravishing violation. Stephen Gosson argued that plays "by the
privie entries of the eare, slip downe into the hart, and with gunshott of
affection gaule the minde, whence reason and vertue should rule the
roste." [5] However, it was in response to critics such as Gosson that Sidney
wrote his *Apology for Poetry* (1581?), a work in which he famously defended imaginative literature by claiming it as a persuasive force that need
not supersede or contradict, but might rather foster and uphold, the higher
mental forces that guided moral thought and action. I will argue here that
in both the *Old Arcadia* and the *Apology* (which appear to have been written around the same time) Sidney attempts to reconceive the relationship
between author and reader by investigating and questioning the concept
of ravishment. At the same time, he attempts to reconceive conventional
relationships between the sexes. For, as I will show, the convergence of
legal and aesthetic meanings in the word "ravishment" signaled a deeper
cultural connection between notions of gendered subjectivity and issues of
representation and interpretation. I therefore begin with an examination
of the models of subjectivity that Early Modern rape law both reflected

and enforced, and then discuss how in the *Old Arcadia* Sidney depicts crimes of ravishment, in order to engage the deeply intertwined problems of the sexual and textual. Finally, drawing upon the *Apology,* I will demonstrate that both in this treatise and in the romance, Sidney attempts to envision new models of textual production by portraying the paradoxical figures of the cross-dressed man and the desiring yet virtuous woman—both of whom seem capable of transcending the forces of textual and sexual violation. Yet, Sidney's attempts to resolve the problem of ravishment and reenvision the roles of author and reader are themselves limited by his own investment in the system of gender relations his works often seek to criticize.

Pleasure and the Will

Sidney wrote his *Old Arcadia* during a period in which the legal meanings of "rape" and "ravishment" underwent a significant transformation. The medieval statutes had applied these synonymous terms both to acts of forced coitus and to crimes of abduction or woman-stealing (one of the original Roman meanings of *raptus*). By confusing or conflating these two types of crime, laws against sexual violation seemed more designed to protect the rights of a woman's father or husband, whose "property" she was, than of the woman herself. By the sixteenth century, however, "rape" and "ravishment" were used in the law to refer only to acts of forced coitus, and seemed intended to protect the rights of individual women.[6] Nazife Bashar has argued that in the Early Modern period, "rape came to be seen as a crime against the person, not as a crime against property."[7] Yet, underlying both medieval and Renaissance law was the assumption that only virginal or chaste women, or women who had value under a system of patriarchal and patrilineal marriage exchange, would refuse to engage in illicit acts of copulation—would, in other words, be capable of becoming victims of sexual violence. Since in all other areas of law women did not gain greater status as "persons" during the English Renaissance, it is more useful to see alterations in rape law not as indicating a new relation between women and property but as part of a Reformation shift in the relative importance of the ideals of virginity and chastity. But a close reading of rape law demonstrates that both of these ideals continued to inform Early Modern notions of gendered subjectivity.[8] Furthermore, the distinction between virginity and chastity was the subject of an early Christian theological debate on the meaning of rape that continued to echo throughout the English Renaissance. Since this debate also addressed the complex relationships between intention, erotic desire, and corporeality—or the body's role in both physical sensation and acts of representation—writers such as Sidney took up the problematic meaning of sexual violation as they reconsidered the interplay of authorial intention, audience reception, and the "body" of the text.

The definitive medieval law against ravishment, the Second Statute of Westminster (1285), was clearly concerned with the value of women as forms of property. It began as follows: "If a man from henceforth doe ravish any woman . . . where she did not consent, neither before nor after, he shall have judgement of life and of member. And likewise where a man ravisheth a woman . . . with force (although shee consent afterward) he shall have such judgement as before is said."[9] Historians have interpreted the statute's strange language of consent "before" or "after" in terms of crimes of abduction. According to J. B. Post, for example, when in its second sentence the statute identified the primary feature of "ravishment" as the lack of "consent before," this was really code for parental consent to marriage. "Consent after," in turn, referred to the agreement of the woman herself to the sexual or marital relationship, an agreement that could be canceled out by lack of "consent before." In this, the statute effectively outlawed elopements and sexual affairs as well as actual abductions or coerced sexual acts.[10] Westminster II, in other words, suppressed women's abilities to exercise their individual powers of consent, and instead attempted to render them the objects of marriage exchanges controlled by their families.

Although statutes against abduction that essentially repeated the injunctions of Westminster II (while further specifying that they protected upper-class women possessing "moveable goods") continued to be passed throughout the Renaissance, by the fifteenth century these laws no longer used the word "ravishment" and its cognate "rape," which instead came to describe acts of forced coitus alone.[11] Yet Early Modern law books continued to quote the language of Westminster II. This was because the statute's temporal notion of consent "before or after" remained relevant to concepts of copulation.[12] For Early Modern rape law was based upon the belief that even if a woman were initially unwilling, an act of copulation could eventually cause her to experience pleasure after it had begun. What the law manuals record is a debate over whether such pleasure could be allied with consent—or what Westminster II termed "consent after." This debate was a version of an early theological argument over the relative virtues of virginity and chastity. On one side, theologians such as Cyprian, Tertullian, Jerome, and Ambrose formulated a concept of virginity in which any experience of erotic pleasure could be equated with sexual consent; on the other side, Augustine elaborated a concept of "chastity" that questioned this equation.

The Christian ideal of "virginity" applied to the physical integrity of the female body but also and more crucially to a woman's lack of all erotic thoughts, desires, and pleasures. Although early Christian theologians advocated perpetual virginity for both men and women, their writings on this virtue reveals that female virginity in particular was allied with both physical and mental integrity or purity—with, in other words, the sense of being materially and spiritually "untouched." In the Renaissance, we find invocations of this ideal in such writers as Juan Vives, who advised that before marriage "maydens should keepe them selves . . . from eyther hearing or seeing, or yet, thinking any foule thing."[13] The assumption that a true virgin possessed an original sexual innocence explains why during this period marital defloration was often described as an act of theft. For example, Puttenham's *Arte of English Poesie* claimed that on the wedding night the husband's duty was "to rob his spouse of her maidenhead."[14] If a virgin was free of all erotic thoughts and desires, then it stood to reason that a bride's first sexual encounter had to be imposed upon her in a coercive act. Furthermore, Dod and Cleaver's *A Godly Forme of Household Government* (1598) suggested that a wife could experience pleasure after this initial "robbery," and that such pleasure was equivalent to consent. These authors advised that "The husband ought not to bee satisfied, that he hath robd his wife of her virginity, but in that hee hath possession and use of her will" (167).[15] Since the word "will" could refer to the genital organs and the desire or pleasure that animated them, Dod and Cleaver's description suggested that a virgin's first sexual encounter, though begun unwillingly, could cause her to experience pleasure, that this constituted an initiation into erotic desire, and that such desire could be read as a form of consent "after." In other words, this account linked a woman's pleasure to her "willingness" to become the "possession" of a man. In the law, such an equation between pleasure and consent appears first in a dictum in a thirteenth-century treatise by Britton, and was repeated in sixteenth- and seventeenth-century manuals for justices of the peace. Based upon the prevalent belief that female orgasm was necessary for conception,[16] these manuals stipulated that "if the woman conceive upon any carnall abusing of her, that is no rape, for she cannot conceive unless shee consent."[17] In other words, a woman's experience of orgasmic pleasure—proved by her subsequent pregnancy—constituted a form of "consent after" that nullified any claims she might make that she had been violated.

Barbara Baines argues that the equation between pleasure and consent was "devoutly embraced by the Renaissance."[18] Yet, while legal authorities in this period continued to cite Britton's dictum, they also acknowledged exceptions that contradicted this view. For example, some manuals asserted that there could be circumstances where, even if a woman experienced pleasure as the result of a sexual assault (and therefore had the potential to became pregnant), this apparent "consent" was not "voluntary and free," and thus should not be considered legally relevant.[19] This

distinction between "voluntary" choice and the condition or sensations
of the body derived from St. Augustine's discussion of rape in his major
theological treatise, *The City of God,* where he argued that "the sanctified body [*corpus*] is the instrument of the sanctified will [*voluntas*],
and . . . if that will continues unshaken, whatever anyone does with the
body or to the body . . . involves no blame to the sufferer."[20] Augustine
developed his definition of rape specifically to oppose other religious authorities who equated female sexual purity only with virginal innocence.
Instead, Augustine emphasized the ideal of "chastity," which could be at-
tained by sexually experienced and inexperienced women alike. According to Augustine, a chaste woman could be capable of feeling desire or
pleasure, but this was irrelevant to her ability to refuse to give her sexual
consent: what mattered was not the state of her body—and its initiation
into erotic sensations or yearnings—but the condition of her will, or her
faculty for moral choice.

The Augustinian paradigm clearly underlay a new definition of rape as
"carnal knowledge of a woman's body against her will" that first appeared
in English law manuals immediately after the Reformation and had become predominant by the end of the seventeenth century. Both Finch and
Dalton cite the 1469 Year Book as the source of their definitions.[21] While
this new definition seemed to constitute a public acknowledgement of
women's rights to self-determination, Augustine's vision of sexuality reveals that the concept of the "will" he developed in relation to sexual violence was tied to specific notions of female subjectivity and virtue that
were different from, yet no less limited than, the ideal of virginity he criticized. In his discussion of rape, Augustine emphasized the complete separation between the will and the body; this differed radically from the
model of intention, desire, and corporeality developed in the rest of *The
City of God.* There he maintained that the will could never be disentan-
gled from the desires and sensations of the material body, which manifested
themselves most saliently in the independent movement of the sexual organs.[22] According to Augustine, this genital motion was God's punishment
for original sin, for Augustine speculated that in paradise human beings
could have moved their genitals in order to copulate through a pure act of
will. After the Fall, however, Adam and Eve discovered that their genitals
had gained a new capacity for involuntary motion:

> "They realized they were naked." . . . Therefore, embarrassed by their flesh's
> disobedience, a punishment that bore witness to their own disobedience,
> "they sewed fig leaves together and made themselves aprons." . . . Thus
> modesty, prompted by a sense of shame, covered what was disobediently
> aroused by lust against a will condemned for disobedience. (XIV.17)

Although throughout his discussion of the Fall, Augustine suggests that the punishment of genital motion was meted out equally to both men and women, it is hard to read descriptions such as the above without thinking of what James Grantham Turner has called "the tragicomic mechanism of erection."[23] Paradoxically, it seems, the Fall brought with it the uncontrollable rise of the male member as a visible sign or gesture that "bore witness" or "gave testimony" [teste] to the involuntary nature of carnal desire. Since elsewhere Augustine describes Eve's body as incapable of such visible motion, it is difficult to understand how women fit into his schema.[24]

In Augustine's discussion of rape, however, it is precisely women's exceptional position—their possession of bodies that could not "bear witness" to experiences of desire or pleasure—that allows him to imagine them as able to maintain a clear distinction between the body and the will. In other words, because Augustine believes that a woman's state of mind could not be expressed in a language of physical movement, he envisions women as having access to a purely private realm of conscience that resists all outward attempts at interpretation. This means that the raped woman is the figure most likely to possess a fully "chaste" will, because she lives the contradiction between public appearance and inward spiritual or Edenic purity. He therefore "consoles" rape victims lamenting the loss of their virginity, "do not be amazed at having lost that for which you were concerned—because it would win people's approval—while you have retained what cannot be displayed before their eyes" (I.28). Similarly, Augustine condemns Lucretia for attempting to prove that she was raped by committing suicide: "since she could not display her pure conscience to the world, she thought she must exhibit her punishment before people's eyes as a proof of her state of mind." For Augustine, Lucretia's self-murder did not end speculation about her chastity but only signified her prideful unwillingness to use her public defilement as an opportunity to pursue a wholly private, spiritual existence.

Because Augustine portrays female desire and intention as essentially unknowable, ultimately his discussion of rape does not so much resolve the problematic relationship between female pleasure and consent as displace it to a region inaccessible even to his own efforts of imagination. This becomes clear at the moment in the *City of God* when he attempts to describe a woman's experience of being raped: "Although [an act of forced coitus] does not destroy the sexual purity retained by the utmost constancy of soul, still . . . it may be believed that the act was committed with a willing mind, since perhaps it could not take place without some pleasure of the flesh." With the passive phrasing of "it may be believed," Augustine leaves open the question of whether it is the woman herself, or those who might judge her from the outside, who would confuse the relationship between the experience of pleasure and the consent of the will. With his speculative "perhaps," he further indicates that he himself is only an outsider who cannot determine whether women necessarily experience pleasure during copulation. At another moment of speculation—when he contemplates the possibility that Lucretia consented to her rapist—Augustine even seems to equate such consent with pleasure and desire. He writes, "Suppose (a thing which only she herself could know) that, although the young man attacked her violently, she, lured by her own lust, consented, and that when she came to punish herself she was so grieved that she thought death the only expiation" (I.19). This description of the slide of "lust" [*libido*] into "consent" seems to contradict Augustine's larger emphasis in his discussion of rape upon the absolute separation between female pleasure and will. Yet, this is not a contradiction he needs to resolve. For he relegates the complex relationship between female pleasure and consent to the inaccessible reaches of the female mind: whether Lucretia consented is something "only she herself could know."

The fact that Augustinian theology underlay the emerging Early Modern definition of rape as "carnal knowledge of a woman's body against her will" explains why the law's acknowledgement of the importance of women's powers of voluntary consent did not mean that the conviction rate for rape increased during this period—indeed, it may have lessened. For the Augustinian view of rape only reinforced women's position as "*femmes couverts*," or "subjects" denied the political and legal potential for meaningful acts of public self-expression—particularly the expression of their sexual or erotic desires and intentions.[25] For example, an Augustinian perspective surfaces in a 1634 letter written by a judge to his superior, in which he counseled him to abandon the prosecution of a rape case. Writing to the President of the Council of the Marches of Wales regarding the case of Margery Evans, the judge Tymothy Tourneur called the Evans case overly "complicat[ed]" and described rape in general as a crime "wherein the proffe of the act of copulacion is but secondary and the disagreement of the woman at the tyme of the act is primarie[,] soe that the issue is not upon the [e]xternall act whether it was done or not but whether it was in the *patiens* voluntary or compulsary."[26] Here, Tourneur describes "copulacion" as an "externall act"; he thus separates acts from processes taking place "in" the woman—processes that define what is "voluntary" or "compulsary." In one sense, this emphasizes the idea that the sexual act affects the woman's body but not necessarily her will. At the same time, however, Tourneur refers to the woman as the "*patiens*," or the Latin legal term for one acted upon: the "external act" of copulation, in other words, is one in which the female body is fundamentally *inactive* or "passive," unable to achieve a movement that would signify a meaningful action. By emphasizing the "external," Tourneur's description therefore envisions the female body engaged in copulation as a spectacle where what can be seen on the surface cannot reveal the woman's internal, mental state and therefore the legal and moral meaning of the act as a whole.

Tourneur's letter further reveals how the Augustinian paradigm constructed relations between the sexes in terms of the problem of knowledge. For Tourneur's description of rape calls attention to another troubling division between the external and the internal: the distance that divides his perceptions of the visible world from his ability to achieve sure, inward knowledge of that world. It is this emphasis upon the relationship between the epistemological limitations of the male subject and the representational limitations of the female that particularly distinguish what I call the Early Modern "dynamic of ravishment." It is also this restrictive constellation of gendered relations that Sidney's writings attempt to move beyond.

"Some Excellent Artificer"

The *Old Arcadia* was written when legal authorities were shifting the meaning of sexual violence away from the ambiguous language of Westminster II and towards a definition that centered on the female will. Sidney's text seems to participate in this project, as it points to the inadequacies of older definitions of "ravishment" while sympathetically portraying its female characters' desires to decide their marriages according to their own choosing. In depicting a trial in which the romantic yearnings of the protagonists are not only thwarted but condemned, the *Old Arcadia* appears to suggest that the law must allow space for erotic and romantic desires that its characters typically express by composing poetry. Yet, Sidney's narrative also illuminates how the conventions of love poetry—most saliently those of Petrarchan verse—are, like the law, centered upon a desire to penetrate to a truth hidden behind the veil of representation. This desire, the romance shows, is indistinguishable from the drive towards sexual violation. Sidney, then, is less interested in reforming the law than he is in questioning and transforming the models of subjectivity and expression that inform it. Since these models are embedded in a set of poetic conventions, the *Old Arcadia* attempts to work out problems of gender, power, and representation by reworking such conventions. For it is through imaginative invention, Sidney argues in his *Apology,* that the "right poet" can move beyond "what is, has been, or shall be" to what "may or should be."[27]

In the trial scene that ends Sidney's romance, the two traveling princely cousins, Pyrocles and Musidorus, stand accused of "ravishment." Arcadian

law uses this term in the same dual sense as Westminster II: while Pyrocles
is accused of attempting the sexual violation of Princess Philoclea, Musidorus is charged with taking her older sister Pamela from the house of her
father Basilius, Duke of Arcadia. Both apparent "ravishments," however,
were actually consensual: not only did the women exchange private vows
of marriage with their lovers, but afterwards Philoclea willingly slept with
Pyrocles, while Pamela willingly eloped with Musidorus. Yet at the trial,
the judge Euarchus makes it clear that ravishment—at least when committed against upper-class women—is primarily understood as a crime
against the women's family and, in this instance, also against the state ruled
by that family (of which the two daughters are the only heirs). Following
the logic of Westminster II that privileged parental consent or "consent before" over an individual woman's "consent after," the judge admits that
while the women may have agreed to the relationships with the princes,
this is not grounds for dismissing the charges of ravishment. Meanwhile,
the princesses' perspectives are literally banished from the trial, for they are
barred from the court and remain in prison. There, they write letters
pointing out the contradiction in using the term "ravishment" to refer to
consensual acts, and demanding that the court acknowledge and honor
their right to choose their own husbands. The court, however, never admits these letters as testimony, and when the trial produces a clearly unfair
outcome—in which the princes are sentenced to death and are only saved
through a miraculous intervention—it appears that a law based on princi-
ples similar to those in England's medieval statutes has little ability to dis-
pense true justice. It may seem, therefore, that Sidney's narrative begins to
uphold a version of rape and marriage law that would privilege women's
individual rights of consent.

Despite Sidney's clear intention to elicit his readers' sympathy for his
unfortunate heroes and heroines, as many critics have noted, the "moral"
of the trial scene is not easy to determine.[28] For readers of the romance
know that during their elopement Musidorus has attempted to rape
Pamela when, alone with him in the "desert" outside her father's lodge, she
falls asleep in his arms. This turn of events undermines the idea that
women acting independently could make binding contracts with their
suitors. When Pamela escapes with Musidorus, she makes the preservation
of her chastity a condition of their elopement, stipulating, "Let me be your
own (as I am), but by no unjust conquest" (173); notwithstanding, once she
is asleep the narrator seems to blame her attempted rape on her decision
to act on her own without her family's approval, for he tells us that "no
vow is as strong as the avoiding of occasions" (177). This scene, which begins when the lovers recite verses to each other, demonstrates that although the conventions of Petrarchan poetry—like emerging Early

Modern definitions of "rape"—seem to center on the question of whether a woman gives or withholds her sexual consent, in fact, the dynamic of ravishment that underlies both discourses works to undermine women's ability to exercise this power.

When we first visit Pamela and Musidorus after their escape, the narrator describes how "Pamela had much . . . pleasure to walk under [the] trees, making in their barks pretty knots which tied together the names of Musidorus and Pamela . . . with twenty other flowers of her travailing fancies, which had bound themselves to a greater restraint than they could without much pain well endure" (174). For Pamela, composing love lyrics and inscribing them upon the barks of the trees represents an attempt to resolve her own contradictory impulses towards erotic "pleasure" and chaste "restraint." The "knots" she carves are therefore efforts to represent simultaneously her virgin "knot" that she will preserve until her official marriage, and the love that already binds her to Musidorus. Pamela is able to superimpose these two images because she reworks Petrarchan conventions from a female perspective. The male poet/lover of this tradition claims to have been "wounded" by the sight of his beloved's beauty, yet also identifies the cause of this wound as her cruelty in refusing his advances. When he therefore finds it impossible to determine whether the manifest beauty of the female body, or her inner virtue that denies access to that body, is the seductive force that originates his desire, this mirrors back to him his own inability to distinguish between the Augustinian forces of will and carnal desire that do battle within him. Pamela, however, portrays herself simultaneously as the lover who suffers from unfulfilled desires, and as the woman whose chastity frustrates those desires. In the first poem she composes she describes her own wound of love as "giv'n to my heart by my fore-wounded ey'n," or the sight of Musidorus, and as a "chosen smart / Which barred desires (barred by myself) impart." In another poem, she then reconciles this division between the powers of outward appearance and inward essence by arguing that her virtue and beauty form the combined qualities that she will bestow upon her beloved:

> my inward parts, and outward glass,
> Though each possess a diverse working kind,
> Yet all well knit to one fair end do pass:
> That he to whom these sundry gifts I bind,
> All what I am, still one, his own, do find. (175)

Although these lines seem to suggest that Pamela's contradictory nature will only be resolved once Musidorus has penetrated to her "inward parts" in a possessive act of defloration, Pamela's poetry instead insists that he should view such a reconciliation in the promise of marriage she has already made to him. She therefore ends her first poem with the lines, "in this growing bark grow verses mine. / My heart my word, my word hath giv'n my heart. / The giver giv'n from gift shall never part." The trees, which seem to hold a static form yet continue to grow, come to embody a vow of love that must be deferred but not denied. Combining her own erotic longings with her faculty for "choice," Pamela therefore positions herself as the subject who can "give" the "gift" of her "heart," rather than a bride who must be seized and only retrospectively grant "consent after" in a relinquishment of her own will for the "use" of her husband.

Yet Pamela fails to realize that according to the Petrarchan paradigm, the fantasy of willful control can only be sustained if the desire expressed in the beautiful words of the poem stands in contrast to the chaste fixity of the medium upon which they are inscribed. To the extent that the marked tree "grows," then, its independent motion replicates the Augustinian vision of the disobedient erection of the male genitals that "bears witness" to an irreconcilable battle between desire and the will. If the beautiful Petrarchan text is instead understood as an inanimate object whose language nonetheless expresses the male poet's desire as if it were its own, it comes to resemble Augustine's chaste-but-raped woman, whose violation signals her possession of an independent will hidden behind her opaque exterior. This, then, leads to the desire to penetrate the artful surface of the poem—and by extension the equally paradoxical surface of the female beloved—to a unified, spiritualized interior associated with Edenic sexuality. Pamela herself describes this dynamic when in her first poem she justifies her act of wounding the flesh of the tree by rhetorically asking it, "Thus cruel to myself, how canst thou crave / My inward hurt should spare thy outward rine?" (174). Here she suggests that if poetic composition represents an attempt to control desire, this can only occur through a fantasy of physically violating a quiescent, unfeeling surface. This suggestion, then, sets the stage for her own rape, for when she sings her next poem, Musidorus's ears are "filled . . . with the heavenly sound of her music, which before he had never heard, so that it seemed unto him a new assault given to the castle of his heart, already conquered." He then sings "in a kind of still but ravishing tune a few verses" (175) that in turn lull her to sleep. In this state, Pamela's body itself becomes "still but ravishing" like his poem, for at one point the shepherd Philisides had said that sleep "the senses up doth shut the senses to preserve." What Pamela's sleep preserves is a spiritualized notion of her own sexual purity, guaranteed by the contrast between her unmoving, unfeeling body and the enthralling beauty it nonetheless radiates:[29]

[Musidorus] thought her fair forehead was a field where all his fancies fought, and every hair of her head seemed a strong chain that tied him. Her fair lids (then hiding her fairer eyes) seemed unto him sweet boxes of mother of pearl, rich in themselves, but containing in them far richer jewels . . . the roses of her lips (whose separating was wont to be accompanied with most wise speeches) now by force drew his sight to mark how prettily they lay one over the other, . . . and through them the eye of his fancy delivered to his memory the lying (as in ambush) [of her teeth] under her lips. . . . And lest this beauty might seem the picture of some excellent artificer, forth there stale a soft breath, carrying good testimony of her inward sweetness . . . [from] that well closed paradise, that did so tyrannize over Musidorus's affects that he was compelled to put his face as low to hers as he could. . . . But each of these having a mighty working in his heart, all joined together did so draw his will into the nature of their confederacy . . . that rising softly from her, overmastered with the fury of delight, having all his senses partial against himself, and inclined to his well beloved adversary, he was bent to take the advantage of the weakness of the watch, and see whether at that season he could win the bulwark before timely help might come. (177)

Here, Pamela's beauty continues to be a seductive power: her hair "[en]chains," her lips offer "force," her teeth lie in "ambush," her breath "tyrannizes," and all together "compell" Musidorus. Like Augustine's fallen Adam, who confronts his own erection as a part of himself whose actions nonetheless seem to obey a force he finds alien and uncontrollable, Musidorus's perception of Pamela's beauty causes "all his senses" to become "partial against himself," threatening to overturn his chivalrous intentions expressed in his vow to her. Yet, in Sidney's text, it is the ability of poetic beauty to blur the boundary between illusion and reality that causes Musidorus's confusion regarding the origin of his desire. Because Musidorus views Pamela with the "eye of his fancy," her physical body seems inseparable from the *blason* in which it is described: "he thought her fair forehead was a field . . . her hair seemed a strong chain . . . her fair lids . . . seemed . . . boxes of mother of pearl." Indeed, the narrator himself says that her image appears to be "the picture of some excellent artificer." While Musidorus seems most likely to be this artificer, since this description is framed as his thoughts and perceptions, he is controlled by the poetic experience his imagination also appears to originate, and that more and more comes to be the language the narrator himself employs. The narrative voice, however, holds out the possibility that since this beauty radiates from Pamela's sleeping body, beyond her frozen exterior may lie a "well closed paradise" of Augustinian conscience in which Musidorus's confusions would be resolved. The only messenger from this elusive realm seems to be her breath, which brings "good testimony of her inward sweetness," invoking a juridical notion of proof as a potential remedy against the seductive powers of art. But the scene's events contradict this idea, for Pamela's breath only increases the enthralling power of her image, bringing Musidorus closer to her body and thereby drawing his "will"—a word that now, taking on the meaning of genitalia, perfectly confuses the forces of desire and intention—into a "confederacy" with her beauty, and "overmastering" him "with the fury of delight." He is then incited to attempt a deeper penetration of her interior by raping her.

This scene seems to represent the corrupting effects of poetic beauty in exactly the terms Sidney attributes to his imagined critics in his *Apology for Poetry,* who call this medium "the nurse of abuse, infecting us with many pestilent desires, with a siren's sweetness, drawing the mind to the serpent's tail of sinful fancies" (34). In that treatise, he contends that poetry's hold over the "fancies" of its audience can make it a force for good. Arguing that art surpasses philosophy as a method of moral instruction, he writes, "the philosopher, with his learned definitions, be it of virtues or vices, . . . replenishes the memory with many infallible grounds of wisdom which notwithstanding lie dark before the imaginative and judging power if they be not illuminated or figured forth by the speaking picture of poesy" (17). In the *Apology,* Sidney offers two alternative visions of authorship that suggest how the poet could therefore create an art that reconciles the faculties of imagination and moral judgement. According to the first of these, the poet encourages virtuous behavior by planting inspiring images in the minds of his audience. Thus, at one point Sidney writes, "I will not deny but that man's wit may make poetry, which should be *eikastike* (which some learned have defined "figuring forth good things") to be *phantastike* (which does contrariwise infect the fancy with unworthy objects). . . . But, what, shall the abuse of a thing, make the right use odious?" (36–37). Earlier, he had given an example of the beneficial "figuring forth of good things" when he described the superior art of the "heroical" poet, "who (if the saying of Plato and Tully be true, that who could see virtue would be wonderfully ravished with the love of her beauty) . . . sets her out to make her more lovely in her holiday apparel" (30). Here, poetry still "ravishes" or reaches its audience through the passions aroused by their imaginations rather than their reason, but it does so in order to use its beautiful exterior to "set out" virtue. If this suggests that a new poetry of love could be created by reforming its conventional imagery, we may notice that the *Old Arcadia's* description of attempted rape reveals that what unites both legal and Petrarchan discourse is the focus of their inquisitive gaze upon the silent, quiescent surface of the female body rather than the "wise speeches" it might produce. This exclusion, then, seems to be what prevents the beautiful woman (and by analogy the beautiful text) from becoming a "speaking picture" who would teach her own virtue to others.

Nevertheless, we also saw how in the moments leading up to the rape, Pamela's own attempts to project such a virtue through verbal expression failed. This narrative trajectory therefore calls attention to another way that legal inquiry parallels the rapacious desire of the Petrarchan lover, for in both cases the dynamic of ravishment is activated through the desire to evade the manipulative force of representation by attempting to move beyond its illusions to a hidden truth or "carnal knowledge" at its source. If poetry is to become a "speaking picture," then, it seems that it must do more than reform the content of poetic conventions; instead, it must question their fundamental epistemology. This opinion Sidney expresses in an alternative view of the role of the author that he elaborates in the *Apology* and attempts to apply in his romance: that poetry is a superior medium for teaching because it engages the imagination while simultaneously signaling that it is a work of artifice that has no claim of truth. Responding to critics who contend that poetry "is the mother of lies," he argues that the poet does not dissemble because "he nothing affirms . . . he never makes any circles about your imagination, to conjure you to believe for true what he writes. [He does not labor] to tell you what is or is not, but what should or should not be" (34–35). We must notice, therefore, that when Sidney describes the ravishing beauty of epic poetry that clothes "virtue," he calls it "holiday apparel," suggesting that what allows the effect of this medium to be "wonderful" is not its ability to allow virtue (an intangible quality that, Sidney implies, can never be "seen" directly) to "speak" through an accurate representation, but rather the way it calls attention to its own status as something out of the ordinary.

The romance's rape scene achieves this effect by employing a narrative voice that weaves in and out of the various discursive registers of the text and the differing perspectives of the characters. This technique allows the text to point to an authorial presence that remains distinct from its representations, and knowable only through an engagement with them. The method suggests that the work of art can only be experienced once its audience has abandoned the distinction between "truth" and "lies," such as in the rape scene's refusal to distinguish "beauty" from an artifice neither entirely imaginary nor completely real, therefore neither a deceptive illusion that must be penetrated to arrive at a hidden truth, nor an entirely accurate representation of such truth. Such a stance, then, creates a space from which to judge the mechanism of "beauty" itself, whose functioning, as we saw, represents the intentions of neither of the scene's characters. For the narrator later tells us that Pamela's "own beauties enforced a force against her self" (265) even as they engaged her lover in a "confederacy" that rendered his senses "partial against himself." Instead, the romance asks its readers to look for meaning in the gap between authorial intention and literary

expression, which will always be grounded in the imitation of a set of conventions that the author did not originate and whose meaning he cannot
completely control. Pointing to the space between author and text as
something that must necessarily exist, Sidney offers it as the arena for an
ongoing process of interpretation.[30] Such a condition of perpetual knowing through unknowing seems to be part of the individual's ideal relation
not only to art, but to life itself. Thus, in its first pages, the *Old Arcadia*
warns its readers of "the vanity that possesseth many who, making a perpetual mansion of this poor baiting place of man's life, are desirous to know
the certainty of things to come, wherein there is nothing so certain as our
continual uncertainty" (5). While this phrase at first glance seems to suggest that since the world is only a fleeting illusion, we should abandon all
attempts at interpreting it, in fact Sidney's paradoxical phrase asks us to
seek certainty in "continual uncertainty."[31]

In the *Old Arcadia,* such a perspective connects to a new way of looking at the development of gendered subjectivity as an ongoing process of
self-creation mediated through fantasy. The romance's hero, Pyrocles,
comes to represent this new view of intentionality and identity, since
throughout the first part of the narrative he courts the closely guarded
Philoclea by disguising himself as a woman. In so doing, he transcends the
"ravishing" effect of beauty that divides the sexes, to achieve a position
from which he can identify with his beloved. Such cross-dressing also
comes to represent Sidney's narrative strategy, since his authorial persona,
like Pyrocles, identifies himself as the source of the text's enthralling effects
while also signaling that his identity in some sense contradicts the significations of his medium of poetic "apparel." At the same time, Sidney's portrayal of Pyrocles's lover Philoclea begins to suggest how women could
achieve a new form of self-expression beyond the dichotomy between
chastity and unchastity that limited the meaning of female consent. Indeed, if the romance's rape scene allows its readers to identify beauty as a
force whose power both precedes and conditions the sexual relationship
between Musidorus and Pamela, it begins to reveal how in Sidney's society, female beauty crystallized women's value as objects of exchange between men in a system of marital relations adjudicated by the laws of
"ravishment." At one point in the *Old Arcadia,* Sidney signals this possibility, when Pamela's mother Gynecia describes her own beauty as "those
moveable goods of nature wherewith . . . my royal parents bestowed me
upon" the Duke (240). But, as I will discuss in the final section of this essay,
Philoclea comes to represent the contradiction at the heart of Sidney's poetic enterprise, as she becomes the figure most liberated from the strictures
of a feminine identity, yet also, ultimately, most confined by the notion that
women must be what they seem. This view is tied to the more restrictive

and controlling notion of authorial intention Sidney at times contemplates in his *Apology*, whereby an inward virtue must become absolutely manifested in an outward representation. It is therefore easier for Sidney to imagine how a cross-dressed man could point to the artificial nature of a feminized "beauty," than to grant such freedom to women themselves.

Impossible Desires

In an early scene in the *Old Arcadia,* Sidney describes a debate between Musidorus and Pyrocles that strongly echoes his own debate in the *Apology* with critics of poetry over the status of beauty. When Pyrocles first tells Musidorus that he intends to adopt the female persona of an Amazon to gain access to Philoclea, this becomes the occasion for a *pro et contra* dialogue on the merits of heterosexual love, in which each friend's explanation of female subordination can be allied with the versions of poetic authorship that each comes to embody. For while Musidorus displays a misogynist view of women as the source of a seductive beauty that leads to men's moral downfall and is connected with ravishment, Pyrocles instead emphasizes that men and women are not inherently unequal, but are made so through social institutions; he therefore offers a way to demystify the allure of beauty associated with the potentially corrupting effects of poetry.

At the beginning of the dialogue, Musidorus warns his friend that since "true love . . . doth transform the very essence of the lover into the thing loved," the "effeminate love of a woman doth . . . womanize a man." This, he argues, leads to immoral behavior, since such love's ravishing power "utterly subverts the course of nature in making reason give place to sense, and man to woman," creating a "bastard love" "engendered betwixt lust and idleness" (18). Contradicting his friend, Pyrocles traces the origin of female subordination to men's "tyrannous ambition," not women's moral inferiority: he argues that although mankind has brought women's "virtuous patience under them, . . . [women] are framed of nature with the same parts of the mind for the exercise of virtue as [men] are" (19); therefore it cannot be immoral for the "essence" of the lover to be transformed "into the thing loved" when that object is a virtuous woman. If his own love is immoral, Pyrocles contends, the source of that immorality lies in himself not his object, for since love is "the highest power of the mind (which notable men have attributed unto it), . . . if love receive any disgrace, it is by the company of . . . lust, idleness, and a weak heart . . . those troublesome effects you say it breeds be not the fault of love, but of him that loves, as an unable vessel to bear such a power" (20–21).

Pyrocles's defense of love almost replicates the argument Sidney offers in his *Apology* against the claim that poetry, like woman, represents a source of corrupting, ravishing beauty that "abuses men's wit, training it to wanton sinfulness and lustful love." Instead, he insists that the love of beauty can lead men into moral action:

> But grant love of beauty to be a beastly fault (although it be very hard, since only man and no beast hath that gift to discern beauty); grant that lovely name of Love to deserve all hateful reproaches (although even some . . . philosophers spent a great deal of their lamp-oil on setting forth the excellency of it); grant . . . that not only love, but lust, but vanity, but if they list scurrility, possess many leaves of the poets' books, yet think I, when this is granted, they will find their sentence may with good manners put the last words foremost and not say that poetry abuses man's wit, but that man's wit abuses poetry. . . . Nay, truly, though I yield that poesy may . . . by the reason of his sweet charming force . . . do more hurt than any other army of words, yet . . . the abuse should [not] give reproach to the abused. . . . [Since] whatsoever being abused does most harm, being rightly used . . . does most good. (36–37)

Here, Sidney argues that if poetry corrupts, this is the fault not of poetry, but of those authors who would use it towards lewd ends. The poet who refuses to "abuse" his literary medium is implicitly compared to the chivalrous lover who would refrain from using violence to corrupt his beloved. Sidney makes clear that in either case the poetic medium itself, like the beautiful woman, should not be held responsible for its potentially negative effects, since it would be wrong if "the abuse [of a thing] should give reproach to the abused." The *Old Arcadia*'s initial contrast between the rapacious Musidorus and the lovestruck Pyrocles compares therefore to the distinction between the bad poet, who allows poetry to "infect the fancy with unworthy objects" and do "more hurt than any other army of words," and the "right poet" who uses this "sweet charming force" to do "most good."

Pyrocles's defense of love defends his plan to dress as a woman. It would seem, then, that if he figures Sidney's right poet, this poet does, on some level, cross-dress. Mark Rose, however, has criticized theories that would treat the disguised Pyrocles as a positive image. Rose points out that in his *Apology*, Sidney describes how "Hercules, painted with his great beard and furious countenance in a woman's attire spinning at Omphale's commandment . . . breeds both delight and laughter" (50). According to Rose, when Pyrocles adopts a similarly ridiculous Amazon disguise, he becomes a living symbol of the "injustice of female rule."[32] Rose fails to note, however, that at this moment in his treatise Sidney argues for the potentially salutary effects of comedy. While he condemns the playwrights of his day for inspiring only the "scornful tickling" of laughter, he contends that in great works of art, laughter and delight can "go well together." Describing the difference between these two emotions, Sidney writes, "delight we scarcely do but in things which have a conveniency to ourselves or the general nature; laughter almost ever comes of things most disproportioned to ourselves and nature." He clarifies this difference by offering the example that "we are ravished with delight to see a fair woman, yet are hardly thereby moved to laughter" (49–50). The mixing of delight and laughter can be read as a version of the coupling of "delight" and "teaching," which he argues throughout the *Apology* is the method literature should use to convey moral truths. In the *Old Arcadia's* rape scene, for example, Sidney uses the "ravishing" effects of poetry to "delight" his readers with an imitation of "the general nature"—specifically the "nature" of female beauty and its effect on male desire—while the teaching function of his text derives from his inclusion of a distanced, ironic narrative voice "disproportioned" from that nature and therefore able to open up a space for contemplation and moral judgment.

Elsewhere in the *Apology*, Sidney identifies this dual position in regard to nature as the proper stance of the right poet. There, he characterizes the poet's struggle to move beyond "what is" or "has been" as the development of a new relationship not only to poetic convention, but to nature itself. He compares the Aristotelian notion of the artistic imitation of nature with the more slavish devotion to nature practiced by the physician or metaphysician:

> Only the poet, disdaining to be tied to any such subjection, lifted up with the vigor of his own invention, does grow in effect into another nature in making things either better than nature brings forth or, quite anew, forms such as never were in nature, as the heroes, demigods, cyclops, chimeras, furies and such like. So as he goes hand in hand with nature, not enclosed within the narrow warrant of her gifts but freely ranging within the zodiac of his own wit. (9)

This description could easily apply to Sidney's technique in the *Old Arcadia*, which not only announces itself as a work of fantasy, but is also famous for its chimerical mixing of literary styles and genres that demand different forms of emotional engagement. Since the *Apology* identifies the portrayal of the cross-dressed Hercules as an example of such successful literary mixture, it makes sense that Sidney's romance also features a cross-dressed male character. In adopting an Amazon disguise, Pyrocles, like the right poet, "grow[s] in effect into an other nature" and "brings forth or, quite anew, forms such as never were in nature, as . . . heroes, demigods, cyclops, chimeras, furies and such like." This chimerical persona allows Pyrocles to go "hand in hand with nature" without allowing himself to be "enclosed within the narrow warrant of her gifts."

As if highlighting how Pyrocles's new identity as the "Amazon" Cleophila mirrors Sidney's right poet, the romance has this character compose its first love poem. This sonnet begins to disrupt the conventions of love lyric to replace a Petrarchan poetics of contradiction with a new poetics of mixture that mirrors Cleophila's chimerical identity. The opening stanza describes how Pyrocles was first assaulted by the "outward force" of Philoclea's beauty, which encouraged his own "inward treason." The next stanza then elaborates upon this image:

> For from without came to mine eyes the blow,
> Whereto mine inward thoughts did faintly yield;
> Both these conspired poor reason's overthrow;
> False in myself, thus have I lost the field.

Contradicting Pyrocles's earlier arguments against Musidorus, here the poem does not depict him as the sole cause of his moral weakness. Instead, it describes how the sight of Philoclea's beauty penetrated his body through his eyes and colluded with his "inward thoughts" in causing his reason to become servant to this vision. The poem then conflates his sight of such beauty with his beloved's intentions, continuing, "Thus is my power transformed to your will." If this would make the supposedly virtuous Philoclea the source of Pyrocles's moral downfall, the poem addresses the problem by positing Pyrocles's gender disguise as a resolution of the distinctions between "inward" and "outward," self and other, continuing, "What marvel, then, I take a woman's hue? / Since what I see, think, know, is all but you?" (26).

Such an ending seems to replicate Pamela's attempt in her romantic verse to reconcile the contradictions in Petrarchan discourse; yet Cleophila's song reaches its conclusion not by adapting this tradition, but by mixing it with a vision of love from another poetic model: Ovid's *Metamorphoses*.[33] That work narrates stories in which an individual's nature could change through the power of desire. Cleophila's poem summarizes its version of this poetics in its opening line, where it depicts "her" as "Transformed in show, but more transformed in mind." The effect of this combination of Petrarchan and Ovidian visions of love is to create a hybrid poetics that corresponds to a hybrid subjectivity. Existing in a space between an Ovidian identity entirely transformed by love, and a Petrarchan identity riven with conflict through its relationship with an alien and unreachable beloved, Cleophila occupies a subjectivity in which she perpetually alternates between the positions of lover and beloved. Thus she complains of being "troubled with love both active and passive," and at one point composes a sonnet in which she laments, "When pity most I crave,

I cruel prove / . . . / What I call wrong, I do the same, and more" (188; 100). Sidney's narrative style also accentuates Cleophila's paradoxical identity, for once Pyrocles adopts his disguise, the narrator refers to this Amazon persona using only feminine pronouns. The romance's audience therefore experiences Cleophila as a female character while also knowing that from a narrative perspective, she is just a disguised Pyrocles. In this sense, Cleophila, like the right poet's text, is "artificial," as her subjectivity defies any clear distinction between reality and illusion. Cleophila herself reveals that the power of imagination allows her to occupy a chimerical identity. When Musidorus compliments his friend on his Amazon persona, Cleophila responds, "if I have any beauty, it is the beauty which the imagination of [Philoclea] strikes into my fancies, which in part shines through my face into your eyes" (25). In its combination of Petrarchan and Ovidian visions of subjectivity, Sidney's text therefore produces a new poetics of identification where the subject is created through an ongoing process of transformation and self-discovery in its engagement in an imaginative relation to an other.

Sidney's narrative suggests that the literary work of art—like Pyrocles's new Amazon persona—is created through such processes of identification: echoing Cleophila's first love poem, the narrator calls attention to his own act of writing by directly addressing Philoclea as an imagined audience and inspiration: "But alas, sweet Philoclea, how hath my pen forgotten thee, since to thy memory principally all this long matter is intended. Pardon the slackness to come to those woes which thou didst cause in others and feel in thyself" (95). The narrator then describes those "woes" that Philoclea "feels in herself," and in this process "causes" his readers to experience them as well. At other moments, the narrator signals more directly that his depictions of the various characters' private thoughts are actually imaginative constructs. For example, describing the moment when Pyrocles and Philoclea are caught in bed together after they have fallen asleep, he breaks off in mid-sentence to offer several possible explanations for why this occurred:

> Whether . . . they were so divinely surprised to bring their fault to open punishment; or that the too high degree of their joys had overthrown the wakeful use of their senses; or that their souls, lifted up with extremity of love after mutual satisfaction, had left their bodies dearly joined to unite themselves so much more freely as they were freer of that earthly prison; or whatsoever cause may be imagined of it. (237)

Moving rapidly through the possible views of sexuality provided by Christian providential narrative, Scholasticism, and Neoplatonism, the narrator at last reveals that all interpretations are produced through acts of imagination, and opens this process up to his readers. Similarly, Sidney invites the "fair ladies" he addresses throughout his romance to regard the text as a mediating garment across which he and they can engage in a mutual process of identification.

Yet, if Sidney's authorial persona remains male (if figuratively cross-dressed) and addresses an audience identified as female, we must ask the extent to which his literary vision allows for the possibility that Philoclea could achieve a level of effective self-representation. Philoclea does not undergo a gender metamorphosis comparable to Pyrocles's; she does fall in love with someone she believes is another woman. When she realizes her desire for Cleophila, she laments, "It is the impossibility that doth torment me; for unlawful desires are punished after the effect of enjoying, but impossible desires are plagued in the desire itself" (98). If Philoclea's homoerotic love is "impossible," her lament seems to suggest that this is because it cannot be "enjoyed" or consummated, a notion that resonates with Montaigne's claim in his essay "Of Friendship" that ideal same-sex relations between men exist "in the desire itself." Such affiliations are ruined by the pursuit of physical union: "*enjoying* doth loose-it, as having a *corporall* end, and subject to society. On the other side, friendshippe is *enjoyed* according as it is *desired*, it . . . *encreaseth* [not] but in *jovissance.*" Yet Jeffrey Masten argues that for Montaigne, "sexual relations between men are incompatible with friendship not because they are sexual *per se,* but because . . . [they are] founded in 'disparitie': of gender, of age, or of 'office' whereas they should be based in 'an *equitable* jouissance.'"[34] Similarly, we may read Philoclea's love for Cleophila as "impossible" not in the sense of being incapable of sexual fulfillment, but as removed from the hierarchical relations that mark heterosexual union: for in defining her love as "impossible," she specifically opposes it to the "unlawful"—and therefore to the power dynamics of ravishment associated with the prohibitions of a patriarchal law.[35]

Such homoerotic longing appears to coincide with the romance's concept of ideal love, for early on the narrator calls this emotion "that wonderful passion which to be defined is impossible, by reason no words reach near to the strange nature of it" (11). The "strange nature" of Philoclea's "impossible" love further seems to derive from its ambiguous mixing of the naturally delightful and the unnaturally disproportioned, as the Delphic oracle implies when it predicts that Philoclea will "with nature's bliss embrace / An uncouth love, which nature hateth most" (5). "Impossibility," therefore, seems to function in an artificial space between truth and falsehood, and explains the contradictory meanings that coexist in the text's coy reminder that "the many duties Cleophila did to [Philoclea] assured her Cleophila might well want power, but not will, to please her" (98). The surface meaning here depends upon a distinction between "power" as potential, and "will" as desire: Philoclea seems to believe that her apparently female lover lacks the genital equipment, and therefore the ability, to "please" her. Nevertheless, this reading is confused by the fact that the word "will" could also mean genitals. If read in this light, the sentence separates the "many duties" of a genital eroticism from the exercise of "power."[36] In this sense, the nature of the body that lies underneath Cleophila's feminine clothing becomes irrelevant, for it is the donning of the clothing itself that appears to constitute the relinquishment of "power," rather than of "will"—a word that nicely conflates the experience of desire and the physical means of its fulfillment.

At the moment when Philoclea accepts her "impossible" love, she also seems to become capable of gaining a new perspective upon the poetics of self-representation, for she returns to a spot where she had earlier written a poem "as a testimony of her mind" upon a "fair white marble stone." Declaring in that poem that the stone's "pureness doth present / My purest mind," she had vowed that "My virgin life no spotted thought shall stain." However, she herself "spotted" the stone by writing her poem upon its surface—a contradiction she only understands when she revisits the poem after realizing her feelings for Cleophila, and finds that "the ink was already foreworn and in many places blotted. . . . Alas, said she, fair marble, which never receivedst spot but by my writing, well do these blots become a blotted writer; but pardon her who did not dissemble then, although she have changed since" (97). Unlike Pamela's poem inscribed upon the "lofty pine," which embodied a fixed promise that she hoped would grow to fruition, Philoclea's original Petrarchan lyric more resembles Ovid's Galatea, who moved from being an adamant portrait to expressing a living desire. In the same way, Philoclea's original poem attempted to represent a static truth, yet it ends up embodying an evolving subjectivity—one that signals its perpetual incompleteness, and therefore its ability to revise its previous meanings without "dissembling." Philoclea's poem, then, avoids the "vanity" the romance warns of in its opening pages, "which possesseth many who . . . are desirous to know the certainty of things to come" (5).

Yet if the love between Philoclea and Cleophila seems to offer a space of neither truth nor lies where the erotic imagination can "range freely," it is important to remember that this relationship is actually founded upon an original deception: Pyrocles's disguise. A more sinister aspect to the notion of "impossibility" emerges, for although Pyrocles's lie releases Philoclea's imagination, it also limits its potential: "taking [Cleophila] to be such as she professed, desire she did, but she knew not what; and she longed to obtain that whereof she herself could not imagine the mean" (49). Because

her imagination is limited, she succumbs to the power of a love she believes is between equals, only to discover that she is actually engaged in a
heterosexual relationship in which her role is to be possessed by the man.
Thus, although Sidney portrays Philoclea as joyous when her friend reveals
his true sex to her, nonetheless she appears hesitant to give up the refuge
offered her by his disguise. She tells him that "when so thou wert . . . my
passions were far fitter to desire than to be desired," and that she will continue to call him by his Amazon name, explaining, "for so I love to call
thee, since in that name my love first began, and in the shade of that name
my love shall best lie hidden" (106–7). After this point, Philoclea seems to
lose the power to express or fulfill her desire, for the first time she sees Pyrocles without his feminine attire, he engages her in a sexual encounter in
which he is portrayed as "fighting a weak resistance that did strive to be
overcome" (211). In this description, the state of Philoclea's consent is
solely represented from Pyrocles's point of view, and depicted as a process
of "ravishment" in which resistance is not clearly distinguishable from desire. Furthermore, as in the comparable encounter between Pamela and
Musidorus, this scene begins when Philoclea composes a song that Pyrocles then answers and supplants with his own poetic *blason,* including the
lines "What tongue can her perfections tell / In whose each part all pens
may dwell?" If here Pyrocles compares his sexual mastery to that of an author whose "pen" masters a quiescent text, it is significant that after this
point, Philoclea never composes verse again.[37]

Philoclea's inability to recognize Pyrocles's artifice accords with the idea
that a woman can only be virtuous if the sexual desire she experiences has
been imposed upon her, rather than originated from within her. Philoclea
herself describes how her new feelings seem to contradict this notion of
virginal innocence when she prays, "if I have willingly made myself a prey
to fancy, or if by any idle lusts I framed my heart fit for such an impression, then let this plague daily increase in me till my name be made odious to womankind. But if extreme and unresistible violence have
oppressed me, who will ever do any of you sacrifice, O ye stars, if you do
not succour me?" (97–98). Here she reasons that if her "will" or "lust" has
caused her to experience this love, she must then be an example of female
sexual vice; instead, she hopes she has been seized by an "unresistible" ravishing "violence" to which she has "consented after." The narrator then
reaffirms Philoclea's hopeful scenario, describing how, confronting love in
her ignorance, she was "surprised before she was aware that any matter laid
hold of her" (98). If this scenario allows her to remain virtuous, it also
makes it difficult to imagine her as an artist, rather than as a work of art:
for if we return to the story of Galatea, we can see that it is only in this
second role that a virginal woman can be transformed into a desiring sub-

ject. In his *Metamorphoses,* Ovid describes the sculptor's lifeless statue as "That of a virgin, truly, almost living, / And willing, save that modesty prevented, / To take on movement" until its creator, through the strength of his love and the assistance of Venus, makes her come to life.[38]

Sidney seems to attempt to resolve the problem of Philoclea's desire in his *New Arcadia,* when he depicts in more detail how she fell in love with her Amazon friend—who in this version is named Zelmane. This description explains how Philoclea could move from the role of audience to that of creator. Because she admires Zelmane, she seeks to copy her; yet in copying her, she unwittingly begins to imitate the gestures of love her admirer offers to her:

> [S]o that as Zelmane did often eye her, she would often eye Zelmane; and as Zelmane's eyes would deliver a submissive but vehement desire in their look, she, though as yet she had not the desire in her, yet should her eyes answer in like piercing kindness of a look. . . . If Zelmane took her hand and softly strained it, she also, thinking the knots of friendship ought to be mutual, would with a sweet fastness show she was loth to part from it. And if Zelmane sighed, she should sigh also. . . . Zelmane's languishing countenance, with crossed arms and sometimes cast up eyes, she thought to have an excellent grace, and therefore she also willingly put on the same countenance, till at the last, poor soul, ere she were aware, she accepted not only the badge but the service, not only the sign but the passion signified. (239)

At first, Philoclea's gestures are not connected to an emotional state: she can "deliver a submissive but vehement desire in [a] look" even though she "ha[s] not the desire in her." She therefore experiences a disjunction between the significations of her visible body and her "inward" desires. In the process of imitating her cross-dressed lover, Philoclea gradually melds the "sign" with the "passion signified." Through imitating a man who is, in turn, imitating her, she unites her will to her beauty by desiring a projected image of that beauty in the feminine disguise of her lover. In a sense, this process remains a version of the transformation of an innocent virgin into a sexual woman through the power of male desire. Yet Sidney complicates this reading by making Pyrocles take the name "Zelmane" rather than "Cleophila" for his new Amazon identity. Pyrocles does so in order to pay homage to a young woman who, out of love for him, had cross-dressed as a boy to be near him. In this long regression of mirror relationships, the *New Arcadia* ultimately locates the origin of Philoclea's desire in a female, rather than a male, character.

We may notice, however, that much as Sidney seems interested in representing female desire as a creative force, Philoclea's mode of self-expression here does not adhere to the chimerical model of authorship he develops in the *Apology* and explores in the *Old Arcadia*'s rape scene, but instead recalls the more rigid idea that the text could "figure forth" a virtue that might then be adopted wholesale by its audience. For although Philoclea confronts Zelmane's beauty as something alien to her, this does not lead her to recognize it as a work of artifice that actually mirrors back to her the potential artificiality of her own body's significations. Instead, she misunderstands the emotion that lies behind the Amazon's gestures, taking them to be expressions of friendship when they are actually manifestations of erotic desire. Her own adoption of these gestures, therefore, allows them to control her, matching her inward "passions" to the outward "signs" of her body in a correspondence that—as we saw when Pamela attempted to represent her "wound" on the bark of the tree—participates in the epistemology of ravishment that drives towards the resolution of appearance and essence. Similarly, Pyrocles's technique of cross-dressing is only a more insidious (and successful) means of venturing inside the body of his beloved than that attempted by Musidorus. In addition, if Sidney also cross-dresses Cleophila/Zelmane for the audience by referring to this character as "she," then to the extent that his (purportedly female) readers buy into this illusion, they, too, seem to be subject to a "ravishment" that does not afford them the distance to judge.

At a key moment in the *Apology,* Sidney describes the role of the author in exactly these coercive terms. Just as God created the natural world through his Word, so, Sidney argues, the "skill of each artificer stands in that Idea or fore-conceit of the work, and not in the work itself, and [the fact] that the poet has that Idea is manifest by delivering them forth in such excellency as he had imagined them." This belief that the work can "manifest" the author's intentions while simultaneously pointing back to him as origin is also an attempt to limit the power of the reader. Far from being free to explore various moral perspectives through the mechanism of their imaginations, readers must interpret the characters' relation to the author's "foreconceit" in the same way as they interpret their own relationship to God, and "learn aright why and how that maker made" them. Rather than occupying the persona of the chivalrous lover, who allows his beloved a space for the exploration of her desire, here Sidney as author instead envisions himself as a force that can control and limit the potential meanings of his text, whose inferior materiality is allied with a feminized nature. For Sidney describes the poet's godlike power over his text as the conquest of a nature whose "uttermost cunning" cannot give birth to individuals as virtuous as those we find in poetic works. With its pun on the slang for female genitals, this description suggests that here we are to take the natural as a realm of sinful materiality that must be controlled or transcended, recalling Musidorus's misogynist association of women with corrupting sensation and men with virtuous reason. More startlingly, by allying the poet's power with that of God, Sidney holds out the possibility that the poet may evade the regime of fallen sexuality and subjectivity—a possibility Sidney describes by evoking Augustine's depiction of Adam's punishment:

> [God,] having made man to His own likeness, set him beyond and over all the works of that second nature, which in nothing he shows so much as in poetry, when with the force of a divine breath he brings things forth far surpassing her doings (with no small argument to the incredulous of that first accursed fall of Adam, since our erected wit makes us know what perfection is and yet our infected will keeps us from reaching unto it). (10)

Here we jarringly return to the moment when Musidorus leans over the sleeping Pamela to attempt to read her breath as testimony emanating from the "well closed paradise" that houses her will. As we saw, in that scene such spiritualized breath represented a fantasy that within the female body there could exist an absolute reconciliation of the will with a material beauty associated with carnal desire. In that scene, Sidney dramatized that such an Edenic sexuality must always remain unattainable in this world of perpetual "uncertainty." In the *Apology,* however, the breath is associated with the power of God himself, that blows through the poet's own body, uniting his authorial intentions to those of the deity. Sidney therefore holds out the possibility that the poet can achieve an Edenic state that collapses the distance between will and representation, and possess an "erected" wit that mimics Adam's prelapsarian ability to control the functioning of his genitalia free from the "infection" of a fallen carnal desire.

The *New Arcadia* breaks off in mid-sentence. Due perhaps to Sidney's untimely death, the unfinished nature of the work may also signal his failure to resolve these two versions of authorship, and their opposed perspectives upon the potential virtue of a poetic "beauty" tied to notions of the feminine. Indeed, if Fulke Greville's account is correct, on his deathbed Sidney himself announced this failure, expressing the opinion that "Even beauty itself, in all earthly complexions, was more apt to allure men to evil, than to fashion any goodness in them" and asking that his *Arcadia* be burnt.[39] As Sidney's last poetic enterprise, the *New Arcadia* seems to register a growing suspicion of the literary medium by using versions of symbolic characterization and action to "figure forth" a moral universe divided between virtue and vice. The danger of ravishment previously posed by Sidney's heroes is displaced onto another set of male characters who abduct the heroines (including Zelmane), imprison them in a castle, and threaten them with sexual violence. The abduction occurs just at the moment when the princesses seem about to exchange vows of love with their

suitors; thus from within a fortress metaphorically representing the boundaries of their bodies and psyches, rather than in physical encounters with
their lovers, the princesses confront the ambiguous terrain of "consent
after." There, they defend their virtue against not only rapacious men, but
Cecropia, a figure of female sexual vice who voices the opinion that there
is no such thing as rape since no woman is really "chaste" or without desire: "'No' is no negative in a woman's mouth . . . [Theseus ravished An-
tiope], but having ravished her, he got a child of her. And I say no more,
but that, they say, it was not gotten without consent of both parties. . . .
For what can be more agreeable than upon force to lay the fault of desire,
and in one instant to join a dear delight with a just excuse?" (533). Although these changes in the plot seem to clarify the text's moral alternatives, the romance abruptly ends just as it appears that Musidorus will
storm the castle while the cross-dressed Pyrocles combats the princesses'
enemies from within. The heroes' attempts to penetrate the female subject—Pyrocles from within, Musidorus from outside—dramatized in the
Old Arcadia, take place in the new version on an allegorical rather than literal level. On this level, however, the plot disturbingly replicates the process
depicted in Cleophila's first poem, which described how Pyrocles's
fortressed subjectivity was ravished by both an "outward force and [an] inward treason"—where a seemingly "unresistible violence" from without
was met by a preexisting desire from within. Sidney—like Augustine before him—was paradoxically forced to confront the portrayal of an Edenic
heterosexual love beyond ravishment that reconciled the divisions between
sense and reason, pleasure and will. He had to envision a woman who
could originate and express her own desire for a man while still remaining "virtuous," and a man who could love a woman without violating or
possessing her. This paradox exists at the heart of Sidney's literary enterprise, which he tries to resolve in his Apology: while morality is tied to a
set of standards that are naturalized as given, the creative impulse that
would teach this morality must move beyond the given to contemplate alternative, and therefore inherently disruptive, possibilities. To the degree
that Sidney fails to achieve such creative "freedom" from the constraints of
a "virtue" that underwrites women's subjection, his text can never sustain
the illusory presence of a "feminine" voice.

    I have attempted here to trace how representations of the feminine
were linked to a developing Early Modern concept of the fictional. In investigating this metaphorical relationship, I have not intended to confine
issues of gender to an abstract realm our society typically associates with
the textual. Instead, I have tried to follow Sidney's Old Arcadia and Apology
for Poetry in using metaphor's status between the real and the unreal, tangible and intangible, to insist upon the imbrication of textual poetics and

sexual politics. This has, I hope, allowed for a "denaturing" of the models of desire that inform these politics. For I have attempted to resist what I see as essentializing tendencies in the work of critics such as Mark Breitenberg, who describes how, in the Early Modern period, masculine desire "appears as the supreme example of self-assertive will *and* . . . the agent of a complete loss of self control . . . the desire to possess leads to a state of being possessed by one's desire." Breitenberg concludes that "Men project [this] conflict onto women or onto their relations with women."[40] Although Breitenberg emphasizes this version of desire as historically and culturally specific, he nonetheless seems to assume that an "anxious" masculine psychology preexists and conditions not only literary representations of desire, but also larger cultural constructions of feminine subjectivity. Rather, in keeping with Sidney's *Arcadia*, I would like to suggest that the idea that a paradoxical masculine desire originates in men and is then "projected" onto women as objects is itself a version of the poetics of ravishment Sidney seeks to avoid; when instead he makes his mutually "ravished" characters attempt to emulate each other, his romance reveals the interdependence of Early Modern gendered identities within a system where one sex "possessed" and trafficked in the other. Sidney's narrative holds out the hope that this realization can allow individuals to explore other possible visions of "nature"; at the same time, however, it also points to how the interpenetration of modes of representation and gendered subjectivity conditioned Sidney's vision of the nature of not only literary, but human, possibility.

Notes

1. Sir Philip Sidney, *The Countess of Pembroke's Arcadia (The Old Arcadia)*, ed. Katherine Duncan-Jones (Oxford: Oxford University Press, 1985), pp. 200–201. All further references are from this edition, and are noted in the text. The original version of the *Arcadia*, known as the *Old Arcadia*, was written sometime between 1577 and 1580; a second, substantially reworked version, known as the *New Arcadia*, was probably written around 1584 and was never finished; W[illiam] A. R[ingler], "Sir Philip Sidney," *The New Cambridge Bibliography of English Literature*, ed. George Watson, vol. 1 (Cambridge: Cambridge University Press, 1974), pp. 355–56. Sidney's sister Mary, the Countess of Pembroke, published the *New Arcadia* posthumously in 1590, appending the ending from the *Old Arcadia* onto the later unfinished version; the *Old Arcadia* itself was circulated in manuscript but was not published, and was only rediscovered by scholars in 1907.

2. Sidney's image of the psyche is derived from Thomas Aquinas's notion of "rapture" or *raptus*. In Aquinas's *Summa Theologiae*, he distinguished between the "higher appetite"—which included the faculties of intention

and reason—and the "lower appetite," which included the senses. According to Aquinas, spiritual rapture came about when God lifted up the higher appetite of the individual in a spiritual embrace, leaving him numb to all physical sensation. Yet, Aquinas also described a second kind of "rapture," which occurred when "the higher appetite is left behind and a man is wholly carried away by what relates to his lower appetite," a state of affairs that could happen when an individual experienced a "passion . . . so intense that it makes away with all use of reason, as happens in those who are mad because of the intensity of their wrath or of their love"; *Summa Theologiae*, vol. 45, trans. Roland Potter (New York: McGraw Hill, 1964), p. 101. Aquinas's theory was an Aristotelian reworking of the Augustinian division between the will and carnal desire, which I discuss below.

3. George Puttenham, *The Arte of English Poesie* (London, 1589; rpt. Kent, OH: Kent State University Press, 1970), p. 207.

4. Thomas Wilson, *The Arte of Rhetorique* (London, 1553), "Epistle," p. 2; "Preface," p. 2.

5. Stephen Gosson, *The Schoole of Abuse* (London, 1579), Sig. B7r.

6. The transition from one definition to another was hardly straightforward; throughout the seventeenth century, we still find "rape" and "ravishment" used to refer to abductions both colloquially and in some law texts. Also, as John Marshall Carter's study of medieval England makes clear, abduction was never a central part of "ravishment," since in this earlier period the vast majority of cases of "rape" and "ravishment" were prosecuted as sexual crimes; only a few cases involving upper-class women made use of the notion of abduction. See John Marshall Carter, *Rape in Medieval England: An Historical and Sociological Study* (Lanham: University Press of America, 1985).

7. Nazife Bashar, "Rape in England Between 1550 and 1700," *The Sexual Dynamics of History: Men's Power, Women's Resistance,* ed. the London Feminist History Group (London: Pluto Press, 1983), p. 41.

8. Clearly the Reformation's valorization of married chastity over perpetual virginity was a significant historical development. However, in Christian theology the distinction between chastity and virginity involved more than questions of a woman's sexual experience, and both virtues continued to be important to the Early Modern imaginary.

9. *The Statutes at large,* vol. I (London, 1618) 13.Ed.1.cap.34.

10. J. B. Post, "Ravishment of women and the Statutes of Westminster," *Legal Records and the Historian,* ed. J. H. Baker (London: Royal Historical Society, 1978), p. 158. For other interpretations of Westminster II, see Christopher Cannon's essay in this volume, "Chaucer and Rape: Uncertainty's Certainties," and Henry Ansgar Kelly, "Statutes of Rapes and Alleged Ravishers of Wives: A Context for the Charges Against Thomas Malory, Knight," *Viator: Medieval and Renaissance Studies* 28 (1997): 361–418, esp. 366.

11. See statutes 31.H.6.Cap.9 [date: 1452]; 3.H.7.Cap.2 [date: 1487]; 4&5.Philip and Mary.Cap.8 [date: 1557]; 39.Eliz.Cap.9 [date: 1597]. These

statutes contradicted the view of marriage held in ecclesiastical law, which privileged women's individual rights of consent. Although the Reformation saw vast changes in understandings of marriage and other matters for ecclesiastical law, in England there was no accompanying reform of the Church court rules or system. Thus, as James Brundage notes, "Marriage and sexual behavior remained subject primarily to ecclesiastical courts whose rules and procedures differed only marginally from those of medieval Catholicism"; *Law, Sex, and Christian Society in Medieval Europe* (Chicago: University of Chicago Press, 1987), p. 572. The medieval contrast Elizabeth Robertson describes (in this volume) between ecclesiastical and common law notions of marital consent therefore also seems to hold for the Early Modern period. For more on Early Modern ecclesiastical law, see Henry Swinburne's *A Treatise of Spousals, or Matrimonial Contracts* (London, 1686). Written in the later sixteenth century, this was an attempt to assimilate both old and new ecclesiastical law for contemporary church courts; see also Martin Ingram, *Church Courts, Sex and Marriage in England, 1570–1640* (Cambridge: Cambridge University Press, 1987).

12. Thus Early Modern rape cases used the Westminster phrasing of "ravishment" against a woman's "will" or "consent." For example, in a 1677 case in Northumberland, Barbary Elder described how her assailant "did hould her handes down by her side & did pull up her cloathes and did ravish her much against her will"; PRO ASSI 45 12/1/20A. As late as 1962, the author of a guide to forensic medicine warned that "a girl out of her first decade is seldom capable of being raped against her will"; K. Simpson, *A Doctor's Guide to Court* (London: Butterworths, 1962), p. 125; cited in Zsuzsanna Adler, *Rape on Trial* (New York: Routledge, 1987), p. 24.

13. Juan Vives, *A Verie Fruitfull and Pleasant Booke, Called the Instruction of a Christian Woman*, trans. Richard Hyrde (London, 1585), pp. 58, 44.

14. Puttenham, *The Arte of English Poesie*, p. 66.

15. Richard Dod and John Cleaver, *A Godly Form of Household Government* (London: 1598); cited in Valerie R. Lucas, "Puritan Preaching and the Politics of the Family," *The Renaissance Englishwoman in Print: Counterbalancing the Canon*, eds. Anne M. Haselkorn and Betty S. Travitsky (Amherst: University of Massachusetts Press, 1990), p. 233.

16. Both Audrey Eccles and Thomas Laqueur argue for the predominance of this view in Early Modern England. While I agree that this theory of conception was influential and clearly informed the written law, the evidence might suggest that it was not as universally accepted as these writers assert. Laqueur develops his theory based mainly on medical and philosophical treatises; though he speculates that "there must have been much local wisdom and a florid oral tradition among women in Early Modern Europe" he concludes that this is something "which printed sources, no matter how popular, can never recapture. They are forever lost to historians." This absence of evidence allows him to argue elsewhere that while "counterevidence must have been readily at hand that women frequently conceived

without [orgasm]. . . . Experience . . . is reported and remembered so as to be congruent with dominant paradigms" (namely, the "one sex" model); Thomas Laqueur, *Making Sex: Body and Gender from the Greeks to Freud* (Cambridge, MA: Harvard University Press, 1990), pp. 69, 99. However, legal records of bastardy and infanticide cases include many instances where accused women claimed they had been raped. I have found several examples of such rape-claims in seventeenth-century pretrial testimony in the counties of Somerset and Essex; while these are too numerous to list here, some others are described in Paul Hair, *Before the Bawdy Court: Selections from the Church Court and Other Records Relating to the Correction of Moral Offenses in England, Scotland and New England, 1300–1800* (London: Elek, 1972); Miranda Chaytor, "Husband(ry): Narratives of Rape in the Seventeenth Century," *Gender and History* 7.3 (November 1995): 378–407; G. R. Quaife, *Wanton Wenches and Wayward Wives: Peasants and Illicit Sex in Early Seventeenth Century England* (London: Croom Helm, 1979). Furthermore, although Audrey Eccles asserts that by the Early Modern period, "it was generally agreed [in gynecological literature] that women had seed, which they must emit in orgasm for conception," some early medical sources present strong claims for a different model of sexuality. One of the most popular textbooks on childbirth in the period, Thomas Raynalde's *The Birth of Mankind* (1545), presented the two-seed theory, yet at another point described female "seed" as serving "no other purpose but only to excite, move, and stir the woman to pleasure" and denied its role in conception; Audrey Eccles, *Obstetrics and Gynaecology in Tudor and Stuart England* (Kent, OH: Kent State University Press, 1982), p. 29; Reynalde cited in Joan Larsen Klein, ed. *Daughters, Wives, and Widows: Writings by Men about Women and Marriage in England, 1500–1640* (Urbana: University of Illinois Press, 1992), pp. 186–87. For some recent discussions of the physiology of female pleasure, see Valerie Traub, "The Psychomorphology of the Clitoris," *GLQ* 2 (1995): 81–113; and Katharine Park, "The Rediscovery of the Clitoris," *The Body in Parts: Fantasies of Corporeality in Early Modern Europe,* ed. David Hillman and Carla Mazzio (New York: Routledge, 1997), pp. 171–94. For an excellent analysis of medieval gynecology, see Joan Cadden, *Meanings of Sexual Difference in the Middle Ages: Medicine, Science, and Culture* (Cambridge: Cambridge University Press, 1993).

17. Henry Finch, *Law, or, A Discourse Thereof* (London, 1627), p. 204. For other legal writers who propounded this view, see, for example, Guilliaulme Staundforde [John Stanford or Staunford], *Les Plees del Coron* (London, 1574), pp. 43–44; William Lambard, *Eirenarcha, or the Office of the Justices of Peace* (London, 1614), p. 324; Michael Dalton, *The Countrey Justice, Containing the Practice of the Justices of the Peace out of their Sessions* (London, 1630), p. 281; Matthew Hale, *Historia Placitorum Coronae. The History of the Pleas of the Crown,* ed. Solomon Emlyn, vol. 1 (London, 1736), p. 628.

18. Barbara W. Baines, "Effacing Rape in Early Modern Representation," *ELH* 65 (1998): 80.

19. This phrase is from Michael Dalton's *The Countrey Justice* (1630). The full passage reads: "If a woman at the time of the supposed rape doe conceive with childe by the ravisher, this is no rape, for a woman cannot conceive with childe, except she doe consent. *And yet* if a man ravish a woman, who consenteth for feare of death or dures[s], this is ravishment against her will, for that consent ought to be voluntary and free" (p. 631; emph. added). Here, Dalton repeats the idea that if a woman experiences pleasure in a sexual attack, this is understood as a form of "consent" that can disprove an accusation of rape. With his "and yet," however, he also offers an instance that contradicts this rule: if a woman becomes pregnant after she "consents" under threat to an act of copulation, such "consent" is not "voluntary and free." In other words, what distinguishes this type of rape is the existence of an initial agreement between rapist and victim to engage in copulation. Dalton argues that because the woman's entrance into this contract was compulsory rather than voluntary, it is not binding. He therefore distinguishes between two levels of consent in the individual woman—the physical or pleasurable, and the contractual or intentional.

20. *City of God,* I:16. The Latin version employed here is from Augustine, *The City of God Against the Pagans,* trans. Philip Levine (London: Loeb Classical Library and Harvard University Press, 1966). My translations are loosely based on Levine and *City of God,* ed. David Knowles, trans. Henry Bettenson (New York: Penguin Books, 1977). Further citations will be noted in the text by book and chapter numbers only.

21. Similar language first appears in the medieval "Year Books" of 1469 and 1505, which described "rape" as "feloniously seizing and then and there carnally knowing [a woman] against her will." Sir Anthony Fitzherbert's *New Boke of Justices of the Peas* suggests, however, that a decisive change in usage occurred during the middle of the sixteenth century. The first 1538 edition lumped together several statutes under the category "Statutes ageinst Ravishers of wimen," including Henry VII's 1487 abduction statute, which did not use the term "ravishment"; in contrast, the first revised edition of the work, from 1554, distinguished the crime of "rape," "which is to ravishe a woman agaynst her wyl," from the category "Takers of women agaynst their wyll." After this, the crimes of forced coitus and abduction tended to be treated separately, and the definition of "rape" was increasingly refined away from the ambiguous language of Westminster II. The 1607 legal dictionary Cowell's *Interpreter* explained that rape was "ravishment of the body of a woman against her will: which is carnall knowledge had of a woman, who never consented thereunto before the fact, nor after." Twenty years later, Henry Finch's legal compendium defined rape only as "the carnall abusing of a woman against her will," and the 1630 edition of Michael Dalton's *The Countrey Justice* similarly described the crime as "a Carnall knowledge had of the body of a woman, against her will," while also including Westminster II's definition of "ravishment." Towards the end of the century, Matthew

Hale would use Dalton's phrasing exclusively in his influential definition of the crime. *Year Book,* Trin. 9 Edward IV, p. 35, fol. 26; *Year Book* 20 Henry VII, p. 17, fol. 7; Sir Anthony Fitzherbert, *The New Boke of Justices of the Peas* (London, 1538), pp. lxxxvi^r-lxxxvi^v; John Cowell, *The Interpreter* (Cambridge, 1607); Finch, pp. 204–5; Dalton, p. 281; Hale, p. 628.

22. Augustine's view of gendered corporeality is actually characterized by a feminine distinction between the will and the body (*corpus*) and a masculine distinction between the will and the flesh (*carnis*), a term that differs from the concept of "body" in some crucial ways. In this essay, however, I have not been able to highlight this difference, which takes us into some complex theological terrain not directly relevant to the topic of rape.

23. James Grantham Turner, *One Flesh: Paradisal Marriage and Sexual Relations in the Age of Milton* (Oxford: Clarendon, 1987), p. 45. Turner points out that "The moment [in the *City of God*] when the first couple's 'eyes were opened' corresponds to the moment in the *Confessions* when Augustine's father notices in the baths that his son is 'pubescentem'; the pagan-humanist father rejoices, in anticipation of grandchildren, at the physical signs of his son's sexual 'intoxication'—though the Christian mother is filled with grief" (44; refers to *Confessions* II.iii.6). He also notes that we can trace the special meaning of the "flesh" for Augustine "via S. Paul to Hebrew semantics, where *basar,* 'flesh', can mean both the whole human being and the erect penis" (43).

24. See his description of prelapsarian intercourse in the *City of God* XIV:26. Although there he described Eve's womb as capable of voluntary motion during childbirth, he did not indicate any physical motion on the part of the woman during copulation itself.

25. Nazife Bashar's study of Home Circuit cases from 1550 to 1700 indicates that as a new Augustinian definition of rape took hold over the course of the seventeenth century, the number of successful rape convictions decreased from 25 percent in the later half of the sixteenth century to 12.5 percent from 1650–1700 (throughout the entire period, the conviction rate was very low: of 274 rape cases, only 45 men were found guilty, and only 31 received the requisite death sentence; thus rape constituted less than 1 percent of all felony indictments; see pp. 32–33). In the only statistical study for an earlier period, John Carter's evidence suggests that in the thirteenth century, the rate was comparable to that of the sixteenth century, with the accused man being found guilty in 21 percent of the cases that were prosecuted. Carter's study also describes a very different definition of rape from the one we find in any of the printed legal authorities of the period. According to Eyre court records, in this period "ravishment" could involve breach of promise as well as cases of forced coitus, and those convicted were fined rather than put to death as legal authorities stipulated. J. M. Beattie's statistics for the period 1660 through 1800 indicate that in the county of Surrey, the conviction rate for rape was also lower than that of the sixteenth century, or 14.7 percent, and was the lowest for

any felony crime; J. M. Beattie, *Crime and the Courts in England 1660–1800* (Princeton: Princeton University Press, 1986), p. 411.

Bashar further shows that the few convictions that the courts imposed were on men accused of raping women assumed to be virgins. Bashar explains this phenomenon by arguing that "Rape of a virgin . . . was regarded as the theft of her virginity, the property of her father to be used in procuring an advantageous marriage. Only the rapes that had in them some element of property, in the form of virginity, ended in the conviction of the accused" (pp. 40–41). I would, however, argue that while the Augustinian notion of "chastity" precluded the possibility of proving rape, when rape was instead envisioned as the violation of an ideal virginity, the courts did admit the importance of physical evidence. Early Modern law saw the destruction of the hymen as a potential representation of the destruction of a woman's sexual innocence. The more violent this act was shown to be, the more it suggested the woman's original sexual virtue. The persistent emphasis upon signs of extreme physical struggle that pervades Medieval and Early Modern legal cases and treatises therefore seems to be tied to the belief propounded by early Christian theologians such as Jerome and Ambrose that a virgin could even defy the injunction against suicide in order to resist the threat of rape, since once virginity was lost the status of sexual and spiritual purity it offered could never be regained. The law seems to have modified this concept to insist instead that cases of rape could only be proven if the woman could show evidence that she had fought against her attacker with a vehemence that risked her own death. Since the loss of virginity was also a loss of material and social worth, crimes of violent defloration were prosecuted as versions of the theft of property. For example, one of the earliest compendia of English common law—the thirteenth-century *On the Laws and Customs of England* ascribed to Henry de Bracton—defined all acts of "*raptus*" in terms of defloration. Although Bracton applied his definition of sexual violence to all women, it appeared under the heading "the rape of virgins" [*de raptu virginam*], and stipulated that a raped woman "show the injury done her to men of good repute, the blood and her clothing stained with blood, and her torn garments." This emphasis on evidence of tearing and bloodstains strongly evokes the image of the destroyed hymen, and Bracton's definition emphasized that "virginity and chastity cannot be restored," and that men convicted of *raptus* should therefore be punished in accordance with the level of the woman's sexual virtue, which he implicitly described as a form of property that could be damaged; Bracton, *On the Laws and Customs of England,* ed. and trans, Samuel E. Thorne (Cambridge: the Selden Society [by] Harvard University Press, 1968), p. 415.

If Early Modern rape law were based upon both the contrasting ideals of virginity and chastity, which corresponded to different notions of the importance of physical evidence, this also seems to shed light on the legal treatment of sexual violence in the contemporary United States. For Susan

Estrich describes a remarkably similar relationship between what are now called "forcible" and "simple" rapes in her book on contemporary American rape law, *Real Rape* (Cambridge, MA: Harvard University Press, 1987). For standards of evidence in Early Modern law manuals, see, for example, E. W., *Statuta Pacis: Or A Perfect Table of all the Statutes (now in force) which any way concerne the Office of a Justice of Peace* (London, 1644) p. 189; *A Manuall or Analecta Formerly called the Compleat Justice* (London, 1656), p. 229; I. L. and T. E., *The Lawes Resolutions of Women's Rights, The English Experience* no. 922 (1632; Norwood, NJ: W. J. Johnson, 1979), pp. 392–93; Dalton, p. 281.

26. San Marino, California, Henry E. Huntington Library MS EL 7400, p. 1. Leah Sinanoglou Marcus discusses the Evans case in "The Milieu of Milton's *Comus*: Judicial Reform at Ludlow and the Problem of Sexual Assault," *Criticism* 25.4 (Fall 1993): 293–327; and "Justice for Margery Evans: A "Local" Reading of *Comus*," *Milton and the Idea of Woman*, ed. Julia M. Walker (Urbana: University of Illinois Press, 1988). The letter appears among the papers of Thomas Egerton, the Earl of Bridgewater, which are now housed at the Huntington Library.

27. Philip Sidney, *Defense of Poesy*, ed. Lewis Soens, Regent's Critics Series (Lincoln: University of Nebraska Press, 1970), p. 12. All further citations will be noted in the text. Sidney's *An Apologie for Poetrie* was written about 1581 and circulated widely in manuscript before being published posthumously in 1595 as the *Defense of Poesy*.

28. Most recent critics have argued that the trial presents the limitations of a law based in idealized and universalizing views of human nature that is cut off from the reality of individual circumstances and human fallibility. See, for example, Margaret E. Dana, "The Providential Plot of the *Old Arcadia*," *Studies in English Literature, 1500–1900* 17 (1977): 39–57; Robert E. Stillman, *Sidney's Poetic Justice: The Old Arcadia, Its Eclogues, and Renaissance Pastoral Traditions* (Lewisburg, PA: Bucknell University Press, 1986), pp. 222–28; Mary Ann Bushman, "Rhetoric in the Courtroom: Sidney's *Arcadia*," *Ball State University Forum* 28.1 (1987): 28; Elizabeth Dipple, "'Unjust Justice' in the *Old Arcadia*," *Studies in English Literature 1500–1900* 10.1 (1970): 101; Stephen J. Greenblatt, "Sidney's *Arcadia* and the Mixed Mode," *Studies in Philology* 70.3 (1973): 274. Ann W. Astell, however, argues that the reader must ultimately assume the judging position of Euarchus in condemning the follies of the other characters—follies that mirror those of the reader him or herself, "Sidney's Didactic Method in the *Old Arcadia*," *Studies in English Literature 1500–1900* 24.1 (1984): 50–51. For a feminist reading of this scene, see Margaret Sullivan's "Amazons and Aristocrats: The Function of Pyrocles's Amazon Role in Sidney's Revised *Arcadia*," *Playing with Gender: A Renaissance Pursuit*, ed. Jean R. Brink et al. (Urbana: University of Illinois Press, 1991). Sullivan focuses on Pamela's ambiguous status as future ruler of Arcadia and argues that because Pamela "is positioned not only above the laws that Euarchus invokes . . . but also outside the restricted feminine code to which [he subjects the other women]" (p. 66),

her role in the trial begins to expose contradictions in the patriarchal positioning of women as "property" that Sidney does not fully address until the *New Arcadia*. Although I accept Sullivan's assessment of the trial as a dramatization of women's powerlessness within a patriarchal legal system, I see Pamela less as occupying a special role than as representing the position of the female heir described in the abduction statutes. For more on Pamela as potential ruler, also see Sullivan's "Getting Pamela out of the House: Gendering Genealogy in the *New Arcadia*," *Sidney Newsletter* 9.2 (1988–89): 3–18.

29. Anne Sussman similarly points out that in this scene, "poetic ravishment is . . . both an antecedent and an incitement to physical ravishment." I disagree with her claim that Sidney celebrates this ravishing poetics both here and in his *Apology*, and her conclusion that the *Old Arcadia* creates a model of sexual violence, linked to the beauty of verse, that is "supposed to be fun"; "'Sweetly Ravished': Sidney's *Old Arcadia* and the Poetics of Sexual Violence," *Renaissance Papers*, ed. Barbara Baines and George Williams (Raleigh, NC: Southeastern Renaissance Conference, 1995), p. 65.

30. My reading resembles Stephen Greenblatt's in that he argues that the *Arcadia* presents its readers with multiple literary "modes" (i.e., the text's various literary styles and genres) in order to place its audience in a position of judgement regarding the moral systems represented by those modes.

31. As Turner suggests, Sidney's theory of the imagination actually owes much to Augustine's emphasis upon the combined powers of emotion, divine grace, and imagination, which could break down the rigid distinction between the "rational" and the "sensual." See *One Flesh*, pp. 31–32, 35, 39. For a discussion of how Sidney's more secular appropriation of the imaginative identification with the divine contradicted contemporary Protestant thought, see Peter C. Herman, *Squitter-wits and Muse-haters: Sidney, Spenser, Milton and Renaissance Antipoetic Sentiment* (Detroit, MI: Wayne State University Press, 1996), pp. 67–70.

32. Mark Rose, *Heroic Love: Studies in Sidney and Spenser* (Cambridge, MA: Harvard University Press, 1968) p. 51; *Defense*, p. 50. Rose gives a more extensive version of this argument in his earlier article, "Sidney's Womanish Man," *Review of English Studies*, New Series 15:60 (1964): 353–63.

33. An article by Maria Teresa Micaela Prendergast called my attention to the interplay of Petrarchan and Ovidian imagery in the romance; see "Prose, Verse, and Femininity in Sidney's *Old Arcadia*," *Framing Elizabethan Fictions*, ed. Constance C. Relihan (Kent, OH: Kent State University Press, 1996). In that article, Prendergast argues that in the *Old Arcadia*, Sidney sets pieces of Petrarchan verse within a prose narrative suffused with Ovidian imagery in order to suggest we abandon the version of gendered subjectivity developed in the former poetic tradition in favor of that of the latter. She maintains too absolute a distinction between these conventions by associating them, respectively, with the romance's use of lyric verse and prose narration. Ultimately, however, Prendergast is correct that

for Sidney, prose becomes the medium most able to accommodate his new notion of the relationship between author, text, and reader. On Ovidian themes in the *New Arcadia,* see Clare Kinney, The Masks of Love: Desire and Metamorphosis in Sidney's *New Arcadia,"* *Criticism* 33.4 (1991): 461–90.

34. Jeffrey Masten, *Textual Intercourse: Collaboration, Authorship and Sexualities in Renaissance Drama* (Cambridge: Cambridge University Press, 1997), pp. 34–35 (quotations from the Florio translation of Montaigne's essay "Of Friendship" are cited in Masten). Writing from the perspective of social history, Alan Bray makes a similar argument, showing that "sodomy" was a term specifically associated with male-male sexual relations across class or age barriers and that such relations between social equals did not necessarily receive the same censure. See "Homosexuality and the Signs of Male Friendship in Elizabethan England," *Queering the Renaissance,* ed. Jonathan Goldberg (Durham, NC: Duke University Press, 1994), pp. 40–61.

35. In suggesting that her love is unrecognized by the law, Philoclea echoes actual English law, in which statutes against sodomy only prohibited male-male sexual relations. Valerie Traub has noted that sex between women was prohibited under Early Modern French law. What was specifically illicit were forms of "tribadism": either the wearing of men's clothing or the imitation of their phallic sexuality through the use of dildos. Traub opposes this prohibition to the more morally acceptable "femme-femme" love in Renaissance English literature. Thus, although she does not make this connection, her analysis suggests that what made certain same-sex relationships unacceptable was their mimicry of or basis in unequal power relations; Valerie Traub, "The (In)significance of 'Lesbian' Desire in Early Modern England," *Erotic Politics: Desire on the Renaissance Stage,* ed. Susan Zimmerman (New York: Routledge, 1992). On the representation of female homoeroticism in terms of the conventions of male friendship, see Janel Mueller, "Troping Utopia: Donne's Brief for Lesbianism," *Sexuality and Gender in Early Modern Europe: Institutions, Texts, Images,* ed. James Grantham Turner (Cambridge: Cambridge University Press, 1993): 194–95. On the "Arcadian" pastoral space as an arena where alternative, non-hierarchical relationships can be explored, see Bruce Smith, *Homosexual Desire in Shakespeare's England* (Chicago: University of Chicago Press, 1991), Chapter 3.

36. In the *New Arcadia,* this scene is immediately followed with a description of Philoclea and Pamela in bed together: "as they lay together, . . . cherishing one another with dear though chaste embracements, with sweet though cold kisses, it might seem that love was come to play him there without dart." *The Countess of Pembroke's Arcadia,* ed. Maurice Evans (New York: Penguin, 1977), p. 245. Sidney portrays this not only homoerotic but incestuous encounter as "chaste," apparently because of the absence of a penis or "dart." Yet, his use of the word "seem" signals the text's inability to decide whether female-female love can be realized on the physical plane,

something reinforced by its juxtaposition of erotic possibilities and their negation: "dear though chaste, sweet though cold." I therefore disagree with Richard Levin's argument regarding the *New Arcadia* that we are supposed to see the love between Philoclea and the cross-dressed Pyrocles as threatening the princess's moral corruption. Levin can only make this argument by ignoring the clearly more dangerous relationship between Musidorus and Pamela, which is foil for the central love plot. As I will discuss below, however, the fact that Cleophila is a cross-dressed man undercuts the image of "freedom" Sidney seems eager to promote in depicting this apparently homoerotic relationship. See Richard Levin, "What? How? Female-Female Desire in Sidney's *New Arcadia,*" *Criticism* 34.4 (1997): 463–79.

37. According to Mary Ellen Lamb, Sidney's image of many "pens" tracing this particular feminine body/text was mirrored by actual reader response, for in the seventeenth century, readers copied this poem into their miscellanies more than any other from the *New Arcadia*. For an alternative interpretation of the relationship between sexuality and textuality, as well as a reader-response analysis of Musidorus's class masquerade, see her "Exhibiting Class and Body in Sidney's *Countess of Pembroke's Arcadia,*" *Studies in English Literature 1500–1900* 37 (1997): 55–72.

38. Ovid, *Metamorphoses,* trans. Rolfe Humphries (Bloomington: Indiana University Press, 1983) Book X, l.251–54. The original Latin reads, "*Virginis est verae facies, quam vivere credas, et, si non obstet reverentia, velle moveri.*" Sidney invokes this story twice in the *Old Arcadia,* at the moments when Pyrocles adopts and then reveals his disguise (see pp. 25, 106).

39. Fulke Grevillle, *The Life of the Renowned Sir Philip Sidney,* ed. Warren W. Wooden (1652; rpt. Scholars' Facsimiles & Reprints: Delmar, 1984), p. 19.

40. Mark Breitenberg, *Anxious Masculinity in Early Modern England,* Cambridge Studies in Renaissance Literature and Culture 10 (Cambridge: Cambridge University Press, 1996), p. 99.

PART IV

READING RAPE:
THE CANONICAL ARTIST, THE FEMINIST
READER, AND MALE POETICS

CHAPTER 12

OF CHASTITY AND RAPE:
EDMUND SPENSER CONFRONTS
ELIZABETH I IN *THE FAERIE QUEENE*

Susan Frye

Confronting the biography of the poet and his poetics directly, Susan Frye establishes the interconnections between Spenser's representations of rape and his own personal anxieties as subject to Queen Elizabeth.

What tongue can her perfections tell
In whose each part all pens may dwell?

—*Philip Sidney, c. 1580*[1]

By the end of the sixteenth century, the predominant meaning of the word *chastity* was exactly as the *Oxford English Dictionary* defines it today, "purity from unlawful intercourse." "Unlawful intercourse" means sexual intercourse outside of marriage, and in the sixteenth century specifically meant a wife's intercourse with someone other than the husband who legally possessed her body. Thus, *chastity* rests on the assumption that women exist as the possessions of men. Within this definition a woman can only be virtuous when acting as male property, a position that ostensibly allows her only limited forms of choice—unless that woman is an unmarried and aging queen. As Elizabeth Robertson and Christine Rose discuss in their introduction to this volume, the degree to which women are perceived as consenting to rape "crystallizes . . . each era's particular understanding of female subjectivity."

Within each era, too, issues of women's consent to the passive definitions offered by rape may alter in the case of privileged women, and especially in the
case of Elizabeth I. Yet her desire to define herself within definitions of the
feminine that allowed her a choice of husband and finally the choice to remain single was perpetually contested by the men who surrounded her—in
many cases, by the same men, like the poet Edmund Spenser, who also
worked to create her image as a semi-divine virgin. It is not surprising, then,
that the language such men used in their attempts to contest and contain the
queen is often the discourse of rape, a discourse that groups the queen with
other women, and then articulates the limited choices all women supposedly
experienced within the legal definition of *chastity*.

While the word *chastity* retains and transmits the logic of female possession, the very existence of this logic presupposes that women will not
always have legal intercourse. As a result, the combined moral and legal expectations of female behavior expressed in *chastity* also imply enforcement—the necessity to claim and reclaim the female body as possession
through rationalization, imprisonment, threat, or rape.[2] Indeed, the meanings of both *chastity* and *rape* emanate from the same discursive structures
surrounding and seeking to define the female body. The primary meaning
of *rape*, "the act of taking anything by force" (*OED*), by the turn of the fifteenth century had been extended to mean sexually "taking" the female
body as a possession without the consent of the possessed. *Chastity* resides
in female inaction; *rape* in male action. *Chastity* and *rape* are bound together
within essentialist conceptions of gender that define the female as passive
and possessed and the male as active, possessing, and enforcing possession.

This article will demonstrate how the poet Edmund Spenser used the
language of Book 3 of *The Faerie Queene*,[3] first published in 1590, to conduct a written rape that sought to enforce the predominant meaning of
chastity as "purity from unlawful intercourse."[4] That Spenser's pen is the
instrument of the rape makes it inevitably metaphoric. At the same time,
the widespread belief that the male poet's pen could possess its subject—
"dwell" in "each part" of a woman's body, as Sidney expresses poetic penetration in the epigraph above—makes the rape of Amoret in Cantos 11
and 12 of Book 3 a general claim that men have the right to possess
women's bodies. More specifically, these cantos offer a metaphoric rape of
the queen herself that claims Elizabeth as the possession of the male poet,
however temporarily, as a response to Elizabeth's political use of the alternative meaning of chastity as "abstinence from all sexual intercourse"
(*OED*). In defining chastity as a political conception that maintained her
autonomy from the male interests surrounding her, Elizabeth and the
painters and masque writers she and her courtiers commissioned sought to
recover Roman and Christian conceptions of female virginity as magical

and sacred, while further defining the queen's chastity as active and self-possessed. Book 3 of *The Faerie Queene* attempts to enforce the meaning of chastity as male-determined and male-possessed by presenting the rape of the figure Amoret, who represents Elizabeth, in front of the cross-dressed knight, Britomart, who also represents Elizabeth, in a poem whose intended reader is Elizabeth, thus making clear that the queen herself is the center of the violence.

Elizabeth's Definition of Chastity

In order to understand the motivation and method of Spenser's poetic rape of Elizabeth, it is necessary to understand her definition of chastity and the courtly dynamics of its representation within which Spenser was working. To reign effectively as a female monarch in a patriarchal society, Elizabeth had to make clear that she alone possessed her body. This proved a tough battle in a political system whose stability was thought to depend on the monarch's production of male offspring. Although Elizabeth's success as queen and the relatively smooth succession of James I eventually proved mistaken the belief that only a male heir could maintain political stability, members of parliament and of Elizabeth's privy council spent 20 years—until the queen was well into her forties—attempting to convince her to marry some mythically suitable male. Since they spent almost as much energy trying to convince her *not* to marry every suitor who was actually available for fear of the political or religious consequences, and since Elizabeth found not marrying to be an effective political strategy both at home and abroad, her marriage—with its thorny attendant question of who would then own Elizabeth—was continually postponed.

Meanwhile, Elizabeth, together with powerful men and interest groups who sought to preserve her as unmarried for their own reasons, turned her virginity into a powerful political idea that was called *chastity* but differed radically from the meaning of chastity as "purity from unlawful intercourse." Her conception of chastity drew on Christian conceptions of a magical and powerful virginity like that of the Virgin Mary. Even as Elizabeth considered the possibility of marriage, she found that her self-representation as a royal virgin was her most effective strategy for evading the control of the many powerful male groups surrounding her.

The queen's chastity was never a fixed idea but was always evolving and unstable, and thus continually open to repossession. Soon after her accession in February 1559, she began fighting for her definition of chastity when she responded to parliament's exhortation that she marry. She declared that "in the end, this shall be for me sufficient, that a marble stone shall declare that a queen, having reigned such a time, lived and died a virgin."[5] A virgin queen could not by definition have a father, brother, or husband. Therefore, she was not in the custody of any male but remained as self-possessed and independent as any woman in the social hierarchy of sixteenth-century England could be.

Once Elizabeth was unquestionably past marriage in the 1580s, during the period that Spenser was working on Book 3 of *The Faerie Queene,* her chastity became the foundation of her contention that, though aging, she was different from all womankind—unique as the phoenix, self-sacrificing as the pelican—and always sufficient in herself to rule. Court painters in royal portraits commissioned by her as well as by the powerful men and women close to her, assigned various forms of royal chastity to her person.

The portraits in which Elizabeth holds a sieve, a series produced from 1579 to the mid-1580s that linked her to the legend of the Roman vestal virgin, Tuccia, associate the queen with the Roman empire as well as Roman conceptions of a sacred virginity. When Tuccia's chastity was questioned, she proved that her virginity remained intact by carrying water in a sieve from the Tiber to her temple. The sieve portraits feature Elizabeth as Tuccia holding the sieve that proves her virginity—presenting, in effect, her own miraculous hymen.[6] The three Armada portraits, which commemorate the defeat of the Spanish Armada in 1588, associate the queen with other Roman imperial symbols while emphasizing that her virginal chastity ensures her intermediary position between God and her subjects. In two of them (the third has been cut down in size), Elizabeth sits elaborately dressed, her head perched on an ornate lace ruff, her right hand on the globe of the world near which sits an imperial crown. Behind her, two scenes show the defeat of the Spanish ships by fire and weather. In what Louis Montrose calls "the demure iconography of her virgin-knot,"[7] the artists have represented Elizabeth's chastity in the bow and single dangling pearl—her "jewel," generally connoting the female genitalia—hanging directly over her genital area to which our eye is drawn along several lines within the composition.[8] The pearl and the two scenes of the Spanish defeat form a compositional triangle that suggests that the queen's chastity forms the connection among the Spanish defeat, the emerging English empire, and her own virginal presence. In both series, Elizabeth's chastity is self-possessed, magical, and sacred precisely because her hymen is intact and she has not been "taken."

Thus, sovereign chastity asserted the queen's intermediary position between God and her subjects as well as between nature and mortals. These portraits did not, however, succeed in silencing other points of view, nor did they form a dominant discourse. Instead, their conceptualizations of Elizabeth's chastity as both source and expression of an active, self-assertive power ran disturbingly counter to prevalent definitions of the feminine as yielding and passive.[9] The queen's conception of herself as an autonomous female body was, Maureen Quilligan points out, at odds with the social construction of the female: "The queen's virginity conflicts with the broad sweep of the Protestant redefinition of the family—and therefore of women and of sexuality itself."[10]

The queen's political definition of "chastity" as magical and self-contained openly contradicted the word's predominant definition as "purity from unlawful intercourse," because it placed the source of her power in herself rather in the male who possessed her. Elizabeth had no intention of being chaste in the usual senses of wife and mother as defined by the masculinist codes of English law.[11] But in not conforming to the norm, Elizabeth left herself vulnerable to being judged by that norm. The conviction expressed in humanist texts from Vives to Baldassare Castiglione and in derivative texts such as *The Mothers Counsell,* or *Liue within Compasse,* that "If chastity be once lost, there is nothing left praysworthy in a woman" is founded not only on a desire to ensure bloodlines but also to contain women within socially sanctioned roles. *The Mothers Counsell* makes clear that the opposite of chastity is "Wantonesse," which "maketh a woman covet beyond her power; to act beyond her nature, and to die before her time"[12]—which is to say that "wantonesse" describes any woman who seeks alternative self-definition—like ruling a country— "beyond her nature." Moreover, according to this definition, the unchaste woman courts violence and death.

Chastity was so central a term in describing the masculinist control of women's behavior that by the end of the sixteenth century the social institution of marriage may be said to have rested on it. The early modern ideology of marriage drew on the medieval tradition of companionate marriage as articulated in ecclesiastical doctrine, law, and commentary. As articulated in Erasmus's *Colloquies,*[13] companionate marriage formed not only an emergent but also a dominant discourse by the close of the sixteenth century, as Margo Todd and Valerie Wayne have convincingly argued.[14] Long before Elizabeth's iconography raised the challenge of self-possessed female virginity, the colloquy *Courtship* attempted to restructure chastity within the bounds of matrimony. In *Courtship,* a young woman, Maria, argues for her virginity and against marriage with Pamphilus, protesting: "But they say chastity is a thing most pleasing to God." Pamphilus counters by firmly incorporating chastity within the sanctified bond of matrimony: "And therefore, I want to marry a chaste girl, to live chastely with her. It will be more a marriage of minds than of bodies. We'll reproduce for the state; we'll reproduce for Christ." He goes on to assure her that such bondage as exists in marriage is like "your soul imprisoned in your body . . . like a little bird in a cage." If one "ask[s] him if he desires to be free. He'll say no, I think. Why? He's willingly confined."[15]

The apparently nonviolent humanist conception of companionate marriage entered the mainstream of English thought through the educational system, which required boys to translate *Courtship* and other marriage colloquies into English. It is not surprising to find that echoes of Erasmus are ubiquitous in Elizabethan culture and present in Spenser's sonnet sequence, the *Amoretti,* in which his speaker makes similar assurances to his imagined bride in Sonnet 65: "Sweet be the bands, the which true love doth tye, / without constraynt or dread of any ill: / the gentle birde feeles no captivity / within her cage, but sings and feeds her fill."[16] Possession—to the point of imprisonment—is implicit in this picture of the bird, as through *her* captivity the male speaker attempts to reassure his beloved that "The doubt which ye misdeeme, fayre love, is vaine, / that fondly feare to loose your liberty" (lines 1–2). In such a marriage, "simple truth and mutuall good will / seekes with sweet peace to salve each others wound. / There fayth doth fearlesse dwell in brasen towre, / and spotlesse pleasure builds her sacred bowre" (lines 11–14). Similar expressions of the perceived relation among marriage, chastity, harmony, and fertility together with imprisonment and possession abound during the period. For example, the pro-Catholic William Byrd's song on marital chastity suitable for wedding parties asserts, "Sound is the knot, that Chastity hath tied, / Sweet is the music, Unity doth make, / Sure is the store, that Plenty doth provide."[17] Like Spenser, Byrd's lines argue the blissful union of chastity and bondage that is her lot if a woman *consents.*

This was not the kind of chastity that Queen Elizabeth had in mind. Nevertheless, in spite of her and her associates' efforts to use chastity to explain and exercise a power both magical and self-possessed, the lawful meaning of chastity was frequently reasserted and then contested at the Elizabethan court, largely through allegorical court spectacles. Spenser, in rewriting Elizabeth's chastity in *The Faerie Queene,* takes as his model the ways that court spectacle used the central figure of Elizabeth to define the queen's chastity. Spectacle at the Elizabethan court included several different forms of performed entertainment; it was sometimes serious and sometimes lighthearted, and it usually involved allegorical figures representing topical ideas of importance to domestic or foreign policy acted out in a particular scene called a "device." A spectacle often featured hired actors as well as members of the court, but it always displayed the talents of its author or sponsor—or exposed them to ridicule. On numerous occasions, especially in spectacles enacting her powerful chastity, the queen played herself. Spenser would have known about these spectacles because he saw them and read them in print or in manuscripts circulated among his fellow Protestant sympathizers.

The most popular narrative of Elizabethan court spectacle, the imprisonment and rescue of a central chaste female figure, makes clear that figures representing chastity appear accompanied by threats, imprisonment,
and the possibility of rape. Because Elizabeth herself and her court had a
considerable stake in representing the queen's power as related to her
chastity, several of these rescue narratives took the form of a figure of
Chastity rescuing another figure of Chastity. (Throughout this discussion
I will use *chastity* to refer to conceptions attached to the word itself, and
the capitalized *Chastity* to refer to allegorical figures representing those
conceptions.)

In one such spectacle, the Rescue of the Lady of the Lake, performed
during the prolonged and expensive Kenilworth entertainments of 1575,
Elizabeth's conception of a magical chastity prevailed. The queen herself
played the figure of a potent, active Chastity, a cosmological force that mediated between heaven and earth, nature and humanity, similar to that
which would later appear in the Armada portraits. The spectacle is preserved in George Gascoigne's *Princely Pleasures of Kenilworth Castle,* whose
text provides us with an account of the device,[18] which features Elizabeth
driving off the forces of rape and mayhem in order to rescue the Lady of
the Lake from the villain, Sir Bruse sans Pitie. Sir Bruse is a rapist who
"sought by force . . . full fowlie to deface" the "virgins state" of the Lady
of the Lake.[19]

To some extent, the Lady threatened by the rapist resembles the young
Elizabeth, who shortly before her accession to the throne was imprisoned
in the Tower and later at Woodstock by her sister, Mary Tudor. To perceive
a close relation between the Lady of the Lake and Elizabeth is not fanci-
ful: even E. K., the unknown commentator on Spenser's *Shepheardes Calender,* whose notes were published as part of the text in 1579, saw a relation
between the queen and the figure of the Lady of the Lake because the
Lady was a marriageable figure of Elizabeth.[20] The Kenilworth device,
however, mainly focuses on the mature, active, and autonomous Elizabeth.
According to this drama, the only hope for the imprisoned virgin lies in
Merlin's prophecy that the Lady "coulde never bee delivered but by the
presence of a better maide then hir self.[21] Elizabeth graciously complies
with the request from Neptune, Triton, and the other gods, "Her to defend
and set at large,"[22] by walking across a bridge. In saving the Lady of the
Lake through "soveraigne maiden's might,"[23] Elizabeth performed the
powerful role of a self-possessed, magical Chastity independent of male
control. This was one of several gynocentric rewritings of the stock masculinist imprisonment and rescue narrative so frequently performed at
Elizabeth's court.

Elizabeth's self-possessed chastity as performed at Kenilworth, however, was not a static conception. Precisely because it carried a political charge, Chastity as an allegory and chastity as a conception were in turn redefined or used to make the political arguments of others. One prime example is the Richmond entertainment that Philip Sidney helped to compose, *The Four Foster Children of Desire.*[24] On this occasion, in order to demonstrate the futility of negotiating a marriage between Elizabeth and the duke of Anjou to an audience that included French envoys, Sidney and other members of the Protestant faction again had Elizabeth play herself as self-sufficient Chastity. In the device, the queen's virtuous figure of Chastity repelled the assault of the Four Foster Children of Desire, whose lances failed to penetrate her—a visible demonstration that Elizabeth's chastity precluded her marrying the French duke. Presumably the queen cooperated in acting this role because she wished to demonstrate to the French audience the extent of the opposition to the marriage that her personal letters to Anjou had been suggesting all along. In any case, at both Kenilworth and Richmond, Elizabeth rescued an imprisoned female who presented an allegorical version of Chastity. At Kenilworth, the rescued female was the Lady of the Lake, imprisoned and threatened with rape; at Richmond, the vulnerable figure was more openly the queen herself, imprisoned and threatened with penetration and possession in a politically unpopular marriage.[25] The major difference between the two spectacles is that the Kenilworth device illustrates how Elizabeth constructed her own chastity that claimed her power and agency, while the Richmond device demonstrates how that construction could be altered to serve the interests of a political faction—in this case, the militant Protestants with whom Spenser is also associated.

The men who wrote or paid for the entertainments, like George Gascoigne or Philip Sidney, also manipulated Elizabeth's political version of her own chastity to stage collective fantasies of the queen as imprisoned and possessed. Chastity as an idea was the intellectual property of any individual or group that found it useful. The enacted images of Elizabeth were not always for her benefit. Narratives of imprisonment, threat, rape, and rescue, whether in court spectacle or *The Faerie Queene,* demonstrated the power of Elizabeth's chastity whether she was audience or participant. But it is important to note that male authors constructed these narratives for a male audience that relished the fantasy of a threatened queen and her counterparts, however momentarily.[26] For the ambitious courtiers surrounding her, the enactment of the elements of possession and enforcement implicit in chastity provided a paradigm of control, at once temporal and physical, for enforcing an entire code of approved female behavior—passivity, silence, modesty, and consignment to a world hidden from the public eye.[27]

Spenser's Definition of Chastity
in *The Faerie Queene*

Spenser's strategy in Book 3 is to accomplish what court spectacle accomplished: using narratives of Elizabeth's self-possessed chastity to screen the reimposition of a male-possessed chastity. He had to go about this project subtly since his epic allegorical poem was his major hope of preferment from the queen. Book 3 in particular addresses Elizabeth as its reader and provides a number of female figures that represent her. Although the most obvious Elizabeth figure, the Faerie Queene, never actually appears in the poem, the speaker and other figures refer to her. Other versions of Elizabeth include Belphoebe, the unapproachable but gazed-upon Amazon; Amoret, Belphoebe's twin sister; and Britomart, the militant enforcer of chastity; as well as Mercilla, the queen of Book 5. Amoret and Britomart further resemble Elizabeth in that they enact the figures of imprisoned Chastity and rescuing Chastity familiar from court spectacle.

Spenser, like Gascoigne and Sidney before him, uses the structures of court spectacle to reclaim the definition of chastity before the combined gaze of the queen and her male courtiers. Spenser attempts this reclaiming through the manipulation of allegory—and the allegory organizing the House of Busirane, and indeed all of Book 3, is Chastity. Throughout Book 3, and particularly in its final two cantos describing the captivity and rape of Amoret, we can examine Spenser's ongoing attempt to redefine and thus confine the queen's self-possessed chastity within the male control of threat, imprisonment, and rape. If Elizabeth could not be controlled by a father or husband, a courtier, or faction, she could still be controlled by the pen—that is, by the masculinist poetics formulated through the conventions of humanism, Petrarchism, and Neoplatonism.[28]

Spenser plays against Elizabeth's definition of chastity beginning with the title of Book 3. That title, "The Third Booke of the Faerie Qveene Contayning, The Legend of Britomartis. Or of Chastitie," stands juxtaposed with the opening stanza of the proem (that is, the poetic introduction) about Elizabeth's chastity, implying at least initially that Britomart's chastity directly corresponds to the queen's and that the poem will reaffirm sovereign chastity. These first lines addressed to the queen seem to name the source of the allegory: Elizabeth is the origin of the Faery Chastity. Yet in the following lines, the speaker asks a puzzling question:

It falles me here to write of Chastity,
That fairest vertue, farre aboue the rest;
For which what needs me fetch from *Faery*
Forreine ensamples, it to haue exprest?
Sith it is shrined in my Soueraines brest,

And form'd so liuely in each perfect part,
That to all Ladies, which haue it profest,
Need but behold the pourtraict of her hart,
If pourtrayd it might be by any liuing art. (3.proem.1)

To paraphrase, the speaker is asking, Why import a Britomart or other figures of chastity from Faeryland when I have Elizabeth's sovereign chastity
before me? Why indeed? I argue that in asking, the speaker points to the
discrepancy between sovereign chastity and Faery chastity—to the gap between a militant, compelling, but unapproachable virtue and a vulnerable,
male-assaulted, and male-protected virtue.

The proem's playful identification of Faery Chastity with Elizabeth and
the speaker's failure to explain why he needs the "forreigne ensamples" of
chastity in effect provide a canceled association between the queen's
chastity and the chastity allegorized in the poem. Indeed, Britomart ac-
quires all the regal, virtuous, and court-validated qualities necessary for a
court spectacle, yet she remains Spenser's allegorical creation, subject to his
notions of female sexuality and its control implicit in the lawful definition
of chastity. It is not Spenser's project to answer his speaker's question
openly. Because Spenser works within yet also alters the meanings of Elizabeth's chastity, in the long run his text works to enforce the legal definition by presenting allegorical narratives of male possession of the female
body and of the violent enforcement of that possession.

As Book 3 progresses, it seems clear that Britomart's self-sufficient chastity
is of the regal kind. She appears in the first canto as an admirably independent figure who defeats Book 2's problem hero, Sir Guyon, and then six of
Malecasta's knights. Nevertheless, Britomart is subject to eventual male control, as figured in the male threats she receives during her search for her destined mate. The narrative simultaneously affirms Elizabeth's independence
and emphasizes her vulnerability. For example, Britomart triumphs in battle
against Malecasta's knights only to be exposed to Malecasta's attempt to share
her bed, after which Gardante gores her side.[29] Faced with these threats, Britomart does not possess—as does one court spectacle's figure of an autonomous, militant chastity—a "heart of stone / That none can wound, nor
pearce by any meane."[30] Instead, Spenser's vulnerable figure of Chastity is attacked both in Castle Ioyeous and the House of Busirane. Although the as-
saults are unsuccessful, Spenser's rhetorical threat transforms the royal
iconography of Elizabeth's chastity. Through analogous threats to other female
figures such as Florimell, whom Proteus confines within the sea, Spenser establishes Britomart's vulnerability as part of his redefinition of chastity.

In creating Britomart as the allegorical figure of Chastity, Spenser simultaneously uses and reconstructs Elizabeth's definition of chastity. To

some extent, Britomart's strengths and behavior allude to Elizabeth, but those strengths are perpetually undermined by circumstance. Even as Britomart retains the advantages of self-defense, disguise, and mobility inherent in cross-dressing as a knight, her strength is mitigated by the attacks on her person. Britomart's disguise, in fact, does not protect her from male control, since cross-dressing as a knight is to a large extent the means through which she will eventually find her future husband, Artegal.

Amoret, on the other hand, has already found her destined mate, Scudamour. Unlike Amoret's twin sister, the Amazon Belphoebe who also figures Elizabeth's Chastity, Amoret is destined for marriage. At the same time, because Belphoebe and Amoret are twins, Amoret must also figure Elizabeth. By the time that Britomart arrives in the midst of Amoret's story, a wicked poet-magician Busirane has separated Amoret and Scudamour in order to imprison and rape Amoret. When Scudamour tells Britomart that he is helpless to save his imprisoned beloved, Britomart, much like Elizabeth in the Rescue of the Lady of the Lake, takes on the task of rescuing a version of herself.

Britomart enters the House of Busirane in order to rescue Amoret from the poet-magician Busirane who has chained her and is raping her both with his words and with a knife plunged into her heart. The knife in Amoret's heart is a displaced physical rape, a violent attempt at possessing Amoret. Although it takes time for Britomart and the reader to realize what is happening in the poem, the third and final description of Busirane's attack that appears when he says his spells backward in order to undo the damage to Amoret's body, makes clear its penetrative nature: "the wyde wound" in her "Her bleeding brest, and riuen bowells gor'd, / Was closed up, as it had not bene bor'd" (3.12.38). I will shortly discuss these lines' concurrent attempt to erase the rape while providing its most physically precise description.

Like the court spectacles featuring chastity as a political conception realized through the virginity of Queen Elizabeth, the Busirane episode defines the chaste captive and the chaste rescuer by pairing them: the captive and rescuer may seem to fulfill opposite roles, but neither can exist entirely without or as the other.[31] Through the similarities between Britomart and Amoret, Spenser revises Elizabeth's royal claim to female independence by first locking up Amoret—a marriageable form of Chastity—and then sending Britomart, another Chastity in need of her mate, to stop the rape. In this way the courtly representations of the queen's independent chastity are transmuted into the two fertile, marriageable figures of Amoret and Britomart.

Threat, rape, and captivity are the interconnected strategies that Spenser uses to enforce the prevalent definition of chastity as legal and moral female behavior within the possession of the male. The House of Busirane containing Britomart and Amoret locates the male threat spatially, within the world of women imprisoned by the masculinist structures of desire. It is the kind of world that Nina Auerbach identifies as "a typical device" within the structures of romantic fiction:"the tale within the tale, collapsing into a series of increasingly claustrophobic vistas, a narrative series of dark passageways."[32] Busirane's first assault on Britomart's royal self-possession occurs within the topography of tyranny and pain she must traverse to reach Amoret.The first room is hung with tapestries illustrating Jove's adventurous metamorphoses, in which the full extent of Cupid's power turns on the orthographic pun of Iove/love/Jove. The speaking pictures illustrate that "love" so dominates the cosmos that the social hierarchy of humankind collapses beneath his power:"Kings Queens, Lords Ladies, Knights & Damzels gent / Without respect of person or of port, / To shew Dan *Cupids* powre and great effort" (3.11.46).The blood-red borders surrounding and uniting these stories of gods and men suggest the violence necessary for domination. As she moves through the house, Britomart must view artwork—tapestries, friezes, statues—that conveys pain and structures—frames, walls, the verse itself—that reinforce the message that love is bondage.

The horror deepens when the inner door of the third room flies open to reveal a processional masque, the entertainment physically confines the central female, Amoret, among the animated forms of masculinist love poetry.Two by two the courtly players step forth—Fancy and Desyre, Doubt and Daunger, Feare and Hope, Dissemblance and Suspect, Grief and Fury, Displeasure and Pleasure.These couples emerge slowly enough for the narrator to provide a lengthy description of each costume's allusive iconography. As I will explain, it is significant that the narrator quickly loses his ability to explicate the rest of the figures or the scene as a whole.Trailing behind the six couples, defined by their physical and metaphoric proximity, walks a figure portraying Amoret, the centerpiece of the masque and, as we later discover, the interior audience of its rhetoric. She holds her heart, removed and pierced, in a basin.

> Her brest all naked, as net iuory,
> Without adorne of gold or siluer bright,
> Wherewith the Craftesman wonts it beautify,
> Of her dew honour was despoyled quight,
> And a wide wound therein (O ruefull sight)
> Entrenched deepe with knife accursed keene,
> Yet freshly bleeding forth her fainting spright,
> (The worke of cruell hand) was to be seene,
> That dyde in sanguine red her skin all snowy cleene.
>
> At that wide orifice her trembling hart

Was drawne forth, and in siluer basin layd,
Quite through transfixed with a deadly dart,
And in her bloud yet steeming fresh embayd. (3.12.20–21)

The masque is repeated on the next night, as it has been for the past seven
months. But before the masque concludes the next night, Britomart dis-
pels the players by striding into the third room. There she finds the "real"
figure of Amoret, whose captivity has been enforced by the love metaphors
of the masque: "both hands / Were bounden fast, that did her ill become,
/ And her small wast girt round with yron bands, / Vnto a brasen pillour,
by the which she stands" (3.12.30). Her breast is cut open and her heart,
instead of being in a basin, is here pierced but unremoved. Unlike the figure of Amoret in the masque, this is the Amoret who has been forced to
witness herself within the horrific procession. Unlike the figure of herself
whose heart is removed, this Amoret has resisted being persuaded or
"moved," despite Busirane's knife in her heart. Thus, the figure in the
masque is Busirane's fantasy of the Amoret he would like to see—the
Amoret he has persuaded to love him. In a moment of insight rare in these
cantos, the narrator explains that Busirane has been writing these
pageants—the tapestries, the musicians and their lay, the masquers, the
house itself—in the blood flowing from Amoret's wound.

And her before the vile Enchaunter sate,
Figuring straunge characters of his art,
With liuing bloud he those characters wrate,
Dreadfully dropping from her dying hart,
Seeming transfixed with a cruell dart,
And all perforce to make her him to loue. (3.12.31)

Like Merlin, also an "Enchaunter" (3.3.17) who writes "strange characters"
(3.3.14), or Sidney, whose pen may "dwell" in any female "part," the poet-
magician Busirane creates a spell to instill certain pictures within the minds
of his audience. Here the picture created for Amoret and Britomart—as
well as Elizabeth—is the rape of a woman through the spell of words written in her own blood.

The assertion that Busirane tortures Amoret "all perforce to make her
him to loue" has been much ignored by scholars interpreting Amoret's
situation, although this "love" is the narrative explanation for the house,
pictures, masque, and Amoret's pain. In much the same way as Richardson's Lovelace will love Clarissa, Busirane loves Amoret and writes his
rape of her in her blood. But this narrative explanation is only the starting place to trace the origins of this horror. We must ask larger questions

about why this violence exists and, indeed, why love is given as the justification for this violence.

In fact, similar questions can be found within the text and, as in the proem, remain unanswered. For instance, there is this speech from Scudamour, Amoret's beloved, who, in Canto 11, bewails the absence of values in Faeryland:

> If good find grace, and righteousnesse reward,
> Why then is *Amoret* in caytiue band,
> Sith that more bounteous creature neuer far'd
> On foot, vpon the face of liuing land?
> Or if that heauenly iustice may withstand
> The wrongfull outrage of vnrighteous men,
> Why then is *Busirane* with wicked hand
> Suffred, these seuen monethes day in secret den
> My Lady and my loue so cruelly to pen? (3.11.10)

Echoing Scudamour, we want to ask, Why a victim? Who permits this suffering, this penning? Who holds the "pen"—the pun that signals the relation among authorship, captivity, and the penetrating penis?[33]

Spenser's Relation to his Narrator

The holder of the pen was once literally Spenser. But exactly how is Spenser the author related to this "penning," this captivity, this suffering, this rape? I suggest that we look at Book 3's narrator and examine why Spenser insists on separating the narrator from full comprehension of Busirane's work and yet allows him an intimate knowledge of the violent details. As I mentioned earlier, the narrator's ignorance of the whole masque scene bears examining because the closer Spenser's narrator comes to the scene in which he describes the poet-rapist, the less explication we receive. As Paul Alpers describes him, Spenser's narrator is particularly unstable throughout *The Faerie Queene:* "We know this is a narration because we sense the presence of a narrator; nevertheless, we cannot assume that he is a dramatically consistent figure."[34] Consistent or not, the narrator usually provides the moral valence or actual explication of events within *The Faerie Queene,* although such explanations tend to complicate rather than clarify.

In Elizabethan spectacle, it is the narrator who delimits the range of possible interpretations of any given allegory. The narrator supplements the interpretive mechanisms of allegory—its correspondence among pictorial, verbal, and musical elements—with his own explication. His glosses form what an ethnographer would term "actor explications," explanations from within the ideology of the pageant's producers. But the semiomniscient narrator of Canto 11, carefully reporting to us what the figures in the murals say, becomes the narrator of Canto 12, standing so close to the masque that he can only provide a confused view of its conclusion without commenting on its unmistakably violent figures.

In the third room of Busirane's house, we discover that the narrator's ignorance of the masque is part of his denial that the rape actually occurred, because he is otherwise privy to a great deal of detail. For example, once the spell on Amoret is reversed, the narrator tells us that Amoret is fully restored. The "cruell steele, which thrild her dying hart, / Fell softly forth" and "the wyde wound, / Which lately did dispart / Her bleeding brest, and riuen bowells gor'd, / Was closed up, as it had not bene bor'd." We are told that "As she were neuer hurt, was soone restor'd," although she is considerably weakened by the experience: "When she felt her selfe to be vnbound, / And perfect hold, prostrate she fell vnto the ground" (3.12.38).

Amoret's release suggests that the narrator has nothing to do with the rape. But is this the case? The narrator's language continues Busirane's cruelties even as they supposedly end, by describing Amoret's violated body in terms that are more like an actual penetration than any description we have yet read. Her "riuen bowells" were "gor'd" and the opening to her heart was "bor'd." Thus, the stanza describing the restoration of Amoret's body provides still another report of her rape. The narrator in fact provides three descriptions, each different enough to constitute a separate rape. The first Amoret that we see is the female figure in the masque, holding her pierced heart in a basin. We discover that she is a projection of the second Amoret, who is tied up. The second Amoret's heart is also pierced, but because of her loyalty to her future husband, it is unremoved. Once healed, this second Amoret becomes the third Amoret who is made a "perfect hole," so that while her violated hymen is restored, the third and most brutal description of her violation is canceled. The instability created by these three versions works to confuse the horror if not to eliminate it.

The way that Spenser's narrator tells the story with a mix of ignorance and lurid detail is part of a cultural and literary pattern in which rape is both obsessively inscribed and obsessively erased. In their introduction to *Rape and Representation,* Lynn Higgins and Brenda Silver note the "obsessive inscription—and an obsessive erasure—of sexual violence against women (and against those placed by society in the position of 'woman')."[35] Since Spenser made the assaulted Amoret and the witness Britomart both figures of the queen, he was especially motivated to construct a text that follows the logic of most literary representations of rape. He is able to construct the violence that counters Elizabeth's strong, autonomous chastity at the same time that he denies that the violence exists. This denial is an open invitation to his readers to participate in erasing the rape. The temptation to do so is undeniable. Even after Amoret's release to fall at the feet of the armored Britomart, whom she assumes is another male, the narrator's stance remains complicitous: rather than excoriate Busirane, the narrator allows him to escape retribution. And although Britomart chains him with the same chain he used to control Amoret, the poet-magician is allowed simply to disappear from the poem. The narrator's supposed ignorance of a crime he eventually denies and the narrator's release of Busirane come directly from Spenser—Spenser needs both to enforce the meaning of lawful chastity and to deny how closely it conspires in rape.

After Book 3 is over, Spenser's narrator returns again and again to Amoret's rape. These fragments of Amoret's history should not, of course, be read as part of the narrative of the Book 3 published in 1590 because they were written as an extension of that story and published six years later. Yet, they illuminate Spenser's unease and suggest a wish both to apologize for Amoret's rape and to contextualize it, just as Busirane has, as a "natural" part of love. In Book 4, the narrator attempts this retelling: in Canto 1, Stanza 1, he observes that no story "more piteous euer was ytold, / Then that of *Amorets* hart-binding chaine," while he "oftentimes doe wishe it neuer had bene writ" (4.1.1). In Canto 2, the narrator tells us that Busirane captured Amoret during the presentation of his "masque of love" at her wedding banquet. In Canto 6, Britomart explains to Scudamour that she rescued Amoret "from enchaunters theft / Her freed, in which ye her all hopelesse left" (4.6.35), lines that replay the violence of the rape.

In the final half of Book 4, the telling of Amoret's rape obscures the agency of the rapist. In Canto 7, for instance, Spenser's narrator links Amoret through the "Great God of love" to other female figures who have experienced love in different forms. Here love is pictured as necessarily violent for all women, as the narrator explains that love's "cruell darts" have pierced the hearts of Florimell and Britomart as well as "Amoret, whose gentle hart / Thou [Love] martyrest with sorrow and with smart . . . / That pittie is to heare the perils, which she tride" (4.7.1–2). Although Amoret suffers the most, according to the narrator, the cause of Amoret's suffering and that of Florimell and Britomart is the same: Love, the emotion that works to justify the male possession of women's bodies. Thus, the seventh canto's retracing of the incident deletes the rapist from Amoret's story by conflating him with other agents of love. By the tenth canto of Book 4, Amoret's rape becomes figuratively enmeshed in the story of her own courtship as Scudamour describes how he wrested Amoret from the Temple of Venus where he first met her. The courtship story comes out as Scudamour and Britomart travel as two knights together for a time. Scudamour explains to Britomart how he penetrated the perils of Venus's Temple, quieted the fears of its hermaphroditic goddess of generation by showing her his shield "with *Cupid* with his killing bow / And cruell shafts emblazoned" (4.10.55), and forced Amoret to go with him in spite of her tears and entreaties, mixed with "witching smiles." As he tells Britomart man-to-man, "sacrilege me seem'd the Church to rob, / And folly seem'd to leaue the thing vndonne, / Which with so strong attempt I had begonne" (4.10.53). Through Scudamour's account, Britomart hears the violence of Amoret's courtship as surely as she has seen Amoret's rape. Thus, these scenes function as a set of narratival mirrors through which Britomart witnesses Chastity—a figure represented by herself as much as by Amoret—constructed through the conflation of love, violent courtship, and rape.[36]

Spenser as Busirane

Literary critics have long sought to illuminate the source of Busirane, his house, the masque, and Amoret's ordeal.[37] In the most enduring reading of Cantos 11 and 12, Thomas P. Roche, Jr. concluded in 1961 that the violence directed against Amoret formed "an objectification of Amoret's fear of sexual love in marriage."[38] In 1970, Maurice Evans read Book 3 as a narrative about "Britomart's growth to sexual maturity"[39] and her encounter with Busirane as central to this growth. Harry Berger's complex readings have undergone subtle redefinition; one article first published in 1971 centers on "the masculine mind wounded first by desire and then by jealousy and envy"[40] as allegorized in the figure of Busirane. Robin Wells in 1983 saw Scudamour as responsible for the violence, "because it is his own lack of faith in [Amoret's] ability to withstand temptation which is the real cause of her torture."[41]

In three of the most recent significant discussions of Spenser in the past decade, Maureen Quilligan, Joseph Loewenstein, and Lauren Silberman read Spenser as using Busirane to expose the violence and misogyny within Petrarchanism, but envisage Spenser as standing outside the horror, unimplicated by his use of court structures and masculinist poetic discourse.[42] In Quilligan's view, Spenser's awareness of the ways that Petrarchan poetics structure love is in part recuperative. Amoret forms part of a "process of redemption" whereby "Britomart learns" "how to speak of love."[43] Loewenstein describes both the *Amoretti* and Cantos 11 and 12 as "tests" of Spenser's "power to reform Petrarchism,"[44] while Silberman discusses Busirane as a "master of Petrarchan sexual politics," whose "mere sadomasochism, the archetypal dualism, is rejected." Loewenstein and Silberman make their observations in the midst of very different though equally provocative arguments. They do, however, share Quilligan's sense that the House of Busirane's violence should finally be constructed as redemptive or transcendent of its cultural milieu. For Loewenstein, Spenser's nuptial poem, the *Epithalamion,* "celebrates the social and psychological redemptions that enable us to leave Busyrane's erotic culture behind." For Silberman, "the text itself creates a reader who . . . transcends the partiality Spenser attributes to men, who, when they write and when the read, praise only themselves."[45]

In contrast, I see Busirane as the figure of all the displaced frustration and violence that Spenser feels toward his queen. Spenser's text is courtly in that it screens the poet's desire for royal patronage behind his praise of her. Nevertheless, violence exists in the relation among its putative author, Busirane, who becomes difficult to distinguish from that elusive poet-magician, Spenser; its narrator, who provides and withholds descriptions and interpretation; and its audience, whether Britomart, Amoret, Elizabeth I, or ourselves. The text's exhibition of the poet's power to turn the celebration and entertainment of his audience into captivity and the rhetoric of desire into rape results in a horror so deep, an anxiety about the relation among sexuality, persuasion, and control so pervasive, that Spenser attempts to dissociate himself from Amoret's abuse.

Spenser had every reason to combine the captivity narrative so central to Elizabethan spectacle with the assertion through a masculinist poetics of his ability to manipulate even sovereign power through love. His selection of the rescue of Chastity expressed in violent reworkings of Elizabeth's iconography suggests his own frustration at not seeing the promise of *The Shepheardes Calender* fulfilled following its publication in 1579.[46] Instead of a rapid Christopher Hatton- or Walter Ralegh-like rise to English lands, court appointments, governmental duties, and patent revenues, Spenser arrived in Ireland a year after the *Calender*'s publication as secretary to Lord Grey, the governor-general of Ireland. Whatever unknown reason accounted for his sudden move to Ireland, Spenser was conspicuously well employed when unemployment was the fate of the truly disgraced. He even prospered: the acquisition of his Irish estates in 1586–87 and the castle of Kilcolman established him as an ostensible member of the gentry. He participated as an undertaker of Munster, renting three thousand acres in county Cork from the crown. Six years after Spenser visited England and was presented at court by Ralegh at the time of the publication of the first three books of *The Faerie Queene,* the privy council recommended him for Sheriff of Cork. Given all this, some Spenser critics have recently begun to question whether Spenser was all that unhappy in Ireland. But if Elizabeth's favorites, including Robert Dudley, the Earl of Leicester, Sir Walter Ralegh, and Robert Devereux, the Earl of

Essex, continually complained about how little they received from their queen and how few of their schemes she was willing to support, I see no reason to think that Spenser was satisfied with his lot. Instead, Spenser, like Elizabeth's more successful courtiers, wanted more in a world whose few paths to recognition and immediate wealth ended in the figure of an aging queen. The frustrations of existing in a society that gave only partial scope to his ambitions can be read in the violence with which he confronts his figures of the queen.

Epilogue on Gender, Violence, and Allegory

Although Spenser's Book 3 presents playful, chivalrous, erotic, bawdy, and finally violent reworkings of chastity, Spenser achieves no fixed redefinition of chastity through allegory. The more he attempts to define gender roles, the more absolute gender distinctions elude the text. His images of lawful chastity generate any number of instabilities: a narrator whose moral vision dims as he approaches Busirane; a poet-magician, Busirane, who shares Spenser's language and talents, who tortures and rapes but escapes punishment; a captive female figure, Amoret, her outline shimmering and indeterminate, now in the masque, now providing the blood-ink from a heart both removed and unremoved, "riven" and yet inviolate; and a rescuing female figure, Britomart, independent in her quest for her destined mate and invulnerable to male attack while cross-dressed as a knight, yet vulnerable to attack within the bedroom and the torture cell.

Spenser's use of the structures of court spectacle itself creates contradictions: Spenser praises the queen while he threatens her analogues; invites her interest but attempts to silence her response; asserts that poets have a power in the land of Faery that figures their power in the real world, despite Spenser's frustrating experience to the contrary. Moreover, he asks the queen to watch as he erodes her representations of self-possession and displaces her authority with the masterly threats underlying the increasingly dominant codes of companionate marriage. Spenser insists on chastity's redefinition by threat, captivity, and rape, even as that insistence generates instabilities that negate any absolute definition of gender roles. The instability of language, and particularly of allegory, renews the very anxieties that have motivated Spenser's attempt to redefine chastity in the first place. As Spenser exposes and explores the tensions among court, culture, and language, he attempts to tighten his grip on definition, forming a discursive site that engenders violence.

In reclaiming chastity through the repossession of the figured queen, Spenser raises unsettling questions not only about his own pressing need to revise the queen's iconography but also about the entire process of defining cultural categories, morality, and behavior. Jacques Derrida's discussion of the relation between violence and writing seems particularly illuminating here if we consider its social consequences in terms of gender roles. Derrida claims that the first violence is the construction of difference: "There was in fact a first violence to be named."[47] Rhetorical violence is inherent in culture precisely because difference is necessary for language to exist: "To name, to give names that it will on occasion be forbidden to pronounce, such is the originary violence of language which consists in inscribing within a difference, in classifying, in suspending the vocative absolute. . . . Out of this arche-violence, forbidden and therefore confirmed by a second violence that is reparatory, protective, instituting the 'moral,' prescribing the concealment of writing and the effacement and obliteration of the so-called proper name which was already dividing the proper, a third violence can *possibly* emerge or not (an empirical possibility) within what is commonly called evil, war, indiscretion, rape."[48]

Initial difference gives rise to a second violence, the attempt to protect distinctions through the institution of the "ethical," in part through the construction of hierarchies and moralities. This safeguarding of difference through morality—in effect, its social enforcement—can in turn give way to a third level of violence that arises "within what is commonly called evil, war, indiscretion, rape."[49]

All three forms of violence within language occur in Book 3 and such violences were as insistently present in the court discourse of chastity as they are in its redefinition. Court discourse was predicated upon an assumed difference between Elizabeth and the rest of humanity—that she was ageless, invulnerable, unique, wise, and independent, a being both gendered and cross-gendered. Spenser's counterdiscourse originated in an assumed difference between all men and all women that uses language to equate the control of the feminine with male aesthetic production. Court discourse promised status and wealth to those who reproduced and developed the imagery of Elizabeth's autonomous chastity, although in practice royal discourse both created and was created by the codified hierarchy of her court. Members of that court occasionally experienced advancement and favor, but more often knew bankruptcy, disappointment, exile, and sometimes even torture and death. Spenser's counterdiscourse promises the joys of heterosexuality, although through a strange assortment of interrupted courtships, missing marriages, and displaced consummations, while enforcing the moral architecture of lawful chastity through the threat, rape, and captivity of his female figures.

When Elizabeth's self-definition and Spenser's essentialist gender distinctions collide, the movement from difference to rape produces Amoret's sufferings for an audience of Britomart, the queen, and ourselves. The happy reunion of Amoret and Scudamour in the 1590 edition, in which they embrace "like two senceles stocks" (3.12.45a) so closely intertwined that they form a hermaphrodite, cannot quietly contain the cumulative impact of the three versions of Amoret's rape. Instead, the rape invites us to interrogate the constructions of difference underlying Erasmus's assurance that "the most holy kynd of lyfe is wedlocke puerly & chastly kept."[50] In *The Faerie Queene*'s enforcement of masculinist codes that naturalize gender differences, Spenser reveals that the ideal of a lawfully chaste marriage instantiates the threat, language, and practice of rape.*

Notes

* This article is a revision of "Of Chastity and Violence: Elizabeth I and Edmund Spenser in the House of Busirane" that appeared in *Signs* 20 (1) (Autumn 1994): 49–78. For assistance with this version and its previous incarnations, I owe special thanks to John Bender, Louis Montrose, Stephen Orgel, Robert Torry, Janice Harris, Karen Robertson, Maureen Quilligan, Margaret Hannay, Louisa Castner, and Elizabeth Robertson. The later version of this article appears as part of chapter 3 in my *Elizabeth I: The Competition for Representation* (New York: Oxford University Press, 1993; rpt. 1997).

1. *Phillip Sidney, The Countess of Pembroke's Arcadia (The Old Arcadia),* ed. Jean Robertson (Oxford: Clarendon Press, 1973), p. 238.

2. On the operation of rape to assert and enforce patriarchy at all levels of society, Susan Brownmiller's work was germinal (*Against Our Will: Men, Women, and Rape* (New York: Simon & Schuster, 1975). See also Terry Castle's analysis of Lovelace's rape of Clarissa for its discussion of rape as patriarchal: "The quintessential act of violence against women, it is that hidden physical threat held over the woman who tries, wittingly or unwittingly, to overstep any of the fundamental restrictions on her power—in any area" (see *Clarissa's Ciphers: Meaning and Disruption in Richardson's "Clarissa"* (Ithaca, NY: Cornell University Press, 1982), p. 117, and on Clarissa's rape, pp. 108–35. The most recent sociological studies on the subject of rape acknowledge this feminist argument (see Larry Baron and Murray A. Straus, *Four Theories of Rape in American Society: A State-Level Analysis* [New Haven, CT: Yale University Press, 1989], pp. 61–94; and Linda Brookover Bourque, *Defining Rape* [Durham, NC: Duke University Press, 1989], pp. 14–58).

3. Edmund Spenser, *Edmund Spenser: "The Faerie Queene,"* ed. Thomas P. Roche, Jr. (1590, rpt. New Haven, CT: Yale University Press, 1981).

4. I am mindful that discussing Spenser as the agent of the text gives rise to various questions of intentionality that have become central to feminist theory, since erasing the author carries the danger of making patriarchal values appear to be part of a natural order. I find useful Robert Weimann's analysis of the relation between social structures such as court spectacle or

royal iconography and the individual author. For Weimann, "the social and the individual perspectives on experience are *within* the poet and the creative process itself, just as they are *in* the reader and form part of the receptive process. Structure is born out of this interaction by which the poet and his audience, also the self and the social within the poet, are all genetically connected. . . . Structure is 'historically given': it accommodates the traditional (or original) modes of rhetoric and mediation between the poet and his first audience, and it reflects or mirrors the form and pressure of the age in which the art work is created" (*Structure and Society in Literary History: Studies in the History and Theory of Historical Criticism* [Baltimore, MD: Johns Hopkins University Press, 1984], pp. 7–8, and see pp. 46–56). For Weimann's literary historian, the biography of the author and the reader are inseparable from the analysis of structure because "the issue of historicity must be discussed on more than one level: not only on the level of what is represented (which would reduce this project to some genealogy of the signified) but also on the level of who and what is representing. The point is to view these levels (the rupture between them as well as their independence) together and to attempt to interconnect the semiotic problematic of signification and the extratextual dimension of representativeness, as involving changeful relations of writing, reading, social reproduction, and political power" ("Text, Author-Function, and Appropriation in Modern Narrative: Toward a Sociology of Representation," in *Literature and Social Practice,* ed. Philippe Desan, Priscilla Parkhurst Ferguson, and Wendy Griswold [Chicago: University of Chicago Press, 1989], p. 30). As Cheryl Walker has pointed out, those who consider an author's biography must remain aware that in discussing the author "we reveal our own epistemological assumptions and our own politics of interpretation by our insistence on a certain notion of subjectivity as speaking" ("Feminist Literary Criticism and the Author," *Critical Inquiry* 16 [1990]: 551–71).

5. Frances Teague, "Marriage Speech," in *Women Writers of the Renaissance and Reformation,* ed. Katharina M. Wilson (Athens: University of Georgia Press, 1987), p. 538.

6. See John N. King, "Queen Elizabeth I: Representations of the Virgin Queen," *Renaissance Quarterly* 43 (1990): 30–74 for a different argument. Although I have not discussed the differences among the sieve pictures, in fact they differ from one another in fascinating ways. The most elaborate of them, the Siena Portrait, forms a complex allegory that, while retaining Elizabeth at the center holding a sieve, includes a variety of figures and enigmatic words that have been interpreted as both upholding and undermining Elizabeth's claims to power through her chastity. See Roy Strong, *Gloriana: The Portraits of Queen Elizabeth I* (New York: Thames and Hudson, 1987), pp. 101–3; Constance Jordan, "Representing Political Androgyny: More on the Siena Portrait of Queen Elizabeth I," in *The Renaissance Englishwoman in Print: Counterbalancing the Canon,* ed. Anne M. Haselkorn and Betty S. Travitsky (Amherst: University of Massachusetts Press, 1990), pp. 157–76.

7. Louis Montrose, "The Elizabethan Subject and the Spenserian Text," in *Literary Theory/Renaissance Texts,* ed. Patricia Parker and David Quint (Baltimore, MD: John Hopkins University Press, 1986), p. 315.

8. For another reading of the composition of the portrait that argues that the queen's sexuality is subdued "in order to proclaim her power," see Andrew Belsey and Catherine Belsey, "Icons of Divinity: Portraits of Elizabeth I," in *Renaissance Bodies: The Human Figure in English Culture c. 1540–1660,* ed. Luce Gent and Nigel Llewellyn (London: Reaktion Books, 1990), p. 18. See also Roy Strong, *Gloriana: The Portraits of Queen Elizabeth I,* pp. 131–33.

9. See Ann Rosalind Jones, *The Currency of Eros: Women's Love Lyric in Europe, 1540–1620* (Bloomington: Indiana University Press, 1990), pp. 11–35.

10. Maureen Quilligan, *Milton's Spencer: The Politics of Reading* (Ithaca, NY: Cornell University Press, 1983), p. 177. My discussion is indebted to the passage quoted and to the section of Quilligan's "Book III and the Gender of the Reader" (*Milton's Spencer,* pp. 185–208).

11. See Julia Kristeva, *Powers of Horror: An Essay on Abjection,* trans. Leon S. Roudiez (New York: Columbia University Press, 1982) on the relation between codes and the feminine. On the relation between the heterosexual order and its enforcement through "its inquisitions, its courts, its tribunals, its body of laws, its terrors, its tortures, its mutilations, its executions, its police," see Monique Wittig, "On the Social Contract," *Feminist Issues* 9 (1989): 11.

12. "R. M.," *The mothers counsell, or Live within Compasse,* p. 7.

13. Desiderius Erasmus, *A ryght frutefull Epystle by the moste excellent clerke Erasmus in laude and prayse of matrymony,* trans. Rychard Tauernour (London, 1532); Desiderius Erasmus, "Courtship," in *The Colloquies of Erasmus,* trans. Craig R. Thompson (1450, rpt. Chicago: University of Chicago Press, 1965).

14. Margo Todd, *Christian Humanism and Puritan Social Order* (Cambridge: Cambridge University Press, 1987); Valerie Wayne, "Introduction," in Edmund Tilney, *"The Flower of Friendshippe": A Renaissance Dialogue Contesting Marriage,* ed. Valerie Wayne (Ithaca, NY: Cornell University Press, 1992). Valerie Wayne pointed out to me that Erasmus's colloquies on marriage formed a crucial part of the humanist curriculum in England throughout the sixteenth century and graciously allowed me to see her work in manuscript ("Introduction").

15. Erasmus, "Courtship," pp. 86–87.

16. Edmund Spenser, *The Yale Edition of the Shorter Poems of Edmund Spenser,* ed. William A. Oram et al. (New Haven, CT: Yale University Press, 1989), pp. 639–40, lines 5–8.

17. William Byrd, ed., *Psalms, Sonnets, and Songs of Sadness and Piety,* in *An English Garner,* ed. Edward Arber (1588, rpt. Westminster: Constable, 1905), vol. 4, p. 85.

18. John Nichols, ed., *The Progresses and Public Processions of Queen Elizabeth,* 3 vols. (1823, rpt. London: Nichols, 1966), vol. 1, pp. 485–523.

19. Nichols, *The Progresses of Elizabeth,* 1: 499. For a discussion of this spectacle as Elizabeth's rewriting of Gascoigne's planned staging of masculinist power in the context of the English intervention in the Netherlands, see Susan Frye, *Elizabeth I: The Competition for Representation* (New York: Oxford University Press, 1993), chapter 2, pp. 56–96.

20. Edmund Spenser, *Spenser's Minor Poems,* ed. Ernest de Selincourt (1595, rpt. Oxford: Clarendon, 1910), pp. 40 and 44.

21. John Nichols, ed., *The Progresses and Public Processions of Queen Elizabeth,* p. 502.

22. Ibid.

23. Nichols, p. 500.

24. Jean Wilson, ed., *Entertainments for Elizabeth,* pp. 60–85.

25. Other examples of the rescue of Chastity by Chastity appear frequently within court spectacle. In 1592, for example, Elizabeth participated in an entertainment in which she released Daphne from the laurel tree she had become while fleeing Apollo. This occurred at the only entertainment described as having taken place at the home of a female courtier, Lady Russell.

26. Eric Mallin, "Emulous Factions and the Collapse of Chivalry: *Troilus and Cressida,*" *Representations* 29 (1990): 165–66.

27. In the past decade, critical attention has focused on the social marginalization of women during the Renaissance and the rhetorical fragmentation that typifies their representation. In particular, Patricia Parker and Peter Stallybrass have discussed women as rhetorical property and patriarchal territory (Peter Stallybrass, "Patriarchal Territories: The Body Enclosed," in *Rewriting the Renaissance,* ed. Margaret W. Ferguson, Maureen Quilligan, and Nancy J. Vickers [Chicago: University of Chicago Press, 1986], pp. 123–42; Patricia Parker, *Literary Fat Ladies* [New York: Methuen, 1987], pp. 126–54), while several of the essays in *Enclosure Acts: Sexuality, Property, and Culture in Early Modern England* ed. Richard Burt and John Michael Archer (Ithaca, NY: Cornell University Press, 1994) discuss how women lived within the confines of such masculinist codes as chivalry, poetry, and the law. These codes were literalized whenever women were physically captured or limited in their everyday activity. These various forms of captivity invite discussion because, as Michel Foucault aptly demonstrated, it is in the practice of confinement that operations of power are most visible (*Discipline and Punish: the Birth of the Prison,* trans. Alan Sheridan [New York: Vintage Books, 1977]). The real or fantasized control of women enacts a patriarchal culture's physical and mental proscriptions upon even the most powerful woman in the realm.

28. By "masculinist poetics," I mean the prevalent codes, such as the topoi of rhetoric and poetry, and narratives, like the captivity narrative of romance, that serve to demark areas of life and language from which women were discouraged and through which women were defined. On the humanist attitudes towards women that helped to disseminate these codes, see Constance Jordan, "Feminism and the Humanists: The Case of Sir Thomas

Elyot's *Defence of Good Women,*" *Renaissance Quarterly* 36 (1983): 181–201. On the central question of the relation of women to male codes, especially language, see in particular Gayatri Chakravorty Spivak, "Displacement and the Discourse of Woman," in *Displacement: Derrida and After,* ed. Mark Krupnick (Bloomington: Indiana University Press, 1983), pp. 169–95; Julia Kristeva, "About Chinese Women," in *The Kristeva Reader,* ed. Toril Moi (New York: Columbia University Press, 1986), pp. 138–59; Teresa de Lauretis, "The Violence of Rhetoric," in *Technologies of Gender: Essays on Theory, Film and Fiction* (Bloomington: Indiana University Press, 1987), pp. 31–50; Luce Irigaray, "Women's Exile: Interview with Luce Irigaray," trans Couze Venn, in *The Feminist Critique of Language: A Reader,* ed. Deborah Cameron (New York: Routledge, 1990). On the conceptualization of male language as generating discourses, see Alice A. Jardine, *Gynesis: Configurations of Women and Modernity* (Ithaca, NY: Cornell University Press, 1985), especially chapter 4, "Spaces for Further Research: Male Paranoia," pp. 88–102.

29. For a careful account of Britomart's narrative as implying "a serious criticism of the Elizabethan cult," see Philippa Berry, *Of Chastity and Power: Elizabethan Literature and the Unmarried Queen* (London: Routledge, 1989), p. 163. Thickstun also notes, of Britomart's eventual marriage, that "such an ending retrospectively redefines female independence by encoding it within the scripts of lawful heterosexual generation" (Margaret Olafson Thickstun, *Fictions of the Feminine: Puritan Doctrine and the Representation of Women* [Ithaca, NY: Cornell University Press, 1988], p. 43).

30. Thomas Churchyard, "A Discovrse of The Queenes Maiesties entertainement in Suffolk and Norffolk . . . ," Short Title Catalog microfilm number 5226.

31. In Canto 12, Stanzas 33–38, for example, the distinction between Britomart and Amoret becomes blurred. The fact that Busirane wounds Britomart as well as Amoret suggests their kinship as both audience and subject. Moreover, the profusion of singular feminine pronouns that refer one moment to Amoret and the next to Britomart serves to conflate them in a single unstable feminine figure that is sometimes rescuer and sometimes rescued, but always the audience of Busirane. For example, when Amoret prevents Britomart from killing Busirane because only he can undo the spell that keeps a knife in Amoret's heart, the two females become one as they listen: Busirane read "and measur'd many a sad verse, / That horror gan *the virgins* hart to perse, / And *her* faire lockes vp stared stiffe on end, / Hearing him those same bloudy lines reherse" (3.12.36; my emphasis). The "virgin" and "her" signify Britomart *or* Amoret, as well as Britomart *and* Amoret. While lack of familiarity with the spell may explain why Britomart's hair stands on end, the "she" who hears these lines as the "same" is Amoret, the only one who has heard the spell before.

32. Nina Auerbach, *Romantic Imprisonment: Women and Other Glorified Outcasts* (New York: Columbia University Press, 1985), p. 10.

33. The use of *pen* creates a running pun that also functions as a reminder of the relation between male creativity and procreativity. At the end of Book 3, the "pen" preempts metaphors of female creativity, even those, such as birth metaphors, often used by men. On the opposition of phallocentric and gynocentric metaphors of creativity, see Susan Stanford Friedman, "Creativity and the Childbirth Metaphor: Gender Difference in Literary Discourse," *Feminist Studies* 13 (1987): 49. Maureen Quilligan suggests that the relation between Spenser and Busirane lies in Spenser's use of Busirane to call attention to poetic strategies, to parody Petrarchan convention. In considering the "penning" of Amoret, Quilligan writes, "Through a multifaceted pun on one word, 'pen,' which completes an extensive pattern of parodic criticism of Petrarchan conventions, Spenser demonstrates the imprisoning nature of this way of talking about love" (*The Language of Allegory: Defining the Genre* [Ithaca, NY: Cornell University Press, 1979], p. 84). In the process, Spenser rises above his imagery.
34. Paul Alpers, "Narration in *The Faerie Queene*," *ELH* 44 (1977): 21.
35. Lynn A. Higgins and Brenda R. Silver, *Rape and Representation* (New York: Columbia University Press, 1991), p. 2.
36. Compare Stephanie Jed's discussion of Lucretia's rape as the heart of the mythic narrative of humanism and republicanism because it is the necessary prelude to the overthrow of Tarquin (Stephanie Jed, *Chaste Thinking: The Rape of Lucretia and the Birth of Humanism* [Bloomington: Indiana University Press, 1989]). Rape stands at the center of the companionate marriage as well, as a form of possession when all others fail.
37. See Thomas P. Roche, Jr., "The Challenge to Chastity: Britomart in the House of Busirane," in *Essential Articles for the Study of Edmund Spenser*, ed. A. C. Hamilton (Hamden, CT: Archon, 1972), pp. 189–98; Maurice Evans, *Spencer's Anatomy of Heroism: A Commentary on "The Faerie Queene"* (Cambridge: Cambridge University Press, 1970); Harry Berger, Jr., "Busirane and the War between the Sexes: An Interpretation of *The Faerie Queene*," *English Literary Renaissance* 1 (1971): 99–121; Robin Wells, *Spenser's Faerie Queene and the Cult of Elizabeth* (Totowa, NJ: Rowman & Littlefield, 1980); Sean Kane, *Spenser's Moral Allegory* (Toronto: University of Toronto Press, 1989), p. 100.
38. Roche, "Britomart in the House of Busirane," p. 195.
39. Evans, *Spencer's Anatomy of Heroism,* p. 166.
40. Berger, "Busirane and the War between the Sexes," p. 99.
41. Wells, *Spenser's Faerie Queene and the Cult of Elizabeth,* pp. 82–83.
42. See Maureen Quilligan, *The Language of Allegory: Defining the Genre;* Joseph Loewenstein, "Echo's Ring: Orpheus and Spenser's Career," *English Literary Renaissance* 16 (1986): 287–302; Lauren Silberman, "Unsung Heroines: Androgynous Discourse in Book 3 of *The Faerie Queene*," in *Rewriting the Renaissance: The Discourses of Sexual Difference in Early Modern Europe,* ed. Margaret W. Ferguson, Maureen Quilligan, and Nancy J. Vickers (Chicago: University of Chicago Press, 1986): pp. 259–71.

43. Quilligan, *The Language of Allegory,* pp. 84–85.

44. Loewenstein, "Echo's Ring: Orpheus and Spenser's Career," p. 294.

45. Lauren Silberman, "Unsung Heroines: Androgynous Discourse in Book 3 of *The Faerie Queene,*" p. 271.

46. Although disappointed and marginalized as a court figure because of his location in Ireland, Spenser continued to function within the court's system of patronage and praise. Jonathan Goldberg has pointed out the paradox of Spenser's position; in spite of Spenser's many complaints in verse about the court, "his fortunes grew; a pension was awarded; over the years there was the patronage of royal favorites, Leicester, Ralegh, Essex" (*Endlesse Worke: Spenser and the Structures of Discourse* [Baltimore, MD: Johns Hopkins University Press, 1981], p. 173).

47. Jacques Derrida, *Of Grammatology,* trans. Gayatri Chakravorty Spivak (Baltimore, MD: John Hopkins University Press, 1976), p. 112.

48. Jacques Derrida, *Of Grammatology,* p. 112.

49. As de Lauretis points out, Derrida's own text seeks to ignore gender even as it cannot help mentioning rape ("The Violence of Rhetoric," pp. 32–33, 46). For another discussion of "the violence of the letter" in a literary work, see Maguerite Waller, "Usurpation, Seduction, and the Problematics of the Proper: A 'Deconstructive,' 'Feminist' Rereading of the Seductions of Richard and Anne in Shakespeare's *Richard III,*" in *Rewriting the Renaissance: The Discourses of Sexual Difference in Early Modern Europe,* ed. Margaret W. Ferguson, Maureen Quilligan, and Nancy J. Vickers (Chicago: University of Chicago Press, 1986), pp. 159–74. Since all of Book 3 is actively engaged in redefining chastity, its general structure may be said to participate in Derrida's analysis of the movement from difference to rape. The book begins with play between signifier and signified, between the forms of Chastity, Elizabeth, Britomart, Belphoebe, and Florimell, and, in the Garden of Adonis, between death and fertility, animal and vegetable, masculine and feminine. But within that range of relations and associations, the feminine is established as existing within male-conceptualized law and nature. As it nears its conclusion, the book becomes increasingly insistent on morality: by Cantos 9 and 10, the text produces Hellenore and Malbecco as transgressors of chastity's code, and their behavior results in the spectacle of their dehumanization.

50. Desiderius Erasmus, *A right frutfull Epystle by the moste excellent clerke Erasmus in laude and prayse of matrymony,* trans. Rychard Tauernour (London: 1532), C6.

CHAPTER 13

SPENSER'S RAVISHMENT:
RAPE AND RAPTURE IN *THE FAERIE QUEENE*

Katherine Eggert

> *The Faerie Queene* oscillates between two ontologically incompatible
> modes of poetry: rapine and rapturous. Rape is associated with inad-
> equate, unsubtle, and solipsistic poetry; rapture, with a poetics of
> shared and sensual delight.

> . . . *men being of wit sufficient to tonder [consider] of these vertues which are in us*
> *women, are ravished with that delight of those dainties, which allure & draw the*
> *sences of them to serve us, wherby they become ravenous haukes, who doe not onely*
> *seize upon us, but devour us.*
>
> —Jane Anger Her Protection for Women *(1589)[1]*

"Ah who can love the worker of her smart?" The narrator of Edmund
Spenser's late-sixteenth-century magnum opus, *The Faerie Queene,*
rhetorically poses this question at one of the grisliest moments in an often
grisly poem, as the enchanter Busirane uses the very heart's blood of his
pinioned victim, the chaste Amoret, to write "a thousand charmes" meant
to capture her affections.[2] Rhetorically—and yet twentieth-century interpreters of the allegory of this situation have often taken the question as one
that requires answering. For some 30 years beginning in the mid-1960s,
the dominant critical trend among Spenser scholars was to describe
Amoret's suffering as an externalized, allegorically expressed form of either

her dread of sexual union with her brand-new husband, Scudamour—
Busirane having kidnapped her at the wedding masque, before the marriage could be consummated—or her shock and shame at the magnitude
of her own sexual desire.[3] In these readings, the "worker" of Amoret's
"smart" thus proves to be not the sadistic Busirane, but Amoret herself.

Only recently have some critics stopped blaming the victim in this
episode and examined it as what Spenser's narrator calls it: an instance of
violence against women, specifically of allegorical rape. For these readers
of the poem, Busirane is indeed the "worker" of Amoret's "smart," and his
transfixing Amoret's heart with a "cruell dart" is thematically related to
other crucial episodes in *The Faerie Queene* in which a woman is either actually raped—the nymph Chrysogone, unwittingly impregnated by the
sun as she sleeps (3.6.5–10); nearly raped—Una, attacked by Sansloy who
"With beastly sin thought her to have defilde" (1.6.3); or physically abused
in a way that figures or anticipates rape—Serena, laid upon a sacrificial altar
by cannibals who view her choicest body parts "with lustfull fantasyes" ob-
scurely both erotic and culinary (6.8.41). Sheila Cavanagh, for example,
cautions us not to read past rape, to dismiss these narrative events as ex-
cusable elements in the service of some larger psychic or moral allegory.[4]
And Maureen Quilligan and Susan Frye have each suggested in connection with the Busirane-Amoret episode that if rape *is* part of a larger
agenda, that agenda is also one of men terrorizing women, this time
through poetry: either as a class of "sadistic sonneteers" working in the Petrarchan tradition of poetically dismembering the lady's fair form,[5] or as an
embittered Edmund Spenser himself, seeking through literary means to
master Elizabeth I, the unforthcoming queen who never granted him the
professional advancement he desired.[6]

My only argument with these innovative and timely studies is that they
presume it is to poetry's advantage to model itself upon rape. That is to say,
poetry is most effective when it both (1) portrays women being sexually
assaulted and (2) describes its own operation as the phallic penetration and
wounding of a defenseless and unwilling subject. In the case of the first
presumption, Spenser's poem surely joins most of the Western aesthetic tradition in being guilty as charged. But it is my contention that *The Faerie
Queene* displays considerable uneasiness about the second presumption.
That uneasiness can be sensed in Spenser's dual usages of the notion of *ravishment*. As opposed to figuring poetry as genital rape, a tool for single-
minded exposure, penetration, and comprehension of a feminized scene,
The Faerie Queene also, if only intermittently, hints at poetry as a vehicle for
rapture, a suffusion of delight that suspends the quest and admits a multiplicity of both erotic and epistemological pleasures.[7] This rapture is felt, I
want to demonstrate, by female as well as male characters in the poem, and

specifically in scenes that a number of Spenser critics have identified as allegories of the writing and/or reading of poetry.

My argument will also depend, though, upon analyzing why these moments of poetic rapture in *The Faerie Queene* are just that, momentary, and why these rapturous instances are enwrapped with discomfiting regularity by brutal invasions of feminine spaces whose force is both rapine and blatantly teleological, always designed to move the quest along towards its end and the narrative towards its conclusion. At stake in my analysis of these rapine episodes is an understanding of not only how violence against women is fundamental to the operation of poetry, but also how such violence furthers the aims of Spenser's particular poetic project, allegory. I draw here from Gordon Teskey's thesis that allegory is inextricably linked to a systematic program of violence. Teskey describes this link as variable, depending on whether we consider allegory as process or product. To allegorize is to enact the violence of wresting whole systems of readable meaning from the inchoate stuff of the material world; but the product of this allegorical effort, the literary work itself, generally succeeds in burying these violent origins under the seamless, quasi-mythographical schema that has thereby been created.[8] Some allegories, however—among them *The Faerie Queene*—are, in Teskey's view, unusually self-aware in that they periodically "draw back the veil of an optimistic, metaphysical illusion to reveal the truth of its origin and the certainty of its undoing."[9] This self-awareness, it seems to me, extends within Spenser's poem to a recognition of what is lost when poetry turns to rape as both its topic and its model. At the very moments at which *The Faerie Queene* violently overthrows modes of rapture in favor of modes of rape, it details the human and poetic costs of such an overthrow, among them the substitutions of inadequate for complex modes of knowledge, solipsistic for shared modes of sensual and sexual pleasure, and obvious for subtle modes of poetry.

Specifically, I propose that critics who have discussed Spenserian rape have wrongly assumed that in *The Faerie Queene,* an act of rape is the subordinate half of a trope. In their view, rape—the physical event—is the vehicle of a metaphor, the tenor of which is unjustly and misogynistically supplied either by the text itself (Sansloy is not a real rapist, he is the assailant of "Una" as signifier of the one true faith) or by critics of the text (Busirane is not a real rapist, he merely reveals Amoret's fear of losing her virginity to her husband).[10] In this assumption, feminist readers of the poem have been rowing the same hermeneutic boat as the critics they critique who attempt to explain rape away; the only difference is that feminists have sought to call attention to the vehicle rather than the tenor of the trope. My thesis, in contrast, is that rape enacts precisely the reverse of this schema. It is not that rape is the ineluctable narrative event for which alternative allegorical concepts (religious, historical, or psychoanalytic) are unsatisfactory and misogynistic textual or critical substitutions. It is that the narrative event of rape itself is a metaphoric maneuver, a substitute action foisted on the narrative in order to conceal or evade a rapturous mode of poetic operation.

I am thinking of metaphor here in the terms deployed by English literary theorist (and near contemporary of Spenser) George Puttenham, who evokes the violence of rapine abduction through his definition of metaphor as "the figure of transport": "a kinde of wresting of a single word from his owne right signification, to another not so naturall."[11] Puttenham shares this sense of metaphor's imposition of force with Teskey, who finds violence at the heart of the "master metaphor," allegory. Teskey, however, describes the victim of this violence as feminine in the sense that matter—including the raw matter of experience from which meaning is constructed—was, for Early Modern Neoplatonists like the ones who influenced Spenser, always figured as feminine: "To be ravished is what Matter secretly wants, so that it may bear in its substance the imprint of beautiful forms."[12] Puttenham's definition of metaphoric violence, though, is more complex, and more apropos to the oppositional modes of rapturous poetry and rapine poetry that I want to elaborate. Puttenham assigns to the before-and-after states of metaphoric violence not the categories of Matter and Meaning, but the categories of Right Signification and Unnatural Signification. In other words, rape as metaphor does not impose order upon chaos by asserting signification where none existed, but rather substitutes its own signifying system for one that is already in place. As Patricia Parker has shown us, it is not only matter that has historically been associated with femininity, but form: particularly a certain type of expansive, seemingly undirected linguistic form exemplified, for instance, by the rhetorical technique of *dilatio,* or by the siren song of lyric poems.[13] As a result, rape's metaphorical vector is meant to redirect our attention not from matter to form, but from one literary form to another. In Susanne Wofford's wonderful phrase, rape enacts the "figurative compulsion" of "right" reading.[14] Although I have no intention of denying that the sexual menace of women is a disturbingly recurrent element in *The Faerie Queene,* my sense is that rape or near rape most often recurs not just as a symptom of patriarchy, but precisely as a mode of worrying over rape's viability as signifying system and over whether that system might be shown up in all its strenuous, unattractive unnaturalness when juxtaposed with the rapturous poetic modes it replaces.

In part, my analysis of these alternative poetic modes is designed to intervene in a long-standing critical discussion about how *The Faerie Queene* passes judgement on the relation between sensual pleasure and poetic beauty. Central to this debate, appropriately enough, has been a location of sexual domination in *The Faerie Queene* governed by not a man, but a woman who takes sexual pleasure at will: Book 2's stunning, aesthetically ornate, and tremendously sensual Bower of Bliss, at whose center the witch Acrasia hangs over her sleeping lover "And through his humid eyes did sucke his spright" (2.12.73). Coming upon this scene, the knight of Temperance and hero of Book 2, Guyon, responds by breaking down "all those pleasant bowres and Pallace brave" with a physical force so intemperately "pittilesse" (2.12.83) that it seems, on the face of it, unsuited to his former unimpeachably temperate self—unless one assumes that Guyon's reaction encodes some kind of warning, one too global to be circumscribed by one knight's signal virtue, against the dangers of aesthetic productions' erotic appeal. As a result, critical response to how Guyon cancels this rapturous poetic reverie has ranged from regret to approval, elaborating on the early reactions of, on the one hand, readers like Herbert Grierson, who declared that "there is no virtue in the mere destruction of the beautiful," and, on the other, readers like C. S. Lewis, who denounced Acrasia's Bower as "artifice, sterility, death."[15] For Stephen Greenblatt, however, critical approval and critical regret of Guyonic violence merely recapitulate two elements already in dialectical relation within the Bower of Bliss episode itself: the renunciation of sexual pleasure, but also the sexual pleasure itself, whose attractions must nonetheless be felt so that they may be renounced. Aligning Guyon's immoderate rampage with the violence that marked both the European encounter with the New World and the sixteenth-century English Protestant campaign against Roman Catholic devotional images, Greenblatt describes such acts of destruction as necessary to the fashioning of the (tacitly masculine) self prescribed by Spenser's culture:

> The violence of the destruction was regenerative; they found in it a sense of identity, discipline, and holy faith. In tearing down what both appealed to them and sickened them, they strengthened their power to resist their dangerous longings, to repress antisocial impulses, to conquer the powerful desire for release. And the conquest of desire had the more power because it contained within itself a version of that which it destroyed: the power of Acrasia's sensuality to erase signs and upset temperate order is simultaneously attacked and imitated in Guyon's destruction of the exquisite Bower.[16]

It is my contention, however, that Greenblatt's sense of the interdependence of the sensual image and its violent overthrow must be modified when we understand Guyon's actions here as an act of rape, and when we further reflect on how, elsewhere in Spenser's poem, rape is associated with a particular poetics. While rape and rapture may both share a quality of intemperateness, *The Faerie Queene* treats rapine poetry and rapturous poetry as ontologically incompatible. Thus, while Guyon's actions may encapsulate the tensions prerequisite to fashioning the Renaissance man, they also prove him astoundingly insensible to the productive, and far more radical, tensions inherent within the poem itself. Proving this case, however, will require turning for awhile from Acrasia's Bower to other episodes in *The Faerie Queene*, ones that also model their narrative action after the act of rape.

We can begin to see *The Faerie Queene*'s association between rape and the avoidance of rapture with the poem's first sexual assault on a woman, that of Sansloy on Una (1.6.2–6). This episode in isolation certainly conforms to Cavanagh's sense that the act of rape too easily digresses, in the narrative and, thus, also in the reader's mind, into far removed and much more "elevated" topics. The name of the rapist, "Sansloy," inspires us to think about rape as a crime against law in the abstract, rather than against a woman's person. Furthermore, Una's fortuitous rescue by fauns and satyrs alludes not only to classical literature but also to the Old and New Testaments, guaranteeing the story a number of typological resonances that necessarily distance our reading from the physical event.[17] Such allegorical opportunities might lead us to conclude that this story, in its evasive maneuvers, is literally *about* rape, rather than rape itself. We must, however, ask ourselves what this story about rape, in all its circumlocution, is doing within the structure of Book 1. Una's plight and rescue are sandwiched between two episodes, contiguous in narrative time, of the Christian hero Redcrosse Knight's feminine imperilment: first, his backdoor escape from the clutches of the duplicitous seductress Duessa and of Dame Pride (1.5); and, second, his reunion with Duessa next to an enfeebling, distinctly Ovidian fountain where, disarmed and "Pourd out in loosnesse on the grassy grownd," he falls prey to the giant Orgoglio, a "monstrous masse of earthly slime" who embodies Redcrosse's surrender to pleasures of the flesh (1.7.7, 9). In this light, Una's near rape seems to be less imperiling—after all, she, unlike Redcrosse, is never endangered by lust again—than is Redcrosse's own susceptibility to Pride's pageantry or to the fountain's delightful and deeply intertextual *otium*.[18] That is to say, rape is not the horrific core at the center of this episode's layered meanings; rather, it is the typological trajectory that diverts us from the true core, which is erotic poetic pleasure. (Just as Una herself attempts to divert her deliverers, those woodland fauns and satyrs, from a sensual, mythological frame of reference when they proceed to "[worship] her in vaine, / And [make] her th'Image of Idolatryes" [1.6.19].)

From this episode one might, therefore, infer that *The Faerie Queene* proposes rape as salvation: from sexual sin, from idolatry, and even from er-

rant readings of figures like Una herself. Rape, in other words, is revelation. Such a supposition might find support in the sixteenth century's primary, legal definition of "ravishment," which, Deborah Burks tells us,
connotes the illegal transport of women as "a crime targeted at propertied
men, through a piece of their property."[19] Kathryn Gravdal traces this definition's origins to the French etymology of the word:

> By the end of the twelfth century, *ravir* can mean to run at great speed; to
> carry off by force; or to be carried off at great speed. *Ravissant* designates, in
> the twelfth century, some one or thing that carries others off by force. But
> as early as 1155, the Latin *raptus* in the sense of abduction brings about the
> shift towards a sexual meaning: *rap* (c. 1155) or *rat* (c. 1235) designates ab-
> duction by violence or by seduction, for the purposes of forced coitus.[20]

Ravishment's dominant connotation, then, is one of possession, of gaining
access, of acquiring power and rights (albeit illicitly). In *The Faerie Queene,*
however, ultimate power is conveyed not by means of possessing property,
but by means of acquiring access to the truth, whether spiritual, moral,
marital, or genealogical. By this logic, rape indeed ought to be a tool of
revelation, willfully entering the dark and vicious place of begetting in
order to see the light.

This, however, proves not to be the case. Instead, as Cavanagh explains,
The Faerie Queene's instances of men invading feminine spaces are anything
but enlightening.[21] I mean here to depart from Parker's assertion, drawn
from Laura Mulvey's theories of filmic scopophilia, that the poem's male
voyeurs manage to gain full visual access to the forbidden female body and
thus perhaps to master their fear of castration.[22] First of all, and as Cavanagh notes, despite its frequent feints at revealing the inner sanctum of
the female genitalia the poem manages never to do so. The most famous
such instance, the stripping of Duessa that proves the beautiful seductress a
loathly hag, modestly refrains from revealing Duessa's pudenda only to
dwell with relish, in a kind of displacement backwards, on a rear view:
"Her neather parts, the shame of all her kind, / My chaster Muse for shame
doth blush to write; / But at her rompe she growing had behind / A foxes
taile, with dong all fowly dight" (1.8.48). Similarly, Serena upon the cannibals' altar is stripped naked only to be bedecked, in the narrator's image,
with a surfeit of surprisingly phallic coverings: "Her goodly thighes, whose
glorie did appeare / Like a triumphall Arch, and thereupon / The spoiles
of Princes hang'd, which were in battel won" (6.8.42).[23] Even in the
episode that most imitates Actaeon's beholding a naked Diana—that paradigmatic Ovidian tale of a man's being able to see all that should not be
seen, even if he suffers death as a result—ends inconclusively: in Spenser's

version Faunus, who spies Diana bathing but lives to tell the tale, sees only a vague "some-what" (7.6.46).

These incidents of literal stripping are fairly rare in the grand scheme of *The Faerie Queene;* the poem is far more devoted to metaphorical penetrations of the female inner sanctum. But even then, penetration does not convey comprehension. As any number of critics have noticed, Guyon seems not to learn anything as he invades the "covert groves, and thickets close" of Acrasia's Bower (2.12.76). His comments to his monitory guide, the Palmer, after he has infiltrated and destroyed this feminine enclosure deal only with the piggish Grill, who, like the "Gryllus" transformed by Circe in Plutarch's reworked version of the *Odyssey,* resists being returned to human form.[24] Spenser's Grill, however, seems to have succumbed to the temptation more of hogwash than of feminine filth, so that for Guyon to learn his primary lesson from Grill's example ("See the mind of beastly man, / That hath so soone forgot the excellence / Of his creation" [2.12.87]) is for him to have forgotten Acrasia and her erotic temptations entirely. Thus even if— as Greenblatt argues—Guyon masters the Bower's allure of erotic release, he nonetheless absorbs none of that allure, even so much as to comment on it. Since knowing the Bower in a sexual sense would be prelude to knowing it in an epistemological sense, inhabiting all its feminine mysteries, Guyon's task—to rephrase John Milton's comment on this episode—is to see, not know, and hence abstain.[25] In a similar episode of invading a privileged feminine enclosure, the knight Calidore is likewise just as stupid about erotic desire as ever he was after he stumbles into a circle of dancing Graces; despite the long conversation that ensues with the poet-figure Colin Clout on what he has seen, he immediately turns once again towards his previous, ill-advised erotic activity, a demeaning contest with a rustic swain for Pastorella's favors (6.10.10–36). (Calidore in this respect is like Faunus, in whom the illicit sight of Diana naked inspires not a sublime vision, as Leonard Barkan defines the impetus of the Actaeon myth, but rather just a "foolish thought" [7.6.46].)[26] And, finally, in the poem's most allegorized version of invading a feminine body, the knights Arthur and Guyon move ambitiously through a castle emblematic of the physical form of its owner, Alma. But even though they travel from her portal as far as her brain, where they read histories of their own ancestors' deeds, even then full revelation is denied to them—Arthur because his chronicle is cut off midsentence, Guyon because his leads up to the unknowable Gloriana, the allegorical version of Queen Elizabeth who, though often referred to in *The Faerie Queene,* never appears (2.10.68, 76).[27]

This evasion of knowing the female body involves more, I think, than a mere fear of feminine sexuality, although such a fear is unquestionably in play in these episodes. Paradoxically, the poem's refusal fully to reveal these feminine hollowed spaces occasionally sustains the sensual pleasure I have identified with the experience of poetic rapture. In such instances, *The Faerie Queene* revises sixteenth-century ravishment by introducing a third definition of the term, one that exists somewhere between the primary one of kidnapping and raping female bodies, and the secondary one— more familiar to the modern reader—of excessive, discombobulatory rapture that takes a person away from herself. In this third term, ravishment is physically felt, located within and upon the body, as it is for the unfortunate victim of the crime. But it is also pleasurable in its sensuality, ecstasy without *ekstasis*. This intermediary definition bears some relation to another sense of *ravishment,* one that was almost out of date in the late sixteenth century but that thus is in keeping with Spenser's habit of employing quasi-archaisms: a state of heightened awareness brought about by being possessed by the Holy Spirit. (The *OED*'s last citation of *ravish* in connection with religious ecstasy dates from 1644.)[28] This kind of mystic transport, however, unlike Spenser's, generally discards the body as a useless or tainted hindrance to delight; thus, the sainted Pope Gregory the Great is praised by the *Golden Legend* for owning a spirit that "let everything go by beneath it, and [that] rose above the transitory to think upon nothing but the things of heaven . . . it escaped the confinement of the flesh by contemplation."[29] Spenser's poem, in contrast, abjures seeing things this clearly, in either the Pauline or the Neoplatonic sense, because to do so would require discarding the material world entirely or burrowing past appealing surfaces into the heart of things. Rather, *The Faerie Queene* displays an unwillingness to give up the tactile and visual pleasures of surfaces and the sensual *frisson* they give. *The Faerie Queene* seeks to preserve, in other words, what Parker calls the association between dilatory poetics and feminine enticement, and what Greenblatt, in relation to Shakespearean comedy, calls the association between fiction and friction, between poetry and the somatic delights of the external surface.[30] But whereas Greenblatt's reading of the transvestite actor's body dwells on the frictional pleasures promised by female interiority, by vaginas designed to be matched with homologous penises, *The Faerie Queene* locates its seductive frictions upon the exterior contours of both poetry and flesh. To use a specific example, *The Faerie Queene* takes seriously the implication that, had Chrysogone been awake during her impregnation by the sun, she might have enjoyed it.

I use this distasteful phrasing not to endorse the notion that women desire to be raped, but rather to suggest that before Chrysogone is "pierst" by the sun she experiences the kind of eroticism of surfaces that I am describing. Having "bath'd her brest, the boyling heat t'allay; / . . . with roses red, and violets blew, / And all the sweetest flowres, that in the forrest

grew," Chrysogone falls asleep before she can feel how the sun initially
continues that pleasurable sensation of nature's gifts caressing her soft skin:
"The sunne-beames bright upon her body playd, / Being through former
bathing mollifide" (3.6.6, 7). Of course the sun does not stop there, and she
is raped while unconscious and later shamed by pregnancy. But briefly,
Chrysogone might feel ravishment as rapture, not as rape. This is a moment
that philosopher Catherine Clément would call "syncope," or the con-
spicuous disruption of the rhythm of linear thought: seizure, delirium, a
missing beat, rationality abandoned in a fit of ecstasy; and indeed it is signaled by a remarkable instance in poetic technique, a rare, syncopated stut-
ter in the pattern of the Spenserian stanza where the internal matching of
lines 4 and 5 is created not by Spenser's usual bravura of a rhyme, but by
sheer repetition: "all naked bare di*splayd; /* The sunne-beames bright upon
her body *playd*" (3.6.7, my emphasis).[31] Although Chrysogone's loss of
consciousness is the end of her rapture, her sleep might be read as the in-
verse of Guyon's famous swoon when he is faced by all the glittering trea-
sures of the cave of Mammon (2.7.65–66): not as a denial of sensual
pleasure, but as a surfeit of it.

This example is meant to complicate Nancy Vickers's influential argument that the blazonic description of the female body is an invitation to
rape.[32] Although this is indeed the sum effect of the Chrysogone episode,
the text's hesitation during the moment of rapture suggests another mode
of sexuality entirely. Other instances in the poem achieve this hesitation by
pausing on the lip, as it were, of feminine enclosures; and although we
might well read in these pauses a justifiable Actaeonic phobia of the threat
women pose to masculinity, I think that such hesitation also hints at how
rapture might replace rape as a model for the interface of human and other
physical bodies. The most abrupt example of this phenomenon, found in
Book 2's blazon of the virgin huntress Belphoebe, is signaled by a poetic
device used only four times in *The Faerie Queene,* a truncated line:

> [She] was yclad, for heat of scorching aire,
> All in a silken Camus lylly whight,
> Purfled upon with many a folded plight,
> Which all above besprinckled was throughout
> With golden ayguylets, that glistred bright,
> Like twinckling starres, and all the skirt about
> Was hemd with golden fringe
> Below her ham her weede did somewhat traine. . . . (2.3.26–27)

By pausing at, then skimming over, the fringed hemline that is metonymic
for Belphoebe's pubic hair at the same moment that it pauses at the chasm

between Stanzas 26 and 27 of this canto, the verse emphasizes, as Philippa
Berry has described it, both Belphoebe's "refusal of any phallic attempt at
the unravelling and decoding of her body" and "an alternative, many-
faceted eroticism, whereby the female body is 'close enwrapped' within itself."[33] Another such pause seems to organize the heart of Book 3's Garden
of Adonis, where the penetrative "bore" that wounded Adonis is mewed
up and where the reigning male presence is thus Adonis himself, whose
erotic contact with Venus seems more like her labial/clitoral rubbing of
him than like his penile invasion of her: "There yet, some say, in secret he
does ly, / Lapped in flowres and pretious spycery" (3.6.46).[34] No wonder
Venus's mount, the geographical and sexual center of the Garden, is described as all bedewed. But Adonis experiences pleasure, too, in fact a state
of everlasting rapture: "There now he liveth in eternall blis, / Joying his
goddesse, and of her enjoyd" (3.6.48). Similarly, the intricate ring of the
Graces' dance upon the poem's other mons veneris, Acidale (a "mount" to
which "*Venus,* when she did dispose / Her selfe to pleasaunce, used to re-
sort" [6.10.8–9]), includes the merrily piping Colin Clout, whose presence
seems not to disrupt the ring but rather to keep time for its continued
dance. Seemingly as a result of his playing, Colin is catapulted from con-
clusive past-tense narrative into the ecstatic stasis of the present tense:

> He pypt apace, whilest they him daunst about.
> Pype jolly shepheard, pype thou now apace
> Unto thy love, that made thee low to lout:
> Thy love is present there with thee in place,
> Thy love is there advaunst to be another Grace. (6.10.16)

And so too is Calidore "long astonished in spright, / And rapt with pleasaunce," at least for the few lines that elapse before he "resolv[es] . . . to
know" what he has seen and breaks the circle, causing the entire spectacle
to vanish (6.10.17).

Calidore's "luckelesse breach" of the Graces' dance, with its pun on
"breech" connoting breaking and hinder body parts all at once, clearly
amounts to a metaphorical rape. But this rape's enactment has a force quite
different from what Teskey describes as the typical operations of allegory,
where meaning is violently imposed on the material (and hence feminine)
world. On the face of it, the Mount Acidale episode conforms exactly to that
pattern, since the Graces vanish only to be replaced by Colin Clout's extended explanation to Calidore of who they are and what they signify. But
Calidore's breaking of the Graces' magic circle serves to discontinue not only
sensual matter but also aesthetic form, since the dance is delightful in its
order and its ornamentation as well as in its intermingling of pleasurable

sights, sounds, and odors. Furthermore, this loss of aesthetic satisfaction is specifically aligned with the cessation of a certain kind of poetics. Colin, identified as the author's poetic alter ego in Spenser's early pastoral poem *The Shepheardes Calender,* responds to the dance's ending by breaking his instrument of song, his bagpipes, in disgust. As in Colin's earlier acting out of this same gesture, the abolition of poetic effort only leads to its reconstruction: in another eclogue in *The Shepheardes Calender,* "Aprill," a different shepherd, Hobbinol, sings the song for us, whereas in *The Faerie Queene* Colin himself renarrates what Calidore has just seen. But because on Mount Acidale Colin's abandoned song celebrates present fulfillment, rather than complains (as Colin did in "Januarye") of vanished love, the reconstruction carries a different weight. Colin's ex-post-facto account—a rather deadening and defensive allegorization—relegates the women at best to the role of inspiring, rather than participating in, aesthetic and especially poetic creativity, as the Graces now are labeled as representing all those social skills that Calidore, the knight of Courtesy, should cultivate: "comely carriage, entertainement kynde, / Sweete semblaunt, friendly offices that bynde, / And all the complements of curtesie" (6.10.23). Similarly, Colin's own "countrey lasse," who stood in the center of the Graces' ring "as a precious gemme, / Amidst a ring most richly well enchaced," no longer conveys a multitude of mysterious sensual pleasures but rather becomes a waxwork figure signifying "Divine resemblaunce, beauty soveraine rare, / [and] Firme Chastity, that spight ne blemish dare" (6.10.12, 27).

The poem's most important meditation upon the contrast between rapine and rapturous poetry, however, occurs in the episode that has attracted the most pointed charges of Spenserian rape: Busirane's transfixion of Amoret (3.12.19–21, 30–31). Cavanagh calls Amoret's victimization an act of "pornographic sadism," and Frye goes even further by assigning Spenser, represented by Busirane as artificer and author, the role of the sadist. Spenser's motive in this representation, Frye asserts, is to design an outlet for "all the displaced frustration and violence that [he] feels towards his queen."[35] Leaving aside the issue of male poets' resentment of a female monarch, I want to dispute Frye's unqualified equivalence of Spenser the poet and Busirane as poet-figure. Rather, in my view Busirane's house ironically enacts the futility of fashioning poetry as a rape. At the same time, though, Busirane's house demonstrates the difficulty of sustaining an alternative poetics of rapture; we get it here only temporarily and in flashes, and only by wading very much against the current of what we "know" to be the evils of this evil place.

The first of these flashes can be seen, contrarily enough, in a notably sleazy piece of Busiranean interior decoration: elaborate tapestries depicting Ovid's version of the loves of the gods, tapestries that all Spenser crit-

ics, from the most to the least traditional, have found morally and psychologically suspect. Although Harry Berger is surely right to argue that Britomart—the female knight whose task it is to rescue Amoret—moves past
increasingly advanced images of masculine sexual perversion as she progresses through Busirane's house, I want to establish that this progress also
proves, as a parallel phenomenon, that the more rapine poetics become the
less likely they are to have the desired effect of seduction.[36] In this pro-
gression, the Ovidian tapestries are the first artistic creations Britomart encounters, and are therefore the most likely to hint at modes of poetic
efficacy derived from sensual pleasure—notably, at least on occasion, the
sensual pleasure of the subordinate female participant.[37] This pleasure, unlike the instances of rapturous poetics I have described above, does not take
place in the absence of masculine penetration of women; in other words,
rape is always a possible element of the scene. Nevertheless, frictional fictional delights are proffered as well. For example, consider the description
of Leda and the swan:

> O wondrous skill, and sweet wit of the man,
> That her in daffadillies sleeping made,
> From scorching heat her daintie limbes to shade:
> Whiles the proud Bird ruffing his fethers wyde,
> And brushing his faire brest, did her invade;
> She slept, yet twixt her eyelids closely spyde,
> How towardss her he rusht, and smiled at his pryde. (3.11.32)

This stanza, ostentatiously expanded from Ovid, not only remarks the skill
of the image maker but also identifies that skill as causing female pleasure,
as it is arguably Leda rather than the swan himself who "smile[s]" at the
swan's "pryde" in this stanza's last line. That pride is more than phallic: it
refers to the bird's self-caresses, which in turn are reminiscent of the floral
embrace of Leda's daffodils. Similarly, if more elliptically, Alcmena seems to
experience sensual enjoyment herself when Jove "Three nights in one . . .
/ did put, her pleasures lenger to partake" (3.11.33). Perhaps these traces
of feminine satisfaction are what impel Britomart to experience momentary rapture herself in this room, as the sight of Cupid's statue, which sums
up the theme of these tapestries' stories, "faire *Britomart* amazed, / Ne seeing could her wonder satisfie, / But evermore and more upon it gazed, /
The whiles the passing brightnes her fraile sences dazed" (3.11.49). Britomart's wonderment depends upon the practically somatic visual effect that
Paul Alpers sees in Spenser's simile describing the tapestries' golden thread,
which "shewd it selfe, and shone unwillingly; / Like a discoloured Snake,
whose hidden snares / Through the greene gras his long bright burnisht

backe declares" (3.11.28): "through alliteration, rhythm, and the concluding 'declares' with its strong rhyme, Spenser makes us feel we are dazzled,
our field of vision filled."[38]

In contrast, the spectacles of the second Busiranean room she enters
hold more intellectual than sensual interest for Britomart. Not only does
she spend time trying to puzzle out the phrases "Be bold" and "Be not too
bold" inscribed over the room's many doors, but her absorption in the
room's decoration, a golden bas-relief detailed with illustrations of "wilde
Antickes, which their follies playd" (3.11.51), is prompted more by curiosity at the chamber's desertedness than by the images' aesthetic effect:

> The warlike Mayde beholding earnestly
> The goodly ordinance of this rich place,
> Did greatly wonder, ne could satisfie
> Her greedy eyes with gazing a long space,
> But more she mervailed that no footings trace,
> Nor wight appear'd, but wastefull emptinesse. . . . (3.11.53)

As a result, when Britomart views Busirane's next artistic production in
this room—a sadistic masque that is the initial presentation of Amoret at
his mercy, her bosom stripped and her heart laid out in a silver basin—we
are not surprised that Britomart as audience remains unmoved, proceeding on to Busirane's inner sanctum "Neither of idle shewes, nor of false
charmes aghast" (3.12.29). This is the case despite—or, I would say, because
of—the masque's appearing as a caricature of how rapine poetry hopes to
infiltrate the object of desire. First of all, the masque presents no woman
taking pleasure in erotic interaction, but rather just a series of standard figures, warmed over from the thirteenth-century French allegory *The Romance of the Rose,* of women's inviting and spurning men's sexual advances
(for example, Hope, Dissemblance, Pleasance, Daunger, Doubt, and
Feare).[39] Second, and more pertinent to my argument regarding notions
The Faerie Queene proves insupportable, the masque imagines that the sexual violation of Amoret will open her up to complete knowability. Amoret
in her masque appearance takes the form, in fact, of a womb dissected and
splayed open at the moment of impregnation—a fantasy of the medical
scientists of Spenser's time who, as Richard Wilson has detailed, were
barred from cutting open inseminated female cadavers.[40] Amoret's bared
breast reveals, through its "wide orifice," her "trembling heart," a female
organ in a visible state of being pierced through.

A gruesome fantasy, indeed. But it is a fantasy that is clearly marked
as emanating not from Amoret's own psyche, but from an excess of
misogynistic authorial zeal. After the entire rout of the masque's allegor-

ical personae has passed, the narrator comments on their status as literary commonplace:

There were full many moe like maladies,
Whose names and natures I note readen well;
So many moe, as there be phantasies
In wavering wemens wit, that none can tell,
Or paines in love, or punishments in hell; . . . (3.12.26)

In the narrator's weary comparison between a procession too elongated and repetitive to "readen well" and the similarly endless number of "phantasies / In wavering wemens wit, . . . / Or paines in love, or punishments in hell," I hear the driest of allusions to hoary literary precedents that, when badly imitated, anyone finds boring: *The Romance of the Rose* again, with its static representations of feminine psychology as "wavering wemens wit"; Petrarchan-style sonnets, whose conventional male lover feels conventional "paines in love"; and—in a glance at how reading such bad love poetry feels—the *Inferno,* with its stultifying eternity of "punishments in hell."

Busirane's poetry is just this awful, and in the end just this inconsequential. Busirane certainly tries hard, as he busily writes charms in Amoret's blood and even seeks to make an authorial imprint upon Britomart when he turns his knife upon her, too. But Britomart's resulting wound is both unreadable and unmemorable as print—"nothing deepe *imprest*" (3.12.33, my emphasis)—which may explain why Amoret remains emotionally unaffected by her own, similar wounding: "A thousand charmes he formerly did prove; / Yet thousand charmes could not her stedfast heart remove" (3.12.31). It seems, then, that the "weake feete" on which Amoret totters through Busirane's masque might belong as much to the measures of Busirane's verse as to Amoret herself (3.12.21).[41] As long as he engages merely in the rapine "sadistic sonneteering" that Quilligan describes, Busirane is doomed to poetic obscurity.

Amoret, thus, is highly mistaken when she assumes that Busirane must produce the same kind of verse to procure her release, curing her by recurrence: "none but hee, / Which wrought [her pain], could the same recur againe" (3.12.34). Britomart, contrariwise, frees Amoret by herself introducing an oppositional poetic mode, forcing Busirane to undo his charms either by reading them backwards or by remaking them entirely—"re-versing" them, as the stanza punningly puts it (3.12.36). For this one stanza the cause and effect of rape are held in equipoise while these new charms are being wrought. Britomart stands with her phallic sword suspended over the magician, even while she herself takes on a resemblance to the spectacle of the raped Medusa with her bristling locks:

"That horror gan the virgins hart to perse, / And her faire locks up stared stiffe on end" (3.12.36).[42] But this scene of poetic rape gives way, under the influence of Busirane's new versification, to one of rapture. Not only is phallic penetration canceled, as Busirane's knife withdraws and his brazen pillar breaks, but Amoret is evidently moved to the point of orgasm, as Busirane's house vibrates into pieces, Amoret's constricting bonds burst open, and "Before faire *Britomart,* she [falls] prostrate" in gratitude (3.12.39). Amoret is subsequently restored to "perfect hole," a locution that reinforces the impression that this rapturous poetry lingers lovingly on the edge of hollow feminine enclosures.[43]

The conclusion of the Busirane-Amoret episode exists in two versions, one published in 1590 to round out *The Faerie Queene*'s first installment of Books 1–3, and the second in 1596, when the poem was extended into Books 1–6. The 1590 ending of Book 3 is notable in that in some ways, it takes even further the equation between poetry and feminine orgasmic pleasure that is asserted at the fall of the house of Busirane. In the ravishment of this 1590 ending, where Amoret is reunited with her husband Scudamour, inside and outside, penetrator and penetrated are so thoroughly commingled as to bear no distinction. On the one hand, Amoret's body still is envisioned as having a prominent interior—"late the prison of sad paine, / Now the sweet lodge of love and deare delight"—and she is "overcommen quight" by a comically erectile "huge affection" (3.12.45a). But, on the other hand, this huge affection is identified as Amoret's own, not Scudamour's; and because his arms are around her in a ring in which she as occupant "did in pleasure melt, / And in sweete ravishment pourd out her spright," she seems the more penile figure in their version of bodily union (3.12.45a). This interchangeability is reinforced by the pronouncement, "Thus doe those lovers with sweet countervayle, / Each other of loves bitter fruit despoile" (3.12.47a), as well as by their embrace's being compared to a statue of a hermaphrodite. (Though I shall have more to say of that hermaphrodite.) Watching them, Britomart is aroused, as well, being "much empassiond in her gentle sprite" (3.12.46a). And finally the "faire Swayns" that are addressed as the 1590 *Faerie Queene* concludes are invited to "cease [their] *worke*"—a noun that recalls penile penetration as *swinking,* as well as Busirane as "worker" of Amoret's "smart" (3.12.31)— so they may "at [their] pleasure play" (3.12.47a, my emphasis). Perhaps in this interval of rapture, this holiday of mutual pleasure, the first installment of *The Faerie Queene* itself is read.

In at least this episode of *The Faerie Queene,* then, rape itself serves to reveal its untenability as a narrative device. Thomas Greene tells us that Spenser's sentence structure is too "tangled and circular," too "subtle and seductive" to convey what Greene calls "virile directness and natural force."[44] But in a poem that depends so heavily upon detailed sensual encounters with ingeniously ornamented surfaces—gardens, tapestries, masques, tableaux, and especially the ornate, convoluted structure of both the smallest and largest units of Spenserian invention, the intensely intricate stanza and the longitudinally complicated knightly quest—the virile directness and force of rape become a mode of closing off what we might term the "textural" erotics, the textured and textual erotics, of such encounters. As I hope I have begun to demonstrate, a poetics of rape demands disdain for this elaborate decoration of nature and of art. Like the sixteenth-century radical Protestant aesthetics with which Spenser had some association (and to which I will shortly turn), rape is a radical gesture of the antibaroque.

My argument, however, must lead me to speculate about how *The Faerie Queene* would look if it fully embraced, and were embraced by, a poetics of rapture. In that case, and as if *The Faerie Queene*'s generic status were not already a knotty problem, rapture would have to be coordinated not only with dilatory and ecstatic verse but also with Spenser's project of Christian allegory. In some ways, the poem does in fact achieve such congruence of mutually poetic and Protestant rapture, in part through Spenser's penchant for folding widely disparate episodes of his poem together, as he does with the poem's two conclusions. The implied end of *The Faerie Queene,* as outlined in the "Letter of the Authors" that brings up the rear of the 1590 edition of Books 1–3, is one that Spenser's unfinished poem never reaches, a reunion of all the questing knights in the court of Queen Gloriana. *The Faerie Queene*'s actual end, at the close of the Mutabilitie Cantos—two new cantos tacked on after Book 6 in the posthumous, 1609 edition of the poem—is a prayer for a quite different reuniting moment, the "Sabaoths sight" of the apocalypse (7.8.2). I have argued elsewhere that the Mutabilitie Cantos' concluding stanzas, when taken alone, deliberately purge the apocalypse of feminine qualities.[45] Here, though, I would like to modify that assertion to acknowledge that a reader with a good memory, or with a copy of the 1590 *Faerie Queene* to hand, might ally these stanzas' recollection of Gloriana/Elizabeth's name (in their evocation of Eli-Sabbath, "God's rest") with Gloriana's feast. Taken together, then, these instances of closure—first, in Gloriana's court; and second, at the end of time—would describe the end of allegory and even the end of the world as potentially feminized, possibly erotic (given Gloriana's status in the poem as the object of Arthur's desire), and certainly somatic. Rape may be, as Stephanie Jed has argued, the foundational gesture of Renaissance humanism, which seeks in part—like Actaeon invading Diana's bower—to discover texts' naked truth, their core meanings, and origins. But in that case, the conclusions of *The Faerie Queene* harbor a strong, if intermittent, strain of antihumanism, both rhetorically and historically: in constructing closure not out of ultimate knowledge, but out of ultimate delight; and in powerfully recollecting the kinds of visions, analyzed by Caroline Bynum, in which women mystics of the pre-Renaissance era modeled their descriptions of the rapturous reunion with Christ at world's end after female sexual ecstasy.[46]

And yet my reference to Roman Catholic religious practice, and women's practice at that, serves as a reminder that even if *The Faerie Queene* locates its primary values in the stuff of sensual poetry, it cannot possibly elide the ideological difficulties of such allegiance, difficulties that are felt in the poem's jostling both against its own history of composition and publication, and against its cultural milieu. In the remainder of this essay, I will discuss these two contexts, internal and external to the poem, as a way of demonstrating how *The Faerie Queene* itself often takes exception to the poetic ravishment I have described. As I mentioned above, instances of rapture in *The Faerie Queene*—even in Book 3, the portion of the poem most interested in accommodating some version of feminine sexuality—are conspicuously short-lived, bracketed or riddled as they are by skeptical or downright averse commentary. Berger has, for example, convincingly established that even the omphalos of feminine erotic satisfaction, the Garden of Adonis, is seeded with allusions to and comments upon a masculine fear of such overpowering bliss.[47] Similarly, the 1590 ending's marvelously sensual embrace of Amoret and Scudamour is qualified in its eroticism by its resemblance to an artistic creation whose "richness" lies not in its ornate embellishment, but in its expense: "that faire *Hermaphrodite,* / Which that rich *Romane* of white marble wrought, / And in his costly Bath causd to be site" (3.12.46a). As Berger remarks, both the heavy-handed Ovidian reference and the aesthetic distance imposed by this intrusive comparison to the unnamed "rich *Romane's*" lavatory installation disengage the reader's own sensual inclusion in the lovers' embrace.[48] Even Britomart herself, we learn, only "*halfe*" envies the couple's "blesse" (3.12.46a, my emphasis). Britomart's unexpected, if partial, retreat from somatic involvement in the pleasures of the scene amounts to the poem's moving towards a mode of literary engagement that separates mind from body, analysis from text, allegorical meaning from literal pleasures.

The Faerie Queene in its 1596 incarnation treats the attractions of "textural" poetry even more warily than this, so that by the time we encounter Colin Clout in poetic rapture on Book 6's Mount Acidale he has become the exception that proves this new rule of the rapine. First of all, the 1590 ending to Book 3 is canceled in favor of one that disallows rapture entirely, as Amoret and Britomart exit the ruins of Busirane's house only to find Scudamour gone. When Britomart and Amoret return to their now unconcluded quest at the beginning of Book 4, then, the poem returns to what Maureen Quilligan has described as allegory's scrutiny of "the slippery tensions between literalness and metaphor": whereas a rapturous poetry would revel in such slipperiness, celebrating the attractions of the literal, Books 4 through 6 successively rein in such revelry to quest for the heart of the matter.[49] In this regard, the pitiless procession through Book 5 of the knight of Justice, Artegall, and his iron sidekick Talus establishes rapine poetics as the paradigm for poetic progress. As I have argued elsewhere, the stripped-down, dour stanzas and plot of Book 5's historical episodes constitute a Spenserian experiment in a de-effeminized poetics, and even if this experiment is something of a failure, the second half of *The Faerie Queene* is never devoted to sensual, rapturous delight with the same intensity as in those flashes in Book 3.[50]

Ironically, then, as *The Faerie Queene* successively unfolds in its 1590, 1596, and 1609 versions into a longer and longer poem, it progressively truncates the extended immersion into pleasure that long poems can provide their readers. For example, the trajectory of the second half of the poem suggests that a reader is, in truth, meant *not* to associate earlier and later episodes in the way that I suggested above: by the time we reach the poem's plea for transcendent rescue *from* the physical world at the end of the Mutabilitie Cantos, we ought to have forgotten Amoret's rescue *into* physical delight at the 1590 ending of Book 3. The poem thus creates the effect, as it reaches its conclusion, of trying to counteract even the unavoidable "textural" somatic pleasures of page-turning and eyeball-shifting, of flipping back and forth to locate or sort out recurring characters and actions, that a reader feels upon handling the impressive physical object that is *The Faerie Queene*—a very materially based "pleasure of the text" that historians of the book tend to ignore when they characterize silent, solitary reading (as opposed to reading aloud in groups) as an abstracted, disembodied activity.[51]

Disallowing the physical pleasures of book-reading itself seems unthinkably extreme, even for the most puritan of late-sixteenth-century moralists—which Spenser certainly was not. Nevertheless, *The Faerie Queene*'s mounting hints of discomfort with even this mode of literarily induced delight point towards the ideological difficulties in which Spenser's poetic strategies had to engage. If *The Faerie Queene*'s rapturous interludes disdain abstract verities in favor of sensual images, they are not only antihumanistic, as I have already argued, but also anti-Protestant. Beginning with the Calvinistically defined religious policy of Edward VI, the Church of England in the second half of the sixteenth century officially disengaged the pursuit of Christian truth from the pursuit of physically felt happiness by implementing a doctrine of iconoclasm, whose practice Greenblatt finds replicated in Guyon's smashing of Acrasia's artful Bower. The connection between religious imagery and Spenserian sensuality has to do not only with *The Faerie Queene*'s rendering as parody some typically Roman Catholic images—for example, as Greenblatt points out, Acrasia's cradling of her lover Verdant summons up the Pietà—but also with the incorporation of the physical into the aesthetic.[52] Like the rapine poetics I have been describing, post-Reformation iconoclasm is meant to provide a vector for escaping the possibility that "higher" meaning could be associated with the human body—as an ingestor of the transubstantiated body of Christ, as a venerable saint, or as a worshiper in a state of ecstatic rapture.[53] How, then, was the Reformed Christian meant to *see* the truth if any devotional object that made a sensual contribution to such visions—from incense and music, to paintings and sculpture, to the penitent's own mortifiable flesh—was to be purged from religious experience? The answer lay in the Reformed church's singular attention to the unadorned word. In the former places of churches' devotional images the reformers erected the Word alone, often literally in the form of the Ten Commandments' being painted on the wall where Christ and the saints had once been represented.[54] But for some, iconoclastic zeal grew so hot that it came to implicate not only painted and sculpted images but also the pictorial image in the mind's eye and, hence, also the image expressed in language.[55] Even the minister in the pulpit had to be wary of embroidering his speech with auditorially pleasing features; the function of his oratory was only to teach, not to delight. A worshiper might thus complain, as Phillip Stubbes did in 1593, that religion had become "nothing else but plain talking."[56] At its most extreme, Reformed iconoclasm aims for a utopian discourse that is, improbably, entirely free of speaking pictures: even Lancelot Andrewes, who favored religious ritual, argues that the idols whose worship is forbidden in the second commandment "signifieth any kind of conception or imagination which may arise."[57] In John Calvin's formulation that "Man's nature, so to speak, is a perpetual factory of idols . . . the mind begets an idol; the hand gives it birth," the hand of idolatrous midwifery might as easily be the hand of the author as that of the sculptor or painter.[58] Francis Bacon, true to form, is the most blunt about this equivalence among the arts: "Words are but the images of matter, and . . . to fall in love with them is all one as to fall in love with a picture."[59]

Churchly iconoclasm was hardly accepted or enforced uniformly in Elizabethan religious thought or action; as Christopher Haigh and Eamon Duffy have detailed, the physical, iconic objects of Roman Catholic devotional practice remained in widespread and not always surreptitious use in England throughout Elizabeth's reign.[60] *The Faerie Queene* itself has nothing good to say about its one professional iconoclast, Kirkrapine (1.3.16–18). Still, the fact that iconophobia was the official policy of the English Reformed church continuously from the 1560s until the 1620s, when Archbishop Laud began to restore the material trappings of worship to churches, obviously presents a dilemma for Spenser's Protestant poetics. Given that Reformed theologians often likened images' seductive appeal to the attractions of a beautiful woman—so that, as dissenting preacher Henry Ainsworth puts it, man potentially "goeth a whoring with his own inventions"—*The Faerie Queene's* pleasing ornaments might indict the entire poem, not just its Duessas and its Acrasias, as a sinful trap.[61] As Greenblatt points out in his discussion of Guyon's smashing of images, "Acrasia's realm is lavishly described in just those terms which the defenders of poetry in the Renaissance reserved for imagination's noblest achievements."[62] Greenblatt's contention, though, is that Spenser evades wholesale commitment to poetic idolatry by continually calling attention to the constructedness of his poetic images.[63] Similarly, Linda Gregerson argues that Spenser manages through the semiotics of allegory to clear his own poetry of such charges: "He combats the idolatrous potential of words not by seeking to divest himself of figurative resources but by delineating a dialectical function for his readership, a function otherwise known as interpretation. . . . The Reformed and reforming rhetoric of *The Faerie Queene* posits a model of readerly subjectivity that owes its contours to an eroticized theory of signs."[64] In other words, the reader of the poem understands that he or she must read the text typologically, construing its undeniable literary pleasures as moral edification. I would dispute Greenblatt's and Gregerson's sense that *The Faerie Queene* so easily has it both ways, subordinating iconophilia to iconoclasm, for in the terms I have laid out that would mean accommodating a poetics of rapture to a poetics of rape. Rather, in my view, the poem schizophrenically careens between these two modes precisely because they cannot be synthesized in dialectical fashion.

This schizophrenia might be read, in part, as a guilty acknowledgement of the way in which iconoclasm not only condemns Spenser's text, but also clears the way for its existence. Roy Strong has proposed that it is during the iconoclastic phase of the English church that secular portraiture first became important in England, as the well-to-do learned to contemplate their current estate and their imminent mortality not in paintings of Christ, but in paintings of their family members living and dead.[65] But my sense is that, for less moneyed classes, the desire for sensual aesthetics had to be satisfied by means of much cheaper media: personal costume, public spectacles like the drama, and, perhaps most subversively, the book of fiction. As Walter Benjamin puts it in his study of baroque allegory, "It was . . . a religious scruple which assigned artistic activity to the 'leisure hours'": having purged the Word of physicality, Protestant reformers forced their parishioners to look elsewhere for the physically evocative word.[66] What I am suggesting is contrary to the scholarly commonplace that English Renaissance literature was spawned from Protestantism, with its demand that every Christian actively undertake exegesis of the biblical text. Rather, it seems to me that English Renaissance literature emerges from the discards of Reformed Protestant dogma, as an alternative venue for sensualized delight.[67]

The Faerie Queene, as Christian epic, thus uneasily straddles iconoclasm and iconophilia, rape and rapture, and not just because such categories are predictably liable to deconstruction.[68] What is at stake is also the proposition that a literary creation might be flagrantly detached from Protestant orthodoxy. Finishing his long poem in Ireland, hemmed in by what he saw as barbarous papist hordes, Spenser could not wholly and finally reach such conclusions. But I would like to suggest, perhaps somewhat perversely given my discussion's emphasis on mutual sensual pleasure, that such a poetry is glimmeringly hinted at in the Bower of Bliss, in Acrasia's utterly one-sided "greedily depasturing delight" of the sleeping knight Verdant. What Spenser gestures towards in this episode, I would like to suggest, is not only the erotically appealing product of a poetics of rapture—a product from which Guyon, as potential poetic consumer, may stand at disapproving distance ("Much wondred Guyon at the faire aspect / Of that sweet place, yet suffred no delight / To sincke into his sence, nor mind affect" [2.12.53]) and that he may eventually reject. For just one moment here, Spenser also allows his narrative voice to inhabit the mind of the producer of rapturous poetry, Acrasia herself. Moving her lips across Verdant's body in the same way that Spenser's stanzas customarily traverse the intricate contours of an ornamented aesthetic object, Acrasia seems to stimulate Verdant, even though he sleeps, to the point of erotic rapture as his "spright" (with its bawdy pun on semen as "spirit") exits his "humid eyes." But meanwhile, Acrasia herself "sigh[s] soft, as if his case she rewd" (2.12.73). We might read that "as if" not exclusively as a condemnation of Acrasia's capacity for subterfuge, but also as an invitation to imagine what Acrasia is really thinking.[69]

My sense is that this reference to Acrasia's way of thinking is so brief because it is so dangerous, far more dangerous than her Bower's erotic appeal alone. In the other instances of the production of rapturous poetry I have cited above, the rapine perspective, signified by the agent who is on the brink of invading the feminine space, is near enough at hand in the poem's narrative that its triumph is never in doubt. (Or, if it is in doubt, as it is when Britomart brings about Amoret's ecstasy through Busirane's "reversed" charms, the episode is rewritten.) Acrasia's pleasure, in contrast, is conveyed in a long, suspended series of stanzas in which Guyon and his moral Palmer seem always to be drawing near the Bower, but never to be actually *in* it.[70] To come closer to her would be to merge with her, an act that would not only force a man to orgasmic surrender but also absorb him into an eternity of feminine poetics. A male Protestant poet of the English sixteenth century, dependent as he was on a lineage of rapine poetry and theology even when he critiqued that dependence, could only gesture towards the mental processes of this wholly rapturous poet, one who did not yet exist. Like Gloriana's feast, and like the fully rapturous and fully embodied ecstasy of resurrected Christians at the world's end, Acrasia's poetry awaits us at the end of infinity; it cannot yet be read.*

Notes

* This essay first appeared in *Representations* 70 (Spring 2000): 1–26. Thanks to Lynn Enterline, Richard Halpern, Norman Jones, David Lee Miller, Elizabeth Robertson, Rhonda Sanford, Mark Winokur, and especially Paul Alpers for their comments and suggestions.

1. Jane Anger, *Jane Anger Her Protection for Women,* in *First Feminists: British Women Writers, 1578–1799,* ed. Moira Ferguson (Bloomington: Indiana University Press, 1985), p. 62.

2. Edmund Spenser, *The Faerie Queene,* ed. A. C. Hamilton (London: Longman, 1977), 3.12.31; hereafter cited parenthetically in the text by book, canto, and verse numbers, or by page number in the case of Hamilton's notes. In all quotations, including those from Spenser, I have normalized the orthography of *u/v, i/j,* and *vv/w* but otherwise have retained original spellings.

3. For Amoret's terror as women's fear of sexual intercourse, see, for example, Thomas Roche, *The Kindly Flame: A Study of the Third and Fourth Books of Spenser's "Faerie Queene"* (Princeton, NJ: Princeton University Press, 1964), pp. 73–88; and Alastair Fowler, *Triumphal Forms: Structural Patterns in Elizabethan Poetry* (Cambridge: Cambridge University Press, 1970), pp. 47–58. Even Harry Berger, Jr.'s subtle account, first published in 1971, of patriarchal horrors in this episode attributes the final incarnations of Busirane's masque to Amoret's own psyche and her desire for Scudamour; see "Busirane and the War between the Sexes: An Interpretation of *The Faerie Queene* III.xi-xii," in *Revisionary Play: Studies in the Spenserian Dynamics* (Berkeley: University of California Press, 1988), pp. 183–84.

4. Sheila T. Cavanagh, *Wanton Eyes and Chaste Desires: Female Sexuality in "The Faerie Queene"* (Bloomington: Indiana University Press, 1994), pp. 2–3.

5. Maureen Quilligan, *Milton's Spenser: The Politics of Reading* (Ithaca, NY: Cornell University Press, 1983), p. 198.

6. Susan Frye, "Of Chastity and Violence: Elizabeth I and Edmund Spenser in the House of Busirane," *Signs* 20 (1994): 49–78, and Susan Frye, *Elizabeth I: The Competition for Representation* (Oxford: Oxford University Press, 1993), pp. 132–35.

404 KATHERINE EGGERT

7. I have argued a more general version of this case about the attractions of ravishment in *The Faerie Queene* in Katherine Eggert, *Showing Like a Queen: Female Authority and Literary Experiment in Spenser, Shakespeare, and Milton* (Philadelphia: University of Pennsylvania Press, 2000), pp. 22–50.

8. Gordon Teskey, *Allegory and Violence* (Ithaca, NY: Cornell University Press, 1996).

9. Teskey, *Allegory and Violence,* p. 31.

10. Cavanagh asserts, for example, that "by suppressing the surface meaning of the poem and leaping immediately to its allegorical intricacies, readers [informed by theology, archetypal theories, or typology] occlude the gender-bias such interpretations rest upon"; *Wanton Eyes,* p. 7.

11. George Puttenham, *The Arte of English Poesie,* ed. Gladys Doidge Willcock and Alice Walker (Cambridge: Cambridge University Press, 1936), p. 178.

12. Teskey, *Allegory and Violence,* p. 18.

13. Patricia Parker, *Literary Fat Ladies: Rhetoric, Gender, Property* (London: Methuen, 1987).

14. Susanne Lindgren Wofford, *The Choice of Achilles: The Ideology of Figure in the Epic* (Stanford: Stanford University Press, 1992), pp. 295–371. Wofford's discussion of *The Faerie Queene,* like mine, explicitly associates allegory with rape, and nonteleological visionary bliss with rapture (pp. 353–71); however, she establishes an absolute gender division—only women characters are raped, only men characters are rapt—that I think does not hold true in the poem, as my ensuing discussion demonstrates.

15. Herbert J. C. Grierson, *Cross Currents in English Literature of the Seventeenth Century* (1929; rpt. London: Chatto & Windus, 1958), p. 54; C. S. Lewis, *The Allegory of Love: A Study in Medieval Tradition* (1936; rpt. Oxford: Oxford University Press, 1959), p. 326.

16. Stephen Greenblatt, *Renaissance Self-Fashioning from More to Shakespeare* (Chicago: University of Chicago Press, 1980), pp. 183–84.

17. For this episode Hamilton points out two biblical allusions: "the Satyrs shal dance" in Palestine after its desolation (Is. 13:21), and "I was delivered out of the mouth of the lion" (2 Tim. 4:17); Spenser, *The Faerie Queene,* p. 87.

18. The fountain episode, as Hamilton's notes detail, alludes to and subtly alters passages from Ariosto and Tasso as well as Ovid; Spenser, *The Faerie Queene,* pp. 95–96.

19. Deborah G. Burks, "'I'll Want My Will Else': *The Changeling* and Women's Complicity with Their Rapists," *ELH* 62 (1995): 763.

20. Kathryn Gravdal, *Ravishing Maidens: Writing Rape in Medieval French Literature and Law* (Philadelphia: University of Pennsylvania Press, 1991), p. 4.

21. Cavanagh, *Wanton Eyes,* pp. 35–41.

22. Parker, *Literary Fat Ladies,* pp. 62–66; Laura Mulvey, "Visual Pleasure and Narrative Cinema," in *Visual and Other Pleasures* (Bloomington: Indiana University Press, 1989), pp. 14–26.

23. Like Medusa's multiple snaky locks in Sigmund Freud's famous reading, Serena's "spoiles of Princes" may well signify her castration after all. But the

point remains that her genitalia are far from revealed. I am drawing from Theresa M. Krier's sense in *Gazing on Secret Sights: Spenser, Classical Imitation, and the Decorums of Vision* (Ithaca, NY: Cornell University Press, 1990) that the stripping and voyeurism scenes in *The Faerie Queene* constitute a debate on the morality of male prurience, but I differ from Krier in that I read the withdrawing of the male gaze not as a matter of benign reticence, but as a comment on the advisability of equating *seeing* with *knowing*. My thoughts on these putative unveilings have been much influenced by Melinda Gough's essay "'Her filthy feature open showne' in Ariosto, Spenser, and *Much Ado About Nothing*," *Studies in English Literature, 1500–1900* 39 (1999): 41–67, an early version of which I read in 1994.

24. Plutarch, "Beasts Are Rational," *Moralia* 985D-992C, ed. Harold Cherniss and William C. Helmbold (Cambridge, MA: Harvard University Press, 1957), pp. 492–533.

25. John Milton, *Areopagitica*, in *The Complete Prose Works of John Milton*, ed. Don M. Wolfe, 8 vols. (New Haven, CT: Yale University Press, 1953–82), 2:516.

26. Leonard Barkan, "Diana and Actaeon: The Myth as Synthesis," *English Literary Renaissance* 10 (1980): 317–59.

27. The gender of Alma's castle is an interesting conundrum, since it has no allegorized genitalia; but see David Lee Miller's account of "The displacement through which genital eros finds its way into representation within the temperate body"; *The Poem's Two Bodies: The Poetics of the 1590 "Faerie Queene"* (Princeton, NJ: Princeton University Press, 1988), p. 174. Dorothy Stephens has convincingly argued, too, that even Alma's brain is a decidedly feminine enclosure; *The Limits of Eroticism in Post-Petrarchan Narrative: Conditional Pleasure from Spenser to Marvell* (Cambridge: Cambridge University Press, 1998), pp. 52–61.

28. *Oxford English Dictionary*, 2d edition, *s.v.* "ravish" 3b. Gravdal delineates the etymological shifts that produce the definitions of "ravishment" I describe here: "When it first appears [in the thirteenth century], *ravissement* means the action of carrying off a woman, but by the fourteenth century it comes to have a spiritual or religious sense: the action of carrying a soul to heaven. From this religious meaning develops a more secular, affective one: the state of a soul transported by enthusiasm, joy, or extreme happiness. *Ravissement* now, in the fourteenth century, refers to the state of being 'carried away' emotionally, a state of exaltation"; Gravdal, *Ravishing Maidens*, p. 5.

29. Jacobus De Voragine, *The Golden Legend: Readings on the Saints*, trans. William Granger Ryan, 2 vols. (Princeton, NJ: Princeton University Press, 1993), 1:172.

30. Parker, *Literary Fat Ladies*, p. 10; Stephen Greenblatt, "Fiction and Friction," in *Shakespearean Negotiations: The Circulation of Social Energy in Renaissance England* (Berkeley: University of California Press, 1988), pp. 66–93.

31. Catherine Clément, *Syncope: The Philosophy of Rapture*, trans. Sally O'Driscoll and Deirdre M. Mahoney (Minneapolis: University of Minnesota Press, 1994).

32. Nancy Vickers, "'The blazon of sweet beauty's best': Shakespeare's *Lucrece*," in *Shakespeare and the Question of Theory*, ed. Patricia Parker and Geoffrey Hartman (New York: Methuen, 1985), pp. 95–115.

33. Philippa Berry, *Of Chastity and Power: Elizabethan Literature and the Unmarried Queen* (London: Routledge, 1989), p. 160. Louis Adrian Montrose sees this evasion of Belphoebe's genital region as an avoidance of the danger inhering in the powerful, virginal body of Queen Elizabeth; see "The Elizabethan Subject and the Spenserian Text," in *Literary Theory/Renaissance Texts*, ed. Patricia Parker and David Quint (Baltimore, MD: Johns Hopkins University Press, 1986), pp. 327–28. For this blazon as not evasion, but an invitation to invasion, see Hannah Betts, "'The Image of this Queene so quaynt': The Pornographic Blazon 1588–1603," in *Dissing Elizabeth: Negative Representations of Gloriana*, ed. Julia M. Walker (Durham, NC: Duke University Press, 1998), pp. 160–62.

34. For the Garden as a locus of feminine eros, see Quilligan, *Milton's Spenser*, pp. 192–97; and Lauren Silberman, "Singing Unsung Heroines: Androgynous Discourse in Book 3 of *The Faerie Queene*," in *Rewriting the Renaissance: The Discourse of Sexual Difference in Early Modern Europe*, ed. Margaret W. Ferguson, Maureen Quilligan, and Nancy J. Vickers (Chicago: University of Chicago Press, 1986), pp. 267–71.

35. Cavanagh, *Wanton Eyes*, p. 73; Frye, "Of Chastity and Violence," p. 69.

36. Berger, "Busirane and the War between the Sexes."

37. I omit consideration of Jove's one male object of lust, Ganymede, whose response to being seized is not elaborated.

38. Paul Alpers, *The Poetry of "The Faerie Queene"* (1967; rpt. Princeton, NJ: Princeton University Press, 1982), p. 10.

39. Berger, in fact, implies that the forms of the masque are so predictable as to be decadent; "Busirane and the War between the Sexes," pp. 179–84.

40. Richard Wilson, "Observations on English Bodies: Licensing Maternity in Shakespeare's Late Plays," in *Enclosure Acts: Sexuality, Property, and Culture in Early Modern England*, ed. Richard Burt and John Michael Archer (Ithaca, NY: Cornell University Press, 1994), pp. 125–26.

41. For this clever reading of "weake feete," I am indebted to Rhonda Lemke Sanford. Lauren Silberman has previously made the point that Busirane's torture has no psychological effect on Amoret ("Singing Unsung Heroines," p. 267).

42. For the connections between the Medusa and the experience of horror, see Marjorie Garber, "Macbeth: The Male Medusa," in *Shakespeare's Ghost Writers: Literature as Uncanny Causality* (New York: Methuen, 1987), pp. 87–123.

43. I obviously disagree with Jonathan Goldberg's argument that this "perfect hole" signifies "the place of loss" and hence embodies "the pleasure of the writerly text of the entire *Faerie Queene*"; *Endlesse Worke: Spenser and the Structures of Discourse* (Baltimore: Johns Hopkins University Press, 1981), p. 11. Feminine enclosures in *The Faerie Queene* may be scary, but they're hardly empty. I might add that it matters not one whit whether the fric-

tional bliss on the brink of these enclosures is induced heterosexually, homosexually, or bisexually. When penile penetration is removed from the equation, such distinctions disappear. For the early modern period's interest in nonvaginal female erogenous zones, see Valerie Traub's fascinating essay "The Psychomorphology of the Clitoris," *GLQ* 2 (1995): 81–113. My conception of poetry as an opaque and ornamented surface, elaborated below, owes much to Traub's work-in-progress on the portraits of Elizabeth Tudor as also suggesting nonpenetrative aesthetic and sexual pleasures.

44. Thomas Greene, *The Descent from Heaven: A Study in Epic Continuity* (New Haven, CT: Yale University Press, 1963), p. 329.

45. Eggert, *Showing Like a Queen,* pp. 49–50.

46. Stephanie Jed, *Chaste Thinking: The Rape of Lucretia and the Birth of Humanism* (Bloomington: Indiana University Press, 1989); Caroline Walker Bynum, "The Female Body and Religious Practice in the Later Middle Ages," in *Fragmentation and Redemption: Essays in Gender and the Human Body in Medieval Religion* (New York: Zone Books, 1991), pp. 181–238; and Caroline Walker Bynum, *The Resurrection of the Body in Western Christianity, 200–1336* (New York: Columbia University Press, 1995), pp. 329–41. Jed's expression "chaste thinking," which she uses to describe fifteenth-century Italian humanist practices of exclusionary philology, has the same kind of double valence for her argument that "ravishment" does for mine. Both terms carry the connotation of sensual contact and disdain for sensual contact; for Jed, "chaste" exists "at the join of two conflicting lexical families of terms, one representing the impulse to touch and the other, the impulse to be cut off from contact . . . on the one hand, words related to touching or the absence of touching—*tangible, contaminate, contact, integrity, intact,* etc., and, on the other hand, words related to cutting—*chastity, castigate, caste,* and Latin *carere* ('to be cut off from, to lack')"; *Chaste Thinking,* p. 8.

47. Harry Berger, Jr., "Actaeon at the Hinder Gate: The Stag Party in Spenser's Gardens of Adonis," in *Desire in the Renaissance: Psychoanalysis and Literature,* ed. Valeria Finucci and Regina Schwartz (Princeton, NJ: Princeton University Press, 1994), pp. 91–119; on this anxiety see also Silberman, "Singing Unsung Heroines," 271.

48. Berger, "Busirane and the War between the Sexes," p. 192; see also Miller, *The Poem's Two Bodies,* pp. 284–85.

49. Maureen Quilligan, *The Language of Allegory: Defining the Genre* (Ithaca, NY: Cornell University Press, 1979), p. 64.

50. Eggert, *Showing Like a Queen,* pp. 32–50. Paul Alpers defines the act of reading the entire *Faerie Queene* as an exercise in forgetting: Spenser "does not expect our span of attention and retention to last for more than about a canto, or at most two"; *The Poetry of "The Faerie Queene,"* p. 125. I would argue that this forgetting, compounded when the 1590 poem is doubled into the 1596 version, has the ideological telos of controlling erotic bliss. See Parker's brilliant discussions of how *dilatio* in the poem is reined in by impulses towards conclusiveness; *Literary Fat Ladies,* pp. 8–35, 64–66.

51. Roger Chartier, for example, implies that only by studying reading as an oral, communal activity can historians "take on the task of retracing forgotten gestures and habits that have not existed for some time"; *The Order of Books: Readers, Authors, and Libraries in Europe Between the Fourteenth and Eighteenth Centuries,* trans. Lydia G. Cochrane (Stanford: Stanford University Press, 1994), p. 9. I owe the suggestion that reading the codex of *The Faerie Queene* is itself sensually pleasurable to Lauren Silberman.

52. Greenblatt, *Renaissance Self-Fashioning,* p. 189.

53. So problematic was the notion of embodied spiritual ecstasy that in finalizing the Thirty-Nine Articles of Faith in 1563, the Reformed church went so far as to omit the 1553 version's scripturally unimpeachable tenet that "at the laste daie . . . to all that bee dead their awne bodies, fleshe, and bone shalbe restored"; E. Tyrrell Green, *The Thirty-Nine Articles and the Age of the Reformation* (London: Wells Gardner, Darton, 1896), p. 320.

54. Margaret Aston, *England's Iconoclasts,* vol. 1: *Laws Against Images* (Oxford: Clarendon Press, 1988), pp. 318–19, 368.

55. See Ernest B. Gilman, *Iconoclasm and Poetry in the English Reformation: Down Went Dagon* (Chicago: Chicago University Press, 1986), pp. 14–30.

56. Phillip Stubbes, *A Motive to Good Workes* (London, 1593), Epistle; quoted in Patrick Collinson, "The Elizabethan Church and the New Religion," in *The Reign of Elizabeth I,* ed. Christopher Haigh (Athens: University of Georgia Press, 1985), pp. 171–72.

57. *The Works of Lancelot Andrewes,* ed. J. P. Wilson and James Bliss, 11 vols. (Oxford: Clarendon Press, 1841–54), 6:128; quoted in Aston, *England's Iconoclasts,* p. 393.

58. Jean Calvin, *Institutes of the Christian Religion,* ed. John T. McNeill, trans. Ford Lewis Battles, 2 vols. (Philadelphia, PA: Westminster Press, 1960), 1:108; quoted in Aston, *England's Iconoclasts,* p. 437.

59. *Francis Bacon: A Selection of His Works,* ed. Sidney Warhaft (New York: Odyssey, 1965), p. 224; quoted in Gilman, *Iconoclasm and Poetry,* p. 29.

60. See Christopher Haigh, "The Continuity of Catholicism in the English Reformation," in *The English Reformation Revised,* ed. Christopher Haigh (Cambridge: Cambridge University Press, 1987), pp. 176–208. Haigh particularly notes the prevalence of such ritualistic use of objects in Lancashire, possibly the site of origin of Spenser's family (p. 206). See also Eamon Duffy, *The Stripping of the Altars: Traditional Religion in England c. 1400–c. 1580* (New Haven, CT: Yale University Press, 1992).

61. Henry Ainsworth, *An Arrow Against Idolatrie. Taken out of the quiver of the lord of Hosts* ([Amsterdam], 1611), p. 43; quoted in Gilman, *Iconoclasm and Poetry,* p. 41. See also Huston Diehl, "Bewhored Images and Imagined Whores: Iconophobia and Gynophobia in Stuart Love Tragedies," *English Literary Renaissance* 26 (1996): 111–37.

62. Greenblatt, *Renaissance Self-Fashioning,* p. 189.

63. Greenblatt, *Renaissance Self-Fashioning,* pp. 189–90.

64. Linda Gregerson, *The Reformation of the Subject: Spenser, Milton, and the English Protestant Epic* (Cambridge: Cambridge University Press, 1995), p. 64.

65. Roy Strong, *Spirit of the Age* (London: BBC Publications, 1975); cited in Aston, *England's Iconoclasts,* p. 464.

66. Walter Benjamin, *The Origin of German Tragic Drama,* trans. John Osborne (1928; London: Verso, 1977), p. 176.

67. My argument thus bears some relation to Debora Keller Shuger's assertion that as Reformed Protestant discourse increasingly rejected humanism's incorporation of pagan philosophy and mythology, it necessarily secularized those arts in which "pagan associations clustered most thickly"; *The Renaissance Bible: Scholarship, Sacrifice, and Subjectivity* (Berkeley: University of California Press, 1994), p. 159. As well, any number of literary critics and theater historians have proposed a smaller version of my thesis by contending that Renaissance drama owes its emergence to the Reformed church's canceling the religious cycle plays. Gilman argues, similarly, that "the creative power of sixteenth- and seventeenth-century literature is released at crucial moments when the visual resources of the poet are challenged by a conception of language disinfected . . . of appeal to the eye"; *Iconoclasm and Poetry,* p. 11. Gilman treats the desire for images, however, as a relatively disembodied phenomenon. Paula Findlen suggests quite the contrary: even in Roman Catholic countries, post-Tridentine sanctions on erotic sacred images corresponded to a proliferation of cheap print pornography; "Humanism, Politics and Pornography in Renaissance Italy," in *The Invention of Pornography: Obscenity and the Origins of Modernity, 1500–1800,* ed. Lynn Hunt (New York: Zone Books, 1993), pp. 49–108.

68. Deconstructive tendencies are inevitable in allegory, which often "[gives] independent mythic existence to a negative term" and thus "risks creating a verbal figure suspended between the states of demon and idol"; Kenneth Gross, *Spenserian Poetics: Idolatry, Iconoclasm, and Magic* (Ithaca, NY: Cornell University Press, 1985), p. 56.

69. I borrow the suggestion that Acrasia's subjectivity is an issue from a seminar paper by Sarah Peterson Pittock.

70. The heart of Acrasia's Bower, where the witch and her lover reside, is depicted in great detail in Stanzas 69–80 of Book 2, Canto 12. In Stanza 69, the Palmer draws Guyon "forward thence" towards the Bower's center. In Stanza 76, however, we learn that the "constant paire" are still moving towards the discovery of Acrasia: they "kept their forward way, / Through many covert groves, and thickets close, / In which they creeping did at last display / That wanton Ladie." It is odd, then, that five stanzas later they still have to draw "nigh" Acrasia and Verdant in order to trap them in the Palmer's "subtile net" (2.12.81).

AFTERWORD

Christopher Cannon

> *Whether a proposition can turn out false after all depends on what I make count as*
> *determinants for that proposition.*
>
> —*Wittgenstein*[1]

Something happens, and there is an aftermath. That act, as it is constituted by the discourses that comprise this volume, is rape, and the aftermath is that set of adjudications and readings which name this act and
give it meaning. But the retrospection employed in such a practice has its
aftermath too. The happening may then be the adjudications and readings
of a volume such as this, whose aftermath is the name and meaning given
to what was done here in the name of representing rape. There are, broadly
speaking, only two possibilities. Our readings may, as we have hoped, be
accepted and confirmed, extended and repeated in relation to other happenings. Or the very procedures we have employed will be explicitly or
implicitly reversed, and precisely what we have read as rape will be read
(again) as not-rape. It is difficult to say which result would count as the
greater failure. If our readings are either reversible or repeatable, it may be
wondered, why are they needed? If what comes after the study of the representation of rape in Medieval and Early Modern Europe is either less or
more of the same, why have we offered such a study at all?

Another way to frame the problem is to notice that, insofar as any historical study is an afterword to prior events, it is not only subject to the
very techniques of retrospection it employs, but it might be said to invite
such appropriation by means of its practice. This vulnerability is nowhere
more clear than in the recent critique of the "scholarly handling of the
theme of rape in literature" by Evelyn Birge Vitz, where it is judged, retrospectively, that retrospection is a defining mistake:

> It is astonishing that we today who are so fortunate should think of our-
> selves as archetypal victims, projecting our sense of victimhood—our poet-
> ics and our hermeneutics of resentment and self-pity—back onto other,
> arguably less happy, eras, and trying to raise the consciousness of women
> dead for eight hundred years to the fact that they were oppressed![2]

Whether Vitz could be right about the audience for a feminist historicism
will be addressed below, but here I want only to notice the way the temporal structure Vitz diagnoses also structures her critique. For Vitz is actually willing to grant, first, that it is "true" that "there has been, historically,
some uncertainty as to how to conceptualize and punish rape," but she is
also sure, second, that "*real* rape is, without question a terrible thing."[3] The
particular question her own argument raises, then, is how *she* knows what
"real" rape is, if she is equally sure that there is uncertainty about how to
"conceptualize" such an act. More generally, in a context where the structure of the afterword is precisely criticized for its projections onto a field
of uncertainty, why is it acceptable for Vitz to project her reality backwards
onto just such an "uncertainty"?

The answer, of course, is that this is the only way rape *can* be "reread."
For Vitz derives her discursive strategy, not only from feminist readings of
representations of rape, but from the discursive structure of rape itself,
where, whether for the purposes of adjudication at law or scholarly "reading," a view must be projected, as an afterword, in order for the happening
in question to have a name—for the event to be "real" and, thus, have consequences at law or to understanding. The homology of method across all
these acts of definition is of course also why Vitz's critique is possible and
endlessly repeatable. It is why we must assume that everywhere that a happening has been read as rape in these pages it can, and doubtless will, be
read subsequently as a "joke" or a "metaphor" (the terms Vitz favors), or as
a "seduction" (the common substitution). In this sense, however right or
wrong Vitz may be about the particular redescriptions she offers, what she
demonstrates most clearly is that, within the structure that governs rape,
this volume has no choice but to provide the prior term that will enable
subsequent reversals.

Such a diagnosis also suggests, however, that the views set out in this
volume are *necessary*, not only so that they may oppose the position articulated by Vitz, but so that they may themselves be repeated within the
structure of the afterword, enabling the dialectic which that structure
makes inevitable, but that at least provides the opportunity for reading not-
rape as rape. Furthermore, if the dialectic in which such adjudications are
caught only exists by means of the reversals it necessitates, then to insist
upon those reversals is also to expose that *inevitability* to some scrutiny. For

it also matters that, even if judgements of rape and not-rape employ the same means, the latter always have (and have had) a higher success rate:

> The one whose subjectivity becomes the objectivity of 'what happened' is a matter of social meaning, that is, a matter of sexual politics. One-sidedly erasing women's violation or dissolving presumptions into the subjectivity of either side are the alternatives dictated by the terms of the object/subject split, respectively. These alternatives will only retrace that split to women's determinant until its terms are confronted as gendered to the ground.[4]

As MacKinnon has extensively demonstrated in the theory from which these words are taken, the proper name for the discursive strategy that allows for the reading of rape as not-rape is "objectivity," since it is only a posture of dispassion that could justify eliminating the affective states of women from political and juridical concern. Therefore, when Vitz constructs a minority position for herself and understands the dominant position to be "feminist" ("in the past few years, the academy . . . has had rape on its mind")[5] she is only calling attention to the wake a very well-contained insurgency must leave in a field of power it tries to disrupt but which it has never really altered. It remains true, in other words, that however similar the procedures employed, the redescription of rape as not-rape will be seen as objective, neutral, and reasonable, while the redescription of not-rape as rape will be seen as subjective, partisan, and feminist. To proffer the kind of readings we offer here is, then, also to try to show how "objectivity" is, just like the view we advance, an "iterable structure," and in that way to try to place its constitutive terms "up for grabs, to initiate the contest, to question their traditional deployment."[6] That is, forcing repetition of an oppressive strategy is itself to smoke out the broader interests that strategy serves, to subvert its dominant position simply by making clear that there are other strategies.[7]

Our analysis is also political, not only as it engages legal categories whose adjudication is more generally the province of the state, but as it is historicist. This volume analyzes representations of rape in Medieval and Early Modern texts in order to expose the structure of the afterword not simply at the subsequent moment, but at the point of the happening, the predicate, the prior. At issue is no particular event, in fact, but the very founding of Western liberal regimes. MacKinnon has also proposed that we imagine that founding as a moment when the gender inequalities basic to medieval law were simply accepted, even as gender was defined out of legal existence, suppressed as a problem to equality and thereby placed out of the reach of legal remedy by the means of standards of equality themselves. What constitutes the sexual politics of the liberal state is, therefore, gender hierarchy

in its medieval settlement precisely as that state imagines itself to have rejected and risen above—to have learned better than—that settlement:

> The strategy is first to constitute society unequally prior to law; then to de-
> sign the constitution, including the law of equality, so that all its guarantees
> apply only to those values that are taken away by law; then to construct le-
> gitimating norms so that the state legitimates itself through non-interfer-
> ence with the *status quo*.[8]

By passing through such imaginings to this earlier state of inequality this
volume proceeds by reversing the structure of the afterword that governs
the regime in which we live in order to examine the determinants which
got us here. Historicism is necessarily provocative when it serves to call attention to the fact that the *status quo*, however noble in its aspirations, is
nothing more nor less than the *status quo ante*.

That teachers of English—and medievalists no less—could really intervene in strategies that have proved themselves so effective and so general
in their conscription, would itself be the most unlikely of propositions
were it not at once possible and necessary to understand rape as a "linguistic fact."[9] This is true simply to the extent that rape occurs by a means
of a kind of "social script," that it may be understood as a kind of "narrative" written by the possibilities allowed to social selves ("conventional,
gendered structures of feeling and action").[10] But, as I have already suggested, rape is a linguistic phenomenon insofar as its happening is always a
function of a subsequent act of *naming*, an "emergence into a pre-existent
language" by which the given happening is allowed to be "real rape" only
insofar as a given reality can be secured within the norms governing "what
can be spoken" and "what is unspeakable."[11] The adjudication of rape, even
under the law, is therefore always a *reading*, and, to that extent, it may even
be appropriately understood as a kind of genre criticism. That is, if genre
may be defined as a "fix on the world," as Rosalie Colie has described it
in another context, then what is most at issue in representations of rape is
not simply what generic conventions should apply to a particular case, but
precisely what that case, once determined, may say about the world.[12] The
representation of the happening that is either rape or not-rape is, then, an
issue of language to precisely the extent that all propositions about the
world are linguistic phenomena. What is finally at issue in such words is
not the constituting set of linguistic facts, then, but truth itself.

The most general concerns of this volume—indeed, of any historical inquiry into the history of rape and its representations in literature and law—
are, therefore, epistemological. Inasmuch as reading a particular happening
as rape involves an awareness of how the truth-value of a proposition is to

be (and has been) determined, what we have articulated in these pages is a theory of knowledge. In explaining how happenings come to "be" rape, we have noticed, along with Charles Pierce, that knowledge is never anything more than the "fixation of belief," that any "inquiry" into a truth is no more than "a struggle to attain a state of belief," which will erase "the irritation of doubt" by satisfying it.[13] The struggle to persuade others that a particular happening is either rape or not-rape is, therefore, as we have argued here, an attempt to *know*. And it is, furthermore, an attempt to achieve such knowledge in a context where truth in general must be recognized as a product of the founding activities of the state, as Nietzsche put it, a "legislation of language" that stills "the most flagrant *bellum omni contra omnes*" by quieting the voices it finds most troublesome. The specific critique we offer is then equally general as it exposes these seedy origins.[14]

> What then is truth? A moveable host of metaphors, metonymies, and anthropomorphisms: in short, a sum of human relations that have been poetically and rhetorically intensified, transferred, and embellished, and that, after long usage, seem to a people to be fixed, canonical, and binding. Truths are illusions that we have forgotten are illusions; they are metaphors that have become worn out and have been drained of sensuous force, coins that have lost their embossing and are now considered as metal and no longer as coins.[15]

A significant component of that sum of human relations condensed into the "truth" is, we have hoped to show, precisely that set of gender hierarchies and male perspectives which describe the truth of rape as not-rape—which "know" that sexual violence did not happen. The exposure of this illusion, the unfixing of this canon, is also an activity that it is appropriate to call "reading." But this is also to say that "reading" may sometimes be neither more nor less than noting in which cases, and for what reasons, some of the very truths we hold to be self-evident are false.

Insofar as Vitz imagines feminist criticism as an attempt to "raise the consciousness of women dead for eight hundred years," she is therefore right about our goals, but wrong about our object. Consciousness raising is certainly the general result these readings of rape seek, for they wish to intervene not simply in what false consciousness wrongly knows, but in the way that false consciousness knows it.[16] Since the happenings we here call rape are constituted *as* rape by the "women dead for eight hundred years," precisely as they knew their own violation (either in life or as representations), it can hardly be their consciousness which requires raising. In fact, the consciousness we understand to be false and which we would most wish to raise is the consciousness of someone like Vitz. For, insofar as we understand her rereading to oppose a vital epistemology precisely as it opposes our inquiry, we understand her to oppose knowing itself. It is, of course, our own knowledge of the intractability of such opposition that makes us expect that the afterword to our endeavor will be the pervasive success of the error Vitz articulates. Which is why, in the name of the truth we describe, the only real afterword possible to this volume is a repetition of the very words that begin it: "Feminist analyses of rape have only just begun."

Notes

1. Ludwig Wittgenstein, *On Certainty,* ed. G. E. M. Anscombe and G. H. von Wright, trans. Denis Paul and G. E. M. Anscombe (Oxford: Basil Blackwell, 1969), p. 2.

2. Evelyn Birge Vitz, "Rereading Rape in Medieval Literature," *Partisan Review* 63 (1996): 280–91 (p. 291). The essay has also been reprinted in the *Romanic Review* 88 (1997): 1–26.

3. Vitz, "Rereading Rape," pp. 288 and 291.

4. Catharine A. MacKinnon, *Towards a Feminist Theory of the State* (Cambridge, MA: Harvard University Press, 1989), p. 183.

5. Vitz, "Rereading Rape," p. 280.

6. Judith Butler, "Contingent Foundations: Feminism and the Question of Postmodernism," in *Feminists Theorize the Political,* ed. Judith Butler and Joan Scott (London: Routledge, 1992), pp. 3–21, esp. p. 19.

7. On the subversive potential for repetition in relation to signifying practices, see Judith Butler, *Gender Trouble: Feminism and the Subversion of Identity* (London: Routledge, 1990), pp. 142–49.

8. MacKinnon, *Feminist Theory of the State,* pp. 163–64.

9. This is precisely the proposal of Sharon Marcus, "Fighting Bodies, Fighting Words: A Theory and Politics of Rape Prevention," in *Feminists Theorize the Political,* ed. Judith Butler and Joan Scott (London: Routledge, 1992), pp. 385–403, esp. p. 389.

10. Marcus, "Fighting Bodies, Fighting Words," p. 390.

11. Marcus, "Fighting Bodies, Fighting Words," p. 389.

12. "A genre-system offers a set of interpretations, of 'frames' or 'fixes' on the world," Rosalie Colie, *The Resources of Kind: Genre-Theory in the Renaissance,* ed. Barbara K. Lewalski (Berkeley: University of California Press, 1973), p. 8.

13. Charles S. Pierce, "The Fixation of Belief," pp. 120–37 in *Charles S. Pierce: The Essential Writings,* ed. Edward C. Moore (New York: Harper & Row, 1972), p. 126.

14. Friedrich Nietzsche, "On the Truth and Lies in the Nonmoral Sense," pp. 77–97 in *Philosophy and Truth: Selections from Nietzsche's Notebooks of the Early 1870's,* ed. and trans. Daniel Breazeale (London: Humanities Press International, 1979), pp. 80–81.

15. Nietzsche, "On the Truth and Lies in the Nonmoral Sense," p. 84.

16. On consciousness raising as a form of feminist political practice, see MacKinnon, *Feminist Theory of the State,* pp. 83–105.

WORKS CITED

Accessus ad auctores, Bernard d'Utrecht, Conrad d'Hirsau: Dialogus super auctores. Ed. R. B. C. Huygens. Rev. ed. Leiden: Brill, 1970.

Adelman, Janet. *Suffocating Mothers: Fantasies of Maternal Origin in Shakespeare's Plays,* Hamlet *to* The Tempest. New York: Routledge, 1992.

Adler, Zsuzsanna. *Rape on Trial.* New York: Routledge, 1987.

Aers, David. "Criseyde: Woman in Medieval Society." In *Critical Essays in Chaucer's* Troilus and Criseyde. Ed. C. David Benson, 128–48. Toronto: University of Toronto Press, 1991.

Ahl, Frederick. *Metaformations.* Ithaca, NY: Cornell University Press, 1985.

Aimeric. *Ars lectoria.* Ed. H. J. Reijnders. In *Vivarium* 9 (1971): 119–37; 10 (1972): 41–101, 124–76.

Ainsworth, Henry. *An Arrow Against Idolatrie. Taken out of the quiver of the lord of Hosts.* Amsterdam, 1611.

Alda. Ed. Marcel Winzweiler. In Gustave Cohen, ed. *La "comédie" latine en France au XIIe siècle,* vol. 1, 107–51. Paris: Société d'Edition "Les Belles Lettres," 1931.

Alda. Trans. Alison Goddard Elliott, 104–25. *Seven Medieval Latin Comedies.* New York: Garland, 1984.

Allen, Don Cameron. *Mysteriously Meant: The Rediscovery Of Pagan Symbolism and Allegorical Interpretation in the Renaissance.* Baltimore, MD: The Johns Hopkins University Press, 1970.

Allen, Judson B. *The Ethical Poetic of the Later Middle Ages: A decorum of convenient distinction.* Toronto: University of Toronto Press, 1982.

———. *Friar as Critic: Literary Attitudes in the Later Middle Ages.* Nashville, TN: Vanderbilt University Press, 1971.

Alpers, Paul. "Narration in *The Faerie Queene.*" *ELH* 44 (1977): 19–39.

———. *The Poetry of* The Faerie Queene. 1967; rpt. Princeton, NJ: Princeton University Press, 1982.

Amsler, Mark. "Genre and Code in Abelard's *Historia calamitatum.*" *Assays* 1 (1981): 35–50.

———. "Mad Lovers and Other Hooked Fish: Chaucer's *Complaint of Mars.*" *Allegorica* 4 (1979): 301–14.

Anderson, Judith. "'In liuing colours and right hew': The Queen of Spenser's Central Books." In *Poetic Traditions of the English Renaissance.* Ed. Maynard Mack and George DeForest Lord, 47–66. New Haven, CT: Yale University Press, 1982.

Andreas Capellanus. *De Amore.* Ed. Graziano Ruffini. Milan: Guanda, 1980.

————. *The Art of Courtly Love.* Trans. John Jay Parry. New York: W.W. Norton, 1969.

Andrew, Malcolm and Ronald Waldron. *The Poems of the Pearl Manuscript.* Berkeley: University of California Press, 1982.

Andrewes, Lancelot. *The Works of Lancelot Andrewes.* Ed. J. P. Wilson and James Bliss, 11 vols. Oxford: Clarendon Press, 1841–54.

Anger, Jane. *Jane Anger Her Protection for Women.* In *First Feminists: British Women Writers, 1578–1799.* Ed. Moira Ferguson, 58–73. Bloomington: Indiana University Press, 1985.

Aquinas, Thomas. *Summa Theologiae.* Trans. Roland Potter. New York: McGraw Hill, 1964, 1970.

————. *Summa Theologica.* Trans. Fathers of the English Dominican Province. 5 vols. 1948; rpt. Westminster, MD: Christian Classics, 1981.

Arnulf of Orleans. *Allegoriae super Ovidii Metamorphosin.* Ed. Fausto Ghisalberti. In "Arnolfo d'Orléans: Un cultore di Ovidio nel secolo XII," *Memorie del Reale Istituto Lombardo di Scienze e Lettere* 24 (1917–39): 155–234.

Astell, Ann W. "Sidney's Didactic Method in the *Old Arcadia.*" *Studies in English Literature 1500–1900* 24.1 (1984): 39–51.

Aston, Margaret. *England's Iconoclasts,* vol. 1: *Laws Against Images.* Oxford: Clarendon Press, 1988.

Atwood, Margaret. "Writing the Male Character." *Second Words,* 1982. In *The Norton Reader,* 7th ed., 1046. New York: W.W. Norton, 1988.

Auerbach, Nina. *Romantic Imprisonment: Women and Other Glorified Outcasts.* New York: Columbia University Press, 1985.

Augustine of Hippo. *The City of God Against the Pagans.* Trans. Philip Levine. London: Loeb Classical Library and Harvard University Press, 1966.

Bacon, Francis. *Francis Bacon: A Selection of His Works.* Ed. Sidney Warhaft. New York: Odyssey, 1965.

Baines, Barbara. "Effacing Rape in Early Modern Representation." *English Literary History* 65 (1998): 69–98.

Baker, Howard. *Induction to Tragedy: A Study in the Development of Form in* Gorboduc, The Spanish Tragedy, *and* Titus Andronicus. Baton Rouge: Louisiana State University Press, 1939.

Bal, Mieke. *Death and Dyssymetry: Death and Coherence in Judges.* Chicago and London: University of Chicago Press, 1988.

Barber, Elizabeth Wayland. *Women's Work: The First 20,000 Years.* New York: Norton, 1994.

Barkan, Leonard. "Diana and Actaeon: The Myth as Synthesis," *English Literary Renaissance* 10 (1980): 317–59.

Baron, Larry, and Murray A. Straus. *Four Theories of Rape in American Society: A State-Level Analysis.* New Haven, CN: Yale University Press, 1989.

Bashar, Nazife. "Rape in England Between 1550 and 1700." *The Sexual Dynamics of History: Men's Power, Women's Resistance.* Ed. London Feminist History Group, 28–42. London: Pluto Press, 1983.

Bate, Jonathan. *Shakespeare and Ovid.* Oxford: Clarendon Press, 1993.

Beattie, J. M. *Crime and the Courts in England 1660–1800.* Princeton, NJ: Princeton University Press, 1986.

Belsey, Andrew, and Catherine Belsey. "Icons of Divinity: Portraits of Elizabeth I." In *Renaissance Bodies: The Human Figure in English Culture c. 1540–1660.* Ed. Luce Gent and Nigel Llewellyn. London: Reaktion Books, 1990.

Belsey, Catherine. *Subject of Tragedy.* London: Methuen, 1985.

Benjamin, Walter. *The Origin of German Tragic Drama.* Trans. John Osborne. London: Verso, 1977.

Benkov, Edith Joyce. "*Philomena:* Chrétien de Troyes' Reinterpretation of the Ovidian Myth." *Classical and Modern Literature* 3 (1983).

Benson, C. David. *Critical Essays in Chaucer's* Troilus and Criseyde. Toronto: University of Toronto Press, 1991.

Benson, C. David and Elizabeth Robertson, eds. *Chaucer's Religious Tales.* Cambridge: Boydell and Brewer Press, 1990.

Benson, Larry D. *A Glossarial Concordance to the Riverside Chaucer.* New York: Garland, 1993.

Bennett, Judith. "Medieval Women, Modern Women: Across The Great Divide." In *Culture and History 1350–1699: Essays on English Communities, Identities and Writing.* Ed. David Aers, 147–75. London: Harvester Wheatsheaf, 1992.

——— and Amy Froide, eds. *Single Women in the European Past, 1250–1800.* Philadelphia: University of Pennsylvania Press, 1999.

Bennett, Pamela E. "'And Shortely for to Seyn they were Aton:' Chaucer's Deflection of Rape in the Reeve's and Franklin's Tales." *Women's Studies: An Interdisciplinary Journal* 22, no. 2C (1993): 145–62.

Berchorius, Petrus (Pierre Bersuire). *Reductorium morale, Book 15: Ovidius moralizatus: De formis figurisque deorum.* Ed. Joseph Engels. Utrecht: Instituut voor Laat Latijn der Rijksuniversiteit, 1966.

Berger, Jr., Harry. "Actaeon at the Hinder Gate: The Stag Party in Spenser's Gardens of Adonis," In *Desire in the Renaissance: Psychoanalysis and Literature.* Ed. Valeria Finucci and Regina Schwartz, 91–119. Princeton, NJ: Princeton University Press, 1994.

———. "Busirane and the War between the Sexes: An Interpretation of *The Faerie Queene.*" *English Literary Renaissance* 1 (1971): 99–121.

———. *Revisionary Play: Studies in the Spenserian Dynamics.* Berkeley: University of California Press, 1988.

Bergren, Ann S. "Language and the Female in Early Greek Thought." *Arethusa* 16 (1983): 1, 2: 69–95, and "Helen's Web: Time and Tableau in the *Iliad.*" *Helios* n.s. 7, 1 (1980): 19–34.

Bernard of Utrecht. *Commentum in Theodulum (1076–1099).* Ed. R. B. C. Huygens. Spoleto: Centro Italiano di studi sull'Alto Medioevo, 1977.

Bernardus Silvestris. *Commentary on Martianus Capella's 'De nuptiis Philologiae et Mercurii' attributed to Bernardus Silvestris.* Ed. Haijo Jan Westra. Toronto: Pontifical Institute of Mediaeval Studies, 1986.

Berry, Philippa. *Of Chastity and Power: Elizabethan Literature and the Unmarried Queen.* London: Routledge, 1989.

Besserman, Lawrence. "The Idea of the Green Knight." *ELH* 53 (1986): 219–39.

Bettenson, Henry, trans. *Concerning the City of God Against the Pagans.* London: Penguin Books, 1972.

Betts, Hannah. "'The Image of this Queene so quaynt': The Pornographic Blazon 1588–1603." In *Dissing Elizabeth: Negative Representations of Gloriana*. Ed. Julia M. Walker, 153–84. Durham, NC: Duke University Press, 1998.

Bevington, David, ed. *The Complete Works of Shakespeare*. 4th ed. New York: Harper-Collins, 1992.

Blamires, Alcuin, ed. *Woman Defamed and Woman Defended: An Anthology of Medieval Texts*. Oxford: Oxford University Press, 1992.

Blanch, Robert J. "'Al was this land fulfild of fayerye': The Thematic Employment of Force, Willfulness, and Legal Conventions in Chaucer's *Wife of Bath's Tale*." *Studia Neophilologica* 57 (1985): 41–51.

Bloch, R. Howard. "Chaucer's Maiden's Head: The *Physician's Tale* and the Poetics of Virginity." *Representations* 28 (1989): 113–34.

———. *Etymologies and Genealogies: A Literary Anthropology of the French Middle Ages*. Chicago: University of Chicago Press, 1983.

———. *Medieval French Literature and Law*. Berkeley: University of California Press, 1977.

———. *Medieval Misogyny and the Invention of Western Romantic Love*. Chicago: University of Chicago Press, 1991.

Blumenthal, Wilfred. "Untersuchungen zur pseudo-ovidianischen Kömodie *Pamphilus*." *Mittellateinisches Jahrbuch* 11 (1976): 224–46.

Boccaccio, Giovanni. *Concerning Famous Women*. Trans. Guido Guarino. New Brunswick, NJ: Rutgers University Press, 1963.

———. *Genealogy of the Pagan Gods*. Trans. Charles Osgood as *Boccaccio on Poetry*. Indianapolis: Bobbs-Merrill, 1956.

Boethius. *Philosophiae Consolationis Libri Quinque*. Ed. Karl Büchner. Heidelberg: Carl Winter, 1977.

Bourque, Linda Brookover. *Defining Rape*. Durham, NC: Duke University Press, 1989d.

Bowers, A. Robin. "Emblem and Rape in Shakespeare's *Lucrece* and *Titus Andronicus*." *Studies in Iconography* 10 (1984–86): 79–96.

Bowers, Fredson. *Elizabethan Revenge Tragedy*. Princeton, NJ: Princeton University Press, 1940.

Bracton, Henry de. *On the Laws and Customs of England*. Ed. and trans. Samuel E. Thorne. Cambridge, MA: Selden Society [by] Harvard University Press, 1968.

Bray, Alan. "Homosexuality and the Signs of Male Friendship in Elizabethan England." *Queering the Renaissance*. Ed. Jonathan Goldberg. Durham: Duke University Press, 1994.

Breitenberg, Mark. *Anxious Masculinity in Early Modern England*. Cambridge Studies in Renaissance Literature and Culture 10. Cambridge: Cambridge University Press, 1996.

Brewer, D. S. *Chaucer*. 3rd. ed. London, 1973.

Broude, Ronald. "Four Forms of Justice in *Titus Andronicus*." *Journal of English and Germanic Philology* 78: 494–507.

Brownmiller, Susan. *Against Our Will: Men, Women and Rape*. New York: Simon & Schuster, 1975.

Brundage, James A. *Law, Sex, and Christian Society in Medieval Europe.* Chicago: University of Chicago Press, 1987.

———. *Medieval Canon Law.* New York and London: Longman, 1995.

———. "Rape and Marriage in the Medieval Canon Law." *Revue de droit canonique* 28 (1978): 62–75.

Bullough, Geoffrey. *Narrative and Dramatic Sources of Shakespeare.* New York: Columbia University Press, 1966.

Bullough, Vern. "Medieval Medical and Scientific Views of Women." *Viator* 4 (1973): 485–501.

Burks, Deborah G. "'I'll Want My Will Else': *The Changeling* and Women's Complicity with Their Rapists." *ELH* 62 (1995): 759–90.

Burns, E. Jane. *Bodytalk: When Women Speak in Old French Literature.* Philadelphia: University of Pennsylvania Press, 1993.

———. "Knowing Women: Female Orifices in Old French Farce and Fabliaux." *Exemplaria* 4 (1992): 81–104.

Burns, E. Jane and Roberta L. Krueger, eds. "Courtly Ideology and Woman's Place in Medieval French Literature." *Romance Notes* 25 (1985).

Burrow, J. A. *A Reading of* Sir Gawain and the Green Knight. London: Routledge & Kegan Paul, 1965.

Burt, Richard and John Michael Archer, eds. *Enclosure Acts: Sexuality, Property, and Culture in Early Modern England.* Ithaca, NY: Cornell University Press, 1994.

Bushman, Mary Ann. "Rhetoric in the Courtroom: Sidney's *Arcadia.*" *Ball State University Forum* 28.1 (1987): 20–28.

Butler, Judith. "Contingent Foundations: Feminism and the Question of Postmodernism." In *Feminists Theorize the Political.* Ed. Judith Butler and Joan Scott, 3–21. London: Routledge, 1992.

———. *Gender Trouble: Feminism and the Subversion of Identity.* London: Routledge, 1990.

———. *The Psychic Life of Power: Theories in Subjection.* Stanford: Stanford University Press, 1997.

Bynum, Caroline Walker. *Fragmentation and Redemption: Essays in Gender and the Human Body in Medieval Religion.* New York: Zone Books, 1991.

———. *Jesus as Mother: Studies in the Spirituality of the High Middle Ages.* Berkeley: University of California Press, 1982.

———. *The Resurrection of the Body in Western Christianity, 200–1336.* New York: Columbia University Press, 1995.

Byrd, William, ed. *Psalms, Sonnets, and Songs of Sadness and Piety.* 1588. Reprinted in *An English Garner.* Ed. Edward Arber, 4:71–93. Westminster: Constable, 1905.

Cadden, Joan. *Meanings of Sexual Difference in the Middle Ages: Medicine, Science, and Culture.* Cambridge: Cambridge University Press, 1993.

Cahoon, Leslie. "Raping the Rose: Jean de Meun's Reading of Ovid's *Amores.*" *Classical and Modern Literature* 6 (1986): 261–85.

Cain, Thomas. *Praise in "The Faerie Queene."* Lincoln: University of Nebraska Press, 1978.

Calabrese, Michael. *Chaucer's Ovidian Arts of Love.* Gainesville: University of Florida Press, 1994.

Calasso, Roberto. *The Marriage of Cadmus and Harmony.* Trans. Tim Parks. N.Y.: Alfred A. Knopf, 1993.

Calvin, Jean. *Institutes of the Christian Religion.* Ed. John T. McNeill. Trans. Ford Lewis Battles, 2 vols. Philadelphia: Westminster Press, 1960.

Cannon, Christopher, "Raptus in the Chaumpaigne Release and a Newly Discovered Document Concerning the Life of Geoffrey Chaucer," *Speculum* 68 (1993): 74–94.

Carson, Mother Angela. "Morgain la Fee as the Principle of Unity in *GGK.*" *Modern Language Quarterly* 23 (1962): 3–16.

Carter, John Marshall. *Rape in Medieval England: An Historical and Sociological Study.* Lanham: University Press of America, 1985.

Castle, Terry. *Clarissa's Ciphers: Meaning and Disruption in Richardson's "Clarissa."* Ithaca, NY: Cornell University Press, 1982.

Cavanagh, Sheila T. *Wanton Eyes and Chaste Desires: Female Sexuality in "The Faerie Queene."* Bloomington: Indiana University Press, 1994.

Chance, Jane. "Chaucerian Irony in the Verse Epistles: 'Wordes Unto Adam,' 'Lenvoy a Scogan,' and 'Lenvoy a Bukton.'" *Papers on Language and Literature* 21 (1985): 115–28.

———. *Medieval Mythography: From Roman North Africa to the School of Chartres, A.D. 433–1177.* Gainesville: University Press of Florida, 1994.

Chartier, Roger. *The Order of Books: Readers, Authors, and Libraries in Europe Between the Fourteenth and Eighteenth Centuries.* Trans. Lydia G. Cochrane. Stanford: Stanford University Press, 1994.

Chaucer, Geoffrey. *The Complete Poetry and Prose of Geoffrey Chaucer.* Ed. John H. Fisher. New York: Holt, Rinehart & Winston, 1977.

———. *The Riverside Chaucer.* Ed. Larry D. Benson. Boston: Houghton Mifflin, 1987.

———. *Troilus and Criseyde.* Ed. B. A. Windeatt, London: Longman, 1984.

Chaucer Life-Records. Ed. Martin M. Crow and Clair C. Olson. Oxford: Oxford University Press, 1966.

Chaytor, Miranda. "Husband(ry): Narratives of Rape in the Seventeenth Century." *Gender and History* 7.3 (1995): 378–407.

Cholakian, Patricia Frances. *Rape and Writing in the* Heptameron *of Marguerite of Navarre.* Carbondale: Southern Illinois University Press, 1991.

Chrétien de Troyes. *Cligés.* Ed. Alexander Micha. Paris: Champion, 1957.

———. *Erec et Enide.* Ed. Mario Roques. Paris: Champion, 1976.

———. *Philomena.* Ed. C. de Boer. Paris: Editions Paul Geuthner, 1909.

Christine de Pizan. *The Book of the City of Ladies.* Trans. Earl Jeffrey Richards. New York: Persea, 1982.

———. *"The Epistle of Othea to Hector": Translated into Middle English by Stephen Scrope.* Ed. Curt Bühler. Early English Text Society, vol. 264. New York: Oxford University Press, 1970.

———. *Epistre Othéa.* Ed. Gabriella Parussa. Geneva: Librairie Droz, 1999.

———. *Le Livre de la Cité des dames.* Ed. Earl Jeffrey Richards. Milan: Luna editrice, 1997.

Church of England. *Certayne Sermons or Homelies (1547) and A Homily against Disobedience and Wilful Rebellion (1570): A Critical Edition*. Ed. Ronald B. Bond. Toronto: University of Toronto Press, 1987.

Churchyard, Thomas. "A Discovrse of The Queenes Maiesties entertainement in Suffolk and Norffolk." Short Title Catalog microfilm 5226, 1578.

Claudian(us). *De raptu Proserpina*. In *Claudian*. Ed. and trans. by Maurice Platnauer, 2 vols. Cambridge, MA: Harvard University Press, 1922.

Clément, Catherine. *Syncope: The Philosophy of Rapture*. Trans. Sally O'Driscoll and Deirdre M. Mahoney. Minneapolis: University of Minnesota Press, 1994.

Cohen, Gustave, ed. *La "comédie" latine en France au XIIe siècle*, 2 vols. Paris: Société d'Edition "Les Belles Lettres," 1931.

Colby-Hall, Alice. *The Portrait in Twelfth-Century Literature*. Geneva, 1965.

Colie, Rosalie. *The Resources of Kind: Genre-Theory in the Renaissance*. Ed. Barbara K. Lewalski. Berkeley: University of California Press, 1973.

Collinson, Patrick. "The Elizabethan Church and the New Religion." In *The Reign of Elizabeth I*. Ed. Christopher Haigh, 169–94. Athens: University of Georgia Press, 1985.

Conrad of Hirsau. *Dialogus super auctores*. In *Accessus ad auctores*. Ed. R. B. C. Huygens. Leiden: E. J. Brill, 1970.

Cooper, Helen. "Chaucer and Ovid: A Question of Authority." In *Ovid Renewed*, Ed. C. A. Martindale, 71–81. Cambridge: Cambridge University Press, 1988.

Copeland, Rita. "Introduction: Dissenting Critical Practices," In *Criticism and Dissent in the Middle Ages*. Ed. Rita Copeland, 1–23. Cambridge: Cambridge University Press, 1996.

Cowell, John. *The Interpreter*. Cambridge, England, 1607.

Cowling, George H. *Chaucer*. New York: E. P. Dutton, 1927.

Crampton, Georgia Ronan, ed. *The Shewings of Julian of Norwich*. Kalamazoo, MI: TEAMS Medieval Institute Publications, 1993.

Crane, Susan. *Gender and Romance in Chaucer's Canterbury Tales*. Princeton, NJ: Princeton University Press, 1994.

Cressy, David. *Literacy and the Social Order*. Cambridge: Cambridge University Press, 1980.

Culler, Jonathan. "Reading as a Woman." In *On Deconstruction: Theory and Criticism After Structuralism*, 43–64. Ithaca, NY: Cornell University Press, 1982.

Curran, Leo. "Rape and Rape Victims in the *Metamorphoses*." *Arethusa* 11 (1978): 213–41.

Cursor Mundi. Ed. Richard Morris. 3 vols. EETS o.s. 57, 59, 62, 66, 68, 99, 101. London: Kegan Paul, 1874, 1893.

Curtius, Ernst R. *European Literature and the Latin Middle Ages*. Trans. Willard Trask. Princeton, NJ: Princeton University Press, 1953.

Dagenais, John. *The Ethics of Reading in a Manuscript Culture: Glossing the "Libro de buen amor."* Princeton, NJ: Princeton University Press, 1994.

Dalton, Michael. *The Countrey Justice, Containing the Practice of the Justices of the Peace out of their Sessions*. London, 1630.

Dana, Margaret E. "The Providential Plot of the *Old Arcadia*." *Studies in English Literature, 1500–1900* 17 (1977): 39–57.

De Boer, C. *Philomena: Conte Raconté d'après Ovide.* Paris: P. Geuther, 1909.

Delany, Sheila. *Medieval Literary Politics: Shapes of Ideology.* Manchester: Manchester University Press, 1990.

———. *The Naked Text: Chaucer's* Legend of Good Women. Berkeley: University of California Press, 1994.

———. "Strategies of Silence in the Wife of Bath's Recital." *Exemplaria* 2.1 (March 1990): 49–69.

———. *Writing Woman: Women Writers and Women in Literature, Medieval to Modern.* New York: Schocken Books, 1983.

de Lauretis, Teresa. "The Violence of Rhetoric." In *Technologies of Gender: Essays on Theory, Film, and Fiction,* 31–50. Bloomington: Indiana University Press, 1987.

De Nuncio Sagaci. Ed. Alphonse Dain. In *La "comédie" latine en France au XIIe siècle.* Ed. Gustave Cohen, vol. 2, 103–56. Paris: Société d'Edition "Les Belles Lettres," 1931.

Derrida, Jacques. *Of Grammatology.* Trans. Gayatri Chakravorty Spivak. Baltimore, MD: Johns Hopkins University Press, 1976.

De Tribus Puellis. Ed. Paul Maury. In Gustave Cohen, ed. *La "comédie" latine en France au XIIe siècle,* vol. 2: 225–42. Paris: Société d'Edition "Les Belles Lettres," 1931.

———. Trans. Alison Goddard Elliott. *Seven Medieval Latin Comedies.* 147–58. New York: Garland, 1984.

Diehl, Huston. "Bewhored Images and Imagined Whores: Iconophobia and Gynophobia in Stuart Love Tragedies," *English Literary Renaissance* 26 (1996): 111–37.

Dinshaw, Carolyn. *Chaucer's Sexual Poetics.* Madison: University of Wisconsin Press, 1989.

———. "Getting Medieval: *Pulp Fiction,* Gawain, Foucault." In *The Book and the Body.* Ed. Dolores Warwick Frese and Katherine O'Brien O'Keeffe, 116–63. Notre Dame, IN: University of Notre Dame Press, 1997.

———. "A Kiss is Just a Kiss: Heterosexuality and its Consolations in *Sir Gawain and the Green Knight."* *Diacritics* 24 (1994): 205–26.

———. "Rivalry, Rape and Manhood: Gower and Chaucer." In *Chaucer and Gower: Difference, Mutuality, Exchange.* Ed. R. F. Yeager, 130–52. University of Victoria English Literary Studies Monograph Series 51. Victoria, BC: University of Victoria Press, 1991.

Dipple, Elizabeth. "'Unjust Justice' in the *Old Arcadia," Studies in English Literature 1500–1900* 10.1 (1970): 83–101.

Dod, Richard and John Cleaver. *A Godly Form of Household Government.* London, 1598.

Dollimore, Jonathan. *Radical Tragedy: Religion, Ideology and Power in the Drama of Shakespeare and His Contemporaries.* Brighton: Harvester, 1984.

Donahue, Charles Jr. "The Canon Law on the Foundation of Marriage and Social Practice in the Later Middle Ages." *Journal of Family History* 8 (1983): 144–58.

Donaldson, Ian. *The Rapes of Lucretia: A Myth and Its Transformations.* Oxford: Clarendon, 1982.

Dronke, Peter. "A Note on Pamphilus." *Journal of the Warburg and Courtauld Institutes* (1979): 226.

Dryden, John. *The Poems of John Dryden.* Ed. James Kinsley, vol. IV. Oxford: The Clarendon Press, 1958.

Duby, Georges. "Aristocratic Households of Feudal France" in *A History of Private Life: Revelations of the Medieval World.* Ed. Georges Duby, 35–85. Cambridge, MA: Harvard University Press, 1988.

———. *Le chevalier, la femme, et le prêtre.* Paris: Hachette, 1981.

———. "Lineage, Nobility, and Knighthood: The Mâconnais in the Twelfth Century," in *The Chivalrous Society.* Trans. Cynthia Postan, 59–80. Berkeley: University of California Press, 1980.

———. *Medieval Marriage: Two models from twelfth-century France.* Trans. Elborg Forster. Baltimore, MD: Johns Hopkins University Press, 1978.

Duffy, Eamon. *The Stripping of the Altars: Traditional Religion in England c. 1400–c. 1580.* New Haven, CT: Yale University Press, 1992.

E., T. *The Lawe's Resolution of Women's Rights.* London, 1632.

Eccles, Audrey. *Obstetrics and Gynaecology in Tudor and Stuart England.* Kent, OH: Kent State University Press, 1982.

Eggert, Katherine. *Showing Like a Queen: Female Authority and Literary Experiment in Spenser, Shakespeare, and Milton.* Philadelphia: University of Pennsylvania Press, 2000.

Elizabeth I. "Marriage Speech," 1559. Ed. Frances Teague. In *Women Writers of the Renaissance and Reformation.* Ed. Katharina M. Wilson, 537–38. Athens: University of Georgia Press, 1987.

Elliott, Alison Goddard, trans. *Seven Medieval Latin Comedies.* New York: Garland, 1984.

Enterline, Lynn. "Petrarch Reading (Himself Reading) Ovid." in *Desire in the Renaissance: Psychoanalysis and Literature.* Ed. Valeria Finucci and Regina Schwartz, 120–46. Princeton, NJ: Princeton University Press, 1994.

Erasmus, Desiderius. *A ryght frutefull Epystle by the moste excellent clerke Erasmus in laude and prayse of matrymony.* Trans. Rychard Tauernour. London, 1532.

———. "Courtship." In *The Colloquies of Erasmus,* 1450. Trans. Craig R. Thompson. Chicago: University of Chicago Press, 1965.

Estrich, Susan. *Real Rape.* Cambridge, MA: Harvard University Press, 1987.

Evans, Maurice. *Spencer's Anatomy of Heroism: A Commentary on "The Faerie Queene."* Cambridge: Cambridge University Press, 1970.

Evitt, Regula Meyer. "Chaucer, Rape and the Poetic Power of Ventriloquism." In *Minding the Body: Women and Literature in the Middle Ages, 800–1500.* Ed. Monica B. Potkay and Regula Evitt, 139–65. New York: Twayne Publishers, 1997.

Ferrante, Joan. *Woman as Image in Medieval Literature from the Twelfth Century to Dante.* New York: Columbia University Press, 1975.

Ficino, Marsilio. *Commentary on Plato's Symposium on Love.* 1484. Trans. Sears Jayne. Dallas: Spring, 1985.

Fiero, Gloria K., ed. and trans. with Wendy Pfeffer and Mathé Allain. *Three Medieval Views of Women.* New Haven, CT: Yale University Press, 1989.

Finch, Henry. *Law, or, A Discourse Thereof.* London, 1627.

Findlen, Paula. "Humanism, Politics and Pornography in Renaissance Italy." In *The Invention of Pornography: Obscenity and the Origins of Modernity, 1500–1800.* Ed. Lynn Hunt, 49–108. New York: Zone Books, 1993.

Fineman, Joel. "Shakespeare's *Will:* the Temporality of Rape." *Representations* 20 (Fall, 1987): 25–46

Finke, Laurie A. "'All is for to selle': Breeding Capital in the Wife of Bath's Prologue and Tale." In *Geoffrey Chaucer: The Wife of Bath.* Ed. Peter G. Beidler, 171–88. Boston and New York: St. Martin's Press, 1996.

Fisher, Sheila. "Leaving Morgan Aside: Women, History, and Revisionism in *Sir Gawain and the Green Knight.*" *The Passing of Arthur: New Essays in Arthurian Tradition.* Ed. Christopher Baswell and William Sharpe, 129–51. New York: Garland, 1988.

———. "Taken Men and Token Women in *Sir Gawain and the Green Knight.*" *Seeking the Woman in Late Medieval and Renaissance Writings: Essays in Feminist Contextual Criticism.* Ed. Sheila Fisher and Janet E. Halley, 71–105. Knoxville: University of Tennessee Press, 1989.

Fitzherbert, Anthony. *The New Boke of Justices of the Peas.* London, 1538.

Fleming, John. "Deiphoebus Betrayed: Virgilian Decorum, Chaucerian Feminism." *Chaucer Review* 21 (1986): 182–99.

Fletcher, Angus. *Allegory: The Theory of a Symbolic Mode.* Ithaca, NY: Cornell University Press, 1964.

Foster, B.O., ed. and trans. *Livy: In Fourteen Volumes,* Volume I, Books I and II. Cambridge, MA: Harvard University Press, 1947.

Foucault, Michel. *Discipline and Punish: The Birth of the Prison.* Trans. Alan Sheridan. New York: Vintage Books, 1977.

Foulon, Charles. "Les Serves du Chateau du Pesme Aventure," *Mélanges Rita Lejeune.* Gembloux, 1969.

Fowler, Alastair. *Triumphal Forms: Structural Patterns in Elizabethan Poetry.* Cambridge: Cambridge University Press, 1970.

Fowler, Elizabeth. "Civil Death and the Maiden: Agency and the Conditions of Contract in *Piers Plowman.*" *Speculum* 70 (1995): 760–92.

Fradenburg, Louise O. "'Oure owen wo to drynke': Loss, Gender and Chivalry in *Troilus and Criseyde.*" In *Chaucer's* Troilus and Criseyde, *'Subgit to alle Poesye': Essays in Criticism.* Ed. R. A. Shoaf, 88–106. Binghamton, NY: Medieval and Renaissance Texts and Studies, 1992.

———. "The Wife of Bath's Passing Fancy." *Studies in the Age of Chaucer* 8 (1986): 31–58.

Frappier, Jean. *Chrétien de Troyes: l'homme et l'oeuvre.* Paris: Hatier-Boivins, 1957.

Freccero, Carla. "Rape's Disfiguring Figures: Marguerite de Navarre's *Heptameron* Day 1:10." In *Rape and Representation.* Ed. Lynn Higgins and Brenda Silver, 227–47. New York: Columbia University Press, 1991.

Friedman, Susan Stanford. "Creativity and the Childbirth Metaphor: Gender Difference in Literary Discourse." *Feminist Studies* 13.1 (1987): 49–82.

Froude, James A. *History of England from the Fall of Wolsey to the Defeat of the Spanish Armada,* Part 6. 1862–1890. Rpt. New York: AMS Press, 1969.

Froula, Christine. "The Daughter's Seduction: Sexual Violence and Literary History." *Signs* (Summer 1986): 621–44. Rpt. in *Daughters and Fathers*. Ed. Lynda E. Boose and Betty S. Flowers, 111–35. Baltimore, MD: Johns Hopkins University Press, 1989.

Frye, Susan. *Elizabeth I: The Competition for Representation.* New York: Oxford University Press, 1993.

———. "Of Chastity and Violence: Elizabeth I and Edmund Spenser in the House of Busirane," *Signs* 20 (1994): 49–78.

Fulgentius. *Mitologiae.* In *Opera.* Ed. Rudolph Helm. Stuttgart: B. G. Teubner, 1970.

Fuss, Diana. *Essentially Speaking: Feminism, Nature, and Difference.* New York: Routledge, 1989.

Fyler, John. *Chaucer and Ovid.* New Haven, CT: Yale University Press, 1979.

Gallagher, Joseph E. "'Trawþe' and 'Luf-Talking' in *Sir Gawain and the Green Knight,*" *Neuphilologische Mitteilungen* 78 (1977): 362–74.

Ganim, John M. "Disorientation, Style, and Consciousness in *SGGK.*" *PMLA* 91 (1976): 376–84.

Garber, Marjorie. *Shakespeare's Ghost Writers: Literature as Uncanny Causality.* New York: Methuen, 1987.

Gardner, John. *The Life and Times of Geoffrey Chaucer.* New York: Knopf, Random House, 1977.

Geoffrey de Vitry. *Commentary on Claudian, "Rape of Proserpina."* Ed. A. K. Clarke and P. M. Giles. Leiden: Brill, 1973.

Geta. Ed. Keith Bate, 13–34. In *Three Latin Comedies.* Toronto: Pontifical Institute of Medieval Studies, 1976.

Geta. Trans. Alison Goddard Elliott, 26–49. In *Seven Medieval Latin Comedies.* New York: Garland, 1984.

Ghisalberti, Fausto. "Medieval Biographies of Ovid." *Journal of the Warburg and Courtauld Institutes* 9 (1946): 10–59.

Gilman, Ernest B. *Iconoclasm and Poetry in the English Reformation: Down Went Dagon.* Chicago: Chicago University Press, 1986.

Glauning, Otto. *Lydgate's Minor Poetry: The Two Nightingale Poems.* Millwood, NY: Kraus Reprint, 1987.

Gold, Penny Schein. *The Lady and the Virgin: Image, Attitude, and Experience in Twelfth-Century France.* Chicago: University of Chicago Press, 1985.

Goldberg, Jonathan. *Endlesse Worke: Spenser and the Structures of Discourse.* Baltimore, MD: Johns Hopkins University Press, 1981.

Goodman, Walter. "Conflicting Attitudes About Rape on Campus." Review of television program "Campus Rape: When No Means No." *The New York Times,* December 26, 1990.

Gosson, Stephen. *The Schoole of Abuse.* London, 1579.

Gough, Melinda. "'Her filthy feature open showne' in Ariosto, Spenser, and *Much Ado About Nothing.*" *Studies in English Literature, 1500–1900,* 39 (1999): 41–67.

Gower, John. *The English Works of John Gower,* Ed. G.C. Macaulay. *Early English Text Society,* no. 81, vol. II. Oxford: Oxford University Press, 1900, rpt. 1979.

Gratian, *Decretum in Corpus iuris canonici*. Ed. Emil Friedberg. Leipzig: Bernhard Tauchnitz, 1879–81.

Gravdal, Kathryn. "Camouflaging Rape: The Rhetoric of Sexual Violence in the Medieval Pastourelle." *Romanic Review* 76 (1985): 360–73.

———. "Chrétien de Troyes, Gratian, and the Medieval Romance of Sexual Violence." *Signs* 17, 3 (1992): 558–85.

———. *Ravishing Maidens: Writing Rape in Medieval French Literature and Law.* Philadelphia: University of Pennsylvania Press, 1991.

———. *Vilain and Courtois: Transgressive Parody in French Literature of the Twelfth and Thirteenth Centuries.* Lincoln: University of Nebraska Press, 1989.

Green, E. Tyrrell. *The Thirty-Nine Articles and the Age of the Reformation.* London: Wells Gardner, Darton, 1896.

Greenblatt, Stephen. *Renaissance Self-Fashioning from More to Shakespeare.* Chicago: University of Chicago Press, 1980.

———. *Shakespearean Negotiations: The Circulation of Social Energy in Renaissance England.* Berkeley: University of California Press, 1988.

———. "Sidney's *Arcadia* and the Mixed Mode." *Studies in Philology* 70.3 (1973): 269–78.

Greene, Thomas. *The Descent from Heaven: A Study in Epic Continuity.* New Haven, CT: Yale University Press, 1963.

Gregerson, Linda. *The Reformation of the Subject: Spenser, Milton, and the English Protestant Epic.* Cambridge: Cambridge University Press, 1995.

Greville, Fulke. *The Life of the Renowned Sir Philip Sidney.* London, 1652. Rpt. Ed. Warren W. Wooden. Delmar: Scholars' Facsimiles & Reprints, 1984.

Grierson, Herbert J. C. *Cross Currents in English Literature of the Seventeenth Century.* 1929. Reprint, London: Chatto & Windus, 1958.

Griffin, Susan. *Rape: The Politics of Consciousness.* New York: Harper & Row, 1979.

Gross, Kenneth. *Spenserian Poetics: Idolatry, Iconoclasm, and Magic.* Ithaca, NY: Cornell University Press, 1985.

Guibert de Nogent. *Monodiae.* Trans. Paul J. Archambault. University Park: Penn State University Press, 1996.

Gunew, Sneja. "Feminist Knowledge: Critique and Construct." In *Feminist Knowledge: Critique and Construct.* Ed. Sneja Gunew, 13–25. London: Routledge, 1990.

Haigh, Christopher. "The Continuity of Catholicism in the English Reformation." In *The English Reformation Revised.* Ed. Christopher Haigh, 176–208. Cambridge: Cambridge University Press, 1987.

Hair, Paul. *Before the Bawdy Court: Selections from the Church Court and Other Records Relating to the Correction of Moral Offenses in England, Scotland and New England, 1300–1800.* London: Elek, 1972.

Hale, Matthew. *Historia Placitorum Coronae. The History of the Pleas of the Crown.* Ed. Solomon Emlyn. London, 1736.

Hali Meithhad. Medieval English Prose for Women. Ed. Bella Millet and Jocelyn Wogan-Browne, 2–43. Oxford: Clarendon, 1990.

Hanawalt, Barbara. *"Of Good and Ill Repute:" Gender and Social Control in Medieval England*. Oxford: Oxford University Press, 1998. Esp. Chapter 8, "Whose Story Was This? Rape Narratives in Medieval English Courts," 124–41.

Hanna III, Ralph. "Unlocking What's Locked: Gawain's Green Girdle." *Viator* 14 (1983): 289–302.

Hansen, Elaine Tuttle. *Chaucer and the Fictions of Gender*. Berkeley: University of California Press, 1992.

Harbage, Alfred and Samuel Schoenbaum. *Annals of English Drama*. Philadelphia: University of Pennsylvania Press, 1964.

Heilbrun, Carolyn. *Hamlet's Mother*. New York: Columbia University Press, 1990.

Helmholz, R. H. *Marriage Litigation in Medieval England*, Cambridge: Cambridge University Press, 1974.

Hemker, Julie. "Rape and the Founding of Rome." *Helios* 12 (1985): 41–47.

Heng, Geraldine. "Feminine Knots and the Other *Sir Gawain and the Green Knight*." *PMLA* 106 (1991): 500–514.

———. "A Woman Wants: The Lady, *Gawain,* and the Forms of Seduction." *Yale Journal of Criticism* 5 (1992): 101–34.

Herlihy, David. *Opera muliebria: Women and Work in Medieval Europe*. Philadelphia: Temple University Press, 1990.

Herman, Lewis. *Trauma and Recovery*. New York: Basic Books, 1992.

Hexter, Ralph. *Ovid and Medieval Schooling: Studies in Medieval School Commentaries on Ovid's Ars amatoria, Epistulae ex Ponto, and Epistulae heroidum*. Munich: Arbeo-Gesellschaft, 1986.

Higgins, Lynn A. and Brenda R. Silver, eds. *Rape and Representation*. New York: Columbia University Press, 1991.

———. "Introduction: Rereading Rape." *Rape and Representation*. Ed. Lynn A. Higgins and Brenda R. Silver, 1–11. New York: Columbia University Press, 1991.

Hindman, Sandra L. *Christine de Pizan's "Epistre Othéa": Painting and Politics at the Court of Charles VI*. Toronto: Pontifical Institute of Mediaeval Studies, 1986.

hooks, bell. "Representing Whiteness in the Black Imagination." In *Cultural Studies*. Ed. Lawrence Grossberg, Cary Nelson, and Paula Treichler, 338–46. New York: Routledge, 1992.

Horner, Shari. "The Violence of Exegesis: Reading the Bodies of Ælfric's Female Saints." *Violence against Women in Medieval Texts*. Ed. Anna Roberts, 22–43. Gainesville: University Press of Florida, 1998.

Howard, Donald. *Chaucer: His Life, His Works, His World*. New York: Dutton, 1987.

Howard, Jean. E. *The Stage and Social Struggle in Early Modern England*. London: Routledge, 1994.

Hunt, Maurice. "Compelling Art in *Titus Andronicus*." *Studies in English Literature* 28 (1988): 197–218.

Hunt, Tony. "Chrétien and the Comediae." *Mediaeval Studies* 40 (1978): 122–24.

———. *Teaching and Learning in Thirteenth-Century England*. 3 vols. Cambridge: Cambridge University Press, 1991.

Ingram, Martin. *Church Courts, Sex and Marriage in England, 1570–1640.* Cambridge: Cambridge University Press, 1987.

Irigaray, Luce. *Speculum of the Other Woman.* Trans. Gillian Gill. Ithaca, NY: Cornell University Press, 1985.

———. *This Sex Which is Not One.* Trans. Catherine Porter. Ithaca, NY: Cornell University Press, 1985.

———. "Women's Exile: Interview with Luce Irigaray." Trans. Couze Venn. In *The Feminist Critique of Language: A Reader.* Ed. Deborah Cameron, 80–96. New York: Routledge, 1990.

Irvine, Martin. "Heloise and the Gendering of the Literate Subject." In *Criticism and Dissent in the Middle Ages.* Ed. Rita Copeland, 87–114. Cambridge: Cambridge University Press, 1996.

———. *The Making of Textual Culture: "Grammatica" and Literary Theory, 350–1100.* Cambridge: Cambridge University Press, 1994.

Isbell, Harold. *Ovid's Heroides.* London: Penguin Books, 1990.

Jacobson, G. A. "Apollo and Tereus: Parallel Motifs in Ovid's *Metamorphoses.*" *Classical Journal* 80 (1984): 45–52.

Jacobus de Voragine. *The Golden Legend: Readings on the Saints.* Trans. William Granger Ryan, 2 vols. Princeton, NJ: Princeton University Press, 1993.

Jardine, Alice A. *Gynesis: Configurations of Woman and Modernity.* Ithaca, NY: Cornell University Press, 1985.

Jed, Stephanie. *Chaste Thinking: The Rape of Lucrece and the Birth of Humanism.* Bloomington: Indiana University Press, 1989.

[Jerome, Saint] Eusebius Hieronymus. *Epistulae.* Pars I. Ed. Isidorus Hilberg. Corpus scriptorum ecclesiasticorum latinorum, 54. Vienna: F. Temsky, 1912.

———. *Letters and Select Works.* Trans. W. H. Fremantle. Nicene and Post-Nicene Fathers, vol. 6. 1893. Rpt. Peabody, MA: Hendrickson, 1994.

John of Garland. *Integumenta Ovidii.* Ed. Fausto Ghisalberti. Testi e documenti inediti o rari, no. 2. Messina and Milan: Giuseppe Principato, 1933.

Johnson, S. F. "The Spanish Tragedy or Babylon Revisited." In *Essays on Shakespeare and Elizabethan Drama in Honor of Hardin Craig.* Ed. Richard Hosley. Columbia: University of Missouri Press, 1962.

Jones, Ann Rosalind. *The Currency of Eros: Women's Love Lyric in Europe, 1540–1620.* Bloomington: Indiana University Press, 1990.

Jones, Nancy A. Rev. of *Bodytalk* by E. Jane Burns. In *Bryn Mawr Medieval Review* (now *The Medieval Review*) 94.11.5. November 29, 1994.

Jonson, Ben. *Bartholomew Fair.* Ed. G. R. Hibbard. New York: Norton, New Mermaids, 1981.

Joplin, Patricia Klindienst. "The Voice of the Shuttle is Ours." *Stanford Literary Review* 1,1 (Spring 1984): 25–53. Reprinted in *Rape and Representation.* Ed. Lynn A. Higgins and Brenda R. Silver, 34–64. New York: Columbia University Press, 1991.

Jordan, Constance. "Feminism and the Humanists: The Case of Sir Thomas Elyot's *Defence of Good Women.*" *Renaissance Quarterly* 36.2 (1983): 181–201.

———. "Representing Political Androgyny: More on the Siena Portrait of Queen Elizabeth I." In *The Renaissance Englishwoman in Print: Counterbalancing the*

Canon. Ed. Anne M. Haselkorn and Betty S. Travitsky, 157–76. Amherst: University of Massachusetts Press, 1990.

Kahn, Coppélia. "Lucrece: The Sexual Politics of Subjectivity." In *Rape and Representation.* Ed. Lynn A. Higgins and Brenda R. Silver, 141–59. New York: Columbia University Press, 1991.

———. "The Rape of Lucrece in Shakespeare's Lucrece," *Shakespeare Studies* 9 (1976): 45–72.

Kaminer, Wendy. *I'm Dysfunctional, You're Dysfunctional: The Recovery Movement and Other Self-Help Fashions.* Reading, MA: Addison-Wesley, 1992.

Kamuf, Peggy. "Penelope at Work." In *Signature Pieces: On the Institution of Authorship.* Ithaca, NY: Cornell University Press, 1988.

Kane, Sean. *Spenser's Moral Allegory.* Toronto: University of Toronto Press, 1989.

Keith, Alison. "Versions of Epic Masculinity in Ovid's Metamorphoses." In *Ovidian Transformations: Essays on Ovid's Metamorphoses and Its Reception.* Ed. Philip Hardie, Alessandro Barchiesi, Stephen Hinds, 214–39. Cambridge: Cambridge Philological Society, 1999.

Kelly, Henry Ansgar. *Love and Marriage in the Age of Chaucer.* Ithaca, NY: Cornell University Press, 1975.

———. "Meanings and Uses of *Raptus* in Chaucer's Time." *Studies in the Age of Chaucer* 20 (1998): 101–65.

———. "Statutes of Rapes and Alleged Ravishers of Wives: A Context for the Charges Against Thomas Malory, Knight." *Viator: Medieval and Renaissance Studies* 28 (1997): 361–419.

Kennedy, Gwynne. *Just Anger: Representing Women's Anger in Early Modern England.* Carbondale: Southern Illinois Press, 2000.

King, John N. "Queen Elizabeth I: Representations of the Virgin Queen." *Renaissance Quarterly* 43.1 (1990): 30–74.

Kiser, Lisa. *Telling Classical Tales: Chaucer and the* Legend of Good Women. Ithaca, NY: Cornell University Press, 1983.

Krier, Theresa M. *Gazing on Secret Sights: Spenser, Classical Imitation, and the Decorums of Vision.* Ithaca, NY: Cornell University Press, 1990.

Kristeva, Julia. "About Chinese Women." In *The Kristeva Reader.* Ed. Toril Moi, 138–59. New York: Columbia University Press, 1986.

———. *Powers of Horror: An Essay on Abjection.* Trans. Leon S. Roudiez. New York: Columbia University Press, 1982.

Kubitscheck, Missy Dehn. "Subjugated Knowledge: Toward a Feminist Exploration of Rape in Afro-American Fiction." In *Studies in Black American Literature.* Ed. Joe Weixlmann and Houston A. Baker, Jr., 3: 43–46. [Cited in Higgins and Silver, 10.]

Kunstmann, Pierre. *Miracles de Notre-Dame de Chartres.* Ottawa: University of Ottawa, 1973.

Laber, Jeri. "Bosnia: Questions About Rape." *New York Review of Books,* March 23, 1993: 3–6.

Lamb, Mary Ellen. *Gender and Authorship in the Sidney Circle.* Madison: University of Wisconsin Press, 1990.

Laqueur, Thomas. *Making Sex: Body and Gender from the Greeks to Freud.* Cambridge, MA: Harvard University Press, 1990.

Laskaya, Anne and Eve Salisbury, eds. *The Middle English Breton Lays.* Kalamazoo, MI: Medieval Institute Publications, 1995.

Lass, Roger. "'Man's Heaven': The Symbolism of Gawain's Shield." *Medieval Studies* 28 (1966): 354–60.

Lattimore, Richard, trans. *The Odyssey of Homer.* New York: HarperCollins, 1965.

Lever, J. W. *The Tragedy of State,* 1971. Reprint, London: Methuen, 1987.

Levi-Strauss, Claude. *The Elementary Structures of Kinship.* Trans. James H. Bell, John R. von Sturmer, and Rodney Needham. Rev. ed. Boston: Beacon Press, 1969.

Lewis, C. S. *The Allegory of Love: A Study in Medieval Tradition.* 1936. Reprint, Oxford: Oxford University Press, 1959.

Lindley, Arthur. "Lady Bertilak's *cors: Sir Gawain and the Green Knight,* 1237." *Notes & Queries* 42 (1995): 23–24.

Lively, Genevieve. "Reading Resistance in Ovid's *Metamorphoses.*" In *Ovidian Transformations: Essays on Ovid's Metamorphoses and Its Reception.* Ed. Philip Hardie, Alessandro Barchiesi, Stephen Hinds, 197–213. Cambridge: Cambridge Philological Society, 1999.

Livy. *Livy.* Ed. and trans. B. O. Foster, et al. 14 vols.: vol. 3. London: Loeb, 1919–59.

———. *The Romane Historie written by T. Livius of Padua.* Trans. by Philemon Holland. London, 1600.

Loewenstein, Joseph. "Echo's Ring: Orpheus and Spenser's Career." *English Literary Renaissance* 16 (1986): 287–302.

Lomperis, Linda. "Unruly Bodies and Ruling Practices: Chaucer's *Physician's Tale* as a Socially Symbolic Act." In *Feminist Approaches to the Body in Medieval Literature.* Ed. L. Lomperis and S. Stanbury, 21–37. Philadelphia: University of Pennsylvania Press, 1993.

Lomperis, Linda and Sarah Stanbury. *Feminist Approaches to the Body in Medieval Literature.* Philadelphia: University of Pennsylvania Press, 1993.

———. "Introduction: Feminist Theory and Medieval 'Body Politics.'" *Feminist Approaches to the Body in Medieval Literature.* Ed. Linda Lomperis and Sarah Stanbury, vii–xiv. Philadelphia: University of Pennsylvania Press, 1993.

Lubac, Henri de. *Medieval Exegesis,* vol. 1. Trans. Mark Sebanc. Grand Rapids, MI: Eerdmans, 1998.

Macdonald, Joyce Green. "Women and Theatrical Authority: Deborah Warner's *Titus Andronicus.*" In *Differences in Women's Re-visions of Shakespeare.* Ed. Marianne Novy, 185–205. Urbana: University of Illinois Press.

MacKinnon, Catharine A. "Feminism, Marxism, Method, and the State: Toward Feminist Jurisprudence." *Signs* 8 (Summer, 1983): 635–58.

———. *Feminism Unmodified.* Cambridge, MA: Harvard University Press, 1987.

———. "Reflections on Sex Equality Under the Law." In *American Feminist Thought at Century's End.* Ed. Linda Kauffman. Cambridge: Basil Blackwell, 1993.

———. *Toward a Feminist Theory of the State,* Cambridge, MA: Harvard University Press, 1989.

Mallin, Eric. "Emulous Factions and the Collapse of Chivalry: *Troilus and Cressida.*" *Representations* 29 (1990): 145–79.

Mann, Jill. *Geoffrey Chaucer.* Atlantic Highlands, NJ: Humanities Press, 1991.

———. "Troilus' Swoon," *Chaucer Review* 14 (1980): 319–35. Rpt. in *Critical Essays in Chaucer's* Troilus and Criseyde *and His Major Early Poems.* Ed. C. David Benson, 149–63. Toronto: University of Toronto Press, 1991.

Marcus, Jane. "Liberty, Sorority, Misogyny." In *The Representation of Women in Fiction.* Ed. Carolyn Heilbron and Margaret Higonnet. Selected Papers from the English Institute, 1981, New Series no. 7, 60–97. Baltimore, MD: Johns Hopkins University Press, 1983.

———. "Still Practice, A/Wrested Alphabet: Toward a Feminist Aesthetic." In *Art and Anger,* 215–49. Miami: Ohio State University Press, 1988. Rpt. in *Feminist Issues in Literary Scholarship.* Ed. Shari Benstock, 79–97. Bloomington: Indiana University Press, 1987.

Marcus, Sharon. "Fighting Bodies, Fighting Words: A Theory and Politics of Rape Prevention." In *Feminists Theorize the Political.* Ed. Judith Butler and Joan Scott, 385–403. London: Routledge, 1992.

Margherita, Gayle. "Some thoughts on History, Epistemology, and Rape." *Medieval Feminist Newsletter,* no. 11 (Spring, 1991): 2–5.

Marshall, Cynthia. "I can interpret all her martyr'd signs: *Titus Andronicus,* Feminism, and the Limits of Interpretation." In *Sexuality and Politics in Renaissance Drama.* Ed. Carole Levin and Karen Robertson, 193–211. Lewiston, NY: Edwin Mellen Press, 1991.

Maxwell, J. C., ed. *Titus Andronicus.* London: Routledge, 1987.

McCall, John P. *Chaucer Among the Gods: The Poetics of Classical Myth.* University Park: Penn State University Press, 1979.

McCracken, Peggy. "The Body Politic and the Queen's Adulterous Body in French Romance." *Feminist Approaches to the Body in Medieval Literature.* Ed. Linda Lomperis and Sarah Stanbury, 38–64. Philadelphia: University of Pennsylvania Press, 1993.

McNamara, Jo Ann and Suzanne Wemple. "The Power of Women Through the Family." In *Women and Power in the Middle Ages.* Ed. Mary Erler and Maryanne Kowaleski. Athens: University of Georgia Press, 1988.

Meiss, Millard. *French Painting in the Time of Jean of Berry: The Limbourgs and Their Contemporaries.* 2 vols. New York: Braziller, 1974.

Miller, David Lee. *The Poem's Two Bodies: The Poetics of the 1590 "Faerie Queene."* Princeton, NJ: Princeton University Press, 1988.

Miller, Nancy K. "Arachnologies: the Woman, the Text and the Critic." In *The Poetics of Gender.* Ed. Nancy K. Miller, 270–95. New York: Columbia University Press, 1980.

Mills, David. "An Analysis of the Temptation Scenes in *Sir Gawain and the Green Knight.*" *JEGP* 67 (1968): 612–30.

Milton, John. *The Complete Prose Works of John Milton.* Ed. Don M. Wolfe, 8 vols. New Haven, CT: Yale University Press, 1953–82.

Montrose, Louis Adrian. "The Elizabethan Subject and the Spenserian Text." In *Literary Theory/Renaissance Texts.* Ed. Patricia Parker and David Quint, 303–40. Baltimore, MD: Johns Hopkins University Press, 1986.

Morrison, Toni. *Beloved.* New York: Knopf, 1987.

Moses, Diana. "Livy's Lucretia and the Validity of Coerced Consent in Roman Law." In *Consent and Coercion to Sex and Marriage in Ancient and Medieval Societies.* Ed. Angeliki E. Laiou, 39–81. Washington, DC: Dumbarton Oaks, 1993.

Mulvey, Laura. *Visual and Other Pleasures.* Bloomington: Indiana University Press, 1989.

Narcisse. Ed. Martine Thiry-Stassin and Madeleine Tyssens. Paris: Les Belles Lettres, 1976.

Newman, Florence. "Sir Gawain and the Semiotics of Truth." *Medieval Perspectives* 4–5 (1989–90): 125–39.

Nichols, John, ed. *The Progresses and Public Processions of Queen Elizabeth.* 3 vols. London: Nichols, 1823. Rpt. AMS Press, 1966.

Nietzsche, Friedrich. "On the Truth and Lies in the Nonmoral Sense." In *Philosophy and Truth: Selections from Nietzsche's Notebooks of the Early 1870's.* Ed. and trans. Daniel Breazeale, 77–97. London: Humanities Press International, 1979.

Noonan, John. "The Power to Choose." *Viator* 4 (1973): 418–34.

Novy, Marianne, ed. *Cross-Cultural Performances: Differences in Women's Re-visions of Shakespeare.* Urbana: University of Illinois Press, 1993

Nykrog, Per. "The Rise of Literary Fiction." In *Renaissance and Renewal in the Twelfth Century.* Ed. Robert L. Benson and Giles Constable. Cambridge, MA: Harvard University Press, 1982.

Ovid. *Ars Amatoria in Amores, Faciei Femineae, Ars Amatoria, Remedia, Amoris.* Ed. E. J. Kenney, 113–200. Oxford: Clarendon Press, 1961.

———. *The Art of Love.* Trans. Rolfe Humphries, 103–78. Bloomington: Indiana University Press, 1955.

———. *Metamorphoses.* In *Les Metamorphoses.* Ed. and trans. Georges Lafaye. 3 vols. Paris: Belles Lettres, 1966.

———. *Metamorphoses* (with Berchorius' commentary and glosses). Lyon, 1518. Rpt. New York: Garland, 1976.

———, *Metamorphoses.* Trans. Rolfe Humphries. Bloomington: Indiana University Press, 1968.

———. *Metamorphoses.* Ed. Frank Justus Miller; 2nd ed. rev. by G. P. Goold, Loeb Classical Library. Cambridge, MA: Harvard University Press, 1977.

———. *Metamorphoses.* Trans. Mary Innes. Harmondsworth: Penguin Books, 1976.

———. *Metamorphoseon Libri I-XV.* Ed. B. A. van Proosdij et al. Leiden: Brill, 1982.

———. *Heroides and Amores.* Trans. Grant Showerman, rev. ed. G. P. Goold. Cambridge, MA: Harvard University Press, 1977.

Ovide moralisé en prose (Texte du quinziéme siècle). Ed. C. de Boer. *Verhhandelingen der Koninklijke Nederlandse Akademie van Wetenschappen te Amsterdam: Afdeeling Letterkunde,* N.S. 61 (1954): 1–400.

"Ovide moralisé." Poème du commencement du quatorzième siècle publié d'après tout les manuscrits connus. Ed. C. de Boer, 5 vols. Amsterdam: Nord-Hollandsche Uitgevers-Maatschappij, 1915–38.

Pamphilus. In *Three Latin Comedies.* Ed. Keith Bate, 61–89. Toronto: Pontifical Institute of Medieval Studies, 1976.

————. Ed. Eugène Évesque. In *La "comédie" latine en France au XIIe siècle*. Ed. Gustave Cohen, vol. 2, 167–233. Paris: Société d'Edition "Les Belles Lettres," 1931.

————. Ed. Stefano Pittaluga. In *Commedie latine del XII e XIII secolo*. Ed. Ferruccio Bertini, 13–137. Genova: Instituto di Filologia classica e medievale, 1980.

————. Trans. Alison Goddard Elliott. *Seven Medieval Latin Comedies,*. 1–25. New York: Garland, 1984.

————. Trans. Ian Thompson and Louis Perraud. In *Ten Latin School Texts of the Later Middle Ages: Translated Selections,* 158–91. Lewiston, NY: Edwin Mellen Press, 1990.

"*Pamphilus, De Amore:* An Introduction and Translation." Trans. Thomas Jay Garbaty. *Chaucer Review* 2 (1967): 108–34.

Pamphilus. Prolegomena zum Pamphilus [de amore] und kritische Textausgabe. Ed. Franz G. Becker. *Beihefte zum Mittellateinischen Jahrbuch* 9: 1972.

Paris, Gaston. "Chrétien Legouais et autres traducteurs ou imitateurs de Ovide," *Histoire Littéraire de France* 29 (1885): 455–517,

Parker, Patricia. *Literary Fat Ladies: Rhetoric, Gender, Property.* London: Methuen, 1987.

Parker, Rozsika. *The Subversive Stitch: Embroidery and the Making of the Feminine.* London: Women's Press, 1996.

Paster, Gail Kern. *The Body Embarrassed: Drama and Disciplines of Shame in Early Modern England.* Ithaca, NY: Cornell University Press, 1993.

Patterson, Lee, ed. *Literary Practice and Social Change in Britain, 1380–1530.* Berkeley: University of California Press, 1990.

Paxton, Nancy L. "Daughters of Lucrece: Shakespeare's Response to Ovid in *Titus Andronicus.*" In *Classical Models in Literature.* Ed. Warren Anderson, Walter Dietze, and Zoran Konstantinovic, 217–24. Innsbruck: Amoe: Institut fur Sprachwissenschaft der Universität Innsbruck, 1981.

Pearsall, Derek. *The Life of Geoffrey Chaucer: A Critical Biography.* Oxford: Blackwell, 1992.

Pfeffer, Wendy. *The Change of Philomel.* New York: Peter Lang, 1985.

Pierce, Charles S. "The Fixation of Belief." In *Charles S. Pierce: The Essential Writings.* Ed. Edward C. Moore, 120–37. New York: Harper & Row, 1972.

Piramus et Tisbé. Ed. F. Branciforti, Biblioteca dell' "Archivum Romanicum," 57. Florence: L. S. Olschki, 1959.

Plucknett, T. F. T. "Chaucer's Escapade." *The Law Quarterly Review* 64 (1948): 35.

Plummer, John F., ed. *Vox Feminae: Studies in Medieval Woman's Song.* Kalamazoo, MI: Medieval Institute Publications, 1981.

Plutarch. *Moralia.* Ed. Harold Cherniss and William C. Helmbold. Cambridge, MA.: Harvard University Press, 1957.

Post, J. B. "Ravishment of Women and the Statutes of Westminster." In *Legal Records and the Historian,* Ed. J. H. Baker, 150–64. London: Royal Historical Society, 1978.

————. "Sir Thomas West and the Statute of Rapes, 1382," *Bulletin of the Institute of Historical Research* 53 (1980): 24–30.

Puttenham, George. *The Arte of English Poesie.* Ed. Gladys Doidge Willcock and Alice Walker. Cambridge: Cambridge University Press, 1936.

Putter, Ad. *Sir Gawain and the Green Knight and French Arthurian Romance.* Oxford: Oxford University Press, 1995.

Quilligan, Maureen. *The Allegory of Female Authority: Christine de Pizan's Cité des Dames.* Ithaca, NY: Cornell University Press, 1991.

———. *The Language of Allegory: Defining the Genre.* Ithaca, NY: Cornell University Press, 1979.

———. *Milton's Spenser: The Politics of Reading.* Ithaca, NY: Cornell University Press, 1983.

———. "The Name of the Author: Self-Representation in Christine de Pizan's *Livre de la cité des dames.*" *Exemplaria* 4 (1992): 217–23.

"R. M." [1636]. *The mothers counsell, or live within compasse.* London: Wright. Short Title Catalog microfilm 20583.

Raby, F. J. E. *A History of Secular Latin Poetry in the Middle Ages,* vol. 2. Oxford: Clarendon Press, 1957.

———. "Philomena praevia temporis amoeni." *Mélanges Joseph de Ghellinck,* vol. 2, 435–48. Gembloux: Ducubot, 1951.

Raine, Nancy V. *After Silence: Rape and My Journey Back.* New York: Crown, 1998.

Reed, Alan and Peter Seago. *Criminal Law.* London: Sweet and Maxwell, 1999.

Remigius of Auxerre. *Commentum in Martianum Capellam.* Ed. Cora Lutz. 2 vols. Leiden: E. J. Brill, 1962–65.

Reynolds, Suzanne. *Medieval Reading: Grammar, Rhetoric and the Classical Text.* Cambridge: Cambridge University Press, 1996.

Rich, Adrienne. *Of Woman Born: Motherhood as Experience and Institution.* New York: W. W. Norton, 1976.

Richlin, Amy. "Reading Ovid's Rapes." In *Pornography and Representation.* Ed. Amy Richlin. New York: Oxford University Press, 1992.

Ridewall, John. *Fulgentius Metaforalis.* Ed. Hans Liebeschütz. Leipzig and Berlin: B. G. Teubner, 1926.

Rieger, Dietmar. "Le motif du viol dans la littérature de la France médiévale entre norme courtoise et réalité courtoise." *Cahiers de civilisation médiévale* 31 (1988): 241–67.

Riley, Denise. *Am I That Name? Feminism and the Category of "Woman" in History.* Minneapolis: University of Minnesota Press, 1988.

Roberts, Anna, ed. *Violence Against Women in Medieval Texts.* Gainesville: University Press of Florida, 1998.

Robertson, D. W., Jr. *A Preface to Chaucer.* Princeton, NJ: Princeton University Press, 1963.

Robertson, Elizabeth. *Early English Devotional Prose and the Female Audience.* Knoxville: University of Tennessee Press, 1990.

———. "Medieval Medical Views of Women and Female Spirituality in the *Ancrene Wisse* and Julian of Norwich's *Showings.*" In *Feminist Approaches to the Body in Medieval Literature.* Ed. Linda Lomperis and Sarah Stanbury, 142–67. Philadelphia: University of Pennsylvania Press, 1993.

———. "Rape in Chaucer." Paper, unpub. draft of MLA 1990 presentation.

Robertson, Karen. "*Antonio's Revenge:* The Tyrant, the Stoic and the Passionate Man." In *Medieval and Renaissance Drama in England IV.* Ed. Paul Werstine, 92–106. New York: AMS Press, 1989.

———. "Discussing Rape in the Classroom." *Medieval Feminist Newsletter,* no. 9 (Summer, 1990): 21–22.

Roche, Thomas. *The Kindly Flame: A Study of the Third and Fourth Books of Spenser's "Faerie Queene."* Princeton, NJ: Princeton University Press, 1964.

Roche, Thomas P., Jr. "The Challenge to Chastity: Britomart in the House of Busirane." *PMLA* 76 (1961). Reprinted in *Essential Articles for the Study of Edmund Spenser.* Ed. A. C. Hamilton, 189–98. Hamden, CT: Archon, 1972.

Rondot, M. Natalis. *L'industrie de la soie en France.* Lyon, 1894.

Rosaldo, Michelle and Lousie Lamphere, eds. *Women, Culture, and Society.* Stanford: Stanford University Press, 1974.

Rose, Christine M. "Woman's 'Pryvete,' May, and the Privy: Fissures in the Narrative Voice in the *Merchant's Tale,* 1944–86." *Chaucer Yearbook* 4 (Summer, 1997): 61–77.

———. "Chaucer's *Man of Law's Tale:* Teaching Through the Sources." *College Literature* 28.1 (Spring 2001): 155–177.

Rubin, Gail. "The Traffic in Women: Notes on the 'Political Economy' of Sex." In *Toward an Anthropology of Women.* Ed. R. R. Reiter, 157–210. New York: Monthly Review Press, 1975.

Saly, Antoinette. "La demoiselle 'esforciée' dans le roman arthurien." In *Amour, mariage, et transgressions au moyen âge.* Ed. Danielbe Buschinger and André Crépin, 215–24. Goppingen: Kümmerle, 1984.

Saunders, Corrine J. "Woman Displaced: Rape and Romance in Chaucer's *Wife of Bath's Tale.*" *Arthurian Literature* XII (1995): 115–31.

Schibanoff, Susan. "Taking the Gold Out of Egypt: The Art of Reading as a Woman." In *Gender and Reading: Essays on Readers, Texts and Contexts.* Ed. Elizabeth Flynn and Patrocinio P. Schweichart, 83–106. Baltimore, MD: Johns Hopkins University Press, 1986.

Schnell, Rüdiger. "The Discourse on Marriage in the Middle Ages." *Speculum* 73, no. 3 (July, 1998): 771–86.

Schotter, Anne Howland. "Rhetoric versus Rape in the Medieval Latin *Pamphilus.*" *Philological Quarterly* 71 (1992): 243–60.

———. "The Transformation of Ovid in the Twelfth-Century *Pamphilus.*" *Desiring Discourse: The Literature of Love, Ovid Through Chaucer.* Ed. Cynthia Gravlee and James J. Paxson, 72–86. London: Associated University Presses, 1998.

Schulze-Busacker, Elizabeth. "*Philomena:* Une Revision de l'attribution de l'oeuvre." *Romania* 107 (1986): 459–85.

Scott, Joan. "Experience." In *Feminists Theorize the Political.* Ed. Judith Butler and Joan W. Scott, 22–40. New York: Routledge, 1992.

Sedgwick, Eve Kosofsky. *Between Men: English Literature and Male Homosocial Desire.* New York: Columbia University Press, 1985.

———. *Epistemology of the Closet.* Berkeley: University of California Press, 1990.

Segal, Charles. "La tela di Filomela e i piaceri del testo: il mito di Tereo nelle *Metamorfosi.*" In *Ovidio e la poesia del mito.* Venice: Marsilio editori, 1991.

Seznec, Jean. *The Survival of the Pagan Gods: the mythological tradition and its place in Renaissance humanism and art*. Trans. Barbara Sessions. Princeton, NJ: Princeton University Press, 1953.

Shakespeare, William. *Measure for Measure. The Riverside Shakespeare*. Ed. G. Blakemore Evans et al., 545–86. Boston: Houghton Mifflin, 1974.

———. *Titus Andronicus*. Ed. Sylvan Barnet. New York: New American Library, 1963.

———. *Titus Andronicus*. Arden Shakespeare, 3rd Series. Ed. Jonathan Bate. London: Routledge, 1995.

———. *Titus Andronicus*. Arden Shakespeare, 2nd Series. Ed. J. C. Maxwell. London: Methuen, 1968.

———. *The Tragedy of Titus Andronicus. The Riverside Shakespeare*. Ed. G. Blakemore Evans et al., 1019–54. Boston: Houghton Mifflin, 1974.

Shapley, Thomas. "Those Who Prey On Kids." *Seattle Post-Intelligencer.* 7 April, 1991: D-1.

Sheehan, Michael. "The Choice of Marriage Partners in the Middle Ages," In *Studies in Medieval and Renaissance History,* n. s. I (1978): 1–33. Rpt. in Michael M. Sheehan, *Marriage, Family and Law in Medieval Europe: Collected Studies*. Ed. James K. Farge, 87–117. Toronto: University of Toronto Press, 1996.

———. *Marriage, Family and Law in Medieval Europe*. Toronto: University of Toronto Press, 1996.

Showerman, Grant, ed. and trans. *Ovid: Heroides and Amores*. Cambridge, MA: Harvard University Press, 1914.

Shuger, Debora Keller. *The Renaissance Bible: Scholarship, Sacrifice, and Subjectivity.* Berkeley: University of California Press, 1994.

Sidney, Philip. *The Countess of Pembroke's Arcadia (The Old Arcadia),* (c. 1580). Ed. Jean Robertson. Oxford: Clarendon, 1973.

Silberman, Lauren. "Unsung Heroines: Androgynous Discourse in Book 3 of *The Faerie Queene.*" In *Rewriting the Renaissance: The Discourses of Sexual Difference in Early Modern Europe*. Ed. Margaret W. Ferguson, Maureen Quilligan, and Nancy J. Vickers, 259–71. Chicago: University of Chicago Press, 1986.

Sir Gawain and the Green Knight. Ed. J. R. R. Tolkien and E. V. Gordon. 2nd ed. Norman Davis. Oxford: Oxford University Press, 1967.

Solodow, Joseph B. *The World of Ovid's Metamorphoses*. Chapel Hill: University of North Carolina Press, 1988.

Spelman, Elizabeth V. "Anger and Insubordination." In *Women, Knowledge, and Reality: Explorations in Feminist Philosophy*. Ed. Ann Garry and Marilyn Pearsall, 263–73. Boston: Unwin Hyman, 1989.

Spenser, Edmund. *Edmund Spenser: "The Faerie Queene."* (1590). Ed. Thomas P. Roche, Jr. New Haven, CT: Yale University Press, 1981.

———. *The Faerie Queene*. Ed. A. C. Hamilton. London: Longman, 1977.

———. *Spenser's Minor Poems* (1595). Ed. Ernest de Selincourt. Oxford: Clarendon, 1910.

———. *The Yale Edition of the Shorter Poems of Edmund Spenser*. Ed. William A. Oram et al. New Haven, CT: Yale University Press, 1989.

Spiegel, Harriet, "The Fox and the Bear: A Medieval Woman's Fable of Rape and its Transformations." In manuscript. (1995).

————. "The Male Animal in the Fables of Marie de France." In *Medieval Masculinities: Regarding Men in the Middle Ages.* Ed. Clare A. Lees, 111–26. Minneapolis: University of Minnesota Press, 1994.

Spivak, Gayatri Chakravorty. "Displacement and the Discourse of Woman." In *Displacement: Derrida and After.* Ed. Mark Krupnick, 169–95. Bloomington: Indiana University Press, 1983.

Stallybrass, Peter. "Patriarchal Territories: The Body Enclosed." In *Rewriting the Renaissance: The Discourses of Sexual Difference in Early Modern Europe.* Ed. Margaret Ferguson, Maureen Quilligan, and Nancy J. Vickers, 123–42. Chicago and London: University of Chicago Press, 1986.

The Statutes of the Realm. 12 vols. London: Dawson, 1963; first published 1810–28.

Stephens, Dorothy. *The Limits of Eroticism in Post-Petrarchan Narrative: Conditional Pleasure from Spenser to Marvell.* Cambridge: Cambridge University Press, 1998.

Stokes, Myra. "*Sir Gawain and the Green Knight:* Fitt III as Debate." *Nottingham Studies* 25 (1981): 35–49.

Stone, Lawrence. *Crisis of the Aristocracy.* Oxford: Clarendon Press, 1965.

Strong, Roy. *Gloriana: The Portraits of Queen Elizabeth I.* New York: Thames & Hudson, 1987.

————. *Spirit of the Age.* London: BBC Publications, 1975.

Stubbes, Phillip. *A Motive to Good Workes.* London, 1593.

Teague, Frances, ed. "Marriage Speech." In *Women Writers of the Renaissance and Reformation.* Ed. Katharina M. Wilson, 537–38. Athens: University of Georgia Press, 1987.

Tenison, Eva. M. *Elizabethan England 1583–1585. Elizabethan England, Vol. 5.* Glasgow: Glasgow University Press, 1936.

Teskey, Gordon. *Allegory and Violence.* Ithaca, NY: Cornell University Press, 1996.

Thickstun, Margaret Olofson. *Fictions of the Feminine: Puritan Doctrine and the Representation of Women.* Ithaca, NY: Cornell University Press, 1988.

Three Ovidian Tales of Love. Ed. and trans. Raymond J. Cormier. New York: Garland Publishing, 1986.

Tilney, Edmund. *The Flower of Friendship: A Renaissance Dialogue Contesting Marriage.* Ed. Valerie Wayne. Ithaca, NY: Cornell University Press, 1992.

Todd, Margo. *Christian Humanism and the Puritan Social Order.* Cambridge: Cambridge University Press, 1987.

Tomaselli, Sylvana and Roy Porter. *Rape: An Historical and Social Enquiry.* Oxford: Basil Blackwell, 1986.

Traub, Valerie. "The Psychomorphology of the Clitoris," *GLQ* 2 (1995): 81–113.

Tricomi, Albert. "The Aesthetics of Mutilation in *Titus Andronicus.*" *Shakespeare Survey* 27 (1974): 11–19.

Vance, Eugene. "Chrétien's *Yvain* and the Ideologies of Change and Exchange." *Images of Power: Medieval History/Discourse/Literature, Yale French Studies* 70 (1986): 42–62.

Vatican Mythographers. *Mythographi Vaticani I et II.* Ed. Peter Kulcsár. Corpus Christianorum, Series Latina, vol. 91C. Turnholt: Brepols, 1987.

————. *Mythographi Vaticani I et II.* Ed. Nevio Zorzetti. Trans. Jacques Berlioz. Paris: Belles Lettres, 1995.

Vickers, Nancy. "'The blazon of sweet beauty's best': Shakespeare's *Lucrece*." In *Shakespeare and the Question of Theory*. Ed. Patricia Parker and Geoffrey Hartman, 95–115. New York: Methuen, 1985.

———. "This Heraldry in Lucrece' face." In *The Female Body in Western Culture*. Ed. S. R. Suleiman, 209–22. Cambridge, MA: Harvard University Press, 1986.

Vitz, Evelyn Birge. "Rereading Rape in Medieval Literature," *Partisan Review* 63.2 (Spring, 1996): 280–91.

———. "Rereading Rape in Medieval Literature," *Romanic Review* 88 (1997): 1–26.

"Vulgate" Commentary on Ovid's Metamorphoses. Ed. Frank Coulson. Toronto: Pontifical Institute of Mediaeval Studies, 1991.

Waith, Eugene. "The Metamorphosis of Violence in *Titus Andronicus*." *Shakespeare Survey* 10 (1957): 39–49.

Walker, Cheryl. "Feminist Literary Criticism and the Author." *Critical Inquiry* 16.3 (1990): 551–71.

Walker, Sue Sheridan. "Punishing Convicted Ravishers: Statutory Strictures and Actual Practice in Thirteenth and Fourteenth-Century England," *Journal of Medieval History* 13 (1987): 237–50.

Wall, Wendy. *Imprint of Gender: Authorship and Publication in the English Renaissance*. Ithaca, NY: Cornell University Press, 1993.

Waller, Marguerite. "Usurpation, Seduction, and the Problematics of the Proper: A 'Deconstructive,' 'Feminist' Rereading of the Seductions of Richard and Anne in Shakespeare's *Richard III*." In *Rewriting the Renaissance: The Discourses of Sexual Difference in Early Modern Europe*. Ed. Margaret W. Ferguson, Maureen Quilligan, and Nancy J. Vickers, 159–74. Chicago: University of Chicago Press, 1986.

Watts, P. R. "The Strange Case of Geoffrey Chaucer and Cecilia Chaumpaigne." *The Law Quarterly Review* 63 (1947): 491–515.

Wayne, Valerie. "Introduction." In Edmund Tilney, *The Flower of Friendship: A Renaissance Dialogue Contesting Marriage (1568)*. Ed. Valerie Wayne. Ithaca, NY: Cornell University Press, 1992.

Weimann, Robert, ed. *Structure and Society in Literary History: Studies in the History and Theory of Historical Criticism*. Baltimore, MD: Johns Hopkins University Press, 1984.

———. "Text, Author-Function, and Appropriation in Modern Narrative: Toward a Sociology of Representation." In *Literature and Social Practice*. Ed. Philippe Desan, Priscilla Parkhurst Ferguson, and Wendy Griswold. Chicago: University of Chicago Press, 1989.

Wells, Robin. *Spenser's* Faerie Queene *and the Cult of Elizabeth*. Totowa, NJ: Barnes & Noble, 1983.

West, Grace Starry. "Going by the Book: Classical Allusions in Shakespeare's *Titus Andronicus*." Chapel Hill: University of North Carolina, 1982.

West's Annotated California Codes. 73 vols. St. Paul, MN: West Publishing, 1954.

Whately, William. *A Bride-bush*. London, 1623.

Wiesner, Merry. *Women and Gender in Early Modern Europe.* Cambridge: Cambridge University Press, 1993.

Williams, Carolyn D. "'Silence, like a Lucrece Knife': Shakespeare and the meanings of Rape." *Yearbook of English Studies* 23 (1993): 93–110.

Williams, R. D. *The Aeneid of Virgil: Books 1–6.* London: Macmillan, 1972.

Willis, Deborah. *Malevolent Nurture: Witch-Hunting and Maternal Power in Early Modern England.* Ithaca, NY: Cornell University Press, 1995.

Wilson, Jean. *Entertainments for Elizabeth.* Totowa, NJ: Rowman & Littlefield, 1980.

Wilson, Richard. "Observations on English Bodies: Licensing Maternity in Shakespeare's Late Plays." In *Enclosure Acts: Sexuality, Property, and Culture in Early Modern England.* Ed. Richard Burt and John Michael Archer, 121–50. Ithaca, NY: Cornell University Press, 1994.

Wittgenstein, Ludwig. *On Certainty.* Ed. G. E. M. Anscombe and G. H. von Wright, and trans. Denis Paul and G. E. M. Anscombe. Oxford: Basil Blackwell, 1969.

Wittig, Monique. "On the Social Contract." *Feminist Issues* 9.1 (1989): 3–12.

Wofford, Susanne Lindgren. *The Choice of Achilles: The Ideology of Figure in the Epic.* Stanford: Stanford University Press, 1992.

Wolfthal, Diane. "'Douleur sur toutes autres': Revisualizing the Rape Script in the *Epistre Othea* and the *Cité des dames.*" In *Christine de Pizan and the Categories of Difference.* Ed. Marilynn Desmond, 41–70. Minneapolis and London: University of Minnesota Press, 1998.

Woods, Marjorie Curry. "Rape and the Pedagogical Rhetoric of Sexual Violence." In *Criticism and Dissent in the Middle Ages.* Ed. Rita Copeland, 56–86. Cambridge: Cambridge University Press, 1996.

Wynne-Davies, Marion. "'The Swallowing Womb': Consumed and Consuming Women in *Titus Andronicus.*" In *The Matter of Difference: Materialist Feminist Criticism of Shakespeare.* Ed. Valerie Wayne, 129–51. Ithaca, NY: Cornell University Press, 1991.

CONTRIBUTORS

MARK AMSLER has taught medieval studies and linguistics at the University of Delaware and Eastern Michigan University and is currently professor of English at the University of Wisconsin-Milwaukee. He has published widely on medieval literature, the history of linguistics, and the history and sociology of English, including *Etymology and Grammatical Discourse in Late Antiquity and the Early Middle Ages* (John Benjamins, 1989). He is completing a new book on medieval literacies and textualities.

ROBIN L. BOTT is an assistant professor in the English Department at Adrian College. Her work has appeared in *Medieval Perspectives* and *Teaching Shakespeare Through Performance* (MLA, 1997).

E. JANE BURNS, Professor of Women's Studies at the University of North Carolina at Chapel Hill, publishes extensively on Medieval French literature, especially Arthurian Literature, and women. Her most recent book is *Bodytalk: When Women Speak in Old French Literature* (University of Pennsylvania, 1993). She is a cofounder of *The Medieval Feminist Newsletter.*

CHRISTOPHER R CANNON, University Lecturer in the Faculty of English, Cambridge, has published articles on Chaucer's life and language, Early Middle English, and is a contributor to the *Cambridge History of Medieval Literature* (1999). His book, *The Making of Chaucer's English: A Study of Words,* was published by Cambridge University Press (1998).

AMY GREENSTADT is Assistant Professor of English at Portland State University. Her recently completed dissertation is entitled "Divine Enchanting Ravishment: The Rhetoric of Rape in Early Modern England" (UC-Berkeley, 2001). She has also volunteered as a rape crisis counselor at San Francisco Women Against Rape.

KATHERINE EGGERT is an Associate Professor of English at the University of Colorado, Boulder. She is the author of *Showing Like a Queen: Female*

Authority and Literary Experiment in Spenser, Shakespeare and Milton (University of Pennsylvania Press, 2000), and of essays on Early Modern authors, new historicism, and Shakespeare on film.

SUSAN FRYE is Professor of English at the University of Wyoming. She has published *Elizabeth I: The Competition for Representation* (Oxford University Press, 1993), and edited, with Karen Robertson, *Women's Alliances in Early Modern England* (Oxford University Press, 1999). Her work-in-progress includes a study of the relation between women's domestic production and their literary production in Early Modern England

NANCY A. JONES is an independent scholar and author of essays appearing in *Rape and Representation* and *Sex and Gender in Medieval and Renaissance Texts: The Latin Tradition* (State University of New York Press, 1997). She is the coeditor (with Leslie Dunn) of *Embodied Voices: Representing Female Vocality In Western Culture* (Cambridge University Press, 1994).

MONICA BRZEZINSKI POTKAY is an Associate Professor at the College of William and Mary, and coauthor with Regula Meyer Evitt of a book on medieval women for Twayne Press, *Minding the Body: Women and Literature in the Middle Ages, 800–1500* (1997).

ELIZABETH ROBERTSON is an Associate Professor of English at the University of Colorado, Boulder. She was a founding editor of *The Medieval Feminist Newsletter*. Her work on Medieval women has appeared in numerous essay collections, and she is the author of *Early English Devotional Prose for Women* (Tennessee University Press, 1990) and coeditor, with David Benson, of *Chaucer's Religious Tales* (Boydell and Brewer, 1990) and the Norton Critical Edition of *Piers Plowman* (forthcoming). She is currently writing about female consent in medieval literature.

KAREN ROBERTSON is the Associate Dean of Students and teaches Renaissance Literature in the English Department at Vassar College. She is coeditor, with Susan Frye, of *Women's Alliances in Early Modern England* (1999).

CHRISTINE M. ROSE, Professor of English at Portland State University, has been a member of the Advisory Board of the Society for Medieval Feminist Scholarship. Her recent work has appeared in *Exemplaria, Chaucer Yearbook, Harvard Library Bulletin, Hildegard of Bingen: A Book of Essays* (1998) and *The Medieval Feminist Newsletter*. She is the author of the forthcoming *Trevet's English Chronicle: An Edition of Houghton Library fMS*

Eng938 and is writing a book on late-Medieval conduct books for female readers.

ANNE HOWLAND SCHOTTER is Professor of English and Chair of Humanities at Wagner College. She has published on the influence of Ovid on Medieval Latin poetry, especially on woman's song and the twelfth-century comedy *Pamphilus.* She has also written on *Pearl, Sir Gawain and the Green Knight,* and Dante. She is coeditor of *Ineffability: Naming the Unnamable from Dante to Beckett* (NY: AMS Press, 1984), and with Christopher Baswell she recently coedited the medieval section of the *Longman Anthology of British Literature.*

INDEX